D0968671

These Our People

HEATH'S SOCIAL RELATIONS SERIES

General Editor: HOWARD BECKER
University of Wisconsin

Family, Marriage, and Parenthood
Edited by Howard Becker and Reuben Hill
Iowa State College

These Our People: Minorities in American Culture
By R. A. Schermerhorn
Cleveland College, Western Reserve University

An Introduction to Public Welfare
By Arthur P. Miles
University of Wisconsin

[IN PREPARATION]

Man in Society: An Introduction to Sociology
By Howard Becker and Don Martindale
University of Wisconsin

Industrial Sociology
By Joseph B. Gittler
Iowa State College

R. A. SCHERMERHORN

THESE OUR PEOPLE

MINORITIES IN AMERICAN CULTURE

D. C. HEATH AND COMPANY

BOSTON

PRINTED IN THE UNITED STATES OF AMERICA

5 B 0

Offices: Boston · New York · Chicago · San Francisco Atlanta · Dallas · London

To Helen
who has sacrificed more
for this book
than I

"WHO WAKES?"

[*Detroit, June, 1943*]

Who wakes now who lay blind with sleep?
Who starts, bright-eyed with anger from his bed?
I do. I, the plain citizen. I cannot sleep.
I hold the torturing fire in my head.

I, an American, call the dead Negro's name,
And in the hot dark of the city night
I walk the streets alone and sweat with shame.
Too late to rise, to raise the dead too late.

This is the harvest. The seeds sown long ago —
The careless word, sly thought, excusing glance.
I reap now everything I let pass, let go.
This is the harvest of my own indifference.

I, the plain citizen, have grown disorder
In my own world. It is not what I meant.
But dreams and images are potent and can murder.
I stand accused of them. I am not innocent.

Can I now plant imagination, honesty,
And love where violence and terror were unbound,
The images of hope, the dream's responsibility?

Those who died here were murdered in my mind.

MAY SARTON [1]

. . .

None the less, he knew that the tale he had to tell could not be one of a final victory. It could be only the record of what had to be done, and what assuredly would have to be done again in the never ending fight against terror and its relentless onslaughts, despite their personal afflictions, by all who, while unable to be saints but refusing to bow down to pestilence, strive their utmost to be healers. [2]

[1] From *The Lion and the Rose*. Copyright 1948 by May Sarton. Reprinted by permission of Rinehart & Company

[2] Reprinted from *The Plague* by Albert Camus, by permission of Alfred A. Knopf, Inc. Copyright 1948 by Stuart Gilbert

Preface

THIS is a minimal text in the sense that it makes no attempt to give a comprehensive picture of minority groups in the United States. Through many years of teaching in the field I have arrived at the conclusion that students approaching the subject for the first time need an analysis which will answer their elementary questions without a mass of detail that too often confuses them. Oscar Wilde's remark is still true, "He who tries to exhaust his subject, usually ends by exhausting his hearers."

Furthermore I am optimistic enough to entertain the hope that if the issues are treated with a minimum of technical jargon, my readers will not be limited to college students, but that businessmen, labor leaders, farmers, clergymen, civic officers, and journalists may find it a useful guide. The volume presupposes little in the way of previous sociological training and defines most abstract terms as they arise. Each chapter begins with one or more examples from actual life that introduce the reader informally to the subject discussed.

It has been necessary to run the risk of making each group unique by giving it a special chapter or section. This is not because the uniformities of their life experience are unimportant (they receive a good deal of attention in Chapter 18) but simply because the beginner in the field approaches the subject most naturally through his previous acquaintance with one or more of the minority groups dealt with in these pages. Pedagogically this is where the reader begins. And this introduction attempts to follow the line of his spontaneous interest.

I have tried to give enough of the social and cultural background of the various minorities so that adjustment problems can be understood in terms of unique historical experiences shared by the members of any group. In doing so I have discovered how uneven the empirical studies of ethnic societies are. Sociologists and anthropologists who recognize the gaps in our knowledge will readily observe where such data are lacking. Perhaps the most incomplete studies relate to the acculturation of specific nationality groups in the new immigration. The current research project on Contemporary Cultures initiated by the late Ruth Benedict will eventually enable social scientists to round out their knowledge more satisfactorily.

The urgency of the minority problem for the general public is such that it is visionary to wait until all possible research is completed. The racist attitudes of the American public are already creating vexing problems for our diplomats abroad. The widespread prejudices taken for granted by so many citizens are a potential explosive that any emergency can touch off. Intergroup tensions are everywhere. We need to use the knowledge we have, however incomplete it is.

Those who are familiar with the field may cavil at the choice of minorities in this book. At the risk of being arbitrary I have selected those with the largest population base, that is, those with whom the average American is most likely to come in contact. In this way any student, whether in the southwest, the northeast, the southeast, or the middle west, can find something relevant to his own experience. Armenians, Syrians, Greeks, Chinese, Filipinos, or Puerto Ricans may quarrel with this selection. Only semireference works like Brown and Roucek's *One America* can attempt to give an account of every possible group. The aim of the present work is to be more discursive, with a smaller sampling of minority peoples, so that their life histories may appear more clearly.

Empirical studies of intergroup relations are growing in number, and many receive attention throughout these pages. In an elementary work it is more important to introduce the reader to monographs and studies already made than to develop a novel set of theoretical formulations. Our survey of ethnic researches already available is designed to be of greatest value for readers approaching the subject for the first time. If this volume becomes the starting point for increased study and informed activity in the field of intergroup relations, it will have fulfilled its purpose.

Although I cannot acknowledge indebtedness to all who have helped in the preparation of this work, I feel bound to express my gratitude to those who read and criticized one or more chapters while the writing was in progress. To the following, then, goes my deepest appreciation: Professor Ira DeA. Reid, Professor Norman D. Humphrey, Professor T. Scott Miyakawa, Mrs. Domenic Grillo, Commissioner Edward Corsi, Mr. Frank E. Traficante, Mr. Z. B. Dybowski, Miss Fern Long, Rev. M. F. Benko, Rev. Andor Leffler, Mrs. V. D. Cahill, Mr. Vlaho S. Vlahovic, Mr. Nathan Glazer, Professor Henry M. Busch, and Professor Gordon W. Allport. Without the many helpful suggestions and friendly criticisms of these readers, this volume would have suffered greatly. I hasten to add that the responsibility, however, is mine and not theirs for any errors or faulty emphases the book may contain.

At the same time I wish to acknowledge the special services of Mr. Joseph Galkin and Dr. Leonard Covello in loaning me books, periodicals, and monographs from their own collections.

Rinehart & Company, Alfred A. Knopf, Inc., and the editors of *Common Ground* and *Phylon* have kindly given permission to quote material on which they hold the copyright.

Thanks go also to Dean Myron F. Wicke of Baldwin-Wallace College for arranging time schedules so as to facilitate the writing, and to Professor L. Guy Brown of Rhode Island State College for his continual encouragement and aid. Especially would I extend my appreciation to Dean Harold W. Browning and the authorities of Rhode Island State College for a research grant during the academic year 1947–1948. And to Professor Henry M. Busch at Cleveland College of Western Reserve University I owe a debt of gratitude for his aid in securing additional secretarial assistance.

Dr. James W. Pugsley of the Baldwin-Wallace College Library and Mr. Francis Allen of the Rhode Island State College Library have given invaluable assistance in finding materials. Sincere thanks also go to the following who aided with the typing: Miss Doris Werme, Mrs. Peggy Aanons Barr, Mrs. Helen Carpenter, Miss Elizabeth Aitken, Mrs. Theresa Galipeau, and Miss Margaret Diamond. Miss Eleanor Bruh also deserves gratitude for giving generously of her time in preparation of the index.

To Professor Howard Becker and Dr. Donald Young go special thanks for the onerous task of reading and criticizing the entire manuscript; their aid in giving perspective to the task as a whole has been invaluable. Finally I must reserve a special niche of appreciation for my wife, whose editorial labors have been beyond praise.

R. A. S.

Cleveland College
Western Reserve University

Table of Contents

INTRODUCTION

RACIAL MINORITIES

THE NEW IMMIGRATION

THE PERENNIAL MINORITY

WHEN PEOPLES MEET

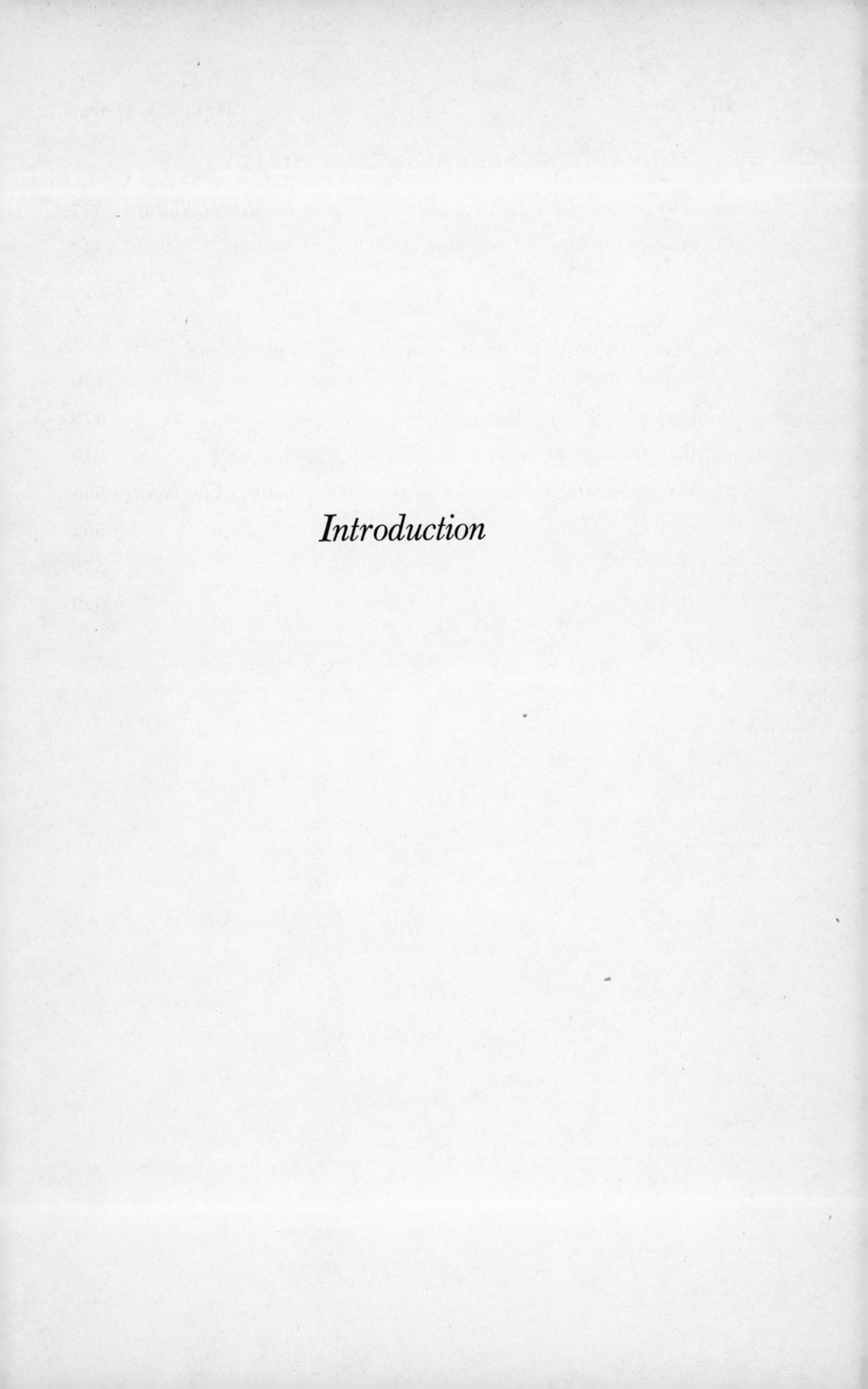

Introduction

CHAPTER I

Why Are Minorities a "Problem"?

BEN SHAPIRO dismayed his parents by getting engaged to a gentile girl. Although his father and mother admitted that Florence was genial and refined and a good homemaker, they could not escape the feeling that their son was betraying them and all they stood for. But with a good deal of grumbling they finally relented enough after the marriage to accept Florence rather grudgingly into the family. Ben was proud of her and entered gradually into her circle of friends. This took him away from his old acquaintances until he belonged to a different social world altogether. He lost more and more contact with the Jewish world, stopped going to the synagogue, and in time visited his parents' home more and more infrequently. Although he and Florence had no children, they were very happy together until the young wife was suddenly killed in an automobile accident. Crushed by his misfortune, Ben moved back with his family and for many months refused to see his gentile friends. He once more began to attend the synagogue regularly and there he became intimately acquainted with Sarah, a daughter of his parents' old friends. One thing led to another and before a year had passed he and Sarah were married. His return to the fold was complete. From this time on, he became perfectly satisfied to remain within the Jewish community, bask in the approval of his parents, and take a deep interest in the rituals and ceremonies of the old religion.

Two college friends, one colored and one white, were motoring home through Ohio and stopped at a café for early morning breakfast. Each ordered coffee and rolls. The waiter looked at them curiously but took their order and disappeared. In one corner a juke box blared noisily. Over the cashier's desk was a sign in letters too small to read from their booth. Being in a hurry, the boys gulped their food and made their way to the cashier's corner.

"That'll be a dollar and a quarter. A quarter for you [indicating the white boy] and a dollar for you [this directed at the Negro]."

"What do you mean? Do you have two sets of prices here?" protested the white student.

The cashier pointed grimly to the sign above his desk. It read: PRICES SUBJECT TO CHANGE WITHOUT NOTICE.

Realizing the futility of argument, the boys paid — and never went back. The sign had its intended effect.

Mr. and Mrs. Ito were returning to California from a three-year confinement in an Arizona relocation center. They were frankly dubious about the kind of reception they would receive in San Francisco, where they had been forced to sell their business at a loss to a white merchant; they had heard rumors from the camp that others had been threatened when they came back to the Coast. When they got off their train in San Francisco, they looked about them apprehensively. To their embarrassment, a group of Marines just back from the Pacific approached them with stern purpose in every move. "Now it is coming," whispered Mr. Ito to his wife. But neither of them was prepared for the Marines' opening sentence, "Hey, Nippon, do you speak Japanese?" The Itos stared at each other, fearing to answer either yes or no. Finally the old man, deciding to brave it out, told the servicemen that he *could* speak it. The Marines grinned broadly and then broke into an excited clatter of pidgin Japanese they had picked up in Tokyo; soon they were all talking rapidly in the language of America's greatest Pacific enemy. The Marines were evidently enjoying themselves in a display of their new-found knowledge. Names and addresses were exchanged and as the Marines finally went on their way with a friendly, "So long, Mr. Ito. Good-bye, Mrs. Ito," the old couple turned back to each other wide eyed. "Who would have thought this could happen?" Relieved, they set out to find their friends and relatives in what was for them a new San Francisco.

Antonio was annoyed with his parents. Every time he earned a dime, they expected him to bring it home, like an infant, and give it to them. After all, they should remember that he was an American now and an Italian no longer. Why should he go to all their clubs and social gatherings when all you could hear there was Italian, and only a dialect at that? Why couldn't he get in with more American friends and learn to be a part of this country? Yet every time he went home, he found the pressure to conform more and more irritating. Before long he met Teresa, a girl his own age, and found that she was having the same trouble with her parents. After comparing notes, they found that they were compatriots in the same struggle to free themselves from the older ways and traditions. It then became the most natural thing in the world that they should join forces and start life anew on their own. By marrying each other, they could get their parents' approval for marrying Italian. Then after satisfying the older generation, they would go ahead and reorganize their lives so that they could live like Americans. It was a "natural."

None of these are imaginary situations; all of them are based on actual cases known through personal experience or newspaper reports. Ben, the Negro student, the Itos, and Tony are not exceptional; they are in many ways representative of minority groups snared in the impersonal clash of forces over which they have little or no control. Each is in a peculiar dilemma because he is a clearly distinguishable member of a minority that remains socially distant from the dominant majority. In popular thinking, individual qualities, personal merit, likability, charm, or leadership seem blotted out by the blurred coloration of group inclusion.

DEFINITION OF MINORITY

What is a minority? For purposes of our study the following definition will prove suggestive, if not exhaustive. Minorities are subgroups within a culture which are distinguishable from the dominant group by reason of differences in physiognomy, language, customs, or culture-patterns (including any combination of these factors). Such subgroups are regarded as inherently different and "not belonging" to the dominant group; for this reason they are consciously or unconsciously excluded from full participation in the life of the culture. Usually the exclusion is at least partly based on historical reasons which differentiate the background of the subgroup from that of the dominant group.

The term "subgroup" signifies a group that is subordinated to the domination of a ruling group, not necessarily a group numerically smaller in size. Thus in South Africa, the Negro population far outnumbers the white but its status is distinctly that of a minority; the same assertion holds for groups of Negroes in many southern communities of the United States or for Mexicans in certain areas of New Mexico. The numerical majority may be treated like a minority and often is.

When we speak of a "dominant group" we mean that group whose historical language, traditions, customs, and ideology are normative for the society; their pre-eminence is enforced by the folkways or by law, and in time these elements attain the position of cultural presuppositions. In Europe it is somewhat easier to recognize the dominant group because it has linguistic, political, and educational power effectively in its hands and usually occupies a well-defined territory. The dominance of the Czechs over the Sudeten Germans or of the Italians over the Fiume Slovenians during the 1930's was clearly marked. In the United States, the dominant group has not had the same conspicuous position. Geographical boundary lines have not coincided with language for any of the federal states. From the first, the thirteen colonies were a cultural mixture of Dutch, English, French, Germans, Scandinavians, and others. But there is little doubt that the major ascendancy finally rested with the Anglo-Saxon Protestant colonists,[1] though the whole matter is obscured by later biological intermixture. It is true that the first imprint of European culture upon the Americas was a Spanish one, and there are scholars who have given primacy to this tradition because of its chronological vantage ground or its permeation of the Pacific culture along the West Coast.[2] But taking the United States as a whole, we find that English became the accepted tongue,[3] English common law became the basis of the legal code, English marriage customs became the prevailing mode, and the philosophy of Locke and Burke was embodied in the American Constitution. The hold of Protestantism, although more subtle, can nevertheless be shown by the fact that a Catholic has never yet been elected President, and the attempt of Al Smith to brave popular sentiment met with a hardening of barriers already firmly set.

HOW MINORITIES EMERGE

What then are the "historical reasons" that have defined the status of minorities? How are minorities formed? Chiefly through power relations. Power may be defined as "the ability to control the actions of individuals or groups, or the exercise of that control." In the former case, the power is potential; in the latter, actual. But even when it is actual, it does not imply violence or coercion unless it is challenged. Power may be embodied in a set of social stereotypes,[4] in persuasion, or in the folkways or systems of etiquette, or it may be enacted into law. Since the exclusive agency of socially justified force is the state, only those elements considered important enough to be enforced by police power receive legal codification.

Minorities come into existence as the product of power relations. They are (1) groups forced into subordination by conquest; or (2) groups captured by force and transported; or (3) migrants accepted for prudential considerations; or (4) groups forced into strong in-solidarity by a shifting of political boundaries. For the most part, minorities in the United States fall into one of the first three types, while those of Europe come chiefly under the fourth. Since our interest will confine itself to the United States, we shall give only passing reference to minority problems of the European type.* And for reasons of space, we shall also exclude the broader questions of colonial policies in Africa, Asia, and the Pacific areas.

IN-GROUP PSYCHOLOGY AND DIFFERENCES

Although power relations are a necessary prelude to minority exclusion, they are not a sufficient explanation of it. The group in power would not exercise control over subordinates without social conditioning of attitudes that make it seem important. It is here that we come up against the universal tendency of all groups to identify social values with their own existence. The simpler societies studied by the anthropologists show this trait most clearly. Whether it is the preliterate band, village community, tribe, or confederation, we find that each thinks of itself as an in-group or we-group. "We" belong; "outsiders" do not. "Our" ways of doing things are right; the stranger's are barbaric. "Our" gods are the true gods;

* See Chapter 9.

those of other peoples are (if supernaturalism is strong) weak or (if supernaturalism is more etherealized) nonexistent. Toward our own members we have duties and obligations of mutuality, helpfulness, and cooperation; they have rights because they are a part of our life, and harming them harms us. But strangers, outsiders, barbarians, and enemies have no rights. In more than one preliterate language the word for "human being" is the same as the name of the tribe. Ergo, the member of another tribe is not a human being and is automatically excluded from fair treatment. Tribal ethics is the root of all ethics. The Sixth Commandment when originally formulated was understood to mean, "Thou shalt not kill (an Israelite). All others — Amalekites, Moabites, and Philistines — are fair game." The same qualifications were extended to other Commandments by cultural presupposition; no one needed to be told as much in words. All *knew* it.[5]

Wherever any group develops the idea that its people are of sole importance and their values the only ones worth cherishing, there arises the trait of ethnocentrism. This social response is a peculiar blend of inner solidarity with outward hostility. The growing complexity of society into national and urban units does not cause ethnocentrism to disappear though it may become diffused. World Wars I and II show that it operates powerfully at the national level. But it is not always so clear that ethnocentrism takes a veiled and potent form in the psychology of class and status groups.[6] By erecting barriers against political, economic, and social participation of "outsiders" it vigorously strengthens the *status quo* and freezes social relations.

Perhaps the most significant result of ethnocentrism is that it singles out and accentuates the cultural and physical differences in those groups that lie outside the range of acceptance. Whether it be language, costume, family customs, diet, modes of address, or forms of etiquette on the one hand, or physiognomy, stature, color, or more visible factors on the other, the dominant group regards these as definitive for each member of the outside group. An ancient proverb has it that "whoever speaks two languages is a rascal," and it will easily be assumed that he who speaks the "wrong" language is a fool, a foreigner who knows no better and therefore is regarded by the ignorant as a threat, or one who is marked down contemptuously as outside the pale. In the United States, separated from its European and Oriental neighbors by two oceans, the need for communication with cultures having different tongues is at a minimum. There is not the desperate necessity of learning two or three languages for commercial transactions, so characteristic of countries like Denmark, Holland, or Poland. Cultural insulation, a product of geographical accident, has therefore been raised to the status of a virtue, in true ethnocentric style. The author has seen, with his own eyes, a United States customs official berating a Slavic immigrant unmercifully on the docks of New York harbor because she could not understand English. Her ignorance appeared to be almost a personal affront, but in his action he was giving voice to the common social definition which the dominant Anglo-Saxon gives to every person who speaks some language other than English. The same tendency affects customs, dress, and diet. In due time the individual who shares these differences from the dominant group is defined in terms of the differences. It is only a step from this definition to the feeling that such distinctions are somehow biologically inherent in the stranger.

Where the variation is one of skin color, shape of face or head, slant of eye, or shape of nose, popular biology seizes upon this heritable distinction and attributes all other features of the person's behavior to inborn traits, in the same way that it attributes the daughter's temper to her mother or the son's lackadaisical ways to a lazy father. "He came by it honestly." Social and cultural traits soon become accounted for by heritable factors. There is, of course, a subtle rationalization involved. If differences in custom, habits of work, manners, and attitudes are a matter of inheritance, then obviously nothing can be done to change the matter and therefore attempts to remedy the condition of minorities are so much sentimental twaddle. If the Negro is by birth half ape, half clown, then more education, better jobs, and decent housing are nonsense. If the Jew is a born egotist, he needs less, not more, of an opportunity to prove himself.

CONFLICT AND ITS DUAL OUTCOME

The power relations between the dominant group and the minority are characterized by continual conflict, whether open or concealed.

On the one hand the dominant group, reinforced by its ethnocentric beliefs, attempts to suppress any and all efforts on the part of the minority to assert itself or to usurp power. On the other hand the minority struggles to make its will felt in society, to challenge and weaken the position of eminence attained by the group with special privilege. In this clash of interests the controlling group develops two modes of response: discrimination and prejudice. The first of these is a behavior pattern, overt and observable. The second is a set of attitudes, beliefs, and accompanying emotions more covert and often quite below the threshold of awareness.

Discrimination may be illustrated by practices such as the restrictive covenant in housing whereby a group of property owners and real estate dealers agree not to sell to Jews, Negroes, Orientals, Mexicans, or other "undesirable elements." This practice is widespread in housing circles though it does not receive any attention in textbooks on economics or political science. Or discrimination may be practiced by college fraternities and sororities that exclude certain minority groups. Or restaurants, hotels, and theaters may train their employees not to admit members of unwanted minorities into their establishments. In the South, these practices reach their culmination in segregation; white and Negro are kept as separate as social communication will admit — with white and colored drinking fountains, white and colored waiting rooms in railroad stations, white and colored coaches on trains, white and colored sections on streetcars, white and colored schools, white and colored churches, white and colored libraries, and so on. Theoretically, discrimination may be practiced without prejudice, as for example in the case of a newcomer into a community who joins the dominant group and acts in Rome "as the Romans do" without sharing the attitudes and feelings of the community but hesitates to break over the lines of discrimination for fear of coming into general disfavor. He may personally fail to share any of the group prejudices, at least to begin with. Gradual habituation to segregating others, however, will eventually have its inevitable effect, and the practices of the society will come to have a normative value so that the proper emotions and feelings are aroused when the folkways are violated. Thus a Northerner who spent five years in the South confessed that after coming back to a northern city he got a rude shock when he saw a white bootblack working over the shoes of a Negro or saw a Negro entering a "white" toilet.

Prejudice, on the other hand, is the psychological component of conflict,[7] which arises when group interest is aroused or threatened. Basically it is a form of ethnocentrism although it may exist in subordinate as well as in ruling groups; it is ethnocentric because it is an expression of group loyalty by which the in-group is elevated through lowering the value judgment on other groups. The real control of social behavior is the opinion of the intimate group to which an individual belongs, and this climate of opinion is as pervasive as the air he breathes. In the conflict of one group with another, it is just as important to have the "right" beliefs as it is to practice the "right" conduct, because both are necessary weapons for rivalry. If a face-to-face group expresses anti-Semitic prejudice and one of its members protests, he is effectively isolated and made to feel a distance between himself and the others.

Popular opinion often sanctions the belief that group prejudice is "natural" in the sense that it is an inherent form of human behavior. This has been clearly disproved by psychological research; children of preschool age play freely with all those of their own age group, regardless of class or color. Personal antipathies of course arise but they are directed against individuals who have obstructed egoistic drives or have had some idiosyncrasy that gave rise to a feeling of dislike. This, however, is not group or cultural prejudice. The latter is learned chiefly by prestige suggestion from teacher, parent, or elder member of the intimate group.

"Mother, Tom says Sam is a Jew. Is he?"

"Yes, he is."

"What are Jews?"

"Well, they are not like other people. You know, they are not Christians."

Innocent and well-meaning as the mother's reply is, she has begun the process of establishing in the child's mind a prejudice or prejudgment that a Jewish boy is "not like other people." Or later she will say, "I wish you wouldn't play with the boys and girls from F Street. They are Jews." The same process may be repeated for Negroes, foreigners, or the "no 'count Smith family." Many prejudices are learned in this fashion, and for this reason they are as natural a part of the mental equipment of the individual as the care and caution with which he avoids automobiles on the street.

One element is nearly always an integral part of prejudice — the stereotype. On the whole the stereotype is a shorthand device for classifying anything whatever. If it is an opinion, a person holding, for instance, the belief that the government should establish new T.V.A.'s might be stereotyped as a radical. Or conversely, one who believes that most taxes should be removed from business after the war would be stereotyped as a fascist.

Our special interest here is the stereotyping of groups. This is done by a rough rule of thumb which has of course some empirical justification. Thus the Negro may be stereotyped as ragged in appearance, rough, loud and boisterous in behavior, or perhaps criminal. Plenty of justification can be found for each of these characterizations in the observation of Negro groups. Only closer acquaintance will show that these rough and ready descriptions are really selective and not representative. The chief quality of the stereotype may therefore be called the technique of pigeonholing, premature generalization, and the economizing of thought. In fact stereotypes are a substitute for genuine thinking about the problem of minorities, either because the data have no interest for the individual or because they are too disturbing. When embedded in prejudice, stereotypes usually take on a derogatory character, as is evidenced by names like "kike," "wop," "hunky," or "nigger." And, most important of all, they obscure individual differences entirely and the person as person becomes a case in the category, a replaceable unit indifferently as good or as bad as any other. Mr. Dohnyani is not a garden enthusiast, a passionate lover of music, a devotee of Molnar, and a skillful politician, but a "hunky." Juan Sanchez is not a warm-hearted and generous friend, an expert with the guitar, the possessor of a rich tenor voice, and the most efficient worker in his community, but a "greaser."

In the social analysis of prejudice and discrimination it becomes clear that neither can be given priority over the other. Both arise by a process of mutual interaction. There are some who believe that prejudice is more often the result of discrimination than discrimination the result of prejudice. This is a thesis that would be difficult to prove, although in areas of well-congealed discrimination and segregation it might be true. With special reference to minority status, however, both prejudice and discrimination are derivatives and protective devices arising from privileged power status which is basically a position of unstable tension and conflict.

THE IDEAL OF OPPORTUNITY AND THE OPEN–CLASS SYSTEM

In addition to the tendencies that make the conflict between groups an irreconcilable one, there has been another element in American life which profoundly influences the social process. We refer to the historical ideology inherited from the French Enlightenment and embodied in the early documents of American history that assert the essential equality of men and the rights derivative from it. The American interpretation of this ideology has been that every individual has a right to develop his potentialities without the interference of class privilege or social partiality, or, to put it into words familiar to all, the right to "life, liberty, and the pursuit of happiness." One of the facts that impress immigrants most profoundly, regardless of the handicaps they have had to overcome, is that in America they do not need to bow the knee or take off the cap to the overlord and that in time they may, with persistence, attain advanced status as a matter of right and not as a matter of special influence or bias. Whatever the actual conditions may have been, America has never given up its official adherence to this ideal pattern, one which James Truslow Adams calls the "American dream" — where each person receives recognition for merit and ability regardless of birth or previous condition of inequality.[8] This ideal, which remained more or less hampered in France by the vestiges of the *ancien régime* and the social habits engendered by it, was reinforced by the peculiar conditions of the American frontier which allowed expansion and consolidation of new population indefinitely for over a hundred years. In spite of the fact that this ideal has given undue emphasis to individualism and to unrestrained competition, it has nevertheless retained much of its original moral connotation.

> To abolish extrinsic inequalities and give each a chance to serve in his own fit way, is undoubtedly the democratic ideal. In politics this is expressed by doing away with hereditary privilege and basing every-

thing on popular suffrage; in education it is seeking an expression quite as vital by striving to open to every one the training to any function for which he may show fitness.[9]

Nor has this been merely an ideal. Under the fluid conditions of American life constant communication, migration, and public enlightenment have churned the people into ever-changing patterns, made possible new and fresh contacts, promoted interchange of ideas and experiences. Under conditions of more settled life class and caste organization develop more firmly; but apart from some eastern and southern areas mobility has been fairly characteristic of American society. Also important is the public school system, which is attended by the overwhelming majority of American children and thus affords an opportunity to mingle with individuals with marked differences in heredity and class status.[10] Our two recent wars have accentuated this shifting of populations with corresponding fluidity of class status. Thus, in spite of the fact that class lines are present and even becoming solidified,[11] there is probably more of an open-class situation in American society than can be found in most countries.[12] This is important because it means that the American ideal has been strengthened by actual empirical observation which shows its translation into actuality. Thus the claim of the underdog to better chances is heard more favorably than, say, in a country like India where caste is so deeply ingrained that the idealistic pronouncements of a leader like Gandhi, impressive though they seemed, met with very little popular response in remedying the lot of the untouchable.

THE VENEER OF IDEAL

The conclusion follows that there is an irreconcilable contradiction between the pure power relations of dominant and minority groups on the one hand and the partly implemented ideal of freedom and equal opportunity for all to which everyone gives partial if grudging allegiance. Gunnar Myrdal has called this "an American dilemma." Historically, however, it has a special significance that is often overlooked. In the growth of Western civilization (including the United States as an end product) group conflict, subordination and superordination, ruler and ruled, privileged group and underprivileged group, or, baldly, pure power relations — all these are hundreds or even thousands of years old. In the words of Max Weber, "Politik ist Kampf" (politics is struggle). It has been only during the last two hundred years that the Western nations, and the United States in particular, have given allegiance to the ideal of freedom and equality. In terms of cultural habits, the practice of granting free opportunity to all is a superficial layer superimposed on the more deeply ingrained habit of group struggle in terms of power. It is almost analogous to the cerebral cortex in the human organism, which has been evolved by nature as a system of control and coordination of deeper-lying involuntary processes. Psychology and physiology show clearly that in times of crisis and emergency, unless that control has been firmly established by continual discipline and practice, the functions of the cortex become subordinated to the glandular and reflex systems. Without wishing to press the analogy too far, we may likewise say that the accumulated cultural habits of thousands of years of reacting to tension and conflict are as yet but imperfectly controlled by a system of ideals so recently developed. The same phenomenon appears in the courts, where a jury will seldom convict a father brought to trial for the murder of a man who raped his daughter. Primitive vengeance is not yet fully displaced by civilized legal processes.

In sum, an individual faced by an emergency is likely to fall back upon emotional habits rather than upon rational ones, and the group will probably react with age-old feelings of self-assertion rather than its more recently acquired stock of brightly shining ideals. It is in the crisis that the group pulls itself together and cries havoc to the outsider. And more often than not the muddle is economic. The Irish who came to the United States in the eighteenth century aroused little or no hostility, but when they turned up by the hundreds of thousands in the late 1840's during the period of temporary decline following the Mexican War boom, anti-Irish feeling arose. These illiterate, poor, half-starved Papists from foreign shores were taking the bread from the mouths of good Americans, and riots broke out against them.[13] Likewise on the West Coast, the Chinese were at first heartily welcomed and put to work in mining camps and on the transcontinental railroads. But in the middle 1870's, after the railroads were finished and a depression set in, the public suddenly discovered that the Chinese were undermining the American standard of living, that they were addicted to awful vices, or simply, in the words of Bret Harte, that "for ways that are dark and for tricks that are vain, the heathen Chinee is peculiar." The Exclusion Act followed. And very much the same cycle was later repeated for the Japanese.

THE GREAT DIVIDE AMONG THE MINORITIES

Returning to the power relations which are the stark reality underlying the status of minorities, we may now take a panoramic view of the problem in the United States. A typology based on power groupings will serve as a guide through the mazes of the problem. To begin with, there are minorities forced into subordination by conquest; [14] this came chronologically first in our history, and the American Indian properly belongs here. Second are the minority groups captured by force and transported for slave labor: the Negro belongs in this category. Third in the list are migrants who are accepted for prudential considerations of various sorts: this class embraces the European, Ibero-American, and Asiatic immigrants.

This, however, gives us only half of the story. If there were no other classification it would be necessary to lump together the Mexican, Japanese, Italian, and Jew as uniform elements in the same problem — which they decidedly are not. Even the novice who considers the difficulty will feel that the first two have something in common which the others do not; and he might want to include the Negro and American Indian as well. In this he would undoubtedly be right: there is a factor of high visibility in these groups due to their racial origins. Precisely what race means is not in question here,[15] but the need for recognizing racial strains as well as power relations is a compelling one if only for the reason that the dominant American[16] public feels more closely related to Poles, Russians, Hungarians, and Yugoslavs than to Negroes, Mexicans, or Japanese Americans. This popular feeling may or may not be mistaken but it must be recognized; and in terms of our future analysis we shall see that it has some scientific justification.

If we accept what the anthropologist tells us about race, we can set up another type of classification which satisfies popular need as well. Taking the four racial minorities having the largest representation in the country, we then arrive at the following outline:

RACIAL MINORITIES

1. The American Indian — by conquest
2. The American Negro — by slavery
3. The Mexican } — by migration
4. The Japanese American } — by migration

The other minorities that deserve examination all belong to the immigrant group, some more and some less assimilated. On the whole the more recent arrivals have found less land and less opportunity awaiting them. It so happens that students of the immigration problem also find that the newcomers that have arrived since 1880 have come more largely from eastern and southern Europe and have met with more linguistic and cultural obstacles in their attempt to become full-fledged Americans. While it will be impossible to describe all these groups, it will make the issue more manageable to treat a selected list of these in order of their size (which does not necessarily mean importance). Choosing the first five as the minorities most likely to be met with in day-to-day relations, we then have in order of size:

THE "NEW IMMIGRATION"

1. Italians
2. Poles
3. Czechs and Slovaks
4. Hungarians
5. Yugoslavs

But the list is not yet complete, for there is another minority which is not racial (though often called a race) and which is not wholly "new immigration," having begun its American history in Colonial times; it cuts across nationality lines and displays a religious difference. At times distinct to the point of divisiveness, at times so indistinct as to be scarcely discernible, this group is yet one of our largest migrant minorities. It is also the world's oldest minority, which has had subordinate status in other countries as well. We refer to the Jews. Although they do not fit into any neat categories, they constitute a source of unbroken interest for the student of social affairs. Any treatment of minority problems that omitted the Jew would miss the focal point of the whole subject.

These, then, are the groups that will receive attention in these pages. They cannot be adequately examined without the aid of the tools and discoveries of social science. When we want to know what the atom is, we turn to the physicist and the chemist and receive an answer as clear as the present state of their knowledge will allow. It will be a premise of this study that no one can know thoroughly what minorities, races, and cultures are until he examines patiently the results of long years of investigation in which anthropologist, sociologist, social psychologist, economist, and historian give their results. Nor can the policies and programs of the future succeed until they are based on the solid discoveries of the social scientist, as bridges and skyscrapers cannot stand without the discoveries of the physicist. We then turn to the first question: what is race?

CHAPTER 2

Facts and Fallacies about Race

WHEN GALILEO, in the seventeenth century, manufactured his own telescope and began to study the heavens, he found that his observations did not agree with the older ideas of astronomy handed down from Aristotle. One day he asked a priest to look for himself and see the evidence that the earth was not the center of the universe; but the priest replied that he had no need to see with the new instrument because the science of astronomy had already been laid down by Aristotle and he therefore knew already what the truth was. Such was the power of tradition that the Copernican idea of the solar system did not penetrate the popular mind until well into the eighteenth century or a hundred years later. After all, everyone could see by looking into the sky that the sun moved around the earth. We may take the opposite for granted today, but not very many would be able to prove it. Most of us are willing, however, to accept the findings of the astronomers and physical scientists without too much opposition.

In the twentieth century, common belief and tradition often stand as far apart from the results of the social sciences as they did from those of the physical sciences in the seventeenth century. Our psychologists tell us that the popular belief is still alive concerning intelligence in people with high foreheads. They have also shown that adults who believed the old legend that intelligent people have high foreheads actually saw persons they thought were intelligent as having high foreheads though measurement showed the exact opposite.[1] Truly we see what our traditions tell us; and if those traditions repeat an error, the public repeats it too. If they are founded on scientific observation, popular belief will follow just as well.

There is, of course, one distinction between the results of the physical and of the social sciences: the former do not often induce the common man to change his opinion about himself and his neighbors or their ways of living together. Hence he can accept them without jarring his thought-habits too much. On the other hand, there is no easy way to escape the feeling that he must alter his conceptions and customs if what the social scientist says be true. And likewise it is easier to examine the social scene for himself without the refined methods developed by research and thus prove to himself that his opinion is equally valid when compared with that of the social investigator. So he may continue to think that men with high foreheads are intelligent because he has seen some of them, even though measurement of several hundreds or thousands of representatives will show that his limited range of observation is misleading him.

It is doubtful whether any set of traditional beliefs in popular thinking is farther removed from the actual empirical data of the social scientists than our racial conceptions. To cite a familiar example: the average American citizen of European descent looks at the Negro and sees that he is of a different color. He reads somewhere that illiteracy and crime are higher among Negroes than among whites. If he is in comfortable circumstances, he has a Negro maid or one of his friends has one; he knows that the girl is simple minded, that stories are told about her morals, and that her family has been on relief. He may work in a concern where Negroes were hired in additional numbers during the war and he therefore has had a chance to hear of or to see many of them who got drunk, bought expensive cars and clothes, and made a lavish display. Now that the war is over, he notes that many of these are right back where they started, with no money, little food, and "filthy" homes. He concludes vaguely, but with conviction, that these Negroes are "just like children" and as a race are incapable of bettering their lot or "living like a white man." This fits in with what his parents have told him — that he must not play with Negro children because they are so dirty and rough or perhaps diseased. Perhaps he has seen an educated Negro once or twice, but of course "there are exceptions to all rules" and the rules remain.

Traditions and experiences of this kind lead to a rough and ready generalization: that there are different races in mankind just as there are different species among animals. Basic to this belief is the inarticulate feeling that different physical characteristics in the various races necessarily cause different attitudes, habits, and degrees of intelligence. Some races are therefore naturally inferior to some others, and the whole thing is really rooted in biological differences. Why or how this is true, our citizen cannot tell, but the notion serves him well as an explanation of the phenomena he actually sees. Take the Jews, now, he says; they aren't exactly inferior in intelligence but they have a peculiar appearance that anybody can spot once he knows them. And they are a greedy, grasping lot who would steal the shirt off a man's back if they had the chance; they have no morals in business at all. If he is asked whether this is due to inheritance, he will probably say it is, even though he may be somewhat doubtful. As for the Mexicans, he can "see" for himself that they are inferior. And the Japs? Well, they are cunning, all right, and shrewd, but they can "live on so much less" than the American that they are a danger and a threat to him in the orchards and farms. And the way those Japs fought! "They are nothing but beasts anyway" so there is no point discussing the matter further. If it isn't a racial trait, what is it?

WHAT RACES ARE

Before classifying the various popular and fallacious theories about race, it will be best to begin bluntly with what the anthropologist says. Not until the individual assimilates scientific conclusions will it be possible to see what is fact and what is fancy in the whole subject.

The anthropologist approaches the problem from both above and below; the view from above may be called a general conception, while the view from below may be termed specific. In the general conception, the anthropologist begins with the biologist's method of classification (sometimes called taxonomy). Thus, just like the biologist classifying animals, he takes the first step:

GENUS: Homo
  SPECIES: Sapiens
    SUBSPECIES: 1, 2, 3, etc.

These subspecies then receive the name of *stocks.* The human species, Homo sapiens, has three main subspecies or stocks known as the Caucasian, Negroid, and Mongolian stocks. Then each of these subspecies has several sub-subspecies.

SUBSPECIES: Caucasian
Sub-subspecies: Nordic, Alpine, Mediterranean, Armenoid, Hindi

SUBSPECIES: Negroid
Sub-subspecies: Nilotic, Forest, Pigmy, Negrito, Oceanic

SUBSPECIES: Mongolian
Sub-subspecies: I. Old World
North Chinese, Malay, Siberian
II. New World
American Indians

In the specific conception, the anthropologist begins with groups that have a homogeneous heritage; i.e., groups that are small and isolated from other groups chiefly by geographical boundaries and that have practiced inbreeding until there is a kind of family resemblance. This genetic group is called the *breed.* There are few examples of this kind left in the world today, but Linton illustrates the type by citing the Cape York Eskimo with something under five hundred persons who have interbred for three hundred years. According to the present hypothesis, many of these breeds who lived close together and began to marry members of other breeds in nearby territory gradually came to resemble each other as well. This gave rise to the type that is now called a *race.* Thus a race, according to the specific conception, is a group of breeds having physical characteristics sufficiently alike so that they can be grouped together into a single type. Race, as defined by this hypothesis, is for all practical purposes identical with the sub-subspecies mentioned above. And finally, a group of races that resemble each other sufficiently would be called *stocks,* the three main ones being, as before, the Caucasian, the Negroid, and the Mongolian. The diagram for the *specific* conception would differ only in its point of reference but in other details would resemble the one presented by the *general* conception above. Hence it would be:

Breeds (genuine biological entities): 1, 2, 3, 4, etc.
Races (groups of similar breeds): Nordic, Alpine, Mediterranean, Armenoid, Hindi
STOCK (a group of similar races): Caucasian

It will now be easy for the reader to follow through the classificatory process with the other stocks. There is, however, one important distinction which belongs to the *specific* conception, and that is that the positing of breeds is at present hypothetical, for none of the pure breeds that make up the races any longer exist. They are inferred entities, and we have good reason for inferring them because of the laws of genetics developed since Mendel.[2]

The question immediately arises: what about the white race, the yellow race, and the black race? The answer is that anthropologists and social scientists in general who are careful of their terminology, never use the terms "black race" or "yellow race" or "white race" because those terms refer more specifically to stocks than to races. Furthermore, it is not entirely accurate to say that the Caucasian stock is composed of white races, because many anthropologists include the Hindi race with the other Caucasian groups, and the Hindi people live in India and have a brown skin. This means that color of skin is less important for the anthropologist, who finds in the Hindi other measurable characteristics very similar to those of the Mediterranean groups. Thus, even though there may be a variant skin color, the other characteristics compel him to call the Hindi a Caucasian race (though it should be explained that this classification does not include all the Indian groups). Nor does the difficulty refer to the Caucasians alone. It is not accurate to call the Mongolian stock the "yellow race," because its color varies from yellow to brown to a kind of copper color among the American Indians. And also among the Caucasians of European descent, color ranges from a light fair skin among the Nordics to a brown or swarthy hue among the Alpines and Mediterraneans. Were the early American colonials more Nordic? Anthropologists do not think so. Dr. Hrdlička of the Smithsonian has made a fairly definitive study of the situation and has come to the conclusion that most early Colonial Americans of European descent were roundheaded and dark.[3] Although the writer knows of no survey of "white" Americans in the United

States, he ventures the opinion that such a study would find far more brunette types than blond. We shall see the significance of this fact later. In the meantime let us emphasize that anthropology knows nothing whatever of "the white race" or "the black race."

It would be false, however, to leave the impression that all the peoples of the world are neatly classified as parts of the three main stocks. A number of groups do not belong clearly to any one of them and therefore must be placed in separate categories. Among these are the Hottentots of Africa (who apparently are not true Negroid people), the Ainu of Japan (a white group who are extremely primitive in culture), the Polynesians of the Pacific (who, even if they are part Mongoloid, have unique characteristics of their own whose origin is obscure), and the Australian bushmen (who resemble a prehistoric type more than they do any modern stock). Although this does not exhaust the list, it includes those that are rated independently by most students of the subject.

CHANGING METHODS IN RACIAL IDENTIFICATION

In the discussion so far, it has been necessary for the sake of clarity and preliminary orientation not to inquire too minutely into one or two terms which must now be examined. For example, reference has been made to "like" or "similar" physical characteristics. It is now important to ask: "like" whom? or "similar" to whom? Do all the students of the subject agree on these features? Here we reach the paradox of scientific research on the question, one which reveals how uncertain the whole question of race really is.

The physical anthropologists of the nineteenth and early twentieth centuries, who were interested in racial measurements, followed the Darwinian conception that a race, like a species, changes very slowly by the process of natural selection in which occasional mutations or changes in the germ plasm appeared, which in turn were either useful or useless in the struggle for existence. Since very few of these occurred in hundreds or even thousands of years, the fixity of racial types was relatively constant. Racial types were then established by making anthropometric measurements of outstanding physical characteristics in a given population and comparing these measurements with those of another. Although the units of measurement were more or less uniform and agreed upon, *the units to be measured were not.* One anthropologist would measure head form, hair form, eye fold, stature, and nose shape. Another would take color of eye, color of skin, head form, hair form, form of face, amount of body hair, lip form, and stature. It is not difficult to understand why they came to different conclusions and turned up with somewhat variant lists of races. Although there was overlapping agreement, there was also a wide area of difference in their conclusions. In fact they came upon the dilemma of all students of nature so neatly stated by Professor C. I. Lewis of Harvard: "The reason why we find nature so simple is not that *she* is simple, but that *we* are simple."

Let us take one illustration for observation. If two anthropologists measured the head form of a group that were medium in shape and neither broad-headed (brachycephalic) nor longheaded (doliocephalic), it would be a question whether the individuals measured were broad-headed members of a narrow-headed race or narrow-headed members of a broad-headed race.[4] The attempt to make nature simple would succeed only by simplifying the answers and silencing questions. Not only did the answers disagree (though they had much in common) but the root difficulty appeared in the further question: which measurements are significant? To this question we have subjective answers, and unavoidably so. The result is that race was what the anthropologist *made* it; his choice of categories determined the result. For a good many physical anthropologists, anthropometric measurements *established* the existence of races; or if the measurements showed a good deal of variability, the results were averaged and the average was called a race. Everyone will recognize the fictional element in this idea; it is much like the "average citizen" or "the man in the street" that one never seems to meet. Montagu calls this method of averaging the characters of a group, stirring them together, and serving them up as a race, the "omelette conception." * [5]

At this point a certain vague uneasiness will undoubtedly arise, and the acute reader can hardly help asking himself: are, then, the races mentioned above on pages 21, 22, and 23 mere construc-

* This is reminiscent of the story about Adam and Eve, who were engaged in the delightful occupation of naming the animals as they went by in procession. "That one's an elephant," said Eve. "How do you know?" asked Adam. "Because it looks like an elephant," ingenuously replied Eve.

tions, figments of imagination, or omelettes? Yes and no. The first list, arrived at as a *general* view, employs chiefly the method of measuring physical characteristics used by the older school of physical anthropologists, with the appreciable difference that it fits in more closely with the biologist's mode of classification of species and subspecies. Those who know their history of biology will recall that older classifications are continually being modified in line with newer knowledge so that, to take one case, a type which was originally classified into three families, seven genera, and seventeen species was eventually assigned to a single species.[6] Science is continually refining its methods, and hence in another ten or fifty years it may be stated that races have a somewhat different position in the taxonomic scale.

However, the second or *specific* classification makes use of a new biological method, that of genetics. The Mendelian principles of genetics tell us that hereditary characteristics are distributed discretely in the germ plasm as unit characters. Thus there is one character for eye color, one for brachydactyly (short-fingeredness), etc. Without going into details of the genetic system, we can say that certain family lines show that specific genes predominate so that a relatively homogeneous set of inheritable characters can be traced. The same is characteristic of inbreeding groups such as the *breed* mentioned above. Linton is correct in saying that the breed is the only genetically homogeneous group in our racial classification. The difficulty is that only the original subdivisions of the human family in their original forms could be called breeds and we no longer know what they were. But if we are faithful to the data furnished by the geneticist, we must at least posit such groups as the true basis for the later, more diversified groupings called races. At the same time, it is only fair to acknowledge with the critics [7] that human breeds are not as homogeneous as animal breeds like terriers, Boston bulldogs, or Newfoundlands. There are no human groups that show such marked uniformity as these, because the same kind of artificial breeding process did not occur.

From the genetic point of view the great fallacy in the idea of the anthropometrist is that his measurable characteristics do not correspond with genetic characters but rather with *aggregates* of these characters. Thus such features as lip form, head shape, hair form, and the like are not due to specific genes (the real units of heredity) but to groupings or combinations of genes. And these combinations are not heritable in regular Mendelian ratios as the unit characters such as eye color, brachydactyly, etc. Until the science of genetics is much further developed than it is at present, it must be admitted that all the measurements of the physical anthropologist refer to the phenotype (observable appearance) rather than to the genotype (genetic constitution of the germ plasm).

There are two other features of racial inheritance that deserve attention if the subject is to be adequately understood. First, migration seems to speed up the process of change in many observable characteristics. Franz Boas should probably be credited with the discovery, for in 1911 he published his now famous report on the changes in bodily form of immigrants and their children in the United States. He found among other factors that the cephalic index (measuring narrow- or broad-headedness) changed appreciably when immigrants were compared with their own children in this country. In general the broad-headed types became more narrow-headed and the narrow-headed groups became more broad-headed, thus tending toward a median position. To make doubly sure, he measured the heads of children born the first year after the parents arrived, then those born the second year, and so on up to the tenth year. The findings were in keeping with the main conclusion, i.e., that those children born later varied more greatly from the original head forms than those born earlier.[8]

Although the scientists were incredulous, Boas' discovery has been verified by similar findings. H. L. Shapiro, comparing (1) Japanese sedentes (residents born in a country) in Japan proper, (2) Japanese immigrants to Hawaii, and (3) Hawaiian-born Japanese of immigrant Japanese parentage, found that the last two groups differed in eighteen out of thirty-five traits, while in fifty traits the male immigrants differ from the sedentes in 73.3 per cent of the measurements and the females in 67.9 per cent of the measurements.[9] In 1943 Marcus Goldstein made a similar study of Mexican immigrants to the United States as compared with the sedentes in Mexico and discovered a considerable increase in stature for the immigrants and their children and a general tendency for most dimensions to increase somewhat.[10]

As yet, the reasons for these modifications are still mysterious: they may exist in climate, diet, or a combination of elements. They do show that inherited types are not fixed but plastic, and that they change far more rapidly than the older anthropology allowed for.*

A second factor that makes for continual racial change is the interbreeding or crossbreeding of types that occurs with migration. The history of the world is a history of alternate migrations. The Mongolians moved from central Asia as far as lower China on the east and as far as Russia and Hungary on the west. Negroid groups crossed to many islands of the South Seas. Arabians mixed with the Africans and carried their conquests as far as Spain. Turks and western Asiatics invaded eastern Europe. A number of Malays crossed to Madagascar and mixed with the population there. Since the discovery of America, mixture of Indian, Spanish, French, some Anglo-Saxon, and Negro has constantly been taking place. These instances could be multiplied manyfold. When crossbreeding continues for several hundred years, totally new racial types may be evolved, which in turn may be mistaken for "pure" types by the uninitiated.[11] Not only does this crossbreeding make for continual modification of types but in the face of all these wanderings and shiftings of population no one can any longer assert that racial "purity" exists unless it be in a few isolated geographical areas. And it would be difficult, if not impossible, to find any Caucasian groups of this nature.

For the most part, the results of constant intercrossing are not so well known as they should be. If one hundred Mediterranean males and an equal number of Mediterranean females were inbred

* This variability must not be regarded as absolute, for there are natural limits to it, as both Goldstein and Boas point out (Goldstein, *op. cit.*, pp. 21–22). Montagu is so impressed with the flexibility of types that he wants to give up the term "race" altogether since for him a race is only a "temporary mixture" of genetic traits (Note 5, *op. cit.*, p. 40). He, together with Huxley and Haddon, prefers to drop the term "race" altogether and substitute for it the designation "ethnic group." (Montagu, *op. cit.*, p. 43; Julian S. Huxley and A. C. Haddon: *We Europeans*, New York, Harper, 1936, p. 83.) However, until the term "temporary" is more carefully defined, it will probably be more intelligible to keep the older word "race" with the qualifications already urged. It is probably Utopian to think that it will disappear in the near future. That the term "race" is needed may be seen from the fact that Montagu continues to employ it, though always bracketed with quotation marks.

today, there is more than a probability that their offspring would contain what appeared to be "pure" Alpine types.[12] With intermarriage of two relatively pure strains for as much as three hundred years, there would not be a single individual of either "pure" type left.[13] There is a common opinion that Africa is populated by "pure" Negroes or a genuinely Negroid stock. This is false. Most native Africans have some admixture of Caucasian genetic strains, having received them from Hamitic groups which are related to the Mediterranean. Conversely most peoples living around the Mediterranean Sea (including the large European population) have some components of Negroid heritage.[14] Furthermore, the Negro population of the United States is even less pure than that of Africa, for Herskovits found, in a sample of 1652 which he examined, that only 22 per cent were entirely unmixed Negro and others showed admixture of Indian or white (Caucasian) characteristics. This finding has been corroborated by studies of Hrdlička, C. S. Johnson, and E. A. Hooton.[15] And since miscegenation (race crossing) has been a common feature of American life, with many light-skinned mulattoes constantly "passing" into the white group, no one knows how "pure" the Caucasian strains in American life are. Lyle Owen raises the question in its most poignant form by proving that by counting back twenty generations every person would have something like a million grandparents.[16] In tracing lineages, the proud inhabitant of Boston or Charleston follows up only a single line in this total background; but though this may be allowed by the genealogical tables, biology does not permit such a narrow selection. All peoples in the stream of civilization are related to some degree.

The history of race differentiation throughout the world can be reconstructed somewhat upon these lines: prehistoric man belonged to a single species, and his similarities were such that he could interbreed with any other sort of man. In this sense the fundamental unity of mankind is a basic postulate. At the same time early man probably had, in various parts of the globe, different colors of skin and possibly of hair; [17] it seems likely that he began with only two of the present blood-groupings, namely, O and AB.[18] This primitive group had a somewhat diversified genetic constitution which later became separated into more distinct strains as groups migrated to different areas and became subject to the effect of isolation by constant geographical separation from their fellows. The more these plural groups were divided and the longer their history of segregation from each other, the more inbreeding took place. Thus plural breeds appeared. These breeds were subject not only to genetic but also to geographical influence, so that those in tropical countries developed through natural selection a darker protective skin coloration. New blood groupings appeared, A as a mutation, probably in western Europe, and B as a variant mutation in eastern Asia.[19] As we know from our knowledge of animal breeding, once a definite genetic mixture takes place, it can never be reversed except by the artificial methods of the stockbreeder. It is therefore natural to assume that these breed types became relatively fixed until conquest and increased migration began the process of admixture. In this process the breeds closest to each other would then show the results of miscegenation, and the coming of large empires and civilizations tended to increase this mixture until population over wider areas showed many likenesses. Thus the stocks began to show certain fundamental or at least phenotypical resemblances that served to set them off from other stocks. When civilizations and empires came into conflict with each other on a wider scale, the mutual crossing became more pronounced and the stocks then began to show the effects of mixture to such an extent that many of the finer distinctions were lost and the relatively clear-cut differences became blurred, especially in the areas where culture contact was greatest. This is the stage man has reached today. In the meanwhile such has been the crossing and intercrossing of types that all blood groups are found in all populations, though differing somewhat in percentage.[20] The process toward unity is therefore intensified.

THE SO-CALLED JEWISH RACE

Because of the popular misconceptions about Jews, it will now be significant to inquire into their heritage. Not only many gentiles but many Jews as well refer to the Jewish people as the "Jewish race." Undoubtedly this idea is based on an established fact, namely, the endogamous nature of Jewish marriage practice (tendency to marry within the group). It is well known both to the public and to students of the subject that Jewish parents bring considerable pressure on their children to prevent them from marrying gentiles.

This practice, carried on for centuries, would certainly tend to fix a "Jewish type," one which many people believe they can identify on sight. It is supposed to be distinguished by such marks as a prominent, usually convex or "hooked" nose; dark and oily skin; black hair, sometimes wavy; and a rather narrow jaw. The composite of these characters gives an individual the "Jewish look" which in popular opinion enables him to be discerned at a glance. Is this impression based on fact or is it, like the belief about high foreheads, based on tradition regardless of fact?

To begin with the nose, which is the center of argument as well as of the face, let us start with the assumption that a convex nose with somewhat flattened tip is found in large numbers in the Jewish population. How would it be possible to account for this? Professor Coon of Harvard advances the idea that the interbreeding of Nordic and Alpine with eastern Mediterranean traits brought in from Palestine helped to establish a new strain, one characteristic of which would be the convex nose of the modern Jew.[21] If we accept this thesis, the Jewish nose is due to a *crossing* of racial strains and not to "racial purity." On the other hand, we know that the Jewish people were not endogamous before the Babylonian captivity in the sixth century B.C. Before this time the Hebrews were not people of pure ancestry, having intermarried with the peoples of Canaan and the regions farther north. Ezekiel, accusing his people after the Exile of being somewhat promiscuous, doubtless spoke the truth when he said, "Thy mother was a Hittite and thy father an Amorite." * This statement is interesting to us today because scholars believe the Hittite belonged to an Armenoid group, and one of the special characteristics of the Armenoid strain was the presence of a convex nose flattened at the tip and tied to the forehead in a straight line. This nose can be seen in many Armenians and some Turks of today. Even if we accept this hypothesis, the result is the same: the Jewish people received their nasal characteristics because of intercrossing and not through inbreeding.[22] If there is such a thing as a Jewish nose, it is not Jewish at all but definitely due to a mingling with other strains. And it is worthy of mention that Melville Jacobs, another anthropologist who has made a serious study

* Ezekiel 16:45.

of the problem, declares that there are more Caucasian gentiles who have convex noses of the "Jewish" type than Caucasian Jews.[23]

The term "Caucasian Jew" should be used in our culture because we rarely see other types. But there are Chinese Jews, Ethiopian Jews, and in fact Jews of many racial strains. Originally the group was Semitic and therefore was Mediterranean with probably Armenoid mixture, and therefore Caucasian. In Europe the two main types are the Ashkenazim or eastern European Jew and the Sephardim who took up their residence in Spain in the eleventh century. There is some evidence that before the Crusades there was much more intermixture of Jew and gentile in northern Europe than during the ghetto period of the Middle Ages and that this continued again after the eighteenth century. Today there are so many variations in measurable characteristics between Jews of northern and eastern Europe, the Caucasus, north Africa, and Arabia that they certainly have no racial identity.[24] In general the Sephardic types are darker of skin and eyes than the Ashkenazim because of Moorish intermixture, while the Jews of the Caucasus have predominantly round heads and the Arabian Jews long heads. In parts of Germany as much as half the Jewish population have blue eyes and appear as fair as their neighbors.[25] For the most part the height of Jews in western Europe and England is greater than among those of Poland, Russia, and the East[26] — a difference which nutritionists will probably ascribe to diet.

At all events, the conclusion seems inescapable that the Jews are not a race in any sense of the term. Even Coon, who believes that the Ashkenazim show distinctive characteristics that are identifiable, refuses to use the term "race" with respect to them any more than he would use it for the English or the French.[27] Of course many of the Jews show similarity in certain features because of endogamous practice, but the same tendency exists in other groups like the southern Italians. It is therefore more proper to speak of the Jews as a people or a cultural group, for it is their social rather than their biological heredity that is distinctive. This will become clear in the section under Chapter 16.

GENERAL CONCLUSIONS

Summarizing the results of our brief survey, we may then conclude:

(1) There are no "pure" races in any civilized country today.[28] Migrations and the mixing of peoples have modified the genetic structure of European, Asiatic, and African peoples to such an extent that even relative fixity of type becomes increasingly difficult to establish as time goes on.

(2) Because of the very nature of his task, the anthropologist can only posit races as hypothetical constructs which are necessary points of reference. He may assume the earlier existence of breeds as a necessary step in his historical argument, but those breeds no longer exist. The more pronounced differences found by the anthropologist are in the stocks — Caucasian, Negroid, and Mongolian — and henceforth in this volume when we speak of racial differences, it will be chiefly those between stocks that are referred to. Since we are mainly concerned with four groups in the American scene where these differences play a visibility role and make them identifiable as minority groups, we shall refer to them as our racial minorities — the Indian, the American Negro, the Mexican American, and the Japanese American. But whenever a common term is needed which applies to these and other smaller groups within the United States, we shall then employ the concept "ethnic group" or "minority." The context should make clear what is meant.

(3) Most of the common or popular ideas of race which are given currency in everyday conversation refer to factors that are not specifically racial. It is inadmissible to refer to the inhabitants of any country or nation as a race. Hence there is no Chinese, British, or French race. People who speak the same language do not form a racial identity either; and therefore it is incorrect to refer to the "Aryan" or "Latin" race or races. Relatively homogeneous peoples (e.g., the Jews) who have a different religion and culture from the great majority of United States citizens cannot be spoken of as a race. Nor is there any hypothetical pure race which has been spoiled by intermixture, as the Germanic, Nordic, or Aryan hypothesis takes for granted.[29] It is equally false to speak of physical types such as the Arab, Irish, or Spanish which are supposedly recognizable, as races. And while color classifications have a limited validity within

the narrow confines of the United States, so that the stocks may be partially separated on this basis, it would be false to judge race by this criterion alone. We have already seen that the Hindi race is brown but belongs to the same stock as the Caucasian. Furthermore, the various Negro-white mixtures within the United States to be found in the mulattoes depend largely on social definition. It is one of the peculiar irrationalities of American tradition that even the lighter-colored mulattoes are classified with the Negro population, whereas biologically they are far more white or Caucasian than they are Negro. In South Africa, where the white population is in the minority, the social definition is very different.

(4) The real difference between groups — and the one which has the most social relevance — is the history, culture, and life habits that have resulted from living as a distinct entity. Any infant born anywhere on the globe has the potentialities for becoming a member of any culture. Fung Kwok Keung, for example, was born of American Caucasian parents who deserted him at the age of three. He was then adopted by a Chinese family who went back to China and remained there till the boy was nineteen. At that age he returned to the United States, where he had some difficulty in adjusting himself because his language, attitudes, customs, and habits were Chinese. It came as a considerable shock to the Americans who met him that he should have "white" features and yet be unable to communicate with them. Finally he entered an Americanization class and began learning English with other foreigners; the difference between him and native white Americans was not in racial but in cultural characteristics.[30] It is the fundamental thesis of social science today that social inheritance plays the primary role in distinguishing groups from each other and that racial differences are of little or no importance *unless they are so defined by the society*.

For instance, South Africa has three population elements: whites (Caucasians), "colored" (mixed Negro and Caucasian), and native blacks or Negroes. There is a marked distinction between the "colored" and the subordinate native groups, since the former have full legal equality with whites. It happens that the black or Negro population constitutes three fourths of the whole, and so the whites are glad to have allies in maintaining their precarious dominance.

Though some of the "colored" are more Negroid than Caucasian, their biological difference is annulled by the legal definition which gives them a position of social eminence.

In the United States the principle is reversed. Though from a biological point of view a person may be so dominantly Caucasian as to show practically no Negroid features, he is socially defined as a Negro if it is known that he has the slightest trace of Negro ancestry. This is the whole point of such books as Sinclair Lewis's *Kingsblood Royal* in which a "white" person discovers traces of Negroid heritage, or William L. White's *Lost Boundaries* where a mulatto family "passes" unnoticed for white over several decades. In both cases the status of the characters changed entirely when the social situation was redefined. In the United States it is advantageous for the mulatto to have the scientific conception of race more widely accepted. His status will be raised with the general realization that he is more Caucasian than Negro.

Another example would be the "pure Spanish" of the Southwest, who are a variable mixture of Spanish and Mexican-Indian elements. As long as the Anglo community define them as having complete Spanish ancestry, they participate fully in all phases of American life. On the other hand, the Spanish American is perhaps less interested in having the scientific view of race prevail, since this would raise many admittedly mestizo (mixture of Spanish and Indian) individuals to the same social status with himself.

The scientific concept of race may be regarded as having two levels: the first is the definition of race characteristics, and the second is the social implication or meaning of race differences. The crucial factors in the second level appear most prominently in the phenomena of race mixture and the realities of social status. Popular views also follow this double pattern as shown in the table on page 36.

If the acceptance of (1) cancels out (4), it then becomes possible for (2) to cancel out (5), though in practice this does not always follow. If (4) and (5) are altered as the result of accepting (1) and (2), the mulatto and the Spanish American would have a different status in society still thinking in terms of (6). Until (3) is accepted, however, (1) and (2) by themselves will have little effect upon (6). For without (3) it is still possible, for example, to define the mulatto as legally equal to the Caucasian and yet segregate the socially "inferior" Negroes. This is precisely what occurs in the case of the mulattoes ("colored") of South Africa.

	SCIENTIFIC	POPULAR
Definition	Racial characters determined by measurement or genetic ancestry (1)	Race determined by striking differential appearance or by "blood" (4)
Borderline cases	If more that half the measurements or genetic characters belong to one race, the individual is assigned to that race (2)	Arbitrary assignment to one race or another, depending on power relations in society. "Mixed breeds" usually defined as lower, but not always (5)
Status	No biological inferiority (3)	Some races inherently inferior to others. They must therefore occupy a lower hierarchical status (6)

In "race relations" or the "race problem" the sociologist is dealing with population units as defined by popular ideology and social contacts in terms of commonly accepted beliefs. The Negroes of the United States are not a race in the anthropologist's meaning of the term. Nor are the Mexicans, nor many Indians and Japanese Americans, who are partly or largely Caucasian. However, the differences between these groups *as a whole* and the dominant Caucasian majority are sufficient so that, for sociological purposes, they can be conveniently classified as "racial minorities." * At the same time, the Jews are eminently Caucasian, and for this reason are not treated as a racial group here, whatever the popular connotation may be.

The problem of inferiority and superiority cannot be understood apart from a discussion of cultural conditioning and its differential effects. It is therefore time to consider this phenomenon, which will occupy the next chapter in detail.

* For an able discussion of this point, see E. B. Reuter, *The American Race Problem*, New York, Crowell, 1938, chap. 2, "Race as a Sociological Concept."

[CHAPTER 3]

Race and Culture

GRACE W. WAS DOING such poor school work that her teacher finally referred her to a psychologist for testing; she failed every one of her subjects except spelling and penmanship, raising the question whether she ought to be kept with the other children in her grade. As the teacher expected, the test came back marked "feeble minded," so Grace was transferred to the "opportunity room" where an ungraded class carried on special work. Here she showed many of the same traits that appeared in her regular class — indifference, failure to answer questions, humorless and stiff behavior, lack of attention, no socializing with the other children, and generally inferior work except for spelling and penmanship. Grace's consistency in keeping up with these two subjects gradually led her new teacher to wonder whether the girl was really feeble minded after all. It soon became obvious that Grace showed signs of panic whenever arithmetic problems appeared, for she refused even to try them.

One day when the teacher conducted a class in arithmetic, she left several arrangements on the board for subtracting, remarking about one of them that it was old fashioned but still usable. She told the class that they could use any arrangement they liked, provided they got the right answers. To her surprise, Grace got to her feet and came up to the blackboard with the timid question, "Could I do that?" "Of course," said the teacher, "if you want to." Grace started to tremble and dropped the chalk but the teacher helped her start on the problem, which Grace finally solved successfully. After it was over, the child went to pieces and sobbed in the teacher's arms saying, "That's the way I did it when daddy showed me but Miss Jones [her former teacher] said I was crazy."

Finally Grace's story came out. She had been sick two years previously when the children were learning to add, and was forced to stay out of school until nearly the end of the year. Then she was promoted with her class before she learned how to subtract. When she ran into difficulty in the sixth grade, Grace asked for her father's help and used the antiquated method he taught her. As a result the teacher derided her before the class and sent her back to her seat in shame. Having a sensitive nature, she began to withdraw more and more from those around her and to give decreasing attention to her studies until the teacher thought her stupid. When given an intelligence test she was unwilling to cooperate with the psychologist and made such an inferior grade that he classified her as feeble minded and sent her to the opportunity room. Fortunately, after her story was known, the teacher kept encouraging her until she was doing normal work again and finally finished grammar school with good grades.[1]

Here is a not uncommon situation where the teacher gave a routine judgment that a girl lacked intelligence because she could not pass her subjects. The intelligence test confirmed the diagnosis, and the child was removed from her grade. So far the whole matter was settled by an appeal to the facts in the case, and everyone was satisfied with the evidence. Yet the conclusions were false. This would never have been discovered without the later accidental revelation of neglected evidence in the child's social history. Instances of this kind have led to increasing caution on the part of social psychologists to pronounce hasty judgments on intelligence without some knowledge of the social and cultural factors involved.* Thus the terms "social feeble-mindedness" or "social retardation" have come into more general use in doubtful cases.

To clarify the picture, what made Grace appear inferior to her colleagues? *First*, she missed some of her necessary training because of conditions beyond her control (illness); *second*, she received a severe shock when the teacher defined her as "different"; *third*,

* By "culture" the anthropologist means the socially acquired habits, skills, and attitudes, together with their material embodiments in tools, artifacts, buildings, etc. For a good discussion see Clyde Kluckhohn and William H. Kelly, "The Concept of Culture" in *The Science of Man and the World Crisis*, ed. by Ralph Linton, New York, Columbia University Press, 1945.

she developed laziness and slipshod work by reason of indifference to school accomplishment; *fourth*, she failed on the intelligence test because of her negative attitude and previous slackening of study habits; *fifth*, the school authorities officially established her feeble-minded status and placed her in the ungraded room; *sixth*, her own reaction to the official verdict led to even more unintelligent behavior. Notice that these items are listed in chronological order of their appearance. That is because all the important evidence is available. *But suppose it is not available* and steps 1 and 2 are lacking. Working at the problem from the other end, an observer could see that her behavior in the opportunity room was unintelligent, that she was classed as feeble minded by school authorities, that she failed to pass the intelligence test with a normal score, and that she did low-grade work in her sixth-grade class. These are all visible items open to inspection and constitute what might be called the outer layer of the problem. Popular thinking, and even that of the unwary psychologist, rarely goes beyond this point.

In the final analysis, then, there are three levels in the determination of intelligence. The first of these is manifest behavior or what the individual actually does in the way of accomplishment. This can be tested and measured so that exact knowledge of it is possible; it changes from stage to stage as the individual matures and hence it will show variation. The second level is that of modifying experiences such as the subject will have in family, school, and group membership and in the cultural variations which he learns from his elders as well as those of his own age. This cannot be measured statistically but only related in a kind of narrative; yet it serves as a necessary check or interpretation of the manifest behavior and helps to make it intelligible. When the modifying experiences are known, the manifest behavior appears as an end product and not simply as a raw fact. The final level has to do with the innate factors of the individual or his capacities and potentialities. Intelligence is a person's native capacity to solve problems with unfamiliar elements. Strictly speaking, this cannot be measured but can only be inferred from accomplishment, taking into account the cultural experience. It now becomes apparent that the most serious error will be to infer the innate factors from the manifest behavior alone. This is precisely why Grace's teachers judged her wrongly: they had failed to take into account the modifying experiences, or the social history. The conclusion is inescapable that *intelligence testing cannot be accepted at its face value until the social and cultural background is used to interpret it.* With this principle firmly in mind, let us now turn to a comparative study of race psychology.

EARLY TESTING OF RACIAL INTELLIGENCE

During the first World War a group of psychologists devised an intelligence test which was given to nearly two million recruits in the American army. This test (known as the Army Alpha) revealed that the Negro draftees showed a consistently lower score when their average was compared with that of the whites. As many as 85 per cent of the Negroes were below the average intelligence of white soldiers when measured by Army Alpha. On the whole this result was in line with general opinion and served to confirm the belief that whites had innate superiority to Negroes in native intelligence. At the time many if not most American psychologists accepted the findings without further questions; one of them, C. C. Brigham, stated on the basis of Army Alpha scores that the average Negro child would be unable to go through a regular grammar school curriculum with a white child and keep up.[2] Similar statements were made by many other psychologists familiar with the test; but since these judgments confirmed the usual belief in Negro inferiority, they served only to put the stamp of scientific authority on it.

Before long, however, the critics set to work. They pointed out that the score of northern Negroes was very much higher than that of southern Negroes; in fact there were six times as many northern as southern Negroes in the A or highest ranking group and considerably less than half as many in the D minus or lowest ranking group. If the test measured only native intelligence, it would be hard to explain why northern Negroes were so superior to those below the Mason and Dixon Line. Beginning a search for the modifying experiences, they suggested that the number of years in school would have considerable influence, especially since the Alpha test was given to literates only. The southern agricultural Negro often attended school only from four to seven months a year as compared with the regular nine months' term of the Negro in northern cities.

Furthermore a greater number of Negroes on the plantation necessarily dropped out of school early to work in the cotton fields and this would mean that they did not retain even as much as they had learned. It began to appear that Army Alpha was more a test of the learning of linguistic items in school than a measurement of innate intelligence.

This is precisely what might be expected on the basis of the previous analysis, for the error of initial acceptance lay in inferring innate factors from manifest behavior, without any interpretation based on the modifying experiences. However, the critics went much farther. Taking the median scores of northern Negroes and comparing them with those of southern whites, they found that the Negroes of New York were 3.5 points higher than the whites of Kentucky, the Negroes of Illinois were 5.2 higher than the whites of Arkansas, and the Negroes of Ohio 7.38 points higher than the whites of Georgia.[3] Clearly the race differentials disappear and are even reversed when the school environment is changed for the better. When confronted with this type of evidence, Professor Brigham examined the whole problem again and set an example of scientific honesty for other researchers in the field by concluding that his earlier results were without scientific foundation.[4] On the whole most of those engaged in comparative testing have now reached substantially the same conclusion, that it is incorrect to make comparisons unless the social and environmental differences are as nearly identical as possible.*

Further evidence comes from the experience of World War II, where two different lines of investigation confirm the same conclusion. Using the Army General Classification Test which replaced the old Alpha and Beta, psychologists discovered that Negroes had larger numbers in grades IV and V, which are at the lower end of the curve; at the same time they noticed that the Army units which had the largest number of whites in grades I and II also had the largest number of Negroes in the same grades, while those with the largest

* Similar conclusions appear for the Army Beta scores which were not based on linguistic items but on performance tests for illiterate and foreign groups. These scores are likewise significantly related both to Alpha levels and to differential expenditures for education in northern and southern areas. See F. L. Marcuse and M. E. Bitterman, "Notes on the Results of Army Intelligence Testing in World War I," *Science* 104:231–2, September 6, 1946.

number of whites in grades IV and V also had the largest number of Negroes in those grades. This was apparently due to geographical distribution in terms of better schooling for the first and less adequate schooling for the second.[5]

The other evidence comes from the teaching of illiterates from both ethnic groups in the army. Here the special methods of instruction enabled illiterates to attain the equivalent of the fourth grade level in about eight weeks' time; at the end of this period, the soldier was either transferred to another unit for regular training or discharged because of inability to keep the pace. Among the whites 84.2 per cent continued with basic military training while 15.8 per cent were discharged; the Negro record was 87.1 per cent who left special training for the regular, while 12.9 per cent were discharged. Thus the learning ability or educability of the Negro was even slightly higher than that of the whites who took the same course. Many psychologists believe that the ability to learn new materials is a more adequate test of intelligence than any other, and on this basis the Negro makes an excellent showing. Even though the group samples were not exactly equal, they show that learning ability is approximately the same in the two groups.[6]

THE ROVING I.Q.

The question then arises: was not the Army Alpha test very inadequate in determining intelligence? If it were possible to use a more standardized test like the Stanford-Binet, would it not be possible to show that the I.Q. remained constant and was unaffected by environmental conditions? If this could be proved, then it would be possible, with more refined methods, to fix the relative intelligence of racial groups.

Without going into detail on the whole thorny issue, research in the field throws some doubt on the fixity of the I.Q. Bertha Wellman and her associates at the University of Iowa made a study of the records of 652 children before and after training in the Iowa preschool kindergarten. The mean initial I.Q. of these children before any training was given was 116.9; after training in the preschool environment the retest showed a mean of 123.5, a gain of 6.6 points. Another group of 232 young children were tested before and after admittance to an orphanage where they had an unfavorable environment such as recreation, play, and other organized activities under the supervision of untrained individuals, and an educational program that was quite unplanned. After retest, this group showed a pronounced trend toward lower borderline or even feeble-minded intelligence. Another group who had been equal before testing but were given preschool training while the others were in the orphanage, gave a quite superior pattern of growth.* Reymert and Hinton tried similar testing on a group of children who were transferred from poor home environments to the Mooseheart Institution for children in Illinois. Although they found no significant differences for the group as a whole, they discovered, when they separated them into age groupings, that the children six years of age or younger made very important gains in intelligence and the others above that age showed very little difference.[7] Burks found that in the more extreme cases a change from an exceptionally poor to a very good environment could raise the I.Q. as much as twenty points.[8] The main conclusion appears to be that the I.Q. can be changed either for better or for worse during the most formative years, say from three to six, and after that time intelligence seems to be more constant. During this period, differences in environment are truly crucial. As Read Bain so convincingly puts it, we may not make a silk purse out of a sow's ear, but we make many sow's ears out of "potential" silk purses and we do it all the time.[9]

In view of these results it is abundantly clear that comparisons of racial intelligence on the basis of testing would be unfair unless environmental backgrounds were matched, especially during the early formative years of childhood before schooling took place. In all the literature on the subject it is practically impossible to find any crucial experiment of this sort and we must therefore conclude that proof of inherent difference on this basis has yet to be made.

ARE MIGRANTS TO THE CITY MORE INTELLIGENT?

It is widely believed that rural dwellers who migrate to the city are those with the most initiative, ambition, and desire to improve themselves and hence are likely to be more intelligent than the

* While criticism of Wellman's results shows that they must be qualified, the studies of Reymert, Hinton, and Burks here noted give enough cumulative evidence to make the variability of I.Q. probable.

country dwellers who stay at home. If this were true, it would be relatively easy to explain the superior showing made by Negroes in northern cities and to show that they were exceptional rather than average in ability. The powerful attraction of the city would single out keen and sharp-witted individuals and leave the dull and stolid at home. Migration would therefore be a selective process.

Actual studies of migration give conflicting evidence on this point. When school records or educational advancement were used as indexes, Gee and Corson in Virginia and Gist, Pihlblad, and Gregory in Missouri found that rural migrants to the city showed a definite superiority of several points over the children who remained at home.[10] Since many children accomplish much less in school than they are able to do, this proves nothing about their native intelligence. Gist and Clark, however, used actual intelligence test scores in the schools (rural high schools) and then ascertained which individuals had migrated to cities and which ones had remained at home. The migrants had an average of four points higher in general intelligence than the group who remained in the country or rural villages. But the authors say quite emphatically that this does not measure inherent differences but rather the influence of home environments or such traits as attitudes, values, ambitions, and special interests that could be satisfied better in urban surroundings.[11] They also point out that even if this were a proof of selective migration in Kansas (which was the area studied), it would not necessarily show that it occurred in other areas. In fact, Sorokin and Zimmerman have shown that for the Minnesota area, it is the home-owning class on the farms that remains in the country and there might be some presumption that they are of higher intelligence because when their children *do* occasionally migrate to the cities, they rise more rapidly in the social scale.[12] Yet the Sorokin and Zimmerman studies do not actually prove that the more intelligent remain at home, either; they only show that there is some presumption that they do so in the Minnesota area.

The evidence becomes somewhat clearer in studies made of rural school children in New York, New Jersey, and Connecticut, for it was found that some of these rural schools employed intelligence tests to rank the children. Investigators then discovered a number of these pupils who had migrated to nearby cities; their score did not show any appreciable superiority over that of the children who remained at home.[13] To come closer to our problem, Klineberg reports on rural Negro children who changed their residences to New Orleans, Nashville, and Atlanta. By giving them the National Intelligence Test, it was discovered that their scores improved in proportion to the years they lived in these cities — from an average of 38.3 for those with residence of a year to 68.7 for those who had lived in urban homes seven or more years.[14] This shows that hereditary traits have little significance in the comparison of migrants and the stay-at-homes but that cultural and environmental changes make a tremendous difference.

This conclusion is reinforced by Klineberg's study in New York. He gave a set of intelligence tests, both linguistic and performance types, to 3000 southern-born Negro children in the Harlem schools of New York City and compared their scores with northern-born Negro children of comparable social and economic status in the same grades. These children were also grouped in terms of their length of residence in New York — the first group with a one-year residence; the second, a two-year residence; and so on. The result was that the children showed improvement in I.Q. scores which correlated almost exactly with their stay in the northern city. On the Binet test, the children who had been in New York one year showed a mean score of 81.4 while those who remained from three to four years showed a mean score of 88.5. With the National Intelligence Test the average score showed the same tendency, and significantly most of the improvement took place in the first five or six years. *Whatever difference could be measured was due chiefly to cultural changes.*[15]

THE TESTED GROUPS: ARE THEY TYPICAL?

One of the pitfalls obstructing investigation of racial intelligence is the choice of samples taken for testing. If the student of the problem selects a group because it will serve conveniently for purposes of his aims, he may fail to ascertain whether it is composed of exceptional individuals or whether it is truly representative of the racial or ethnic group as a whole. For example, in the case mentioned above on page 41, it is not difficult to show that some Negroes are superior to whites if the Negro sample is taken from those states which have better schooling and where the Negro is given comparatively equal opportunity in school work and if on the other hand the white group chosen for comparison is taken from areas where there is a dual school system and therefore whites receive less in the total of expenditure per child. Much has been made of the low school budgets for Negroes in the South, and there is no denying the figures; but few have pointed out that the southern whites also fall far below the national average, partly as a result of keeping up two separate school systems. The national average expenditure per school child was $74 in 1935–1936; the average for southern whites in ten states was $49.30 and for southern Negroes $17.04. Thus compared with the national average, the southern white is a selected group as well as the southern Negro. On the other hand the average in such states as New York and California was well above the national average, running $115 or higher.[16] Children from schools in these states would also be a select group; so much so that five hundred Negro elementary school children tested in Los Angeles obtained a medial I.Q. of 104.7, which was somewhat higher than the white children with whom they were compared.[17] Yet no one would conclude that Negro children as a whole had higher intelligence than white children because of this selected sample.

The same principle applied to other ethnic groups. For example, the Army Alpha test showed immigrants from northern Europe to be superior in intelligence to Italians from southern Europe. Yet those who have studied the immigration problem thoroughly make it quite clear that the German and the Italian migrants do not come from the same social strata in their home communities abroad but that there are many more Italians from the peasant and day-laborer class in Europe,[18] which would mean a correspondingly meager opportunity for schooling and literacy. On the whole many of the immigrant groups are quite atypical samples of the national peoples they represent.[19] An unprejudiced study of racial types in Europe shows that there is no clear superiority of one over another but there is marked superiority of urban over rural types when given intelligence tests.[20] And while it was true that Danish girls in Racine were superior to Italian girls in New York, little or no difference was found between Danish girls in Copenhagen and Italian girls in Rome.[21] This reinforces our principle that background factors must be equated or else the atypical character of a tested group will give striking results that are really due to the sample.

ATMOSPHERE OF THE TEST

Anyone who has ever taken a test will admit that the personality and attitude of the investigator will influence the result considerably; he may awaken special interest or simply pursue his objective doggedly but with no exercise of the imagination. The individuals being tested may be aroused to extraordinary effort or they may show listlessness and go through their tasks perfunctorily. The tester may explain well or poorly, may put his hearers in a receptive mood, or may presuppose a lot of knowledge they do not have. Because of his unfamiliarity with the group and its ways of thinking, he may unwittingly take for granted a type of response which is quite foreign to them. Among the Australian blacks, one such investigator was taken aback because they expected him to help them with the answers; it was always their habit to help each other when in difficulty, and if one man knew something which another did not, the first man always helped the second. They naturally felt that Porteus (who was giving them a problem to solve) should give them as much aid as possible. Likewise while Klineberg was investigating the behavior of the Dakota Indians, he discovered that it was considered impolite for anyone to tell his knowledge in the presence of someone who was ignorant of it; this would tend to "show up" the ignorant man and so it was tactfully avoided. The result on intelligence testing is obvious. Similarly with those Indians who have the habit of doing unfamiliar tasks slowly and with thoroughness, they quite fail to respond to anyone who tells them to finish their test as quickly as possible.[22] The attitude toward speed in their culture is quite at variance with the accelerated American tempo of urban life.

The very unfamiliarity of the stranger who comes into a neighborhood to test a group whom he does not know and who may be of a different race, nationality, or culture, often sets up an invisible obstruction to good results. Let the reader, if he belongs to the dominant white group in the United States, ask himself how well he might respond to such a test if it were supervised by an American Indian, a Japanese, or a Negro. Or as Linton imagines the situation, let him picture himself writing Chinese characters with Chinese writing instruments, timed by a Chinese psychologist with a stop watch.[23] To show what differences occur under these conditions, a Negro psychologist procured the aid of a white colleague and they tested alternately a group of white and a group of Negro college students. They found that the Negro students had an I.Q. on the average six points higher when tested by a Negro, and the white students a similar average of six points higher when tested by a white psychologist.[24] It would therefore seem important to know what the conditions of the test are before placing too much reliance on it. Variation of rapport between the experimenter and the subject makes an appreciable difference.

Summarizing briefly the results of racial testing, we may state that considerable difference has been found between native white Americans and Negroes or native whites and American Indians and much less difference between native whites and the Oriental immigrant. These differences cannot be assumed to be innate; it is true that no one factor accounts for the variation in racial intelligence as discovered by the tests, and yet when all factors are taken into consideration — social and economic status, family background, cultural habits, inadequate sampling, variations in amount and quality of schooling, overemphasis on linguistic items in the tests, differences in motivation and rapport — all these items together probably account for what differences there are in different ethnic groups.[25] Unless every one of these elements can be equalized before testing, the burden of proof belongs to the one who insists that there is any inherent difference. The testimony of psychologist and anthropologist alike makes it safer to assume equality than inequality, and this assumption rests on solid evidence.

RACE AND CIVILIZATION

There is another formidable problem still facing the student of race problems: is it not true that racial superiority is clearly reflected in the type of civilization which each race creates for itself? As we look over the nations today, the so-called civilized peoples seem to be found in Europe and America while the darker colored races are still on the road to learning Western technology, scientific method, the political lessons of democracy, and the refinements of living. Although it might appear that this view of things could be destroyed by travel and intercommunication, it is still firmly held by many thousands or even millions of troops who have spent time overseas and are only too glad to get home to the "comforts of civilization" and to "living like a white man" again. And it must not be inferred that it is only the uneducated who have held these opinions: the idea of Nordic supremacy has been championed by Gobineau in France and by W. H. Chamberlain (a Germanized Englishman) in Germany. After they established the theoretical basis of Aryanism, it was later elaborated by the Nazis, who spread it all over central Europe. In America, Lothrop Stoddard and Madison Grant made the doctrine popular, and it still lingers on in mild but attenuated form in the writings of Ellsworth Huntington, the geographer.[26] The whole conception is most plausible provided that one selects historical examples very carefully and overlooks the contrary evidence. However, the scientist who is worthy of the name always interests himself in negative evidence — Darwin stated flatly that it is his first and primary duty—and therefore it will be necessary to search out not merely all the historical examples that prove the superiority of "white" civilization but also those which show the inadequacy of such a view.

To begin with, there is as much variation within racial and stock groupings as there is between them. A comparison between the civilization of a citizen in Rome and a wandering Bedouin of the Arabian desert would show a considerable variation in the Mediterranean race. Is the difference due to race? If so, there should be a uniform superiority. In the western hemisphere it is instructive to take the ancient Mayas of central America or the Incas of Peru with their highly developed culture and compare them with the American Indians of California who were so primitive that they lived chiefly on acorns and even refused to copy the maize culture of the nearby Pueblos and the Mexican tribes. Yet the two groups belonged to the same stock and were related racially. Or the Chinese mandarin of Pekin or Hankow may be placed beside the primitive Siberian tribes who live in tents even though they dwell in the cold arctic regions, have even failed to develop adequate snow houses as the Eskimos have, and rate among the world's simplest peoples. Yet the two groups belong to a racial strain that is equally Mongolian;

hence it is hardly their race that stamps one as superior and the other inferior. (We will not raise the question here whether this superiority is more fictitious than real.)

This, however, does not dispose of the Nordic question, for it may still be asked why it is that in the northwest part of Europe and in America which was settled from that area, there is the highest development of our present industrial civilization. A flippant answer would be that the two greatest wars in history have also been fought by countries with a dominant Nordic or at least Alpine strain. But that reply would fail to meet the problem squarely. It is more to the point to ask what was happening to the Alpine or Nordic peoples during the period of the Greek or Roman civilizations. More than one scholar has pointed out that the basis of our Western society was laid in these two ancient cultures which were predominantly Mediterranean; indeed they looked upon the northern Nordics as wild boors who might in time see the light of civilization. And from their limited standpoint, it is easy to see where they made a mistake. We must ask, however, whether our viewpoint today is not equally limited to the era in which we live. Does the temporary material superiority of the Nordic and Alpine in our era guarantee that it will continue permanently, as the Greeks and Romans believed their empires would continue? Any view of this kind depends entirely upon where we slice our history. If we slice it at the beginning of the Christian era, we would reach a very different conclusion. Any type of superiority that exists is therefore relative to a particular century or era.

It is also relative to the geographical area as well as to the limited historical epoch. When the European traders and missionaries started their travels to China, they were given a very cool reception because they were so uncouth and barbaric according to Chinese standards. One scholarly Chinese observer who met a number of Jesuit priests in his travels wrote a friend of his that these "ocean men" from the West were a beastly lot for they had hair on their bodies like the monkeys of southern China, and that they were shrewd and clever enough but that it would take considerable patient training before they could be taught the rudiments of human behavior such as would befit a gentleman.[27] Later on in the eighteenth century when English merchants had established trade with the Chinese, the latter set up rules regulating the behavior of all traders who had anything to do with the English so that the Western barbarians would not contaminate the superior Chinese. It was forbidden for Hong merchants to be in debt to foreigners; on no account could Western traders hire Chinese servants; Europeans were prohibited from using sedan chairs; no foreign traders were allowed to row on the river except at specified times three days a month when they were accompanied by a Chinese interpreter who was held accountable for their misdeeds; when the trading season was over, all Westerners had to leave Canton; a few Europeans who lived at Hong factories were forbidden to leave the grounds or compounds outside — these were about 300 by 500 feet in size, and if a trader strayed off them, it meant certain death. In Japan the luckless Caucasian fared no better; there the Dutch traders were not allowed to enter Japan proper but had to stay on Deshima Island near Nagasaki. Once a year they had to trample a Christian cross in the presence of a Japanese official; and annually all Dutch traders were forced to pay a visit of respect to the Shogun's capital to cut capers for the entertainment of the Court, who laughed heartily at these pale-faced baboons from abroad.[28]

It is naturally easy to retort today that the tables are turned and the Occidental is making Japan step to an even harder tune. At the same time it is a restricted view that takes the contemporary vantage point and insists that it will last forever. Even though Japan has lost all supremacy in Asia, it is by no means certain that China will not seize it and continue to consolidate her gains until she forges ahead. Racial supremacy in history is not a final stopping place but a temporary halt; and when the perspective is one of centuries or thousands of years instead of a generation or two, the whole picture changes. The military and technical superiority of the lighter colored peoples has hardly lasted two centuries — which in historical time is brief indeed.

In point of fact, when the thirteen major civilizations of history are reviewed, it becomes clear that each one of them required the presence of two or more races and none could be accredited to a single race alone.[29] Professor Toynbee, who has given an exhaustive study of the evidence, makes this point unmistakable. On the basis of his study, which is the most complete one ever made of comparative history, he also concludes that there is no absolute criterion for the superiority of one civilization over another and hence all civilizations must be regarded as equal to each other in value.[30] This disposes pretty effectively of the notion of racial superiority in any one of them.

With perhaps one exception, the Negroid, Toynbee concedes that every race and stock has contributed to these major civilizations.[31] On the face of it, this would seem like adequate proof that the Negro strain was permanently inferior in its creative contribution. Yet before that conclusion is accepted, we must face the contrary evidence. What is necessary to the growth of urban empires with development of writing, higher technical exploits, and increasing trade? Most students of the subject agree that it is culture contact — the intermingling of peoples and cultures which comes about as a result of increased communication and consequent diffusion of ideas, inventions, and arts.[32] Where this interchange of elements appears, new stimulus to creative effort arises and a constant borrowing of cultural traits goes on. If anyone were to account for the apparent superiority of European culture over others in the last two hundred years, he might give the likely answer that it was due to the two inventions of gunpowder and printing. Yet both of these were first invented by the Chinese.[33]

If the same kind of investigation of Africa be made, it is soon discovered that the interior of Africa has been cut off from the main streams of diffusion (and hence from interstimulation) by two important geographical barriers. First, there are few good harbors on its seacoasts; and second, there is a lack of navigable rivers that reach far into the continent, the sudden drop from a high plateau to lower land causing huge falls in the rivers. Central Africa was thus nearly cut off from the outside world, almost as much as the wild Nordic tribes that roamed the northern forests during the early history of Rome. In the more northern regions of Africa there was more intercommunication; this led to the growth of three large empires, Ghana, Melle, and Songhay, all of which probably surpassed the little kingdom of Israel at its height except possibly in literary accomplishment. These kingdoms could have been the forerunners of a large African civilization had it not been for the intrusion of the slave trade before further progress could be made; from that day to this, slavery has set back African progress beyond measure, and the colonial empires of European powers helped to arrest development further.[34]

African culture, then, has progressed unevenly because of geographical and historical elements, but it would be unwarranted to assume that this was due to inherent inferiority. Speaking objectively, all we can say is that Africa is the last continent as a whole to enter into the main course of civilization and that she has done so under conditions that prevented her growth and the possibility of her taking a place side by side with other peoples. Furthermore this statement assumes that the present view, which starts from a contemporary *now*, may determine what will happen in the future. If, however, we recall with Toynbee that civilizations have existed in the world for only six thousand years at best and that the astronomers tell us human life will be possible on this planet eighty-three million times as long, then the slowness of Negroid people to enter the arena of civilization seems insignificant and throws no light whatever on their future accomplishments.[35] On the other hand their contributions to literature, art, the drama, music, and science less than a hundred years after their enslavement in America show that when they are drawn into the current of culture contact they can move forward with astonishing rapidity.

One by one the arguments for racial superiority or inferiority are falling before the white light of science. Anthropology, psychology, sociology, and history all attest that inherent differences in intelligence and achievement cannot be proved. It is true that there are many variations in the actual accomplishments of individuals from different racial strains, and yet when these are analyzed, they are found to depend on social and environmental considerations. The manifest behavior varies; the inherent abilities are as nearly equal as refined analysis can discover. It is culture that makes the man, not race. As Franz Boas declares, if we select the best third of humanity on the basis of intellect and personality, every race will be represented.[36]

Racial Minorities

CHAPTER 4

The American Indian: *A Preliterate Culture*

SUPPOSE YOU are given vast social power over the life and limb of Mr. Dubois on the condition that you change his whole way of life. Let us assume that he is a lawyer in middle life and it now becomes your task to make him over into a physician. You have money and police power at your disposal, and you make plans to enter him in medical school so that in three or four years he will begin a totally new profession. Just as you are laying your plans for this momentous experiment, the agency which has given you the power makes a further request. Before he is transformed into Dr. Dubois, you are courteously asked to make a further change in his life; it seems that he is now a Catholic, but at the end of the process you must also see that he is a Protestant in good standing. This will probably make you squirm a little, for it complicates the problem and forces you to change the relatively simple arrangements you had first set up. But let us conjecture that you are not totally discouraged and that you go on with your revised program, wondering how you can arrange for religious training in a denominational institution where he can at the same time receive his premedical and medical training. You are just beginning to make schemes for changing his whole circle of friends to reinforce his new role when you receive another message from the agency, telling you that they feel the program will have more value if you will change his nationality too. He is now a Frenchman, and they feel that you can improve the experiment if you do not mind adding one more feature — to turn him out an Englishman. By this time your impatience has grown to deep resentment. How can you be expected to take a French Catholic lawyer and turn him into a conventional English Protestant doctor?

That will mean that his language and citizenship will also require modification, a job that looks too formidable to tackle. As you look over his case history, you discover that his family has no English blood or ancestry, that he does not know a word of English, that he comes from a long line of Catholics, and that his father, grandfather, and great-grandfather were all lawyers. You find differences of professional habits, religion, language, food preferences, traditions and customs that would possibly cause consternation in British society, differences in political outlook, and finally to top it off, you find that Mr. Dubois comes from a tiny, isolated village in Provence where his family had lived for centuries, and you are asked to make him at home in a London environment. Why not give the whole thing up as a bad job?

This is a little piece of fantasy thinking, no doubt, but it is interesting to see how far we could press the whole matter. Suppose it were a question of transforming not merely the individual but his entire family. And as though that were not enough, we might add his village community and see what could be done with them as a viable social group. The more items we add, the more impossible the experiment appears. And when we finally exaggerate the figure still further, we would reach the end of the trail by selecting a group of savages on a South Sea isle and ask what would be necessary to metamorphose them into a group of middle-class suburbanites merrily playing bridge and worrying about keeping up with the Joneses. As the whole picture becomes more fantastic, one thing becomes clear: the greater the cultural gap, the more difficult the task of change becomes. If you were given a choice, you would probably prefer trying to make an Englishman out of a Frenchman rather than make an Englishman out of a South Sea Islander. The former have at least some language elements in common, they are both acquainted with the uses of an industrial society, they share certain political ideas that go back to the Romans, and they have a similar professional ideal. Such is not the case when we compare the South Sea Islander with the Englishman. You will probably express the difference by saying that the French and English are civilized while the South Sea inhabitants are not. How shall we describe them? The anthropologist has largely abandoned the word "primitive" (for those people probably have a history as long as our own) and prefers the relatively neutral term "preliterate."

PRELITERATES AND THEIR WAY OF LIFE

Generally speaking, preliterate societies are those in which no written language exists, so that all happenings are passed along through the medium of the spoken word; the old men have been called the walking libraries of the tribe. Kinship and village groups hold the society together; a simple economy is practiced, food gathering, hunting, or a rudimentary agriculture. There is usually a profusion of religious beliefs and ceremonies accompanied by witchcraft and magic. Homes, tools, and material equipment are largely handmade with patterns that are constantly repeated even though they show individual variation. The preliterate spends most of his time out of doors, and his language is filled with nature imagery. Most of all, he is resistant to change; his forefathers developed ways and means of maintaining a balance with climate, topography, game supply, soil fertility, neighboring tribes, and supernatural beings. Anyone who disturbs this delicate balance commits a mortal offense against his people, his ancestors, and his gods; as a renegade he suffers ostracism, punishment, exile, death. After wrestling bitterly with nature for centuries, the tribe does not feel that it can allow any deviation from the accustomed ways, and though occasional innovators appear, they find the task of getting their ideas accepted a rough and thorny one. Persistence and tradition are methods of survival and to threaten them is tantamount to endangering the entire society. Life together is largely a face-to-face relationship, and social control through gossip and ridicule is usually enough to keep the solidarity of the group. The culture of the preliterate society is sufficiently simple and homogeneous so that the task of the anthropologist who studies its way of life has been compared to that of the cytologist in biology who examines the cell as the most elementary form of organization in living beings. Similarly the study of the preliterate community shows us the microcosm of all societies as an aid to better understanding of more complex and "civilized" groups.

Since most white Americans live enmeshed in a highly mechanized, industrial, urban society, they rarely come in contact with the preliterate. A few dwellers in the states of Oklahoma, the Dakotas, Wyoming, Idaho, Nevada, or New Mexico know about the Indian reservations and have brief contact with the American Indian. Now and then a tourist in the Navajo country or driving down the Tamiami trail may catch a glimpse of these peculiar "natives" who are as much a curiosity as though they were in a zoo. The weary motorist may allow himself a few moments of vague wonderment — why don't these people become civilized when it is to their obvious advantage to do so? For any popular view, the "civilized" is certainly "better" than the savage. Yet the traveler might find himself embarrassed to explain this lucidly to the people of the Bikini Islands who have moved away so that the white man can experiment to see how much his new toy, the atomic bomb, can destroy at a single blow. In other parts of the Pacific Islands, these preliterates frequently tell the whites they are happier as they are and ask to be left alone. They do not need to work for money because their crops furnish them with what they need; they have no clothes, for the climate makes them unnecessary; they do not accept the white man's tools since they have always been able to get along with their own; they do not want schools because their old men can tell the youth how to get along in their little world; they have no desire for hospitals, for if too many people were saved from death, their islands would be overpopulated and the food supply would run short. They gape at the track fields erected by whites and wonder whether these contests of the white man may not be symbolical of his civilization, since they involve running around in a circle without getting anywhere.[1]

Returning to our mythical task which we proposed at the outset, we see that it is faced with another obstacle when the preliterate is involved: not only are his ways, customs, and habits different from those of "civilized" humanity but he does not want to change. The very nature of his society forces him to resist any alteration in his way of life; having had centuries of success with his own mode, he will persist in it to the end. Those who want him to revamp his existence may call him stubborn; for him, only tenacity and courage keep him on his course. To ask why he does not want to become civilized is to ask a question such as, "Why doesn't the Frenchman want to be English?" or "Why doesn't the Catholic want to become

Protestant?" except that the differences here are profounder and are the product of millennia of experience.

CHARACTERISTICS OF INDIAN CULTURE

It has been more or less consciously assumed by the dominant white culture that constant association of the Indian with the new settlers in America would soon make him indistinguishable from his neighbors. Where two groups of different culture live side by side in close relationship, there is a good deal of borrowing on both sides of language, customs, habits, technology, and ways of life. This process of acculturation, as it is termed by the anthropologist,[2] is unavoidable, although it operates at variable rates of swiftness dependent on such items as strength of tradition, initial similarity, or degree of hostility between the two cultures. In the history of Indian acculturation Charles Loram declares that there are two groups of acculturers on the white man's side of the ledger: (1) informal acculturers like traders, many or most missionaries, farmers, and employers of Indian labor. For the most part, these acculturers know nothing and care less about Indian culture. So far as they are concerned, the sooner the Indian becomes assimilated the better, and if he does not do so it is because he is ignorant, backward, lazy, or stubborn. At least he "ought to know better," and it is "his own fault" if he does not want to make the effort. Then there are (2) formal acculturers who respect Indian culture, such as many officials, some missionaries, educators, and thoughtful Indians, as well as anthropologists. They want to see the process go on slowly and selectively, applying to it both science and social intelligence.[3] By and large, American policy has been dominated by the mentality of the first group, with the result that the white man's attitude toward the Indian has alternated between opposition and hostility, neglect and paternalism, or overprotection.[4] All these policies have ignored the fundamental consideration — the unique characteristics of Indian culture as established by centuries of living before the arrival of the white man.

What, then, are these characteristics? It will be impossible to name more than a few, but some of them are crucial in understanding Indian life and culture. (1) To begin with, the Indian is primarily an outdoor person who has lived close to nature and who prefers living in the open even at the cost of some discomfort, provided he can have direct contact with sun, moon, rain, the stars, animal and plant life, and the simple necessities that go with such a life. Indians are irrepressibly rural.[5] Consequently they are not attracted to the white man's cities or to the impersonal, mechanized life that is so often characteristic of great urban agglomerations. Generally the Indian is not interested in making his life complex for the sake of more intense or sophisticated satisfactions. There have been times when the thrust of sudden change has catapulted him into affluence, as when oil was discovered on Indian lands in Oklahoma. Under these conditions the life of the Indians has been violently disrupted and quick deterioration has set in. Some Osage Indians who had "originally assigned or inherited rights" in land drew fabulous sums from oil payments, starting with a minimum of $13,200 a year.[6] One squaw bought a $1200 fur coat and a $3000 diamond ring, paid a $4000 installment on a California house, bought $7000 worth of furniture, lent $1500 to a sister, and put $12,000 into Florida land. Another Indian and his wife bought $18 worth of strawberries in a store, sat down on the sidewalk, and ate them all at once.[7] Many Indian braves wrecked $5000 Cadillacs in a ditch and bought others rather than have them repaired.[8] Needless to say, much of this profligate spending was encouraged and abetted by white traders and salesmen who urged the new luxuries upon the wealthy tribesmen for a substantial profit. These exceptional conditions only serve to point up the contrast between the *nouveaux riches* and the great mass of Indians, many of whom preferred semistarvation on their scraggly reservations rather than enter the white world where they would necessarily begin a new life of competition and struggle to succeed as individuals. On the reservation, they have a life in the free open air and can maintain many of their simple tribal ways, their language, and their customs.

(2) Originally most of the Indians have been hunters and fishers, although a sizable group has engaged in a rudimentary agriculture.[9] Arctic, subarctic, and Great Plains regions were almost exclusively occupied by hunters, while the Indians of the eastern woodlands supplemented hunting by meager farming. California and the Rocky Mountain areas had chiefly plant gatherers. Only the Five Civilized Tribes of the Southeast (Chickasaws, Choctaws, Creeks,

Cherokees, and Seminoles) carried on extensive agriculture, and they were not wholly settled because they continued to move when the fertility of the soil was exhausted. A small number of Southwest Indians, Pueblos, Navajos, and western Apache, also practiced a simple kind of farming as their chief means of subsistence.[10] For many of these tribes, pushed back into the life of the reservation, Elkin's comment on the Arapaho applies without serious qualification — that they engage in agriculture mechanically but their hearts are not in it.[11]

(3) The Indian is used to a "natural economy" or one in which the search for food is for the near future, where there is no great surplus. As Loram puts it, the preliterate will work hard for food and clothing but not to have money in the bank.[12] He is not used to routing his economic satisfactions through the indirect and abstract channel of money but has been close to a subsistence and barter economy. Preferring the simple to the complex, he has retained a feeling for the neat outlines of economic units requiring a minimum of legal or political definition: skins, baskets, blankets, knives, weapons, and measures of grain.

(4) Communal ownership by the tribe, clan, or great family is more natural to the Indians as a whole than private ownership. When the white man came, there were probably about one million Indians in the areas now occupied by the United States [13] and this meant a thinly scattered people. All peoples with a low population density are likely to have landowning units larger than that of the family. A not untypical condition is presented by the western Shoshoni where water, seed, and hunting areas were all free, not owned at all. But as soon as anyone worked with these areas, they became the property of the individual or family doing the work.[14] It is easy to see that where an area is inhabited by migratory game, individual ownership of land is impractical. And where there is farming, it is also not likely that there will be much extension of individual property unless there is another method of improving the soil than letting it lie fallow.[15] Such groups as the Hopis, who carried on agriculture for centuries, managed land ownership by clans.[16] Tendencies toward individualism were found most often among the groups living in washes or river bottoms.[17]

(5) Because of his simple economy and dire necessity, the Indian

was an economic conservationist in contrast with the white newcomer who exploited and used up the natural resources at a wasteful rate.[18] When there was a limited supply of game, the hunting grounds would be roughly apportioned among tribal or clan units so that the more powerful tribes would not encroach too freely upon the elementary needs of their neighbors. The decline of the Plains Indians is related very directly to the removal of their economic base through indiscriminate hunting carried on by ever-increasing numbers of white settlers.

(6) In his thinking the Indian is a synthesist, not an analyst. He does not indulge in the sharply outlined abstractions so common to the scientific thought of the white man; he does not separate nature and man, the natural and supernatural, the organic and inorganic. Almost all his thinking is done in terms of wholes rather than parts,[19] thus giving his ideas an aesthetic, childlike simplicity quite in contrast to discursive thinking. Among the western Apache, for instance, hard, pelting rain is called "male rain," while gentle, mild rain is entitled "female rain." [20] This nature imagery dominates the thinking of the Indian and makes it difficult for him to understand the more harsh and impersonal terms common to an alien culture.

(7) Most Indians are trained from a very early age to endure pain without flinching and to repress their feelings in the presence of others. To an outsider, therefore, they appear to be stoical and unfeeling where the situation would seem to call for expression of the emotions in laughing or crying or the display of pain reactions. Woodworth's experiment on white and Indian subjects, for example, showed that the Indians would give less evidence of pain when a stylus was applied to the skin.[21] In the dances of Plains tribes tortures were systematically applied to each young brave, holes pierced in the flesh and sticks thrust through the wounds, and the leader hung from these sticks with his feet barely touching the ground. Only after passing such an ordeal would the youths be fitted for the life of a warrior.[22] In social groups the Indian placed much emphasis on dignity and silence, often waiting many minutes before expressing himself; and when he did so it was with a sort of ceremonial oratory and eloquence that would befit the occasion and lend embellishment to the simplest meeting or assembly.[23]

THE IMPACT OF WHITE CULTURE

The power relations which made the Indians a minority were the realities of conquest.* As soon as the white man arrived, it became evident that he was not interested in penetrating behind the veil of reserve and taciturnity of the red man to his inner preferences and values; the white settler was chiefly interested either in using his new neighbor to his own advantage or in eliminating him from possible competition in peopling the continent. The Spaniards who came first found that they needed labor to man their huge estates or encomiendas and pressed the Indian into service. But as they proceeded north from Mexico into Texas and the great Southwest, they found it increasingly difficult to manage the fiercer tribes of the plains and eventually limited the scope of their conquest.[24] At the same time the Spaniards left behind them two things that later enabled the Indian to protect himself a little longer, the horse and a new land system. Before the white man came, the Indian had no means of locomotion except walking or running, although he might occasionally use dogs to pull a simple travois. But as Coronado's horses escaped and roved over the plains, the Indian found that he now had a new technique of warfare to use against the enemy, and before long, horse stealing became a fine art. It is said that the introduction of the horse among the Plains Indians was as great a revolution for that culture as the invention of steam or the locomotive in European culture.[25] A reform of the Indian land system urged by Bartolomé de Las Casas prohibited the further spread of the encomienda and allowed rights in communal land to the original inhabitants with the rule that the Spanish settlers could not encroach upon them within a thousand yards.[26] These Laws of the Indies, as they were called, were not the result of pure altruism, for they helped to curb the power of the encomenderos; but nevertheless they have had far-reaching effects. John Collier, former Commissioner of Indian Affairs, has this to say of them:

> So strong, so mature, so victorious were the effects . . . of the policies represented by the Law of the Indies, that the subsequent policy of our own government was impotent to overturn them. Through the years from 1850 to 1929 the storm of atomization — the exhaustively

* Cf. Chapter 1, above, p. 7.

searching policy of destroying Indian society — tore into shreds the Indian life of our Great Plains, of Oklahoma, of many other regions. The storm beat in vain against the pueblos; the banner of the Law of the Indies was floating there still.[27]

The colonials of the eastern coast probably had more to do with equipping the Indian with guns, for the Spaniards forbade the possession of them by the red man.[28] With the aid of the new weapon, the Algonquins and Iroquois were forced to enter a new kind of hunting competition with the white man, cutting down the game supply and hence their own means of subsistence.[29] At the same time the white man began to play off one tribe against another, a process that was aided by the disunity of the Indians and the split between the British and the French. Thus by turning the new weapons against each other, the red men unwittingly aided in their own extinction.

Another feature which the Indians borrowed from white culture was the drinking of intoxicating liquors. The ancient Aztecs did have such a drink called pulque, whose effects were so devastating that laws were made to suppress its use. When the Spaniards came, they abolished the old laws but the situation became so serious that they had to be reinstated. The only other Indian tribes that gave certain evidence of imbibing fermented drinks were the Apache and the Pima, who occasionally used them for ceremonial purposes. It seems well established that most of the tribes on the continent when the white man arrived did not have the practice of drinking either fermented or spirituous liquors,[30] and their sudden introduction to them in the seventeenth century led to such wild and ungovernable behavior that most colonies finally prohibited their sale.[31] This did not prevent dishonest fur traders and others from continuing the practice, and the illegal traffic took a considerable toll; both white and Indian leaders raised their voices against liquor selling with little relative effect.[32] With the coming of the Indian reservation, the situation escaped the control of the legal authorities[33] because Indian laws on the reservation did not apply to the white man, and the ordinary laws of the United States did not apply to the reservation. Thus the whisky trader could carry on his trade quite openly without fear of interruption. We are told that the term "bootlegger" originated in this period of United States history.[34]

During the early period of colonization, the white settlers themselves were a minority and carried on extensive diplomacy with Indian tribes to set up working relations which would be satisfactory. Because of misunderstanding on both sides, these temporary provisions were often violated and open warfare was common. The growth of the newer population pushed the original inhabitants farther and farther back into the wilderness and wiped out hunting lands that were the basis of the Indian's whole existence. One chief disagreement was the notion of private property in land, a concept quite foreign to the Indian's mind. That a piece of paper could give legal title to land which was needed by all for food could hardly be grasped by a people who held to communal rights so fiercely. Even with the later arrangement of recognizing the sovereignty of certain tribes and making treaties to ratify agreements, there was still bewilderment over the fact that land could be claimed by new settlers when it had belonged from time immemorial to the Indians themselves. This bewilderment gave place to resentment and bitterness when the Supreme Court decided that a treaty of this kind had no greater validity than an Act of Congress and hence could be abrogated by a similar Act.[35]

It is significant that the United States government established an Indian Office in 1824 under the War Department, for the problem of dealing with the Indian was considered at this time to be chiefly a military one.[36] The country was still largely unsettled and a rapid conquest of the Indians would allow the white population to open up more territory for their own use. Treaties permitted the Indians to continue living on the areas ceded by agreement; but as soon as the white man had settled his own free land, he began to demand that of the Indian, or to invade it — sometimes with government aid — or to persuade the government to revoke the treaty. The lands on which the Indians were now given some rights came to be known as reservations, and they stood squarely in the pathway of the pioneer who wanted new land. Although a few tribes in the northeast were left unmolested on their lands, the usual method of solving the growing conflict with the Indians of the East and South was to move them to Indian Territory just south of Kansas.[37] Later the Osage, Kaw, Otoe, and Pawnee tribes from the western prairies were also moved to the same areas.[38] On the whole the new policy of placing the Indian on the reservation was prompted by the blunt recognition that it was cheaper to feed him than to kill him; [39] it was estimated that every regiment equipped to fight the red man had cost $2 million and all the campaigns of a year had succeeded in liquidating only a few hundred men.[40] In 1870 it was calculated that the Indian wars cost the government $1 million for every dead Indian.[41]

Over these reservations were placed a group of white agents who were to administer the affairs of each tribe in accordance with the rules of the Indian Bureau at Washington. These agents were indifferently chosen, many of them being political appointees who were "deserving" and for whom some job had to be provided by party leaders.[42] So difficult was it to find honest and able agents that for ten years the nominations for these positions were turned over to church organizations — a plan followed by so much bickering and quarreling that it had to be abandoned.[43] By 1880 it was realized that the reservation policy often pauperized and degraded the Indian without raising him to the level of "civilized" status; hence it seemed better to establish a method whereby Indians would be brought into more frequent contact with whites and thus be prepared as soon as possible for a new mode of living. This was the reform motive. Mixed with it was also the very evident desire to view the lands of the Indians as "really" belonging to the white man's government in spite of the "rude" agreements or treaties that had been made heretofore. When such sentiments were expressed quite freely by Indian agents and by prominent government officers, the popular pressure behind such a move can be appreciated. This was the predatory motive.

The first of these two motives was embodied in the so-called Dawes Act or General Allotment Act of 1887. The general purpose of this Act was to provide ways and means whereby the Indian could become a good, responsible, individualistic landowner and farmer as quickly as possible and could thus be "freed" from tribal ways and customs. It provided that every Indian would eventually be given an individual share of the reservation in which he lived, the size being anywhere from forty to two hundred acres. He could then hold this land for twenty-five years during which it was not supposed to be sold and at the end of that time he would have fee patent and the recognized status of managing his own affairs. At last the Indian was to be given a chance to become "assimilated." As soon as he was given an allotment, separated himself from his tribe, and "adopted the habits of civilized life," he was considered to have the full rights of a citizen.[44]

The predatory motive also received its due. Amendments to the Dawes Act in 1891, 1902, and 1907 provided more and more ways in which individual ownership in land by the Indian could be leased, alienated, or sold.[45] Pressure on Congress by farmers and ranchers resulted in declaring large areas of the reservations "surplus" land since they were not in immediate use by the Indians, and these were sold at bargain prices.*

THE PERIOD OF DECAY

This new policy which was to liberate the Indian and give him a place in American competitive culture proved to have results that were quite contradictory to the original aim of the Dawes Act. It finally appeared impossible to legislate the red man into becoming a white man, even in a period of twenty-five years. A preliterate does not change the habits of a thousand years in twenty-five, although it is understandable that those who attempted to carry out the policy might believe in its success, divorced as they were from scientific understanding of mores and habits carried on by peoples different from themselves. Many Indians were confused by the new property system — the fact that an imaginary line divided what belonged to them from what belonged to a neighbor — for was it not all a part of the tribal heritage? How could one live on this little portion of land when the old camping ground still held the lure of "home"? Others were bewildered because they now had to farm

* One of the most flagrant cases of the seizure of land occurred in California, where the federal government made treaties with 119 tribes from 1851 on. By the terms accepted, the Indians gave up claims to something like half the area of California in return for 7 million acres which would return to them under perpetual ownership. Caucasian groups put such pressure on Congress that the Senate never ratified the treaties, but this was kept secret from the Indians even by agents of the Indian Bureau who knew the facts involved. The result was that although the Indians kept their part of the agreement (believing the treaties ratified), they eventually had to stand by and see every acre of the 7 million sold to whites. Cf. John Collier, *The Indians of the Americas*, New York, Norton, 1947, p. 224.

the land like the newcomers, when all they knew was the hunt and the chase. Still others had practiced a rude sort of communal agriculture and could no longer count on the help of neighbors nor work side by side with them. Some were given allotments on grazing land too dry for successful farming, and poverty soon overtook them. The Blackfeet of Montana tried planting crops year after year but soon discovered that the season was so short that their plants were frozen before they could reap a harvest.[46]

Before long there was only one way out for many if not most of those who had received allotments, and that was to lease or sell to the white man. In the grazing country the white rancher was more than willing to come in and lease dozens of holdings until their combined size would make cattle raising profitable. For an individual holding he would pay anywhere from ten to twenty dollars a month [47] and still make a profit, for during the twenty-five years the land was held in trust there were no taxes on it. In better areas where the Indian did not know how to use modern methods of farming and had little chance to learn them, the whites would lease individual holdings all over the reservation until the whole was "checkerboarded." Or occasionally, after the Dawes Act had been sufficiently amended, actual sale to whites became possible, and with no knowledge of how much land was worth per acre the Indian succumbed to the prospect of having several hundred up to a thousand dollars all at once. Being utterly unprepared by experience to manage such sums, and unprotected by all but the most friendly agents, he soon wasted the money and became wholly dependent on the Bureau, where rations were given to keep the situation in control. Thousands lost their land and other thousands held land on which the leases brought less than enough for subsistence. And at the end of the road there was enforced idleness among little clusters of people huddled around the agencies waiting for interminable handouts. These "rural slums" [48] have been unknown and unheralded, although they exist in patches throughout the Great Plains area.

In 1887 there were something like 139 million acres of land on Indian reservations. By 1889 one fifth of this had passed to white ownership, and by 1933 there were only 47 million acres left. This was the most barren and least promising area so that there was no motive to allot it.[49]

The new form of life could be expected to have a lethal effect, and so it proved. Even with the first change to the reservation the death rate rose quite suddenly. On one reservation it removed more than 10 per cent of the population in two years. A continuance of this rate would have wiped out the tribe entirely in some fifteen years.[50] The general rule for most of the reservations for many years was a death rate higher than the birth rate.[51] This decrease in population continued until 1900, when it was arrested; in 1901 the Indian population was down to 269,388.[52] In addition to inadequate diet, the chief enemies of Indian health were tuberculosis, trachoma, infant mortality, and syphilis. By 1924 the problem was finally recognized by the establishment of a Division of Health in the Office of Indian Affairs.[53] Even today the tuberculosis death rate is ten times greater among Indians of rural areas than among whites, and the infant mortality of the Indian nearly twice that of the white infants,[54] while the average life expectancy for Indians is thirty to thirty-four years as compared with sixty to sixty-four for the country as a whole.[55]

The tribes which probably suffered less than others from the allotment policy have been especially those of the great southwest areas, such as the Navajo, Pueblo, and perhaps also the western Apache.[56] On the whole the larger tribes have maintained themselves better than the smaller ones. Lorimer claims that the Cherokee (now in Oklahoma) and the Dakota probably have more people today than when the white men came.[57]

During the same period the system of education carried on by the Indian Office was largely a boarding school regime. This meant that the children were taken away from home at the age of six and removed to a school where their hair was clipped and where they were given uniforms, a cot to sleep on, and a locker for a few belongings. In many cases the children were then turned over to one of the Christian sects in charge of their education and were taught from the same textbooks used for white children everywhere, except that much time was first spent teaching them English. The children were forbidden to use their own language. Under pretext of teaching them a trade, the teachers saw to it that they performed all the manual labor on the school grounds, including janitorial service, and occasionally a little garden work in gangs.[58]

For the most part these activities did not prepare the young for economic self-sufficiency on the reservation and often estranged them permanently or temporarily from their parents. Carlisle and Hampton schools were exceptions to the general rule, for they had an "outing system" in which Indians learned farming and housekeeping.[59] The majority of the Indian youth went back home to the reservation rather than participate in white culture which accepted them only as menials. Among the Sioux two thirds of the boys from school went back to the reservation and among the other one third, half eventually went back.[60] This was fairly representative of other tribal members, although it is true that more boys went away from home among the California and Oklahoma Indians. Among the latter, however, those who remained away from home usually went into Indian service, which is certainly as much a part of Indian as it is of white culture. Furthermore, in Oklahoma the Indian youths found much more acceptance in white culture than they did elsewhere.[61] Many of those who returned home on different reservations became "marginal" personalities, unable to participate freely in white society though educated in its ways, and unable to enter fully into the life of their own people, of whom they sometimes became ashamed. They thus formed a cultural detritus of large proportions, existing in a kind of social no man's land of their own.

ACCULTURATION

It has already been shown that the meeting of Indian and white cultures has resulted in continual modification of preliterate habits and customs. In many cases the change came with such swiftness that Indian society was wholly disrupted and destroyed. Unfortunately we do not have any complete studies to enable us to observe this process throughout the period of historic contact of the two societies. A really thorough study would follow the various factors of change in chronological order: the groups that did the borrowing and their motives in making the change, the comparative receptivity of the groups, the shifts in form and meaning with each change, and the time needed for the integration of the new with the old.[62] Linton states that the borrowing of material artifacts such as tools, utensils, and the like usually comes first, followed by the adoption of behavior patterns and finally the transfer of philosophical or religious ideas.[63]

One thing seems certain and that is that acculturation proceeds more smoothly and with less disrupting effect where there is less friction between two groups and where their cultures already have much in common. Linton says, conversely, that acculturation is least liable to occur when the subordinate group is hostile but has little chance to stage a revolt. In this case there is a kind of passive resistance and a nostalgic clinging to old ways.[64] These conditions fit the situation of the Indian remarkably well and help to account for the continual antagonism toward accepting the ways of the outsider which is fairly characteristic of the folk culture. On account of historic disparities of contact, internal differences, and variations of hostile relations, there have been many divergences and uneven forms of acculturation.

In some cases the Indian has been able to turn the white man's ways to his own use and make successful adaptations. For example, the Fox tribes arranged for purchase of land in Tama, Iowa, the only case in which the Indians did so, and were thereafter protected by the white man's own property laws of ownership. The Fox was one of the few tribes that had hereditary chiefs in a village unit; their intertribal affairs were settled by the chiefs in council. They could carry on their agriculture very much as they did before, and were then allowed a breathing space of time in which to adapt themselves more fully to white ways.[65] Most of the Fox still consider their ways superior to those of the whites even though they depend on the latter economically.[66] On the other hand the Arapaho, who were decimated by the removal of their hunting animals, were given an opportunity to live on the Wind River Reservation side by side with the Shoshoni, who were their traditional enemies. Today they live in a separate culture there with segregated churches, schools, and even stores.[67] Their old habits of mobility, practiced on the plains for centuries, are now channeled into the habit of paying frequent visits and a tremendous enthusiasm for the modern automobile.[68] On this reservation the Arapaho were expected to become farmers, although cattle raising would have been more suitable for the land available since even whites found difficulty in farming in the vicinity.[69] The Arapaho farmer who has been educated with whites and has accepted much of the new attitude is straightforward and aggressive when meeting his white neighbors but modest and quiet among his own people. Even though he might like to attain white standards on his own farm, he is frequently afraid that his own people will think him overbearing. His Arapaho neighbors carry on traditional "shame behavior" or submissiveness with white strangers and this is now heightened by the fact that they think the white man is too domineering. Of course, the attitude is often misinterpreted as weakness, but as a matter of fact the Arapaho often feel resentful underneath.[70]

DIVERSITY OF DEVELOPMENT

It is a common mistake to class all Indians together as essentially alike. At one end of the scale are the Five Civilized Tribes (Choctaws, Chickasaws, Creeks, Cherokees, and Seminoles) which are the most successfully assimilated of all the Indian groups.[71] Two circumstances have aided in their relatively swift acculturation. First of all, they had a more complex and highly developed agriculture and material culture than most of the tribes on the North American continent and were thus more nearly like those from whom they borrowed new artifacts. Sequoyah, a Cherokee genius, invented an alphabet with eighty-seven characters, thus helping to make his tribe literate.[72] Another factor was the settling of the Five Tribes in Indian Territory, where they naturally took the lead because of their advanced material culture. Frontier conditions led to their natural position of leadership and they carved out a considerable name for themselves in Oklahoma. So marked has been their prestige that they have succeeded in breaking down an age-old taboo against intermarriage with the white population. Probably nowhere except in Oklahoma is there quite so much boasting of Indian ancestry, a factor which is much less noticeable in other parts of the United States.

At the other end of the scale have been the Indian tribes of the Southwest, where the preliterates solved their problem largely by withdrawal. Most of these tribes were never very warlike, probably because they were too small, like the Pueblos. This group has kept its own culture completely.[73] An examination of the Hopi people among these pueblo dwellers shows that they have maintained most of their old ways with considerable integrity, although some white influence has touched the fringes of their life.[74]

Between these two extremes lie the other tribal societies — matrilineal, patrilineal, hunting, or agricultural. Many of them are defeated, apathetic, and listless; others, resigned and stoical; and still others continue to make plans for the future by blending the white man's culture with their own. The impact of Christianity upon the life of Indian America can be seen by the following figures: of the 360,000 Indians of the United States * about 100,000 are Catholics, 100,000 are Protestants, and 160,000 either have their old traditional religious forms or are indifferent.[75] This of course lists membership on the basis of formal adherence to Protestantism and Catholicism and does not take into account the various syncretistic forms in Christian belief nor the modifications in the old pre-Columbian religion.

Most of the Indians resist change in their ways of life according to the usual preliterate pattern noted above. When there is an "agency to individual" relationship on the reservation, it hastens the "deculturation" of the Indian. If he tries to live as a day laborer but compromises by engaging in his other Indian group relationships, he is branded as a failure by the agent, who speaks of him as "going back to the blanket." [76] As soon as the Indian begins to use land for making money rather than subsistence, he becomes more assimilated, lives more like the whites, and tends to become separated from his own group.[77]

THE INDIAN REORGANIZATION ACT

The peculiar legal status of the Indian can be inferred from the paradox of conferring citizenship upon all Indians by the national Congress in 1924, while on the other hand the government still had guardianship over thousands of acres of Indian property. In spite of the new federal law, the individual states still had the right to regulate the qualifications for voting, and some of them denied this right to Indians in spite of the fact that they now had citizenship. † [78] How the Indian could be a ward of the government and

* This figure does not include Alaska. When the latter is included, the population increases to more than 400,000. Cf. Clark Wissler, "The American Indian," in *One America*, ed. by F. J. Brown and J. S. Roucek, New York, Prentice-Hall, 1945, p. 21.

† In 1947 most states abandoned restrictions on Indian voting, but Arizona and New Mexico by continuing to disfranchise their Indian population raised

simultaneously a full-fledged citizen is one of the delightful legal fictions with which abstruse minds have wrestled manfully ever since.

It was not until 1929 that the policy of allotment and disruption was gradually nullified. At that time Commissioner Charles J. Rhodes started boldly on a new program which reversed the tendency of the previous forty-two years. First of all the new administration severely restricted the sale of Indian lands, a process which culminated in 1934, when it was totally stopped.[79] At the same time the new administration began to favor a more tolerant policy toward Indian art, religion, and culture far in advance of its predecessors.[80] Not least important of the changes wrought by Commissioner Rhodes was a complete revision of the school system and the appointment of educators qualified to put through a program more in accord with Indian needs.[81] The health program was also strengthened and given more support.

With a change of administration in 1933 these policies were carried out more fully and with greater coherence by the new Commissioner, John Collier, who had the advantage of having served as Executive Secretary of the Indian Defense Association, where he had done intensive research and field work on Indian problems. Mr. Collier felt that if the government drew up a comprehensive program for the Indians it would have to consult the tribes themselves. Under his direction, questions were sent to members of all the reservations, their answers noted, and a basic bill drawn up for congressional action. This bill was submitted to all Indian tribes before going to the legislative chamber, and in addition congresses of Indians were held from coast to coast to discuss the various provisions needed for a permanent reorientation of policy.[82] In 1934 the bill, known as the Indian Reorganization Act (I.R.A.), was passed. Under it all allotments were to cease immediately, "surplus lands" not yet leased or bought by whites would be transferred to tribal

---

protests among returned veterans. See *To Secure These Rights*, Report of the President's Office, 1947, p. 40. In the summer of 1948 the Supreme Court of Arizona reversed an earlier decision and allowed the Indians to vote, and a federal court declared it unconstitutional for New Mexico to disenfranchise Indians living on the reservation. As a result of these two decisions all Indians in the United States have the franchise for the first time in history. See *The Nation* 167:171, August 14, 1948.

ownership, and further provision was made for obtaining more land if necessary. According to this policy a tribal council becomes a kind of corporation or executive committee for the management of the land, empowered to borrow money from the government as credit for cooperative cattle raising.[83] The Reorganization Act provided that its basic conditions could be accepted or rejected individually by each tribe, operating by secret ballot.[84] A new plan for Indian civil service was added to the bill, whereby Indians could be educated for executive positions and professional vocations.[85] It also became possible to teach Indian languages in the schools, along with the revival of native arts and crafts.[86] Both adults and children were given back their constitutional rights to choose a religion of their own, including the indigenous Indian religious forms and practices.[87] An improvement in the health services resulted in a 55 per cent decrease in the Indian death rate by 1945.[88]

Perhaps the chief feature of the reorganization policy is the combination of modern scientific equipment and skill with the older communal habits of living and working together which are natural to the Indian. Many cooperatives have been formed among the tribes, supporting such economic units as a salmon cannery, a group of tourist cabins, a community dairy, an oyster center, a municipal water project, and numerous cattle associations. The Jicarilla Apaches have developed a wholesale and retail cooperative along the lines of successful agricultural cooperatives.[89] Irrigation projects on a tribal basis, such as the Blackfeet have accomplished in conjunction with the Indian Service, have made it possible to get water for their crops in dry, barren areas.[90] Chief Counsel Haas of the Indian Bureau reported that $7 million had been advanced to various corporations and tribes between 1934 and 1947 and that $4 million due for repayment in 1947 came back to the government with a loss of only $1000. A record like this is considerably better than usual in common business practice. The number of beef cattle nearly doubled in fifteen years while the income from livestock increased from $1.3 million to over $21 million under the I.R.A.[91]

There have been many difficulties connected with the new program. In the first place, no provision has been made to unify land holdings which were fractionalized by the old hereditary laws. Under those laws a holding was divided equally among the heirs, until after a generation or two an eighty acre plot might have thirty-nine living heirs each with amounts varying from a tenth of an acre to nine acres. Conversely an individual could inherit equities in several allotments so that after the second or third generation the complication was so terrifying that the legal fictions bordered on the fantastic.[92] Although the original plan of the Reorganization Act provided measures to change these conditions, this portion of the bill was removed.[93] It became necessary to adopt a dual policy of setting up a new system of tribal lands and, parallel with it, full recognition of the antiquated fractionated individual holdings. This has burdened the Act with a severe contradiction which is used by foes of the policy to discredit the Indian Service as a whole.[94]

Another perfectly natural misunderstanding of the reorganization policy comes from those critics who are unacquainted with cultural anthropology and the studies of Indian habits and customs. It is that the new program is "forcing" a form of socialism or communism upon the Indian by government ukase.[95] Although this overlooks the right of any tribe to accept or reject the policy, as already mentioned, it seems to assume that the Indians are basically competitive and individualistic, an idea which is utterly at variance with the findings of responsible students of Indian affairs. The actual operation of the law has proved a stimulus to cooperation between private enterprise and tribal operation in accordance with forms of social labor familiar to the Indians. Even the United States government is still socialistic enough to hold many basic oil reserves for the benefit of the American people as a whole, and many conservative Senators were unwilling to give the office of Secretary of the Interior to a man suspected of violating this policy. On the other hand there seems to be some evidence that officials of the Indian Office put considerable pressure on many tribes to vote for the new Act, and in many cases the vote was close. Where a tribe rejected the I.R.A., even by a small majority, it automatically lost many benefits, including (from the reports of some Indians) the favor of administrators.

Then there is a somewhat different criticism which insists that the expense of buying new lands for the Indians is unnecessary as long as there are areas which the tribes are "not using." The charge is brought, for example, that since the passage of the Reorganization Act, $2 million a year has been spent for Indian lands while there were still many acres which the Indian has leased to the white man.[96] In view of the history of the allotment policy we can see that this criticism cannot be taken seriously, since the original allotments made the same fundamental assumption that the Indian was basically an entrepreneur who could develop the land like any individualistic farmer. Since he was unable to live up to this expectation and could not farm the land successfully without generations of training, he leased it to whites who took advantage of his poverty and ignorance. The lands which are left cannot support adequate ranching and cattle raising without being enlarged, as good land-use-planners have abundantly shown.[97]

It is also urged that those Indians who have made the greatest advance toward assimilation have been those who have had the least connection with the Indian Office, the example being the Five Civilized Tribes.[98] This statement fails to take into account the variations in tribal culture and generalizes the advanced culture of the Five Civilized Tribes into a condition which exists among Indians as a whole. It has already been shown that these groups were exceptional rather than the rule and that any workable program must take into account the great majority of the tribes, which have a simpler culture and definitely preliterate patterns of living. Any policy which treated the Navajos, Sioux, Hopi, and Arapaho on the same basis with the Cherokees would be doomed to failure.

A similar difficulty arises from the unevenness with which many individual Indians (mostly half, quarter, or lesser bloods) prepare themselves to enter into the white man's culture and remain there. In many tribes this has become a serious problem which complicates the task of any policy set up for their benefit. Among the Sioux, for example, many of the younger men (and women as well) have moved into the white world and taken defense positions, while others have gone into military service.[99] There are many of these, and some older men too, who are eager to get off the reservation and who have the skill and training that will equip them to take their place in the white world. A few of the tribes underwent rapid changes during the second World War, especially in the Southwest. Among the Navajos some 12,000 engaged in war work and 3600 entered the armed services. Some of the Pueblos travel daily to work in the Los Alamos Atomic Bomb Project in New Mexico. After the war the Navajos sent a delegation to Washington asking for more educational facilities for their 20,000 children, only 6000 of whom now have schools available. In 1946 the Papagos tribe in Arizona broke a precedent by electing a council of youth to represent them (chiefly war veterans already more familiar with the ways of the white world than their elders at home). Among the Indians of the entire country 30,000 entered the armed services and 45,000 worked in war industries. The impact of these new contacts on their culture will undoubtedly speed up the process of acculturation. Yet it would be false to infer that this group, which is less than one fourth of the entire Indian population, betokens a sudden transformation of tribal life.[100] It is this group who are likely to be vocal enough to write to the politicians and congressmen and give the impression that they would like to be "liberated." This will naturally lead many political representatives to take their part in the honest conviction that they are typical of the Indian as a whole. Are they?

In a recent study made of the Sioux or Teton-Dakota Indians by a staff of competent researchers, it is asked why Dakota young people prefer to stay on the reservation; and the answer is found in the solidarity of their family life.[101] There is no evidence that conditions are not the same among other Indian tribes, many of which have had less contact with the white world than the Sioux. Here again is the apparent assumption that the transforming of Indian semipreliterates into assimilated members of the American white community is a matter of a few years — an assumption made under the allotment policy which has proved so disastrous. It seems realistic to accept the conclusions of a more serious student of Indian affairs, Louis Balsam, who declares that to adjust the Indian to complex modern conditions probably another one hundred to two hundred years will be needed.[102] For this reason a revival of tribal autonomy and its combination with modern scientific techniques seems to be a program which at least faces up to the major problem. However, Collier says the chief aim of I.R.A. in the long run is the ultimate disappearance of federal aid or supervision.[103] But of course this means a strategic retreat all along the line, a subtlety which is misunderstood by large sections of the public and its political representatives. Perhaps the minor attention given to adequate interpretation of the reorganization policy in popular terms accounts for some of this misunderstanding.

It must not be supposed that reorganization policy has not raised serious problems of administration which must be settled in the future. For example, the Indian who is largely assimilated because of more complete acculturation is now faced with the dilemma of a return to tribal ways or of renouncing the Indian community completely and adopting white customs and culture.[104] For him there seems to be no middle ground.

Another problem is that of autonomy. Although tribal councils are being formed, their power is limited and the chief authority is still that of the superintendent of the agency. So far as the schools are concerned, the members of the tribe still have little or no voice in their management, the personnel of teachers, the curricula, or practical relation of the subjects taught to the future life of Indian youth. Although the constitutions of each tribal unit are supposed to be decided upon by the Indians themselves, there seems to be evidence that many of these are formulated in Washington and the superintendents of agencies given the responsibility of seeing that they are adopted by the tribes under their charge.[105] The chief shortcoming of government strategy in the past has been continual change of policy which has confused the Indian beyond measure. There has also been the tendency for the government to make more promises than it has been willing to carry out, a policy precisely the opposite of the Canadian which has been cautious in making promises but has then given more than the administrative Act called for.[106] Nothing would be better calculated to give the Indians of the United States more confidence than the adoption of this kind of strategy.

Another and opposite mistake would be to assume that the I.R.A. will somehow be able to perform the miracle of solving all future Indian problems without further readjustment. The fallacy of this position can be observed by noting conditions among the Navajo Indians in 1947. The reduction of their sheep raising during the war led to widespread suffering as the food supply became limited and cash incomes were curtailed. Surplus food supplies were sent in by the federal government, and the Federal Security Administration deemed it necessary in October, 1947, to announce that New

Mexico and Arizona must provide public assistance benefits to Indian aged, children, and the blind or forfeit $5 million a year in federal grants being given to those states.[107] The disruption of Indian economies resulting from the war poses many problems not envisaged by the I.R.A. and will doubtless call for various emergency measures in the future. Similar short-time aid will be necessary under any program whatever.

The bedrock conditions still exist. Assimilation is not a short-time process and it cannot be forced. The question still remains whether it will not be more fruitful to recognize the diversity of Indian culture and foster it by furnishing the conditions under which it can bloom again. Is American society ready to recognize the right to be different, to have values and goals which are pluralistic rather than uniform? If so, is the public ready to support a program which will encourage and foster these values for another century or two, after which the Indian will be ready to become a more integral part of American society but on his own independent terms? Or will the insistence on racial and cultural superiority lead to continuous disruptions of Indian life in the future as in the past? In case the conviction of superiority is somewhat ingrained and dogmatic, it will be helpful to consider the words of a resolution adopted by the Indian members of the Toronto–Yale University Seminar Conference:

> *Whereas*, representatives of the Indian race have participated in this Conference, devoted to a search for solutions of the Indian problem, be it therefore *Resolved*, that we Indians appreciate having been invited to take part in the Conference and by way of returning the compliment we wish to assure the Conference that you, our white brothers, will be invited to participate in any conference that we Indians may call in the future for the purpose of finding solutions to the white man's dilemma in a social and economic order that has, during the past decade, gone on the rocks.[108]

[CHAPTER 5]

The American Negro: *His Broken Culture*

THE VISITORS from Yankeeland drove their car into a southern city where they intended to observe a small Negro college. As they stopped in the outskirts to get their bearings and inquire directions at a filling station, they asked the proprietor where C— College was. "C—?" he said in surprise. "I didn't know there was such a school here." When they then explained that it was a Negro college, the proprietor's face froze. "No, sir, I don't know anything about it," he barked gruffly and went back into the station. Seeing a Negro boy working on a tire at the other end of the gravel, the driver went over to him and made further inquiries. "C— College? Yes, *suh.* Just follow this road to the left till you come to M. Avenue, take that out to the streetcar line, and follow that left till you come to the railroad tracks. Then it's over on the right. You cain't miss it, suh." Following these instructions to the letter, the driver reached his destination in a matter of minutes. He had also received a preliminary lesson in the separation of white and black society. To test it out further, on longer acquaintance with the city, he asked for directions from the more educated elements of the white community and was received with the same blank stares and with professions of complete ignorance not unmixed with indifference, surprise, or half amused resentment that anyone should suppose the fact to be worth knowing. He tried the same experiment with a considerable number of Negroes, both of the upper middle class and the lower socioeconomic levels, and rarely failed to get the right answer.

The implications of this simple occurrence are many for an understanding of the Negro community. First of all there is a wall of social distance separating Negro and white culture; this wall, like some permeable membranes, permits some circulation in one direction, from blacks to whites. Negroes work as domestics and laborers in the white areas of the city and are more or less familiar with the activities and institutions of white society. But the membrane is impermeable from the other direction, for nearly all white people remain within the confines of their own community, where the Negro is a visitor and worker rather than an inhabitant. The two cultures remain separate and parallel * with the Negro culture developing in a segregated area under a white influence which is occasional and sporadic, an influence which must be adjusted to the interests and values of an all-Negro society operating under restrictive patterns. Thus even though the forms of white society are often adopted by the Negro minority, the meanings will be altered so as to keep their congruence with Negro customs and folkways.[1] Another inference from this incident is the generalized attitude in all levels of white society toward the institutions of Negro advance. A college furnishes an opportunity for climbing up the ladder of success and thus for improving the status of many Negroes. Since the very presence of this institution contradicts the stereotype of the lowly, apathetic day laborer, it is treated as though it did not exist. Cultural silence is quite as significant as cultural pronouncement.

HOW THE NEGRO DIFFERS

We have already seen that the various minorities do not differ in native endowments but chiefly in social heritage.[2] Although the American Indian, the Mexican, the Negro, and the Japanese American show racial differences in body build, pigmentation, type of hair, and contour of head, not one of them can be strictly called a race.[3] Most of the Negroes brought to this country are from the relatively homogeneous group of Negroid stock called the Forest Negroes,[4] chiefly from the western equatorial coast of Africa. During the early period of slavery it might have been correct to call them the Forest Negro race, but today this designation would also be inaccurate since the great majority of American Negroes have some admixture of white blood.[5] Whenever the terms "race" or "racial" are applied to the group, this ambiguity must therefore be kept in mind; the

* See Chapter 6 for evidences of sharing in a common culture.

only accuracy left in the terminology is a relative one — the American Negro may be spoken of as a racial group only in phenotypical contrast with the dominant Caucasian and with other non-Caucasian minorities. Cultural history makes him for good or ill indisputably an American.

At the same time it gives him a different social base from which to operate and a different channel in which he can develop his talents. Like the Indian, the Negro appeared on the American scene as a preliterate and yet he came from western African cultures which could not be called rude or simple as compared with other preliterate societies. They were complex agricultural groupings with considerable social stratification and (as the distinguished student of African culture, Herskovits, affirms) "comparable in many respects" to the medieval culture of Europe, which had no machines and was barely literate in restricted class groups.[6] It is suggested by Herskovits that the southern plantation owner could very well have used the Indians for slave labor and that he failed to do so because the simpler agriculture of the Indians did not fit them for disciplined gang labor in the way that African culture did.[7] This is made all the more probable by our observation that the Indian usually mixed hunting activities with farming and hence lacked vicinal stability.[8]

Unlike the Indians also, the Negroes were forcibly transported and enslaved so that they were placed in a permanent lower status. Thus they became a minority as the result of different power relations.* Since African slaves did not remain together in tribal units, they lacked the social reinforcement of old customs and manners which have given the Indian remarkable resilience in resisting the patterns of a white man's civilization. Slavery atomized the Negro and forced him to make his adjustment either as an individual or in groups that were alike in only the broadest terms.

If we compare the Negro with the Mexican, we find other striking differences. In spite of the disorganizing influences at work in the Mexican community north of the border [9] there has been one bond denied to the Negro, a common language from the homeland.[10] For the most part the Negro made his way in the new land by the use of an unfamiliar tongue, the language of his white masters. And, unlike the Mexican, he did not come of his own volition.

* Cf. Chapter 1, p. 7.

In other respects we may note a considerable contrast with the Japanese or Chinese Americans, since the latter brought with them a historic, well-knit, and integrated culture from another land. The Japanese, for example, had undergone enough westernization to develop state sovereignty together with many technological and political patterns from the Occident. They came to the United States two or three centuries later than the Negroes. Their background gave them a fierce sense of nationalistic pride and they could often count upon diplomats, the Foreign Office, or even the direct intercession of a home government in their behalf.[11] In addition to a common language and civilization, the sense of belonging to one of the great powers heightened their social self-esteem.

Finally, in addition to the divergences already noted the Negro unlike the later European immigrant was a marked man in the American society. While the newcomer from Europe could gradually slough off his old-country ways and by climbing the social ladder establish himself securely in American society and become an indistinguishable part of it, the Negro found himself unable to perform the same feat. Although he could polish his manners, refine his language, educate himself, and improve his economic status, he carried with him a brand of his lowly past more conspicuous than the star of David — his color. High visibility has usually closed the door to social preferment.

THE FALLACY OF THE CULTURELESS MAN

It is true that the Negro slave was torn from his tribal moorings, separated from those of his own language and traditions, and as a consequence lost most of his social heritage. His adjustment to American ways and customs was facilitated by the fact that he was usually placed on a small plantation where he was in close contact with his white masters. Only 10 per cent of the slaves in 1860 were owned in groups of more than one hundred each, and less than 25 per cent of all slaves were owned in groups of fifty or more. Nearly one fourth of all slaves belonged to owners of less than ten slaves.[12] If this picture seems typical of the Old South (and there is good reason to believe that it is), working on large plantations was exceptional rather than usual. On the smaller plantations which were his usual habitat, the Negro was given opportunity to make a quicker adjustment to American culture, to pick up the language and ways of life shown him by his masters. It is also important to recognize that most slaves worked for small owners of middle class or lowly origin, so that very few of them had any contact with the polish and refinement of the plantation aristocracy.[13] In the great majority of cases work habits were crude, there was little machinery, and most of the labor was done by hand or with simple instruments like the hoe. What the Negro absorbed was chiefly white frontier folkways. He was valued chiefly as a labor unit, and any sentimental attachment which he might have had for the new culture was strongly inhibited. The master set the tasks to be performed, and monotonous drudgery represented largely what the white world had to give.

Nevertheless it is not accurate to conclude that the Negro was stripped of all his cultural lineaments or that his old ways of life were totally destroyed by the impact of slavery. Many students of the question have prematurely reached such a conclusion and have given it wide currency in the literature on the subject. Both Negro and white scholars have helped to perpetuate the error, many of them outstanding authorities in the field. E. B. Reuter,[14] E. F. Frazier,[15] E. R. Embree,[16] and others [17] have helped to build up the conception of the Negro as torn from his African heritage and left culturally naked in the new land until he began to take over the ways of the dominant Anglo-Saxon.

A closer comparison with African cultures has helped to modify this extreme view, although a large element of truth is still contained in it. In a way it is the whole burden of this chapter to show that the culture of American Negroes has been shattered largely by the peculiar conditions under which it has made its way in the western hemisphere. But if we start from the basic realities, it is necessary to realize that many traits from the older society still lie embedded in American Negro culture today, though often only in broadest outline. In those areas where the slaves actually outnumbered the whites, such as the Sea Islands off the coast of South Carolina, Lorenzo Turner of Fisk University has found as many as four thousand African words in the vocabulary of the Gullah Negroes.[18] Tonal registers are found for African words with marks for high tone and low tone, as well as the sliding intonation $\sim$.[19] Even cursory acquaintance with Negro speech reveals this cadence: "Ain't *nothin'* I cain't do." The sliding intonation could be placed over the word "nothin'." Similar differences in accent and rhythm of music and dance have been found which have become famous in American blues, spirituals, jitterbugging, and the like.[20] Secret cooperative societies were common in west Africa, and after emancipation of the slaves in the United States they sprang into existence under the acculturated form of the Negro lodge, which certainly has a different meaning for the Negro than the white lodge does for the dominant society.[21] Some of the hairdressing styles common to Africa were also kept in the new world.[22] Considerable emphasis on funerals and "being buried right," with the funerals held long after the burial, seems to come from older African custom, especially in Dahomey.[23] Money offerings laid in the coffin or on a plate by the coffin are also common to both old world and new world Negroes.[24] Cooperation in agricultural labor was common in Africa and this was often paralleled on the plantation and in the gang labor that survived slavery.[25] Many other examples of the same kind may be found in the researches of Herskovits.

HOW ACCULTURATION TOOK PLACE

The general idea that the Negro was largely a cultureless man tends to make him a passive recipient of the white man's culture, a presupposition which is not in accord with social psychology. It seems more accurate to say that Negroes in the United States began with emotions, attitudes, and behavior patterns already channeled in their own society. These secondary drives largely determined the direction of interest in the new culture and resulted in selection, reshaping, and modification in accordance with basic needs and habits. The acculturation of the Negro thus proceeded in accordance with (1) his already channeled interests which helped to determine the elements considered important for imitation or adaptation; (2) rebellion against those repressive measures that prevented adequate and free expression of the personality; (3) permissive patterns of the dominant group; (4) coercive patterns of the dominant group; (5) compensation through overdevelopment and elaboration; (6) intragroup tensions arising from the external pressure exerted by whites. All of this presupposes the background of inferior or semicaste status defined by the white society, who in turn showed considerable indifference toward what went on within the Negro community so long as it did not endanger white domination. White folkways included toleration of social usages which reinforced the current stereotype of Negro inferiority but inhibited any features that challenged the stereotype.

The process of adjustment forced the Negro to adopt a relatively new technology, a different set of economic patterns, and later, other political forms as well. Yet even in the days of bondage the master was much less likely to supervise leisure hours and spare-time occupations such as religion and amusements.[26] As long as it did not interfere too directly with the slave's labor, natural interest (under the permissive pattern) could develop in these areas.

Although the six factors of acculturation mentioned are separable for the sake of convenience, they did not operate singly but as variables which combined in different ways. In order to observe their operation, it will be convenient to examine certain aspects of Negro life to see how the incorporation of new ways of living actually occurred. This will give a more adequate understanding of the special features of Negro culture in the United States.

RELIGIOUS LIFE

It is already clear that the permissive patterns of the white man allowed the Negro to develop unique modes of response in his religious activities.[27] For this reason he was able to construct religious institutions especially fitted to his own needs. More than any other feature of his life, he has come to regard his churches as peculiarly his own — a tendency noted by most investigators of the subject.[28] One tendency which has been particularly pronounced is for the Negroes to affiliate themselves with the Baptist church — so much so that a well-known southern aphorism has it that if a Negro isn't a Baptist, someone has been tampering with him. This can be accounted for in terms of several acculturative factors. To begin with, a prevalence of river cults in Africa made the Negro peculiarly susceptible to ritual and ceremony connected with streams of running water. Priests of the river cults in Africa were especially esteemed and as a group were so resistant to slavery that many of them were sold to prevent their leadership from disrupting the relations with whites.[29] This may be of some significance in accounting for initial interest in the cult. Of more importance was the fact that American Baptists were not only zealous in preaching their gospel to the slaves but gained adherents in large numbers very early in the history of slavery. By 1793 there were something like 73,471 Baptists in the United States, one fourth of whom were Negroes; in 1806, one third of the Baptists in the state of South Carolina were Negroes. Furthermore the Baptists allowed more leeway and freedom for the Negroes to have their own churches and ministers.[30] This was partly due to the fact that the congregational form of church organization permitted each church to choose its own religious leader and manage its own affairs. At all events it is evident that the permissive pattern of the dominant group was strongly influential.

In the case of revivalistic cults with their phenomena of religious seizure, similar forces have been at work. For many years this shouting religion was attributed to the influence of white evangelistic sects which were imitated by the Negro, while the retention of these practices was explained as a social lag in the insulated Negro culture which was, by reason of segregation, prevented from mingling with modern crosscurrents of thought and action.[31] However, even granting this sequence of events, we would still have to account for the Negro's original interest and selection of these religious practices rather than others. It is now possible, because of more extensive African researches, to give this aspect of the problem more adequate attention. It comes to light that in west Africa religious dancing is a common feature of many cults. This dancing takes place until the devotee is possessed by the deity. Priests with their esoteric knowledge take the lead, and others join in until they are overcome by the effect of hypnotic rhythm. There is clapping of hands and beating of drums while spectators gather to see one after another in the circle submitting to the powerful force of the seizure. The drummers do not stop until all who are under the spell have recovered. In this ritual there are initiates and novices, the former training the latter until they know how to bring themselves under the spell. Enjoyment rather than decorous behavior is the keynote of the ceremonies, with spectators joining in the clapping of hands.[32] It is not suggested that these forms were brought unchanged into the American environment, but they undoubtedly helped to account for the Negro's interest in the nearest analogue that could be found in the new home and probably had much to do with the shaping of revivalism along the lines already familiar to him. When taking part in the new cult practice, the African would naturally retain certain forms of behavior, attitudes, and emotional expression which gave vitality to his older customs. While adopting some of the newer forms of shouting, singing, and praying he would still give them a coloration peculiarly his own. After visiting smaller sects of both white and colored groups, Powdermaker notes that a larger part of the Negro congregation participate, that they have more rhythm and less convulsive or jerky movements, and that they also seem to show more spontaneity and freedom in entering into the service.[33]

The permissive pattern was not the only one at work, however. During the period of slavery whites were usually present to observe Negro ceremonies, and a considerable effort was made to separate the congregations of freemen and slaves.[34] Thus some coercive regulations were enforced, and some of these were retained after emancipation by being internalized in the personality of the Negro preacher, who often urged his hearers to keep well within semicaste lines. He was often the go-between linking the dominant community with his own flock, and he justified his work in terms of keeping vagrant members in line with the controls set up by whites. Furthermore, even after slavery there were members of the Negro group who constantly reported the activities of the churches to whites.[35] Under this somewhat rigid arrangement it was natural that otherworldliness should develop as a compensation through overdevelopment and such has been the characteristic pattern of Negro preaching and belief in most churches up to the present day.[36] As long as it keeps its major interest in the next world the Negro church, particularly in the South, receives general commendation from the white community and is left to develop in its own way when the religious leadership is credited with having the right attitudes.[37]

In the background, of course, the pattern of rebellion was never wholly submerged. During the period of Reconstruction many Negro preachers adopted the role of political leaders, and even before this Negro churches in the North served as regular stations in the underground railroad to freedom in Canada.[38] And it must not be forgotten that in the spirituals an indirect expression of the cry for freedom could not be downed:

Go down Moses,
Way down in Egypt land,
Tell old Pharaoh,
Let my people go.

This *double entendre* always had deep meaning for the Negro though it was passed over by the dominant community as "quaint" or "colorful."

In some respects the Negroes apparently took over the practices and policy of white churches bodily. Most of them adopted Protestant forms from a predominantly Protestant environment, including the wide variety of schismatic divisions that mark the life of Protestantism as a whole. At the same time they continued the differentiation of the religious community in terms of "upper class" and "lower class" churches, with Presbyterian, Congregational, and Episcopalian predominating in the upper crust.[39] Yet here there is a likeness with a difference, for intragroup tensions among the Negroes resulting from external white pressure have tended to fractionate the group into smaller and smaller divisions represented by the "store front churches" common to urban centers. These organizations are so named because many of them hold their meetings in abandoned stores or in some cases at the home of a member. Drake and Cayton report that in Chicago 75 per cent of the Negro churches are of this type,[40] most of them having less than twenty-five members. The pressure of the white group upon the Negro community seems to have a double effect. In the first place, it tends to weaken institutional controls because they are instinctively felt as a barrier to freedom of action and belief. On the other hand, in order to assert this freedom the race leader is unwilling to accept subordination under another in his own group. This results in greater factionalism and a multiplication of leaders, at the cost of the number of followers. (As we shall see, this is not a process restricted to the church.) When this process occurs, a reappearance of an older type of action common to an earlier period makes its way to the light. The leader is now charismatic, that is, he establishes his dominance because of his extraordinary qualities, which enable him to arouse enthusiasm among his followers.[41] Whether we should trace this to a universal human tendency that gives the charismatic leader more prominence whenever legal or institutional forms are weak or whether it should be traced more specifically to the prevalence of this form of Negro leadership in Africa and during the early period of slavery — a tendency fostered by conditions within the segregated Negro culture — is an issue that cannot be determined with certainty. At any rate those who were given authority, even among the slaves, were those who had special prowess among their own people, such as magical powers or physical strength.[42] This is one of the natural forms of leadership everywhere and it is at least a defensible thesis that this inclination has been kept alive by the peculiar conditions under which the Negro lives.

HABITS OF LABOR

We have already seen that the Negro had a pattern of cooperative agricultural labor in his own background that prepared him well for the life of the plantation.[43] In the older accounts that told of the Negro's accommodation to slave practices it was often assumed that the vassal was naturally docile and obedient; in fact docility and obedience were attributed to racial qualities inherent in the Negro.[44] It is true that the adoption of servile behavior was a natural accompaniment of slave, as it was later of semicaste, status; equally true that this has persisted into the twentieth century. Undoubtedly it happened that many who played this role became so habituated to it that it finally submerged the rest of the personality. This does not mean, however, that the Negro submitted tamely to the regime of the plantation or that he failed to protest against his servitude, as James Truslow Adams asserts.[45] The researches of Herbert Aptheker have shown that there were scores of insurrections against white masters from 1790 to 1860 and even later.[46] He relates that from 1830 to 1860 about two thousand slaves a year escaped through the underground railroad.[47] The Negro's reaction to enforced labor also expressed itself in acts of indirect aggression like sabotage and carelessness, which resulted in deliberately wasted fields, damaged tools, and economic loss to the plantations.[48] Other ways of contravening the labors imposed by the white man were feigning sickness, self-mutilation, and flight to the swamps.[49] While the latter is represented by Aptheker as a form of strike, with escaped Negroes holding out until their demands for better food, better clothes, or fewer beatings were met, it may equally well be regarded as a form of escape which would hurt the master even though the Negro himself suffered as a consequence. Escape was often the only weapon at hand, and its use in recent years by domestics and others who walked off the job at a critical moment shows that it became an accepted pattern of passive resistance — usually to extra work or unjust conditions — which, because of the coercive patterns of white domination, could not be expressed openly. This type of walking off the job, though met with dire headshakings and contemptuous comments on "irresponsibility" and "laziness," served the Negro well because it was a release that fitted with the common stereotype. If the words of Housman's poem can be torn from their context, the colored worker could have mused:

> I, a creature, and afraid,
> In a world I never made.

It was precisely this feeling that the world of work in the new world was made by others for their own uses and that he was expected to be a willing contributor to the enrichment of an alien group that helped to define the attitude of the Negro toward labor. This applies with less cogency to those who were trained to be artisans or skilled laborers, many of whom were freed or bought their freedom. Not work itself but the *meaning* of work was totally different for the vast majority of Negroes.

It must be remembered that the Negro has labored in an atmosphere where the culture and the subculture of economic life have been contradictory and have tended to cancel each other out. The dominant economic mores which constitute the culture call for individual effort, initiative, competition, and a gradual climb from lower to higher levels. Within this larger area the colored worker also had to make his adjustment to the subculture of segregation within which there were special obstacles to the achievement of economic independence. In general the stronger the influence of the subculture of segregation, the weaker has been the response to the demands made by the competitive or wider culture. Before emancipation, the only Negro who could rise in the social scale was the skilled worker in iron, woodcarving, carpentry, or masonry who already had his freedom. These, who lived in the cities, were able to win for themselves an ever-increasing status in the community comparable to others. During the Civil War when Negroes migrated in droves to the Union Army, many were given the opportunity to become self-supporting with farms or plantations of their own; the results were salutary. Released from the handicaps of alien restrictions, the great majority of them successfully responded to the demands of independence and initiative, with only about one seventh dependent on the government for subsistence payments.[50] In the Reconstruction era, the sudden advent of freedom was a heady wine and many celebrated the new era by a temporary refusal to work at all.[51] Others received such low wages for accustomed plantation work (in one case as low as $1.25 a growing season plus a peck of dry corn a week) that they were finally forced to take subsistence payments.[52] The extent of unemployment during this disorganized and turbulent period can be gathered from the fact that the Freedman's Bureau distributed 21 million rations in a period of four years.[53]

As the period of states' rights returned to the South, the Negro exchanged the badge of slavery for that of semicaste and share tenancy. Too much attention has been given to the attempt in this period to disfranchise the Negro, and too little to the new and artificial restrictions imposed upon his occupational mobility. Some of these were not stated in law but rather were buttressed by it, such as the new forms of tenancy in which paternalistic patterns prescribed the relations between owners and tenants, the commissary system with its increasing burden of debt, and restrictions on any attempt of the plantation worker to seek redress from his superiors. In the industrial field special legislation was introduced to segregate certain industries from the influx of Negro workers, while in the skilled crafts white labor organizations adopted a policy of excluding colored workers. Finally, as C. S. Johnson shows, the only place where the dominant culture of competition and ascendancy was allowed full play was in Negroes' work and service for other Negroes.[54] Up to World War I, the entrance of Negroes into northern industry was uneven and sporadic. Until recent years the role of the labor union has been to exclude them from membership, and this has meant that only jobs at the bottom of the scale have been available.

The result of these subcultural restrictions has been a broken economic culture for the Negro. The rural Negroes of the South are, many of them, still attached to the soil and continue doggedly with their labor,[55] which provides little more than a bare subsistence. Others, drawn to towns and cities because of slightly greater opportunities and considerably greater freedom from white pressure, nevertheless show little rivalry among themselves for positions that might be open to them,[56] assuming perhaps that no one can "beat the game" or climb much higher. Furthermore, the practice of recommending a friend or relative for a vacated position is so common that it may serve to keep rivalry at a minimum. This tendency is in turn aggravated by the segregation of white from Negro culture, so that the white man thinks of substituting one Negro for another in terms of replaceable parts rather than in terms of seeking out a more responsible and efficient laborer.

In the industrial field the tendency has been to use Negro labor for menial and unskilled positions but to use white workers at machines. This has apparently followed the assumption that Negroes are mentally unfitted for such work, although the constantly changing practice of many production centers, especially in World War II, has indicated that under conditions of the proper training Negro labor operates successfully in this field.[57] However, in the South, and to some degree in the North as well, certain types of jobs are defined by the culture as "Negro jobs" or those in which Negro labor can be used without serious repercussions from other workers.* The chief restriction placed upon promotion has been in those cases where managerial or supervisory functions are concerned; in these, subcultural lines of exclusion are still strongly drawn. To the extent that these barriers exist, they give rise to either apathy or protest against artificial restrictions on the job ceiling. In the former case, they serve to underline the current stereotype of the "lazy worker," while in the latter they fix attention on the "trouble-maker" or the "uppity" individual and result in either discharge or transferral or some sort of repressive action.

The intragroup tensions arising from this subcultural situation

* This is not to overlook the constant encroachment of whites into types of work formerly performed by Negroes alone, a tendency most pronounced during the depression of the 1930's and accounting for much of the unemployment among southern Negroes. At the same time it made possible a greater amount of trade union organization in the South.

appear most clearly in the realm of Negro business, where the trader serves his own people. Since about 1910 a powerful ideology of supporting "race" business has been built up as a matter of folk pride. At the same time there is considerable complaint on the part of the Negro businessman that he is not given the trade that is due him. Insufficient support is due, in large measure, to segregated business: the Negro merchant cannot start with the same amount of capital and therefore cannot buy in large quantities; he is obliged to cut down on his help and therefore offers inferior service; he is often unable to get the choice locations which are obtained by white merchants; and he must compete with national chains which undersell. All these items tend to drive customers to the stores of competing white businessmen instead of to his own, for race pride by itself is not sufficient as a motive for buying. On the other hand, it often leads to much mutual recrimination between the Negro customer and his fellow merchant, one asserting that he cannot get the same service or the same prices in stores run by members of the race, while the other berates the would-be customer for failing to give support until such time as the situation would be more equalized.[58]

THE NEGRO FAMILY

On the west coast of Africa the family is polygynous (one male mating with several females) and tied up with larger kinship groupings like the consanguine or great family and the clan or sib.[59] In this respect the past history of the African family has much in common with that of the European family, which had a polygynous form in the Dark Ages,[60] especially in the upper classes. In Africa, however, marriage arrangements were made almost entirely by the two families of the bride and groom, and wider social sanction was not necessary.[61] Usually the woman who had economic independence could leave her husband whenever she wished, as indeed, sexual independence of women everywhere has followed economic independence.[62] In the polygynous family the children of the same mother tended to be together more, though under certain circumstances they shared the same father with children of other mothers. The tendency, however, was to have closer relations with the mother than with the father, a pattern which established initial interest and direction for family groupings in the United States.[63]

When brought to America, the slaves were sold at the convenience of the trader and the plantation owner. Husband and wife, mother and child, were either separated or brought together or sold in groups as the planter wished. Often enough they were forcibly removed from each other and the one to be sold first would be the stronger or more skilled. Family relation was of secondary importance commercially. Nor was it true, as one tradition has it, that mothers and their children were regularly sold together,[64] for in advertisements for runaway slaves it would be stated that the fugitive might be going to see his mother who belonged to another master, or that a mother had several children now belonging to someone else.[65] One of the chief humanitarian objections to the slave trade was that it so often cruelly separated the mother from the children.[66] On the plantation the father's function was biological rather than sociological because he had nothing to do with the care and rearing of the children. He did not have to furnish food or shelter or clothing since this was left to the slave owner. Nor did he take the responsibility of rearing or discipline, for these were the function of the mother. Under these conditions the father was an appendage to the family and was not integrated into its activities as in the more conventional family; to all intents and purposes the mother with her children constituted the family.[67]

There was no single pattern of domination on the plantation which determined the relation between mates or between mother and children. In some cases the slave was mated with the partner his master found for him; resistance was impossible, whatever his previous family connections.[68] In others, the plantation owner very definitely used certain slave women for breeders, and these were given lightened work in favor of a regular succession of child bearing.[69] In other cases the slave woman, though pregnant or having recently borne a child, was nevertheless forced to work under penalty of severe punishment.[70] Perhaps a more common policy was to let matters take their own course in the slave quarters and give little or no supervision to mating.[71] As one planter expressed it, the slaves might have as many wives as they liked so long as it did not lead to discord.[72] Under other conditions the plantation owner would be more concerned about the propriety of family relations and give orders to the overseer that marriages be performed for each slave union and that no plural matings be allowed.[73] Although this would seem to encourage monogamous practice, it could be considered by the Negro as only one more restriction imposed from the white man's world and therefore to be lightly regarded. This was even more likely to be true if the master inconsistently sold the wife or the husband separately. At least we are sure that slave marriages had no standing in the law and therefore could easily be annulled with the master's consent, which could be obtained without difficulty.[74]

For the most part, then, plantation life contributed to a weakening of Negro family structure since the solidarity of father, mother, and children was considered no more important among most planters than that of the domesticated animals owned by them.[75] Added to this was the crossing of the color line by white overseers and owners which the Negro male was powerless to prevent. This was partly due to the excess of males among both Negroes and whites in the South during the period of slavery and partly to the law, which did not allow slaves to be witnesses against whites in any court action.[76] In some cases sexual relations between white men and colored women led to special privileges for the latter and hence to higher status.[77] In others it led to shame or resentment on the part of white men or their wives so that concubines or their mulatto children or both were sold to get rid of the offending image.[78] But whatever the reaction in the white man's society, the pattern of miscegenation (sexual relations between two racial groups) had its influence by arousing the reflection that sexual experimentation resulted from privileged power position; no doubt it also led to the feeling that white insistence upon strict marital standards for the Negro was merely for the purpose of satisfying an artificial moral ideal which could be regarded as far removed from the realities.

With the coming of emancipation the adoption of new family types depending upon the responsibility of the husband was a slow process. In the first place the habits and customs of the plantation tended to perpetuate themselves among both sexes. The men, accustomed to having the children supported by the plantation owner and cared for by the mother, continued to leave responsibilities largely on the mother's shoulders. The women, finding that this type of husband did not give them the support they needed, developed more independent attitudes with regard to mating; in many cases they failed to desire permanent attachment with the added burdens it might place upon their shoulders.[79] Consequently the retention of the maternal family among Negroes has been most marked, though it is accompanied by such a wide variety of types that it furnishes a unique gamut of practices.*

As a result of these historical experiences, acculturation in Negro family behavior has been uneven and irregular. Presenting some of the more familiar types will help to visualize the situation. The one most commonly noticed by observers in contrast with the surrounding white culture is the maternal type in which the mother is the acknowledged provider and disciplinarian. Frazier and King estimate that this probably includes from 20 to 30 per cent of all Negro families, the proportion depending upon factors such as lower class status, southern environment, and urban environment, all of which make for a higher ratio.[80] The maternal family separates into four subdivisions. Four other mixed types may be added. Finally the egalitarian type occurs also. This gives nine types altogether.

1. *The Unmarried Mother type.* These mothers are not the "sinned against rather than sinning" group but those of lower class origin who can see little future in either single blessedness or marriage with a husband unable to find enough work to support the family. Quite deliberately they engage in regular courtship behavior until they have found a father for their children; then sooner or later the couple separate and go their own way.[81] Group solidarity supports the mother in this decision, for if she is not promiscuous and has no quarrels or fighting occurring on her account, she is accepted with the other married women of the community, and her children are regarded as legitimate. They also acknowledge their fathers in the same way that other children do, without stigma.[82]

2. *The Deserted Mother type.* In this case the realities are much the same except that the marriage originally had more public sanction. Particularly among southern lower class Negroes it is likely to be common-law marriage which is casually accepted by the com-

* The sex ratio of the Negro population in 1940 was 95 males to 100 females, in contrast with the native white ratio of 100.1 to 100. The Negro excess of females gives the male a greater variety of choice but restricts that of the woman. Cf. Paul H. Landis, *Population Problems, A Cultural Interpretation*, New York, American Book, 1943, p. 254.

munity.[83] The constant traveling of Negro males in search of better work opportunities often makes them disinclined to return to family responsibility. The result is a deserted wife and children, even though the husband had no premeditated desire to leave them.

3. *The "Quasi Family."* Here there is a male head and a series of wives and children. Some of the children and grandchildren who do not adjust themselves to the new mother drift away, and the more dependent or the more congenial stay at home. The various separations may be given the name of divorce but there is little evidence that they require any formality.[84]

4. *The Divorced Mother type.*[85] It is impossible to separate this absolutely from the Deserted Mother type because of the informality with which marriage bonds are broken when they are unsatisfactory. Legalized divorce is uncommon in southern rural areas because of the costs and because recourse to white justice is naturally shunned.[86] Deserted or unmarried women often report themselves to be divorced or widowed.[87] Those who have informal divorce are probably the largest number and make up an important ratio of the maternal family. Those who have legal divorces are in the small minority and are probably upper-middle or upper class women for whom the economic struggle is not quite so difficult.

5. *Mother-in-law Dominance type.* In this type the father is unable to secure adequate support for his family or does not live up to the expected role of a husband in some way. The wife's mother, as a result of her daughter's disappointing marriage, may then attempt to regulate the life of the family. Since she may have been dominant in her own family, her experience gives her an added satisfaction in setting things to rights in her daughter's family. This is still an example of maternal dominance but it is one generation removed.[88]

6. *"Artificial" or Partly-related-and-partly-unrelated type.* This group lives and functions together as a single family, although there are many individuals in it which were not progeny of the original union. Some may be related, others adopted. There may be a history of two or more past marriages as in the Quasi Family, with children from each, and older relatives or younger children who are either adopted or are the offspring of one of the group. This family is generally stable and responsive to more conventional patterns and the members conduct themselves accordingly.[89]

7. *The Widowed Mother type.* Here the mother is somewhat older and takes full care of the children, who are soon able to furnish their own support. Most of these families tend to resemble the more conventional family since they have had regular paternal support for many years. In this respect the type differs from the Unmarried Mother, Deserted Mother, and Divorced Mother types and is far more stable.[90]

8. *Male Dominance type.* It is impossible to establish this kind of family without regular economic livelihood, and hence it is more likely to occur where employment is permanent, that is, among the semiskilled who retain their positions, salaried employees, and middle class groups.[91] Usually the Male Dominance family follows the more conventional American pattern and is found in those groups who have opportunity to respond more sensitively to the acculturative process. Thus it is found more frequently in upper class groups where the family is in line with dominant American mores. There is also evidence that more equality between the sexes is present in upper class Negroes.[92]

9. *The Egalitarian family.* Among the smaller professional group, especially where women have business, artistic, theatrical, or educational careers of their own, the family reflects whatever joint patterns of authority are most feasible for its individual needs. Like the Male Dominance type it assumes the common forms of upper class equalitarianism anywhere. In fact, all of our nine types may be found in urban culture to some extent also.

In general as we follow these family types from the first to the ninth, we are ascending the class ladder, though there are exceptions to the rule. Among the lower classes, illegitimacy and a certain casualness toward the marriage bond are most common.* Motherhood is highly respected and desired but marriage is not.[93] Since the institutional controls are weak, either the husband or the wife will often resort to violence to reinforce the unstable relationship. At the same time there is a kind of perennial suspicion that the partner is playing false.[94] Adoption of children is common and helps to

* In many respects a similar pattern appears in the lower class groups of the community at large, where premarital and extramarital relations are common. Cf. A. C. Kinsey, *Sexual Behavior in the Human Male*, Philadelphia, Saunders, 1947.

compensate for the constant breaking up of families.[95] Most significant of all, the economic background conditions the family form inexorably. In a Georgia study, Charles King found that two thirds of the maternal families under his observation had mothers who earned from $1.00 to $3.99 per week. This necessitates putting the children to work at an early age to help support the family. At the same time it means that in turn they will repeat the pattern of the unstable family as they grow up, unless new opportunities arise. By means of census figures, King has also shown that decrease in the number of maternal families occurs with increase in living standards. Thus he says of the Negro, "As his occupational efficiency and stability increase, the tolerance of illegitimacy declines."[96]

COLOR DISTINCTIONS

One interesting form of acculturation is the development of a semiclass system within the Negro community based on color differences. There seems to be considerable evidence that mulattoes and those of lighter color were given special privileges on the plantation, doing housework rather than field work, being given more education, and often receiving their freedom.[97] This may have resulted from the biological relationship of these mulattoes with masters or prominent whites. At any rate, when slavery passed, a closely knit group of lighter colored Negroes formed a pretty well defined upper class, many of them becoming teachers, lawyers, doctors, or authors. Starting without the handicaps of the darker group, they were able to become outstanding leaders highly respected by the Negro community and able to serve in a liaison position by reason of greater acceptability among whites. Both the permissive patterns of the dominant group and the compensatory patterns of the more submerged group combined to create a heightened color-consciousness favoring those of lighter rather than those of darker skin. Before long, a kind of color hierarchy developed in which prestige and acceptability went with a near-white or light brown skin.* This color pattern has become widely known and has received much comment from both Negroes and whites.[98]

* An older mulatto woman once told the writer that until she moved from Charleston to a newer southern city, she had never allowed a full-blooded Negro to enter her home.

On this issue a word or two of caution is necessary. It is unquestionable that a rank order somewhat in line with color is present in Negro society, with lighter colored Negroes receiving preferential consideration. This may be seen from the widely adopted practice of darker men of achievement marrying lighter colored wives [99] and the better marriage prospects of lighter skinned females in general.[100] Another indication of the tendency appears in the difficulty encountered by darker colored women in obtaining employment above the menial occupations,[101] and in social cliques formed on a color basis.[102] It would be correct to infer that evidence of lighter color is more important for females than for males, since the female group is more likely to emphasize the ritualistic formalities of "society." As in all status distinctions there is often the tendency to substitute an unquestioned symbol of this kind for achievement, and for those who are excluded to retaliate with epithets or derogatory criticism. As one middle-class girl put it to an inquiring psychologist, "A light person will call you 'black' long before a white person will."[103] And another girl complained that if she were dark, her husband would call her black, and if she were light he would say, "you half-white thing you," so she couldn't win.[104] Thus while the primary pattern stressed the high rating of the lighter colored, a strongly developed secondary pattern condemns any such pretensions and thus helps to right the balance. The upshot of the two contradictory influences is to make those at both ends of the color scheme somewhat ashamed,[105] with those at the lighter end remaining passively acquiescent in a system from which they derive many benefits, while those who are darker either react with belligerent attitudes or are expected to do so. This stereotype, of course, reinforces the tendency.[106]

There is evidence, however, to show that this whole color complex is in a transitional stage that is undergoing many modifications; certainly it is anything but final. Years ago when the lighter skinned or fair individual had more prestige than today, it was the figure of the mulatto that was continually used in advertisements for hair and beauty preparations; today it is the light brown figure that appears. The Negro group in Chicago, for example, is beginning to build up a "cult of the brown-skinned woman" and to refer to itself as "Bronzeville."[107] This represents a crystallization around a midpoint in the color scale, one which is favored by the actual changes in the community itself.[108] As Negro society passes from its early, undeveloped stage where the very possession of a lighter skin automatically conferred prestige, to a more mature period in which achievement among its darker colored members is more and more common, there will be less tendency to associate lighter color with esteem, and the old pattern will die out.[109] As ability begins to count more than color — as it already does among the males — the rise of darker skinned individuals who possess the capacity for advancement will operate against a class system based on lighter color.[110]

SUMMARY

Our brief examination of the Negro in America has shown the development of a broken culture resulting chiefly from four major factors which have had considerable influence on the Negro's development without having an equal effect on white culture. These four factors are slavery, emancipation, fixed class status, and high color visibility enabling the Negroes to be singled out as "different." Slavery broke the mold of the old African culture almost completely, allowing only a few generalized elements to remain; it forced the Negro to adapt himself to new ways as an individual rather than as a viable tribal group. There were few or no "cultural islands" where he might maintain old traditions, language, and customs within a framework of social solidarity, as the Indian was able to do. Thus his acculturation was forced at a more rapid pace than was characteristic of other American minorities. This fact of course brought with it many incongruities and discordant elements from the standpoint of the dominant culture. Slavery compelled the development of a religious escapism, separate religious congregations and policies in line with basic African needs, the special importance of charismatic leadership, and the focalizing of community values in the church. Fixed class status and social isolation helped to retain these features in Negro life long after many had been superseded by other patterns in the dominant community. Slavery also aroused habits of apathy, contravention, or direct resistance to labor patterns so often regarded as imposed from the outside with no corresponding gain to the producer himself. Sabotage, escape patterns, or in some cases appropriation of lesser forms of portable property, became the accepted modes of antagonism in an attempt to right the uneven balance of economic reward. At the same time the unimportance of the father's economic responsibility became a dominant pattern of masculine behavior under the slave regime, as did also the assignment of primary duties to the mother in any family unit. Continual miscegenation and disregard of the master for regularized sex relations among the slaves weakened the family structure so that casualness and informality became characteristic attitudes toward the conventional family.

Emancipation, being a sudden access of freedom, was a source of further disorganization. In religion it cut the congregations off more completely from white paternalism and supervision. While this was a welcome relief to the Negro, the increased pressure of segregated restrictions resulted in increasing rivalry among colored leaders and therefore in almost unlimited schism. In the economic area emancipation meant a swift change from dependence to independence at a time of increasing unemployment and poverty. In this atmosphere the pattern of white domination and paternalism again came to the fore, creating new legalized peonage on the land; while in the cities more and more exclusion of the Negro from industrial or skilled trade occupations became the rule, with resulting irregular work habits and drifting about in search for jobs. All this in turn had its effect upon family life. On the plantations many of the patterns assumed in slavery days were continued through social inertia; in the cities the unstable employment of men helped to continue the dominance of maternal families.

The enforced social distance between racial groups meant that Negro culture gradually began to develop a separate though related community life. In this society social adaptation lagged behind that of the dominant group as a result of lesser participation in the culture as a whole. Immediate color visibility made distinctions easy to draw so that the great majority of Negroes could be stereotyped and defined without difficulty. Under these conditions the broken culture would continue to evolve more slowly than the "outside" society. Older patterns were then perpetuated, even after the original causes for their appearance were no longer present. The retention of religious, economic, and family responses was often more comfortable because it was more familiar. Customs become deeply ingrained in an environment separated by social lines of division. To the outsider these customs and traditions often appear as the distorted image of the dominant culture; a historical review of their origin, however, shows the causes responsible for their appearance and retention. It also shows that as opportunity and education become equalized, the two groups become more and more indistinguishable in actual accomplishment. The color line, however, still remains.

[CHAPTER 6]

The American Negro: *The Southern Picture*

"THAT'S THE WAY it was," mused the white-haired grandfather who had once been a slave. "When freedom came, one white Secesh man might shoot if you tried to git away, and another would take you to the underground and say, 'God bless you, you poor black devil.' Even some of the poor whites would help you if you took 'em something you stole, 'cause they had to eat like anyone else and 'most everybody was hungry then. Some of 'em would turn you in and some would give you a hand. Reckon it ain't much different from what it is today." [1]

It is clear from this narration that the old man who speaks is revealing central features of Southern folkways and customs. Whatever the characteristics of institutional patterns (which are largely stable and predictable), they are mediated to the individual through personal qualities and actions. And it is these intimate, personal, and nonpredictable responses that largely determine the social patterns throughout the South. Many of the apparent paradoxes and inconsistencies that strike the outsider will be resolved when they are approached from this frame of reference.

RURALISM AND LOCALISM

These peculiarly personal relations or primary-group realities arise from the fact that the South is today dominantly what it has been in the past, an agrarian culture.* [2] The old plantation which set the tone of the economy, even though it did not encompass the

* The term "South," as it is used here, is identical with the region which Odum calls the Southeast and includes Kentucky, Virginia, Tennessee, North Carolina, South Carolina, Georgia, Florida, Alabama, Mississippi, Louisiana, and Arkansas. See his *Southern Regions of the United States*, chap. III.

whole, was a little world of its own and as near a self-sufficient community (except at market time) as one would be likely to find. Here the planting, the harvesting, the carpentering, the spinning and weaving, the butchering, and the preserving were carried on in the way that the master and his mistress ordered. Everyone was known to everyone else, and even though the rigidities of the slave system prescribed many of the rules, they depended, as did the law everywhere, upon their interpretation and administration by the master. If he were kindly, so was the plantation community; if he were rough, irascible, brutal, whimsical, or arbitrary, his plantation reflected his personal qualities. Some plantation owners were efficient, some were improvident, some exacting, while others let the overseers manage everything without check or hindrance. In the latter case, then, the personal character of the overseer rather than that of the planter himself became the norm to which everything was referred. "Ol' Carney won't like it" or "Ol' Carney won't mind" became the only law that most slaves ever knew. In those areas where plantations were few the settlements were so small that personal-social relations [3] remained the dominant ones.

In this rural atmosphere occurred the same patterns that occur in rural cultures everywhere. A man was soon known for what he could do, and his traits of initiative, ambition, special skill, and peculiar behavior were common knowledge. He stood out in the community for his abilities or his lack of them. But one thing was sure: he was recognized as an individual. Even though the unalterable relation of slavery stood firm, each colored worker had his own reputation, which largely coincided with fact. Charley could pick more cotton than five other hands, while Bunch could keep everyone in a good humor; Jack could make the finest cabinets this side of Memphis, but Lillie never could cook. Toward all those who had their obvious failings, the ruralite had the typical mixture of tolerance and intolerance belonging to those who live in the same community and hence must learn to live with each other. The community life was therefore a blend of interactions between the dominant planter or overseer and the recognized peculiarities of each slave, so that each came to recognize through long experience just how far the other would yield before resentments became too strong. Just as the owner found that too many beatings would make Tom so sullen that he would not work, so Tom found that too much slackening on the job would bring more beatings. The slave who was caught in the grip of the "peculiar institution" naturally developed means of getting his desires by indirection, sometimes to the point of a fine art. Even today, on Mississippi plantations, we are told that the older colored workers get many things without asking for them directly "just by raising a situation so that the traditions make him [the planter] fork over." [4]

In addition to this intimate personal relationship, there was its extension into community life which goes by the name of localism. Although things might be done differently on another plantation, the feeling was that here, on this land, we do things our own way. "Maybe at Tiptonville 'they' do it one way, but here at McDowell 'we' always do it *this* way. Sheriff Gaines has held office for twenty-five years and he must know everyone in the county; we've never had much trouble here. How could anybody else do what he's doing? That must be a stranger in town; did you hear how he spoke to Mr. Crawford? Guess he doesn't know Mr. Crawford's the biggest man around here!" And so on. This unique sense of belonging to the community with social control a function of tradition and the peculiar relations that have grown organically for many years is the special badge of localism. The Confederacy and the long war which followed, tied these interweaving localisms into the larger localism which is the mind of the South, without entirely obliterating the separate localisms of towns and villages. Even the larger cities of the South seem, to one brought up in the impersonal urbanism of the North, to have retained this local flavor and the informal networks of acquaintanceship that go with it.

PATERNALISM

Bound up together with the rural-localism pattern goes another strain, separable in thought but not in operation. In every rural community there are Mr. Big and Mr. Little, who form two very different types of white man. Originally Mr. Big was the successful farmer and subduer of the wilderness, who added land to land until his property became the center for larger and larger groups of slaves. But unlike the aristocracy of Europe the plantation owners wrested their holdings from a stubborn frontier and became the self-made men of the new world. Also unlike the European, Mr. Big and his plantation were surrounded by relatives and friends who had not climbed so high as he had but who might do so at some later date. Both before and after the war of 1861–1865 he came to be the leading citizen of the nearby village or town. His word was naturally more weighty than that of Mr. Little, for realities are stronger than laws. The courthouse was soon filled with men who were convinced that Mr. Big's requests were perfectly reasonable and that he knew best what should be done with the county. There was nothing sinister about this; it was only a recognition of what counted and what did not count. When the slaves were freed, Mr. Little came into more power but the old informal dependence did not disappear; it was now modified only by the fact that there was a common bond of being white men between them. And so far as possible Mr. Little adopted the patterns of dominance when dealing with the common outsider, the Negro. After all he was related to the Bourbons: he had the surname of at least *some* Mr. Big, and never in all the world could he mention his family except in terms of its highest representative. The late Clarence Cason, a prominent Alabama author, referred to himself as a member of the middle class but he remarked with irony that probably no Southerner before him had ever made such a statement.[5] At any rate the patriarchal attitude adopted by the planter toward his slaves and later toward his tenants, both white and black, has tended to become the fixed attitude of all whites toward the Negro himself. The continued use of Negro maids for domestic service perpetuates this relationship in the cities, where ordinarily it might seem out of place.

Although there are many ramifications of these attitudes among the whites themselves, it is the outcome for Negro-white relations that interests us here. For southern tradition defines these relations in the terms of the master-servant pattern as the only stable condition in which the white community feels secure. This is the basic meaning of the standard phrase that the Negro should keep "his place." In keeping with the southern folkways, no higher praise can be given to a Negro than the comment that he knows his place. If he shows the proper deference and humility, he not only preserves the equilibrium of the society but also gives the white man an agreeable sense of status by oiling the social machinery which in many respects is in a state of near-breakdown. In a sense all the legal restrictions that bear on the life of the Negro community — the segregation codes, the crop lien laws, the poll tax, or the prohibitions of intermarriage and the like — all stem from the desire to keep this basic paternalistic pattern fixed between the white and Negro groups. In this atmosphere the free Negro, like the old slave, gets his desires not in the form of well-defined and predictable rights (for there are no rights under paternalism) but rather as protection and favors that result from temporary indulgence. If at any time a colored man shows that he thinks of his ambitions and rights in the same terms as those of the whites, then protection is withdrawn and violence takes its place. But again, it is an arbitrary, personal matter and depends upon the individual qualities of the policeman, judge, landlord, public official, or white leader in the community. To be more exact, it is the personal characteristic of the leader in interaction with his own status within the local situation. If he is secure in the knowledge of irreproachable status, he can afford to be generous and may gain further prestige by his generosity; but if his position is insecure, he will insist upon hard measures so that no one will question his status.

RESULTS OF PATERNALISM ON NEGRO BEHAVIOR

By establishing a personal role of dependence with a white man, the Negro can often solve his most pressing life problems. In the rural areas the favorite cropper or field hand can often prosper beyond his fellows and even exercise considerable authority over them because of his protected position. This may be called the alliance pattern. The Negro establishes an alliance with a planter or with a professional in the town; by doing errands or favors for his white ally (and sometimes this includes reports on what the Negro community is doing), he then becomes known as a "good nigger" in the white world even though he runs the danger of being castigated as a "white man's nigger" in colored society. In the uncertain world of shifting attitudes and relationships he now has a secure and protected status so that life becomes predictable and safe. By showing sufficient subservience and flattery toward his ally, he can often get ahead even with a lack of more substantial qualities. In the cities the same mode of adjustment often appears, especially in the courts.

Negroes discover that if they have "their white folks" come down and speak to the judge, they will get results. This, of course, presumes that the whites are impeccably dressed and speak patronizingly to the Negro himself in the court session. Often enough this will win a suspended sentence when nothing else will.[6] Nor is this type of behavior confined to lower class Negroes alone; deferential and adroit actions to exploit paternalism that spot the weaknesses of the dominant white occur among Negro college presidents and professionals as well as waiters and servants.[7] The alliance pattern is a powerful agent to be reckoned with in the southern Negro community, although it is selective and applies to a minority within a minority.

The other results of paternalism are more widely spread and affect the entire Negro population in varying degrees. As another example we may take what may be called the devitalized work pattern. Wherever the Negro is employed, the paternalistic relation stands in the background and defines the basic realities of the situation. In order to keep his "place" he has a differential wage to begin with, for it is out of keeping with the folkways for a member of the subservient racial group to receive the same wage as the dominant white. Oddly enough the rural Negro shows less of a comparative discrepancy in this regard than the urban, for the income of white families in the rural South is about twice as high as that of the rural Negro, while the urban white family has an income about three times as high as the urban Negro.[8] This, however, is not the whole story. In the employer relationship the aim is to keep the basic paternalistic pattern of personal indulgence, arbitrariness, or occasional brutality rather than the better defined system of rights. Responsibilities are often poorly fixed and the work has fewer demands in the way of efficient, measurable standards and more demands in the form of traditional insistence on subservience. The Negro who shows ambition, initiative, and a desire to "get ahead" thus comes into conflict with the historic demand of keeping in his "place" and receives less favorable attention from his white employer than the one who makes a proper showing of humility and flattery toward his employer even though it is coupled with indifferent or mediocre work. Since this dependency pattern produces social and sometimes even economic rewards superior to those received by the ambitious worker, the latter draws the only conclusion possible and tends to fall in line.[9] It is probable that this very transition to lower work standards not only serves to confirm the current stereotype of the Negro as "lazy and shiftless" but also gives further social satisfaction and enhanced status to the white by "proving" white superiority. Probably this older paternalistic pattern keeps more of its original flavor in the area of domestic service than in any other; the wages are low but the evidence of master-dominance-generosity is kept alive by allowing perquisites to "tote" home in the form of food, clothing, furniture, or anything usable. Here again, the personal indulgence pattern is preferred to that of rights, and it is joined with a similar lowering of work standards. The devitalized work pattern is thus a direct outcome of the deeply entrenched paternalism of the entire South.

One of the most significant effects of the whole paternalistic complex is the dual role it thrusts upon the Negro; in fact it may even be called a dual ethic. In the uncertainty of the situation where dealing with whites is necessary, the Negro is at once suspicious and obliging. On the whole it is safer to keep one's suspicions to oneself and, as much as possible, to tell the stranger what the latter would like to hear.[10] Thus every southern Negro carries with him two roles either of which can be turned on or shut off at will. There is one type of ceremonial behavior and a set of ideas to match which may be used for social intercourse with members of the dominant community. It is composed of a liberal sprinkling of "yes sirs" or "yes ma'ams," of "cap" or "boss," of drawling humor or deep ignorance, as the situation demands. Although the white mistress in her kitchen feels that she knows a great deal about the personality of her cook, the latter tells only what she thinks her employer ought to know about life in the colored areas across town. While the mistress knows her cook only in work relations, the latter knows her and other whites in a much more intimate way through observing the details of family life, and under the dependency role the maid may conceal a "comprehension which is unsuspected and far from mutual."[11] When the southern white asserts that he "knows" the Negro, it usually means that he knows the ceremonial role or the "framework of etiquette"[12] which the Negro actually assumes in his presence. In fact when he speaks off the record, the white man in the South may confess to the feeling that Negroes keep something from him.[13]

Behind the screen is the other role or the one the Negro plays in his own community; it is at once more natural and more compensatory. He refers to the out-group as "white folks," "those ofays," or "crackers," and gleefully tells of encounters in which he worsted them, not without a trace of artistic embellishment which is duly discredited according to an unwritten understanding. If one of these conversations is overheard by a white, it may lead to misunderstanding and rumor of a damaging kind. For example, some Negro boys enter a five and ten cent store, make a purchase with every show of propriety, and then as they go out, one boy begins to badger the purchaser with, "I'm surprised at you, trying to hold hands with that white girl." The bantering goes back and forth in the role that the Negro reserves for his own group. In this case, however, it is heard by a white man, who then passes on the rumor that Negro boys are molesting white girls by trying to get familiar with them.[14]

A more serious aspect of the dual ethic is the role of self-protection from acts committed by white men that might be injurious to the Negro. This mode of concealment gradually extends toward both petty and serious offenders against the law. Anyone arrested has the status of a martyr in the Negro community and the word "criminal" rarely occurs in their vocabulary because the individual apprehended by the law is thought of as a mere unfortunate; in cases of necessity he is defended by every means possible. The matter does not stop there, however, for not only does this produce a dual ethic among the Negroes but it leads directly to a dual ethic in Southern society, in which violation of accepted codes evokes no condemnation within Negro society and even comes to be expected by whites. To go one step further, the white society then defines Negro behavior as shot through with criminality; in turn the individual who is regarded as criminal will frequently act like one because there is nothing to lose.

SOUTHERN POVERTY AND THE NEGRO

So far we have considered only the southern mores but it must be realized that they are a reflection of the economy, which is still only 32 per cent urban in a nation which is predominantly urban.[15] Although World War II has made some changes, it has not altered the basic pattern.[16] Ever since the days of Reconstruction the South has had insufficient income or capital to bring its economy up to the levels of other areas. To begin with, the plantation owners who were left after a devastating civil war were not merely unwilling to have the Negroes occupy a position of competition in agriculture (something which would have taken considerable time and investment to attain) but were quite literally unable to pay wages and thus had to offer a part of the crop as an incentive to keep the plantations going.[17] Furthermore the heavy hand of tradition kept cotton, corn, and tobacco as the familiar crops and labor as the chief resource. The upshot was a perpetuation of a semifeudal economy with crops that exhausted the soil very quickly and thus led to eroded lands. This was a vicious circle, for it resulted in a more deeply entrenched poverty. By the 1930's the South could calculate that half its arable land was bereft of topsoil and in many areas at least half was no longer cultivable.[18] In order to make this land productive, the South was forced to use twice as much fertilizer as all the rest of the nation combined.[19] The vicious circle continued by slowing down technological progress; as long as land and labor were cheap, it was better to take a chance on the price of cotton with the old methods than to install machinery. Consequently the South multiplied its deficiency in such items as tractors, electric motors, gas engines, electric lights, piped water, automobiles, motor trucks, and telephones.[20] This meant that income and wages lagged from 30 to 50 per cent behind the national level, manufacturing was retarded, with the insufficient markets available, and wages were correspondingly lower. Thus in the peak year before the depression the South had only about 13 per cent of the industries and wage earners, the value of its manufactures was only 9.1 per cent of the national total, and the wages paid to industrial workers constituted only 8.4 per cent of the total wages paid throughout the nation.[21] Not only the industrial income but the agricultural income was below the average of that in all other national regions.[22]

Although this analysis could be extended almost indefinitely, the important consideration for any study of the Negro is that by 1940 two thirds of the entire Negro population of the United States was resident in the South. Or to use exact figures, out of a total population of 12,865,518 Negroes in the nation, 8,169,000 were in southern areas (or the Southeast).[23] This means that many Negroes make their adjustments to American life in an area not yet fully industrialized but operating under a semifeudal economy, an area where wages and incomes are lower than in other regions, and incidentally an area whose chief resource is still its man power rather than its capital. The net reproduction rate of the South was 1.49 in 1930, which was higher than that in any other part of the nation.[24] Since the population replacement figure is 1 and most urban areas are considerably below this figure, the importance of the South as a population replenishment center can hardly be exaggerated. This holds for both Negroes and whites. Even though there was a considerable migration to cities of both racial groups during the 1930's (as much as 2.25 millions), the southern farm areas still showed a gain of one third of a million population.[25] The Negroes at the bottom of the economic ladder migrated more extensively than the whites,[26] but even with this trend there were almost twice as many Negroes in rural areas as in urban areas throughout the South by 1940. Migrations of World War II altered the Negro rural-urban ratio so that 60 per cent of American Negroes were in cities by 1947.[27]

Since the Negro on the land more nearly represents the southern picture than the Negro in the city, how does he fare in agricultural regions? A study of a representative sample in Alabama shows that three fourths of those who began as croppers never rose above that level and only one tenth rose to be owners. Furthermore these cropper families "broke even" in about 45 per cent of the years they were cropping, lost money during about 30 per cent of the years, and showed a profit in something like 25 per cent of the years.[28] Thus during three fourths of the time they spent on the land they earned enough either for a bare subsistence or for a subsistence plus debt, with no money whatsoever to spend. While tenancy among both white and colored farmers increased up to 1930,[29] from that time on the Negroes have lost ground and been pushed into an even lower status, i.e., that of mere field hands.[30] This change, which came under the Agricultural Adjustment Administration, seems to have proceeded through two stages.

In the first stage, the need to keep up the price of cotton by acreage reduction promised cash payments if this policy were carried out. During the first part of this process, the landlord felt quite justified in taking the checks of his croppers and applying them to the debt which they usually owed him. Of course this meant that A.A.A. payments were going directly to landlords instead of to croppers. When complaints arose over this policy and the payments began going directly to sharecroppers themselves, then dissatisfaction occurred among owners.

This led to the second stage, which depended on a legal interpretation of a clause in the A.A.A. Act providing that a reduction in the number of tenants could be made when "justified from the standpoint of sound management" and in this case "the stipulation preventing an increase in the amount of payments to the landlords shall not apply." At this point localism and paternalism stepped into the picture. The administration of the Act, which was left to county agents and a local committee, drifted into the hands of the largest landowners in the neighborhood (the smaller owners and tenants or croppers seldom being represented) and this committee was quite willing to testify that the larger owners or planters were "justified from the standpoint of sound management" in reducing the number of tenants. Consequently, increased payments to local landlords became legalized while more and more croppers were thrust out of the system.[31] In the Southeast and Southwest, 193,700 Negro cropper farms disappeared between 1930 and 1940.[32] Some of the men became day laborers and others drifted to the cities or migrated out of the region.[33] Some, of course, found a place on the relief rolls. Even with all the suffering entailed, the net result may have been salutary for those who found more satisfactory means of employment.

ECONOMIC ALTERNATIVES AND THE NEGRO

Under the present attitudes it appears that whatever choices are made in the southern economy, the Negro can expect little betterment in his position. Four possibilities present themselves. (1) There may be a continuation of the traditional agriculture under the plantation system with no diversification of crops. Although the war brought many changes, this is still a genuine possibility. Under this older system the birth rate will be so high that southern farming can offer employment to only half the boys that grow up on these farms.[34] Since the rural areas keep the high birth rate, social welfare will be dependent on nonagricultural employment. If this does not materialize, wages for farm labor will be lowered and the living standards of the Negro will be depressed. Incidentally it also means retarding the effects of mechanization as well.[35]

(2) There may be a shift from one cash crop to another in the general economy; in fact there is considerable evidence that this has already occurred. Corn, cotton, and small grains have decreased while tobacco has shown a tremendous increase. In Georgia alone it has increased 2500 per cent in thirty years. These "within changes," however, presuppose the already existing social structure; that is, they make it possible to employ unskilled labor which is poorly paid. Any change to livestock or dairy farming is considered unlikely because training is necessary to make it successful, and this would immediately change the status of farm labor and alter the social structure.[36] So a conservative change of this kind leaves the Negro in a different occupation, perhaps, but his economic condition remains basically the same.

(3) On the larger plantations new forms of mechanization may become economically profitable. In fact, with the inevitable alteration of the cotton market following the war there may be no alternative except this.[37] And when it is possible for seven men operating "robot" harvesters to do the work of three hundred ordinary workers in fifteen hours,[38] it requires little skill to calculate that the other 293 workers will not find employment in agriculture but will be forced to seek their economic future in some form of industrial occupation. This will mean that the Negro plantation hand or cropper could be swiftly pushed out of farming areas and into a more or less uncertain labor market.

(4) Openings for displaced rural workers may come since more complete industrialization is not only a possibility but a probability. Already reports show that industrial building is proceeding at a fairly rapid pace since the end of the war.[39] There is no evidence, however, that this will equal the wartime investment of $7 billion in contracts with the accompanying all-time unemployment low of 80,000.[40] In some ways even a larger investment would be needed,

for during the war a sizable element of the population was drawn out of the labor market into the armed services. If the movement toward industrialization proceeds gradually, as appears to be the case, there will still be the problem of providing enough positions for both white and Negro workmen. Furthermore, if these new developments are socially defined in terms of southern industry for southerners, as had been the case with the textile industry,[41] it may lead, as it formerly did, to the exclusion of Negro workers almost entirely.

THE SOUTHERN URBAN NEGRO

Between 1930 and 1940 the Negro population of the Southeast and Southwest decreased from 6,395,000 to 6,289,000 but the Negro urban population increased from 2,966,000 to 3,616,000.[42] While most of the rural loss was from migration to the North, a minimal portion of it went to southern cities.[43] Although most of the Negroes made the change for the sake of new opportunities in industrial employment, they have usually had to remain as unskilled workers or servants.[44] It is true that they have been represented in practically all types of industry and service,[45] but usually they are distributed through many kinds of occupation in relatively marginal capacities rather than being concentrated in any one.[46] The nearest approach to convergence would be in tobacco factories; hand trades; trucking, transfer, or cab companies; wholesale or retail trade; professional service (within their own group); amusement; and laundries.[47] In addition, of course, would be the large number in domestic service. Although in the older period the Negro was protected in certain jobs by tradition which defined them as menial or racial occupations, the tendency has continually been for other groups to push into these lines of work, particularly during periods of intense competition or depression.* [48] While the war changed this picture temporarily, it probably will not alter the basic realities.

Once in the southern city, the Negro finds both advantages and disadvantages. The increasing anonymity of urban existence makes it easier to escape the personal scrutiny which served as a social control in the smaller community; it eliminates almost entirely the danger of lynching, which exists chiefly in rural areas; it brings

* Cf. Chapter 5, p. 96, note.

added excitement and stimulation of acquaintance with new commodities, new amusements, and better educational opportunities; it makes possible a different kind of occupational mobility and a chance to try one's hand at various types of work. Diversity of experience in all fields becomes the order of the day. On the other hand the southern urban Negro soon finds that this new diversity demands money at every turn. Whereas on the plantation he might go from one year's end to the next without much cash of the realm, getting his fun by hunting, swimming, or going to suppers, picnics, and socials where he could contribute his share in kind, now he has dance halls, honky-tonks, or taverns where he is nobody if he hasn't a few coins to jingle. Jobs are not too easy to find and they never seem to supply enough for the endless claims on his petty cash. In the city it is even necessary to buy food nearly every day instead of charging it at the commissary and forgetting about it. Then there is rent at the end of the month for a little box with a curtain separating one family from another, and the necessity of running out in the yard to haul in water and wood.

For the urban migrant there are also new mores to be learned. It is not so easy to find a "protector" in the city as it was in the more personal atmosphere of a small rural community. Drifting from one work opportunity to the next, the Negro may find little difference in wage levels but a considerable difference in the impersonality of labor relationships. Accustomed to a paternalistic type of interaction, he often prefers those jobs where someone will be "good" to him rather than those in which he must fit himself into uniform work standards or demands. He therefore perpetuates the pattern that keeps him in a dependent condition. Other folkways that require new adjustment are the forms of segregation that vary not only in different cities but in many areas of the same city. In going to a theater, he has to discover which movie house will admit colored patrons and which one will let them into the balcony by a little side entrance.[49] He learns that the rest rooms in a filling station are not for Negro use but there are separate ones in the railroad station that are available.[50] If he goes to one railroad terminal, he may be served at the counter in the white waiting room; but in another terminal in the same city he may not enter the white waiting room for any purpose whatever and must stay in his own.[51] In riding a streetcar, he is supposed to sit in the rear, but he soon finds that this is a flexible procedure with many exceptions. If he is in the white area of town, he may have to leave the streetcar by the rear door, but in colored sections he finds it permissible to leave by the front.[52] In hotels, restaurants, public auditoriums, banks, post offices, stores, and other institutions for the public, he must learn the prevailing etiquette and make it second nature, or suffer legal penalties. It soon becomes apparent that he must never enter a public library unless it is a branch especially provided for Negroes which usually does not have good reference facilities.[53]

If he is looking for a place to live, he finds that his choice is considerably restricted by community custom. In general his lack of economic means will make it necessary to find housing in a disorganized area or slum where rents are sufficiently low to allow him a foothold. If this area becomes overcrowded and he desires to move into an area already occupied by whites, he finds that a restrictive covenant prevents the move; it is not a matter of the Fourteenth Amendment or equality under the law but rather a question of real property law in which each jurisdiction can decide for itself — and all southern states uphold the covenants.[54] This means that the Negro and his family make their adjustment to an urban environment by living in one or two rooms with little or no privacy, surrounded by hordes of other low-income families in an area of clip joints, taverns, concealed or open prostitution, and often considerable violence. With the uncertainty of income that goes with his unprotected position, with the lack of small-community control to which he is accustomed, and with the constant demands made upon his marginal income, the line between legitimate or socially recognized means of gaining a livelihood and those which are more questionable becomes more and more thin. Many of his neighbors are coming into sudden affluence by "stringing along with the right people." Now and then by wagering a few cents someone will hit the jackpot. His turn will probably be next and before long he contributes a few cents a day in the hope that "policy" or "the numbers" will bring quick returns. The biggest thrill of the afternoon comes when the policy car roars around the corner and collects the daily bets. Since "everybody" is placing bets, he would be foolish not to try. Don't both the Methodist and Baptist preachers play the numbers regularly?[55] Negro business leaders say that without the numbers their business would suffer too much.[56] It is still better to get "on the inside" and work with the "big shots" by selling chances throughout the community. At first this merely supplements a meager income but before long it may be a more lucrative occupation than other forms of labor. Furthermore it has the inestimable advantage of allowing the individual to work chiefly with those of his own kind where he is free from the uncertainty of response in the white world; or if he does sell to whites, it will be with those who treat the seller with some indulgence. By removing both the social and the economic stresses and strains, the numbers do offer an almost irresistible opportunity.

Before long, other chances to engage in occupations that bring in easy money will appear and he will grasp them with alacrity. Status in his own community is rarely achieved by the business and professional leader, since the road to that kind of success is long and thorny, involving special qualities and considerable education. To climb to the top in one of the borderline occupations does not require much training but only loyalty and the capacity for friendly intercourse. Since policy kings and others provide many jobs for the community, he often finds it easy to be accepted and to climb the ladder of opportunity. Before long he may be in a position where he can be generous and pass out a few jobs on his own account, while he can have more luxuries and buy a home,[57] give liberally to churches, clubs, or agencies for the advancement of the race, and retire early as a respected member of the community.

CONTACTS WITH THE LAW

In the urban environment generally, whether southern or northern, the main contacts with white people are of three kinds: casual, economic, and criminal.[58] Although the Negro attempts to separate himself as far as possible from the legal system, since the latter is entirely managed by whites who use it to their advantage, and although he feels no loyalty to the legal order in which he had no share as a political outsider,[59] he nevertheless finds it impossible to avoid the police and the courts altogether. In the southern cities that have curfew laws, through ignorance or some unavoidable delay he may be forced to stay out on the streets later than the prescribed hour and find himself thrown unceremoniously into jail.[60] At other times he may find himself accosted by the police for no reason whatever except to while away a few hours of tedium; if he does not give the proper responses or allows himself to be goaded into heedless action, he will be beaten up and arrested without further ado.[61] In case he is driving an automobile, a minor infraction of traffic rules, holding up the line of traffic, a trifling accident, or anything else which brings him to the attention of a white policeman will frequently lead to insults, arrest, beatings, or fines; he finds that in most cases a Negro is presumed guilty until proved innocent.[62] The word of the white policeman is always accepted by the court against the word of a Negro defendant even when supported by Negro witnesses.[63]

The whole position of the Negro vis-à-vis the law cannot be understood except in the context of southern mores. The police are functionaries not only of justice but of the racial code which is an unwritten law. The view of the white officer is that he is to enforce all written regulations including the provision that there shall be no "disturbances of the peace." This latter provision includes all violations of race etiquette, so that all well-recognized southern customs together with the local variations "become extensions of the law." [64] When it is remembered that policemen are recruited from the classes in the community with low education and insecure economic status and from the group that are frequently forced into competition with Negroes for unskilled positions, it becomes apparent that the exercise of authority over Negroes is more than a routine matter and is one in which resentment, vengeance, and the satisfaction of "proving" superiority take many sadistic forms.[65] Furthermore, the southern elected judge enforces the law and imposes fines or imprisonment (or the chain gang) in terms of local community sentiment.[66]

Moreover the tradition of law has tended to rest lightly upon the shoulders of the South as a whole, where the rural folkways, never far removed from the old frontier psychology, encourage a distrust in any authority above the bare minimum needed to hold the society together.[67] The tendency toward private violence, growing up in the backwoods country, has been perpetuated as a persistent element in the attitudes of private citizens. This extends not only to private offenses but to public ones as well where the individual is less interested in the claims of abstract justice as meted out by the courts and more interested in the immediate personal satisfaction of swift vengeance that can be seen here and now.[68] Even today there are in the South laws against carrying concealed weapons but none prohibiting buying or selling arms; [69] with the result that large sections of the population are armed for "emergencies." One effect is that the southern regions of the United States lead the country in the statistics for homicides [70] for both whites and Negroes.[71] Since the urban population is strongly affected by rural customs, this element is an underlying pattern for urban criminal behavior. Being deeply embedded in the white community, the trend toward violence naturally has considerable influence over the Negro's conduct toward other Negroes as well as in his dealing with whites. And it must not be forgotten that the attitude of "shoot first" is also an integral part of the policeman's psychology. When this frame of mind is prevalent on both sides of the racial line, the result is that each feels rightly insecure and resorts to violence as self-defense, while being defined by the other group as "bad." Thus the policemen proceed in pairs into areas where there are many "bad niggers," and on the other hand the Negroes know which policemen are "bad" and if a situation begins resolving itself to a showdown, will not hesitate to shoot and run.[72] It is hardly surprising that in this explosive situation the number of police officers killed by Negroes and the number of Negroes killed by police is uncommonly large.[73]

This statement must not be interpreted to mean that open hostility and aggression against whites in general is the accepted pattern; open expression of this idea, apart from the special cases noted above, would be suicidal. It is much more likely that the continual repression of open enmity against the all-powerful whites results in freer fighting within the subordinate racial group,[74] since it can be kept on an individual basis without arousing sanctions on a community-wide scale. Coupled with this is the knowledge that the white man's law will take less cognizance of Negro crimes against other Negroes; and this reinforces the pattern of individual vengeance more powerfully.[75] Thus the unilateral submergence of one racial group results in more violence between Negro and Negro.

SOCIAL CHANGE AND VIOLENCE

Southern culture, as noted above, is largely organized around such social patterns as paternalism, localism, and color subordination. As long as these patterns are stable, without too much infringement, a certain equilibrium results. It is not, however, a static equilibrium but a dynamic one which is continually upset by individuals or groups who fail to accept the current definitions of their "place" and overstep the lines of etiquette or ceremony that hold the unique southern configuration together. Where this occurs, there is a regular and sanctioned social form of behavior for whites, which consists of using intimidation or physical attack to keep the pattern intact — not only for the sake of the individual concerned but as a rationalized protection for the entire society.[76] For any infraction of the rules the white man is justified in taking direct action into his own hands, the theory being that a periodic show of force is necessary to keep the *status quo* intact.[77] This would, of course, not happen unless some gain occurred for the dominant group; Dollard mentions three — economic, sexual, and prestige.* [78]

Yet a distinction must be made between the intimidation that occurs occasionally or sporadically in terms of individual or special events and the more widespread conflict that arises when social changes threaten the entire fabric of the cultural web. The former is a result of more or less accidental or local disturbances; the latter takes place when the impersonal forces of the society at large upset the old familiar balance and present the dominant whites with a novel set of patterns that contradict their normal expectations. Where social norms are shattered by events beyond individual control, there is confusion, bewilderment, and then a concerted effort to re-establish the old norms by violent action.[79] Lynchings and extralegal violence may thus be represented as an effort on the part of the dominant community to regain the old controls that have been at least partially disrupted by deep-lying changes in the social structure. Historically the three most important changes of this kind in the South have been Reconstruction, periods of severe depression, and the aftermath of wartime changes. Lynching became

* Dollard shows that the sexual gain was chiefly for white males, who could molest Negro women while preventing the Negro male from interfering.

a time-honored custom in the first period,[80] and a correlation of increase of lynchings with a decrease in economic prosperity has been pointed out by Hovland and Sears.[81] During the period of depression, from 1931 to the late thirties, the change in status occurring among whites often forced them to compete with Negroes for jobs that previously were for colored workers only. Not infrequently this led to downright killing of Negroes to eliminate competitors.[82] The era following World War I saw an upsurge in the number of lynchings [83] and widespread acts of terrorism against the Negro throughout the South.[84]

Taking into account this broader picture of race relations, it is not difficult to predict the rise of increasing conflict under certain specified conditions. This whole aspect of social causality becomes more vivid and realistic when it is reviewed in terms of recent events fresh in the memory. World War II and the succession of events following will serve to illustrate the general thesis.

World War II not only accelerated social change in the South but intensified a type of change which blurred the older distinctions between the status of the dominant group and the status of the subordinate one. A brief listing of the changes will make it clear that every one threatened the existing hierarchy of society and that each therefore appeared to be a psychological crisis. There were Negro soldiers in uniform, and all men in uniform were socially defined as deserving special respect. Northern Negro soldiers in southern camps not only were ignorant of the subcultural etiquette patterns but were openly hostile to them. There were Negro officers who rated salutes by white privates in the military culture. Thousands of Negro domestic workers left their jobs for defense positions when it was a matter of prestige to aid the war effort. The salary of Negro workers in factories and shipyards was far above anything they had ever earned before — and money changes status. Many other thousands of Negroes took the opportunity to migrate into other regions, many of them openly expressing convictions that they would not return.[85] The war against Hitler became a war against Hitlerism and therefore against the doctrine of racial inequality. The ideology of democracy with which the nation fought the war was frequently interpreted as having some relevance to the participation of Negroes in American life, in total disregard of the historic patterns of racial segregation so painfully built up by southern culture. The constant crowding of Negroes into new areas because of migration or the increased mobility following economic affluence caused many minor clashes in forms of public transportation which was more crowded than ever before. A southern editor even advocated abolition of the segregated pattern in the carriers of his own state to solve the problem.[86] Under the F.E.P.C., Negro workers employed for the war effort received the same pay as white workers, and in the military services the situation was the same. After suing a Texas court for being refused suffrage in the Democratic primary, a Negro doctor had his appeal taken to the Supreme Court, where he was sustained. This was perhaps the most serious breach in the solid wall of segregation, and it meant a break with long-established precedent.[87]

The general effect of these changes due to wartime conditions was to increase the tension between the races, with violence rising slightly during the war period but held in check by the larger concerns of the nation. One mild form of this tension was the multiple rumors about increased Negro molesting of white women, rumors about the insolence of Negro domestics to their former employers after they earned more money, rumors of "Eleanor Clubs" supposed to be encouraged by Mrs. Roosevelt, rumors of Negro communities gathering ice picks for attacks on whites, rumors of race riots that never materialized, rumors about Negro assertion of equality rights in travel, rumors of outside agitation, and so on.[88] The number of lynchings increased slightly [89] but, on the whole, large-scale racial violence did not occur.[90]

The year following the close of the war brought about an abrupt relaxation of the control that characterized the war period. Violence, which had been repressed up to this time, now appeared from one end of the South to another. The Ku Klux Klan came out into the open with a drive for membership, with ceremonies that attracted thousands of onlookers. Paradoxically, elections of that year sent to office extreme upholders of traditional southern custom and those who spoke most openly against the Negro at the same time that the first contingent of Negroes had the chance to vote. A "race riot" in Columbia, Tennessee, resulted in the shooting of four officers and two white civilians and the maiming of dozens of Negroes in mass arrests.[91] The number of lynchings increased markedly over the wartime record.[92] One of them, in Monroe, Georgia, involved the multiple killing of two Negro men and their wives; another involved a Negro veteran whose face and body were burned with a blow torch after the veteran had received a severe beating.[93] A Florida town marshal was brought to court for beating a Negro prisoner and forcing him to drown himself in a nearby river.[94] A Negro veteran was removed from a bus near Aiken, South Carolina, by three policemen who beat him and gouged out his eyes.[95] Other examples could be multiplied.

There is considerable evidence that much of the violence in the postwar period is directed especially against the returning Negro veteran who does not fit into the usual pattern of the submissive Negro. In the Columbia case, a Negro veteran and his mother were sought out by a mob from a nearby rural area that had been denuded of its Negro labor by the war. Many returned veterans preferred to stay in Columbia with the "52-20 Club" collecting more from the government than they could earn on nearby farms. A good many of these Negro veterans had learned a different set of manners while in the army and were no longer as servile as the local population felt they should be. Before the rioting took place, many of the local whites were heard to remark that it was high time these Negroes be taught a lesson and "be put back in their places." This was the background of the Columbia affair. Interviews with returned Negro veterans in Georgia told the same story. One of them declared, "They're exterminating us. They're killing Negro vets and we don't have nothing to fight back with but our bare hands." Another remarked, "I'm in the 52-20 Club. Twenty bucks a week from the folks over at the unemployed place. But those white folks burn up over having to give us that twenty bucks and one fine day the cops will grab me and haul me to the jailhouse. They'll say I was drunk and one of them farmers will go my bond for about three or four hundred and I'll have to go over on his place and work it out. If they want you to work for them, that's the way they get you."[96]

In addition to these forms of brutality and intimidation, there has been the formation of a new brand of native fascism, the Columbians. Too radical for the Klan, who dissociate themselves from the Columbians' tactics, the latter have organized to prevent Negroes from buying homes in mixed areas and propose a program to deport all colored people from the United States. This organization, equipped with the paraphernalia of military uniform, with special insignia, and with an undisguised program for national dictatorship, has significantly taken root in the South as its first step, though there is evidence that it is supported and guided by leadership in the North.[97] A general inference from the beginnings of this organization is that it can take root more easily where there is definite resentment against swift changes in the *status quo* for Negroes, and the South is therefore chosen as the area where the most initial progress can be made, particularly in a postwar epoch.

[CHAPTER 7]

The American Negro: *The Northern Picture*

JACK FELT UNEASY. He was in a rut and he knew it. Twice a week regularly he left for his sleeping-car job, made up the beds, stayed up nights, and slept as he could on the train during the day. Most of his time seemed to be spent pacifying travelers who wanted everything from a drink in the middle of the night to bridge tables for an easy game. Some of them were willing to pay and some of them weren't. He knew several ways of putting them in a position where they almost had to, but every time he did so he felt like a cheap slave. Twice a week to New York where he took over his two by four room and slept solid until time to come back; twice a week back home for those oases of comfort and understanding that were getting too familiar; in fact they threatened to become as humdrum as his job. Mabel was tired of it all too. She wanted to go out with him as other wives did with their husbands but usually he was too tired or else he was gone. Her bridge clubs had begun to pall on her lately and she never was much of a churchgoer. Maybe she was two-timing him and he didn't even know it; but he didn't want to think about that. He saw some slick chicks himself every time he was in New York, and once or twice he had given them a whirl. Certainly Mabel had plenty of chances every day when she went up to 47th and South Park. But why go into that? Both of them were on a treadmill and both of them knew it.

This wasn't quite what he had in mind when he went to Fisk and came out with a brand spanking new diploma. Of course he wouldn't have gone there if it hadn't been for Biff; he and Biff went to high school together and when Biff said he was going to Fisk, he had to go too. Nearly broke his health going through because ma couldn't help him after pa disappeared. But waiting on tables and working for country clubs weekends and as a redcap in the summer time gave him a chance to make the grade. Of course there was a little debt of $400 at the end, but he'd paid most of that off now. He and Mabel had made some wonderful plans back there in Nashville, and not one of them had paid off. He would be a big insurance salesman and buy her a lovely house all fixed up the way Doc Brown had his. He even got a good start but the company folded up in the depression and there were too many other guys who wanted to do what he'd done. If Mac hadn't come along that Monday after he'd had his second eviction notice and offered him a chance to get in the Pullman game, where would he be now? In fact, where *was* he now? Just where he was ten years ago only maybe the union had made it a little better. But he would never get any higher and there wasn't any use kidding himself. Once in a while he'd feel better at a Phi Beta Sigma meeting or dance, getting together with the boys and forgetting everything else. Anyway he was better off than some of these poor devils who had to have a shot of rotgut for a good time or these "club men" who tried to act so dicty * when everyone knew they had no manners to begin with and wouldn't know Jack London from Richard Wright. That's a laugh — a Pullman porter complaining about the lack of culture of his fellowmen; just where? . . . back in the squirrel cage again. If he didn't watch out, he'd get bald trying to push his head against the ceiling; it certainly didn't give any.

However typical this sample of urban Negro life in the North may be (and in more than one sense it is unrepresentative), it does give some indication of the modes of adjustment called for by the shift of habitat from the original area of Negro population in the rural South to the largely urban and industrial North. While absolutely fixed status has disappeared, lending a rosy glow to the North as a haven of refuge, the personalistic, paternalistic pattern has also been replaced by the impersonal anonymity of city life and a wall of indifference on the part of white society. The Promised Land is discovered to be a semiarid desert of fierce and unyielding competition with an initial handicap. In place of an almost unrelieved economic misery, a new and surging hope appears, only to be dashed to the ground with monotonous regularity.

* "Stuck up."

The hope is there. Dr. L. D. Reddick of New York City indicates four ways in which the general condition of the Negro in the North differs from that in the South:[1] (1) In his attempt to get equal rights, he is supported by the law. (2) He has the vote. (3) The North has no historical tradition such as that of slavery and Reconstruction, that interferes with generous impulse. (4) The educational level of both Negroes and whites is generally higher. No doubt the third of these factors is the most potent, for it allows the color line to break here and there. Segregation is not absolute in public conveyances, libraries, museums, or stores; in fact it hardly exists. In theaters, restaurants, schools, and parks the line is badly bent but still existent, while in hotels and housing areas it is practically as strong as ever.

Whatever the advantages, there is also a basic uncertainty about status for the Negro migrant from the South. The familiar landmarks of segregation are gone, and he has to learn a new social map. Which theater, which restaurant, which hotel, or which bathing beach will admit him without question; which will ignore him; which will make the claim that everything is already reserved; and which will treat him abusively? Only experience will tell. The social situation is no longer tightly structured; it is highly ambiguous. Usually a personality confronted by unstructured situations of this kind reverts to older and more traditional habits. For the Negro this would mean a return to the etiquette of his subordinate status as he learned it in southern society. Yet he is prevented from using his familiar habits for two reasons: (1) he came north for more freedom and therefore feels that he can no longer act as a submissive underling; (2) his Negro friends in the North will jeer at him if he continues to act like an "Uncle Tom." He is thus cut off from his past, with an uncharted sea before him. Pilots are few and the voyage is long. His only method of learning is to make mistakes and eventually eliminate them, one by one. Perhaps the most common reactions are overcaution or overaggressiveness, both responses to uncertainty. Long residence in the North cannot eliminate these entirely since the rapidity of social change in urban areas alters status continuously without warning.

Economic opportunities of more diverse types are opening up with the war pushing the door open several notches, so long as upgrading is not expected too seriously. By using the vote, the Negro has a chance to alter his conditions and this keeps hope alive. It is a new world and in some ways a promising one where unremitting struggle may eventually show results. No doubt some day . . . .

MIGRATION

Although there was sporadic migration of Negroes from the South to northern cities after the Civil War, the number was small until about 1890. From that time to 1930 the movement of Negroes out of the South grew with each decade with the exception of the period 1900–1910. The so-called "great migration" came during and after the first World War when immigration to the United States was cut off and the need for more labor in foundry and factory became great. In fact, from 1920 to 1930 the loss to the South was 615,000, with Georgia, South Carolina, and Mississippi losing most.[2] This migration had two foci: one in the cities of the East, New York, Philadelphia, Baltimore, and Washington (Washington being "North" in a restricted sense); the other being in the Middle West at Chicago and St. Louis. The chief tides of migration to the eastern cities of the North came from the Atlantic coastal states, while the movement to Chicago and St. Louis came for the most part from Mississippi, Tennessee, Alabama, Arkansas, and Louisiana. Cities like Detroit and Cleveland did not follow quite the same regular pattern but received migrants from both the eastern and western areas of the South.[3] It might be expected that during the period of depression and unemployment of the 1930's, the stream of migration from the South would stop. Although there was a decrease in absolute numbers, there was no letup.[4] Chicago alone received 43,000 during this epoch.[5] By 1940 the North had nearly four million Negroes and the tide was still coming.[6] Although not all of this was urban migration, the movement into rural areas was so small as to be negligible. Even by 1930 the largest Negro city populations were not in the South but had moved across the Mason and Dixon line to New York, Philadelphia, and Chicago.[7]

During the early period of the war boom from 1940 to 1942 there was little relative movement of Negroes, chiefly because they were not integrated into the newer types of employment. Dissatisfaction with the delay in giving Negroes defense positions when the country as a whole was vociferously demanding more man power led to the organization of a March on Washington, largely under the leadership of A. Philip Randolph, President of the Brotherhood of Sleeping Car Porters. This finally led to a conference between President Roosevelt and Mr. Randolph, after which the Fair Employment Practices Committee (better known as the F.E.P.C.) was set up for the purpose of preventing discrimination in employment "regardless of race, creed, color, or national origin." Gradually the bars were let down and a new migration of Negroes to production centers was on.[8] During the war years 750,000 Negroes crossed state lines to one industrial area after another.[9]

This war migration followed a different pattern from all the others, for this time it proceeded fanwise from southern rural areas (and sometimes urban) to the Atlantic and Gulf Coasts, the Pacific Coast and the Great Lakes region.[10] Some of this was simply a reshifting of position in the southern area with large numbers of migrants going to Charleston, Hampton Roads, and Mobile. In the Great Lakes area, the two largest production centers showing greatest increases in Negro population were Detroit–Willow Run and Muskegon, Michigan;[11] the Detroit area alone gained about 80,000.[12] The largest change in the traditional pattern of migration, however, came in the even larger influx of Negroes into the West Coast cities of Los Angeles, Portland-Vancouver, Seattle, San Diego, and the San Francisco area. Between 1940 and 1944 these cities showed a total increase of 121,000 for a gain of 113 per cent.[13] The largest proportional increase was in the Portland-Vancouver area, which went to 437 per cent; the largest absolute increase was in the Los Angeles metropolitan region, which picked up 59,000.[14] Another feature which complicates the total migration picture of the war years is that this time many migrants moved from one northern area to another, or from the central North to the Far West. Over 100,000 trekked from northern and "border" states to other areas, perhaps as many as 50,000 to the Far West.[15] Smaller numbers of migrants followed the more traditional pattern from South to North and settled in such centers as Chicago, Cleveland, Pittsburgh, Philadelphia, and New York. Eighty thousand went to Chicago alone.[16]

Although from the standpoint of geography it is inaccurate to treat the West Coast and the other areas outside the deep South in the same category, yet it will be convenient to treat them all together as constituting a similar environment for the Negro. It is the social rather than the purely geographical environment that plays the most important role for our problem, and although recognizing certain inherent difficulties in this classification, we shall consider all states in the Pacific area together with those above the Mason and Dixon line as "North." [17]

THE NORTHERN IDEOLOGY

While the attitude of the typical southern white man toward the Negro is clear cut and vigorously expressed, that of the northern Caucasian has a distinctiveness of its own which is not often recognized. Basically it is a form of escapism. The Southerner meets the race problem head on, while the Northerner believes that if he gets away from it as far as possible it will no longer exist. In the South it is impossible to flee from the situation. It is omnipresent; there is probably no rural area and no metropolitan center which does not contain a sizable number of Negroes. But while the white man in the North was forming his attitude on the question in the later nineteenth century, he could do so in the absence of any direct contact with Negroes themselves. The typical northern ideology thus appeared in a social vacuum or, if that be too exaggerated a figure, in a lily-white atmosphere. The attitudes and conceptions that developed before the great migrations of Negroes into northern metropolitan centers have remained fundamentally unchanged in spite of transformed social conditions. They constitute a major social lag in our culture. "The Negro" was regarded in the abstract or in a southern setting which was equally abstract for the white man of the North. This abstract Negro who lived somewhere else had been freed after the Civil War and he "should" have the same justice and the same rights that any citizens have. Of course, it was really the task of the South to give these to him and if Southerners would obey the laws of the United States, there would be no difficulty. In fact a few more laws abolishing lynching and the poll tax might be a good thing, for they would show that we "meant business" in bringing about justice for Negro citizens.

On the other hand, the ideology affirmed, equal opportunity for the Negro "should" be granted by white men everywhere, provided that any movement toward this end were initiated by the whites rather than by the colored people themselves. Of course the Negro should have the chance to prove himself in the economic world so long as he was not in too obvious competition with whites. Naturally a white man would not ordinarily employ a Negro except at unskilled or domestic labor because he was best fitted for this type of work and would often do it for less. So far as education goes, Negroes should have the right to go to any school whatever, unless they become too numerous; then it was better to let them have one of their own because they "preferred to be among their own kind." If they showed signs of promise, they should also have the chance for a college education provided that they kept out of the fraternities and sororities, where they might associate with whites. Negroes should have every opportunity for self-improvement that anyone else has although they should not intrude themselves where they were not wanted, into social clubs, country clubs, amusement resorts, academic societies, or churches.

It is even granted in the northern ideology that a Negro has the right to marry a white person so long as he does not marry into "my" family, where it might prove embarrassing. In politics he may expect to run for office and hold any position provided he represents his own people. And the Negro should have the right to buy or rent any property he wishes as long as he stays out of areas where people do not want him. In public life the Negro ought to have opportunity to stay at the same hotels and eat in the same restaurants with whites so long as he does not frequent those in which he will be too conspicuous, i.e., those most popular for the whites. With regard to its results, the northern ideology accents subordination while it minimizes segregation.[18] Internally it is composed of moral idealism with a touch of complacency, indifference unless circumstances force the issue, withdrawal to prevent occasions that might test a real concern, and practical ignorance of the Negro as a human being or of his culture as a subject for research or understanding.

Historically it is also significant that while the basic attitudes toward the Negro were formed in a rural setting throughout the South, they have crystallized in typical urban casual contact all over the North. In the fluid mass society of a metropolitan center the average person engages in work more or less routinized, travels in crowds, eats in crowds, gets his amusement in crowds, and even works in crowds. The kaleidoscopic experiences of the day are so multiple and varied that he soon protects himself by a stylized callousness and indifference to everything except the most violent impressions. In this milieu constant jostling and contact with others make little or no impression, so long as they do not provide him with occasions of surprise or wonder. With his jaded taste he soon loses the ability to notice the most obvious occurrences unless they take on the color of the sensational. It is true that he has a broader acquaintance with life than his rural counterpart, but much of this is vicarious — he reads about it in a newspaper or a book, or perhaps sees a play. To the city dweller the Negro is simply one of many stimuli fleetingly glimpsed in the day's hurry but not an object of personalized feelings.

While the Southerner may know an individual Negro as a domestic servant or laborer and develop the restricted intimacy of the master-servant relationship, the northern urbanite knows "about" the Negro from his vicarious experience. In fact he reads far more about him than the southern white does, can tell about his struggle for advancement, name some of the outstanding race leaders, discuss glibly *Mamba's Daughters* or *Anna Lucasta*, and show in general a pretty sophisticated understanding of the "race problem." He knows what areas of the city are occupied by Negroes, can tell something of their housing difficulties, their crime and delinquency, and shows acquaintance with some of their outstanding institutions and societies. The evening newspaper has given him a superficial acquaintance with many such details. At the same time his impression of all these related items falls into place along with the rise in divorce, the high price of butter, the new freeway, the chances of a Republican comeback, and the local Masonic convention. Unless he is living in a neighborhood either contiguous to or in danger of being invaded by Negroes, he adopts a casual attitude toward the whole matter. While the status system of the South is so organically unified that any southern white feels a personal responsibility to see that it is upheld for all whites as well as himself, the urban dweller of the North disregards any change in Negro-white relations unless it affects *his* club, *his* church, or *his* family.[19]

RESIDENTIAL CONCENTRATION

During the period of the heavier migrations it became apparent that the northern ideology was simply the parallel of social action on the part of the whites. Movement of Negroes was to the areas where small colonies of older colored settlers had already established themselves, in Chicago just below 22nd Street and in New York around 59th Street between Seventh and Eighth Avenues.[20] As more and more migrants moved in, the white community began to evacuate the area where Negroes concentrated, avoiding the problem by escape and thus establishing a pattern. As long as direct contact was largely avoided by easy stages, the question of overcrowding for new settlers and the necessity for confronting new problems could be ignored. In part it was the frontier method of settling an issue, by seeking out new ground where there was no issue and, if necessary, moving again.

This pattern was applied somewhat differently in Chicago and in New York and by implication in other northern cities. Most of all the difference was due to two variant patterns of settlement. In Chicago there was a simple expansion of the original community toward the south and east,[21] or what Gibbard calls "contiguous expansion."[22] The original Negro area in New York, however, became so overpopulated that a few dissatisfied renters were able to find real estate dealers in Harlem who were willing to let some of them get into the area already in a real-estate slump. As a few more began to move into the area, the whites began moving out in droves, leaving more and more flats and tenements available for colored occupants.[23] This "noncontiguous expansion" eventually accounted for the almost solid Negro population of present-day Harlem. A 90 per cent concentration of Negro population in specific areas with a scattered settlement elsewhere is characteristic of northern cities.[24]

Usually these concentrations are in "central colonies" located near the center of the city, where property values are high on account of the anticipation of expanding commercial areas downtown.[25] Older homes and residences of bygone grandeur are cut up into small flats of one or two rooms and receive practically no care or improvements. Apartments or flats already present are divided and redivided until every inch of space is used. Dilapidation of these neighborhoods is rapid and they become the center for a tremendous increase in taverns, gambling dens, pool rooms, and hangouts for the underworld. In both Chicago and Buffalo the Negro found his area of settlement either mixed with or next to the most prominent vice sections of town.[26] Since the expanding edges of these colonies do not change as rapidly as the pressure of population from within, the entire section soon becomes an "artificial neighborhood." It is artificial because the various economic and occupational groups within the Negro community are forced together into the same dwelling units or the same block — the educated and uneducated, the better salaried and the unemployed, the respectable and the criminal.[27]

The rapidly expanding Negro communities on the West Coast have shown a similar pattern. The only one of considerable size or with a fairly long history of development has concentrated in the Central Avenue district of Los Angeles, with secondary concentrations in other parts of the city.[28] In Seattle the major area of settlement in the Madison Street district is supplemented by three smaller concentrations in other parts of the city.[29] In San Francisco a variant on the main theme is provided by Negroes moving into the neighborhood left vacant by the relocated Japanese and sharing the overcrowded "little Tokyo" with white in-migrants. This section now has twice the number of residents it had when the Japanese were occupying it.[30] Portland, however, settled the Negroes chiefly outside the city in vast housing projects instead of in central areas; now they form a colony largely excluded from community affairs and even from the vote.[31]

It is within slums like this that the Negro makes his first adjustment to the North and to the new conditions of his life. In central colonies or overpopulated areas he rears his family, has them educated, seeks for employment, finds his amusement and recreation, tries to maintain his health, and worships his Maker. Bound together with ties of solidarity along with others making the same effort under the same disorganized conditions, he finds his place in the constant shifting and reshifting of the social process. He seeks with his fellows for ways and means of "advancing the race" through political or social action. The longer he plans for new methods of improving his economic foothold, the larger the number of new migrants and competitors becomes. If he has middle class ambitions, he will translate these into a new move to the outskirts of the community or to some protected section where he can have more control over his mode of life.

HANDICAPS OF HEALTH

In view of these conditions it soon becomes apparent that the urban environment is lethal to Negroes. Today, some twenty-five years after the major migrations began, the tuberculosis death rate for Negroes in selected northern cities is about five times that of the white population.[32] Infant mortality rates, though not showing the same sharp differential, are all strikingly higher among northern urban Negroes than among whites. In 1940 New York had 33.4 infant deaths per 1000 births among whites, while the ratio was 56.4 among Negroes. Chicago had corresponding rates of 27.3 and 38.8; Philadelphia, 37.5 and 59.1; Detroit, 35.6 and 53.0; and so on to the lowest differential, in Los Angeles, of 34.1 to 37.8.[33] The number of childless families is very great, in fact so great as to demolish completely the usual stereotype of high Negro fertility. In northern cities, the Negro childless families run as high as 50 per cent.[34] It would seem that this is not entirely due to the usual factors operative in the urban environment such as the change of sex ratio, delay in age of marriage, the rise in the standard of living, and the growth in knowledge of contraceptives, but to the factors selective in Negro areas such as high incidence of sickness, disease, poverty, and inadequate housing combined with the usual urban influences. The compounding of these elements brings about striking differences in the two racial groups. And not least of all the effects of "central area" living is the high incidence of venereal diseases; in Chicago alone seventy-five cases per thousand Negroes were reported in 1942 as compared with three per thousand among whites.[35] In Cleveland the corresponding figures for March, 1943, were 21.4 and 2.1.[36] Continual residence in vice areas, the necessity for taking in boarders and lodgers outside the family, and the general ignorance of the factors responsible for "bad blood" as well as of prophylaxis are in large measure responsible. The weaker institutional structure of the Negro family makes it possible for all these causes to combine more effectively in raising the incidence of the disease.[37]

NEW ACTIVITIES

Although the line is not an absolute one, the shift from southern to northern areas brought with it opportunities for self-expression in two fields of activity that were new to the Negro. These were, in order of their appearance, politics and trade union participation.

Before taking for granted that political activity was always permitted to Negroes in the North, we must correct this misconception. With the exception of all New England states (apart from Connecticut), no northern state permitted the Negro to vote until the passage of the Fifteenth Amendment in 1870, attempting to force the issue in the South, resulted in the change of voting laws in northern states. In a sense the franchise for Negroes was thus a by-product of the whole Reconstruction program.[38] There is also some evidence of gerrymandering to nullify the Negro vote in certain areas.[39] Nevertheless the practice of allowing the franchise is so firmly established that it is pretty well taken for granted in most northern areas. With a southern background of nonparticipation in politics, the Negro in urban areas followed at first the pattern most common to other ethnic groups, that of placing his vote where the most pressure or the most tangible results dictated.[40] He did not, however, lose his special loyalty to his own group with the years, as European immigrants and their children often did, but increased and intensified it.[41] As his own leaders came into prominence, both in party organizations and in representation on the ticket, there is evidence of mixed attitudes on the subject.

One investigator found while interviewing lower class Negro girls that many of them were doubtful about voting for Negro politicians because of a suspicion that they might prove incapable or untrustworthy. Middle or upper class individuals would certainly not show this hesitation.[42] During the period from 1942 to 1946 an editorial in a large Negro publication complained that recent migrants from the South had by the thousands neglected the opportunity even to register, let alone vote.[43] If this situation is at all representative, it suggests that the early period of becoming adjusted to the new life of the North is one in which political habits are not quickly learned. Too often there is apathy toward both white and Negro candidates or toward issues of great importance tc the colored community such as the agitation for a state F.E.P.C. law. The voting habits of the Negro electorate are not uniformly consistent; there is a low proportion of voters in Detroit and a much higher one in Chicago, in fact higher than the white average for that city.[44] The long tradition of party organization in Chicago, with considerable friendly interest shown by the machine politicians in getting Negroes political jobs for votes, may have had considerable influence. It was said of Big Bill Thompson, the former mayor, that he gave so many jobs to Negroes that people called the city hall "Uncle Tom's Cabin." [45] To a lesser extent the same policy was followed by Mayor Kelly.[46]

There are times, as in Harlem, where an independent with wide appeal like Adam Clayton Powell, Jr., could show sufficient power to make other Negro candidates withdraw in his favor; Powell got votes from members of both parties in his aldermanic race.[47] If such a candidate becomes known as a fearless champion of new economic opportunities for Negroes and shows results (as Powell did), he may then become a national figure with prestige enough to win easy support in a Congressional race. Even though Powell finally ran on the Republican ticket, it was plain that the man used the ticket and not vice versa.[48] With the appearance of a stronger militancy during the war, the Negro has become politically more aroused in all areas of the nation. Much of this new awareness is due to the tireless efforts of the Negro press.[49]

In one way Powell's colorful career illustrates the internal changes and divisions of Negro politics very well. His first election as an independent shows the fluidity of the Negro vote which has developed largely since the New Deal,[50] and the bargaining power inherent in the situation. His second election, under the Republican banner, reflects the traditional loyalty to the party of Lincoln; this is a deeply seated pattern in Negro voting to this day, a loyalty that evokes memories of the first representative to Congress ever elected by Negroes, Oscar De Priest.[51] It is true that as soon as city machines change hands, the Negro underworld and its "shadies" are forced to shift their allegiance in order to keep proper protection.[52] And in spite of the tremendous swing of Negro voters to the New Deal in the 1940's, when northern urban areas were largely in the hands of Democratic machines, this changing was always sharply watched by militant leaders to see whether it brought concrete returns. Negro Republicans and newspaper editors have not failed to make the point that the southern wing of the Democrats has more than its proportionate share of power in Washington and points with alarm to any allegiance with "the party of Bilbo and Rankin." Similarly they point effectively to New York State and New Jersey enacting a local F.E.P.C. law under Republican leadership while the Democrats counter with a similar F.E.P.C. law in Massachusetts under a Democratic machine.

Most important from the Negro's standpoint are the economic results of party loyalty — the number of appointive and elective jobs, more and better housing, and increased economic opportunities depending on legislation. A small group depends on party affiliation for its favors, but more and more the leaders are making increasing demands on city, state, and national administrations for measures that improve economic life. On this issue the leaders are agreed, but as yet there is no leadership strong enough to unite all factions into a balance-of-power unit which will swing toward the party that promises most. On the whole "Negro leadership is factional and competitive leadership," with the Negro playing his part largely through alliances.[53] He is thus in a position to command promises but not the fulfillment of those promises.

The coming of the Negro to the North has meant greater opportunity for industrial employment and consequently for union activity. The latter has come much more slowly than the former. In fact, many Negroes made their first advances into industry as strikebreakers. By this means many of them got a permanent foothold in meat packing, steel, railroad work, in teamsters' and machinists' occupations, coal mining, and in baking and confectionery work.[54] While this introduced them into different occupations, it also created a certain amount of distrust among white workers. In general, craft unions have discriminated either tacitly or openly against Negro workers, and industrial unions have been more favorable.[55] The usual practice in the former group was to segregate the Negro into special locals without voting powers,[56] although there were some unions that by express provision in their constitution or rituals refused to admit any but whites. The proportion of Negroes employed in manufacturing had shown a steady growth up to the

1930's but reached a new low by 1940.[57] The chief introduction to the new union activity came mainly after the war boom of 1941–1942, when opportunities began to multiply.

The process of getting more Negroes into unions was often begun by upgrading those who were already in but who accepted seniority in an unskilled status without demanding any rights of promotion. In case after case management tried to upgrade Negroes to defense positions but met opposition from local members of the union even though the national or international organization was in favor of nondiscrimination. Again and again a conference of management with national representatives of the union resulted in their order to the local to allow the new arrangement. This in turn made room for other Negroes to come in and take the places of those who had been promoted.[58]

The increase of Negro workers in war industry can be seen from the proportions of nonwhite workers employed from 1942 to 1945. For all industries the ratio changed from 5.8 per cent to 8.2 per cent. Most rapid development came in agricultural machinery, where the proportions changed from 1.9 to 6.0; in aluminum, from 7.1 to 13.5; in communication equipment, from 0.7 to 4.9; in tanks, from 2.2 to 13.0; in tires and inner tubes, from 3.3 to 9.5. In the more traditional fields such as iron and steel foundry products the proportion grew from 18.6 to 25.4.[59] This meant in most cases full membership in the union, though discrimination was not entirely eliminated. Probably the C.I.O. industrial unions had the fullest participation of Negroes because, after the original resistance to their acceptance, the locals finally began to practice fuller integration and inclusion of Negroes on the job, at union meetings, and in social affairs. Many Negroes were elected to positions of both local and national responsibility, and the Negro community became friendly to the C.I.O. because of the visible benefits it had brought them. Often the Negroes were slow to enter and take part; many of them, in fact, did not attend union meetings at all.[60]

In other cases where a joint labor-management committee cooperated to the fullest extent and where meetings, dances, picnics, bond drives, and rallies were sponsored without discrimination, the Negroes entered into all activities regularly.[61] Under these conditions the Negroes lost some of the resentment resulting from their exclusion during the early period of the war and felt united in the entire war effort. At the same time many of them gave voice to the feeling that the expression of democracy in day-to-day relations is something that transcends the importance of an increase in economic opportunities.[62]

On the other hand there is justifiable anxiety in the postwar period because the unity of wartime was brought about under conditions that could easily be temporary in their effects, a willingness to forget differences for the sake of national morale. The Negroes are keenly conscious of the fact that their gains have been most important in wartime — during both World War I and World War II — and they are concerned about the loss of seniority that comes with peace as well as about the slow change of public opinion back to normal levels. Having tasted a large measure of public participation in labor and community activities, they remain potentially dissatisfied with anything short of the fuller status granted during the height of the nation's emergency.

CLASS STATUS

Although a large number of Negroes live in artificial neighborhoods, there is also a tendency for the colored community to become differentiated along lines of occupation and position. Sometimes these areas are defined in terms of "upper" and "lower" neighborhoods, or "best areas," "mixed areas," and "worst areas." In the central area of Cleveland, for example, East 55th Street is more or less a dividing line between the "lower" and "upper" groups. Research workers declare that it more or less separates groups showing differences in "class, culture, and interest."[63] In Chicago the "worst areas" are bounded on the south by 32nd Street, the "mixed areas" are bounded by 47th Street, and the "best areas" spread from 47th to 71st Street with the exception of the Midway.[64] Similar patterns are found in other cities with large Negro communities, both establishing and reflecting the class lines of the group. These areas correspond roughly with various social factors such as rents, quality of housing, educational differences, and social activity in clubs and the like, and to a lesser degree with delinquency and mortality figures.[65]

Occasionally the division is not ecological but historical, as when the "old settlers" view with alarm the influx of newcomers and bewail the passing of the old days when conditions were supposed to be idyllic,[66] after the well-established American tradition.

More important than the location of lower and upper class neighborhoods are the patterns of living developing in terms of position in the Negro community. The whole configuration differs considerably from that of southern cities or from corresponding occupational and class differentiations among whites as a whole. The relaxing of restrictions on the vertical mobility of Negro workers in the North as compared with the South, brings about a much wider distribution of social forms with many subtle refinements and niceties of shading. But the class distinctions among Negroes have a different meaning and relative significance than they have for whites, largely because the former have only about 23 per cent of their number in occupations on or above the skilled level, while the whites have something like 60 per cent on or above that level (these figures are for males only). Thus certain persons with high status in the Negro community would rate much lower among whites; for example, Pullman porters with considerable education, like the one cited at the opening of this chapter. Among Negroes they might be either in the upper middle class or the upper class, depending on their education. Teachers would generally have the same rating, while most of them would probably have rather lower middle class status among whites. Social workers would be comparable to teachers. Again, postal service workers and civil service employees, who would certainly be in the lower middle class in the white community, often attain positions of considerable influence and leadership among Negroes, for their vocation carries with it a tradition of steady employment and a protected status that has made it long coveted as a kind of "upper" occupation. Another contrast appears in the "shady" occupation or one which is not defined by tradition or legitimacy. While "shadies" are not usually admitted to the social sanctums of the upper class Negroes, they have a kind of upper class organization of their own and are probably more tolerated on other social levels than would be the case in white society,[67] especially if they adopt the manners and conventions of respectable society or if their wives have prestige qualities such as money, light color, or higher education.

On the whole the lower class [68] is characterized by a carry-over of attitudes and modes of behavior brought from the South, a greater tendency to follow without anxiety an accommodative or stereotyped role with respect to whites, [69] a more unsteady and mobile employment status, and a fairly casual attitude toward family and institutional controls.[70] This group may be roughly divided into (a) those whose behavior and motivations are orientated toward "respectable" and middle class goals and (b) those who are more disorganized by the hazards of living at the poverty level. Among the latter are those who are apathetic and rebellious by turns but have made no permanent adjustment, and those who have crystallized their relationships into an underworld pattern. It is often noticeable that the denizens of the underworld are better off financially because their income is not derived from traditional occupations.[71] As for those who identify themselves with the world of more stabilized, middle class living above them, many identify themselves with the church and its moral standards for the attainment of respectability that is not found in other institutions.[72]

Psychologically the lower class group is less disturbed by anxiety due to racial membership, and accepts its position with some of the uncomplaining stolidity of the southern group. "He that is down need fear no fall; he that is low, no pride." Typical of this is also the acceptance, even by lower class secularized persons, of the church's judgment on them; the absolute line between sinners and saved leaves them in the sinner column. They placidly admit the fact though at times they show by their attacks on the church that they are vaguely uneasy about belonging to the sinners.[73] They have a larger number of maternal families [74] and the women are forced to take affection on male terms or get none, with the result that there is a constant movement from marital status into "available" status.* [75]

There is a considerable amount of sex delinquency, and in some groups of younger individuals a boy is a "sucker" when he escorts a girl for a month without pressing his advantage to the limit.[76] A direct pursuit of pleasure in its available forms is characteristic, a *carpe diem* philosophy; parties have cards, alcohol, and hot music as the chief ingredients.[77] In a large number of cases families are

* The factor of the sex ratio enters here again.

divided on the religious issue, with the women supporting the church and the men taking no interest.[78] In such cases sexual affairs do not result in ostracism; the chief conflict comes in the attitudes of the children, who are torn with ambivalent feelings, continuing to have affection for one parent or the other but having irritation or disgust at the general state of their family relations.[79] Some of these children not only consciously reject family standards when others are presented in school and the wider society but, if there is acceptance of a higher pattern, they also gain the ambition that goes with it and bring pressure to bear on the parents to move out of the neighborhood, since the battle to keep the ideology of "striving" is a losing one in a slum environment.[80]

In the middle class a somewhat different pattern of attitudes and behavior is found. Perhaps the chief criterion is the desire to get ahead or to plan for the social advancement of children in the family.[81] Those who have attained this status have usually done so by overcoming such important obstacles that much of their attention and energy is spent in creating and improving a kind of social ratchet that will move forward but not back. In common with other peoples and groups that have been submerged, the Negro urban middle class is preoccupied in a compensatory way with this problem. In general it involves the drive for home ownership;[82] the attainment of and emphasis on a greater amount of education; the seeking and attaining of more steady employment in occupations that afford some security; "moving north" or to a "better city" — more recently to the West Coast or any area "where one can live"; elaborating an extensive club life and the social whirl, with considerable lavishness and conspicuous consumption (in Chicago alone there are 800 to 900 of these clubs);[83] a fierce unwillingness to accept the stereotyped role of the Negro in society (illustrating what Kardiner calls the "anxieties mobilized");[84] and a greater awareness of prestige differences, which includes an increased sensitiveness to color variations.[85]

The upper class in urban Negro areas, while it is at the pinnacle of success within the race, is nevertheless somewhat isolated and ingrowing. It is largely composed of those whose incomes range from $5000 to $10,000, which means that on this basis it is about on a level with the middle class whites.[86] It is also marked off by higher educational status; in fact it illustrates to some degree the pattern already noticed — its educational level is higher than its occupational level.[87] It is composed largely of business and professional leaders who give service to those of their own race, with the exception of a limited few who are well enough established to have white clients as well. Like upper classes everywhere, it is conservative in its dress, tastes, and politics, although it is more tolerant toward radicalism than a corresponding upper class group in white society.[88] Its churches are predominantly Congregational, Episcopalian, and Presbyterian rather than Baptist or Methodist.[89] In its social activities it draws the line against "shadies" who want to be admitted and against racketeers, the uncultured, or the notoriously immoral. This prohibition, although it is set up against those of questionable reputation in the adult world, does not apply to their children.[90] Upper class clubs are more informal and casual, with less ritual and flourish than those of the middle class.[91]

Most of the upper class members actively support causes and organizations for "the advancement of the race" in one way or another.[92] During business and professional hours they have contact with people of all ranks and grades of society, but in religious and social activity they form a congenial circle into which outsiders are not admitted. In many cases they also shun contacts with whites to avoid embarrassment or the jeopardizing of relations between the two groups, and for this reason they are doubly isolated.[93] In a word, they are encysted in a racial situation that does not make for full integration.[94] Upper class members are at a halfway point in society where they criticize both the lower class Negroes and the whites quite freely among themselves, the former for activities that "set back the race" and the latter for superimposing obstacles in the way of racial advancement.[95] In their position they also come in for a good deal of criticism from those below them in the social scale within Negro society, especially if they seem to show signs of snobbishness, overrefined behavior, or too little concern for the Negro community when they represent them in various forms of interracial contact. It is fairly common for upper class members to express distrust of interracial meetings and to assert that they do not "get anywhere." [96] Part of this distrust may be due to the uneasy feeling that other Negroes will expect too much from these meetings and hence it will not reflect any credit upon them to attend without some tangible effects to show — and these are rarely forthcoming.

The continual agitation of the leaders to do everything in their power to "advance the race" began as a thin stream but has now become a mighty torrent. Until this rise of militant action is understood, the full measure of the whole interracial situation today cannot be understood. It is to this that we now turn.

CHAPTER 8

The American Negro: *His Rising Militancy*

BEFORE THE CLOSE of World War II a Negro leader addressing his people urged a new program. "Leave the South! When victory comes, it will be the sign to begin the greatest migration in America's history. Since the South treats the Negro with cruel bitterness, she apparently does not want the darker people there. Don't stay where you aren't wanted! Turn your back on Egypt and old Pharaoh. This war has been a war of migration. Millions of Russians moved back into Siberia and millions of Chinese to the interior provinces. Why should we not turn away from the land that has been the scene of our oppression? The early American colonists left Europe because they could not breathe free air any longer. Can we do less? Come to the land where you have a chance! It may be hard going at first, but even those who are hungry to begin with will know that they are free. They will know that there is no lynching, and no one to tell them they can't vote. Schools, hospitals, and homes are better. Even the slums are better than the old shacks of the poor sharecroppers. Let the migration begin with the million Negro soldiers mustered out of the armed forces. Three fourths of them are from the South. Why should they go home? They can use their separation pay to bring their families north. Let the rest follow them. We need not be afraid that it will ruin the economy of the northland any more than the millions of immigrants did; most of them stayed in the North and in so doing helped to build it into a better and more progressive industrial center. Four cities will feel the major impact of the migration — New York, Chicago, Detroit, and Los Angeles. It will be no new problem for them to take in large masses of immigrants, and they can do it without altering the basic patterns of their urban life. Let those who think that trouble will result remember that the Negro vote will constitute a powerful weapon to hold over the heads of city officials. The 'mature new Negro' can wield this like a sword. By leaving the South the Negro would do more to emancipate that area than anyone else could do. No longer would Southern politicians be able to hold back the tide of democracy for fear the Negro would share in it. The white worker would have a chance to rise, and on the way he would begin to appreciate his fellow colored worker. The Mason and Dixon line might even disappear in time. Let us deliver this blow for democracy and freedom!" [1]

The significant fact about this appeal is not that it is representative of Negro beliefs and attitudes on the interracial situation — as it decidedly is not — but that it could be urged with great seriousness by a popular leader who is both the pastor of the largest Negro church in the United States (the Abyssinian Baptist Church of Harlem) and also a representative in the halls of our national Congress. Adam Clayton Powell, Jr., who uttered these sentiments, is proving to be a symbol of the desperate need of the twentieth century Negro to find a practical program that will energize and motivate him in his search for a new freedom. Even a temporary and makeshift goal, if it is large enough and grand enough to fill the imagination, is better than none at all.

MASS ENTHUSIASM

To the eye of the social psychologist, this situation appears as the indubitable symbol of a rising mass society and its crowd behavior. The mass is characterized by a loss of personal intimacy so typical of large cities, and by a compensating substitute of enthusiastic crowd contagion. Ordinary or traditional controls are lacking, whether of the job, the family, or the institution. Mass behavior is therefore more likely to occur in a disorganized or less conventional society when its structures, for one reason or another, become more fluid and changeable and when the stabilizing effect of well-established norms with leaders to enforce them has disappeared. Temporary and transitional goals take the place of long-time calculation [2] and these appear in the form of slogans, suggestion, persuasion, emotional appeals, and other forms of irrationality.* [3] If collective insecurity grows, as in a period of depression or a widespread loss of status,[4] mass behavior becomes more pronounced and passes beyond the stage of talk and slogans to definite action of a more militant kind. The impulse to action is crystallized by leaders who may urge the necessity of working through established channels in a concerted, rational program or by those who propose to create new organizations around themselves, many of them psychopathological types, demagogues, or shrewd masters of psychological appeal.

Sometimes there may be a mixture of the two approaches. The second is more popular from the standpoint of mass appeal even though it is short lived; it creates "gesture adults" [5] with substitute goals and symbols which are satisfying for the moment and which capture the crowds. Where one leader fails, another takes over, often with the same crowd. The symbol used by the leader is a rallying point for "spontaneous group integration" which means a temporary utopia.[6] If this utopian phase is followed by the removal of the initial dissatisfactions that made it attractive, the movement will die. If it is followed by a relatively loose organization, it will carry on for a short time; if the organization is more strict, it may command enough cohesion to effect permanent changes or to become a regular feature of the society. This in turn depends on the nature of leadership; if it is resourceful, adaptable, able, and intelligent, the movement may continue beyond the leader's death or removal from the scene. If his chief claim to prominence is personal magnetism, then his following may disappear quickly as soon as he goes. All this in turn depends on varying social conditions and the amount of social security or insecurity fostered by them.

We thus have a situation with four variables: (1) the shifting base of socialized security and controls, traditional, institutional, economic, or ideological; (2) the relative satisfactoriness of symbols, beliefs, goals, and ideals in the proposed program; (3) administrative or organizational stability, i.e., "soundness" in varying de-

* While the broad aim may not be irrational, since it implies improving social conditions, the atmosphere of contagion itself is not conducive to rationality, since it encourages ephemeral goals which melt rapidly. Defeats may cause quick loss of morale.[7]

grees; (4) the potentialities of leadership, whether pathological, demagogic, or charismatic on the one hand, or rational, flexible, and institutional on the other. Although we might go through the entire list of permutations to indicate the many possibilities in the situation, we shall dwell on only one feature. As the first variable changes so that there is widespread collective insecurity whether of status or of norms and economic bases of living, the entire situation becomes dynamic and mass movements will occur even though the other three variables are weak and undeveloped. The change will also create a mass atmosphere or mass situation in which emotion, belief, and action become contagious and highly charged with immediate significance.

THE GROWTH OF PROTEST

During the years of slavery the opportunities for insurgence against oppression were difficult to find, but sporadic and spontaneous revolt could not be prevented. Sabotage and uprisings were far more frequent than traditional history records,[8] although they could not under the conditions of the time lead to any organized movement. Even during the days of Reconstruction, while temporary political leadership sprang up among the southern Negroes and was effective locally, the illiteracy of the common people did not make a fertile soil for any sort of concerted movement. Here and there remarkable leaders arose [9] but their names did not become household words and their influence was soon cut off by the rising tide of reaction and disfranchisement that followed.

Immediately after this came a period of "lone voices" that spoke for the entire racial group, giving utterance to the aspirations and desires of the people. Outstanding among these were Frederick Douglass in the early period and Booker T. Washington some time later. They represented the northern and the southern approaches to the whole racial issue: Douglass was the fiery orator who pressed uncompromising demands for increasing freedom for the Negro; Booker T. Washington took the path of realistic compromise, urging the Negro to "let down his buckets where he was" and develop manual or technical skills as a solid foundation for future progress. The measure of influence exercised by these two men can be gauged from the fact that nine out of ten rural Negro schools in the South will have pictures of them on the wall.[10] A poll taken in 1946 among prominent Negro educators, in which they were asked to tell what they thought were the five "greatest books on race relations," showed a preference for Washington's *Up From Slavery* and Frederick Douglass' *Autobiography*, with the latter significantly leading.[11] The significance of the "lone voice" period was that it implanted a greater sense of race pride and race consciousness by means of vicarious achievement. Many of those who had never read a line of either Douglass or Washington came to feel a greater unity and sense of participation through the prestige of these leaders, and this feeling provided a cultural atmosphere in which a greater and more effective protest could make itself heard.

Nevertheless the cleft between the two ideas of advancement represented by these men grew steadily wider. Although Booker T. Washington was the acknowledged leader of his people for years and had given many of them new hope, there were many who did not forget his speech at the Atlanta Cotton States and International Exposition in 1895 where he said, "In all things that are purely social we [the two races] can be as separate as the fingers yet one as the hand in all things essential to mutual progress. . . . The wisest among my race understand that the agitation of questions of social equality is the extremest folly and that progress in the enjoyment of all the privileges that will come to us must be the result of severe and constant struggle rather than of artificial forcing."[12] The more sensitive members of the Negro community began to feel uneasy. Did this statement mean that the Negro must give up all demands for his rights, accept segregation permanently, and put his faith only in economic advancement which was restricted on all sides by special legislation and discrimination? More serious was the criticism arising from a new voice which was to become representative of the Negro intelligentsia, that of W. E. B. Du Bois. In 1903 he published his book, *The Souls of Black Folk*, in which he pointed out that Mr. Washington's speech at least temporarily gave up "political power, insistence on civil rights," and "higher education of Negro youth." Du Bois showed that the result of Washington's program seemed to be more loss of the Negro vote, more civil laws enforcing his inferiority, and steadily diminishing funds for Negro higher education.[13] Although there may have been no direct connection between the two, Du Bois insisted that Washington's pronouncements had made the task of reaction easier.[14] From this time on, the militant note in Negro protest became more and more the dominant one, although at first the great masses were not affected.

Informed public opinion came largely from the efforts of the Negro press in the early part of the twentieth century. This laid the foundation for a more vocal protest spearheaded by the radical *Guardian*, published in Boston by William Monroe Trotter from 1901.[15] The *Chicago Defender* and *The Crisis* soon followed, the latter edited by Du Bois himself. These and other Negro newspapers gradually prepared the Negro public for rallying to the cause of Negro betterment and advancement in all fields. The stage was already set by the increasing literacy of the Negro community, from 42.9 per cent in 1890 to 69.6 per cent in 1910.[16]

Though before this the wrongs and humiliations of the group were known by only a few, they now were trumpeted far and wide. Every lynching, every beating, every instance of injustice in the courts, every clash with whites — all these and many more were given headline reinforcement for the Negro reading public. On the other side of the ledger every success of an outstanding Negro in art, literature, politics, business, the professions, and education aroused great pride. So also did the social achievements in club and society life of prominent Negroes or near-prominent ones. Whenever a new court decision in favor of extending Negro rights was announced, it would receive major attention both in the headlines and in the editorials.

In spite of the many divisions within Negro society, a new feeling of sharing together in the fortunes of the group came to overshadow the internal schisms so far as public utterances and opinions were concerned. As yet much of this was negative and resistive. It was the solidarity of the suffering wronged. It did not have a program except protest and more protest, or chipping away at the wall here, or cracking it there. But even though the contribution of the Negro press was highly charged with denunciations and sensationalism, it accomplished a new self-awareness and race consciousness. As yet the ideology was not fully formed, but it was forming. It took the events of the first World War and its aftermath to crystallize many of these vague aspirations into a more solid shape.

FUNCTIONAL ORGANIZATIONS

During these early years of the twentieth century the two outstanding Negro organizations, representing restricted functions on which there could be minimal agreement, were organized. Both were interracial from the beginning and limited in scope, neither of them obtaining mass support. But the need to crystallize some of the major demands of Negroes had become compelling particularly among the Negro intelligentsia and professional leaders. Paradoxically both organizations began on the initiative of whites, although the major work was carried on by Negroes themselves after organization began.[17] These two institutions were the National Association for the Advancement of Colored People, popularly known as the N.A.A.C.P., and the National Urban League. The former absorbed most of the intellectuals of the "Niagara Movement" which had been opposing the conceptions of progress urged by Booker T. Washington, with W. E. B. Du Bois as its leading voice.[18]

The fundamental task of the N.A.A.C.P. was to make a frontal attack on prejudice against the Negro by furnishing legal means for the redress of wrongs in the courts and for the continual enlargement of rights under the American Constitution. With this went a continual program of ceaseless agitation in *The Crisis*, an official publication of the N.A.A.C.P., edited by Du Bois himself. It meant a continual process of investigating "race incidents," publicizing their importance for the community at large, and furnishing legal talent for the defense of Negroes whose fundamental rights under the Constitution had been abridged. It meant calling for renewed action and propaganda for more and better schooling, for new political participation both in voting and in holding political office, for anti-lynching laws, and for improved status of the Negro in the armed services.

In certain cases the N.A.A.C.P. fought to prevent the extradition of Negroes wanted for crimes in southern areas where there was evidence that they would not receive an unbiased trial or would receive a verdict calling for an excessive penal sentence. It has fought against segregation in most of its forms, though in recent years it has gone farther in this direction than Du Bois himself, eventually causing his resignation from the organization.[19] Wherever the law allows equal rights, the N.A.A.C.P. has fought against discrimination, whether in housing, job opportunities, employment in federal services, or health services and education. It has aroused the Negro community to protest against all these forms of discrimination. Yet at the same time it receives inadequate financial support to carry on a program in which the rank and file cooperate in other ways.[20] Its membership among Negroes is still small (estimated membership about 400,000) and it is doubtless true today, as a Negro sociologist declared in 1940, that the Negroes who have never heard of the N.A.A.C.P. or the Urban League are probably in the majority.[21] It is, however, a mark of social respectability and race pride for upper class Negroes to belong to and support the organization.[22]

The National Urban League, beginning in the period from 1906 to 1911,[23] is an organization which attempts to aid Negroes in adjusting themselves to urban life, primarily in the field of employment and industrial opportunity as well as in related problems like housing and vocational guidance. It has served as a center of mediation between the Negro worker on the one hand and employers or labor unions on the other. While its primary task has been to enlarge the area of Negro employment through consultation and pressure on union locals and personnel managers, it has also had an important responsibility in helping Negro workers get special training that would enable them to meet their job opportunities more successfully. Until recent years the Urban League has not engaged in much political activity but has done its work quietly and without fanfare. Its position of mediation has given it an administrative responsibility that is somewhat removed from the more vocal protest and reformism of the N.A.A.C.P. or the Negro press. Its program is not largely financed by the Negro community, and in an increasing number of cases it has found its support from Community Chest contributions or welfare organizations.[24] Since the Urban League is responsible, at least to some degree, for the success of the workers it recommends to prospective employers, it has been forced to take on the somewhat onerous task of preparing unskilled and uneducated labor for regular and exacting standards. For example, a pamphlet, *Succeed on Your Job*, prepared for Negro workers, urges responsibility in these terms:

M en do not argue on the job. Do your work quietly, quickly, and pleasantly.
A lways be on time and give your boss a full day's work. Do not lay off.
K eep your mind on your work. Do not clown on your job. You were not hired to entertain. Be observing. Offer helpful suggestions.
E arn the name Efficient, Responsible Worker. Be friendly. Do not look for "favors."

G et acquainted with your fellow workers. Work with them and not against them. Join the union in your plant.
O nly abuse comes from profane language. Plain, direct American is more effective.
O rganize your thoughts and habits. Have a schedule. Follow it. Clear thinking avoids many accidents.
D ress neatly. Eat correctly. Over-indulgence slows you up. Every man-hour counts.[25]

The urging of duties as well as rights upon the Negro community has unavoidably meant that the Urban League is less popular than the N.A.A.C.P. although its services are more concrete and more rewarding to a larger number of citizens in an immediate way. Membership in the League or contributions to its work are not so widespread among upper class Negroes as they are in the case of the N.A.A.C.P.[26]

MASS MOVEMENT

We have noted above that mass movements are likely to have their origins in a period of collective insecurity. Such a period arrived after World War I when the preliminary spadework of arousing the Negro masses had already been accomplished to a great degree by the Negro press and to some extent by the dramatic labors of the N.A.A.C.P. During the war the Negro soldier had been subjected to new forms of discrimination in the armed services, in many cases to attacks by white civilians upon Negroes in uniform, as well as to the more serious types of resentment by southern white soldiers who reacted violently against any new forms of status achieved by Negroes in military service. After the war came a new wave of violence against the Negro in the form of beatings, lynchings, and other murders.[27]

Into this period of turmoil came a new "black Messiah," Marcus Garvey. Although his birthplace was Jamaica, Garvey began his campaign in Harlem for a new and grandiose plan for Negro Americans. With a shrewd knowledge of popular psychology he began to organize his Universal Negro Improvement Association or U.N.I.A. under the slogan "Back to Africa" or "Africa for Africans." Although Garvey did not have much formal education, he had done wide reading in his trade of printer and was able to exploit his journalistic knowledge of the Negro's past in such a way as to develop race pride. He talked of the glorious history of the Negro, his colorful potentates in Africa, the heroes of slave revolts, the dramatic leadership of Toussaint L'Ouverture of Haiti. Again and again he extolled the growth of Negro business, which he claimed was soon to cut itself off from white capital. Playing on race pride he gave special prominence to everything black: he would have only black men as officers in his organization, spurning those whose skins were lighter; some of his utterances on race purity matched in fervor and doctrine the more rabid speeches of the most unreconstructed Southerner.[28] He created a new flag for the black peoples of the Americas and Africa — red, green, and black [29]; he talked of the day when every pale face would be driven out of Africa [30]; he anathematized the United States because no black man could ever rise to be the President of the country [31]; he organized a Negro merchant marine known as the Black Star Line and sold shares to his followers at five dollars each.[32] Finally he created a black religion with a black God, historians who reinterpreted the Biblical writings, and an African Orthodox Church with a Negro divine as primate (Bishop G. C. McGuire) presiding over a service to "canonize" Jesus Christ as the "Black Man of Sorrows" and the Virgin Mary as the "Black Madonna." [33] He saw to the manufacture of black dolls for Negro children.[34]

As his meetings became larger and larger, he welcomed delegates from South America, the West Indies, and Africa itself. He organized high parades full of pomp and pageantry, in which he wore a brilliant costume of purple, green, and black, with gold braid and white plumes on his hat, acknowledging the applause of his followers as His Excellency, Provisional President of Africa.[35] His plan to lead all the Negroes back to Africa received, by an ironical twist of fact, open support from the Ku Klux Klan and related organizations. This bothered the mighty leader not a bit, for he turned these blasts into a boomerang by asserting that the Klan was a real friend since it helped the "race" recognize that it could not exist with the white man and would have to seek a course of its own. Everywhere the Garvey movement gained momentum till at the height of its power it claimed six million followers throughout the world, a number which an official of the organization later reduced to two million dues-paying members and four million interested sympathizers.[36]

This was a true mass movement. It capitalized on insecurity and used slogans, suggestion, and a grandiose utopian scheme of colonization and resettlement in a land that was to be the Negroes' very own. The enthusiasm of the people was whipped to fever pitch by crowd meetings, parades, rallies, speeches, slogans, and fervid appeals to race pride through the publicity organ *The Negro World*. It had popular support from the common men who were not touched by the more rational appeals of ordinary traditional institutions, men who had no chance to participate in the concerns of the Negro intellectuals, the "forgotten" men of the Negro community. A spontaneous urge to follow the Black Moses filled literally millions of hearts in a society that "paid them no mind." Among all these uncounted hosts came a stirring of hope for a new day.

In the end the movement proved to be a flash in the pan. Before long Garvey came under investigation of the federal government and was brought to trial for fraud. One of the Black Star Line ships had already sunk in a passage to Cuba, and the others proved worthless. Although it was estimated that Garvey had taken in $10 million, he declared at his trial that he had only $40 in the world and some shares of stock. He was convicted by the court and sent to the Atlanta penitentiary. Though he made a brief attempt at a comeback later, he was finally deported to Jamaica. After a short stay he went to London, where he died in poverty.[37] To the outsider the fiasco was over. But not so for the Negro community; here the memory of the man who promised great things, the one who had tapped Negro popular opinion as no leader in America had done, was not forgotten. The intellectual leaders among the colored people found here a powerful force which they had failed to harness, for though many tried for a time to ignore or explain away the whole movement, they were unable to do so.[38] In spite of the fact that the residue of the Garvey movement in the popular mind is something of a mystery,[39] it may be conjectured that it left a consciousness of solidarity on the one hand and a greater cautiousness about commitment to similar schemes in the future.

MASS REACTIONS IN THE DEPRESSION

In the next period, during the depression years of the 1930's, the Negroes suffered another form of collective insecurity. In that epoch their morale reached a low point which called for a new mass movement of hope and improvement. It is perhaps an indication of the sad lesson of bitter experience that no other messiah appeared to lead the masses to a promised land. Instead came a local flurry of interest in a minor prophet who claimed to be God — Father Divine — whose chief claim to fame was the very earthy and satisfying one of providing his "angels" with food, clothing, and lodging.[40] In the proper sense of the term, this was hardly a protest movement but rather a religious cult with obvious economic advantages. It had no political program, did not appeal to a national or international audience, and held out no glittering promises of a new empire for Negroes. Although Father Divine's appeal brought in a few former Garveyites,[41] it did not have the same universal attractiveness.

Instead of a broad national movement, a whole series of sporadic outbursts and spontaneous activities of a local character, aimed at local goals, usually immediate ones that promised a brief measure of economic relief, marked the depression period. Most of these local movements were centered in the cities, where millions of Negroes were filling more than their share of the relief rolls. As those in central areas here and there looked around them, they noticed something that had struck their attention before but only fleetingly. They observed that in the colored sections of town white merchants who had been doing business there for years and who now appeared to be the only members of the community who were able to take money out of it, were dependent on local or neighborhood trade. Another observation made by the Negroes, with minds now sharpened by the miseries of unemployment, was that these stores and businesses did not hire Negro employees.

In a community largely employed, this feature of the situation might arouse no more than passing comment; but where 30 to 50 per cent of the neighborhood could find no work, this discovery came as especially poignant. Why could the white merchant go on with business as usual, taking advantage of the fact that staples of life were necessary to his customers, and still refuse to employ men of color? The wave of discontent in community after community crystallized into action, and the slogan, "Don't buy where you can't work" became a new fighting symbol.[42] The use of picketing and the boycott became common, and this form of social pressure developed several new militant organizations like the Colored Clerks' Circle in St. Louis, the New Negro Alliance in Washington and the Future Outlook League in Cleveland. In some cases these organizations cooperated with agencies already set up in the community; the leadership in St. Louis, for instance, was largely from the Urban League and cooperated with its "block plan" program [43] as well as with the labor unions.[44] This meant that the leadership was educated, trained, and followed the tendency of working through already channeled institutional interests. This was the general pattern followed by the New Negro Alliance, the Harlem Committee on Employment (which later became the Greater New York Coordinating Committee for Employment),[45] and the Vanguard League of Columbus, Ohio.

On the other hand there were numerous organizations more informally led which mushroomed in and out of existence in northern cities. Some of these lasted only as long as an immediate crisis and died out with the winning of minor objectives. Others remained in existence a few months or a year, using the boycott and picket on occasion and serving to channel the emotions of the neighborhood into sporadic aggression in defense of Negro economic interests. For the most part these lesser spontaneous organizations were headed by untrained but natural leaders who were admired in their own locality for their open defiance of existing employment practices and their ability to organize effective public demonstrations. These smaller groups did not usually operate in conjunction with other institutions but carried on a spirited amateur guerilla warfare of their own. Since they could win only limited objectives, most of them showed a high mortality. Probably the only one which has lasted up to and through World War II has been the Future Outlook League of Cleveland, led by Mr. John Holly, who has operated quite independently. In fact the Future Outlook League has organized a local labor union, through which it dispenses jobs to its members. In the Garvey tradition it avoids white influence or cooperation, preferring to rely on the strength of popular Negro participation.[46]

In general the effect of the depression was to limit both messianic and social objectives of the Negro protest. At the same time it strengthened in-group feeling through the ever-increasing protest of Negro newspapers and the sense of accomplishment in smaller organizations working for employment gains. Incidentally it promoted action groups of the interracial type. Most of all it focused attention on the economic area as the sphere where most effective advance could be made and thus laid foundations for the war and postwar psychology.

WORLD WAR II

As the defense period approached in 1941, the Negro community became more and more concerned about the failure to integrate colored workers in the new production centers. In Michigan, for example, out of 26,904 defense positions, 22,042 were barred to Negroes, and the figures for other areas were similar.[47] With the new sensitiveness to job discrimination developed through the depression and with the consciousness of strength developed through mass action, Negro opinion began to crystallize around the March on Washington idea, led by A. Philip Randolph.[48] Although previous movements had been local and limited, the March had the cooperation and coordinated powers of the N.A.A.C.P., the National Urban League, Negro civic and church organizations, and trade unions.[49] The plan envisaged fifty thousand Negroes on the White House lawn July 1, 1941, to demand employment in defense industries. The impact of a new crisis welded the Negro community together in a nation-wide unity, acting as a single pressure group on the federal government. This was an entirely new phenomenon, and though the resulting Executive Order 8802 which established the national F.E.P.C. was a concrete and tangible result that gave evidence of some success, the Negro community was both disappointed and bewildered at the outcome; disappointed because their show of strength was not actually carried out, and bewildered because the March did not materialize and the achievement of the goal came with suspicious ease.[50] Furthermore, experience showed that the law could easily be circumvented.

With the coming of Pearl Harbor and the early defeats of the Allied Powers at the hands of the Japanese, the Negro experienced a sort of irrational pleasure in realizing that colored races had shown themselves capable of winning strategic battles against the white man. It was a temporary mood, to be sure, and Negro loyalty to the United States was real; at the same time it was felt that if the darker peoples lost in the long run, they would at least have given the white colonial powers a lesson that might bear fruit.[51] For those who regarded the war from the European angle, especially those trained in the more radical leftist movements, there was the vocal conviction that the war was largely between two imperialisms, one Nazi or fascist, the other capitalist.[52]

In general the attitude of the Negro people in war participation was one of acquiescence, with mental reservations. They were not impressed with the many war slogans made by liberal white leaders such as "A Century of the Common Man," "A People's War," "A War of Liberation," or "One World." Leaders who urged them to support the war did so on the basis that to fail would be to "alienate the Negro people from the very progressive forces whom they must win as allies." [53] This was a limited basis on which to build Negro morale, and needless to say it did not affect the rank and file very greatly. The latter were more likely to be affected by the transfer of Negro combat troops to work battalions, by the violence of race clashes near southern cantonments, by constantly reported brutality of white M.P.'s against colored personnel, by the segregation of Negro troops in special units both at home and abroad, and by other similar occurrences. All of these received headline attention in the Negro press along with the cynical slogan that gained nation-wide attention — the inscription on the tombstone of a Negro soldier, "Here lies a black man who died fighting a yellow man for the protection of a white man." [54]

The war produced a ground swell of militant Negro sentiment which has penetrated into the psychology of the lowly as well as the great. In the atmosphere of the Negro community today it is not popular to declare oneself for slow and gradual reform or to urge caution upon the leaders as was so often the case in premigration days. Although in the South this attitude is still to be met with [55] and has considerable influence, the leader who makes bold and challenging speeches — in the Negro community — is still the one who draws most applause. Both in the South and in the North unmitigated scorn is bestowed on the "Uncle Toms" or "handkerchief heads" who perpetuate the old ways of behavior and there is a genuine, if sometimes concealed, admiration for the "race leader" who speaks the aims of his people fearlessly, regardless of consequences. The compromising leader may often carry the ball for limited gains, but he does not get the headlines or the glory. Often enough he may receive severe criticism for "selling out" from the more vocal members of the community. The war has brought about a new stage in the Negro psychology where *aggressiveness in behalf of rights and privileges is given full-hearted support by the masses while compromise is scorned.* This pattern, which appeared sporadically during the early years of the twentieth century, is today the *dominant note* in the Negro population and has come out into the open. The war has brought with it a new solidarity and a new consciousness of strength, one which cannot be trifled with. Failure to recognize this new psychology by the nation at large is analogous to the failure of an engineer to calculate the strength of materials in erecting a building. Excessive moralizing or viewing with alarm is about as successful as attacking a battleship with a pea shooter. Social growth on a scale as large as this can be guided but not uprooted without more serious results for society at large.*

* At the same time white leaders need to recognize that inflammatory utterances and claims are often exaggerated simply as a method of softening up public opinion so that better terms are possible when negotiations reach an end. Those familiar with trade-union tactics will find the situation familiar and easy to understand. Those who are not, make the mistake of accepting all militant statements at face value and withdrawing hastily from race relations when they come up against radical demands. It is unrealistic to expect the Negro leader to make cautious and conservative statements when Negro public opinion is vociferously pressing for increased gains at any cost. No one can expect a leader to destroy the basis of his own leadership. Yet full consideration will show a basic willingness to accept practical compromises so long as they involve real gains for the "race." White negotiators must then be prepared for the Negro leaders to exaggerate this progress for the approval of their own group. The real conclusion is that the radicalism of Negro leadership is a sort of trade-union rather than Communistic radicalism. It is not subversive, though it is frequently noisy. Anyone disturbed by such agitation will have a difficult time cooperating with Negroes today.

In the development of this social militancy there is something analogous to, though not identical with, the process of revolution. The student of revolutionary movements makes it clear that these sudden changes in social direction do not occur where oppression or exploitation has completely submerged a people; in that case there is only resignation and compliance. Revolt or uprising occurs only where there is "hope, not despair." [56] The parallel with war and postwar conditions for the Negro is only too plain. Although, as one tenth of the population, he cannot hope to stage a full-scale revolution, he nevertheless has passed from a period of docility and resignation to one in which he has been more fully integrated into American society as a whole, has fought side by side with white soldiers and sailors, worked side by side in war plants, lived side by side in housing projects, and found new economic and political opportunities opening on every hand. He has tasted the strength of national, political, and economic victory and found it sweet. A new hope has been born and with it a surging impulse to press forward to make that hope a permanent acquirement rather than a temporary success. The social momentum of this hope cannot be minimized; it must rather be reckoned with. It is also significant that this hope is directly in line with the "American creed" [57] and the war aims which were an ideology shared by the entire nation.[58]

PLURALITY OF GOALS

Although the emotional unification of the Negro people is largely an accomplished fact, there is no indication that the forces of protest have yet focalized on any single, comprehensive program or that any single leader, in the manner of Marcus Garvey, has reappeared to channel their aspirations in one direction. It may be that this will not happen for many years to come. But the general outlines of major goals now considered important by most Negro leaders and receiving support from the rank and file would surely include:

(1) A continued attack on all forms of segregation whether in housing, employment, the armed services, public carriers, or public places like hotels, theaters, restaurants, parks, swimming pools, playgrounds, or tourist camps. The fight for withdrawal from the white community, so passionately waged by Garvey, has really been lost. Today the American Negro speaks up for integration with

the entire community, not for separation from it.* [59] No stereotype is more effective in arousing resentment among Negroes than the epithet "Jim Crow." If any institution, any issue, any practice of the white community can be tagged with the label Jim Crow, that in itself is sufficient to condemn it. Accepted more and more under duress in the South, it is fought openly and continuously in the North. As an example, the proposed erection of an "interracial hospital" in the central area of Cleveland is vigorously opposed by the local N.A.A.C.P. for the reason that it will preclude the acceptance of Negro doctors, internes, and nurses in other hospitals and bring about a purely Jim Crow institution,[60] as they claim has happened with Sydenham Hospital in New York City.

(2) Corollary to the attack on segregation comes a new increase in coracial groups in many areas. During the war there was some demand for a volunteer unit in which members of various races and groups could cooperate,[61] and considerable stress was given to the mixed units where relationships were satisfactory.[62] A good deal of favorable attention goes to nonsegregated housing projects which have developed harmonious relations between whites and Negroes, such as the Pioneer Homes of Elizabeth, New Jersey, with 333 white families and 72 Negro families, or the Jane Addams project in Chicago which is 70 per cent white occupied and 30 per cent Negro.[63] It is certainly significant that 46 per cent of the new war housing has been jointly occupied by Negroes and whites.[64] Interracial activities in which no discrimination occurs receive considerable favorable publicity, such as the coracial camp sponsored by Dr. Thomas W. Patrick, Jr., near Roscoe, New York.[65]

(3) There is recognition that a drive for new opportunities is always strategically allied to economic issues. One reporter visiting a Negro mass meeting in Detroit heard a preacher say, "We've had enough of the gospel of 'dem golden slippers.' What we want is the gospel of thick-soled shoes." His statement was greeted with hearty applause.[66] The churches have become a forum platform for

* Drake and Cayton report the community "ambivalent" on this issue [67] and show that Negro leaders, particularly politicians, have a vested interest in segregation. Yet they agree that Negro newspapers unanimously oppose it.[68] Since they also have a vested interest, it may be asked why they oppose it. The answer is, because public opinion will not let them do otherwise.

the community where all organizations may have their say, and in recent years this has included many labor unions and left-wing groups as well.[69] Negroes are agreed on the issue of the job ceiling and heartily join in the efforts to break it.[70] While this was originally a program largely operating through existing institutions like the unions and the Urban League, today it is taking on an increased political character in the call for an extension of F.E.P.C. into various states.[71] It is probably true to say that reliance on political strategy has become more prominent than more direct action through labor unions and the methods of the 1930's; another depression, however, might tell a different story. But the extent of the political attack may be recognized from the fact that forty-nine different bills for an F.E.P.C. were introduced in twenty state legislatures in 1945.[72]

(4) Another issue, closely related to that of segregation, is the whole matter of restrictive covenants. Although segregation of housing areas by law is prohibited, private agreements between realtors and home owners specify in the deed to a home that it will not be sold except to Caucasians; in some cases leases designate specific groups or individuals to whom a house may not be sold.[73] Suits to break these provisions began before World War II, with the movement spearheaded in Chicago.* [74] During the war, however, the whole attempt to break the power of restrictive covenants which so frequently keeps the Negro community in urban ghetto areas, became a nation-wide concern and was given extended publicity in Negro newspapers. It has become a primary issue for Negro public opinion, as shown by the Negro Digest Poll in which colored citizens were asked, "Are race restrictive covenants justified?" Results were [75]:

	YES	NO	UNDECIDED
North	0%	96%	4%
South	1%	95%	4%
West	0%	98%	2%

In this poll the southern attitude shows very little difference from that of the North. On the other hand, white opinion is shown to be almost exactly the reverse [76]:

* California also claims some priority for this development.

	YES	NO	UNDECIDED
North	89%	5%	6%
South	96%	1%	3%
West	90%	5%	5%

This is therefore one issue in which Negro public opinion deviates perhaps most sharply from that of the dominant whites. During the years 1941–1945 the rising tide of attack on restrictive covenants may be observed from the fact that there was practical unanimity of judgment among Negroes on the issue. Since this matter is largely in the hands of the courts, a determined effort to appeal cases to state supreme courts and eventually to the federal Supreme Court developed.[77] Behind this movement is a solid mass of Negro support. The climax came on May 3, 1948, when the Supreme Court decided that judicial enforcement of restrictive covenants violated the Fourteenth Amendment. Voluntary adherence to such clauses is still effective but it cannot be enforced by law.*

(5) "First class citizenship" is a slogan that has become increasingly popular as a rallying point for Negro militant action. Apart from the segregation issue, Rayford Logan expresses this program as follows:

Equality of opportunity
Equal pay for equal work
Equal protection of the laws
Equality of suffrage
Equal recognition of the dignity of the human being.[78]

Here, as elsewhere, the emphasis is increasingly upon political action. The abolition of the poll tax in Georgia and the ruling of the Supreme Court that the white primary is illegal have stimulated an interest in the use of the ballot that surpasses all expectations. In spite of obstacles 100,000 of the 200,000 qualified Negro voters of Georgia cast their vote in the primary of July, 1946.[79] A lesser number were qualified and voted in the Texas primary.[80] In spite of the attempts to restrict the number of Negro voters and the threat to abolish the primary, setbacks in the South are probably temporary.[81] The growing political strength of the Negro in the North is already a matter of record; by 1946 he had two Congressmen at Washington.

* Cf. L. Miller, "Right Secured," *Nation* 166:599–600, May 29, 1948.

In state and local governments the Negro has gradually been enlarging the number of office-holders from the colored community, a process that bids fair to become cumulative. As John H. Burma has put it, "Today's Negro is neither silent nor self-effacing. He will not, and can not, be ignored. . . . He is a second class citizen, but he will work and fight with all the means within his power until he can proudly say that he is an American, citizen first class." [82]

Another movement to form mayor's committees or community relations committees in northern cities following the Detroit riots will be given attention in a later chapter.[83]

SOCIAL TYPES IN THE NEGRO PROTEST

In his reaction against white domination, the Negro has developed certain social types, each of which employs unique methods and techniques to deal with the problem. In an enumeration of these types (together with more ingratiating and accommodative ones) Samuel M. Strong has presented the following, largely in terms of the Negro's own opinion:

(1) The "bad nigger." This type, usually from the lower class, nevertheless refuses to accept the social definition of himself as submissive or as a person who "stays in his place." If crossed, he will fight to the finish with a wild fury that is blind and reckless. Although he may commit crimes against white people, he is, more frequently than not, admired by those of his own class for his independence. Upper class Negroes, however, are not likely to approve of his unintelligent methods, although the younger element, even among students, are divided on the issue, some of them maintaining that the "bad nigger" is a credit to "the race." [84]

(2) The "race man." On the whole this leader is of somewhat higher class status though not well educated. He is aggressive and ambitious in presenting programs for "the race" and is eager to start new organizations, clubs, or societies for the purpose, all under the guise of race betterment. Either this leader is anxious to become known and thus to have prestige as a promoter of race advancement — largely an egoistic purpose — or his program suffers because his knowledge of society and social institutions is insufficient to make it an effective force. Usually the "race man" has little more than local influence.[85]

(3) The "smart nigger." Here is an individual who is able to manage his relations with whites in such a way that he or the race comes off victorious without full awareness on the part of the white who is managed. There are many varieties of this shrewdness, of course. The upper class group are likely to use the term "smart nigger" to mean a cunning, crafty fellow who gets his way by artful maneuvers. Another type recognized by the Negro community is both firm and shrewd in his dealings with whites and is able to get his way without losing self-respect or the respect of his group.[86] This type will be variable in class status.

(4) The "race leader." Such a leader has sufficient education and training to have a carefully prepared program, is capable and skilled in the art of accommodation, but escapes the stigma of being disloyal to "the race" when he compromises. His sincerity is attested by the fact that he does not use his leadership for personal gain but cares only that his program for race betterment be carried out. He is both aggressive and successful in promoting his ends. Naturally this type will be somewhat higher in the class scale, and his influence may be either local or national.[87]

(5) The "race woman." Some of those who have been most successful in the leadership of "race" causes have been women. The "race woman" not only cultivates race pride but is talented and forceful in presenting the demands of Negroes to the white community, often being able to succeed where a man cannot. When she attains full stature as a leader, she is often given more trust and confidence by the colored rank and file than the male leader.[88] This is hardly surprising in view of the high position given to mothers in the Negro community.

Both "race men" and "race leaders" may rise from local to national fame as their prestige grows. As this happens, the lines usually diverge so that "race men" become leaders of Negroes, while "race leaders" are leaders of whites and Negroes in race relations. A. Philip Randolph began as a "race man" far superior to the usual leaders in that category, rose to national prominence, and finally reached a position where he could poll a sizable Negro vote in a political alignment. Walter White of the N.A.A.C.P. and Ralph Bunche of the United Nations staff are "race leaders" who act as mediators between Negroes and whites, spending even more time in the white community than in the Negro. Neither White nor Bunche could poll more than a negligible number of votes in the Negro community if running for office. They do not have the "grass-roots" status as Randolph does, yet they are regarded by many whites as leaders with mass support. It would be more accurate to say that leaders like White and Bunche accomplish more *for* Negroes than *with* Negroes. There are other "race leaders," of course, who do retain closer affiliations with the masses.

CHAPTER 9

Mexican and Spanish-speaking Americans: *A Mixed Culture*

A ROW OF PARKED CARS stood by the elementary school in a northern city as the parents came to take their children home. For several days the occupants of the automobiles had noticed a short, swarthy man acting queerly as school let out. He seemed to be hiding first behind one car and then another, peering toward the school. If challenged, he would seem confused and then run behind another car, where he kept his diligent watch on the children with no apparent purpose. Alarmed by his peculiar behavior, the parents finally notified the policeman at the next crossing. Soon an officer arrived to question the stranger; the man's broken English was so unintelligible that he was taken to court, where charges of loitering were made against him. Not until he had lodged in the city jail for two days was his story at all clear; then his wife appeared with a social worker to explain that he meant no harm to anyone. He was only a Mexican industrial worker on a night shift at one of the city's largest factories. Worried by his daughter's sudden adoption of American ways, he had come to the school to spy on her to discover whether she walked home with boys. If she did, he was going to refuse permission to attend school any longer. His objection was based on his own cultural heritage from Mexico, where segregation of the sexes was the rule and coeducation would have been a shocking affront to conventional practices. Only with difficulty had he been persuaded to let his daughter go to an American school at all, and apparently he felt that his traditional male discipline in the home would suffer unless he made certain that she was not taking on "loose" American ways on the way home from school. In old Mexico his word was law; so after his arrival in the American city he became increasingly anxious as his methods of control were challenged. By the time he was noticed, he was too disturbed to care about appearances in his attempt to re-establish restraint over his daughter.

Of course the court records in this case would simply designate a "Mexican arrested for loitering." Multiply this by many more cases in which culture conflict is the basic difficulty and it becomes apparent why the Mexican arrest rate is high as compared with that of other immigrant and ethnic groups.[1] Although this instance represents only one rather simplified type of cultural conflict, there are many of a more serious sort noted below, all complicated by the general lack of cultural participation in American life, a defect which is perhaps as serious for the Mexican American as for any other minority group.

PEOPLES OF MEXICAN DESCENT: DIVERSE GROUPINGS

The actual population figures for all those of Mexican descent in the United States are highly inaccurate for two main reasons: First, much of the Mexican immigration during the years 1910 to 1924 was entirely unrecorded because there was lax enforcement of registration in line with the policy of employers in the Southwest who needed a steadily increasing force of "cheap labor." Second, many of the Mexican migratory workers in both southern and northern states have not appeared on any census rolls because of the difficulty in making accurate registration. Hence the unofficial estimate of the National Resources Planning Board made in 1938 is probably more accurate than the official census figures of 1940. The former gave the number of Mexicans or persons of Spanish-speaking ancestry as about three million,[2] while the latter totals the "people of Spanish mother tongue" as 1,861,400.[3]

Although it may be convenient to lump together all those of Mexican descent in this way, it is actually misleading since it gives the impression that the entire group is homogeneous. Such is far from the case. Beneath this statistical uniformity is a welter of diversity: peasants who have kept their way of life relatively unchanged for three hundred years; railroad and industrial workers whose cultural forms are undergoing radical transformation; middle class storekeepers in states clear across the Union from California to Ohio; senators and governors from New Mexico; migratory workers in Texas, Colorado, and states farther east; and scores of others.

Of all the groupings into which persons of Mexican descent may be conveniently brought together, the most useful is probably classification by length of residence. For Americans unacquainted with the great Southwest and its history, it is necessary at the outset to recognize two major divisions: Spanish Colonials, and Mexican Americans of later immigration. The former is the only sizable group in America attaining minority status in the European manner through a shift in political boundaries.* The Spanish Colonials, most of whom reside in New Mexico, are from the standpoint of history the oldest group of inhabitants of European ancestry in the United States as we know it. These descendants of the Spanish conquistadors and the Mexican Indians began to settle in the region now known as New Mexico in the sixteenth century,[4] establishing small communities for agriculture, sheep raising, and trade with the Indians. After the Mexican War, this entire group was annexed and given full citizenship rights by the treaty of Guadalupe Hidalgo.[5] The Spanish Colonials (also called Spanish Americans or Hispanos) today form about half the population of New Mexico,[6] with estimates of their number varying from something under the 221,740 [7] of Spanish tongue in that state to an unofficial calculation of 260,000.[8] This would make the number of Hispanos roughly one twelfth of all individuals of Mexican descent; the rest or Mexican Americans came by immigration rather slowly until about 1910 and then rapidly until the middle 1920's or 1930, although it must be remembered that a sizable proportion of the whole were born in the United States after that time and hence are American citizens. The Colonials and the immigrants, however, make up two very distinct strata among the Spanish-speaking peoples of the United States.

Another major division is occupational. Here there are three dominant groupings, with smaller representation in a smaller, minor category. Most workers of Mexican descent are either settled agricultural workers or migratory laborers or unskilled industrial operators; a smaller percentage are engaged in trading, white collar occupations, or the professions. While these are the major occupa-

* See above, Chapter 1, p. 7.

tional groupings, they do not have fixed boundaries since many laborers leave one category for another fairly often. Agricultural workers in depressed areas may temporarily join migratory groups, and industrial operatives may do the same. On the other hand migratory workers may return to a "home base" in an industrial community where they find temporary work for the winter. Job turnover is usually high and mobility extremely common. At any given time a Mexican American will belong in one classification, but during a different season or year he may be in a different category altogether. On the whole the Mexican American may be called America's most unsettled minority, in spite of the fact that many thousands have made a stable adjustment in single communities. It is impossible to give numerical estimates for any one of these occupational groupings, though the Hispanos of New Mexico make up the great bulk of the settled agricultural people.

The people of Mexican descent who are American citizens fall into three categories: the Spanish Americans, the immigrants of the first two decades in the twentieth century who have been naturalized, and the children who have been born of the entire immigrant population. This means that the age range varies considerably; among the Spanish Americans every age group is represented, the naturalized Mexican Americans range in age roughly from forty to fifty, and the children are represented in a younger group from the early twenties downward. While it is statistically probable that the younger group of citizens is the largest of all, there are no exact figures obtainable to clarify their numerical proportion.

Still another grouping may be made on the basis of geographical distribution. From this standpoint it is clear that the great bulk of the Latin American population is in the Southwest, for five states — Texas, California, New Mexico, Arizona, and Colorado — have 85 per cent of the total, based on the census of 1940.[9] Texas had the highest number, with California second and New Mexico third. Northern states with the highest concentrations were Illinois, Kansas, and Michigan.[10]

The racial composition of this minority is considerably mixed. At the most, only about 300,000 Spaniards migrated to Mexico during and after the Conquest, and nearly all of these were single men.[11] By intermarriage with the Indian population they changed the composition of the people to that of a mixed group or *mestizos* until the latter group today comprises about 60 per cent of the whole population of Mexico.[12] Part of this was due to the royal Spanish policy of encouraging miscegenation and legalizing it [13] as well as erecting a social fiction that aggressive mestizos were to be called "white" so that the latter would side with the creoles (American-born Spanish) instead of with their darker brothers.[14] On a purely scientific account, therefore, the great majority of Americans of Mexican descent are undoubtedly mestizo, though the Hispanos in New Mexico probably have less Indian blood than other groups in this country.[15] We have noted above that the Indians of Mexico as well as those of the United States are an offshoot of the Mongolian stock considerably modified by migration and later isolation. Since the Spaniards were predominantly of Caucasian Mediterranean ancestry, their complexion was somewhat darker than that of racial groupings in northern Europe but there was considerable variation. Hence a mating of the two groups resulted in offspring now of lighter, now of darker hue. It is a common belief among Mexicans today that every family has a "blanca" (light one) and a "prieta" (dark one).[16]

The popular definition of these differences is at variance with the scientific, and no explanation would be complete without some notice of it. There are at least three widely current variations on the theme of race difference. One is found in southern California where many of the Spanish Americans were settled before those of northern European ancestry came in. These old settlers are called by the inhabitants "pure Spanish" while the later Mexican immigrants are entitled "pure Indian." The shoe pinches slightly here because many of the older Spanish American families with their proud heritage intermarried with the northern Europeans or "Anglos" as they were called, and there is little disposition on the part of either to admit any Indian intermixture in their heritage.[17] A second definition is to be found in New Mexico where the early Colonials insist on the term Spanish American, though the percentage of Indian ancestry among them must be considerable.[18] Even though the mixture is somewhat less than it is among the later Mexican arrivals (as is doubtless the case), this does not make a distinction between the two absolute. Finally, the Anglo in New Mexico often fails to make any distinction at all and calls the Colonials Mexicans, thus implying that there is no essential difference between the old settlers of the state and the more newly arrived Mexican nationals. This leads to an even more determined effort of the Colonials to insist that they be called Spanish Americans.[19]

HISPANOS OF NEW MEXICO

It would be easy to make out an argument on paper for the advantageous position of the Spanish Americans in New Mexico. Comprising about half the population of the state and 80 per cent of the population of seven counties,[20] they have full political rights and have elected representatives to the state legislature and the federal legislature and several governors.[21] Spanish as well as English is recognized as an official language in the state of New Mexico.[22] The Spanish American community has its own school teachers, lawyers, doctors, and merchants. There is no official segregation, and restrictive covenants do not occur in real estate, the price determining who gets the property.[23] Any mention of prejudice in writing or in public is taboo. A psychologist at the University of New Mexico who attempted to set up a social-distance scale to measure the attitude of Anglos toward Spanish Americans aroused such a storm of protest in the Hispano community that his test had to be abandoned and he eventually lost his position.[24] Spanish is now taught in the elementary grades from the fifth on, and the use of the language is becoming more and more widespread among the Anglos. Relations are probably as friendly between the two groups as between any other dissimilar cultures in the United States. Much of this has been built up by constant interaction and accommodation until it has reached a sensitive balance.

It would be false, however, to present this as the whole picture of the Spanish American in New Mexico. What is often forgotten is that the middle class or white collar group among the Colonials is a thin veneer over a larger mass of people who are still living in the seventeenth century culturally. The dominant majority of the Spanish Americans does not consist of the merchant, the school teacher, the politician, or the professional, but of the peasant mass. This peasant, still practicing ways of agriculture that he inherited from the Mexico of many centuries ago, has lived chiefly in the agricultural counties of the state and isolated from the concerns of the dominant culture. The peasant culture was originally a blend of communal practices following the Indian tradition with the feudal pattern of old Mexico — partly Aztec, partly Spanish in its mode of organization. It was a subsistence rather than a competitive economy. The concepts of landholding were less precise than those of the Anglos who emphasized title, for the Spanish Americans emphasized use and occupancy.

Although the treaty with Mexico specified that all land grants made by that country would be respected by the United States, the federal government at Washington did not bother to enforce the provisions to the letter in such a distant place which was not even a state of the Union until 1912 (up to that time it was a territory only). The result was similar to the various treaties with the Indians.[25] When a competitive culture with precise definitions of ownership came into contact with a semicommunal culture having only a vague set of legal abstractions, it was like a contest between a man with a rifle and a man with a blunt club. The man with the rifle got possession of the best land while the man with the club got what was left — often land not best suited for peasant economy. In Taos County all the original grants were lost to the Anglos; four of these were community grants and five were transferred to individuals.[26] Recently the federal government, in a move to restore to the Indians some of the land they had lost, took over much of the old land that had been set aside for the Spanish Americans.[27] Thus one minority was aided at the expense of another.

The subsistence economy, in which the enlarged family is the unit of ownership, work, and control,[28] has meant a lag in machine technology with consequent impoverishment. The average gross income from farms in Taos County is less than $600 a year and this amount seems to be decreasing, with the land getting poorer.[29]

The retention of older medical practices and superstitions and reliance on the *curandero* (herb doctor) and the midwife [30] have kept health conditions low except for a few experimental projects. While the infant mortality of the United States is 51 per 1000 live births, the New Mexico figure is 125.9; in Taos County, with a larger percentage of Spanish Americans, it is 147.9 per 1000 or almost three times the national average.[31]

In the schools a similar pattern prevails. The origin of the school problem is found in the attitude of the Anglos that the Spanish Americans be given the same kind of schooling that is given to all children of the United States. Neither the Anglo community nor Congress took into account the different background of the Spanish Americans so long as they were within the boundaries of the United States, although this difference in background was given much attention in Puerto Rico and Cuba beyond our borders.[32] The Spanish American child who goes to school must begin with English the first day, and although he does not speak it at home, he must continue the whole of his schooling in English. The result is that he learns by rote and regards the whole process as artificial; his learning of English is very imperfect as it would not be if he were started in the vernacular and given a gradual introduction to English forms of speech.[33] (This, by the way, is the method employed in Puerto Rico, where the results are better but still leave much to be desired.) Education is not really adapted to the bilingual situation and there is little recognition of the fact that the Spanish Americans, unlike many immigrant groups, do not abandon their native language for English.[34] The result is that they are handicapped by imperfect English when they try to enter the larger community and thus further cultural isolation is encouraged.

Poor linguistic training also means that Spanish Americans leave school earlier than other children. More than half the Spanish-speaking children are in the first three grades; and in all grades above the first, over 55 per cent of these children are over age.[35] To complicate the picture further, the expenditure of school funds is much higher in Anglo that in Spanish-speaking communities. In 1937–1938 New Mexico spent $55 per school child, but in those areas with the highest per cent of Spanish Americans the state spent only $35.[36] The average salary of rural elementary school teachers is $800 a year; that of the rural teachers in Taos County is about $600 a year.[37]

Although the numerical strength of the Spanish Americans prevents official segregation, a kind of informal separation is practiced. Some have drifted to the cities, where they are usually found in the ranks of unskilled labor. White collar jobs are scarce and even bilingual stores refuse to hire them.[38] Separate churches are preferred, largely because of the difference in language.[39] Segregation in the schools, though officially banned in the state constitution, nevertheless works out on a kind of informal basis since there is a certain measure of residential segregation; this will mean one school primarily for Anglos and another primarily for Spanish Americans.[40] Since the Hispanos drop out of school earlier than the Anglos, there are fewer of them in the high schools and still fewer in college or in the state university. Some students prefer to attend elsewhere, for in the University of New Mexico the Hispanos are excluded from fraternities or sororities.[41] There is little contact of the Spanish Americans with the Anglos in social groups, dancing, or recreation; most of it occurs in business or politics.[42] The Elks and Rotary exclude the Spanish Americans almost entirely.[43] In general the more Anglos there are in a given community, the stronger the prejudice against the Spanish Americans, though this is not expressed openly.[44]

The community of Hispanos in New Mexico is an unused national asset. As long ago as 1912, E. D. M. Gray pointed out that the Spanish American student or citizen, by training for business and diplomacy, could become an intermediary between the United States and Latin America.[45] With the cultural background of a Latin American heritage, and specialized training in the folkways and stateways of our broader culture, such a leader would give invaluable service to the United States in its Pan-American activities. Not the least of his services would be the proof to the Latin American countries below the border that the United States is not the stereotyped imperialistic gringo whose superiority complex makes understanding impossible. A similar refrain is echoed by Dr. Joaquin Ortega of the University of New Mexico, who speaks of that state as a "bridge between the two Americas."[46] For Dr. Ortega the special significance of New Mexico is to be found in the relationship potentially present between the Spanish Americans of that state and Mexico just across the border. If this relationship is to be one of confidence and mutual understanding, the natural source would be found in those Americans on this side of the border who have cultural ties with old Mexico. The developing of these ties would bring about a closer political understanding on both sides of the Rio Grande.

THE IMMIGRATION PERIOD

Although there were a few persons of Mexican descent who filtered across the border before 1910, the real influx came between that year and 1930 when the best estimates place the number at about 1,050,296.[47] This figure, however, is complicated by two factors. (1) A large number of immigrants made illegal entry and therefore were not counted but only estimated. During this period a new type of smuggler or "coyote" facilitated illegal entry by charging less to get the immigrant over the border than he would have to pay for a visa or head tax.[48] (2) Countless immigrants returned to Mexico without registering when they left the United States. This group was required to register with Mexican authorities but not with those on the northern side of the border. Thus the United States figures for Mexicans who left for Mexico during the peak years of immigration 1920–1925 showed only 38,740, while the Mexican figures showed 489,748. Gamio concludes that the latter figures are more accurate, but the continual movement north and south across the border indicates that immigration was not always a permanent change. In fact if the Mexican figures are accepted, there was not a single year from 1920 to 1925 in which the number leaving the United States was not greater than those entering.[49] Of course many of the men both with and without families entered and re-entered many times, some remaining here permanently, others in Mexico.

Probably the three main reasons for migration of Mexicans to the United States were (1) lack of economic opportunities at home; (2) unsettled political and religious conditions; (3) the lure of higher wages in the new land. As for the first, the concentration of land ownership in a few hands was greater during the Diaz regime from 1900–1910 than in any other country of Latin America.[50] Even after the reforms preceding 1930, 70 per cent of the workers in Mexico were agricultural and of these 69.9 were tenants, share-croppers, or laborers and hence did not own their land.[51] Further-more, even when a Mexican laborer began paying for a piece of land, revolutionary or other disturbances might prevent him from acquiring full title. Again, those suspected of subversive activities were continually under suspicion and often preferred to leave the country.[52]

It is interesting that the largest migration to the United States came from that area of Mexico where there was the largest concentration of land in the hands of big proprietors, with the peons obliged to emigrate periodically.[53] This was also the area where religious rebellion developed sufficiently to disturb public relations, i.e., the states of Jalisco, Michoacan, and Guanajuanto in the *mesa-central.*[54] North of the border new economic opportunities grew rapidly, so that there was an extraordinary demand for unskilled labor in the Southwest — for railroad workers and miners; for cultivators of beets, winter vegetables, and cotton; for unskilled hands in iron foundries, cement factories, packinghouses, and small manufactures.[55] Thus the Mexican worker came not only because he could better himself but because he was needed and wanted.[56] This latter statement can be proved by the large number of labor contractors for industrial or agricultural interests who scoured Mexico for laborers, promising them good jobs at high wages.[57] The *enganchistas* or contractors worked hand in glove with the *coyotes* and brought innumerable workers over the border without visas,[58] thus raising insuperable problems for those who later wanted naturalization and could not reveal their mode of entry without exposing themselves to the danger of deportation.[59] If there were any doubt of the need for these workers during the 1920's, it could be quickly dispelled by observing that the proposal in 1925 to put Mexicans on a quota basis was emphatically opposed by industrialists who demanded the labor.[60] It would probably not be an exaggeration to say that for the Mexican the *pull* of opportunity was even greater than the *push* of poverty or unsettled conditions.[61]

THE CULTURE BROUGHT BY THE IMMIGRANT

Although there have been no anthropological studies of ordinary Mexican communities, most researches having been made on mixed Spanish and Aztec elements with minor attention to the more native blend of Indian patterns with the Spanish, Ruth Tuck gives a valuable picture of the village background in central Mexico.[62] Immigrants come chiefly from towns over 3000, which are urban by Mexican standards.[63] At home they lived in a town or village community and went out to the country to work, following a more or less communal pattern of labor as in many European countries.[64]

The laborer was a jack-of-all-trades, knowing something of sowing, reaping, cultivation, the preparation of food, carpentry, the care of animals, and often the making of many household utensils or clothing.[65] Family ties were strong and a patriarchal family tradition prevailed. Instant obedience to elders was part of the code, and infraction meant punishment.[66] The order of authority in the family from top to bottom would be father, mother, son, and daughter.[67] Boys in the smaller towns frequently married at fourteen or fifteen, when they would take over the duties of a man and care for a family.[68]

Separation of the sexes was rigidly followed and women were never supposed to leave the house without an escort.[69] Something like common-law marriage was usual among the poorer classes before one could afford a church wedding.[70] Boys were expected to get their sexual experience early with the few girls of the community who were easy with their favors.[71] The practice of keeping mistresses in addition to a regular household was preferred (in the European manner) to the serial monogamy so characteristic of the United States.[72] The family lived in a small house, often of adobe and of not more than three rooms where persons of different ages and sexes slept on mats stretched out on the floor. Thus a lack of family privacy was accepted as a proper sort of intimacy.[73]

The Mexican laborer lived in a folk society largely governed by oral tradition in which the folkways and mores were passed down by word of mouth. Though acquainted with the written word, he did not often have any chance to use it and hence it was important only for commercial contracts or the occasional signing of his name.[74] The usual taboos and superstitions of a small community governed his life: pregnant women were to be shunned; the evil eye brought misfortune or death; and the use of folk remedies cured disease.[75] Much of the Mexican's Catholicism was pagan [76] and he found it easy to combine deep religious fervor with hostility toward the church or the priest.[77] The Mexican laborer also had his own distinctive foods, tortillas, gorditas, enchiladas, tamales with a liberal use of chili, and special sauces like *mole* that might be used for festivals. Corn and beans were the most common vegetables, and tortillas made from corn meal constituted the staple dish for every day. Coming from a noncompetitive economy, he did not save money,[78] and any surplus from his land gave him the excuse to sell in the open market place where he could enjoy the pleasures of social intercourse. He loved the various fiestas of the year in which the entire community participated and socializing became a fine art. He looked up to the man of prominence in his community, the *patrón*, as the source of authority and even referred to the deity as *El Patrón Arriba* or "the big boss up above." [79] Within his own groups there were social distinctions but no real classes; there were the *decentes* or respectable people, and the *cualquieras* or those of no account.[80] In his own country he remained fixed on the soil of his community and did not migrate from place to place [81]; his people had lived on the same ground for generations or centuries.

ADJUSTMENT AND ACCULTURATION

When the Mexican immigrant came to the United States, he found that the kind of life he lived in the home country was of little value to him economically or culturally.[82] His introduction to American life was in the role of unskilled or contract labor where he had the added handicap of beginning without knowledge of the English language, American laws, currency, folkways, and mores. Accustomed to work by the job or by natural units of labor like finishing the plowing of a field or completing the building of a house or shed, he now found that he must work by the hour and fit himself into an impersonal schedule with little chance to loiter. Lacking vitality after the long trip and being exhausted from his own labors at home, he found his energies consumed and he often lost interest in his work, became sick, laid off for a few days, or returned to Mexico. His employer, who was interested only in the eight hour work period, branded him as inefficient or lazy when the real problem was the learning of a totally new set of work habits.[83] Finding that the wages which seemed so high from the vantage point of the mother country were less remunerative in terms of the American standard of living, he adapted to the new situation by means of the patterns he knew best. With a bare pittance from day to day he therefore lived in the immediate present, much as he had done in Mexico.[84] Forced by economic circumstances to come by himself and send for his family later,[85] he found himself at first in a group with an unbalanced sex ratio and no satisfactions of family life. When the family did come, conflicts immediately arose with the American pattern. Playground fights would occur because Mexican children spoke Spanish in a group with Anglo-Americans; Americans, being indifferent linguists, did not like the sound of another tongue.[86]

But the most important change in family living came as a result of the new cultural influences, for mobility breaks up the older consanguine ties, coeducation prevents the sheltering of the girls after the old pattern, and American ideas about women undermine male authority.[87] The most pervasive element that disrupts family ties is the simple fact that before long the children have more knowledge of American culture and its demands than does father or mother. This means that in line with the Mexican ideas of male dominance the oldest boy soon becomes a new source of authority in the household. Knowing American ways as he does, having a better acquaintance with the language and customs than his father, he soon becomes the mentor and guide to the younger children and even to father and mother. The reorganized hierarchy of the Mexican American family is therefore son and father occupying relatively equal positions above the mother, with the daughter climbing up to a status more or less equal with the mother.[88] Although this is a common mode of organization, there are many variations and gradations. Some families more closely approach the American standard of partnership between husband and wife, with considerable freedom among the children. To attempt this pattern, however, is dangerous since it may result in much instability. The great bulk of families follow a more conservative course; only the few take the more daring and modern method.[89] The Mexican American community is tolerant of individual differences and experimentation, recognizing different adaptations with the remark, "That's the way they look at it." Those who make a successful combination of Anglo-American and Mexican patterns will often speak of "having the best of both ways." [90]

Although family life, language, and food habits probably resist change longer than any other elements of the Mexican culture transplanted to the United States,[91] there is evidence that all are being modified. Even though there may be a preference for Mexican dishes, they are now supplemented with such American items as hamburgers, peanut butter, jello, baker's bread, cookies, etc.[92] Spoken Spanish is becoming highly Anglicized with addition of many

English words, and Spanish American editors of various journals predict that in ten years most of their news will have to be printed in English.[93] There is more hybridizing of language among the Mexican American immigrants than among the Hispanos, who are somewhat more isolated from mobile contacts, at least in the rural areas.

Another difference between the Spanish Colonial and the immigrant is found in the appellation preferred by each group. The person who migrates from Mexico is not complimented when called "Spanish" for he tends to think of the Spanish in the traditions of the old country as the *gachupín* or "spur-wearer" and hence an exploiter. The few individuals in Mexican American communities who try to fit in with the Anglo view that they are "Spanish" are ridiculed among their own people as pretenders. The real Mexican is proud of his mestizo origin and speaks grandly of *la raza*, by which he means the Mexican mestizo.[94] On the other hand, the Hispanos insist on being called "Spanish."

There are numerous status differences among the Mexican Americans and they tend to follow well-defined lines in terms of mobility, occupation, and economic position. At the bottom of the scale are the migratory workers and agricultural laborers, who are the most mobile. A railroad worker will make the proud statement, "I never picked an orange in my life." [95] The lowest of the migratory workers are the "wetbacks" who make illegal entry across the border for the first time; they are so ignorant of American ways that they cook on open fires in front of their shelters because they do not know how to use the oil stoves provided for them.[96] It is estimated that 25,000 to 30,000 of these come to the northern beet fields or the Texas cotton areas.[97] There are thousands more (though figures are difficult to obtain) that migrate every year from one part of Texas to another [98] or from Texas, Arizona, and New Mexico north to the harvests of Oklahoma, Kansas, and the beet fields of Colorado.[99] Others go farther north to Ohio and Michigan.[100] Many of these migrants are forced to travel with their entire families in order to make sufficient earnings to pay for the trip and help tide them over the winter — usually in Texas. Working in separate groups or gangs, they often have less chance to become acquainted with American culture than the more settled laborers in agriculture or industry and hence lag behind them. Their children have little opportunity for normal schooling and tend to follow the pattern laid down by the head of the family. In northern industrial communities the settled Mexican Americans put a considerable social distance between themselves and the incomers from Texas, who are considered "no account." [101]

Among the more settled communities there is a kind of twofold class division: an upper group of "big people" who have succeeded in terms of American middle class standards, together with a disorganized fringe; and the large mass of common people, with *their* disorganized fringe.[102] On the whole the latter group have little hope of climbing to the usual level of the American middle class but have as their main goal the father's regular occupation and employment in shop or factory.[103] Their ideals are therefore those of the American working class family.

In his health practice the Mexican American is becoming more Americanized; only the older families use the older magical forms of cure or depend on them. More reliance is now placed on proprietary medicine and clinics. Likewise the Mexican mixture of pagan and Catholic elements (especially an intimacy with local saints) has been replaced with nominal churchgoing, engaged in more regularly by women than men.[104]

INTERACTION WITH THE DOMINANT COMMUNITY

The general position of the Mexican American immigrant cannot be fully understood without some account of the "climate of opinion" or the social definition of him by the dominant Anglo community. Throughout the Southwest he is generally regarded as having a status above the Negro and the native Indian but below that of the native-born white American.[105] The various prejudices against him are largely in terms of color or language differentiations. For the most part, the very darkest skinned Mexican will meet with somewhat the same exclusion that the Negro experiences. A man of medium dark skin will be able to find service in a lower class restaurant frequented by poorer Anglos but could not do so in a more expensive dining place. A light brown skinned Mexican cannot get accommodations at one of the better hotels, although a light skinned one may do so especially if he speaks fluent English.[106] Only experimentation on his part determines where he will fit in. In order to define the situation more exactly, many proprietors of stores, hotels, or restaurants place signs in their windows: "White Trade Only" — thus making a clear distinction that tends to slow up acculturation and to throw the Mexican back upon his own society. The forms of segregation practiced are informal and casual, without the legal reinforcement practiced against the Negro in the South. The result, however, is similar: two parallel cultures with little awareness on the part of the Anglo as to what is happening on the other side of the indifference curtain. Since there is both high mobility and a relatively low wage scale for most Mexican Americans, the results are visible in several ways.

One of the most important processes of segregation is to be found in the school system, where local geography favors one system for Anglos and another for the Mexican American. It is true that if the child does not have an obvious mixture of Negro or Indian blood, he may attend school with the "white" children. But this affects a small percentage. The usual practice, for example in Texas, is to have segregation of Mexican American children, particularly in the lower grades. Since a similar segregation of Negroes occurs, this means in practice a three-way school system. In a good many communities this also means that segregation brings with it inferior facilities for the minority group. This segregation breaks down somewhat in the higher grades or high school,[107] the probable reason being that fewer Mexican Americans are found at these levels. The economic disadvantage of the group, combined with its cultural differential, means that fewer children attend. The estimate is that at least one fourth of school-age children are not attending school and many more attend irregularly. Probably more than half the children are in the first three or four grades, while those in high school are less than half the number that might be expected. In twelve districts this is reduced to one fifth.[108] In San Antonio, where the Mexican community forms between one third and one half of the population, there are 3000 children of school age who have never attended school, and nine tenths of the illiterate are of Mexican origin.[109] For those who go to school, either in Texas or in other parts of the Southwest, the same bilingual difficulty in learning is experienced that occurs in the case of the Spanish American in New

Mexico.[110] The real difficulty is for the child to obtain more than an elementary grasp of English, particularly since there is restricted opportunity to practice it in the life of his own community.

Segregation affects housing and health in much the same way that we have noted for the Negro. For example, in San Antonio 56 per cent of those who lived in substandard houses were Mexicans; 72 per cent of the deaths from tuberculosis were among the Mexicans; and the latter had an infant mortality rate of 120 per 1000, which is one of the highest in the United States.[111] The chief cause of death among Latin American children in Texas is diarrhea, which results from an exceptionally heavy growth of bacteria such as that from open sewage. The extent to which this affects Mexican children can be judged from the figures for deaths from diarrhea in San Antonio for 1944: eight Anglo children and 226 Mexican children perished from the disease.[112]

The frequency of slum or substandard living conditions also has an effect on the social behavior of the younger element. In 1938, 55 per cent of all juvenile arrests in San Antonio were of Mexican children.[113] The discrimination experienced by these adolescents has given rise to cultural maladjustments, some of which take on the air of compensatory bravado. Play groups of boys (called *pachucos*) gather together for any form of recreation they can find. To make themselves look distinctive many have affected the "zoot suit" with drape coats falling to the knees and pants with peg-topped bottoms hiked up to the armpits. These boys let their hair grow long and comb it back in two wings meeting at the back of the head in a topknot, adding to this the crowning glory of a broad-brimmed hat. Accoutred in these outfits, the pachucos sallied forth during the war, especially in Los Angeles, driving jalopies and raising the kind of disturbance characteristic of adolescents. Having high visibility, these groups received exaggerated publicity, especially after the "Sleepy Lagoon" murder at a mud hole used by the boys for a swimming pool resulted in conflict with servicemen of Los Angeles. A mass raid by the police followed, with indiscriminate arrests of hundreds of Mexican youths and a kind of pogrom by mobs of servicemen who attacked zoot suiters in streets, theaters, and taverns. The police did not interfere with this primitive sport. Actually the chief need of these adolescents was more recreational outlets and greater participation in the community; repression did not touch the root of the difficulty.[114]

It is significant that the delinquency pattern of the Mexican differs considerably from that of the Negro. In spite of the high rate among Mexican American boys, the cloistering of girls has resulted in an almost total lack of female adolescent delinquency,[115] and the same phenomenon appears in the small number of arrests among older Mexican women.[116] This contrasts markedly with the Negro maternal family and its greater freedom for girls. It has been noted that the delinquency rate among Negro girls is much higher than that of white girls though lower than that of Negro boys.[117]

DISORGANIZATION AND PARTICIPATION

Most of the Mexican Americans in the United States have reached a cultural plane so different from their way of living in their country of origin that they would find readjustment to Mexico difficult if not impossible.[118] On the other hand they are kept from cultural participation in American life by invisible barriers that are none the less real in spite of their mysterious submergence in the folkways. Latin Americans have had their web of culture torn in great gaping holes and are forced to mend them with any materials they can find.[119] For those who are unable to accept new ways or are shut off by the curtain of indifference, there is only a half-world to live in, a *Zwischenwelt* between the old and the new.[120] The price of failure to assimilate is underprivilege,[121] and the price of underprivilege is the inability to assimilate.

A good case can be made out for the hypothesis that as economic, political, and civic opportunities increase, the immigrant community begins to function more smoothly with the larger society; but while they are increasing, disorganization, crime, and general apathy exist. Miss Tuck has pointed out that the elements which increase the disorganized fringe in the Mexican community are such factors as depression, unemployment, a "repressive civic policy," and discredited leadership. When the opportunities to rise in the social scale (after the tradition of vertical mobility in the American community) increase, the disorganization in the minority community lessens. But when the "pull at the top" decreases, the minority group becomes disrupted again. For example, the pachuco groups began to decrease as war jobs became available, as pride in the achievements of war heroes grew, and as legal barriers broke down. Thus it is the social forces in the dominant community that largely determine what happens within the minority group.[122]

That the behavior of Mexican Americans is a reaction to that of Anglos in the community is shown by the recrudescence of delinquency and crime in the San Antonio area when the economic opportunities of the war period disappeared. The juvenile officer remarked that this was largely due to the increase in "race prejudice, retaliation, jealousy, and interracial fear." The number of rape cases among Mexicans increased although the Anglo girls involved were either professional or amateur prostitutes. Mexican attacks on Anglo-Americans drew heavy sentences while similar attacks on Mexican Americans brought a verdict of acquittal. One Anglo boy who killed a Mexican American youth was acquitted in a jury trial although he admitted having the gun and firing it. The local newspapers gave no news whatever on the Anglo-American attacks but gave special notice to the delinquency of Mexicans. The only news of the former appeared in the Spanish language papers. It was these same papers that first printed stories about a Mexican American staff sergeant who won the Congressional Medal of Honor but was refused a cup of coffee in a Texas restaurant. Another anecdote told of a Mexican American soldier who had traveled through Mexico on a good-will tour sponsored by the United States Army but was thrown out of a café on his return to the United States.[123]

These reports in the Mexican American press arouse the community to excited antagonism and help unite them in opposition to the dominant Anglos, much as we have noted in the case of the Negroes. On the other hand they create bitter aggression among the younger element, who refuse to accept subordinate status. The returned veterans of Bataan[124] and the Pacific are outspoken in saying that they did not fight for an opportunity to return to the ghetto. The lack of new economic gains will make them explosive.[125] One-sided reports in the Anglo-American newspapers, with a suppression of all items that might be derogatory to the dominant community, add fuel to the flames. There is little evidence that this trend is lessening; in fact it seems to appear in other areas of the Southwest, where the newspapers even refuse to print facts that are uncovered in public trials.[126] The peculiar penchant of public opinion for "retaining dramatic untruths" [127] is an element in repressive civil policy that increases disorganization among the Mexican Americans.

LEADERSHIP IN THE COMMUNITY

In order to attain fuller integration with American life as a whole, it is necessary that new leadership be developed throughout the Mexican American community. This is a delicate matter for, as we have seen in Negro life, this too often becomes the basis of division within the group. At least five types of leadership can be distinguished:

(1) The charismatic or "natural" leader whose ability is based on personal magnetism and the knack of getting his colleagues to follow him. While these leaders have had considerable influence, they have the defects of their qualities which are an intimacy with the group, a limited vision with respect to outside contacts, and lack of status in the dominant community which might enable them to accomplish more for their own people.[128] The small following which each of these "natural" leaders builds up for himself means that cooperation between them is difficult and factionalism is common.[129]

(2) The accommodating leader, called by his own group the *explotador* or exploiter. During the early history of immigration this was often the only type of leadership obtainable by the Mexican American community. The Negroes would have called it an "Uncle Tom" variety, and although it had some influence with the Anglo-American group, much of this was clearly in line with stereotypes of the Mexican group and couched in such terms as "my people are so backward." [130] It thus gave the Anglo the opportunity to separate the leaders from the mass and label them "high type" in order to reinforce the commonly held opinions about Mexicans as a whole.[131]

(3) Consuls from the home country, who often emphasize the "old ways as the best" and thus encourage a sort of nostalgic nativism. Although this attitude has its uses in preserving the pride of the Mexican for his home country, it is also a definite bar to assimilation in the new environment. The term for this ideology is *Mexicanismo* and for the immigrant it too often becomes a "warm relaxing bath" in which he can immerse himself after an exhausting and unsuccessful struggle to become assimilated. In many cases it

actually supports those forces that are hostile to the Mexicans in the American community.[132] Miss Tuck suggests that the consuls would aid their compatriots more in their new country if they encouraged more study of the history and achievements of the homeland, together with special rewards and honors to those who accomplished the most in the United States.[133]

(4) Professional and business leaders. These often have attained positions of responsibility and power through their own efforts, usually through increased education and knowledge. Their very success, however, has estranged them from their own group, for in order to keep a high level of competence, many of them feel forced to think and act in terms that the great majority do not understand.[134] It is significant that money is not enough to give status in the Mexican community if it has been made through gambling or the underworld.[135] On the other hand a person who is a professional, an editor, a school teacher, or one of the "big people" or *señores grandes* has an unquestioned place in the respect of the group.[136] The main difficulty here is that only a man who has the welfare of his group at heart and is not open to the epithet "explotador" can retain his standing very long.[137] The others remain at some social distance from the group when they feel that to maintain their own social standards they must live in a little society of their own or cross over to the dominant group entirely. Too often this has resulted in an isolation of the mass from its leaders. The gap between the common people and this type of leader is still very great and calls for some alignment that will permit more interaction so as to serve the community without at the same time calling for inordinate sacrifice on the part of the leaders.[138]

(5) Temporary political leaders. These are a variation of the "natural leaders" and arise when some special issue calls for neighborhood unity — it may be to get legal rights to swim in a community pool, or to vote for a new school, or to remove some sore spot of local discrimination.[139] By reason of their enthusiasm and acceptance in the neighborhood they are able to get out a substantial vote for the immediate aim. When the task has been carried through to completion, they sink quietly into the background.[140]

While the Mexicans do not socialize as freely as the Negroes, having fewer clubs and organizations, there are a few societies that deserve mention. One of these is the Confederación de Sociedades Mexicanas, a federation of Mexican insurance groups which helps to celebrate Mexican national holidays in the extreme Southwest.[141] Another group having a broader membership and participation is the League of United Latin American Citizens, founded in Texas in 1929, and having as its aim the Americanization of Mexican Americans, the promoting of better English, the exercise of the franchise, and social recreation in many communities.[142] This organization, which is known by its alphabetical symbols of LULAC, edits a publication in English known as the *LULAC News* in Laredo, Texas. The officers in various parts of the Southwest are known as "District Governors" and have shown considerable leadership in civic affairs.[143] The extent of their Americanization may be judged by the fact that they boldly form "Ladies' Councils" and do not confine their activities to men alone.[144]

A recent unification of Latin American Service Clubs throughout the Southwest into a new organization called Community Service Clubs, Inc., shows the development of an institution somewhat resembling the Urban League among Negroes, its purpose being to render service to Latin Americans in the United States by "promoting the health, welfare, and education of Spanish-speaking people in the United States; setting up and administering student aid for needy and qualified Spanish-speaking youth; and planning, organizing, and rendering social services to Spanish-speaking people in the United States." [145] This organization issues an English publication, *Pan-American News*, as a stimulus to political thought and action; it is published monthly at Denver, Colorado. A somewhat older organization, largely fraternal in nature, is the Alianza Hispano-Americana for the Spanish American citizens of Arizona and New Mexico. As might be expected, their monthly publication is chiefly in Spanish thereby preserving the old culture, though recent issues show more and more English influence. Bearing the name of *Alianza* it is published in Tucson, Arizona.[146]

A PRECEDENT FOR THE FUTURE

During World War II the need for man power in the United States became particularly grave, and though there was some illegal entry stimulated by agricultural employers as noted above, a new pattern began to emerge. This took the form of an agreement between the United States and the Mexican governments to allow the importation of Mexican nationals into the United States under supervision. The agreement provided that "Mexican workers were not to be engaged in military activities, were not to be subjected to discriminatory treatment (as outlined in Executive Order 8802 of June 25, 1941), were to be assured transportation to and from their homes and subsistence en route, and were not to be used to displace other workers or be employed for the purpose of reducing wage standards in the United States." [147] The program was administered in the United States under the aegis of the Farm Security Administration.[148] By January 1, 1945, about 80,000 Mexican workers entered the United States, chiefly for agricultural and railroad labor [149] as a contribution to the war effort. The non-agricultural workers were further protected by a stipulation that 10 per cent of their wages were to be deducted for savings when they returned home. Extent of the aid from these Mexican nationals can be judged from the fact that they contributed ten million man days of agricultural labor to the United States in 1944 alone.

This pattern of labor recruitment, while not without attendant difficulties, has nevertheless pointed the way toward a new form of inter-American cooperation. A mutual plan of this sort, if employed in the future, may make it easier for the Mexican Americans already in the United States to face assimilation without the handicaps of continual disruption by floods of newcomers who are unprepared to take their own place in American life and thus jeopardize the adjustment of Mexican Americans already here.

[CHAPTER 10]

Japanese Americans: *A Historic Culture Acclimatized and Traumatized*

IT WAS DECEMBER 7, 1941. A Japanese American girl attending one of the West Coast universities writes her experience. "That Sunday morning my roommates and I had 'slept in' and in fact had to dash in order to get down on time for dinner. As we entered the waiting room, there was a hushed silence all of a sudden and every eye seemed to center upon me. I had no idea what it was about, so I tried to disregard it. Shortly, A— made her way through the crowd and said that she was sorry about the terrible news and that she knew exactly how I felt and 'I'm sure that everything will turn out all right.' I was completely in the dark as to what this sympathy was about until some of my other friends came up and asked me directly whether I had heard the news a couple of hours ago. And then it came out. All through dinner I couldn't think of anything except of the effect this war would have on Mother and Dad, who were both Japanese aliens. What would happen to them?

"Reports in the newspapers after that showed that leaders and some members of the Nihon-jin Kai [the Japanese Association of America] were being rounded up and taken into custody by the F.B.I. My father did not hold any of the executive positions in the Association, but was nevertheless an active member. He was President of the Japanese Hotel Association of P— which, however, was a purely business organization for the purpose of assisting the various Japanese hotel owners and leasers in technical matters concerning the regulation of their property. But I was afraid that the F.B.I. would 'pin' that fact [on him] in order to round him up because he was an alien. For the next few weeks I was phoning Mother long distance several times a week to inquire as to the whereabouts of Dad. The only sign of the police at home was the fact that two plain-clothes men were assigned to the hotel for only two days to watch those who came in and went out. Nothing happened. . . .

"On the other hand, there were a few townspeople who did not like the idea of the *Nisei* being free to go to town without any restrictions put on them. Once when A— and I were in the bank, a couple of farmers . . . pointed to us and remarked aloud, 'What are they? Japs, Chinese, or Filipinos? Sure hard to tell 'em apart. But if they're Japs . . . .' Another time just before the curfew ruling had been put into operation, B— and I were coming home from the movies, and we were followed by a young newsboy yelling, 'Are you Japs? If ya are, ya'd better get outa here. My ma told me to hate all you Japs!' He kept skipping along behind us continually repeating that over and over again. Finally as we approached the corner and were crossing the street, the little boy remarked disgustedly with his hands on his hips, 'Now look what ya made me do — I'm a whole block away from my regular beat!' And off he went."[1]

The dramatic story of Japanese American evacuation and relocation has been told many times and is now familiar to the American public. What is less well known is the matrix of social and cultural factors in the lives of Japanese migrants to this country and their effect on adjustment and assimilation. What sort of people are the Japanese, their racial composition, their customs, habits, and ways of thought? As Orientals are they so different from the Caucasians of America that they constitute an element that is incapable of assimilation? Except for Americans on the West Coast, they have been little known by most of our citizens, although through the process of relocation and resettlement they have become somewhat more familiar to citizens in central or eastern areas. But this acquaintance is slight and tends to be superficial so that the historical elements are hazy and blurred. A brief review of the salient facts is thus necessary before mature judgment can be passed on the problem of this tiny minority of 120,000 in American life.

RACIAL BACKGROUNDS

The Japanese are chiefly of Mongolian stock, and their islands have received migrations from the north, central, and southern mainland of eastern Asia in ancient history (largely undated). The greatly predominant Mongoloids came to Japan from two sources, one group from Malaysia and southeast Asia,[2] and a much larger number via Korea on the mainland.[3] In addition to these were three very small groups, the Kumaso, the Ainu, and the Negrito. The Kumaso were the aboriginal inhabitants of the southern island, Kyushu, while the Ainu were the original settlers of the main island of Honshu. These two were variations of an obscure Caucasoid type with especially heavy facial and body hair. The Ainu still exist as a separate group of 15,000 [4] or more in relative isolation from other Japanese in a state of undeveloped culture. Evidence of some intermixture is found in some Japanese with relatively heavy beards.

In southern Japan the occasional appearance of a kinky-haired individual has led to the conjecture by anthropologists that there may have been an early strain of Negritoes on the islands or that the Malay strain was mixed with the Negritoes.[5] This, however, has had relatively little influence on the physical type of the Japanese as a whole. They resemble the Koreans and Malays more than they do other Mongolian types and tend toward short stature (averaging five feet four). Traditionally the slender, narrow-headed types have been linked with the nobility, while the stocky, broad-headed individuals are supposed to be of peasant stock. This is not scientifically valid, however.[6]

Japan was thus a racial mixture much as was Great Britain on the other side of the continent, except that one was a composite of many Mongolian strains while the other united a number of Caucasian types.

THE JAPANESE ETHOS

Of all the immigrants to the United States perhaps none were further removed from some of the typical American culture-patterns than the Japanese. Their Oriental culture, developed through centuries of feudalism, set up a series of attitudes, customs, and habits which distinguished them from Europeans, Mexicans, and other

Orientals such as the Chinese.* An understanding of these inner springs of motivation and behavior is necessary for an analysis of the Japanese American "problem" and immigrant attitudes. To clarify this situation, it will be convenient to enumerate five major differences between the Japanese culture and that of America.

To begin with, one of the central motives of Japanese existence is the feeling of obligation; this is not merely obligation in the ordinary sense of the English word "duty" but in a much more comprehensive sense. Obligation, expressed by the Japanese word "on," means an indebtedness because of the heritage passed on to an individual by those older, wiser, or superior to the self. It means that continuity between one generation and another is to remain unbroken and that everything done for a person by another produces a debt that must be repaid with unswerving devotion and loyalty.[7] Repayments of *on* are analogous in character to our repayment of a debt; the obligation constantly hangs over one and demands strict accounting.[8] In its original form this *on* is a kind of filial piety which stresses the never-ending task of children, who must work hard at their obedience to discharge the enormous debt they have to their parents for all the sacrifices and inconveniences the latter have undergone for them. Later on, the bringing up of the children's children is considered a further discharge of *on* to the former's parents.

Since the pattern of society is hierarchical with lower and higher grades of authority, it follows that *on* is also the obligation due to one's superiors in general. This *on* may be owed with no offense because by definition the superior in the hierarchy as well as in the family has *ai* or affection for his dependents. *Ai* refers exclusively to the love from above to below and seems to be an extension of family paternalism to feudalistic and authoritarian controls.† [9] Within the family there is also a hierarchy after the patriarchal pattern, the father at the apex. He gets first service at meals, has his bath first, and receives proper obeisance or bows from the rest of the family, which he acknowledges with a slight nod.[10] The elder brother is next highest in authority; then follow the other brothers, mother, and sisters.[11] Family needs outweigh individual

* As we shall see, this is a purely relative matter.

† It is worth mentioning that it was Japanese feudal society itself that shaped the family into a more patriarchal type.

desires, and the father or elder brother has responsibility for the house and especially its honor.

Obligation or *on* calls for repayment and this is of two kinds. The first is *gimu* or limitless repayment, one which is never fully paid. The individual owes *gimu* to the emperor and nation, to his parents and ancestors, and to his vocation. Then there is *giri* or limited payment, to be made with full exactness and with some time limit. On the whole, *giri* is of two kinds. One is "to the world" — the exact duties prescribed as owing to a liege lord, to one's affinal family (one's in-laws or those related by marriage), and to others from whom *on* is received because of special services. The other is "*giri* to one's name," which involves such matters as keeping proprieties, the duty to admit no failure or ignorance, and the clearing of one's reputation through feuding or vendetta.[12] These two types of *giri* have a different emotional content, for *giri* to the world is a sort of contractual obligation which does not "come from the heart." It might be translated as those duties paid to others if one is to be respectable in the eyes of society. All these duties are well regulated by conventional rules and are candidly referred to as the kinds of repayment "hardest to bear." [13] One of the worst things that can be said of an individual is that "he is a person who does not know *giri*."[14] The other type of *giri* or "*giri* to one's name" is probably considered less onerous because it has as its object the defense of personal honor and thus has an intimate spiritual value with which the individual identifies himself. That there is a difference is clear from the fact that this type of *giri* is known as "*giri* outside the circle of *on!*" At all events, the theory underlying it is that it is just as much a right act to repay insults as to repay benefits. To even scores is to balance things; otherwise "the world tips." [15]

The second feature of the Japanese ethos is the attention given to control and the planned quality of life.[16] The Japanese learns the proper etiquette, the respect rules, and the types of address to be given to each person in the family hierarchy where all the rules are strictly observed.* [17] Since rules for proper behavior are all planned, excessive emotion is out of place; cursing, weeping, or loud laughter

* This does not mean that the family atmosphere is strictly formal, as Benedict would imply. Many Japanese testify to casual and fun-loving patterns in the home.

would show that a person did not anticipate events and therefore act calmly as he should.[18] Self-discipline is one of the cardinal virtues and it is pushed to what would be considerable extremes in Occidental eyes. In this discipline there is no self-sacrifice involved; no one in Japan feels sorry for himself because of rigorous restrictions he places upon himself. In fact it is the general view that only by this method does one "get the taste of life" or enjoy it.[19]

The method whereby this strict training is given to the child differs from American rearing. The Japanese give most freedom to babies and to the aged. The child is allowed to have considerable liberty in the home until after he goes to school for two or three years, and from then on he submits to more strenuous forms of family discipline. If after this time the child does not gain the approval of other groups in the community, he disgraces the name of the family and may be ostracized. Few cultures punish the child so severely as the Japanese if he brings dishonor upon the family name; the whole family will turn against the child so that he has no refuge. Neither the world outside nor the world within the home will shelter him; he is then forced to accept family rules implicitly. Some of the flavor from simpler societies is present here, for with the Japanese ostracism is worse than violence, and ridicule is the worst form of punishment.[20]

This brings us to the third element. Japan emphasizes shame in her culture while the United States tends to emphasize guilt.[21] The horror of failure to observe conventions and rules is deeply ingrained, so that shame is the root of virtue in Japan. The man who is responsive to shame will automatically follow the right path, he will live in his right station in life, observe the conventions of hierarchy, and be a model for those who come after him. The person who has brought shame upon himself, his superior, or his emperor can acquit himself only by suicide, which is the ultimate way of clearing his name.[22] Shame is the painful awareness of failure to fulfill one's obligations, or of the lack of order in one's relations. It is also a mode of response to social stigma and there is a well-known Japanese proverb that "if there were no society one would not need to respect oneself."[23] The emotion of shame thus telescopes and focalizes all the duties and restrictions of society on the individual and keeps him sensitive to social demands with a supremely powerful motivation.

A fourth contrast of Japanese with American ways appears in the more concrete area of work and vocational patterns. The serious overpopulation of Japan restricted the size of farms to something like three acres for the average family.[24] As a result, the Japanese farmer developed a remarkable knowledge of soils, fertilizers, methods of land reclamation, and modes of intensive cultivation quite in contrast with the lavish expansionism of the American pioneer.[25] By a combination of highly disciplined labor and a knowledge of intensive cultivation, the Japanese were able to enter areas of California regarded by the white man as uncultivable — sections like the Imperial Valley and the Delta country or the waste timber lands of the northwest — and from the inhospitable soil they wrested new green fields and orchards or vineyards.[26] A good deal of California's remarkable fertility is due to these methods of cultivation, which in some cases increased fruit and vegetable yields three and four fold.[27]

Finally the Japanese set up group habits of labor demanding social cohesion and solidarity in contrast to the individual initiative of the American Caucasian. In Japan itself the agriculturalist found it impossible to achieve a living from the soil without help from the entire family and a mutual exchange of services and cooperation with other farmers in the district.* [28] Since obedience, loyalty, and conformity were more important to the Japanese than individualistic traits, the farmer was often able, by obeying the orders of the superior in his district, to accomplish far more than he would have been able to do alone. This group solidarity, transplanted into the United States, made a massive economic phalanx quite in contrast with ordinary American methods of conducting agriculture and business, though not with other immigrant customs.

During the early period of Japanese immigration the home country treated her emigrants as colonists, and the Japanese Association became a sort of unofficial branch of the government. It maintained bureaus in California cities, registered the Japanese, kept a regulatory hand on them, and advised the home government on their problems.[29] In addition to this, early comers were organized under bosses in

* Similar trends may be observed in other Oriental societies and among European peasant groups. But the Japanese group-cohesion in America was accentuated by Caucasian distrust and suspicion.

labor camps. The ranchers of the California area could call these camps at any time and specify what kind of work was needed and the number of men required, and pay for their services at a flat rate without having to keep them on their land permanently. This sort of employment exchange was maintained for and by the Japanese themselves.[30] By obeying orders, the Japanese laborer realized a great advantage because the organization did much of his thinking and planning for him. In San Diego County a series of droughts for three years drove most white farmers out, but the Japanese remained. Their cooperative association or those who had money, loaned to those who had losses; Japanese stores and shops advanced credit to those who needed it; and Japanese banks loaned money to their countrymen on easy terms. Thus the colony was able to last out the drought because of their cooperation and ability to work together.[31]

A PEOPLE OF DYNAMIC AGGRESSIVENESS

The American native whites thus came face to face with a relatively new quality in immigrants, a quality that was somehow disturbing. Perhaps the best term for this characteristic is dynamic aggressiveness. How did it happen that the Japanese possessed this to a degree noticeable to American eyes? The hypothesis that will be advanced here would account for this inherent dynamism in terms of an interaction between (1) social traits brought to America from Japan and (2) elements present in the American community or derived therefrom.

Probably the social traits developed in Japan that proved most significant were, as already indicated, a highly developed disposition of obedience and obligation, heavy self-demands involving the giving up of free impulse, a pride in name and the bringing of honor to one's family, and an unusual cohesive organization of the group. These in themselves are sufficient to produce tension and dynamism of enormous power.[32] In important matters the Japanese is trained to lock up desire and live after the expected pattern imposed by the society. These social traits might be introduced into a milieu that would minimize their effectiveness; but instead they entered an atmosphere of prejudice and a definition of the Oriental as somehow of an inferior race.[33] In addition the West Coast of the United

States, particularly California, was not a homogeneous society but an aggregation of unstable elements: mining, fishing, pioneer agriculture, and a marked lack of consensus characteristic of frontier cultures.* [34] In a community like California where law and order were poorly developed, a solidly compact group could operate most effectively in contrast with the ineffectual cooperation of the American groups, which were often at cross-purposes with each other. Both the prejudice and the loosely organized nature of the new land served to heighten the quality of dynamic aggressiveness among the Japanese, and this became evident in the intensification of personal and national pride and a very natural desire to show that Orientals were capable of achievements superior in quality. Being more sensitive to criticism and shame, the Japanese have developed more tension than the Chinese, and in some ways this has been a disadvantage in the broad arena of public opinion.[35] The Chinese had capacity for persistent labor but were not numerous enough to develop equal efficiency in mutual aid.

The resemblance of the Japanese group to the Jewish minority has been noted by Professor Park, who comments, "A group which is small in numbers, intimate, compact, and well organized, as is the case with the Jew and the Japanese, has, in the long run, great advantages in competition with a larger and less organized community. If there are already racial prejudices, this kind of competition intensifies them."[36] (Though this similarity exists, it is well to remember that the methods of the two minorities were employed in disparate fields, those of the Japanese largely in agriculture and the forms of trade connected with it, those of the Jews chiefly in urban centers.)

The impetus and momentum with which the Japanese have pushed their enterprise in America are legendary. As a concerted group they have made demands for better working conditions, conducted strikes at times when they would most embarrass the ranchers or fruit farmers, and refused to accept low standards. Leaders of the groups demanding Japanese exclusion from California complained that the incomers were not willing to work for wages but sought to

* We are not overlooking the large corporate farms of California. They were developed by relatively few individuals operating under frontier conditions but on a large scale and on the individualistic pattern.

gain control of farms and crops.[37] Owning one's own land was an acceptable ideal — until it was practiced by an Oriental. The success with which the Japanese pursued their economic gains has been shown by E. K. Strong in a sample of 1457 first generation newcomers. He found that during their first five years in the United States, 80.7 per cent were common laborers while twenty years later only 46.1 per cent were in this class, the rest becoming chiefly owners, managers, or tradesmen.[38] Colonel Irish commented that the incoming Chinese were condemned for their vices but the Japanese for their virtues.[39] What the native Caucasian abhorred was not Japanese inferiority but Japanese superiority.

Combined with this aggressive character is a quality that appeared contradictory to the American observer, namely, the self-sufficiency and reserve with which the Japanese carried on all dealings with outsiders.* J. Merle Davis attributed this to the long social conditioning of feudalism in a land of rivalries honeycombed with espionage, where the individual soon learned to protect himself from strangers by cultivated impassivity.[40] This natural reserve and the habit of withholding oneself appeared paradoxical to the American when coupled with the intensive drive to get ahead that is so characteristic of the Japanese newcomer. In this respect the parallel with the Jewish minority clearly breaks down, since the latter showed rather a more heightened emotionality. It may be conjectured that the native Caucasian gentile found the latter easier to understand and closer to his own habits of thought. Intense ambition combined with exquisite politeness and self-sufficiency, on the other hand, would be more disconcerting.

THE IMMIGRATION PROCESS

From the standpoint of the American community on the Pacific Coast, the Japanese came in during the 1890's to fill the gap left by the official exclusion of Chinese labor in 1882.[41] New opportunities for unskilled laborers were opening up, particularly in the more unproductive agricultural regions. On the Japanese side of the ledger there were several impelling reasons or motives that drove

* The emotionality of the Japanese, so apparent to an insider, is often unobservable on casual contact. Prejudice and discrimination forced the Japanese to repress their feelings even more in America than in their homeland.

the Nipponese from their homes to seek their fortunes elsewhere. Although the traditional attitude of the government was to discourage emigration, this ban was finally lifted for students in 1871 and for laborers in 1884.[42] The primary cause of emigration was economic, though it was not the most impoverished and ignorant group that migrated, for they could not afford to pay their fare, but rather the ambitious middle class farmers who were caught between the upper and nether millstones of the Japanese agricultural system.[43] Their motive to escape to an area of greater opportunity was strengthened by encouragement from agents licensed by the Japanese government to assemble labor emigrants either under contract or otherwise and by the "golden stories" of a few individuals who had become fabulously wealthy in the new land.[44] In addition to this was the desire to escape military service since the conscription law of Japan provided that males of twenty were to enter a compulsory military training for three years, this provision remaining in force for all who could not serve until they were thirty-two years of age.* [45] There were also many who began as contract laborers in Hawaii but on hearing of better opportunities on the mainland changed their residence as soon as they were able to do so.[46]

LaViolette divides the history of Japanese settlement into three main periods: (1) the frontier period from 1870 to 1908; (2) the family-building period from 1908 to 1920; (3) the second-generation period from 1921 to 1941.[47] During the frontier period the great bulk of immigrants were young men, and the number of females was negligible.[48] From 1905 to 1907 a series of attacks on Japanese immigration were made by a small but well-organized group of politicians and citizens in California. This also included a move to segregate Japanese in the public schools. In order to stop this agitation and at the same time to avoid wounding the sensibilities of Japanese government officials, President Theodore Roosevelt stopped further Japanese immigration from Mexico, Canada, and Hawaii by executive order, and entered into the so-called Gentleman's Agreement with Japan which was to stop further movement of Japanese labor into the United States as a voluntary act on the

* This meant of course that large numbers of Japanese immigrants were definitely antimilitaristic and hence out of sympathy with the later imperialistic aims of the home government.

part of Japan.[49] Unfortunately this agreement was never made public and did not have the authorization of Congress (no doubt, to avoid offending proud Japan); and while it gave the impression that immigration was to be stopped, it did allow immigrants to bring wives to this country as well as "former residents" and "settled agriculturalists."[50] The number of arrivals in the United States was therefore cut in half from 1907 to 1908 and during the following year became a small trickle [51] of about 3000 a year.

The family-building period from 1908 to 1920 was one in which many single men in the United States sent home either for their wives or for brides who would marry them on entering the United States. The customary mode of arranging these marriages fitted well into the traditional forms of Japan where most marriages are arranged by families rather than by individuals.* The immigrant would write to his relatives at home asking them to arrange a marriage, and the exchange of pictures became a part of the usual procedure. These arrivals became known as "picture-brides," many Americans concluding that the exchange of pictures was a prelude to romantic attachment on the part of the mates. Such was far from the case, for the romantic ideal is not the customary mode of behavior in Japanese society; loyalty and obedience to parents includes submission to their choice of a mate for the individual.[52] As in all familial societies there were many ways of modifying the system in accordance with individual taste.

The result of the picture-bride system was to stabilize the Japanese family in the American community, since the presence of a one-sex society has elements of disruption and disorganization only too clearly shown in other cases.[53] It allowed more normal living for the Japanese immigrant and also served to hasten the change from migratory or gang labor to more settled occupations of farm or business.[54] On the other hand the continual appearance of more and more picture-brides at Pacific ports became a source of uneasiness to popular opinion, and inflammatory reports in the newspapers exaggerated it to a new avalanche of Orientals swamping California with a "yellow peril."[55]

Recognizing the danger in this agitation, the Japanese of the West Coast went out of their way to petition the home government

* Note the similarity to European practice in Chapters 11–14 below.

in 1919 to deny any more passports to Japanese women. The following year the Japanese government acceded to their request, and migration of picture-brides was stopped at the source. This became known as the "Ladies' Agreement" of 1920.[56] Parenthetically it is well to remember that figures for incoming Japanese during the period 1911–1920 should also be balanced by those outgoing or returning to Japan. When this is done, the difference between the two figures shows that the balance remaining in the United States was not large. During this era there were 87,576 arrivals and 70,404 departures, which leaves a balance of only 17,172.[57] Up to 1930 about two thirds of the population growth in the Japanese community was due to natural increase and not to immigration. Moreover, that natural increase was only about 9 per cent higher than that of the total population,[58] thus contradicting the popular stereotype that the Japanese "breed like rabbits," a claim that has been made about many other immigrant groups in this country. This 9 per cent difference was largely a reflection of the predominantly rural composition of the Japanese community. In this respect it simply reflects the usual characteristics of rural population.

The period from 1920 to 1924 could be called the period of increasing rejection by the American community. California passed the strengthened Alien Land Law in 1920 prohibiting those "ineligible for citizenship" the right to own or lease land for agricultural purposes.[59] By 1922 the Supreme Court of the United States declared in the Ozawa case that a Japanese was not a "white" person and hence was ineligible to citizenship.* When Congress was considering the 1924 immigration law which would limit entry to the

* The original Naturalization Act of 1790 restricted citizenship applications to "any alien being a free white person." At that time only immigration from the east was contemplated and no notice was given to possible Asiatic applications. By 1870 this law was amended in line with the Fourteenth and Fifteenth Amendments to include "aliens of African nativity and persons of African descent." Even by this time no attention was given to the Oriental problem, so that between 1870 and 1882 a number of Chinese and some Japanese were actually naturalized without any serious question being raised. The Chinese Exclusion Act of 1882 specifically barred further Chinese naturalization but left the Japanese question still open. The Ozawa case of 1922 finally settled this problem on the basis of the original "white person" clause. Cf. M. R. Davie, *World Immigration*, p. 328. This shows the racist character of the American tradition embodied in law. In principle it resembles the later "Aryan" restrictions of Nazi Germany.

United States on a quota basis, Senator Shortridge of California presented an amendment to exclude "all aliens ineligible to citizenship" from further immigration, based on the Supreme Court decision of 1922.

Although opposed by the press and public opinion outside of California and by the State Department, which feared international repercussions, the quota law with the Shortridge amendment passed by a substantial majority.[60] From that time to the present, Japanese immigration to the United States has been effectively stopped. Citizenship restrictions do not apply to second-generation Japanese born in the United States because the basic law of the latter is *jus soli*, under which anyone born in the United States or its territories automatically has citizenship status.* Had the quota law of 1924 permitted a specified number of Japanese immigrants each year on the same basis that was granted other countries, it would have meant something like 100 per year [61] and would have avoided singling out one country whose immigrants were excluded on purely racial grounds.

The exclusion of Japanese by the law of 1924 had important consequences both in the sphere of international relations and in the life of the Japanese community in America. It provoked the wildest antagonism in all Asia as well as in the Japanese public and strengthened the growth of those militaristic or antiforeign elements in the Japanese government which culminated in Pearl Harbor.[62] At home the effect of the law was to bring about ingrowing tendencies and a slower rate of assimilation among the first-generation Japanese settlers but an increase of political activity among the younger citizen generation.[63] In fact the history of the Japanese community from 1921 to the present might even be called the period of conflict

* Most countries, including Japan, have the *jus sanguinis* in which the citizenship of the child follows that of the father. The United States, as an exceptional case, has the *jus soli*. This meant that early second-generation Japanese in the United States had dual citizenship because of conflict of laws. However, a Japanese ordinance of 1924 allowed the child of a migrant in a foreign country to assume citizenship there if his birth was not reported to the Japanese consul. The Japanese parents were so eager to take advantage of this that an estimate taken from relocation centers in 1943 showed that "as a result of their own efforts, the Japanese in this country have reduced the number of dual citizens by 85%"; *The Case for the Nisei*, Brief of the Japanese American Citizens League, n.d., p. 17.

between generations, since the gap between them has steadily widened.

THE JAPANESE COMMUNITY

The immigrants born in Japan who came to America at an adult age are known as Issei; their children born in the United States are called Nisei (these terms are both singular and plural). Another smaller group, born in the United States but sent back to Japan to be educated, are given the title Kibei. Family mores in this country followed those of Japan in most respects, with patriarchal rule and general male dominance. Children are given the discipline usual in a patriarchal family and are trained to honor the family name at all costs.[64] A rather strict sexual segregation is the rule, and considerable conflict developed in homes where the Nisei began to follow the American pattern of social dancing.[65] There is also much friction resulting from the adoption of American courtship customs by the Nisei since the parents believe that only an arranged marriage is respectable.[66] A number of compromise patterns have resulted, such as superficial conformity to parental plans with the reservation that the Nisei has the right to stop the process at any point by refusing to go farther.[67] Ross and Bogardus list four types of Nisei marriage: the conformist, the compromise, the sudden-love type, and the "miaikekon" or "interview" type.[68] The latter is denied the status of a distinct type by LaViolette.[69] Perhaps a more adequate way to describe the situation would be to construct a scale from the Japanese type to the American romantic type. Most marriages would fall today toward the latter end of the scale.

There is very little intermarriage of Nisei with Caucasians since the mores of the group do not sanction it.[70] The consanguine pattern is followed by many families, particularly those in more isolated communities; this means that the bride lives at the home of the groom's parents.[71] Some family instability occurred during the early years because the Issei were often undecided whether they ought to remain permanently in the United States or not,[72] although this factor has gradually lessened in importance. On the whole, however, the strict social controls of the Japanese family have kept the group strongly integrated and brought about an almost nonexistent delinquency rate among Nisei children and adolescents.[73] This also meant that during depressions members of Japanese families were rarely or never found on the relief rolls, the presumption being that this would bring disgrace on the family name.[74]

On the whole, the educational level of the Japanese community is high. By 1930 the Issei showed an average of eight years of schooling in Japan while the Nisei were chiefly high school graduates and many were attending college.[75] By 1942 the educational level of the Nisei was considerably above the level of the native white population.[76] The Issei parent is usually eager to educate his children and may work longer hours to give them educational advantages.[77] In addition to the American program of education, the Issei had set up the *gakuin* or Japanese-language school as a sort of self-defense against the exclusion policy of American society, a cultural protection whereby they could assure their children some training in the history and cultural ideals of Japan. It also aided the parent in communicating with the children. While these *gakuins* were operated after public school hours so as not to interfere with the American pattern, they were not uniformly successful because the Nisei saw less and less reason to attend them, going only out of dutiful obedience to their parents' wishes.* The Japanese language was learned very imperfectly in the *gakuins*, and the schools were not re-established after World War II.[78]

The prestige structure of the Japanese community followed lines that were familiar from the homeland of the immigrants. At the top of the social scale stood the Japanese consul, who represented the home government and who symbolized in his person the authority of the emperor. Families whose culture was still dominantly Japanese gave him deference and respect as a member of the Japanese authoritarian classes; he served as the official functionary on all important occasions. Other more Americanized groups regarded him with amusement, annoyance, or scorn. We have already seen the effect of consular authority in the case of the Mexican immigrant; for the Japanese this element was perhaps more important because of the hierarchical pattern of their older semifeudal society. The consul was important as the go-between in all matters affecting the interests of community members and Japan. Diplomacy required consideration of his feelings. Some Nisei were hostile, however, if the Japanese representative were unable to speak English well and

* Notice a similar pattern below, Chapters 12 and 13.

thus help to protect them in the American society.[79] Most Japanese, however, had no contact whatever with consular representatives.

Somewhat lower in the status scale were the *kaisha-in* or "company people," who were business agents of large Japanese corporations in this country. Most of them had higher salaries and lived on a plane of living quite above and beyond that of most Issei or their children. Although many of them came from the middle classes in Japan, their peculiar position in the American scene placed them in a more exalted, high class status. A good share of them held themselves somewhat apart from their countrymen in the United States and often they did not mingle socially with the immigrant population. Another reason why the *kaisha-in* had an importance quite out of accord with their numbers is that they also acted as employers of immigrant group members; since there was no discrimination here against people with Japanese faces, employment by the *kaisha-in* furnished a sort of protected economy where Nisei could feel safe, even though remuneration was not always equal to American standards.[80]

Apart from these two groups, social distinctions in terms of status played a rather secondary part in the Japanese community, although the tendency to stratify along American lines of economic success became more marked as time went on.[81] All these patterns, of course, were characteristic of the subculture before World War II. It is yet too early to determine what effect relocation and the defeat of Japan will have on the immigrant community.

At first there was a close connection between vocational patterns and the concentration of Japanese in various Pacific Coast areas but this gradually changed as the Issei grew older. It is already clear that the great bulk of Japanese in this country began as agricultural laborers and at first this meant that they resided chiefly in rural areas. For them, as for other minority groups, the first World War proved to be an era of economic advance when many became established in the hotel business, cleaning and dyeing, or food marts.[82] Certainly the movement toward urban centers was well marked by the 1920's and kept increasing until 1940 when urban inhabitants comprised 54.9 per cent of all Japanese in the United States.* [83]

* This is almost exactly the urban percentage of the population as a whole. See Kolb and Brunner, *A Study of Rural Society*, Boston, Houghton Mifflin, 1946, p. 20. The concentration of Japanese in Los Angeles County was also comparable to the percentage of Californians in that county.

Though there was a tendency for the immigrants and their children to disperse into other areas, cultural as well as economic forces helped to keep them concentrated. For example, it is perfectly clear that the Japanese consuls encouraged concentration even after immigration ceased.[84] In the cities, the Japanese were largely concentrated in "little Tokyos" as a result of both economic and cultural forces and the practice of restricted covenants that prevented them from buying or leasing property outside their own areas.[85]

By 1941 the Japanese on the farms grew about 42 per cent of the produce crops in California, raising from 50 to 90 per cent of crops like tomatoes, peppers, celery, spinach, strawberries, cucumbers, cauliflower, and artichokes. Urban occupations were chiefly wholesale and retail services connected with the organization of the market for these products.[86] Working on truck farms often near to the cities and appearing with greater frequency in urban markets, the Japanese had a visibility ratio out of proportion to their actual representation in the population. Their undoubted success in truck gardening and greenhouse growing obscured their lack of interest in other occupations and gave rise to the stereotype of undercutting the Caucasian in the market as a whole.[87] Also overlooked was the fact that, as their standard of living approximated more and more the American standard, this type of competition began to disappear.

The suspension of Japanese immigration has resulted in an almost total cleavage between Issei and Nisei as reflected in their population pyramid; in fact the figures show clusters of individuals in the age ranges 15–25 and another from 45 to 60, the females appearing more largely in the 40–50 age group and the males from 50 to 60.[88] This has resulted in a gap between generations which is probably more sharply drawn than in any other minority group. The Issei had more loyalty to Japanese traditions and ways; many were highly nationalistic, insisted on deference behavior, patterned their farming or business on an authoritarian mode of control, often insisting on wage scales or standards much lower than those prevailing in the dominant American community; approved of arranged marriages, took for granted a consanguine family relationship rather than an individualistic one, and reinforced their attitudes through a powerful group of elders, the Japanese Association of North America. This Association combined the functions of town council, chamber of commerce, and social service agency, and had a considerable control of jobs and patronage.

On the other hand, the Nisei had almost contradictory attitudes and wished to emphasize their duties and rights in political America. To this end they formed an organization of their own, the Japanese American Citizen's League (known as the J.A.C.L.), to encourage voting, political participation, and solution of problems especially pressing for the second generation. Since the Issei were not trained in democratic procedure or the franchise, the J.A.C.L. from 1921 began to operate as a political pressure group; one special result of its work was the obtaining of citizenship for veterans of World War I who were not born in the United States and who belonged to the Japanese community.[89] It also labored to remove civic disabilities for its members and to combat discrimination. On the whole it was a popular organization with the younger members of the Japanese group, having fifty chapters throughout the nation by 1941.[90] Yet it had relatively little power or political influence among the immigrants as a whole because the lack of experience was crucial, the youthfulness of the members was a handicap in Japanese eyes, and it could offer little protection or economic aid to its members because they had as yet little status in their occupations. It showed its weakness by the fact that it took an entirely neutral stand on the issue of the Sino-Japanese war which preceded Pearl Harbor.[91]

RELOCATION

When the United States went to war with Japan in 1941, the Japanese community in the West suffered a profound shock from the evacuation of its members *en masse* by military order. No other minority group in the United States experienced a traumatic condition of this sort, and the total effect on both Issei and Nisei is still to be determined.

By 1940 the Japanese population in the United States was 126,947 and their concentration on the Pacific Coast meant that the great majority of them were in prohibited military areas. Eventually 109,300 persons of Japanese ancestry were evacuated into various internment centers.[92] How did it happen that this mass evacuation was ordered? After Pearl Harbor, the F.B.I. moved swiftly to intern the older Japanese leaders who seemed to have unquestioning loyalty to their mother country.* Most of those who were detained proved to have positions in business or in associations or organizations that would make them possible leaders of fifth column activity.[93] A Naval Intelligence officer writing just before the outbreak of war reported that in his opinion, 85 per cent of the resident Japanese population were loyal to the United States. During the same period, an investigator for *Collier's* who made a thorough study of the situation gave a similar report and announced that neither the Army nor Navy nor the F.B.I. believed the situation to be dangerous to military safety since the few disloyal Japanese were already under surveillance and would be rounded up immediately in case of war.**[94]

Why, then, was the decision made to intern all those of Japanese ancestry on the West Coast? Two factors seem to be chiefly responsible: first, a wave of war hysteria seems to have been deliberately fostered by a small minority of anti-Japanese agitators in California — a campaign that changed the atmosphere from one of sympathy toward resident Japanese to one of hatred and ill-founded rumors.[95] Almost on a single day the radio, the Hearst newspapers, and various politicians began a campaign of propaganda based entirely upon rumor to oust the Japanese. Denials of sabotage from F.B.I. and Intelligence Service were not printed. False rumors were. This spread clear across the country, even to New York newspapers.†

Second, the decision with regard to evacuation was left to General J. L. DeWitt, who was partly influenced by the more vocal minority that demanded total expulsion. Just as effective in determining his decision, however, was a totally unscientific ideology of race held by General DeWitt himself. His statement showed clearly the force of this idea, "The Japanese race is an enemy race and while many second and third generation Japanese born on United States soil, possessed of United States citizenship, have become 'Americanized' the racial strains are undiluted."[96] If this means anything, it seems to

* Paradoxically this did not mean anti-Americanism for most of them. A real ambivalence of feeling was involved.

** There has never been proof of any Japanese sabotage whatever on the West Coast. See *Impounded People, Japanese Americans in Relocation Centers*, Department of the Interior, War Relocation Authority, Washington, D.C., Government Printing Office, n.d., p. 37.

† The author is indebted to Professor T. S. Miyakawa of Boston University for this information.

imply that racial inheritance determines belief as well as physical type. On the basis of this ideology, General DeWitt made his decision determining the fate of 100,000 people, and the entire group, both citizens and aliens, received discriminatory treatment wholly on the basis of their race or ancestry, a procedure which was avoided with respect to every other alien group in the United States. And in no other case was this treatment meted out to citizens.

The haste with which the relocation process was organized meant that the Japanese had to dispose of properties and holdings to anyone who would buy. The government agencies that were set up to deal with the Japanese did not accept responsibility for custodianship and urged them to sell as quickly as possible. Bradford Smith, who has made a considerable study of the problem, estimates that of those who had anything to lose at least 95 per cent suffered economic loss ranging from small sums to thousands of dollars.[97] No attempt whatever was made to protect their property.

The work of relocation took place in two stages: during the first, the evacuees were taken to assembly centers, usually race tracks or fair grounds where horse stalls were hastily made into rooms of about 9 by 10 feet for the average family.[98] Single persons were haphazardly placed with others or thrust into family circles unknown to them. The function of these assembly centers was to provide a temporary halting place for those who were to be interned more permanently as soon as quarters could be erected by the War Relocation Authority, a civilian agency created to supervise the detained Japanese. The usual period of residence in these centers was several months, 215 days being the longest period.[99]

The second stage comprised detention in relocation centers (ten of them) in the states of California, Arizona, Idaho, Wyoming, Colorado, Utah, and Arkansas.[100] There were from 8000 to 16,000 in each of these centers, which were a series of barracks surrounded by barbed wire, each family being given a cubicle about 20 by 25 feet with eating arrangements in community dining halls.[101] Although it was announced at first that there would be self-government in the centers, a later announcement by the War Relocation Authority announced regulations limiting all elective offices to Nisei.[102] The rules also forbade the use of the Japanese language either in public meetings or in center newspapers, and this further strengthened the hold of the Nisei group, at the same time widening the already existing gap between generations.[103] The J.A.C.L. became more and more powerful in the relocation centers until by the end of the war they constituted the most influential organization in the community.[104] The rulings by the W.R.A., however, led to many difficulties and were finally honored more in the breach than in the observance. In Tule Lake Center, California, the Council or official body of the relocatees was controlled by Nisei but the block meetings were held by Issei. This led to a stalemate.[105] A similar situation arose in the Poston, Arizona, Center where the Issei referred somewhat contemptuously to the "child council" who were, by their standards, working only for their own interest and not for that of the people in Poston.[106] The reversal of leadership which occurred during relocation was a revolutionary change in Japanese community life which would have required a much longer time except for the sudden disruption of the war. Furthermore, no matter how well trained, Japanese were always subordinate to the Caucasian staff, even though the latter might be lacking in education.

On the whole, relocation life disrupted the family since common dining halls, laundries, and social activities fostered the primacy of age groups.[107] Children and adolescents escaped from parental supervision during most of the day, returning only at night to the primary group, with a resulting upsurge of youthful delinquency.[108] Hasty marriages contracted just before the relocation period became subject to the disorganizing effects of camp life with its lack of privacy and gave rise to predictions of an increased divorce rate in the postwar period.[109] The enlarged freedom of the camps gave many Nisei an opportunity to escape from the bonds of the familial group with its more conservative influences and to assume a veneer of smart sophistication and premature adult behavior.[110]

On the other hand the reverse tendency also occurred because the bitter disappointment following internment caused other Nisei and Kibei to identify themselves still more closely with their parents and their type of culture. While this did not signify a lack of adjustment in the relocation center, it nevertheless foreshadowed an increasing problem for the Nisei after returning to American life. The continual use of Japanese in spite of all restrictions had its effect, for as one Nisei put it, "I used to speak English with a Japanese accent; now I speak Japanese with an English accent." * [111]

The problem was still further accentuated by the W.R.A. questionnaire asking all relocatees about their loyalty to the United States. If the Issei said they were loyal, they automatically renounced all protection since they would thus lose their Japanese nationality and the protection given them under the Geneva protocol. On the other hand, since American law did not allow them to become citizens, a declaration of loyalty to America gave them no legal protection under our laws. If the parents could not answer with an unqualified yes, their children hesitated to do so, for it became quite clear that all "disloyals" would be separated from the "loyals" and sent to the Tule Lake Center in California. To affirm one's loyalty to America thus meant separation from parents. The number who declared themselves "disloyal" in order to remain with their parents was quite large, as might have been expected. Furthermore, Tule Lake looked better to many Japanese than the "outside," where according to many newspaper reports they might have a hostile reception. "Disloyalty" had two major advantages: it meant security in camp and it meant freedom from military service.[112] About 19,000 of the Japanese out of 100,000 (including Issei, mostly older persons) requested repatriation or expatriation,[113] although the motives for doing so were extremely mixed.

It is quite certain that most of those classifying themselves as "disloyal" would not have done so under ordinary circumstances. It is equally certain that many who did are finding the adjustment in the post-relocation period more difficult and have had their assimilation into American life retarded. The defense of such individuals by the Civil Liberties Union in 1946 has led the courts to take a somewhat lenient view of the matter for those who refused induction.[114] The W.R.A., by a coincidence regretted later, provided at the same time for enlistment of the Nisei in the 442nd unit. Many were quite willing to fight but insisted they should be under the same Selective Service as other citizens and not in a segregated unit of their own.†

* A considerable number ended with a broken pidgin or "campese" (comment of Professor Miyakawa).

† Supplied by Professor Miyakawa.

The problem has been eased somewhat by the outstanding combat record of the Nisei who did enlist to see duty in the 442nd and 443rd infantry divisions. The total number in the armed forces finally reached 30,000.[115]

Evacuees did a large share of the work at the relocation centers and were allowed wages of $16 a month for nonskilled workers and $19 a month for skilled ones such as doctors, lawyers, and engineers.* [116] In addition, supplementary clothing allowances of $3.75 monthly for adults and $2.25 for children were given.[117] Schools and churches both operated on a full-time basis. At Poston Center, about one year after its establishment, 230 high school seniors were graduated and received their diplomas.[118] Both Nisei and Caucasian teachers were employed. Churches in the centers were maintained through the sponsorship of the Protestant Church Commission for Japanese Service which supplied equipment and Caucasian religious workers who sought out and utilized the services of Japanese pastors in camp.[119] A large number of Buddhist organizations were also formed. Regular social service agencies were set up in relocation centers and staffed with Caucasians from outside. The recreation program was largely managed by Nisei leaders though nominal direction was still in Caucasian hands,[120] again with a salary differential weighted against the Nisei. Movies became a very popular source of recreation, though seating arrangements were either primitive or nonexistent.[121] Institutional forms like the Boy Scouts and the Y.M.C.A. maintained many of their functions for male youth.[122]

The movement from centers to the outside became known as resettlement and began with the issuance of work permits for agricultural and industrial labor in the western states.[123] Students were granted leave to attend colleges and universities, chiefly in the Middle West.[124] Others, who were unable to get releases since they could not get employment, were aided by church groups who established hostels in major cities like Des Moines, Chicago, Cleveland, Cincinnati, Washington, Detroit, Philadelphia, Minneapolis,

* This meant, of course, inability to keep up insurance or mortgage payments, amounting to a further confiscation of property. At the same time Caucasian employees, often of lesser ability, were receiving salaries as high as $6000 a year. (Supplied by Professor Miyakawa.)

and Brooklyn.[125] The W.R.A. allowed release to those who were accepted by a hostel administration, and the evacuee could travel to this new center, get board and lodging at nominal cost, and find aid in securing employment. Because of the activities and encouragement of the hostels, thousands of Japanese have taken their place in cities throughout the country and have found new homes far removed from the West Coast.

The military ban on returning to the Pacific area was lifted in December, 1944, with the announcement that all relocation centers would be closed by the end of 1945.[126] The process of dispersion into the American community, in marked contrast to the original concentration, resulted in some Japanese resettlement in forty-eight states and the District of Columbia.[127] In some of these areas, the Japanese American community cannot exist without "taking in each other's washing," as at Denver. In other cities like Cleveland or Des Moines they are fairly independent of other Japanese, carry on their economic occupations as individuals, and have achieved economic security.[128] As of March 20, 1946, when the last relocation center was closed, the W.R.A. reported that of the 109,300 relocated persons, 51,000 settled away from their former homes while 57,500 are again in the West Coast states. For the remainder, between 7000 and 8000 were returned to Japan under expatriation or repatriation proceedings and a few are still held in Department of Justice detention camps.* [129] The largest group outside the Pacific area today is in Chicago, which has received 20,000.[130] Another community of considerable size is found in Utah, where there were 8309 by the end of 1946.[131] In most of these settlements the presupposition that the members will go back to the West Coast seems to be taken for granted, although a realistic appraisal by Japanese leaders themselves seems to indicate that this is unlikely.[132]

While the trauma of relocation is largely past, the impact of the uprooting will not be fully revealed for many years. Meanwhile one student reports, "I have found that there are other minorities besides our own group which have similar problems; that there are vast opportunities to be found in other parts of the country besides the West Coast; that the little Tokyos of California have

* Some of those returned to Japan and all those in the Department of Justice camps are not included in the original figure of 109,300.

been broken up *; that the Nisei have had a greater chance to assimilate and make friends with the Caucasian people than ever before in their lives, and thus to create a most favorable mutual understanding between the two groups." [133]

AFTERMATH

Not only did the Nisei servicemen make an outstanding contribution in the European Theater of Operations but in the Pacific areas as well. General Bissell has made the statement that the Nisei intelligence work in the Pacific saved thousands of American lives. Colonel Moore maintains that in the Buna operations alone the Nisei saved several thousand lives. A good many of these veterans came home to find their property escheated by the state, while the parents of those who were killed had their property confiscated under the Alien Land Laws of California without any compensation.[134]

The only satisfactory study of the returned evacuees to the West Coast has been made by S. F. Miyamoto and R. W. O'Brien of the University of Washington in the Seattle area. It shows that compared with 1940 about two thirds as many Japanese are now resident in Seattle, though part of these have come from other areas and were not previous residents. Contrasting with prewar conditions, a larger percentage of the group is employed by Caucasians and in a more diversified group of occupations, both skilled and unskilled. Many are employed for the first time as porters, janitors, chambermaids, bus boys, power operators in clothing manufacture, pressers, and even as foundry workers. A good many more have the advantages of union membership with increased pay, and others are increasingly accepted in white collar positions either in government agencies or private (Caucasian) firms. On the other hand some of the older forms of enterprise have been largely disrupted; the only exception is the hotel business, which is firmly re-established. But many other forms of business such as cleaning and dyeing and the management of vegetable and fruit markets and produce houses have been lost. Most of those who have re-entered business are largely confined to serving the rather narrow market of the Japanese community itself.[135]

* An overstatement; some were partially restored.

The New Immigration

[CHAPTER 11]

The Italo-American: *The Latest Arrival*

"DID YOU HAVE a good time last week?" Nicola looked up and down the street to be sure that no one heard him. Then he said cautiously, "Sure I did. It's the big event of the year. Of course I skipped school. That's always good." He grinned.

"Tell me what happened."

"Well, you know that everyone in our neighborhood takes part in the festival. To tell you the truth, we have a lot of fun getting ready. Even though it's a lot of work too, we don't really mind. Americans don't have anything like it and I think they're missing something. During the Feast I feel closer to my folks than I do any other time of the year. This time we were more responsible than ever because my dad is president of the 'Sons' [Sons of Italy] so he and I worked together every night getting everything set. He didn't say much but I could see that he was glad I could help him like I did. Of course that wasn't all, either. Mr. Maccalucci and I got the kids down at the settlement to dance the old dances too. Maybe you think that wasn't work for a gang that's been doing nothing but jitterbugging. Anyhow, during the three days of the Feast we all went around to each other's houses and ate and drank till we couldn't stand up any more. You should have seen Giuseppe. He was comical. Everywhere he kept falling asleep just when things got interesting. Now I doubt if he remembers half of what went on. We had plenty of fun, but I'm glad that none of the kids from High School saw me." [1]

Nicola represents, in this illustration, the cultural conflict more or less typical of second generation Italian youth living in two social worlds. Today the Italian has become a familiar figure, though he is even yet imperfectly understood by the dominant "Americans." In considering the Italians, we are turning from those minorities with high *visibility* (due to differential non-Caucasian traits) to the minorities of *audibility*. Japanese, Mexicans, Indians, and Negroes are quickly identifiable by sight, but the European minorities of the "new immigration" * can be recognized for the most part either by language or by name. Customs and traditions, to be sure, differ from those of the native white stock of northern European ancestry, but the initial distinction is usually made in terms of language.

Racially all European elements of the American population are composite, mixed and related in the great Caucasian family whether they be Poles, Yugoslavs, Hungarians, Italians, or Scandinavians, or Jews.[2] It is important to remember that all the inhabitants of the United States are descendants of immigrants — even the Indians. The great bulk of our immigration, however, has come from European shores and consequently in the broad sense America is and always has been an aggregate of groups of minorities. But the inhabitants of the country have not been satisfied to leave the problem there: distinctions and discriminations have arisen between one group and another. Since the older form of European aristocracy was not applicable in a pioneer country, a new way of defining status arose, namely, length of residence. From early colonial days, both in New England and in the South, a line has been drawn between "old settlers" and newcomers. And in the broader national field of immigration, the same distinction appears between the "old" and the "new" immigration. Our concern here is only with the minorities of the latter.

THE NEW IMMIGRATION

It might well be asked how it is possible to draw the line between older settlers and newcomers as long as immigration continues. Would there not be a continually shifting line or area with changing conditions so that immigrants who were once on the unfavorable side of the line would eventually change over and indulge in the luxury of stigmatizing their fellows for coming over on a later boat

* The term "new immigration" will be clarified in the following section.

than themselves? The answer is yes; this is precisely what did occur down to the 1880's when those of English ancestry bewailed the coming of the Irish, and the Irish the coming of the Germans. But most authorities on immigration are agreed that 1882 was a kind of great divide separating an earlier mass migration from northern and western Europe on the one hand and a similar influx of eastern and southern Europeans on the other.[3] In that year the United States embarked on a policy of "selection-by-rejection" in its first federal immigration law and in the Chinese Exclusion Act.[4]

Before the 1880's America was traditionally the "asylum of all the world," the safe haven to which the poor and oppressed of all lands who were willing to work might come.[5] President Lincoln and the Republican Party of 1864 approved the establishment of a system to foster immigration, and the Congress of that year passed a bill entitled "An Act to Encourage Immigration."[6] Why then did the attitude of Americans change after 1880, and why did more immigrants begin to pour in from southeastern Europe?

The main reason was the rapid rise of industrialism, with a sudden demand for new workers. Those who were coming from northern and western Europe followed the traditions of their countrymen who came before them and entered agricultural occupations (with the possible exception of the Irish). Oftentimes the very fact that they had relatives in this country tended to draw them into small towns and farming communities rather than into the cities and industrial centers where there was a crying demand for labor.[7] But this was not all; the countries of northeastern Europe were themselves undergoing a similar wave of industrialism and tried to discourage emigration because of the need for laborers at home. Their own labor unions and organizations were gradually raising the standard of living so that emigration appeared to be more of a risk than it had been before.[8]

Just as important for the rapid increase of immigration was the preference of American employers for workers of other nationalities as a source of cheaper labor. The discrepancy between living standards in America and in southern or eastern Europe was still great enough so that small wages from the American standpoint looked big to the peasant in far-off Poland or Calabria. It was also to the advantage of the American employer to have a new source of labor as yet untutored in the ways of labor union activity. Many immigrants were brought in under contract as strike breakers,[9] and others were played off against each other on the basis of language or traditional hostilities carried over from the European scene.[10]

Of course the shift in origin from northwestern to southeastern Europe did not come suddenly; to be exact, its starting point was roughly the 1880's, with its peak coming in 1907.[11] At any rate, the language, nationality, and cultural differences in the southeastern Europeans were in greater contrast to American culture so that antiforeign feeling and discrimination began to grow against them. The "Latin and Slavic element" came in for a considerable share of vilification and abuse; this wave of resentment became sufficiently strong to result finally in new Congressional Acts restricting immigration in 1917, 1921, and 1924.

The general purpose of these Acts was to discriminate against those of southern or eastern European origin without actually naming them openly. This was done by the "national origins" clause and a quota system whereby immigrants from any country were admitted on the basis of the number of their nationals already in the United States. In the 1924 Immigration Act, sometimes known as the quota law, the annual quota from any one country was to be 2 per cent of the number of foreign-born individuals from that country resident in the United States according to the census of 1890.[12] The effect of the law was to restrict immigration both absolutely and selectively: selectively, because the number of foreign-born in the census of 1890 was predominantly from northern and western Europe.

The motives and attitudes behind the Act were such as to define the southeastern European immigrants as a specially recognized minority in our midst; this social definition has become traditional in American public opinion and may now almost be called a part of the national ideology.* [13] It portrays the United States as a white-Anglo-Saxon-Protestant civilization somehow fighting against hordes of "foreign" or "colored" elements which threaten to destroy its pristine purity. That this picture is not entirely a figment of the

* For an account of the scholars who helped to popularize this belief see Carey McWilliams, *A Mask for Privilege, Anti-Semitism in America*, Boston, Little Brown, 1948, pp. 56–77.

imagination is shown by an analysis of short stories and advertising copy in popular American journals: the major characters are white, Anglo-Saxon, or Protestant and the minor or criminal ones belong to other nationalities, races, or religions.[14]

ITALIANS: A PROFUSION OF LATECOMERS

We are beginning the consideration of national minorities with the Italians, because they are numerically larger than any other group in the new immigration. When compared with the immigrants of all other southern and eastern Europeans, from 1820 to 1930, the Italians preponderate with 4,651,195 entrants, a far greater number than from any other country.[15] The nearest contender is Austria-Hungary with 4,132,351; but under older passport regulations many of those who entered from "Austria-Hungary" belonged to nationalities now recognized as distinct, such as Czechs, Slovaks, Hungarians, Yugoslavs, Poles, or Russians. If the numbers of foreign-born Italians and their children in the United States today are totaled, the figure is roughly six million.[16] It is therefore evident that the Italians have the largest homogeneous group of all nationalities that have entered the United States since 1880. (In the older immigration, the Germans had the highest number.)[17]

What is perhaps not so often realized is that the Italians also arrived latest among the new immigrants.[18] The peaks of immigration came in 1907 and again in 1913 just before the first World War.[19] In 1924 Antonio Stella computed the average length of residence of different nationality groups and found that at that time the Italians had an average of seventeen years in the United States as compared with thirty-four years for the English, fifty-one years for the Irish, and thirty-eight years for the Germans.[20] The Italian foreign-born population of 1890 was only one seventh of the number in 1910 and one ninth of that in the 1920's.[21]

Problems of adjustment, acculturation, economic livelihood, and assimilation have therefore been accentuated for the Italians in more potent form than for other nationality groups. Free lands were gone, the frontier was dwindling to a vanishing point,[22] and the chief opportunities were mainly in common labor on the railroads or in other unskilled industrial jobs. Although the Italian group has spread from one end of the United States to the other, their lateness of arrival has largely been responsible for the fact that even by 1940, nearly 88.5 per cent of them lived in urban communities.[23] New York, as the chief port of entry, today contains one third of all the Italians in the United States and is the largest Italian center in the world, Rome not excluded.[24] Cities like Newark and Providence are 32.7 and 35.8 per cent Italian,[25] while throughout the country as a whole there are something like three thousand Little Italys in various urban centers.[26]

Since the Italians arrived "too many and too late," they were forced to take the jobs and housing areas that no one else wanted and thus to make their adjustment to American folkways under exceptionally difficult circumstances. Although about 85 per cent of the immigrants had agriculture as their major occupation before coming to America, only about 15 per cent were able to go into agriculture after their arrival.[27] In city after city the Italians moved into slum areas vacated by other nationalities. In New York they occupied a section notorious for being the worst tenement district in the city, one that called forth the wrath of Jacob Riis and other reformers.[28] Likewise in Chicago the Italians moved into sections left practically untenantable by other groups, and even in the 1920's about 75 per cent of Chicago Italians were slum residents.[29]

Coming to America as unskilled workers, the Italians did not join the labor unions until a comparatively late period, preferring to work with their own group or under an Italian "boss." [30] In many ways their entrance into the broad stream of American life was delayed considerably beyond the period characteristic of the usual immigrant.

NORTHERN AND SOUTHERN ITALY

Early in the nineteenth century Metternich remarked that Italy was not a country but a mere geographical expression. It is certain that the major division between the Italy of the north and that of the south shows important contrasts. The northern area was in continual contact with France, Germany, and Switzerland, was highly industrialized, had a well-developed middle class, was the forefront of the movement for Italian unification known as the *Risorgimento* (1860), and in general became the spearhead of modern and progressive movements. The northern Italians from that day to this assume an attitude of superiority over southern Italians, who are largely agricultural.[31] Parenthetically, the immigrants from north Italy to America arrived before those from the south. They had already reached positions of prominence in the American scene by the time the Neapolitans, Calabrians, and Sicilians arrived and could therefore continue to look down on their fellow nationals in the United States. This situation meant that the southern Italians here received little guidance from those who had come before them.[32]

In the area south of Naples, the peasant engaged in a desperate struggle for existence. Climatic conditions were unfavorable. Most rains came in the autumn, when it was too late to water the crops and when vegetation was scarce. Erosion of topsoil was therefore common. Hot dry winds like the sirocco and the favonio blew up from the African deserts at the very time when crops were maturing.[33] The scarcity of water was unbelievable; oftentimes it would be hauled for miles and sold in small measures.* [34] Most of the soil was poor, having been exhausted by centuries of feudal cultivation in large estates. In times past the inhabitants practiced deforestation in order to use as much land as possible, thereby making the erosion problem more serious.[35]

The landholding system aggravated conditions for the *contadino* (peasant). Even at the end of the nineteenth century practically all the land in southern Italy belonged either to the barons or to the church. When feudalism was officially abolished and the lands sold in order to get a more equal distribution, the larger proprietors got the lion's share. The poor often had to sell their property for taxes, since they lacked capital to keep it productive.[36] Absentees got half the land but about two thirds of the value. Much of it was bought for speculative purposes and sold many times.[37] The best land around the village came to belong to the baron; so the *contadino* was forced to lease land farther away and thus be removed from any immediate access to his soil. Everyone in the community lived in the village, and the peasants would have to arise at 3 or 4 o'clock in the morning in order to walk out to their little strips of soil by daybreak.[38] At night after an exhausting

* Dr. Covello tells of traveling through southern Italy in 1938 and reports that every hotel shut off its water pipes by 9 P.M. and no protests could bring a glass of water after that hour.

day's work they had to walk back, often up steep slopes to the town perched high on a hill or mountain.[39]

Because of the confusion resulting from the breakup of feudalism, legal tenure of land was uncertain and titles were not guaranteed. The opportunities for fraud were numerous. The many taxes were collected from the peasant before the crop was gathered and sold (the time when he had least money).[40] If he wanted to borrow money, he had to pay from 25 to 50 per cent interest and so debt was common.[41]

The old system of inheritance, in which the first-born son obtained the property, gave way to *frazionamento* or the division of property among several members of the family.[42] This eventually made holdings so small that they were no longer profitable. A speculator would then come and buy up the strips, leaving the peasant without any land of his own. A form of sharecropping that became common enabled the peasant to provide for his family's support with half the crop. The *mezzadria* or crop-sharing contract was never recorded and so there was no official record, only a verbal arrangement.[43] This gave the landlord or *gabelotto* (overseer of an estate) a chance to drive hard bargains at the beginning of the season and to squeeze the peasant still more at harvest time.

The influence of the geography of southern Italy was exceedingly important. Apart from Naples and the Palermo area, the entire region is so cut up by mountain ranges that each valley is separate from others and isolated. This tended to keep society static, to develop localism and provincialism.[44] Cut off not only from easy communication with other agriculturalists but also from the currents of industrial change in the North, the peasants of southern Italy carried on a type of agriculture not very different from that of Roman times. Poverty and bad roads prevented the importation of machines,* and the *contadino* thought them impious; anyone who employed them was going "ahead of the Eternal Father." [45]

After the *Risorgimento* the officials of north Italy attempted to make their country a first rate power; the result was that they squandered their resources in Africa while neglecting the southern

* Jerre Mangione who visited the peninsula in the 1930's reports that in all his time in Sicily he failed to see a single modern farm implement. See his *Mount Allegro*, Boston, Houghton Mifflin, 1942, p. 272.

areas of Italy proper.[46] Their policy was to treat the South much like a colony, to increase the tariff on industrial products but to leave the agricultural areas unprotected from competition.[47] Under these conditions the backwardness of the South, already solidified by historical and geographical causes, was perpetuated when competition with other agricultural countries reduced profitable markets at home and left the overpopulated portion prostrate.[48]

In a sense Italy was a microcosm of Europe as a whole, for her first emigrants to the United States came from the north and west; but as soon as these sections were progressively urbanized and industrialized, there was greater opportunity for local labor at home and emigration was checked at the source. During the years 1876 to 1900, north Italy provided more than two thirds of the total Italian emigration to the United States.[49] With unification and the newer economic trends, the tide to America shifted until it was mainly from south Italy. By the time the quota law began to operate, southern Italian immigrants to our shores finally numbered more than four fifths of all the Italians in the United States.[50] Something like a fourth of these were from Sicily.

For practical purposes, then, any consideration of the Italian minority in the United States must deal with the southern Italian group. It is probably true that the "typical" Italian in America is not representative of Italy as a whole but of the economically depressed areas; in this impoverished section, the struggle for existence stimulated emigration as the only escape from an intolerable situation. The southern Italian comes from a distinctive subculture in his home country, and any description of his manner or way of life presupposes this selective interest.

SOUTHERN ITALIAN CULTURE

The life of the southern Italian peasant was one of economic hardship, social isolation, outdoor living, and monotonous routine punctuated by an occasional festival.

Social stratification divided the community into four classes. (1) The *Dons* or *galantuomini*, who were the nobles, landed gentry, professionals, and the clergy. This upper class controlled most of the social and political life of the village and kept a link with the outside world through travel and association. All connections with the government in Rome were made through members of this class. (2) The *artigiano* or artisan class, including craftsmen and small merchants. Tailors, barbers, shoemakers, masons, and storekeepers were representative. Their numbers were so small that they hardly constituted a middle class but corresponded roughly with that position. They participated in political and administrative affairs of the village and gave their children an elementary education. (3) The *contadini* or peasants, who leased their tiny plots of land or in some cases owned them. Most of them had little opportunity for schooling or civic participation, and their main occupation was tilling the soil. (4) The *giornalieri* or landless day laborers who had no plots of their own but were forced to migrate from estate to estate seeking daily work for wages.[51] Most of them were employed only about 120 days out of the year, and their poverty was severe.[52] The worst fate that could happen to a *contadino* was to lose his status and become a *giornaliero.*

The day laborer was practically a social outcast. He was addressed by his first name or by *tu* (a mark of familiarity). Now and then he would be jokingly called *Santu* (saint) because he had no worldly goods.[53] The *contadini* did not want their children to intermarry with the day laborers, who were *cafoni* (low-brow). *Giornalieri* made up over half the males in agriculture in southern Italy during the period of emigration.[54] The great bulk of the rest were *contadini.*

In south Italy the peasant usually lived in a one-room house located within the confines of a village, sharing his room with such farm animals as pigs and chickens. If he was fortunate enough to have two rooms, the animals occupied the second.[55] In spite of this fact, practically all the peasant houses were swept and clean, the chief obstacle to cleanliness being the smoke from cooking which begrimed the walls. On ceremonial occasions like weddings or baptisms the *contadino* would whitewash the walls. Although he had a great love for flowers, he was unable to indulge his taste because his land was so far away and his cramped living quarters did not allow space to be used for this purpose. Bouquets for weddings, cunningly contrived to look like flowers, were actually candies arranged in flowerlike shapes.[56]

Since the peasant's title and tenure were uncertain, he gradually lost the love of the soil and became *homo oeconomicus*, whose chief interest in it was profitable operation. The ancient term for cultivating the crops was *governare* (rearing or nursing) and this could be applied to an animate object. By the time the peasant left for America a different term became common: *lavorare il terreno* (to work the land).[57] In the same way the aim of the *gabelotto* or overseer for the absentee landlord was not productivity of the land but driving hard bargains with the *contadini* to increase his own profit.[58] To the peasant the members of other classes were enemies, given to *sfruttamento* (exploitation). This term included the priests in many cases since they either came from the wealthy class or supported them in any contest with the lower. Peasants felt that the spiritual leaders should not enter political affairs.[59] The *contadini* took no part in the *Risorgimento* and were apathetic to political change.[60] Officials in the town were usually from the North and the peasant felt that there was collusion between them and the landowners.[61] Yet while the peasant seldom revolted and usually appeared listless in political affairs, he constantly lived in a state of "latent revolution." [62] Emigration served as the safety valve for possible revolutionary tendencies, and one scholar has remarked that emigration rather than the *carabinieri* (police) abolished brigandage in Basilicata and Calabria.[63]

FAMILY AND VILLAGE

In this environment the south Italian had direct acquaintance with primary groups only: the family and the village. Of these two, it was the family to which he gave unquestioning allegiance.

In general there were two main divisions in family life: (1) the *famiglia* or large family, including both blood relatives and in-laws up to the fourth degree — this was larger than the typical consanguine family, which is usually composed of blood relatives only;[64] (2) the marriage unit, which comprised husband, wife, and children. When the southern Italian uses the word family, he signifies the *famiglia;* the only way in which the marriage unit receives significance is in its relation to the larger group. By the time a given marriage unit is the oldest living household group within the *famiglia*, it then assumes more importance, since the head of this unit is the *capo di famiglia* or head of the larger related group.[65]

In the fierce and unremitting struggle with nature and an unfriendly class system, the haven of refuge was the *famiglia*. Solidarity within the family was necessary for the stability of social life. One who did not belong to the family group was a *forestiere* or stranger. The large family was a world within a world, a unit surrounded by "strangers." [66] Obligation to members of the family was absolute; to strangers, limited or nonexistent.[67] Each person felt responsible to the family rather than to the community.[68] There were even times when a person performing a benevolent act to a nonfamily member would be regarded as weak headed. "Has this man no family that he should benefit strangers?" would be the question.[69] There were times, of course, when a neighbor died and all those living nearby would give aid with money or gifts; in general this seems to have been less sympathy for the person than a way of supporting the family pattern.[70] And charity or *pietà* to beggars or monks was a way of heaping up merit in the supernatural world.[71]

The word *amico* (friend) was rarely used in southern Italy. Friendship with nonrelatives did not involve much intimacy; confidences were shared with family members but could not be given to strangers.[72] The Italian in America translates *paesano* as "friend." But the term *paesano* in Italy was simply a member of one's home community and implied acquaintance only. The meaning of this word became greatly enlarged after the Italian came to the United States.[73]

The *onore della famiglia* (honor of the family) was the touchstone of conduct. The reputation of the individual mattered less than that of the family. If a boy or girl did not behave well, the *capo di famiglia* was blamed for not controlling him and upholding the family honor.[74] But the term had another meaning as well. In another context the *onore della famiglia* also signified the unique way of life practiced by a particular family. It might indicate a special chivalry for women, or the opposite; it might involve insubordination to official authority; or it might concern something so trivial as buying animals of a special color. Whatever it was, it constituted the family's "little tradition" which was respected and observed by every member. When a girl married into another family, she was expected to adopt their "little traditions" and be wholly loyal to them.[75]

There is a common belief that the Italian family was patriarchal. There is much to support this view. Not only is the father the recognized head of the house but the brothers dominate the sisters. In south Italy anything large and fine is *maschio* (male). Girls were not allowed to leave the house unchaperoned by father, brother, or a male relative. It was traditional that only "bad" girls walked alone. After the age of seven, girls were not allowed to be idle or play games; they had to learn how to carry on the domestic tasks of the household in preparation for an early marriage. Poverty of the family meant that everyone had to work as soon as possible. It was the ambition of every mother to see her daughter *sistemata* or settled as early as possible. Some of these marriages occurred as early as at the age of fourteen years.[76] After the traditional seven-day honeymoon, the male was supposed to drop all gallantry and assert his authority over the young wife.[77] The husband usually distrusted the wife in their early years of married life; there was danger of infidelity and also the possibility that she would be more loyal to her own family than to his.[78] To marry young was to assure success in bringing up a wife according to one's own ideas.[79]

On the face of it, the Italian family gave the impression of absolute male dominance. Yet the evidence is not conclusive. At a distance all dark colors look alike but closer examination will show important shades that do not appear to a casual observer. It is significant that in south Italy paternal authority lasted only until the father showed that his strength was weakening; then one of the sons took over the authority.[80] The father's domination was based on fear, and this fear departed as soon as the patriarch lost his strength.[81] The boy who showed authority over his sister was encouraged by his father, but when he was in the house with only the mother and sisters present, the mother would intervene. Thus the brother showed two forms of behavior toward his sisters, one when the father was present and another when the mother alone was there.[82]

If the Italian family was purely patriarchal, why did the husband turn over all his earnings to his wife and retain only an allowance?[83] Or why was it that in Apulia (a province of south Italy), the relatives of the wife could come and punish the husband of one of their girls simply because he had beaten her?[84] In the family feuds which were as common in southern Italy as they are in the Kentucky mountains, the sons felt it their duty to avenge the family honor, but the father seldom did. And when the sons desired a blessing for this dangerous task, they came to the mother and not to the father — at least in Apulia and Sicily.[85] Sicilians were allowed to make fun of old men but never of old women.[86] The mother's subservience was an imposed pattern but underneath she had a good deal of authority, especially within the household.[87] In certain homes the mother has been the strongest person, dominating the other members of the family without question; yet to her neighbors she will tell how virile her son is, how she cannot do this or do that because the son would not like it. At home she may slap him and order him around without the least compunction.[88] An ancient proverb from south Italy has it, "If the father is dead, the family suffers; if mother dies, the family cannot exist." [89]

There is considerable evidence that male authority in south Italy has superseded an older form of matriarchal society. In Sicily there were a number of matriarchal survivals: the wife could dispose of her property as she wished, and if she died childless her dowry would be claimed by her sisters.[90] The dowry always remained the personal property of the wife in any case. It is therefore suggested that the extreme jealousy of the male in southern Italy and Sicily is compensatory, that it marks a certain insecurity in the male role.[91] At least the patriarchal role is qualified more than common belief would have it. Covello notes that in the areas where cattle raising is the main occupation, the wife is more subservient to her husband; but where the chief crop is composed of small grains, the wife has more authority. The origin of these differences is still obscure.[92] Certainly the woman had more authority in Sicily; and in Sicily women traditionally do not work in the fields.[93]

The closest ties outside the family were to the *compare* (godfather) and *commare* (godmother). They were accepted into the family circle as insiders, except that it was not the custom to confide in them to the same extent.[94] A person who was *compare* was not always a true godfather but might be best man at a wedding or the sponsor of a child's confirmation. Thus there were degrees of *comparaggio* (relations to a *compare*).[95] On the whole the wife had less tendency to accept friendship ties outside the family than the husband.[96]

Outside the *famiglia* the only social bonds were with the village. Since the confines of the church parish and of the village were the same, the church became the religious expression of the local group, not a separate institution. The two words which express this localism of culture in south Italy are *campanilismo* and *paesano.* The former refers to all those living within the sound of the church bell (the bell tower being the *campanile*), and may be translated "village-mindedness." [97] A *paesano* is a fellow villager. The small community was a primary group with local customs, folkways, festivals, saints, and a local dialect frequently incomprehensible to dwellers in the rest of Italy.[98] The political, social, and religious boundaries of the village and its environs were the horizon of the peasant. His masters did not want him to see beyond, and in time he did not care.

The tiny community faced inward to such an extent that it was completely circumscribed; marriages were endogamous, for the peasant believed that it was dangerous for his son or daughter to make entangling alliances with strangers.[99] Town endogamy was expressed by a proverb, "Marry girls and buy cattle from your own town only."[100]

The mental horizons of the peasant were also limited. Schools in southern Italy were of the poorest kind, with little or no equipment, no heat, and no hygienic facilities.[101] Roads were lacking in most areas, and transportation was out of the question. Although there were compulsory attendance laws, officials in the village of the *artigiano* or *galantuomini* class were not interested in enforcing them. Peasant children were simply not expected to go to school; they were *cafoni.* Instances occurred when one dared to go, only to be jeered out of the building.[102] When allowed to go, the children of the *contadini* received an inferior education, for Italy of that day spent twice as much on higher education as it did on elementary.[103] Authorities were not interested in extending popular education for who, then, would do the work? The peasant himself saw little use for it; the need for literacy was not apparent in the village, where it was uncommon to write letters or use books and magazines.[104] The father saw no reason why his boy (and even less his girl) should attend school when he might work at home and help increase the family income.[105]

Thus in 1901 the average illiteracy for the southern provinces of Italy was about 70 per cent for males. This average includes the larger cities and it can therefore be inferred that the figures for small towns must have been higher. For females the illiteracy rate was greater still; Basilicata, for example, had an average rate of 94.7 per cent for women.[106] In a good many cases, however, the census takers avoided the villages and so the statistics are not accurate.[107] The common opinion among the peasants was that a child should be *buon educato* (well-mannered or well brought-up but it was a manner of indifference to be *buon istruito* (well instructed in book learning).[108] The chief aim was to have the child learn how to work so that he could help support the family.

The religious outlook of the peasant was also narrow and confined; Foerster makes the significant comment that about 50 per cent of the religion was festivity and the other 50 per cent superstition.[109] It is important to remember that the people of south Italy became Christian by decree rather than from conviction. This helps to account for the retention of numerous ancient religious practices.[110] Blunt shows that pagan customs were taken over bodily into Catholic practice with little modification. The *lares* and *penates* became the household saints; ancient gods and goddesses used as figureheads for fishing boats later appeared as madonnas or saints; and the place for pagan statues at the entrance of the home became a niche from which a madonna or saint guarded the household.[111] These saints were simply a new version of the old Roman gods and spirits of woods and rivers; in this transformation, the worshippers perpetuated a sort of informal polytheism.[112] The functions of the different saints vary in different localities: some have healing qualities, some will bring a good husband, some provide a good death, etc. In addition to these, each town has a patron saint who is protector of the village.

Supernatural forces received fully as much attention as natural ones. Anything unusual was attributed to mystical influences in a human guise.[113] The most common example was the *mal'occhio* (evil eye), a vague influence that brings bad luck. The perpetrator is not a special type of person, as in some of the other superstitions.[114] One of the likely occasions evoking the *mal'occhio* was any unguarded exultation or joy, boasting, or pride. Particularly was this true if a person expressed admiration for a child without saying at the same time *Dio benedica* as a means of warding off the possible bad luck.[115] Wearing amulets or making the sign of horns could also avert the evil eye. Since witches were abroad during the night hours, leaving the windows open was an invitation for them to enter the house; hence the way to sleep was with doors and windows tightly closed. Those who forgot the old superstition would rationalize the practice by saying that the night air was naturally bad.[116]

In contrast the festive side of religion was a time of merrymaking, a release from hours of grinding toil. Perhaps the most popular was the celebration of the day sacred to the patron saint of the village, when the procession carried an image through the streets and gifts were thrown on the wagon bearing the statue. Sicily had thirty-seven festivals a year in addition to other holy days; at each festival the village spent huge sums of money, and the amount of display was in marked contrast to the poverty of the participants.[117] Some of these festivals have been transplanted to the American scene, the largest, in honor of Our Lady of Mt. Carmel, being celebrated every July 16 in East Harlem, New York City. On the eve of this occasion as many as 300,000 people gather in a few square blocks around the shrine adjacent to the East River Drive.[118] The story opening this chapter refers to a smaller instance of the same kind.

The Catholic church in southern Italy was not usually dependent upon its communicants for regular gifts to carry on its ministrations, but at the time of the great emigration the status of the church was changing. It had lost most of its lands and began to find its support elsewhere, sometimes from the municipality and sometimes from the *galantuomini*. But the peasant paid very little.[119] Church services were informal: there was little solemnity, much noise, whispering, sneezing, giggling, and coughing. Most of the people had to stand throughout the service. Many paid no attention to the ceremonies, and a few slept.[120]

Men in the middle range of life were not expected to pay as much attention to the church as the women, children, and old people. The conception seemed to be that the young still had to learn devotion, and the old needed to prepare for death.[121]

The priest of the village was often enough a *paesano* who had grown up with the members of the congregation and could therefore supply a type of service especially suited to the needs of that particular community.[122] He encouraged local beliefs where he did not share them, and in this he received the support of the hierarchy. If he opposed superstition, there was a danger of losing the people; thus superstition was accepted as a lesser evil than defection and neglect of religion.[123]

Distrust of government, which was both distant and tyrannical, led to a quality of life much prized particularly among the Sicilians, *omertà*. This trait was a kind of self-reliant manliness; a man who had it could look out for himself. Since the police were considered enemies, the man with *omertà* would handle his own affairs and see justice done without the aid of authorities or courts, who too often seemed to get the wrong man. Since institutional controls were weak, they were replaced by a more personalized form of justice similar to that of vigilante justice in the pioneer days of the United States.[124]

Male associations established to get some form of justice in spite of the tyranny and inefficiency of the government were in many cases a dire necessity. Since the only reports of their activities have come from those who regarded them as brutal and lawless, without knowing anything of the intimate local affairs in which they operated, the impression has been that they were mere criminal gangs. The secrecy in which they operated sometimes made it possible for them to indulge in illegal activities, but the people felt safe with them and not with the police.

Sometimes an organization like the Mafia of Sicily punished violations of Mafist honor and practiced extortion or kidnapping. Yet if we are to believe reports of insiders, these acts were punishments for individuals who had committed crimes against innocent and respectable people and who had gone undiscovered by the police.[125] The worst misdeed, according to Mafist codes, was to report offenses of any kind to the police authorities; therefore criminals outside the organization would also be protected. Each local association or *cosca* was more or less independent of others in the established localist tradition; rivalry between two of these associations or even between members of the same group often occurred. None of the *cosche* was large, though their influence was out of proportion to their size.[126]

PSYCHOSOCIAL TRAITS OF SOUTHERN ITALIANS

The way of life practiced by simple peasants and fishermen accentuated certain traits at the expense of others. The almost hopeless conditions under which the *contadini* had to labor have given them a dogged persistence tinged with patience, docility, and resignation.[127] Daily and monotonous activities channeled their interests into the immediate present; the south Italians tend to reject what does not bring immediate gain. But even though the utilitarian trend is strong,[128] it extends to the future in one special respect: the passion to save. On other shores they showed little sense of labor solidarity at first; their interest was to work as individual toilers who sacrificed everything for their families. Their initial rejection of close ties with other workers was simply a function of their intense desire for savings (the striker loses his little hoard).[129]

The southern Italian was not ashamed to show his emotions, whether joy, sorrow, disgust, or anger. The frustrations of daily work, constant exploitation, and social inferiority often resulted in aggressive behavior which sprang up quickly [130] but as quickly subsided.[131] When the peasant's emotion came to the surface, it showed an immediate urgency, a momentary enthusiasm or anger which as suddenly cooled.[132] There was a personal sensitiveness on the part of the Italian male, the coming of a moment when a decision meant all or nothing.[133]

The southern Italian had a passion for flowers. D'Angelo in his first years in the United States as a young immigrant commented on his impression that all Americans were unfeeling people. In New York he did not see a single man who put a twig of sweet basil over his ear "as the men — real men — of our town do on summer evenings." [134]

In the arts, Italian music shows primarily dramatic or melodic rather then reflective forms; it has sudden changes of mood just as the people themselves have.[135] As for the festivals, whether they are the cause or the result of the people's deeper impulses, they reflect their love of display. As an individual, the Italian prefers to be an actor rather than a passive admirer; he identifies himself with actors or singers and enters into their ardent emotions with tremendous urgency.[136] He cannot sit idly by but feels impelled to go through the emotions himself. Thus the humdrum of his daily existence is punctuated and accented by moments of fervor that heighten his sense of participation in life. These moments come to have an intrinsic importance or finality.

A related trait is the flair for telling stories. Since many of the best raconteurs speak only in the bosom of the family, this characteristic is often unnoticed by others. During the recital, the storyteller will pile climax upon climax and emphasize the tale with vivid gestures, grimaces, or long pauses for effect.[137]

The alternation or wavy pattern in the emotions manifests itself in the southern dialects through heavily accented vowels and variations in pitch or tone. Eloise Griffith has commented that they do not *speak* the language, they *caress* it.[138] The wholeness with which individuals enter into their emotions is also shown by gestures which are used for expressiveness rather than meaning; these gestures often employ the entire radius of the arms or bend the entire body for effect.[139]

EARLY ADJUSTMENTS TO THE UNITED STATES

The Italian migration to America, like that of other countries, was composed at first chiefly of males. Even more than other newcomers (the Slovaks possibly excepted) the southern Italian expected and desired to go back to his native village where he could establish himself in better circumstances. Typically, the opinion of the rest of the world was a matter of indifference; but to succeed in the eyes of the *paesani* was to achieve for the only audience that mattered. The passion for saving, already noted, was in the beginning directed chiefly toward the goal of a return to Italy.

Such was the economic standard of the old home environment that transplanted Italian immigrants, even with large families, saved as much as $5 a week from a $15 wage. If the savings were not used for return passage, they could be sent to relatives or used for buying property in the United States rather than for raising the immediate standard of living.[140] But the sex ratio remained high; even by 1930, the number of foreign-born male Italians outnumbered that of females 139.4 to 100.[141]

Since many of the first men did not have relatives or friends in the United States and were unfamiliar with its language, money, and customs, they placed themselves in the hands of an intermediary, the *padrone* (boss). This boss was of Italian origin but knew American ways sufficiently to do innumerable services for his fellow countrymen with less experience. In some cases he advanced passage money to those who wished to make the trip, and allowed them to work off their debt on jobs which he secured for them. In this he was repeating an old American custom, familiar since colonial days, of practicing a form of indenture. In other cases the *padrone* contracted for the labor of men from south Italy, arranged for their passage, and collected a commission from both employer and worker. Frequently enough he made arrangements for rooms and board, banking, trading, and personal service.[142] Then again he secured special privileges with an employer in exchange for supplying a gang of workers. He often became the commissary man who furnished the laborers with the staples of life while they were working in gangs outside of the large cities. He would either run the camp store or put it in charge of a trusted subordinate. In a good many cases, this led to open exploitation of the new workers; if work was scarce, married men often lost their jobs first because the single men spent more at the commissary. The most welcome worker was the one who kept the games going, for then the beer would flow freely. The loser had to buy the drinks. Those who tried to save money would often find that they were charged with as much debt as a person who spent freely, since the latter brought more profit to the *padrone*.[143] Only as the men became capable of handling problems of their own employment was the power of the *padrone* broken.

Many of the lone males at first lived in boardinghouses with *paesani*, bachelor quarters where the first adjustments to American life occurred.[144] For a time fully two thirds of the newcomers were males, and the abnormality of living in a one-sex society, whether in a boardinghouse or working with a labor gang, made itself felt. Unaccustomed to urban conditions, overcrowding, and anonymity, the immigrant found that normal restraints were no longer adequate. Savings that first found their way regularly to the family in Italy, gradually decreased in size.

The disproportionate number of males would naturally tend to increase intermarriage with other groups. Evidence is conflicting on this point. Carpenter's early study shows that Italians headed the list for endogamy for all groups of foreign born in the 1920 census.[145] Drachsler asserts that the low exogamy of the Italians is exceeded only by that of Jews and Negroes.[146] Other writers like Bercovici estimate that intermarriage of the Italians has been quite extensive; by the 1920's, he contended, between seven and eight million people in America were of part Italian parentage.[147] Even as early as the 1870's in Boston the Italian men showed more than usual interest in Irish girls, though their women were secluded from Irish men.[148]

The fact probably is that intermarriage was exceptional and due to unusual circumstances. Most of the Italian men faithfully followed the customs of their village and married within the group. Some found a wife before leaving home and then sent for her. Others wrote back asking their parents to arrange a marriage with a girl from the home community. A few who lived in boardinghouses sent home for picture brides.[149] After part of a family had settled in America, it became common custom to send for other members so as to have as many of the *famiglia* together as possible. As the stream of immigration increased, the colonies in cities became poly-nucleated into little knots of *paesani* or family groups. One street would have villagers from a tiny community in Basilicata; another, fellow townsmen of a hamlet in Avellino; and still another, residents from two or three neighboring villages in Siracusa (Sicily).[150]

The dialect, cooking habits, and religious practices were continued without a break from the homeland. In the early years the Italian *wanted* to live in insulated communities.[151] In any one of these Little Italys it was dangerous to break the customs of the old village because the individual ran the risk of being *sparlato* (badly talked of). To live better or worse than the rest of the group as a whole brought considerable criticism.[152]

There were other reasons. Living in colonies enabled the new-comers to cushion the shock of transplanting a rural culture into urban life, and a foreign society into an American one. Habits of communication in restricted groups made for an intimate sense of enjoyment which had its place in reinforcing the personality against the disorganization of the slum areas in which the group was forced to live.[153] While this socialization was not shared with outsiders, it nevertheless formed the positive though obverse side of the se-cretiveness with which the Italian was charged. It also presented a haven where prejudice and discrimination against "foreigners" could not penetrate, where a person was not a "wop," a "Dago," a "guinea," but a human being.

THE ZIGZAG OF ACCULTURATION

At first, apart from the boardinghouse, the Italian did not have any social life of his own, though he mingled informally with the people of his own neighborhood. But as the pressures of American society became greater, he felt the need for some protection and help. The answer to this need was the mutual aid society or benefit organization to reduce the risks of sickness, accident, and death which were ever present.[154] At first these were largely dependent on the old family feeling or localism and some were organized by individuals who felt a special need for prominence in the community. Made up of *paesani*, these societies charged from 50 cents to $1 a month and in case of sickness would pay $6 a week or $200 at death.[155]

During the early years of the twentieth century, hundreds of these societies came into existence. Gradually their functions broadened from insurance and protection to social activities. It was not long before the small size of the organizations revealed their weakness; mergers then occurred to conserve what had already been invested. In Chicago alone the number of benefit organizations among Italians decreased from about four hundred to two hundred between 1912 and 1927. The increasing stringency of insurance laws forced many more to disband or else incorporate under new mutual benefit laws of the state, and this resulted in their joining larger and better established fraternal insurance organizations. Examples of the nationwide types are The Italo-American National Union, The Order of Sons of Italy of America, and The Venetian Fraternal Order.

As these larger groups brought together more individuals from different parts of Italy, they found themselves developing a newly awakened patriotism for their old homeland, a realization for the first time that they were all Italians and not merely villagers or provincials. At the same time that their economic and insurance techniques were becoming more Americanized, they were paradoxically recognizing themselves to be more thoroughly Italian.

Parallel with the growth of mutual aid practices was a new sense of solidarity resulting from a series of sensational crime scares connected with the Black Hand extortions and murders of the 1907–1911 period. Although these operations seemed to be connected with older Mafia patterns (and were so regarded by the American public), the organization in its Americanized form was just as unknown in Italy as Tong warfare of the American type was in China.[156] The very term "Black Hand" was coined by Carlo Barsotti, editor of the Italian journal *Il Progresso Italo-Americano*, for the express purpose of avoiding the word *Mafia*, which would have obscured the resemblance between the newer urban crime pattern and the typical racketeering of American cities.[157] There is evidence that not only Sicilians and Italians but members of other groups hid themselves under the Black Hand cloak to carry on illegal activities.[158]

In addition to the public outcry over the Black Hand, sensational publicity appeared in the newspapers about homicides in the Italian community. The average American was unaware of the fact that the rate of criminal convictions in the Italian community was approximately the same as that in other foreign-language groups and was actually less than that of native-born whites.[159] While crime against the person was higher, other crimes had a much lower incidence, e.g., drunkenness, forgery, disorderly conduct, and the like.[160] One reason, plausibly advanced by Seabrook for the fact that Italian homicides received more attention, was that the southern Italian was more dramatic and theatrical in the commission of them or showed more propensity for bandit codes which made headlines and sold more copy for avid newspaper readers.[161]

Whatever the cause, the native white American soon built up a stereotype of the Little Italys as seething hotbeds of crime. This erroneous opinion provoked a surge of defense and solidarity among the Italians themselves, a new "consciousness of kind" expressed through the publications of all organizations and furnishing reams of indignant copy in Italian newspapers throughout the country.[162]

The Sicilians, Neapolitans, and Calabrians thus became conscious of their common destiny as Italians in America, though without losing their individualistic traits or family solidarity. Pride in their home country was intensified by the exploits of Garibaldi and by the feelings engendered by the first World War. The national spirit which had never penetrated to their home villages, or at least to the lower classes, here began to quicken and enlarge.[163]

Simultaneously with this awareness of a common heritage came the tremendous enthusiasm for the two hundred thousand Italo-

Americans who served in the armed forces of the United States, fighting side by side with Italy against a common foe.[164] In the mutual feelings engendered, patriotism for both the old and the new country reinforced each other. After the Immigration Law of 1924 when further arrivals from Italy were largely cut off, the consciousness of kind became intensified in the growth of an "Italian vote" in political elections. The very forces that heightened self-feeling and distinctness also encouraged a new group participation in civic life.

In religious matters it must not be forgotten that the immigrant from south Italy often showed considerable independence of the priest.[165] For a period after his arrival in the United States the newcomer either found himself separated from the church altogether or under the care of Irish priests whose ways were as foreign to him as those of native-born Americans. In the 1890's the Italians in Chicago, for instance, had only one church of their own and so habits of passive acquiescence or neglect became common.[166] Added to this trend was dislike for the American custom of supporting the church liberally with gifts, a habit quite foreign to the folkways of the peasant village. The suspicion of mercenary motives in the church has been dominant in the defection of many worshippers.[167] The general tendency to make religion "less a matter of daily concern" than do the Irish or the Poles is noticeable.[168] The bringing in of Italian priests has changed this pattern considerably since the early days.*[169]

In the spoken language a newly coined Americanized Italian became a sort of *lingua franca.* Sometimes it affected the newspapers also. "Storo" became the word for store; "olzoppare," for hold-up; "mascina," for machine or automobile; "gliarda," for yard; "grosseria," for grocery; "ghelle," for girls. "Bosso" replaced the older *padrone* for boss, "barra" meant bar, and "ganga" was

* Mangione relates an incident of his boyhood in Rochester, New York, when he and his brother attended a Roman Catholic church served by an Irish priest. During the ceremony the priest rebuked an older Italian woman for giving so little to the collection. To his horror, Mangione heard his brother shout, "You can't do that! She's a poor woman. She can't afford any more!" Both of the boys postponed going home after church, for fear that the parents would punish the brother severely. To their great surprise, on their arrival, the brother was treated like a hero not only by father and mother but by the rest of the neighborhood. Cf. Mangione, *Mount Allegro*, Boston, Houghton Mifflin, 1942, pp. 75–77.

used for gang.[170] The adoption of American words and phrases into a new patois showed the steady and continuing effect of hearing English spoken. A similar modification of language occurs in all nationality groups throughout the United States and is one symbol of the transition from foreign to American status.

The number of Italian newspapers continued to be large in the 1930's and 1940's. During World War II there were 130 Italian newspapers in the United States, most of them weeklies.[171] An adequate study of the Italian press is not available, but indications are that the newspapers, like the publications of other nationality groups, include more and more English in their columns to attract younger readers.[172] Results are not striking, however, for few of the second generation take the time to read these periodicals.[173] Too many of them are still edited by first generation literati whose nostalgia for older Italian ways puts them out of step with the youth they are trying to interest.[174]

THE LADDER OF ADVANCEMENT

The dogged individualism and fierce desire to save which the Italian immigrant brought with him from his own shores, fitted well into the new environment of intense competition. At first these traits were reinforced by the older tradition that all earnings in the family should be turned over to the parents. Immigrants were eager to have their children learn a craft or trade, for this was the familiar method of social advancement which they remembered from the home country.[175] The custom of withdrawing the children from school at the earliest legal age in order to have them work for the family has been most marked, tending to keep many Italians in relatively limited occupational groups.[176]

However, the pattern of resisting school influences is not uniform. In the areas where there are large concentrations of Italian-speaking people, neighborhood opinion will support the parents and the old traditions of introducing boys into full-time jobs as early as possible. No peasant in Italy ever supported a boy twelve years of age; he was helping the family by that time. Compulsory education was resisted because it would wean the children away from home ideas, and without these notions of obedience and loyalty the parents did not see how they could control their children.[177]

When the immigrant accepted the fact that he was going to stay in America, he began to adopt a new family pattern. In the 1920's Italian parents in New York began the accommodation process by saying that they had *Americani* children, so what good were they until they were older? They might as well be in school instead of doing nothing. As the children neared working-paper age, both they and their parents changed. Boys and girls tended to become more passive toward school and to lose interest. Parents reverted to their original Italian ideas and talked of their poverty and the duties children should have to their parents. When the mothers began to "cooperate" with the schools, it was often to see that education did not carry their children too far from home ideas. But the mores of the *contadini* clashed more with the school than with any other American institution.[178]

On the other hand in those areas where the Italians were fewer in number or sparsely scattered through the community, school patterns were more quickly assimilated. Experienced high school teachers declare that the attitude and behavior of second generation Italian students has undergone a great change since the 1920's.[179]

During the first period of adjustment, parents pointed to those in the colony who had made rapid success in small trading or industry even though their educational background was meager. This tendency gradually changed so that boys at least were given more opportunity to choose new occupational fields, though not without long family discussions and advice from older members whose conceptions of a vocation were taken from old country customs. It is quite common, however, for a father to react against his own occupation and prepare his son to follow a different one.[180] A comparison of the occupations of Italian fathers in 1916 and in 1931 showed that the percentage of common laborers dropped from 50.4 per cent to 31.4 per cent, and a similar comparison of bridegrooms for the same years showed a drop in the percentage of common laborers from 32.5 to 10.6.[181] An increase in the number of chauffeurs, clerks, salesmen, bakers, mechanics, plasterers, and butchers showed that the occupational structure of the group in New York City is rapidly approaching the national norm.[182] Though data are not available, it is probable that this trend is similar, or even more marked, in other areas where contacts with a wider culture are more numerous.

In the South, the Italians have formed the backbone of the fishing and the fruit-growing industries and have also been active in tobacco and sugar cane growing; only a few went into cotton cultivation.[183] In fishing, the Sicilians lead all others in San Francisco,[184] while the northern Italians have established themselves in wine making throughout the state of California.[185] Italians in New England and the East have made a flourishing business out of truck gardening.[186] The community has many success stories with the familiar rags-to-riches theme; the number of millionaires rising from obscurity is surprisingly large.[187]

Eventually the Italians entered the labor movement and were heading many locals during the late 1920's.[188] Perhaps one of the most powerful union groups in the country today is Local 89 of the International Ladies' Garment Workers' Union; its membership is almost wholly Italian, and its executive secretary, Luigi Antonini, is a familiar figure in labor circles.

In spite of his background the Italian is learning organization rapidly, so that the list of Italian societies is tremendous. New York has an Italian Typographical Union, an Italian Medical Society, the Rapallo Association (lawyers), an Italian Chamber of Commerce, an organization of Italian Social Workers, an Italian Actors Union, an Italian Athletic League, and many others.[189]

In a generation, the Italian has forged ahead in politics. At first his *prominenti* or "natural leaders," with a small personally loyal following, were tied up with Irish machines who pitted them one against another to keep them subordinate. As education and skill in effective leadership have developed, Italians have become more powerful in the political arena, going across party lines to vote for their own candidates. It is significant that in New York the most effective Italian political leaders have been LaGuardia and Marcantonio, both of whom are nonparty men.[190] A different situation exists in Rhode Island, where the Italians, voting the Democratic ticket, put their own candidate, Governor Pastore, into office. The political club is now a potent factor in the Italo-American community and cuts across all the old lines.[191]

In addition to these advances the Italians have had outstanding success in music, organizing many orchestras and opera companies, notably the San Carlo Opera.[192] The American Federation of Musicians is largely composed of Italians down to the present day.[193] In architecture, sculpture, the fine arts, and the industrial arts, a small but vigorous group have contributed work of high quality.[194]

The tradition of higher education is making great strides in the community as it becomes apparent that white collar occupations require college preparation. Until recently most of the Italians in the professions in America came from the nonpeasant group like the *artigiano* class.[195] This too is gradually changing as the pressure of American conditions forces on the parents a new orientation of values.

A NOTE ON RELIGIOUS LIFE

Although the great majority of Italians in the United States are regarded as Catholics, this view is an oversimplification. A small minority have broken away to Protestantism, chiefly to Baptist and Methodist churches. Are the rest fundamentally Roman Catholic? Dr. Tolino, after considerable study of the problem, concludes that of the six million population of first, second, or third generation, about one third are probably "good Catholics," i.e., attend church regularly and go to confession. This would be two million. On the other hand, something like one sixth are outside of the church altogether, have had no religious instruction, and receive none at the present time; in other words, about a million. Then half of the entire group get partial instruction in the Roman Catholic tradition but do not go to church regularly or attend confession except occasionally. In the familiar phrase, they are not "good Catholics." The community has bantering names for those who attend only on certain days. The ones who go to church on Christmas are called "Natalino"; on Palm Sunday, "Palmina"; and on Easter, "Pasqualina."

Dr. Tolino estimates that among the three million, a very small minority remain faithful to the church. If these figures are correct, about two thirds of the Italian community are either outside the Roman Catholic church entirely or have a minor or nominal relation to the institution. Even in those areas where the Catholic Italian parishes have schools, it is often the case that only one fifth to one half of the children actually attend. The canonical parishes (not allied with any nationality group) close the door to children from the "national" parishes. Whether this is the result of prejudice or not, it is difficult to say. The fact remains that today the majority of Italo-Americans have little connection with the church;[196] this secularizing process is due in large part to the urbanization of the Italians, as already noted.

THE SECOND GENERATION

What of the children of the Italian immigrant? Their position in American life has thrust culture conflict upon them. They lacked the protective loyalties their parents had to a small but compact group in Italy, or the familiarity and congeniality their older relatives had with the *famiglia*. Whether they reflected upon their position or not, it was a marginal one [197] in which they were urged by school companions and the promptings of their playmates to leave the older cultural traditions behind and enter into the full stream of American life. On the other hand their parents, who spoke to them in Italian, served Italian food, and kept Italian customs, drew them back into the current of the old ways. One culture at home and another outside — usually Italian was spoken at home and English elsewhere — how was it possible to be loyal to both?

Nor was the problem simply one of duality. The children of immigrants, while attracted by American norms and ways of life, were also made to feel that they did not belong to America, that they were not "American"; prejudice and discrimination thrust them back into their old surroundings where they actually did not want to go. An example from a true life incident will make the situation clear.

> I had grown to love the church, because we lived next door to one and then across the street from one. The priests dropped in to my father's jewelry store for a visit and chat quite often. I felt very close to the church. My parents sent me to an exclusive private Catholic school during the "dangerous period" 13–16. [There] my maiden name was changed to an Anglo-Saxon one by the Mother Superior. She of all people! This resulted in quite a traumatic experience for me which took years to overcome. However the ground was fertile from previous repressed conflicts with parents and spasmodic changes of environment. I was at that age when I began to wonder if "they" were right. "We" were different. "We" were "wops," "dagoes." Then as I observed that others of my Italian friends were getting along quite nicely, I began to think it was I. What was wrong with me, anyway? [198]

Child, in his study of the marginal Italians, pictures three major types of reaction to this problem: the rebel reaction (from Italian culture); the in-group reaction (to Italian culture); and the apathetic reaction which involves either escape or withdrawal from the situation and refusal to maintain a strong initiative.[199]

The rebels want to be considered American, dissociate themselves from everything Italian, and keep their background hidden. They find themselves labeled "Italian" anyway, but in spite of obstacles keep trying to be Americans in the manner of their own age group. Frequently they are hostile to anything Italian or disparage it so as to leave no doubt where their real feelings are. If the rebels are parents, they tend to project their own difficulties or frustrated desires forcibly on the children.[200]

In contrast the in-groupers are especially eager to claim membership with the Italian group, to participate in it fully. They prefer the intimacy of a small, homogeneous subculture to looser-structured participation with a larger American group. They separate themselves from American symbols and traits by showing either hostility toward them or a decided preference for Italian parallels. Their chief associates are always in the Italian group and frequently they work hand in glove with the politicians for Italian victories. Their preference for Italian ways is accompanied with so much tension that it often shows compensatory signs.[201]

The apathetic group make a more passive adjustment to their conflict, avoiding situations where nationality is important and minimizing their membership in Italian society in order that Americans of older stock will not think that they give any significance to their past. Sometimes they even make joking use of "wop" or "guinea." But there are mixed feelings about their dual status; at one time they affirm, at another deny, their duality. This lack of consistency is sometimes accompanied by an increase of anxiety but rarely of aggressiveness. By treating the subject of culture conflict lightly, by deprecating it, and avoiding it as much as possible, the apathetic group seeks to rob it of any special significance.[202]

Even though Child's study applies to male adolescents only, it has significance for adult groups as well. While it uses only two categories, one of participation (the in-group type) and the other of attitudes (the rebel and apathetic types),[203] it is nevertheless suggestive, if not all-inclusive. Further study is needed to determine the variations that occur with different class status; for example, those who have already achieved a fairly comfortable middle class position in American society may simply accept the norms of the white collar group as a natural preference without rebel attitudes. Those whose parents had already reached a middle class status would accentuate this preference. On the other hand children of parents in unskilled occupations might show more of the rebel reaction if they were striving eagerly for advanced positions.

As Italians climb the scale into higher status, they tend to take on not only the behavior patterns of the new stratum but also its prejudices. This is an indubitable proof of their Americanization. At the beginning Italians showed less resistance to the residential invasion of Negroes than to that of nationality groups such as the Irish. Negro and Italian areas were frequently found next to each other, or in mixed areas where both lived together without serious friction.[204] Reports from the second generation, however, show that the typical American prejudice toward Negroes is proceeding apace as a part of the natural process of assimilation. As one Italian child reported to Covello in East Harlem, his community was a good place to live in. "Without Puerto Ricans and Negroes, it would be swell." [205] In many cases, of course, the marginal Italians are moving into areas of the city where Negroes are not found. For example, Corsi states that by 1942, less than 40 per cent of the Italians in New York City were living in little Italys.* [206]

* Orrie Van de Visse, in a spot check of the Italo-American community of Cleveland following World War II, indicated that the solidarity of the Italian family group is breaking down more since the war, partly because of increasing contact with other groups in industry, the changing attitudes of children regarding other groups, and the loosening of parental authority. Another important factor making for independence of the youth is the added ability to find employment. The religious life of the community has been somewhat strengthened as a result of the benefits given to servicemen by the church. The first generation are coming to see the importance of education for their children, and consequently the youth will have a better chance for more training beyond high school. Thrift will not allow them to reject the opportunities of the G.I. bill. The second generation group are breaking away from Italian organizations and joining clubs of mixed nationalities or groups. They want to lose the identity which living in a nationality area gives them. This will certainly lead to rapid abandonment of the area when marriage occurs.

VANISHING MINORITY STATUS

With their gradual absorption into American life, the Italians like other nationality groups are beginning to lose their distinctness. Six out of ten from Italian stock in America have been born in the United States, and one out of the other four has been in this country since childhood. An estimated 80 per cent of Italians now speak English.[207] The Order of the Sons of Italy has dwindled from a peak of 300,000 members to about 100,000. Younger leaders are in positions of responsibility for reorienting the program, and younger priests are serving in the church.[208]

Before World War II, Mussolini enjoyed great popularity among the Italians of the United States, although this was largely due to the increased prestige of the home country as reflected in American public opinion. It was an occasion of sorrow for the community when it became obvious that this country would eventually be pitted against their old homeland. To stave off the inevitable, the Italians grasped the sentiment of isolationism, gave Senator Wheeler and Lindbergh great ovations, and generally expressed the opinion that this was not America's war. Many opposed war because it would mean increased discrimination against Italians in America, and others simply wanted to stay out of trouble. As one remarked, "I came to this country for peace, and all I get is war, war, war!" [209]

As the United States became more and more involved, Italian public opinion tended to follow the trend of American sentiment. *Il Progresso Italo-Americano* and *Il Corriere*, the two most important Italian dailies in the United States, became avowedly anti-Fascist during the war.[210] A measure of Italian loyalty to the adopted country can be noted from the fact that although they had the largest alien group in the United States — nearly 700,000 [211] — yet out of this entire group only four thousand were taken into custody temporarily and only 112 were interned during the war.[212] The rest were given absolute freedom.

The number of servicemen of Italian parentage in World War II was 400,000 or twice the number in the previous war.[213] For a while during the war, Italians dropped the support of some things that formerly received considerable aid. In New York, for example, both the Leonardo da Vinci Art School and the Italian Welfare League had to close. But with the coming of peace a greater feeling of belonging to America occurred on the part of the servicemen who had participated in the fighting not as Italians but as Americans.

In the years preceding and during the war more Italians applied for naturalization than members of any other nationality group.[214] With the realization that the homeland no longer furnished a possible haven for nostalgic desires (an attitude furthered by the rapid growth of Communism in Italy) the Italian entered increasingly, with full participation, into all that America had to offer, realistically accepting his place as a full-fledged member of our society.

CHAPTER 12

The Polish American: *Peasant Patriot*

JAN SAT by the kitchen stove reading *The Rover Boys*. Behind him his mother bent over the table, spoon in hand, tasting the soup she was preparing for the Boleslawskis' supper. Getting warmer and warmer by the fire, Jan wriggled his toes luxuriously as he followed hair-raising exploits with increasing satisfaction. Suddenly the door slammed and Jan made a swift move as if to hide the book, but it was too late. His father's shadow darkened the doorway of the kitchen and a bass voice boomed, "What kind of trash do you have there now?" Reluctantly Jan passed over the book into his father's hand, knowing that the gates of wrath would soon be opened. He did not have to wait long.

"This is the last time I tell you," the elder Boleslawski shouted. "Don't ever bring such books in the house again. I positively forbid you to get them. Isn't it bad enough to have a son who is good for nothing but to keep his nose in a book without having him come home with this cheap American junk?"

Jan said nothing. He was trying to calculate how he could manage in the future. It would be hard, but he'd do it all right.

"Do you hear me? Who are you anyway, forgetting your fine Polish traditions, never speaking a word of our beautiful national tongue unless you have to? Is this why I sent you to parochial school, so that you would grow away from your own parents? You learned Polish there. Why don't you use it? Anyway I never want to see another of those cheap books in this house."

A plan formed itself in Jan's mind. The next afternoon when he visited the branch library in the neighborhood, he renewed *The Rover Boys* but craftily took with it an English translation of Sienkiewicz' *Quo Vadis*. Arriving at home he hid the former but kept the latter with him and was reading it when his father started to play cards with several of his men friends. Before long his father's eye wandered from the cards to where Jan sat; with a tremendous stride, Boleslawski reached his son, snatched the book out of his hand, and was ready to throw it on the floor when Jan spoke.

"Look what it is first!"

Dubiously the father examined title and author and there was no question about it. His face softened.

"See, men, Jan has brought home a good Polish author — Sienkiewicz! I didn't know he was put into English. Maybe Jan can read some to us — no?"

His friends shouted their approval and Jan began with some misgivings. He soon found that many words were difficult, the sentences were long, and he stumbled frequently. In a few minutes the men had had enough; but in succeeding evenings his father made him read aloud again. Each time it became easier but his father tired of it long before the book was finished.

Yet a curious thing happened. Here was a new kind of adventure story. It had its obscure passages and some spots were a bit difficult for a lad of twelve, but Jan found that the Sienkiewicz gave him a delight he had never had before. Something in it answered to an inner need that had always been dormant. He went back for another Sienkiewicz and then for other Polish authors. He realized suddenly that he was a Pole and that these men had been Poles too, that they expressed something larger than he had ever known. At school he began to be proud of his Polish background and raised his hand quickly whenever the teacher asked a question about his national history or origin. The backward glance had sent him forward. How it happened he never knew but the spark had kindled a new interest which remained with him years later when he wrote of his childish experience.[1]

Though few of the second generation have had such a fortunate experience, and it is not typical, yet it represents a possibility which, once realized, throws considerable light on the adjustment of the American Pole.

THE SLAV

For the Pole is a Slav, and it is characteristic of the Slavonic peoples that their culture has been truncated, repressed, and allowed to grow only sporadically or even in secret. Of the various groups in Europe all the Slavs have gained national and cultural autonomy very late,* with the result that they have developed a fierce pride in their languages and institutions that must be felt to be appreciated.

The average American has only a vague image in his mind when he hears the word Slav. For some it means a race, for others a nation, while for the more initiated it still connotes a hazy conglomeration of peoples "somewhere in eastern Europe" and thus includes erroneously the Hungarians, the Rumanians, or even the Greeks.

All these conceptions are incorrect. The word Slav, or its synonyms Slavonic and Slavonian, refers to a group of people using related languages but it has no connection whatever with race.** The Slavs have been in Europe since the sixth century, spreading northward as far as the Arctic Circle and westward as far as central Germany. A great belt of non-Slavic peoples, including the Austrians, Hungarians, and Rumanians, separates the northern from the southern Slavs. Again, what are really northern Slavic peoples can be subdivided into eastern and western groups, in Davie's manner, as follows: [2]

EASTERN SLAVS: Great Russians, White Russians, Little Russians or Ukrainians
WESTERN SLAVS: Poles, Wends, Czechs, Slovaks
SOUTHERN SLAVS: Slovenians, Croatians, Serbs, Bulgarians

Before the outbreak of World War I (the period of greatest emigration to the United States), the Slavs, with the exception of the Russians, organized themselves into smaller territorial units and on the whole avoided the pattern of empire building.[3] It is true that Poland had a mighty kingdom in the fourteenth century, stretching from the Baltic to the Black Sea. This tremendous expanse is sometimes regarded as normative by Polish nationalists but in the long history of the Slavic peoples it stands out as exceptional. It is probably an oversimplification to suggest, as Seton-Watson does, that the Slav lacks aggressiveness and that this is the chief cause of

* With the possible exception of the Russians.

** The term "Slavish," while sometimes used, is not accurate and should be discarded.

his disinclination to form empires.[4] It seems likely that if all the Slavs had spoken a single language, their pre-eminence in Europe would have been more marked. But from the first they divided into areas where each group became semi-isolated from the others and developed its own dialect or colloquial forms of speech and its own culture and traditions suitable to its geographical domicile. The breakup of their initial unity, along with the lack of natural boundaries that might have protected them from other cultural groups, resulted in their subjugation by larger empires, particularly the Austro-Hungarian, the Russian, and the Prussian. Their strategic position between these three growing units of power in eastern Europe made their country a battleground of innumerable wars and the victim of partition among the contending dominions. To a lesser degree the same can be said of the Czechs, the Slovaks, and the southern Slavs.

The resemblance between various Slavic nationalities is not, however, a racial one. While Ripley maintains that they seem to be an offshoot of the Alpine type, practically every variation in the Caucasian stock can be found among them. They are longheaded, roundheaded, tall, short, some lighter, some darker in color, with almost every shade of eye color from brown to blue, though the lighter tints predominate.[5] As Seabrook graphically puts it in his description of the Poles in the United States, "They simply look like people."[6] The stereotype that the Slavic face always shows a marked tendency toward high cheekbones is simply untrue. Their only deviation from other Caucasians is in language, history, culture, and traditions.

Perhaps the most significant of their social determinants is the fact that they have been subject peoples who by reason of their subjugation have entered somewhat late into the nationalistic stream of European culture. The whole belt of Slavic states with which the American is familiar was formed after 1918, whereas the great majority of migrants came to the United States before that time. It is also important that about 70 per cent of the Slavs who migrated to the United States from 1899 to 1908 were from the Austro-Hungarian Empire while only 25 per cent came from Russian regions.[7] Along with others of their own language groups, each aggregation of Slavs arriving on United States soil, whether Czechs, Poles, Slovenes, or Serbs, came as suppressed nationalists who firmly believed in the eventual emancipation of their compatriots from centuries of submission; most of them had seen their own language prohibited or restricted at home and had experienced a governmental policy of enforced assimilation. In their journey from Europe to America they exchanged a harsh, brutal, and repressed minority status for a milder one that was unfamiliar.

MIGRATION OF THE POLES

There were Poles in the Jamestown Colony during the early settlement of America; and the names of Kosciusko and Pulaski, who served in the American Revolution, are familiar to all.[8] Miecislaus Haiman divides the history of Polish immigration into three periods: (1) the colonial period (1608–1776), when the newcomers were chiefly artisans and adventurers; (2) the period of political immigration, when the intelligentsia — small numbers of soldiers, noblemen, writers, and political exiles — began to escape from Europe because of oppressive conditions at home (1776–1865); (3) the period of economic immigration — the one with which we are chiefly concerned (1865 to date) — when the group was largely composed of peasants and unskilled workers.[9] Since the economic period was the one which brought the great bulk of migration to the United States, a word about the background of the Polish newcomer at that time may help clarify the picture.

During the nineteenth century the Polish people were living under three regimes — these had been established by the third partition of Poland in 1795 — the largest group under Russian domination, the second largest under Prussia, and the smallest group in Galicia ruled by Austria. The economic migration began in the regions of Prussian Poland, that is, in Upper Silesia, the area around Poznan and West Prussia. Although the land was fertile, the Poles were in the position of either small proprietors or landless peasants living under feudal subjection to Prussian lords. During the middle and late 1870's there was considerable persecution under the Bismarck "Kulturkampf" policy, a crop failure in 1876, a new Prussian conscription law, and general unsettled conditions. At the same time knowledge about the successful migration of many Germans and a few Poles to the United States added fresh stimulus to the desire of the landless peasant to escape. The movement spread from Prussian Poland to Russian Poland and finally to Galicia.[10]

For the most part the Poles from Russian areas came with the fewest advantages. Educational standards were low and poverty was severe. The Russians pursued a policy of denationalizing their Polish subjects so that the latter were usually unable to read and write their own language, having gone to Russian schools when they went at all. At the opposite end of the scale were the Austrian Poles, who had greater advantages, went to school longer, and were given semi-autonomy in the Austro-Hungarian Empire so that they sent representatives both to their territorial government and to the parliament in Vienna. Politically they were the most self-conscious and articulate of all the Poles, and Galician leaders formed the spear-head of later Polish nationalist movements. The Prussian group, forming a kind of median position, were neither as underprivileged as the Russian Poles nor as strong in leadership as the Galicians.[11]

The actual number who migrated to the United States is somewhat in doubt, because of the fact that they did not come with passports from Poland but from Prussia, Austria, and Russia. There were also a considerable number of Polish Jews that migrated at the same time, some of whom were counted in with the Polish Christians. Since we are treating the Jewish minority separately in a later chapter, this group will not be considered here.[12] The greatest number arrived in this country in the period from 1900 to the first World War, in this respect paralleling the Italian entry. The year 1912–1913 was the peak of immigration in which 174,365 Poles were admitted into the United States.[13] There was, however, a larger bulk of earlier immigrants among the Poles than among the Italians, and a greater number of the former went into agriculture on their arrival. It is estimated that 90 per cent of the Poles who migrated to the United States since the Civil War came from agricultural regions. Even today 75 per cent of the population in Poland proper is agricultural.[14]

How many Poles are there in the United States? This is more difficult to calculate for the Poles than for the Italians, for the reasons mentioned. As early as 1910 the Polish National Alliance estimated that there were approximately three million, while the American Association of Foreign Language Newspapers put the figure at three and a half million; at the same time the Polish press gave four million as the correct number.[15] In 1945 Professor Roucek estimated that there were about four million in the United States, while Dr. Stefan Wlowzczewski says the figure should be much higher.[16] Furthermore, these estimates do not indicate whether the second and third generations are included. Comparing all these figures, we conclude that Olszyk's computation of 1940 is probably as close to the mark as any and it will be accepted as approximate — five million.[17] This would bring it directly below the Italian figure and make the Polish minority the second largest in the new immigration and the third largest as a whole.[18]

In the United States the Poles have settled most thickly in the area from Wisconsin east along the Great Lakes region through Pennsylvania and New York State to New England. The city with the greatest number of Polish inhabitants is Chicago, with more than half a million. At the opening of the second World War it was the second largest Polish city in the world, led only by Warsaw; today it may well be the largest. Other cities with large Polish populations are Buffalo and Detroit with about a quarter of a million each, Milwaukee with 150,000, and Cleveland with 100,000.[19] The mining areas of Pennsylvania are also thickly dotted with Polish settlements.

THE PEASANT BACKGROUND

Whether they came from Prussia, Russia, or Austria, most of the Polish agriculturalists had lived in regions where a feudal economy was still largely practiced. Even though serfdom was practically abolished, the land had chiefly three classes: (1) estate owners who had from four hundred to one hundred thousand acres each; these landlords did not do manual labor but managed their estates with considerable personal supervision; (2) the small landowners, heads of families with from three to several hundred acres; some worked their land with only the help of their own family members and a few hired hands; (3) at the bottom of the social scale, the landless agricultural workers who had nothing of their own but were hired at a pittance by the owners of estates or small farms.[20] It was members of the two lower classes who migrated in greatest numbers. Perhaps the enumeration of the emigrants from Russian Poland in 1912 may be taken as fairly typical. In that year about 50 per cent of those who left for America came from the landless peasants, while something like 27 per cent belonged to the small landowning class.[21]

Sometimes a landless peasant would work on one of the Prussian estates and be allowed an acre and a half for his own use so that he could raise enough vegetables to supply his family. For working on the estate he would receive in addition $20 a year and at harvest time a bushel of wheat, a bushel of peas, and twelve bushels of rye with which to make bread, etc. He and his entire family would live in two rooms of a large, square eight-room house, divided into four portions, each of which would be occupied by a different family. This house would be built of clay and straw, with one window to a room. The larger of the two rooms for each family would center on the fireplace, which would furnish all the heat available in the winter. Laundering would be done by the mother at the nearby creek, the clothes dipped in the water and then flailed with a wooden paddle. During the winter this process would be more difficult since the ice had to be broken in order to get at the water. The food from day to day was monotonous, usually black bread with soup made of the vegetables the family raised, or some of the year's supplies taken at the harvest. The whole family ate out of the same soup kettle, and often enough there were no plates at all. Easter and Christmas brought white bread with potatoes, cabbage, and peas, or if the family were lucky enough to have a pig, some ham, smoked inside the fireplace. The white bread was not from pure white flour, however, but from "middlings," the best flour going to the Pan * or shipped abroad. From a nutritional point of view, however, this was an advantage.

The only break in the steady round of daily toil came during the holidays — at Christmas or Easter when there were special celebrations, at harvest time, or when someone in the family was married. At such times the feasting was carried on with abandon.[22]

Among the landed peasants, conditions were somewhat better. Of course the farms, unlike American ones, were never entirely in a single piece but were scattered in fragments over a considerable area. Even though the peasant lived in a small village and was forced to go from one section of his farm to another, this did not seem to be, from the standpoint of the community, any great handi-

* Lord or proprietor; equivalent of German "Herr."

cap. It was the way things always had been, and it was accepted passively after the manner of the peasant.[23]

On the whole the peasant seems to have been less isolated in his own village or community than the southern Italian. Villages were closer together and the system of transportation was more developed. One result was that the dialect differences between Poles of one region and those of another were much less marked than they were among the Italians and therefore the tendency to settle in America in terms of the old geographical units was much less important. In other respects, however, the parallel between the two groups is instructive in spite of the differences.

Whereas the south Italian was a member of two main primary groups, the family and the village, the Pole in Europe had membership in several primary groups with different functions: the family, the village, the parish, the commune, and the *okolica* or "the country around," which for convenience' sake is termed the community.[24] The Polish family, in contrast with the Italian, emphasized all blood and law relationships usually to the fourth degree, while the husband, wife, and children formed only a single element in this larger group. In this greater unit (even larger than the consanguine, since it emphasized law relatives) the individual with the most power and authority was the husband of the oldest couple having the most children and grandchildren.[25] In other conjugal groups belonging to the large family the husband and wife were controlled by those of the superconsanguine group; a strong feeling of family solidarity kept them together since the group as a whole was judged by community opinion.[26] Within the conjugal units the parents were responsible for the actions of the children and exercised strong authority over them, the relations generally being based on respect rather than love. (In general it has been only bourgeois or higher class societies that could afford the luxury of romantic love as a regular norm.) Here too the father retired when one of his sons was better able to manage the homestead than he was; the favorite child took over the management of the farm — in central Poland the eldest son, in the southern mountain areas the youngest son, and in some cases the one with the strongest personal qualities.[27] The result was a smaller stem-conjugal family within a larger superconsanguine family.

Since Polish society is mainly patriarchal, the life history of the son is important for an understanding of the whole culture pattern. The first stage of his life is that of childhood, in which he has practically no rights but is under the tutelage of his parents. In the second period he is able to do the work of an adult but is still unmarried; during this time his work contributes to the family support and any earnings he has must be turned unhesitatingly to the father. When he proceeds to the third stage and marries, if he is the one to carry on the family farm he then receives a considerably higher status, his private life is less controlled, and he begins to share responsibilities with the father. His brothers also have a higher status when they are married; but since they often move from the circle, they do not share in all the planning. Finally when the father retires, the son takes over the entire supervision of the farm and begins to exercise a more and more potent authority, culminating in an absolute supremacy by the time of the father's death.[28] Every young person is supposed to marry, and his mate is chosen by the family in accordance with their status. Sometimes the marriage is arranged by friends, relatives, or the *swaty* or professional matchmaker. It is permissible, though not highly approved, to marry someone in an adjoining village but exogamy with respect to nationality or religion is regarded as a grave offence.[29]

Promiscuous sexual relations are not tolerated by the Polish peasant community, and all conversation between a boy and a girl when there are no others present must keep free from sexual allusions, though in a group ribald remarks are considered permissible. There is not the extensive chaperonage system for young women so characteristic of southern Italy, and the patriarchal tradition seems to be somewhat weaker. Illegal sexual relations before marriage are condemned and marriage is usually insisted upon if they occur. Extramarital relations are severely prohibited, whether for men or women, and it is bad form to speak in public about sexual relations within marriage itself.[30] On the whole, sex is not considered impure but rather a matter of private interest within the conjugal unit which, as a part of newly developed adulthood, is kept from public discussion entirely.

Besides the family the peasant participated in other primary groups. (1) First was the village, in which relatives and lifelong acquaintances formed a natural unit of interest; where talk of crops, weather, family relations, unusual happenings, and events of supernatural importance formed the daily round. (2) Partly coextensive with the village was the parish, a larger replica of the patriarchal family, in which the priest was the natural leader. Regular meetings at the church kept alive the religious emotions and a social solidarity that was renewed on Sundays, saints' days, Christmas, Easter, christenings, weddings, and burials. The religious societies of the parish gave the individual a greater sense of participation than he had in other social groups outside the family. In general Polish Catholicism is predominantly social rather than mystical in character.[31] It is true that the church was largely state supported [32] and hence did not depend too directly on the gifts of its parishioners.* This fact, however, did not seem to have the effect of loosening the tie between the individual and the ecclesiastical organization even when the latter was transplanted to America, where continual support was necessary. The large numbers of men as well as women who were devout worshippers,[33] in the home as well as in the church, indicate that Polish piety was a deep-seated attitude.

While a considerable amount of superstition and magic remained in peasant religion, it was always kept subordinate to the power of the priest, who was obeyed implicitly, for his words were those of Jesus and his authority inviolable.[34] Lacking political training on the whole, the people regarded the priest as the only leader they could trust, and this attitude they brought with them to their adopted land. It is perhaps significant also that Poland did not experience the Counter Reformation as the western European countries did; the type of Catholicism developed in Poland was therefore more authoritarian and appealed more to faith and less to reason than the type developed in France, Belgium, and western Germany, where competition with the forces of the Reformation and the Enlightenment gave it a different cast.

Two results of this religious pattern are significant for the immigrant. One was that the priest resisted any efforts on the part of his parishioners for an accounting of the money donated to the church, not because he could not give it but because it would some-

* Particularly in sections under Austria and Prussia, which had a concordat with the Vatican. In Russian areas the Poles had to support their own church.

how be a questioning of his authority.[35] The other was the tradition that the church belongs to God and then to the saint for whom it is named, not to the parish. This view strengthened hierarchical control not only in Poland but later in the United States.[36]

In addition to parish activities the peasant took a limited part in the life of the commune or restricted local government in Russian Poland. Although theoretically this was supposed to be a kind of limited political responsibility, in practice it was circumscribed by bureaucratic controls of the larger state. It functioned only in a routine way. Much more important, from the standpoint of social control, was the *okolica*, which included all those villages and groups near enough to each other to permit public opinion to operate through face to face contacts and gossip. To flout such opinion was equivalent to social suicide.[37]

One characteristic feature of Polish life was the prominence given to the intelligentsia. On the whole, the intellectual aristocracy played a greater part in Poland than in many other European countries. In the first place since the bourgeois or middle class was not strongly developed, a large share of the traders, merchants, or businessmen came from the Jewish community and were therefore outsiders from the standpoint of the Polish Christians. This fact, combined with the great influence of the nobility, cast a certain shadow on financial or commercial occupations while on the other hand manual work was more highly esteemed. Secondly, the intelligentsia were regarded with strong favor because they helped to keep literature, art, and culture alive even though the national group was submerged politically. A member of the intellectual elite was therefore something of a hero.[38]

As for Russian Poland and to a lesser extent Prussian Poland as well, the political regime was conceived as a distant, mysterious, and arbitrary order that could be influenced only by personal manipulation and was even then unpredictable.[39] As soon as emigration began, the state asserted its repressive power by attempting to prevent any outflow to America.[40] Generally, the Pole, like the southern Italian, regarded the government as a coercive force operating from a distant source, and his antipathy toward it was increased because it tried to assimilate him forcibly into an alien culture and to forbid him the use of his own language and institutions.

EARLY IMMIGRATION AND POLISH AMERICAN INSTITUTIONS

Although the number of Polish immigrants was not large until the 1880's, a few agricultural colonists with their families came before that time and found a place in American agriculture. Among them were the groups that founded Panna Maria in Texas during the 1850's; Polonia, Wisconsin, in the same decade; and Parisville, Michigan.[41] The increase of the tide can be observed from the fact that 7000 came in 1860–1870; 34,000 in 1870–1880; 99,000 from 1880 to 1890; and 236,000 from 1890 to 1900.[42]

As the number kept increasing, a tendency toward more male immigration and scattered settlement became characteristic.[43] The trend toward the cities began in the seventies and eighties, and 90 per cent of the Polish Americans live in cities today.[44] Before long individuals from the same provinces began to draw together in nucleated centers,[45] occasionally forming the boardinghouse complex which we have noted already among the Italians. These centers gradually formed in each city a Polish colony known as the Polonia.[46] Engaging in manual labor of an unskilled type and knowing little of the language or customs of America, the immigrant was naturally drawn toward others of his own kind. Even though he endured some of the discrimination shown to all foreign groups, he nevertheless actually found freedom in relative absence of pressure to assimilate him, and he began to organize with great fervor.[47] At first in many cases he imagined himself an exile from the old world rather than an immigrant in the new.[48]

The Polonia was organized in two chronological stages. A preliminary period of transition and orientation gave way to the forming of a mutual benefit organization or "society." The members of the community who had forged ahead economically were often the leaders in the new group. Before its formation there were often collections for the poorer members of the colony bereft by death or misfortune; naturally the affluent were expected to give more substantially. The impulse to put this benefit on a more businesslike basis (parallel with the later development of the community chest) motivated the leaders to form, with all other members of the colony, a society to which each person would contribute a regular share of his earnings and from which he would have the privilege to collect benefits as a matter of right rather than favor when conditions became too difficult for him to manage alone. This insurance principle, however, did not eventually constitute the main purpose of the organization but only its formative principle.[49]

In time the society became a sort of social club that arranged dances, musicals, dramatic entertainments, lectures, and other events in which members of the colony could participate, using their own language and customs. As the community grew, Poles from all three sections of Poland came together and found a common life,[50] thus enlarging the boundaries of the village or province in the old world. As the group began to congregate more and more in a single area, other nationalities would gradually move out and leave homes or tenements vacant, dwellings which were soon appropriated by more incoming Poles. In some cases Polish real estate agents hastened the process by organizing a campaign to buy up more property for Polish families.[51]

The second step of the colony was to organize the Polish parish. Like other nationality groups predominantly Catholic, the Poles on their arrival in America found themselves attending churches in which their own language was never heard and which were often shepherded by Irish priests. Sometimes, as for example in Detroit, the incoming Poles who migrated from Prussia to get away from German dominance could find no other Catholic churches in which they might worship except German parishes. Paradoxically their very familiarity with German even made this an advantage during the early years of adjustment to American life.[52] The colony did not consider this any more than a temporary arrangement, however, and soon began to press for their own priests. The benefit society now became the foundation for the parish and this formed a new primary community with the church at the center, somewhat like the older parish in Poland. The devout parishioners soon furnished the money to erect a church of their own, and relations became more stabilized. The sacrifice necessary to build a national church in the Polonia seems incredible today. A not untypical example occurred in St. Joseph's Parish of South Bend, where unskilled laborers in 1877 contributed $22 per family to the church. In a good many cases this amount represented something like one half of the monthly income for the family.[53]

The tendency to congregate grew even stronger. A large number of saloons, banks, stores, steamship agencies, and undertaking parlors came into being to serve Polish customers.[54] In passing it is of interest to note that Polish Jews do not usually move into Polish neighborhoods even though the ties of language might naturally take them there.[55] This may be due partly to the fact that they do not care to restrict their clientele to a single nationality group and partly to the tendency in Poland to keep them restricted or segregated from other aspects of Polish life, a tendency they could escape in their new environment.

The pattern of cooperative family work was modified to suit American conditions. As soon as possible each child would have a job of his own, contributing all his earnings to the family pool. Many Poles were thus able to forge ahead economically at an accelerated rate. Many working hands in the same family would sometimes bring in a weekly income of $135 to $150 at a time when wages were low by present-day standards.[56] The head of the family with a peasant background often showed a passion for saving and thrift which enabled him to own property or a small business in a few years. Agricultural habits aided this process when the city-dwelling immigrant would find a small piece of land on the outskirts, work with his sons in the factory or foundry, and spend his spare time raising a garden or a few chickens and perhaps a hog. Autumn would find the family laying in provisions for the winter: twenty to forty bushels of potatoes, a barrel of flour, a barrel of herring, and a whole dressed hog. These staples would enable the family to save still more for the future.[57]

While the advantages of this style of living were obvious to the transplanted peasant, he did not always realize its results in terms of the children's future. Leaders of the Polish press complained that children would leave school early and go to the factory, that some of them went as early as eleven and thirteen.[58] Accordingly, the number of youth entering higher educational institutions or the professions was considerably curtailed, with results that can still be observed.[59] Furthermore the custom of turning over all earnings to the head of the family became a bone of contention between child and father as soon as the former became Americanized and demanded new rights.

During the early period of migration, many of the older religious customs were kept in force. Not infrequently the whole family would gather in the home at eight o'clock before a picture of Our Lady of Czestochowa or Our Lady of Seven Dolors and, led by the father, recite the prayers.

The Christmas Eve supper of *wigilia* would be served as soon as a star appeared in the sky. Wisps of hay under the tablecloth symbolized the manger, and the feast would begin with a breaking of the wafer or *oplatek*, followed by an exchange of good wishes and a forgiving of grievances. Late at night would come the midnight Pastoral Mass or *Pasterka*, followed by the singing of carols or *Kolondy*. It is reliably reported that the Poles were the first to sing carols on the streets of Detroit.[60]

On Good Friday children would be awakened by parents, who tapped them with a rod in memory of Christ's scourging as they said the words "*Rany Boze*" (the wounds of God). The people would eat nothing but a bit of bread and water all day and in the afternoon they would walk to the church where a "tomb of Christ" was prepared for all to see. On Holy Saturday a member of each family would take prepared Easter food — sausage, ham, veal, painted eggs, and cakes — to be blessed by the priest. On Easter morning each would greet the other with "Christ is risen, Alleluia," to which the response would be "Verily he has risen, Alleluia." After high mass at the church each family would then have its Easter feast, using the food blessed the day before. A lamb of butter in the middle of the table would serve as a centerpiece. As a regular ceremonial the father would begin the feast by sharing an egg with each member of the family.[61]

Among the institutions in the Polonia one of the most important was the parochial school, which was usually built soon after the church. The parents frequently took the position that children grew too rapidly away from them and from the stabilizing influence of Polish customs when they entered public schools. Desiring some means of cushioning the sudden culture shock to the younger generation, the parents and the priest saw to it that the Polish language was taught as well as something of the history and culture of the home country.[62] The efficacy of the parochial school in keeping the children under control of the parents is certainly not to be minimized, though the Polish content in the curriculum gradually decreased as the community became more Americanized.[63]

One of the criticisms leveled against the parochial school was that a disproportionate amount of time was given to learning the catechism and a much shorter time was allowed for reading, writing, arithmetic, and geography. As a result many children who spent six or seven years in a parochial school could hardly pass an examination for the fifth grade in a public elementary school.[64] Paul Fox, author of *The Poles in America,* states it as common knowledge that children going from a Polish parochial school to a regular public school invariably had to drop back a grade or two.[65] On the other hand Catholic authorities, particularly Father Kruszka, deny this criticism and even assert that Polish American children are advanced when they transfer.[66] The anticlerical Polish newspaper, the *Kuryer Polski,* began agitating this issue between 1910 and 1912 with the proposal that the Polish language be taught in the public schools of Milwaukee along with German. Catholic leaders regarded this as a program to destroy the parochial school system and bitterly resisted it. Neither side would yield. In 1912 Archbishop Messmer of the Milwaukee archdiocese issued a decree forbidding all Catholics to read the *Kuryer Polski;* the newspaper rejoined with a damage suit for $100,000, which was thrown out by the courts.[67] Since then the Polish parochial system has not been successfully challenged.

Although the Polonia was to outward observation a united community, still its hold on the people did not have the coherence or force of the old peasant village or *okolica.* The members of the Polonia had frequent contacts with each other but they were also immersed in a wider society with different values, ideals, and purposes. Its members spent many hours a day in factory, shop, or place of business, in high school, or in casual contact with members of the larger American community. What served as a strong social control in Poland became weakened in America by the loss of social reinforcement outside the local group. Even within there were also members whom Znaniecki calls "secessionists," whose interests differed from those of the majority. Many a national home or *Dom Polski* was founded by a group of these secessionists, but the institution was more like an American club with ballroom, assembly rooms, a bar, and perhaps a theater.[68]

NATION-WIDE ORGANIZATIONS AND INFLUENCES

Before long the purely local character of the Polonia was no longer sufficient, and the demand to combine all Polish Americans in a common body of interest began in the latter part of the nineteenth century. From the first the strongest of these organizations was the Polish National Alliance, which in 1880 united the efforts of local fraternal orders or societies by giving them a rallying point. Its purposes as originally stated were, "To lay [the] foundation for an institution that would work for the material and moral amelioration of the Polish element in the United States by means of a reserve fund. To such institutions belong Polish homes, schools, and all welfare organizations . . . Protection of the Polish immigration . . . Adaptation of the immigrant to American citizenship . . . Commemoration of Polish historic events." In addition there were death benefits — $500 at the death of a member and $300 at the wife's death.[69]

The Alliance was organized as a secular and nonsectarian group with no religious qualifications for membership. In addition to its stated aims, it seems to have promoted a patriotic national (if not nationalistic) Polish spirit. One of the main difficulties of the often untutored immigrant was ignorance of the culture and historic past belonging to his own people; for self-respect he needed a fuller knowledge of the importance which his own background had for him.[70] Besides giving him this, the Alliance furthered the idea that the Poles in this country could in a sense be a strong and integral part of the Polish nation that was to be reborn.[71] This did not mean lack of allegiance to the United States but rather a demand, growing out of political freedom in this country, that this be utilized for the benefit of Poles in Europe who were still under the yoke of foreign domination. Both in Europe and in America the Poles of the new world were referred to as "the fourth province of Poland," and it was the only province where political agitation for Polish independence could operate without hindrance. Economically it was best able to furnish funds in behalf of the Polish cause. In the freer air of America the Polish National Alliance took the immigrant, often without a well-developed Polish national spirit, and helped to create in him a new patriotic consciousness. As we shall see, this process was tremendously aided by the Polish press in the United States.

Significantly enough, the Alliance was led by the intellectual elite who, as remarked before, enjoyed considerable prestige and respect among the Poles in the homeland for their service in keeping Polish culture viable. In America they continued the same function, had a superior press, and founded a college of their own, Alliance College, at Cambridge Springs, Pennsylvania, in 1912.[72] Their chief newspapers are the *Dziennik Zwiazkowy* (*The Polish Daily Zgoda*) and the weekly *Zgoda* (*Harmony*) which is distributed to all its members throughout the country.[73] By the late 1930's the Alliance was still the largest Polish organization in America, having 300,000 members.[74]

Although something like 90 per cent of all the Poles in America are Catholic, so that the membership of the Alliance was overwhelmingly in the church, many clerical leaders were not satisfied with an organization in which the religious element was not pre-eminent. In 1873 an informal federation of parish leaders came together to join their efforts in promoting religious unity among the Poles. They called themselves the Polish Roman Catholic Union. At first the Union failed to thrive and became inactive. A few months after the Alliance started its career in 1880, however, Rev. Vincent Barzynski with several other priests revived the Union at least partly to balance the secular influence of the Alliance.[75] Its purpose, however, was not purely negative; its positive aims were to preserve Polish national culture in its religious forms, to keep the integrity of Polish parishes from absorption by the hierarchy, and to resist a too rapid Americanization of church members which might result in a neglect of familiar religious usages.[76]

While not emphasizing patriotic motives in quite the same way as the Alliance, the Polish Roman Catholic Union nevertheless had many aims that tended to overlap those of the rival organization. The most important was that of preserving Polish national culture in the United States. For a time there was considerable strife and bitterness between the two organizations. The Polish American who wanted to become identified with one or the other was often caught in a dilemma. If he joined the Union, the members of the Alliance would say of him that he was no true patriot; whereas if he joined the Alliance, the Union would accuse him of being untrue to his religion.[77] For some time the programs and policies of the Union seemed to follow or imitate those of the Alliance, which had more adherents.[78] Up to 1939 the Union published the *Dziennik Zjednoczenia* (*The Union Daily*) and the *Narod Polski* (*The Polish Nation*), a weekly delivered to all its members. In 1939 the former of these suspended publication.[79] The membership of the Union in 1937 was 170,000.[80] The rivalry of these two leading organizations gradually moderated as the Alliance came more strongly under church influence and grew more conservative.[81] In 1935 the Union began a new venture by founding its Archives and Museum in Chicago, now the only Polish museum in the world.[82]

Another society of some note is the Falcons, a gymnastic society formed in Poland during the nineteenth century, later establishing branches in the United States. Their first hall or public building was erected in South Bend in 1898.[83] Then there are the Polish Association of America, the Polish Union in America, the Polish Alma Mater, and the Polish Army Veterans' Association.[84] In addition many organizations sprang up during World War I and World War II to give aid to the Polish cause abroad, but since these have played a transitory role, they will not be enumerated here.

No account of Polish life in the United States would be complete without mention of the press and its function. Olszyk lists the purpose of the Polish press as *first*, to keep alive unity and understanding among Polish immigrants; *second*, to inform them of the duties and advantages of American citizenship; and *third*, to bring news of fellow Poles and their activities in Poland and throughout the world.[85] Like other foreign language newspapers, the Polish press was uneven in quality. Barsczewski asserts that tavern keepers or butchers with ambition would get a yearning to become publishers, hire compositors and editors as they would clerks, and go into the newspaper business.[86] Bankers and financial leaders often established journals in order to have a medium for advertising special businesses such as steamship agencies or real estate or loan companies.[87] Most of the associations had their official organs, some of which have already been mentioned. In other cases individual priests here and there began publications in which religious and personal motives were variously mixed.[88] A small socialist faction had a number of organs with a limited circulation. The *Kuryer Polski* of Milwaukee was strongly anticlerical, and the Catholics fought back with the *Nowiny Polskie* or *Polish News*.[89]

The mortality rate of the papers was high: from 1870 to 1900, one hundred and fifty publications were begun and by 1905 only forty-nine were still in existence.[90] In spite of the faults inherent in such a diversified press, the Polish newspapers accomplished several important things: they helped preserve a relative purity of the language so that it did not become a dialect or a form of pidgin English (of course some Americanisms did creep in); [91] they helped raise the literate standards of the great masses who had been denied the use of their mother tongue in Europe; [92] they gave the people an introduction to American life that they could understand; they served as an agency for factional partisanship and helped preserve national pride in the homeland which was translated into practical aid in the formation of an independent Poland. In this latter task not only anticlerical but Catholic and socialist elements played their part. Nationalism and patriotic feelings were never absent from the columns of the Polish press.[93]

As the colonies became more and more Americanized, the number of readers who could understand English steadily increased, and this meant a weakened dependence on the columns of Polish publications. During the depression of the 1930's national advertisers withdrew their support from foreign language newspapers in general so that there was a tremendous decline in revenue.[94] In 1930 there were 129 Polish publications but by 1938 this had been reduced to sixty-eight, only ten of which were dailies.[95]

POLES IN AMERICAN AGRICULTURE

From the time of the Panna Maria settlement in Texas, there have been small Polish agricultural colonies in different parts of the United States, chiefly in the Middle West and New England. Since the Polish farmer had a natural love of the soil, he usually made a marked success in the new environment. Bercovici remarks that second generation Polish youth in the agricultural regions of Michigan, Wisconsin, Minnesota, and Dakota planned to stay on the farms and were attending agricultural schools in large numbers so as to prepare themselves to carry on more efficiently. This situation contrasts with the usual native American pattern of leaving the farm for the city at the earliest opportunity. Furthermore, Polish farmers did not sell their land in times of inflation, believing that the soil would eventually be worth more to them than the money they would receive for it.

Polish farmers have cleared an estimated area of two million acres throughout the United States.[96] Accustomed to back-breaking labor in old Poland, the immigrant came with a willingness to work painstakingly in a manner usually surpassing that of his neighbors. Content at the same time to live on a standard simpler than that of the native American, he frequently accomplished feats that seemed almost miraculous to those of a different tradition. His success with truck gardening near the large cities appears in the history of a small colony like Florida, New York, where the Poles built up an onion industry unparalleled in that area.[97] Here they have also kept many of the traditional ceremonials and festivals of old Poland. The farmers, for instance, bring their seeds to be blessed in a springtime ceremony at the local Catholic church. Then each family tries to get its seeds planted first. With the 1939 harvest the community began a traditional festival called "The Festival under the Trees," with dancing, feasting, and merrymaking in old colorful peasant costumes.[98]

One of the most striking successes came in New England, where the local farms had been largely exhausted and the flight to the city had seriously depleted the supply of farm labor. A few enterprising landowners discovered that by recruiting Polish laborers they could keep their farms productive because the newcomer was accustomed to hard work and did not make the same demands for easier conditions that the native born often did. Beginning with 1908 more and more Polish immigrants were recruited for such labor. Although at first they were hired help, they soon inferred that the increasing prosperity of the Yankees was due to Polish efforts and thus began to ask themselves the question, "Why not work for ourselves?" With savings they would buy a few acres of unimproved land and by dint of persistent labor bring these scrub areas into cultivation. They soon began to make a success out of crops best adapted to the soil, such as tobacco or onions, both of which require a great deal of individual cultivation. Throughout the Connecticut Valley from 1909 to 1921 the foreign stock (most of which was Polish) increased by 38 per cent while the native population remained stationary.[99] Under these conditions the standard of living changed slowly while the immigrant consolidated his economic forces, increased his holdings, and established a regular relation with the market. By 1929, only one third of the Polish inhabitants of Sunderland, Massachusetts (a more or less typical community) had attained a plane of living where they used birth control or opposed women and children's working in the fields.[100] But through the years, large areas of New England once counted uninhabitable had been reclaimed by Polish labor.

During the depression of the 1930's, lower prices of farm lands enabled many Polish Americans to escape from the city and its more restrictive form of industrial labor. Using their small savings, they made down payments on farms on Long Island, in New York state, and in New England and worked hard and were satisfied with a fairly low standard of living so long as they could be on their own soil. Soon they were paying off their mortgages and becoming independent.[101] One generalization often made about the Polish American is that he has, more frequently than not, a desire to own land.[102] It appears likely that this applies with more force to the first generation newcomer than to his children, who are brought up in an urban environment and subject to the diversified cultural influences of American life.

ACCULTURATION AND THE SECOND GENERATION

The discerning reader will have noticed that the Polonia in America was not a purely Polish institution. It was really an amalgam of Polish Catholic institutions and values on the one hand and American urban, industrial, and democratic conditions on the other.[103] From the very first the Pole had a fierce, even pugnacious love of his new country. So long ago as 1879 Henryk Sienkiewicz wrote that it was dangerous to speak disparagingly of America in the presence of an American Pole.[104] It may be conjectured that the full range of his patriotism and nationalistic feeling for Poland did not reach its height until it was stimulated by Polish organizations and the press in the United States. From the first, however, the immigrant's cultural heritage was soon reduced to a minimum. Rev. Joseph Swastek, paraphrasing Turner, says that the American environment found the immigrant:

> a Pole in dress, attitudes, skills, traditions, language, and modes of thought. It stripped off the garments he wore and arrayed him in American clothes. It fed him American instead of Polish food. It directed him to an industrial metropolis or a mining town more often than to a farm. It shut him up in a factory or a pit, away from the bright sun he had worked under all his life. It forced him to learn the use of his hands all over again and to develop new skills. It made him discard his time-honored usages and attitudes. In short, the American environment upon first contact with the immigrant stripped his heritage down to the essentials.[105]

On the other hand, it must not be supposed that this acculturative process was purely one sided. Culture elements from the Polish American community have had silent and largely unrecorded effect on American life as well. The strong religious devotion that the Pole has for his own type of Catholicism has had its influence on American ecclesiastical organization, forcing it to recognize a wider diversity and flexibility in its activities than would otherwise have been the case. The fact that 80 per cent of the Polish families in Chicago owned their own homes before the depression of the 1930's and that most of them still had these homes afterwards is not without its effect on economic mores.[106] And to take a more trivial example, Cameron claims that after the large influx of Poles to Detroit, they were influential in changing the style of hats from derbies to soft felts.[107] If this can be independently substantiated, it should give American males reason to be unusually thankful for Polish influence!

Since the majority of the first Polish immigrants were unskilled workers in factories, foundries, mines, or construction trades, they naturally came into early contact with the American labor movement. On the whole, except perhaps in the mining areas, they have been somewhat resistant to participation in labor unions. In 1911 it was estimated that out of 300,000 Polish Americans in Michigan, only 5000 had labor union membership, and this is not untypical.[108] Several elements in the background help to account for this: an unsympathetic attitude toward non-Polish organizations, an antipathy toward high dues that would make a cut in personal savings, and the unfriendly attitude of many priests toward labor, which was assumed to have socialistic leanings — all of these had their influence.[109]

In mining towns, however, where the need for labor solidarity is great, Polish elements have joined other foreign groups to strengthen labor unions. In one area where they predominated, they formed a "singing union" and marched along the valleys to and from work singing Polish songs.[110] Even here loyalty to the labor group is merged with love of Catholicism. In many homes the picture of John Mitchell, head of the United Mine Workers, used to hang on the wall along with pictures of the saints.[111] At a later period the saints shared the wall with President Franklin D. Roosevelt.[112]

There are, it is true, radical leaders in the Polish community like Leon Krzycki, but they are without substantial influence.[113] The Pole is by cultural affiliation violently anti-Communistic. He has always been an enemy of Russia and does not forget the older days of czarist domination; he has seen the Bolsheviks invade his country; and being a Catholic, he regards Communism as the anti-Christ.[114]

Some of the early influences of the slum areas of American communities had their inevitable disorganizing effects on both first and second generation. On the first, the change from a peasant primary community to the impersonal atmosphere of an urban community loosened controls so rapidly that even the Polonia did not offer a sufficient substitute. Znaniecki maintains that the disappearance of the large family, weakness in controlling all aspects of the individual's life, and the novelty of American legal standards were most influential in making many families unstable.[115] The loosening of old controls and a new mobility hastened the emancipation of the sexual interest in the direction of promiscuity, while American law, interfering between husband and wife, enabled one or the other to use legal means in a quarrel against the other. Divorce and separation consequently increased.[116]

As for the second generation, the children in America did not always or even frequently engage in common work occupations with the parents as was the custom in Poland. Diversity of occupation brought with it diversity of interest, and a division in the home began. Where the child was closer to American cultural standards and values, as in areas where he attended the public school rather than the parochial, he had to mediate between the parents and the community. This gave the child a sudden authority and dominance quite out of line with usual parental discipline, and the home lost its educational influence. Cut off from this restraining control, children too easily found an outlet in delinquency, which was fairly common in the younger members of the second generation. The girl who was forced to turn over her earnings in Poland understood the reason why: it would eventually be returned to her in the dowry and in the meanwhile the custom was part of life in the cooperative large family. In America the large family disappeared, the tradition of cooperation was often shattered, and assurance of a dowry at the time of marriage became problematical. The increased stimulation of city life also made home and "foreign" culture uninteresting. Since it was possible to have a separate life outside the home, the desire for recognition or "getting even" with parents gave rise to defiant behavior in seeking new experience that was often illicit.[117]

In the meantime those who devoted themselves to the delinquency problem among second generation youth were often forced to put pressure on both the Polonia and the American community. Mrs. Josefa Kudlicka of Buffalo reiterated tirelessly to the native-born Americans that in twenty years not a single *adult* Pole had been arrested there. Most important of all she made the point that the better elements of the native American stock and of the immigrant stock never met each other and hence could not cooperate on any program for dealing with second generation delinquency.[118] Giving a sidelight on the devious ways of acculturation she told of one boy who bragged to her one day, "We're getting Americanized real fast now. D'you hear about the two Polish boys that got arrested for counterfeitin'? You didn't? Why all they used to get us guys for was stealin' coal. We sure are gettin' somewhere!" [119]

Evidences of the increasing incorporation of American elements into the cultural experience of the second generation were accumulated for a sample of Polish American young people (American born) of eighteen years or over in 1929. In this study Carpenter and Katz showed that their sample group obtained about half their schooling in the parochial and half in the public school.[120] About 70 per cent of the youth approved the complete authority of parents over adult children and yet 90 per cent asserted that the child should be independent in choosing a vocation.[121] As the investigators assert, "Culture behavior changes more rapidly than rationalized culture attitudes." [122]

Probably the same influence is at work in another response of the younger group, since three fourths declared themselves in favor of a separate Polish community life while only one fourth maintained that the Poles should spread out and lose their identity in the larger American scene.[123] Fifty-six per cent of the group agreed to this statement: "Poles should speak Polish in their homes, subscribe to both Polish and American books, and speak English in their business and daily contacts." On the other hand 37 per cent subscribed to the following: "The Poles should speak mostly English, subscribe mostly to American newspapers, read mostly American books, but should retain some Polish for the value it has in maintaining Polish culture and traditions." [124]

Now, twenty years later, would this or a third generation group reverse these percentages? We have no definite study to inform us, but acquaintance with third generation Poles shows them to come nearer to the second of these two ideals. Even in the 1920's the young people of Polish descent were not in favor of endogamy; only 10 per cent said that a Pole should not marry anyone but another Pole, while 41 per cent said there should be no restrictions provided the individual married a white American or another Pole.[125] The group as a whole were more familiar with American than with Polish history though 56 per cent observed seven typical Polish customs.[126]

The waning of the Polish national spirit in America has been observed by Dr. Karol Wachtl, who comments that even first generation immigrants who came to America before World War II did not show much interest in joining the Polish army in England that was to fight against Germany to help free Poland. Refugees and dignitaries from recent Poland did not do so either, and a good many of them were not even interested enough to work or speak in behalf of recruiting for the cause. As for the younger Americans of the third and fourth generation, he declares that they have no enthusiasm for Polish nationalism at all. No one is really to blame for this state of affairs, since it is a natural result of living in America.[127]

Although by 1942 the Polish American communities in the United States had 831 churches, 553 elementary schools, 71 high schools, 6 colleges, 4 seminaries, 34 hospitals, and 146 other institutions [128] (not including the 118 churches of the Polish National Catholic Church), this picture of strength is hardly accurate without the qualifying observation that Polish culture is being more and more thoroughly displaced by American practices. Swastek summarizes these changes convincingly, and if these processes are visualized in every Polish American institution, the inner weakness of each can be appreciated. He says of the modern Pole, "He contracted mixed marriage with little regard for religious or national difference. He restricted his family circle to the popularly prevailing size. He sought less the guidance of the priest and regarded the Church with the mind's calculation rather than the heart's desire. He did not hesitate to move from the Polish community or to transfer his affiliation from a national to a territorial parish. He sent his children to public as well as parochial schools. He enrolled, not infrequently under a changed name, in organizations and societies outside the community." [129]

From the standpoint of group survival, perhaps the most significant of these assimilative factors is the reduction in the size of family and increasing exogamy. In 1935 Stouffer showed that the Catholic birth rate was dropping more rapidly than the non-Catholic.[130] The following year Robinson's study of the birth rate in Polish and Italian colonies indicated that the reproduction rate in the first generation was twice as large as in the second generation. In Robinson's data it appears that the decline among native whites of Polish descent is more rapid than among native-born whites as a whole.[131] When this tendency is coupled with the trend toward marrying outside the group, it does not take much imagination to conceive the end result or its effect on Polish institutions. The preservation of Polish culture and values today is being carried on largely by older members of the community.*

* Social studies of Polish communities have not yet appeared since the end of World War II, but a spot check of a small working-class sample in Cleveland with data from social workers and housing officials, revealed the following trends in 1947. The Polish community as a self-contained entity is rapidly becoming absorbed into wider concerns. There is no rallying point for the group as a whole such as the Feast of the Assumption of the Blessed Virgin in the Italian area. The second and third generation youth (particularly those who have seen war service) are interested in nationality organizations only for socializing. Younger people use Polish in public only on those occasions when they do not want others to know what they are talking about (e.g., group leaders at the settlement). In general the Polish group remain less within nationality lines in dating and marriage than the Italians of a comparable sample in Cleveland. Marriages

When Paderewski visited the United States during the First World War to obtain funds for the rehabilitation of Poland, he commented ruefully that there were four million Poles in America but not one millionaire.[132] Whether this is true after the Second World War it is difficult to ascertain, but superficial observation leads the onlooker to conclude that the accumulations of great wealth in Polish America probably do not equal those among the Italians, for example. If this hypothesis can be verified, the question may reasonably be raised: what factors caused the difference? Without wishing to attempt a definitive answer, we may at least suggest certain factors that appear to be influential.

The lack of a well-established middle class in Poland has already been remarked, as well as the consequent attitude that manual labor has more dignity than commercial occupations. This cultural pattern tends to repeat itself in the United States; as a Polish farmer

---

outside the nationality are common. Younger people ally themselves with "Americans" and tend to regard their parents as members of a minority.

The solidarity of the Polish family has been even more seriously broken by wartime situations, by employment of women in industry, the housing problem, and the consequent freedom of children. Children are living less with parents after marriage. The sharp distinction which the younger people make between their American ways and those of the father and mother often hinder invitations to visit school programs or exhibits. "They won't be interested." Often they are not invited. One break in the pattern came when it became popular for girls to wear babushkas; this sometimes resulted in an increased number of invitations for mothers to attend their affairs (the shawl on the head being less conspicuous). There seems to be an increasing number of younger people who prefer public to parochial schools; while many yield to their parents' wishes in this regard, others resist and if they attend the public shools, they try to lose their identity with the Polish group.

On the other hand the church has been strengthened by the war. Special masses were held for the servicemen, and the church took an active interest in all families of soldiers and sailors. Most of the young people attend frequently and go to confession regularly. The priests have retained the confidence of the community. Even though there are inter-nationality marriages, inter-faith unions are still rare.

There is less pressure on the younger children of the family to quit school and go to work; the pressure to finish high school comes from both home and church. The ex-servicemen of the area are taking full advantage of the G.I. Bill of Rights and going to colleges, universities, or technical schools. There is evidence that cultural habits of thrift have made many of these students reluctant to pass up this opportunity. In turn it leads them into the wider stream of the community and away from the Polish home base. (Study made by Orrie Van de Visse, Spring, 1947.)

said of a Polish grocer in Sunderland, Massachusetts: "I don't see why he should work easily and not raise onions and soil his hands as I do and why his wife should sit around on the porch while my wife works in the field." [133] It also seems to be true, as Dr. Wachtl observes, that the Pole is proud but subservient. His humility leads to relatively rapid Americanization [134] and yet if the humility remains, it may mean a greater attention to consolidating and strengthening one's own enterprise than to any emphasis on competition with other firms and a desire to surpass them in size. The American delight in the gigantic is not consistent with this humility or cautiousness. As one priest remarked of the Poles in the United States, "They are leaders in their own community but more or less self-conscious when they get outside their own group." [135] This trait would be congruent with the feeling that a trade or business should be kept within a manageable size where personal supervision could be exercised. However, further light on the problem is needed.

WARTIME ADJUSTMENTS

During both World Wars Polish communities in the United States were profoundly affected. In the first, American Poles watched with dismay while Austrian Poles and Prussian Poles were forced to fight Russian Poles on Polish soil and at the cost of destroying Polish property.[136] But at the close of that war, they had the satisfaction of seeing their fatherland reborn, even with the undoubted democratic weaknesses that appeared in its structure and operation.[137] In the second war they saw Poland a battleground again, almost complete destruction of homes and property, and loss of life running into millions of its citizens. They saw Poland become the laboratory for experimental killings by the Nazis, and then looked on helplessly while nearly two million Poles were deported to the Soviet camps of Siberia. In the war of 1914–1918, the Polish community in America sent 300,000 of its sons into the armed services, and in the Second World War 800,000.[138]

The political ramifications of these momentous events are too complex and detailed to permit of discussion here but it is probably accurate to say that most Poles in America today regard the present government of Poland as a puppet regime under control of Russia, Poland's traditional enemy, and hence they regard the homeland as still unliberated in spite of the tremendous sacrifices and suffering endured by the European Poles. The Polish American Congress has organized an American Relief for Poland in which aid for rehabilitation of Poles at home and displaced Poles abroad is being carried on. Though it is doubtful whether that organization, as it claims, speaks for "six million Americans of Polish descent" [139] (since this number is larger than the more conservative figures for Polish population in America and since there are opposition groups of smaller size that take an independent stand, while most of the younger generation are scarcely concerned with the problem to any great degree), nevertheless to the extent that the Polish American group is articulate, this certainly represents a majority opinion of those who are really concerned with the problem of Poland. Probably Dr. Wachtl represents the more thoughtful elements of the community in his conclusion: "We are worth more as American citizens than as a group of immigrants poorly tolerated . . . We can do more for Poland as American citizens than as immigrants . . . Even though we are Americanized, we do not want to be Anglicized. We should preserve the older national sentiments and spirit." [140]

CHAPTER 13

Czech and Slovak Americans: *A Dual Culture*

"WHERE ARE you going, Joe?"

Struggling with his mackinaw and racing for the door, Joe only grunted in reply.

"Hold on a minute, young man," said his father sternly. "I asked you a civil question. All I want is a civil answer."

"Frantisek wanted me to go out with him tonight," replied Joe.

"And what does 'out' mean, can you tell me that?"

"Oh, you know what we do on Thursday nights at the high school, Dad. Just basketball practice."

"So that's it again. I thought so. You're always ready to go out and play basketball but when it's time to go over to Bohemian Hall and get ready for the Slet,* you're usually some place else. Isn't that it?"

"Well, who goes to the Slet except our Czech friends? A lot of the boys are dropping out, you know that. Basketball is an American game."

"American is it? Aren't we all good Americans? Does it make us any less Americans when we go to Sokol ** meetings and learn to have a sound mind in a sound body? To learn the beautiful exercises given to us all by Miroslav Tyrs — isn't that something good? A lot of Americans would be better off if they did the same."

Joe looked at the floor. "Oh, what's the use, Dad? We've gone over all this so many times before. Anyway the Sokol isn't meeting

* A gymnastic celebration sponsored by the Czech organization known as the Sokol.

** The Sokol (Falcon) gymnastic society has a long history of nationalistic sentiment behind it.[1]

tonight and basketball helps build the body too. Coach told me the other day that if I kept on practicing the way I am now, he'll make me a regular forward. Wouldn't you like to have a Vopicka representing the family for Wharton High?"

Mr. Vopicka looked startled for a moment. Then he smiled. "Well, since I don't know anything about the game, how can I know what you're doing? Anyway you can't get the same good out of it as a good stiff night practicing with the Sokol."

"Yes, I can, Dad," exclaimed Joe excitedly. "And you can learn about it too. Come on now, I want you to make me a promise. If I get on the team, you will come and see me play. The other kids are always bragging about their fathers and mothers in the gallery. Why should I be any different? I'll explain the game to you if you'll only come once. Why, if you do that I'll bet you'd keep coming back. It's really exciting, you know. If I get on the team that'll be three Czechs out of five. Wouldn't you like to see the Czechs making good in America?"

Mr. Vopicka laughed long and loud. "Make good, is it? So that's the way to win your way, I suppose. We used to think when we came here — it was misguided, of course — that work had something to do with it. Good hard work. Now I learn from my own son that you can do it by playing. If I had only known that I could have played my way into owning this house, and maybe having some money in the bank."

"Now Karel, don't make fun of the boy," said a mild voice in the doorway. "He does well in his lessons too."

"I know he does, Milada," replied Mr. Vopicka, "but he hasn't learned how to work yet. How can he expect to make his way when he knows nothing about earning a living? When I was his age, I could mend any machine in the village."

"And don't forget that you came here so that you could do more than that; so you could save up enough to live well and maybe make it easier for our boys than it was for you. The young people here don't go to work so early. But most of them live longer," said the mother.

"That's right, Mom. Don't you think you could get Dad to come over with you to a game if I get on the team? I know I can do it. And some day I'll show that I can do other things too."

The parents laughed indulgently. "Well, run along, Joe," said his father. "Only I think you ought to go to Sokol too. That's the only tie we have left now with the old country and you know how much we love it."

"Well," said Joe uncertainly . . . But before he had said another word, he grabbed his cap and ran out into the night, slamming the door behind him.

The Czechs and Slovaks are usually considered together because of their union in Europe since World War I. But the roots of the difference between the two go back to the old Austro-Hungarian Empire from which they emigrated to America. Like the Poles, both Czechs and Slovaks left an area under foreign domination rather than a nation of their own. Nearly all emigration occurred before 1918, when the present Czechoslovakia was formed into a nation having its own sovereignty. But the chief difference between the Czechs and the Slovaks (who speak different though closely related languages) derives from their separate cultural histories.

The Czechs (or Bohemians — the two terms are interchangeable) lived under the direct domination of the Austrian crown; the Slovaks were ruled by the Hungarians or Magyars. Both were Roman Catholic from early times but the Czechs experienced an early movement of the Reformation under the leadership of John Hus, who became both a religious and national hero in the fifteenth century. By 1618 only one tenth of the Bohemian population was Catholic [2] but the Counter Reformation, which was a military as well as a religious movement, culminated in the Battle of White Mountain, the defeat of the Hussite nationalists, and eventually a new Catholicizing of the area. The coercive means employed were effective, for by 1914 the Austrian census enumerated the Czechs as 96 per cent Roman Catholic, 2 per cent Protestant, and 2 per cent Jewish.[3] There is considerable evidence that this Catholicizing was superficial and that adherence to the church was largely nominal, with a strong undercurrent of resentment.

In the political field the Czechs were able to win for themselves a greater amount of freedom; after the creation of the Dual Monarchy in 1867, they gained the right to schools taught in their own language and to representation in the Imperial Reichstag.[4] The result was that Czech immigrants to the United States had the lowest illiteracy rate of all the newcomers from southeastern Europe (3 per cent), being surpassed only by the Scandinavians.[5] In fact the illiteracy rate in Bohemia itself was less than that of the native born in any state of the union in America.[6]

In addition to these unique experiences, the Czechs participated in the new industrialism to a much greater extent than the Slovaks. By the early part of the twentieth century, Bohemians played a major role in the development of manufacturing and trade. Thus by 1908 Czech immigrants to America had as high as 25 per cent skilled workers, in contrast with the South Italians who had 11 per cent.[7]

The Slovaks, on the other hand, began with a quite different background. Under the rule of the Hungarians from the tenth century until 1918, they were a minority people in a land ruled by a minority.[8] Living in the northern part of Hungary, they occupied the least fertile areas in the hill country north of the Hungarian plain.[9] Pushed back into a land with poor and stony soil, they carried on a rudimentary agriculture but very little industry. Since the aristocracy was composed chiefly of Hungarian overlords, the Slovaks were practically the entire peasant class of the region and had little opportunity to escape from the provincialism of their native villages. Strongly Roman Catholic from early times, they suffered under the impact of the Hussite wars in the fifteenth century and came to regard both Protestantism and the Czechs with considerable suspicion if not actual enmity.[10] What Protestantism they did absorb came from Calvinist and Lutheran movements in Hungary, and this was not affected by the Counter Reformation. The result was paradoxical; by the time of the first World War, census enumeration showed a greater percentage of Protestants in Slovakia than in Bohemia, although the Slovaks showed a greater loyalty to their Catholicism than the Czechs to theirs. By that time something like 70 per cent of the Slovaks were Catholic, 5 per cent Greek Catholic or Uniat,*

* The Greek Catholic or Uniat Church resulted from the efforts of Roman Catholic missionaries to bring the Ukrainians and Ruthenians into the Roman fold. A compromise was reached in which the Uniats agreed to accept the authority of the Pope and the *filioque* clause of the creed in return for permission to continue using the Byzantine rite, communion in both kinds, and marriage for the lower clergy.

and 25 per cent Protestant.[11] The Slovak emigration to America was overwhelmingly Catholic, however, and they are therefore regarded by most American students as having a predominantly Catholic culture.

Another important feature of Slovak life in Europe is Magyarization. From the nineteenth century the Hungarians, alarmed at being rulers and still in the minority numerically, attempted to suppress the use of all languages in the public schools except the Hungarian. The result was that Slovak secondary schools were closed and the Slovaks were forced to attend Magyar schools. The Hungarians forced many Slovak publishers out of existence, took over the Slovak museum, and imposed fines for the use of Slovak by the people.[12] Since the peasant children attended school irregularly and for a short time (in the manner of all peasant children), educational standards were low. Twelve of the Slovak counties noted by Balch before 1910 had over 50 per cent illiteracy [13] and many others were little better. The only road to preferment for the young Slovak was to accept Magyarization and to rise to professional positions as a Hungarian rather than as a Slovak. In the well-known pattern some of these leaders became "plus royaliste que le roi," [14] turning their backs on everything Slovak and bringing their own countrymen into even more contempt. In short, to be a confessed Slovak in Hungary meant to belong to a despised people who were poor, uneducated, and without hope or leaders. As for political experience they had none whatever, as Slovaks. Stodola maintains that since the Slovaks who left for America were the most enterprising, the potential candidates for political leadership at the time the Czechoslovak Republic was formed in 1918 were decidedly small in number.

Although it may not have been entirely an accident of history that brought these two peoples together to form a new nation — after all they occupied adjacent areas, spoke closely related languages, and fraternized together in their opposition to Austro-Hungarian rule — their subsequent unity was one of aggregation rather than of fusion, and they are considered together here because of historical reasons rather than because of their unity. We shall see that similar conditions existed in Yugoslavia as well. It will therefore be more convenient to consider their emigrations separately rather than as a single movement. This division also does justice to their diverse patterns in order of entry as well as to the differences in culture and behavior.

THE DEVELOPMENT OF CZECH IMMIGRATION

Were it not for the fact that the peak of Czech immigration came in 1907, it would be possible to make out a case for the contention that the Bohemians should not be considered a part of the new immigration at all. The earliest arrivals came long before 1880, the time usually set for the beginning of the tide from southeastern Europe. It is probably more accurate to say that the Czechs form the bridge between the old and the new immigration, for some of them began the journey to America in the early years of the nineteenth century and the first sizable group came in after the political disturbances of 1848.[15] Actually, the Czechs themselves had an old and a new immigration, the peak of the former coming in the years 1870–1880 and the larger peak of the latter in 1904–1908.[16] In the earlier group, most of the newcomers were peasants from the southeast and southwest portions of Bohemia, where feudalism and poverty had taken a heavy toll of lives.[17]

In addition to political reasons, which were really of secondary importance for most of this early emigration, the redivision of lands after 1848 caused much hardship and helped to stimulate the movement out of Bohemia.[18] The California gold rush in 1849 brought a few immigrants,[19] and the lifting of restrictions on emigration in 1861 gave the steamship companies an opportunity to compete for trade.[20] Complete freedom of movement was allowed by the Austrian government after 1867 and emigration increased to about 4000 a year. The passing of the Homestead Act after the end of the Civil War in the United States also played a part in accelerating the trend of the times.[21] The introduction of a compulsory conscription law by the Austrians in 1867 estranged many Czechs and furnished a further reason for escaping what most Bohemians felt to be oppressive conditions.[22]

Whatever the accessory reasons for leaving Austria might have been, there seems little doubt that the chief motivation was economic. The great estates of Bohemia were in the southeast and southwest, and it was in this region that the peasant found the poorest living conditions of all.

THE BOHEMIAN BACKGROUND

Peasant dwellings in Bohemia had stables and living quarters together. There were only one or two rooms in a house, each with a bare table, tile stove, brick oven, benches by the wall, a feather bed on a solid stand, earthenware crockery, iron pots and kettles, a bare floor, and whitewashed walls hung with religious pictures or sometimes a clock. The diet was monotonous, usually consisting of potatoes, cabbage, and rye bread. On rare occasions there would be meat. The family might kill a goose or a pig and top off the special meal with *kolace* or stuffed buns. Fields were laid out in strips or blocks after the medieval manner; they were usually planted with rye, flax, barley, potatoes, cabbage, and peas and were tilled and harvested by hand since there was no machinery. Each family practiced a subsistence economy, making its own clothing, soap, and household articles. Women engaged in fine lace making and the embroidery of their highly colorful costumes to wear at festivals. In villages and towns many skilled occupations developed, such as weaving, harness making, cabinet making, barrel making, smithing, and masonry.

Among the peasants there was a more highly differentiated class system than, for example, in Poland. At the top of the ladder was the *sedlak*, who owned from thirty-five to seventy or more acres and had his own horses. Below him was the *chalupnik* (cottager) who had about five or six acres and hired his own beast or plow. Farther down the scale was the *baracnik*, a poorer peasant who owned two or three acres with no beast or plow; usually he eked out a precarious living by working for a *sedlak*, *chalupnik*, or landlord. Lowest of all was the landless peasant or *nadenik*, who worked by the day and contracted with anyone who would buy his labor. More emigrants to America came from the *chalupnik* class than any other; these were often skilled workmen who let wife and children carry on the farm work while they plied a trade at home or somewhere else in the village. Jerabek comments that this class felt economic pressure from above and below but had sufficient economic reserve and ambition to be able to migrate.[23]

Practically all the social life of the village was centered at the inn or *hostinec* on weekdays and in the church on Sundays and holy days.

At harvest time or in the spring there would be a *beseda* or festival social gathering with much dancing and merrymaking.[24] The influence of the *hostinec* or tavern became more powerful in America than any other form of socializing.

The church in the Austro-Hungarian Empire was supported by taxes and everyone had to belong nominally to some church to be properly registered in the census.[25] Although there was no Germanization in wholly Czech communities,[26] there were probably few villages that did not have a good many German residents, and bilingualism was necessary to carry on many business or political transactions. The older Czech traditions were shared by most of the people: a memory of a once independent kingdom when Bohemians were masters in their own land; Hussitism and anti-Catholicism; and a generalized antagonism toward Germans or Austrians and contempt for the foreign landlord.[27] However, hatred for the Austrian probably never reached the virulence of the Polish hate for the Russian, and certainly nationalistic feeling was highest in the cities.[28] Successful accommodation to the Austrians was fairly common and neither Czechs nor Austrians made special efforts to enforce endogamy; intermarriage was frequent.

While the early migrants to America came largely from towns and villages, a slow but perceptible change in the economic life of Bohemia gradually brought about a new orientation. From 1850 to 1900 industrialism began to reorganize Austria. At first the factories were largely in the hands of Austrian capital, but the Czechs began a secret boycott of the Germans which proved to be highly effective. At the same time the Czechs put their meager savings into cooperatives and slowly built up industries which were patronized as a part of the nationalistic campaign. What actually developed was a series of small plants or industries with their own skilled workmen or independent craftsmen, operating on a modest scale with a well-integrated but hardly class conscious labor movement.[29] As news came from America that economic opportunities were greater there, these skilled workmen or craftsmen began to work their way across the Atlantic and after their arrival were far better equipped to find a preferred place on the economic ladder.

In Austria itself, the new industrialism brought a wave of urbanization which suppressed many of the folk customs practiced by villagers. Constant intercommunication between city and country helped bring about cultural homogeneity and a disappearance of peasant modes of life.[30] Since the great bulk of emigration to the United States came after this urbanizing process, it becomes clear why the Czech brought less provincialism and fewer peasant folkways to America than the immigrants of other nationalities. It is probably this factor that leads Balch to comment that the Czechs resemble the immigrants from northwestern Europe of the old immigration.[31]

One unique feature of Czech immigration was the advice and guidance which the seasoned immigrants gave the newcomers. Leader of this development was Joseph Pastor, who spent several years in America and then opened a steamship agency in Hamburg where he published a monthly periodical to disseminate accurate information about the new land and about the actual experiences of those who had already arrived. He sent out 1550 questionnaires and printed the answers during 1888 in the journal *Czech Settlements in America* (*Ceske Osady v Americe*). To help regulate the quality of immigrants coming to American shores, he also wrote a letter published in *Czech Settlements* declaring that the Americans did not want bums who came only to take money back to the old country with them but men who would become permanent citizens. Pastor warned his countrymen that America would one day find it necessary to restrict immigration and that all Czechs must be careful not to get on the proscribed list.[32] Whatever the effect of this advice may have been, statistics show clearly that the great bulk of Bohemian immigrants came as whole families, the sex ratio being almost even with only a slight preponderance of males.[33]

THE CZECHS IN RURAL AREAS

Unlike some of the other ethnic groups, the Czechs as a rule did not settle in mining or factory regions or engage extensively in unskilled occupations.[34] It is already clear that most of them were prepared to enter either agriculture or the skilled trades, and since their arrival was earlier than the great mass of the new immigration, they were able to find land without great difficulty. Around 1870 a few Czechs did visit the coal and steel districts of Pennsylvania, Ohio, Indiana, and Illinois, but they soon drifted away from them to farms.[35] In the Great Plains areas, Bohemians arrived early enough to take advantage of the Homestead Act under which a person could take 160 acres, live on it for five years, and get the land free. During the pioneer days of the 1850's and 1860's the Czech settlers lived in dugouts carved out of the sides of ravines, in sod houses, and in log cabins.[36] The first rural dwellers went to Wisconsin and Iowa and later migrated from those states into Nebraska.[37] About the same time a large colony was founded in Texas, chiefly composed of immigrants from Moravia.* [38] In making these first settlements, the Czechs often followed in the footsteps of the Germans who had come before them.[39] This is not difficult to understand when it is recalled that the Czechs were familiar with the German language, having learned it in school. Furthermore the customs and habits of the Germans were familiar and the Czechs felt at home among them, with much old-world hostility dropping away as soon as it was clear that each group could have an equal chance in the new land.[40]

There have been two major studies of Czech farming communities, both of which show that they have been more than moderately successful. The first covers a Czech colony near Petersburg, Virginia, which came in to farm land that was languishing under the old plantation economy. The new farmers revitalized agricultural methods by persevering, arduous toil, by using the labor of an entire family including the mother, and by supplementing their earnings with industrial labor, peddling, woodcutting, or domestic work. Families were close knit and there was no serious problem of delinquency with all the members working together on a cooperative task. In spite of the fact that the wives worked in the fields, they did not have a subordinate place in the household but were regarded as partners with the husband in the family economy; the wife took over the management of the farm at his death. Social stratification being what it was in Virginia, the Bohemians were not integrated into community life even in the third generation and there was little intermarriage.[41] This, however, is not characteristic of the Czech Americans as a whole.

The second study is Lynch's investigation of the "comparative average stability" of the Czech farmers in and around Prague, in

* It is customary to include the inhabitants of Moravia with those of Bohemia as Czechs.

Lincoln County, Oklahoma, as compared with the native-born farmers of that region. The Czechs are superior on nearly every count. In a cotton area, they have a higher number of owners and a smaller number of tenants; they cultivate more land per farm, use more cover crops, have more outbuildings with more improvements, and own better homes. They showed less mobility during the depression years; in fact the population loss for the county as a whole was ten times as high during the 1930's as it was in the Czech communities. One of the factors making for success in Czech agricultural areas was the part played by lodges and benefit organizations. For the native white farmer in Lincoln County, the town is regarded as a detached center for trade and transportation; for the Czechs, it is the focal center of group life since they belong to social organizations other than the church from two and a half to ten times as often as control groups from native white areas.[42]

While these two studies may not be wholly representative of the major areas occupied by Czechs, which are chiefly in the Middle West, the account by Bercovici of his travels through Wisconsin regions inhabited by Czech farmers shows that the major tendencies found in Virginia and Oklahoma are paralleled in the Great Lakes area.[43] It is significant to note that some old-world features are retained longer in rural than in urban areas. For example, the Czech farmers wear their native peasant costumes on festive occasions quite frequently, particularly at weddings.[44] The immigrants also have more opportunity to christen towns with names from Bohemia: in all there are six named Praha (Prague), three Plzens (Pilsen), and seven Tabors. This in contrast with the Slovaks, who have few rural settlements and only two with old-world names — Slovaktown, Arkansas, and Masaryktown, Florida.[45] Another evidence of European culture appears in the use of the Czech language for the publishing of farm journals, a feature unknown in other ethnic groups.[46]

On the other hand, culture assimilation tends to occur with great rapidity in the agricultural regions. One evidence of this is frequent intermarriage; probably the Czech marries outside his group as frequently as any other nationality. He rarely marries Latins or other Slavs but more often Germans or those of northwest European extraction.[47] The Slovaks seem more inclined to marry other Slavs when going outside their own community.[48] Another important influence hastening participation in American life is the fact that Czech farmers send their children to high school and college in large numbers.[49] This may have a good deal to do with accelerating the process of intermarriage itself. In spite of the tendency to train the children away from the farm, Capek reported in 1920 that a larger percentage of the second generation was engaged in farming than was present in the first generation — 43 and 32 per cent respectively.[50] It is doubtful whether this trend has continued into the 1940's but there are no figures available to prove or disprove it. On the whole, however, it is important that about half of all the Czech immigrants eventually engaged in agriculture, a proportion much higher than that of other nationalities.[51] This has undoubtedly been a stabilizing factor in the adjustment of the immigrant to the new land.

THE CZECHS IN URBAN AREAS

Like other nationalities, the Bohemians who settled in urban areas formed colonies with their own people where the transition to full participation in American life could be made with a minimum of culture shock. There is some evidence that during the early days of the migration to the United States they set up their homes near the edge of the city, as they did in Cleveland, where they could have a semirural environment and enjoy their own gardens.[52] The later waves of migrants after the 1880's came from a more highly industrialized environment and settled down in American cities where their special skills could be utilized.[53] Here too they followed in the wake of the Germans; [54] as a matter of record, the first newspaper to be started by a Czech was published in German in Milwaukee and carried the name *Flug Blätter*. Its editor was therefore able to appeal to both a Czech and a German constituency.[55]

During the 1850's the Czechs in New York fraternized with their Slavic confreres, the Poles, using the same fraternal halls and sharing feasts, weddings, concerts, and dramatic performances. Much of this was due to the accident of European history that gave them a common enemy, Austria.[56] The idyllic situation lasted until 1871, when the Czechs sent a delegation to welcome the Grand Duke Alexis of Russia, "our brother Slav." This recognition of an enemy whom the Poles regarded as more hostile and dangerous than any

Austrian, put an end to the friendly relations of Czechs and Poles. The latter seceded from all organizations they had entered with the Bohemians, and the Czechs moved from the Lower East Side to the East River near 50th Street, spreading north as far as 80th Street.[57] This later Czech section was something like old Prague, with tunnels, high stone steps, cobblestones, balconies, vaulted alleys, and sudden elevations.[58] From this time on, the Czechs developed their own societies and organizations separately from other ethnic groups. On the whole the Slovaks have fraternized more with their brother Slavs than the Czechs; [59] a completely Slovak community is rare, for mixed in with the group are usually Poles, Croatians, or Russians.[60] It should also be noted parenthetically that the Czechs have a special hostility toward the Irish.[61] This was partly due to the strong tie the Irish had with Catholicism and partly to the fact that the Irish often had positions as foremen for the industries where the Czechs first found employment.

In Chicago, the largest Czech center, the original settlement in 1852 was on the northern outskirts at the present southern boundaries of Lincoln Park. Later ones, however, were found in more crowded sections not far from the Loop, the third (called Praha) being particularly crowded with an eventual population of 10,000. Other typical Chicago colonies were called by such characteristic Bohemian names as Plzen (Pilsen) and Vinohrady (Vineyard).[62] Like other foreign-born newcomers to Chicago, the Czechs started near the center and gradually worked their way to positions near the outskirts. Horak shows that three factors were responsible for their mobility: (1) population density pushing out from the center; (2) loss of property values near the center; and (3) love of the open air and more land.[63] To this may perhaps be added the prestige value of living away from the more crowded tenement quarters as the group became more Americanized.

It has already been emphasized that the Bohemians came with a large proportion of skilled workmen. One example is the cigar makers, who settled in New York after a considerable apprenticeship in Austria. As early as 1873 about 95 per cent of the Czechs in New York City were engaged in cigar making.[64] By 1920 this percentage had shrunk to less than fifteen.[65] Few of the skilled artisans in the trade rose to be manufacturers or magnates, preferring to carry on their trade in the manner to which they had been accustomed.[66] In fact it was some time before the Czechs departed from a kind of working-class philosophy; they preferred to channel their ambitions in line with the steady and profitable work of the trade and even kept their sons in that group. This was also characteristic of the piano makers, of whom the Czechs had a large number.[67]

Often a certain culturally developed modesty kept the Czech from attempting to make any record outside his own group. Roucek notes the large number of both Czechs and Slovaks who do not move outside their colonies but attempt to rise in the social scale *within* the colony.[68] Although a professional class eventually did develop, it seemed more natural for the Czech to engage in vocations of trade and small business that were at first popular within his own group. By 1900 a survey of Czech merchants in the Chicago area showed tailors were most numerous, then saloonkeepers and grocers.[69] Like the Poles, the Bohemians have to this day developed few millionaires and scarcely any parvenu class.

The acculturation of the Czechs in urban areas was accompanied by peculiar difficulties dependent upon the European background. The linguistic problem was a severe one since English has an idiom far removed from the Bohemian and is much less inflected. During the early days the parents spoke the European language in the home, and the oldest children usually understood it well enough to carry on acceptable conversation although their attempts at English in school or in the American community might lead to derisive comment and the usual appellations of Bohoes, Bohunks, Cheskey, or Bootchkey.[70] Later, children learned less and less Czech until the youngest knew hardly any at all and by this time the parents were able to speak to them in English.[71] The housing conditions in the city were such that difficulties in the way of assimilation were increased. Miller comments that the Czech in New York seemed to prefer poorer living conditions if he could only procure better food.[72] Consuming habits required adjustment. One symptom of the newcomer was a certain recklessness in buying. Many luxuries were displayed in the shop windows which were unfamiliar to the immigrant fresh from Europe, and when he received his first money in the new land, he spent it freely. This was especially true of the women.[73] Significantly enough, the women knew meat values from the European background but were not equally acquainted with clothing values and would frequently splurge their earnings on perishable items. They showed great fondness for the installment plan. Furniture was bought on time, and for a short period in Chicago dealers reported as high as two thirds of the stoves would be repossessed from the Czechs.[74] These symptoms of maladjustment, however, were temporary.

Other patterns were affected by habits brought over from Bohemia. Accustomed to living in one room, the housewife would keep a single room in her American home in perfect order but neglect the rest. Living entirely in the kitchen was fairly common before Americanization set in. It was also routine at first to have eleven to fourteen children born, with only four or five living; but increased medical care, partly supervised by Czech women physicians, cut this death toll considerably.[75] Other survivals noted by Roucek are owning a large house but living in one room, generally the kitchen; buying pianos but not using them; and ordering gaudy furniture as a result of sales pressure by enterprising salesmen.[76]

All this was during the greenhorn period. Habits of thrift and saving were quickly restored as the Czechs started on the road to financial independence. Savings and loan companies organized by Bohemians were soon doing a thriving business. Horak notes one common pattern followed by many immigrants. A family would buy a one story house and continue payments on it until the debt was wiped out. Then a loan would be made to build a second story, which was rented. Eventually the rent paid off the second debt, and then rooms in the back for a store or for more tenants would be constructed as a more permanent investment.[77] Although whole families would contribute their earnings to help in the struggle for financial independence, it is significant that the Czechs did not make their children go to work early but encouraged them to continue into high school. Very few worked below the legal age and the great majority continued until the end of the high school period, even without legal requirement.[78]

The influence of cultural patterns from Bohemia continued in another respect: the first important social center for Czech immigrants was the saloon, where the workingman could meet his colleagues over a glass of beer and relax in a manner familiar to the habitués of the *hostinec* in Bohemia. During the early days these saloons were the open forums of the community where political philosophies of all kinds were given a public airing. Steiner comments that the immigrant used to spend hours of his time in the tavern discussing Bakunin and Tolstoy but later, with Americanization, would take up his leisure hours chiefly in attendance at baseball games or prize fights.[79] Religious discussions, too, were common, and it was often said that where two Czechs came together there would be a religious argument. Many of the triumphs of the freethinking movement started as debates in the taverns. Most of the lodges, clubs, and social organizations were first formed in the saloon.[80]

As soon as these larger organizations began to develop, they established national halls, and these soon broke up the saloon's monopoly of social life.[81] There were two major types of organization: the benevolent associations, which paid benefits and provided a sort of insurance; and the nonbenefit organizations like the gymnastic societies, theatrical clubs, and choral societies.[82] Although the first of these societies was organized somewhat earlier, the best known is the C.S.P.S. (commonly called Chesspass), which was founded in St. Louis in 1854 as a freethinking benevolent organization. The letters stand for Cesko-Slovansky Podporujici Spolek or the Czech Slavic Benevolent Society.[83] The popularity of C.S.P.S. made it the most rapidly growing society, with branches in all cities east of the Mississippi and in many rural communities as well. Affiliated with it was the Jednota Ceskych Dam or the Union of Czech Women, the largest women's organization.[84] While the non-Catholic organizations have been greatest in point of numbers, several Catholic benevolent societies were also organized. The most important of these is the Czech Roman Catholic First Central Union in the United States (Ceska Rimsko-Katolicka Prvni Ustredni Jednota ve Sp. St. Americkych) and its sister organization for women.[85]

Of all the nonbenefit societies the *Sokol* has proved to be the most popular. In Czech the word means "falcon." The history of the organization goes back to Europe. When the Austrian government forbade the Czechs to have any political organizations, Miroslav

Tyrs, a professor of philosophy, conceived the idea of escaping the ban by forming a gymnastic society somewhat after the manner of the German Turnverein.[86] With the motto, "A sound mind in a sound body," he helped to establish Sokols in all parts of Bohemia and Moravia where young men (and young women as well) gathered together and performed gymnastic exercises in unison to the accompaniment of music. These exercises were standardized so that several organizations could meet and perform as a unit. Such an assembly was called a *Slet.*

At the same time, these Sokol societies were the seedbed of revolutionary activity against the Austrians and thus had considerable sentimental and patriotic significance. The Catholics in general were strongly opposed to the Sokol because it based its search for freedom on early traditions of Hussitism.[87] In the United States, however, the Sokol was so popular that in spite of its connection with the freethinkers and anti-Austrians, the Catholics themselves organized a Catholic Union Sokol.[88] Its popularity, however, was not very great, and it attracted few members. Most American Sokol societies take great pride in keeping up the traditional exercises after the original manner, and many of them send delegations to Prague on the occasion of a national *Slet* in the capital of Czechoslovakia.

It was in the cities that the Czech newspapers found their first following. The earliest of these was the *Slowan Amerikansky*, founded in 1860. Still more important in its influence was the *Slavie* of Racine, Wisconsin, which merged two other papers in 1861. The editor of this organ, Charles Jonas, wielded a powerful editorial pen, and when he took the side of the Democratic Party in 1872, such was his influence that most of the Czechs followed him in support of the Democrats.[89] Somewhat after the manner of the Poles, the Czechs expressed their factionalism in two main camps, the Catholic and the anticlerical groups. The *Pokrok* was the first anticlerical newspaper, beginning its short career in 1867; it was answered by the *Katolicke Noviny* in the same year. For several years a member of the Czech community was almost forced to choose which camp he was in and give it his major support, with the newspapers whipping up public opinion. When the *Noviny* perished, it was replaced by the *Hlas* of St. Louis. The *Pokrok* was succeeded by the *Dennice Novoveku* of Cleveland. Before 1891 the latter was the official organ of the C.S.P.S. but it passed out of existence in a merger at the death of its editor, Vaclav Šnajdr (Schneider).[90]

In 1934 Roucek reported that there were eighty-two Czech papers and forty-one Slovak, of which eleven were dailies. Although English sections were printed during the 1930's, these seemed to be unsuccessful.[91] By 1945 this number had shrunk considerably to seventy-four papers for both Czechs and Slovaks, ten of which were dailies; of the latter the Czechs published six and the Slovaks four.[92] Thus in ten years the Americanization process reduced the number of publications by more than one third.

The division among Catholics, Protestants, and freethinkers, though it is the major cleavage among the Czechs, is only one among many. Those who have examined Czech-American life from within comment frequently on the many factions present and on the enjoyment the Bohemian gets from a rousing argument. For many Czechs a good disputation is part of the spice of life, and most of the antagonisms of the group are channeled into this verbal rather than physical form.[93] This has meant, at least since the early period, that there is little political unity as a group since no cause can enlist all of the multiplicity of loyalties.[94] The chief exception has been the nationalistic cause which will receive more attention below.

THE SLOVAKS IN EUROPE

In their own homeland the Slovaks make up a numerically small Slavic group, having only about three million altogether.[95] Though they are racially mixed, like the Czechs, Balch notes that they have two predominant facial types, the rounded configuration and the more sharp, lantern-jawed type.[96] Professor Radosavljevich in his monograph on the Slavs has this to say of them: "The Slovak is of a soft, pliant disposition and industrious character . . . He has a quick and adaptive mind, an eye for the picturesque and the beautiful, a certain inborn dignity, and a fire of soul that may make him formidable." [97]

The Slovaks live in a hill country to the north of the Hungarian plain on the poorest soil of the region. They are largely peasants,[98] or were in the late nineteenth century. Not only were they at that time in bondage to the Magyar landlord but they lived in an area where deforestation helped to eliminate much of the valuable topsoil and impoverish their region.[99] Of the few who did not work directly on the land, a small number engaged in wire working and the making of tinware.[100] In the latter occupation they were known all over central Europe.[101]

In their own section of Hungary the Slovaks clustered in villages of shingle-roofed houses built in rows, usually of brick but plastered or painted, now and then with patterns on the walls.[102] From these villages the men walked to their field allotments, often on a sloping hillside in stony soil, to till the crop. Each village had its own distinctive costumes, some for every day and others for festive occasions, with bright colors and embroidery. The men wore tight-fitting trousers braided with loop designs, sometimes even working in white linen and still keeping clean. Sheepskin coats were their protection from the weather. The women wore knee-length boots and blouses and skirts of intricate design, the latter long or short depending on the village. Young girls wore their hair put up in braids.[103]

Families were patriarchal. The church served as the religious and social center of the village, much in the Polish manner. Of all the festivities weddings were perhaps the most hilarious, with several days of feasting and drinking.[104] The folk music of the Slovaks is proverbial and much of the work was carried on to the accompaniment of songs; [105] it is said that they have fifteen thousand folk songs in all.[106] Like many other peasant Slavs, the Slovaks engaged in somewhat excessive drinking.[107] It was the custom in northern Hungary for the large landowner to run his own distillery and give the Jewish traders the only right to sell liquor. Since the Jews were often the only educated men in the village, they also did legal work and gave advice, and hence it was necessary for the peasant to have recourse to their services. It was frequently the political thing to do to be "in" with the Jewish trader, and this meant to buy his liquor.[108] The system led to many abuses, among which was overindulgence in such spirits as the potent plum brandy or *slivovic.*

The extensive Magyarization of the nineteenth century has already received attention. Although a law allowing the use of native languages was passed in Hungary during 1868, it was soon nullified.

Slovak secondary schools were closed and the Slovaks were forced to attend Magyar schools. Fines were imposed for the use of the Slovak language. During the 1870's to the 1890's, Slovak children were in some cases deported to Hungarian regions to be Magyarized.[109] The usual thing was for the child to attend elementary school only for four winters and then take up his work in the fields.[110] Before 1875 there was an extensive migration of the intelligentsia, chiefly to Croatia and Serbia, though some went to Prague.[111] Thus the great names of the Slovak people gained their fame outside their own region, leaving Slovakia leaderless except for the priests.[112]

Among the reasons for emigration the economic motive was probably the strongest, although there was also an attempt to avoid conscription into the army, resentment of Magyarization,[113] and news of successful adaptation to American life by other Central European peoples. There was also a patriarchal law in Slovakia which made a son dependent till the death of the father and thus reduced the chances to rise in the economic scale.[114]

THE IMMIGRATION PERIOD OF THE SLOVAKS

It has already been noted that the Czechs who migrated to America came chiefly with their families. The background of the Slovaks made this course impossible since their extreme poverty enabled only single men or married men without wives to migrate for a considerable period.[115] Often the Slovak who emigrated without his wife would go to America and expect to return permanently as soon as he earned enough money. Some of them did follow this pattern, while others would remain in the United States and send for their wives and children or pay a last visit to the home village and take their families back to America with them. So many of these early migrants made the return trip that they were counted in the immigration census two or three times; this has made accurate accounting of the actual number almost impossible.[116] Furthermore the Slovaks were not enumerated as a separate group in United States immigration figures until 1899, being included under the Hungarian group before that time.[117]

The migration of men without families led to the same adjustment process among the Slovaks that was characteristic of the Poles and the Italians — the formation of boardinghouses where the men lived a semidormitory existence on a cooperative basis until each could save enough money to bring a fiancée or wife and children to the United States.[118] The loss of these young men must have been felt keenly in Slovak villages, for Stodola maintains that those who left were the most enterprising of the peasants.[119]

In the early period of migration it was significant that a good many Slovak girls crossed the Atlantic alone and found positions in domestic service upon arrival. As one Slovak woman said of a former maid who had gone to America, "She wears a hat . . . And she says the master is so kind he bids her good morning before she has spoken to him." [120] The number of single women migrating probably did not affect the total sex ratio appreciably, however, for from 1899 to 1923 men were about 66 per cent of the total Slovak immigrants and women 34 per cent. It is admitted that some of these men were counted more than once because of re-entry.[121]

The first years of considerable migration were 1873 and 1880,[122] and from that time the number entering the United States rose to the peak of over 50,000 in 1905, gradually dropping to almost zero in World War I, gaining a new spurt of 35,000 in 1921, and slowing down after that period.[123] Since Slovakia was a tiny country or area to begin with, the results are startling: about one third of all the Slovaks in the world now live in the United States.[124] This is in contrast with the Bohemians, who have only about 10 per cent of their population in this country.[125] The Immigration Commission rightly pointed out in 1911 that the actual rate of Slovak immigration was higher than that of any entering group (proportional to the original number in Europe), with the possible exception of the Jews.[126] This does not mean that the Slovaks made up an especially large proportion of immigrant aliens admitted, for even in their peak year of 1905 they were only 5.1 per cent of all immigrants that entered the United States.[127]

THE SLOVAK IN AMERICAN LIFE

For the most part the Slovak entered at a time when frontier or agricultural lands had been pre-empted by earlier arrivals, and his usual destination was therefore industry or mining. At the same time he found that wages were higher in the city and that the women could find employment in industry or domestic labor.[128] For a group of unskilled workmen, therefore, the urban centers constituted the largest opportunity for a secure existence. Immigration figures show that 95 per cent reported themselves as unskilled or "miscellaneous" as against 4.9 per cent skilled and 0.1 per cent in the professional group.[129] The cities with the largest Slovak concentration, in order of size, are Cleveland, Chicago, New York, and Pittsburgh.[130] Youngstown has the highest *proportion* in the larger cities,* 10.4 per cent of its citizens reporting to the census of 1920 that Slovak was their mother tongue.[131]

Although Cleveland has the largest Slovak-speaking population, Pittsburgh is regarded as the main center of the ethnic group. That city is the chief urban center for the largest collection of Slovaks in any state, Pennsylvania containing about half of the million Slovaks in America during the 1940's.[132] There are, to be sure, several hundred Slovak farmers in Pennsylvania, Connecticut, Ohio, Minnesota, Arkansas, Virginia, and Wisconsin,[133] but their number is negligible compared with those in the mining and industry of the Pittsburgh area.

In mining communities the Slovaks often had to live in company homes. Even in this unpromising environment they responded quickly to opportunities for better living conditions and were unwilling to accept low standards except as a temporary arrangement.[134] Both here and in the cities the desire to return to Europe sometimes slowed the rate of assimilation, and so also did the habit of many second generation children in following the occupation of the father.[135]

On the whole the Slovak communities formed separate units or colonies rather than joining the Czech communities, since the culture and interests of the two groups were divergent. In those cases where the Slovaks mingled with others, it was usually with Slavs from different parts of Europe, particularly the Poles.[136] Though they often migrated at least partly to escape Magyarization, there is some evidence to show that they mingled with the Hungarians (they were lumped together in the common American stereotype as "hunkies") since they at least understood the language and did not feel any threat to their security in a fairly close relationship while

* Though Whiting, Indiana, a smaller city, is nearly half Slovak; Zahrobsky, *op. cit.*, p. 54. For full reference see footnote 113.

in the United States. One evidence of this relationship is found in the fact that the first Slovak benefit society was the Persi Uhersko-Slovensky v Nemoci Podporujici Spolek (First Hungarian-Slovak Sick Benefit Society), formed in New York during the year 1883.[137]

The little Slovakias in the cities have been organized much after the manner of the Polonia among the Poles. After the boarding-house, the first institution to be set up was the church and then the parochial school.[138] Although the Slovaks are predominantly Roman Catholic, they also have other affiliations. In a good many of the colonies, the Roman Catholic church was founded first and later a Greek Catholic or Protestant.[139] The first Slovak Catholic parish was St. Joseph's in Hazelton, Pennsylvania.[140] In the parochial schools, Slovak is often taught, though some of them have instruction entirely in English.[141]

In spite of the fact that many of the colonies began in areas where housing conditions are of the worst (in Chicago the stock-yards, for example),[142] the Slovaks have forged ahead steadily toward home ownership. It is reported of the Chicago colonies that the majority of the Slovaks in that city have either bought themselves a frame cottage or are buying one. This process is aided, as in the case of the Czechs, by local ethnic building and loan associations.[143] Although no important studies of home life have been made, it has been noticed by more than one investigator that the rise in the position of women has been particularly rapid.[144] At first the children did not receive higher education in great numbers but now an increasing group is attending high school and college and beginning to enter the professions.[145] Thus the number of intellectuals, which was small in the early years,[146] is steadily growing. During the first years, and even down to the 1920's, the Slovaks largely depended on editors and priests as their most prominent leaders[147] but this is no longer true. Loyal to their faith, a great many still accept the leadership of the local priest without question.

In labor unions the Slovak has played a relatively passive role. If necessary, he accepts the union; if not, he works without it rather than organize.[148] On the whole the ambitions of the vast majority have been security on the job and independence with home ownership. One prominent organization, formerly socialist, is the Slovak Workers' Federation, which is composed largely of those who are not affiliated with any church. This group has two national homes in Chicago and has published a Slovak-English dictionary and two books, *How to Obtain Citizenship* and *How to Fight Booze.*[149]

The Slovak community is quite highly organized, partly because of a sense of release from the ban on any sort of concerted action among them in Hungary.[150] Probably the most important national organization is the National Slovak Society, founded by P. V. Rovnianek in 1890; its popularity can be judged from the fact that fourteen years later it had 512 lodges and over 20,000 active members.[151] Today this society has chapters in most of the large cities of the Middle Atlantic and east north central states, with some in the Middle West. The National Slovak Society requires as a condition of membership that a candidate become a citizen of the United States within six years from the date of joining.[152] Other organizations are the Pennsylvania Slovak Union, the Evangelical Slovak Union, the Slovak Catholic Sokol, and the Slovak Gymnastic Union Sokol,[153] and many singing societies and dramatic clubs.[154] Fraternal and benefit societies of all Slovak-Americans were reported in 1946 as having $250 million of insurance in force and as having made death or benefit payments of $2 million.[155]

Although the Slovaks are probably more united as a whole than the Czechs in America, it is not uncommon to find a considerable amount of factionalism or rivalry between different groups in the same city or society. Roucek tells of the situation at Lansford, Pennsylvania, where 5000 Slovak voters could easily swing the balance of power but were rarely unanimous. Any candidate from the Slovak colony could have been elected if group unity had prevailed, but usually the candidate belonged to one of the many rival factions and would be voted down by members of another faction.[156] In local elections the voting is split, although national issues find them largely in the Democratic camp.

Though the Slovaks were forbidden to read newspapers in Hungary, they seized upon them with avidity after migrating to the United States. Twenty years after the Slovak newspaper was established in Pittsburgh, there were nearly as many organs of public opinion in America as there were newspapers in all Hungary.[157] This first paper was the *Amerikansko Slovenske Noviny* (*American Slavonic Gazette*) and the first editor was Jan Slovensky. Later

P. V. Rovnianek became one of the editors. He also published the *Slovak Daily*.[158] As might be expected, the number of papers was highest in the 1930's; it has been decreasing since that date as noted above.

INTERRELATIONSHIP OF CZECHS AND SLOVAKS

Although the Czechs and Slovaks have had an independent nation since 1918, the bond between them has been somewhat like the French marriage of convenience — defendable on utilitarian grounds but sometimes lacking in inner loyalty and conviction. The two peoples were not together except for the briefest of periods until after World War I. Both history and cultural experience had molded them in different directions.[159] Since the fifteenth century the Slovaks have been suspicious of the Czechs, who took vengeance on the Catholics in the Hussite Wars.[160] On the other hand some of the Czechs no doubt felt that the Slovaks who sided with the faith of the Catholic oppressor deserved no consideration.

The historical divergence of rule suffered by the two peoples gave a natural advantage to the Czechs, who developed under freer institutions and in a land with more economic prosperity. This initial advantage allowed the Czechs to migrate earlier and avail themselves of opportunities in America which were closed to later comers like the Slovaks.

The features that turned the scale in favor of the Czechs both in Europe and in the United States were: (1) a high literacy; (2) political experience, which fostered democratic tendencies; (3) a greater percentage of skilled workmen and professionals; (4) higher standard of living; (5) tutelage in German culture, which was already regarded highly in the United States as well as in Europe. To these may be added another which applied to the American environment: early entrance made agricultural operations possible. Nor should sheer weight of numbers be disregarded; the Slovaks have from time immemorial been forced to take a subordinate position because of their small population. In the United States, numerical superiority was maintained by the Czechs, who have about twice as many representatives as the Slovaks.[161]

All these historical factors have ensured the Czechs more rapid assimilation into American life; they were able to enter at a higher rung on the economic ladder, develop a greater diversification of occupations, and remain less statically fixed in industrial centers or dilapidated areas. Mobility of all sorts has been fostered and a more rapid rate of intermarriage with other groups in American life.

Though it is predicted by Roucek that the present quota system for American immigration will cut off Czech and Slovak arrivals sufficiently so that the ethnic communities may disappear by the 1950's or 1960's,[162] yet the rate of assimilation will of necessity be more rapid among the Czechs than among the Slovaks. In 1922 Miller predicted that it would take the Czechs another generation to become assimilated, and the Slovaks two generations.[163]

The relation between the two peoples in Europe, and later in America, is somewhat reminiscent of that between the North and the South in the United States: on the one hand the industrial giant with his prosperity, education, and plethora of leaders, assuming that to consult the backward Southerner would be a mere waste of time if progress were to be made; on the other hand, the agricultural younger brother feeling that he was powerless to compete on equal terms with the industrial giant and therefore keeping to himself rather than be disregarded or outvoted.

For reasons of this sort the Czechs and Slovaks have not lived together in colonies or engaged in many mutual activities in the United States. Not until World War I, when the independence of a homeland appeared to be more than a possibility, did they begin to work together. The Bohemian National Alliance, which was founded in 1915 to promote Czechoslovak independence, was finally joined by the Slovak League, a federation of organizations in the Slovak community.[164] The Czechs even sank other differences within their own group when Rev. Oldrich Zlamal (now Monsignor Zlamal) brought the Catholic party into a united front working for the birth of a new republic.[165] Without the mutual support, loyalty, and financial aid given by the American Czechs and Slovaks, it is highly probable that there would have been no Czechoslovak Republic. No money was accepted from any foreign power; such were Masaryk's orders. "This is our revolution and we must pay for it with our own money."[166] The foundations of the new government were established in the so-called Cleveland Agreement of 1915 and the Pittsburgh Pact of 1918, in which prominent Czechs and Slovaks both joined.[167]

The end of World War I and the formation of the new republic put an end to the fraternal unity of the Czechs and Slovaks both in America and Europe. The old cleavage returned, this time magnified by the Slovak claim that autonomy had been promised them in the Pittsburgh Pact which they regarded, as Roucek puts it, as "a constitutional act." [168] Although it was nothing of the kind, it was a sort of solemn promise that "Slovakia will have its own administration, its Diet, and its courts . . ." It also stated that this agreement would be enlarged or altered "by mutual agreement." [169] The Slovaks in the new republic charged — and in this they were given ample support by their compatriots in America — that the changes made by the Czechs in the new government were not made by mutual agreement.

When the Czechs put troops into Slovakia in 1919 to protect it against the Communist, Bela Kun of Hungary, they found that there were not enough educated Slovaks to fill the needed administrative posts or to man the schools. Consequently they felt justified in using their own citizens to aid Slovakia in progressing to a position more nearly equal to that of the rest of the country. The Slovak autonomists were not satisfied with this arrangement and have agitated the question of an autonomy within the country ever since. During World War II this controversy enabled the Germans to take advantage of the situation, drive a wedge between the two peoples, and give Slovakia a "free" status within the German orbit. For a time the Slovak League of the United States declared that it would prefer Hitler to Beneš,[170] a phrase strongly reminiscent of the French cry, "Rather Hitler than Léon Blum." Since that time the differences between the Czechs and the Slovaks have, as Kalijarvi says, "considerably quieted." [171]

Under the new Czechoslovak government set up after World War II (before the Communist coup of 1948), the Slovaks had far more governmental power in their hands (except for foreign relations) [172] and President Beneš reported that the Czechs "must and do understand" that they cannot prevent the Slovak idea of "decentralization and local government." * [173]

* At the same time the Slovaks still have the feeling that the use of the hyphen between the terms "Czech" and "Slovak" is a symbol of recognition that relative equality exists between the two groups, that it is true historically as a rec-

Incidentally, it is of interest to Americans that 100,000 United States citizens of Czech and Slovak ancestry served in our armed forces during World War II.[174]

The fast moving events in Czechoslovakia since 1945 have resulted in alternate hope and despair among Czechs and Slovaks in the United States. The formation of a new government with President Beneš at its head, with strong political ties binding it to Russia, was defended by Czechs as the only possible answer to the potential rebirth of Germany. On the other hand, a larger number of Slovaks have been restive at the signs of Communist infiltration. Other nationality groups have been quick to reveal the danger of close cooperation with Russia. For two years or more the Czechs pointed with pride to a free press, free elections, unrestricted travel, and continued prosperity as indications that the new experiment was working well. When seizure of power by Gottwald and the Communists occurred early in 1948, many could not resist the temptation to taunt the Czechs with "we told you so." In some cases this situation has widened the breach between Czechs and Slovaks in America. Those who had defended President Beneš, however, felt the full impact of the change. Before World War II the Czechs lost support of the Western powers at Munich; there appeared to be no alternative but alliance with Russia. When that proved a prelude to absorption in the Communist orbit, the Czechs became more fully aware than ever of the impotence of small nations caught in a balance of power squeeze. Despair mixed with nostalgia has replaced hope for the mother country.

---

ognition of the duality of culture that is present among them.[175] The term Czechoslovakia as a single word creates antagonism in a Slovak. It would be comparable to Swedenorwegia, Amerocanadia, or Austrohungaria.[176] While this objection seems valid enough, the official designation (unhyphenated) has been followed here.

CHAPTER 14

The Hungarian or Magyar American:
Exponent of Honor and Sociability

Julia was out of sorts again. All morning she flitted from kitchen to living room to bedroom, making a pretense of work but getting nothing done. Ever since breakfast she wore a puckered frown, spoke in monosyllables to her mother, Mrs. Koteles, and muttered ceaselessly to herself. Something serious was brewing beneath the surface, and the mother with patience born of long experience simply waited until an outburst would clear the air. Presently it came.

"Mother, why do we have to live here?"

"Here? What do you mean, Julia?"

"Oh you know what I'm talking about. Here in this neighborhood where nobody has more than three or four rooms and it gets so hot in the summer we can't breathe."

"It's just as hot anywhere in the summer," replied Mrs. Koteles mildly.

"No it isn't; not out in Hawthorne. They have big lawns out there and shade trees. Any time you want you can go to the swimming pool and cool off; but did you ever hear of anyone going swimming around here — unless he drove twenty miles up the river somewhere?"

"But how could we move to a place like Hawthorne? You know very well we couldn't afford it."

"Afford it, afford it!" Julia's eyes flashed darkly. "What has Daddy been saving his money for all these years if he couldn't afford to give us something better than this hole? Honestly, sometimes at high school I'm so ashamed when we go with Ben or Ruth or

Margaret to their homes and have a good time. You know I can't ever bring them here, or any other of my American friends. What would they think of this two by four dump? We couldn't dance because there isn't room. We couldn't sing songs around the piano because we haven't got any piano. I doubt if you could get one in here even if Daddy would get generous and shell out — which he won't."

"Now Julia, that's no way to talk about your father. Think of all the nice clothes he got you this year."

"That's just it, mother. I've got the clothes but I haven't got anything to go with them, nothing to back them up, if you know what I mean. I'd rather have a better home any day and live in rags. Then at least when a nice fellow brought me home from a dance I wouldn't have to get off in the next block and then sneak up here when his car was out of sight. Maybe you think that's fun but you don't know how it tears me to pieces every time I do it. I'm so ashamed I just want to die, that's all, just want to die!" Julia's sobs could no longer be restrained and she began to moan.

"Now listen, dear," her mother soothed, her quiet voice belying the uncertainty within. "You know that we are comfortable here. We're out of debt, we eat well, you have nice clothes, and Denes has got a raise at the shop."

Julia's voice became hysterical. "Denes is a clod. That's all he'll ever be. Sometimes I can't see how he is a brother of mine. All he wants is to get some Hungarian girl who will be a good cook for him and he will be perfectly satisfied. Do you think that's what I want? Not me. I want to get a man that's going places and I'll never even have a chance as long as we live over here where nobody would ever look for a decent girl. And don't tell me we're comfortable. I'll *never* be comfortable as long as we're on this street, and you know it."

Mrs. Koteles sighed. "Well, just keep quiet about it a little while. I'll speak to Matyas and see what he thinks. You know how he hates to go into debt."

"But Mother, tell him about the building and loan. He used them once to get this place. But now he seems to forget they ever existed. Couldn't he go to them again like he did before? If he could sell this house, he'd have something to start on. And work on his pride. Tell him he could have a place as nice as the Romans have or the Bujakys or the Nagys. He likes the Nagy family. Maybe it would help if you'd play them up a little. Oh, Mother, if you'd only make him see the light, I'd be so everlastingly grateful to you. And I'll bet you'd like living in Hawthorne too. You could have a decent kitchen with a little ventilation instead of that awful box you cook in now, smack up against the brick wall of the next house. Maybe you could look out on a garden while you were doing your work. Wouldn't we all like that?"

"Well, we'll see. While you're out tonight, Matyas and I will have a little talk. Maybe, maybe."

The next year found the Koteles family in Hawthorne, and the Americanization process was correspondingly accelerated. In this instance, as in many others, the spearhead of change appeared in the girl of the second generation, a pattern of some frequency in all immigrant groups, but especially marked among the Hungarians.[1] Of course this does not minimize the other factors at work in the assimilation of the Hungarian minority but serves to introduce a characteristic feature.

THE MAGYAR PEOPLE

Among the peoples coming to America from southeast Europe, the Hungarians are perhaps the least understood. One of the most common misconceptions about them is that they are Slavs — an idea which would be vigorously repudiated not only by them but by the Slavic peoples themselves. The Magyars have existed as an island of non-Slavic people surrounded by a sea of Slavs like the Slovaks, Ruthenians, Poles, Croats, and Slovenians for many centuries. And although we shall use the terms "Hungarian" and "Magyar" synonymously throughout the discussion, a distinction can be drawn between the two for clarification. Strictly speaking, "Hungarian" refers to any member of the Hungarian nation or former Kingdom of Hungary, regardless of religious or linguistic background. For example, Hungarian Jews claim to be Hungarians first and Jews only by religion.[2] Furthermore the country of Hungary received many immigrants in the eighteenth century, encouraging some of them to come by giving them land tax free.[3] This brought in both Germanic and Slavic peoples who settled on the Hungarian plain, became assimilated, and were absorbed as "Hungarians." But they were not Magyars in the narrower sense of the term, because that appellation is usually reserved for the original inhabitants who migrated as nomads to the area now known as Hungary from western Asia in the ninth century of our era.[4]

But from the first the Magyars were a mixed not a pure ethnic strain. Their history can be traced back to the Ural stock through the so-called Man'si-eri and to the Altaic through the Ogurs and the Turko-Bulgars. Thus they were originally a mixture of the eastern branch of the Ural (Finno-Ugric) peoples and the western branch of the Altaic (Turkic) peoples and are only distantly related to the Mongols with whom they are often too closely identified.[5] Since no other tribes of the same stock shared territory in Europe as far west or north, the Magyars found themselves separated from their neighbors by language, and this cultural heritage has kept them nationally isolated to the present day. Although the Finns have a related language of Finno-Ugric origin, the Magyars and Finns cannot understand each other.[6] Ethnically speaking, the Magyars are all those who are directly descended from these original tribes and who as a result speak the Magyar language and share its cultural background and customs.

In strict usage, therefore, the terms "Magyar" and "Hungarian" are not identical, but this is not the whole story. Intermarriage with Slavs, Rumanians, Germans, Poles, Austrians, and Jews of various nationalities has created a curious amalgam of peoples in Hungary so that there is no clear physical type. The immigration of the eighteenth century increased a trend that had already existed. But since the Magyars and their language were both politically and culturally dominant in Hungary proper, it happened quite naturally that individuals and groups of other nationalities or strains threw in their fortunes with the ruling group and even came to belong to the heroes of Magyar history. Miklos, who defended Hungary from the Turks in 1566, was a Dalmatian or Yugoslav; Petöfi, the most famous Magyar poet, was a Slovak; and Prohaszka Ottokar, a famous bishop of the Catholic Church, was also a Slovak.[7] Thus a Magyar, as we shall use the term here, is any individual who identifies himself with Magyar culture and language, regardless of origin. And, perhaps somewhat arbitrarily, for this study the name

"Hungarian" will be employed for the same group of individuals who come from Hungary and identify themselves with the Magyar language and culture. At times, when Hungarian immigration is referred to, the term may have a somewhat broader connotation, though the context should make the meaning clear.

It should now be evident that the racial characteristics of the Hungarian are greatly mixed. Huxley and Haddon claim that the great majority of Magyars today are "Eurasiatic Alpines" with some Nordic intermixture.[8] This would mean that broad-headedness predominates, but examination will show many narrow-headed types. Coloration is as variable as in western Europe, though brunettes are probably more frequent than blonds. On the whole the Magyars thus show racial characters similar to those of all other Europeans, and any Mongolian traits are so vestigial as to be extremely rare.

THE HUNGARIAN BACKGROUND

The nomadic and colorful past of the Magyar has left its mark in spite of the fact that he settled down in an agricultural plain where farming became the main occupation. The tone of Hungarian life has been set by the aristocracy or feudal rulers who won their large estates on horseback and with the sword. Even as late as the 1930's a foreign visitor could remark that an aristocratic landowner would prefer a visitor who was an expert marksman to one who was an intellectual.[9] The sense of adventure, kept alive in the aristocracy, has permeated other elements of Hungarian life to such a degree that one of their intellectual leaders in America has characterized their ethos as "imaginative emotionalism." [10] Regardless of class, all elements of the population are alike in seeking a kind of spontaneous sociability; [11] part of this is due to gypsy influence, since the Hungarians kept up a symbiotic relationship with the gypsies for many hundreds of years, the latter representing part of the Magyar character that lay dormant under the more exacting regime of the agricultural labor they undertook because of geographic realities.

Another feature of the ethos resulted from the linguistic isolation already mentioned as well as from the success of Hungarian arms. It was a kind of "disdainful attitude" toward surrounding peoples and a fierce assertion of Magyar honor and pride.[12] At least this was the way it appeared to outsiders, though the Magyar himself experienced it as a kind of "collective sensitiveness." [13] This pride underlay the romantic nationalism of the people, led to exploitation for many years by the upper classes, and made it possible to keep Hungary feudal long after other nations had abandoned the pattern.

The class system has been very rigid for hundreds of years. It consists of five main classes, though each of these has its subdivisions: the titled nobility, the untitled lesser nobility or gentry, the intellectuals (including professionals and what we would call "white collar workers"), specialists in trade or industry (tradespeople and artisans), and peasants. In older times the professionals were excluded from the upper class but in the twentieth century they are included. The reason is that many of the gentry were forced for economic reasons to enter the professions and they continued to be known as "gentlemen" or *uri emberek* in distinction from the common people or *nép*.[14] An aristocrat or large landowner possessed 30,000 acres or more. The largest owners, the Esterhazy family, held 221,241 acres, a domain larger than the whole of Ireland.[15] In a predominantly feudal country like Hungary there were many who felt that only the aristocracy and the peasant really counted,[16] that all other classes were essentially parasitical or certainly of minor importance.

The peasants were subdivided into five lesser classes, from the servants on landed estates to the small farmers at the top of their scale. It is from the peasant group one step removed from the top that many immigrants came to America, the so-called *törpe birtokosok* or small proprietors who owned from two to eight acres apiece.[17] This was not enough for earning a living and they were ground between the upper and nether millstones. Since they still had more than the day laborer class, they were able to leave Hungary.

Most of the folk customs were unique in each town, though there were some that were more widely observed. One of these was the *kalaka* or the "bee," at which groups would gather to aid one of the peasants in harvesting, grape picking, pig killing, corn husking, or spinning. There were also vintage festivals and feasts in honor of pig killing that were carried on throughout country districts.[18]

Thus the work of the peasants, although it was hard and difficult, was nevertheless accompanied by festive qualities that helped to break the monotony. Many feast days of the church were celebrated

(Hungary being about two thirds Roman Catholic); [19] among the most celebrated were St. Lucza's on December 13th,[20] the "Blessing of the Fields," and the May Tree or *Május Fa* ceremony. Among the peasantry there were also many superstitious observances or ceremonial acts (*jeles napok*) that served to assure better crops or good fortune. For example, the flocks must be driven to pasture on St. George's Day. At Vep the cattle are beaten with elder branches and green twigs while a chain with eggs is set before their stalls; this means that their feet will get as strong as the chain and that the poor who get the eggs will pray for the cattle. In the Gocsej region it is sometimes the custom for the peasants to run around their houses nude in order to rid the dwellings of rats or vermin.[21]

The family life of the country dweller is not noticeably different from that of the surrounding Slavic peoples. It has a strongly patriarchal strain and the conception of honor is early instilled in the young men. Perhaps one unique feature that requires emphasis is the consideration for aged people; they receive special privileges and respect. The father is very autocratic and expects to receive unquestioning obedience from his children and to a lesser degree from his wife. A little of the old feudal pride is retained by every family head, a feeling of dignity that forbids him to receive without giving.[22]

In addition to the peasants there were the tradesmen and artisans, many of whom also migrated to foreign shores. Perhaps the most significant feature of their socioeconomic life was the tendency toward specialization. Guild practices from the past were continued in a new organization set up during the nineteenth century called the *ipartestület*. This was a kind of syndicate in a given industry and included master workmen, journeymen, merchants, and manufacturers. The syndicate was bound to give a master workman lodging and food for twenty-four hours if he came to its headquarters in any town on his travels.* He then worked for a trial period of eight days, in which he could not be dismissed and could not leave. If his work was satisfactory, he made a contract which included a provision that fifteen days' notice must be given by him if he wanted to leave or by the company if it intended to use his services no longer. Under this system workmen wandered from city to city

* This does not imply that all master workmen were itinerant.

and were usually sure of finding some labor as long as times were good. Some of them who came to America reported that they had worked in at least ten cities in Hungary or Austria before migrating; thus their mobility was an accepted mode of life which was simply continued in the United States.[23] There was a high degree of specialization. A painter apprentice, for instance, had a choice of becoming a gilder, a sign painter, a painter and decorator, a carriage painter, or a room painter.[24] Again, there were two kinds of butchers: the general butcher and the pig butcher, the latter being lower in status.[25]

As for the intelligentsia, though they were few in number and, until after World War I, a minority of those migrating abroad, they comprised managers, engineers, doctors, lawyers, and journalists. The important feature of their psychology was their consciousness of social distance from the common people or *nép*.[26] In the larger cities, particularly Budapest, they moved in a world of their own which was often regarded by the outsider as representative of Hungarian life as a whole. The artists, writers, and musicians of this circle were more cosmopolitan in outlook than the rest of the population; their achievements made Hungary known abroad so that for foreign observers they *were* Hungary. But not at home. Among the Magyars their achievements were regarded with a sort of benign satisfaction since they gave the country a good name abroad and furnished enrichment of culture in theaters, concert halls, and universities. But they were only the jewels in the crown; the gold itself was still composed of the aristocratic families who composed the real rulers and arbiters of political and social destiny.

The intelligentsia was largely composed of two elements: the gentry who had lost their estates and were forced therefore to become civil servants, army officers, scholars, officials, or professional men; and many of the Jews, who had carried on commercial transactions when the nobleman had felt it beneath him to soil his hands making money. By the middle of the nineteenth century, the restrictions on landowning for Jews were removed and industrialism gave them a new opportunity for developing the economic resources of the country. Their enterprise was one of the important factors helping to build the magnificent capital city of Budapest.[27]

Many of the Jews were dissatisfied with commercial pursuits, however, and turned to scholarship, music, art, medicine, and the law. They thus converged with the stream of gentry making their way into the same occupations. This fact may account for some of the anti-Semitism to be found in Hungary, particularly in the large cities where competition is most evident among the professional class. On the other hand the situation leads the Jewish intellectual to greater self-identification with Magyar culture as a whole since opportunity for full development is opened up. Thus we have already remarked that officially a Jew is a Hungarian of Jewish faith; if he is a converted Jew, he takes over the intense nationalism of all other Magyars and may even begin to inveigh against Jews.[28]

MAGYAR IMMIGRATION

The great bulk of Hungarian immigration to the United States came after 1890, although there were a few who came before this time. History records a few scattered names in colonial times and over a thousand following the abortive attempt at revolution in 1848. These were mostly noblemen who were forced to flee for political reasons and who played an important role during the Civil War as officers for the Union forces.[29] Most prominent of these early leaders was Louis Kossuth, the apostle of free government who was received with wild enthusiasm by the American public as an international hero. The memory of Kossuth is still green among all American Magyars, and countless statues and memorials have been erected in his honor. Another prominent nobleman who became famous was Laszlo Ujhazy, who founded the colony of New Buda in Iowa.[30] These early aristocrats, who were antiroyalist and strongly liberal, had great influence on the later immigrants, many of whom came to America with political convictions much more conservative or reactionary. They established the American Hungarian political tradition and gave their compatriots an entirely new conception of liberty for which they themselves had been exiled.

The main stream of immigration began, however, in the 1880's and 1890's. We have already seen how the Slovak exodus began during the same period. For a time the emigration from Hungary was chiefly Slovak.[31] How much this influenced the later Magyar movement has not been investigated but it probably had considerable bearing. Economic conditions in Hungary were anything but tolerable. Even as late as 1907, the peak year of the emigration, the wage of a farm laborer (including board) was only twenty-two cents a day. Properties of the giant landowners were increasing in size, leaving less and less for the peasant; figures show that three hundred owners had one fifth of all the land.[32] Even more important was the drawing power of industrial America, where vast fortunes were being made and the call for labor was insistent. The expense of travel was often paid by railroads, large industries, or coal mining companies.[33] Sometimes these foreign workmen were shipped in as strikebreakers; the Homestead Mills, for instance, subsidized the German Missler shipping agency to bring in Hungarians at the time of their major strike.[34] The famous industrialist Frick imported Hungarians to work in the coke ovens of Connellsville and Leisenring before 1900.[35]

Once a few families came to the United States, they wrote their relatives and friends in Hungary telling them that there was "plenty of work for plenty of good money," and the fever began.[36] The exact number of Magyars who came to this country is impossible to discover for several reasons. In the first place it is already clear that a Magyar cannot be distinguished on the basis of race or even linguistic traits but in a sense must be defined subjectively, i.e., in terms of the cultural ideal to which he is devoted. There were many "twilight nationals" [37] who changed their loyalty as they went from, say, a Slovak to a Hungarian community. If they spoke both languages, they might claim to be Slovaks as long as they were with the Slovaks but Magyars while in the company of the Hungarians.[38]

Another difficulty is the census practice of enumerating individuals as "of Magyar mother tongue." The practical reasons for this measure seem to be self-explanatory, and yet the technique was a fallible instrument. Rev. E. D. Beynon, pastor of a Hungarian church in Detroit, attempted to discover how accurate such a classification would be by asking fifteen people at random in his church what language their grandparents spoke. Only one said Magyar. Yet all of them reported themselves to the census taker as "of Magyar mother tongue." [39]

Finally, at the port of entry when an immigrant was asked his nationality, many Croats, Ruthenians, Slovaks, and Rumanians reported themselves Hungarian and were so classified. The official figures are therefore quite inaccurate. From 1899 to 1913 the immigration figures for the Magyars came to 401,123.[40] The highest figure given in the official census for the number of persons "born in Hungary" appeared in 1910, when it reached 495,609. This number had dropped to 290,228 in 1940.[41] Perhaps the safest estimate for the number of Hungarians of the first and second generations in the United States for 1940 would be the one given by Balogh as from 1.5 million to 2 million,[42] though the lower figure is probably nearer the actual number.

In many ways the early migration in the 1890's and the following decades was similar to that of the Slovaks. It was composed of the unskilled working class or the so-called "stunted laborers."[43] Like the Slovaks, also, the great majority were males. The census of 1910 reported a sex ratio of 160.8 males to 100 females.[44] The Magyars also developed the boardinghouse complex in ways similar to the Poles and the Slovaks, for this was a satisfactory way to protect their earnings. Even after establishing families, many of them supplemented the family income by keeping roomers or boarders.[45] Since the early immigrants arrived too late to share in the agricultural development of America and since many of them had been brought to this country by industrial firms, they were to be found chiefly in heavy industry, railroading, and mining at the beginning. At the same time they kept up their mobile habits and continued to move from city to city in search of better wages and working or living conditions. The Delray Hungarian colony of Detroit has been composed chiefly of those who moved there from similar communities in Pittsburgh, New York, Toledo, Cleveland, or Dayton.[46] Many would migrate back and forth from mining areas to Detroit, and when times were bad would go back to mining.[47]

By 1930, eighty-two per cent of the foreign born of Magyar tongue were listed as of urban residence.[48] The figures for 1930 show that the states with the highest Hungarian populations were, in order, New York, Ohio, Pennsylvania, New Jersey, Illinois, and Michigan. During the same year the cities with the highest concentration of Hungarians were New York, Cleveland, Chicago, Detroit, and Philadelphia.[49] Other cities of great importance for their Magyar communities are Pittsburgh and Bridgeport. Cleveland is known as the "American Debrecen" since this is considered the most typically Hungarian city.[50]

ADJUSTMENT TO AMERICAN LIFE

Although the great bulk of the early Magyars who came to America were unskilled laborers, the character of the immigration gradually changed and with it the problem of assimilation into the American culture. As the flood of immigration increased, other classes came in greater numbers: first the independent farmers or peasants, then tradespeople and merchants and the middle classes.[51] The drain on Hungary's man power was so great that the Manufacturer's Alliance of that country decided to take steps in 1906 to bring workmen back from America.[52]

In the 1930's a random sample of Hungarians in Detroit were asked their occupation before coming to the United States. Out of this sample of 1023, only half reported that they had been agriculturalists or engaged in unskilled labor.[53] If this is at all representative of Hungarian communities elsewhere — and other evidence seems to confirm it — the changing nature of the immigration can be easily observed. A more pronounced change came after the First World War, when another wave of immigration consisted chiefly of the professional classes, ministers, professors, doctors, and artists who fled the necessity of remaining under other governments as stipulated by the Treaty of Trianon.[54]

Although the latter group on the whole had less difficulty in adjusting itself to American life, yet this was not uniformly true. Each occupational group had its own difficulties, which have been studied in some detail by E. D. Beynon in his account of occupational adjustment in Detroit. He shows that the early unskilled laborers found the whole problem most difficult, particularly since they had no special skills and were forced to live on the water front between two major industries in a blighted area where conditions were disorganized by the presence of a red-light area.[55] Other nationality groups opposed their coming and for a time they were outcast.[56] This picture shows many similarities to the first Hungarian settlements in Pennsylvania, New York, Ohio, and New Jersey.

The Magyar workman thus began with several initial handicaps. First of all, the English language was a formidable barrier because it is markedly different from the Magyar in every way. Even though he had had some schooling in his own country — the illiteracy of the Hungarian newcomers was only 11.4 per cent [57] — at first he felt keenly the need of a Hungarian colony to mediate between him and the American community. The peasants, accustomed to socializing in their work, found factory labor and mining monotonous and without flavor. The more skilled workman who was used to the protection of his syndicate found the American habit of hiring and firing without advance notice cold and heartless. Pride in his name and responsibility to his family made him pursue his work with vigor; employers were uniformly well impressed with their Magyar workmen as being conscientious and thorough.[58] Nevertheless the immigrant felt that something was lacking and soon sensed the need for an outlet where his emotionalism and sociability could be satisfied.

The first institution to meet this need was the saloon; but the saloon * had so many functions that it deserved another name. The first were general stores, restaurants, meeting houses, and banks. They were quite undifferentiated as economic institutions and not only sold real estate but served the purpose of community centers.[59] Here the Magyar could eat his favorite foods — goulash, chicken paprikosh, stuffed cabbage, and rye bread; sip some Tokay; listen to gypsy music; and hear the raconteurs tell of life in Hungary or the hardships of the long trek to America, tales interspersed with sly humor or heavily larded with sentiment.

In cities like New York, where social stratification in the Magyar community was more pronounced, the café served as the center of social activity. Here the differentiation was greater, as it was in Budapest. Each had its own clientele, one for artists and musicians, one for shopkeepers, and one for professionals and white collar workers. In the words of one observer, café life whispers to the Magyar, "Business be damned." [60] Perhaps a more accurate interpretation would be that the Hungarian in the café and the saloon felt himself a whole man again, after experiencing a workday in which only a segment of his personality was called into play.

Certainly these early experiences were influential in holding the

* In Hungary the village *kocsma* or inn played a part similar to the Czech *hostinec* mentioned above, Chapter 13, pp. 298–299 and 307.

Magyars together as a distinct people. Hungarians have a marked group consciousness and like to live where they can have dancing and social life of the Hungarian type. Often they will ride for hours on the streetcar in order to share their recreation with other Magyars.[61]

THE CHURCH

Hungarian life has traditionally centered around the church. This trait has continued in the United States.[62] As soon as family life began to assume more normal proportions, the Magyars in each community tried to organize a parish where they could worship according to their traditions and customs. Up to 1894 there was no religious liberty in Hungary; everyone had to belong to some church recognized by the state and support the church into which he was born.[63] Since the church was not supported by a foreign power, as among the Czechs, resentment against clericals of an oppressive regime did not produce such a wave of freethinking in America, although it did lead to considerable independence of thought.

Steiner notes that the Magyars in America were unique in their frank criticism of the priest and at the same time genuinely loyal to the church.[64] The statement is made on good authority that the Magyars have a larger percentage of Protestants than any other group in the new immigration.[65] If this is the case, it may be inferred that there was proportionally a larger percentage of Protestant immigrants than Catholic, since the latter make up two thirds of the religious communicants of Hungary. Although no figures are available, the facts seem to be that the Catholics outnumber the Protestants among the Hungarians in the United States but only by a narrow margin. Nor must the Greek Catholic Church be overlooked. In Hungary the Transylvania settlement was apart from the rest of the country; the dialect is different and this, as well as geography, helped to isolate the group. Many of the Transylvanians are Greek Catholics, like the Rumanians, and some of them in this country attend Rumanian churches and become Rumanized.[66] Those who organize their own Greek Catholic churches are somewhat isolated from the rest of the Hungarian community here as in Europe.

The late 1880's and the following decade saw the establishment of many churches and parochial schools. The first of these, and the oldest Hungarian church in the United States, was the St. Stephen Roman Catholic Church of McKeesport, Pennsylvania.[67] The large number of Protestants in the Free Hungarian Reformed Church (which keeps more to the older Hungarian controls), the Reformed Church in America (which is largely new world in character),[68] and the Lutheran and Presbyterian churches have had only a negligible number of parochial schools. The church, however, served as a new religious and social center for the community. Pastors and priests who were brought from Hungary to shepherd their congregations became influential leaders, though discord sometimes followed when they applied authoritarian methods in vogue from their older European parishes. Oftentimes these spiritual leaders had little sympathy with the democratic ideals of America and found the atmosphere too informal, casual, or downright disrespectful. As a result, a good many of them returned to Hungary somewhat disillusioned with their American sojourn. One such priest reported to Steiner more in sorrow than in anger that in Hungary people would stop when they met him on the street and kiss his hand as a mark of respect but that in America the children on the street would greet him gaily with "Hello, Father!" and go on their way with no more ado.[69] On the other hand, priests and ministers from Hungary who have become more Americanized and are undisturbed by criticism have established themselves as undisputed leaders in the Magyar community.

There is also a considerable number of Hungarian Jewish synagogues in the larger cities, most of them orthodox. A more liberal congregation has been established in New York under the name of *Uj Feny*, and its rabbi, Dr. George Lanyi, is prominent in Hungarian cultural activities. An outstanding member of the congregation, Dr. Albert B. Mark, is one of the directors of the American Hungarian Federation.[70] The Jews enter freely into the life of the Hungarian community in the United States as in Hungary, and their pride in being members of the community is not dimmed. They are accepted freely into the life of the colony in a way which would be impossible in, for example, the Polish group. Balogh makes the comment that the Hungarian press in America is favorable toward Jews but this is not so true of Hungarian vocal opinion when Jews are not present.[71] Since this statement was made after World War II, it may reflect some of the anti-Semitism tapped by Hitler in Hungary during the war years.

Although freethinking and secularism have not been so prominent among the Hungarians as among the Czechs, they have nevertheless made themselves felt. On the whole they seem to exist more among the upper and professional classes and give evidence of indifference rather than of protest against clericalism. In this sense a breaking away from the church has considerable prestige value among the leadership of the Magyar community.

SOCIAL ORGANIZATIONS

From the very first the mutual benefit society has been a prominent feature of Hungarian life in the United States. Many of these societies were begun even before families were well organized and when men lived together in boardinghouses. A group of them would club together and contribute a portion of their weekly earnings to build up a fund that could be used in case of sickness or death. While many retained a local character, some have assumed national proportions, especially the Verhovay Fraternal Insurance Association, founded about 1890. It reported a membership of 50,000 and assets of $6 million by 1945.[72]

Joseph Balogh in his analysis of the Hungarian social organizations divides them into three main types; (1) fraternal insurance, (2) cultural, and (3) charitable-cultural. Although the Verhovay Association properly belongs in the first division, its many activities have included cultural and recreational features as well. For example, in McKees Rocks, Pennsylvania, it joined the Hungarian Society and the Literary Society to establish a national Hungarian home which could be used for meetings, plays, concerts, dances, and parties.[73]

Numerically the fraternal insurance organizations are the largest (this includes the sick-benefit type of organization) and are completely national in character. This means that they insure only members of the ethnic group and do not cater to outsiders.[74] While the earlier sick-benefit or insurance companies had many social accompaniments, they are now losing more and more of their social character to other organizations and becoming more purely financial in type.[75]

The sick-benefit societies are often affiliated with a church and show a trend toward permanence.[76] About 80 per cent of the fraternal insurance companies examined in Allegheny County, Pennsylvania, enrolled Jews; the rest discriminated against them.[77] It is the sick-benefit type of fraternal insurance group that enrolls only nationals; some of the others that are more like old line insurance companies write policies for Slovaks, Czechs, Rumanians, Russians, English, and Italians. On the other hand the sick-benefit groups are chiefly composed of older Hungarian-born members, and their numbers are dwindling rapidly.[78]

The cultural organizations are the next largest in size, their chief purpose being to preserve a kind of "old Hungary" in the midst of America and thus help to give the immigrant familiarity in a strange world.[79] At least that was their original intention — giving plays, concerts, and social gatherings in which features of Magyar life and art were prominently emphasized. In greater Pittsburgh during the 1940's, however, only half of the cultural organizations limited their membership to Hungarians, the rest having mixed groups. One reason is that the society had to pay for an expensive license to serve liquor on the premises and thus members from other groups were welcomed to help defray the cost.[80]

The charitable-cultural organizations are the smallest of all, almost entirely local, and composed of about two thirds women.[81] Their purposes are to keep alive various elements of Magyar culture and to serve as fund-raising organizations for worthy causes. They are less permanent than the cultural organizations and reach a smaller proportion of the Hungarian community.[82]

From the first these social organizations have been fostered by working-class elements. Although many of their members have risen from the ranks into positions of prominence and leadership in the wider American community, the organizations have remained largely what they were so far as the cultural atmosphere is concerned. The leadership has been pragmatic but untrained and often tends to further personal ambition.[83] Professional people do not make good leaders of the group because their methods and suggestions are often not understood (or misunderstood or misconstrued) by the working-class members.[84] Pride and honor are so important that one or two individuals can hold up changes in the program by an intransigent attitude.[85]

The older Hungarians do not take into account the demands of the second generation nor are they usually willing for anyone to experiment with social innovations. Preserving the old ways is such an important ideal that any change seems a betrayal. This has meant, however, that both professional groups and the younger generation are more and more estranged from Magyar associations; as a result they are being more rapidly assimilated into American culture than other elements of the Hungarian community. There seems to be the fear on the part of older leaders of social organizations that if they yield to second generation viewpoints, they will lose control of the organizations or be deposed to subordinate positions. This fear has sometimes led to an out-and-out attempt at autocratic domination, which in turn is resisted.[86]

From the earliest years there have been attempts to organize a unified movement that would bring together the efforts of all organizations on behalf of a well-integrated Hungarian community. Such movements failed in the 1890's because of factionalism and disagreement.[87] The whole matter was therefore dropped until after the first World War, when a democratic parliament of American Hungarians was called together in Buffalo in 1929.[88] For a time the American Hungarian National Federation formed by this meeting was a going concern and united the efforts of all Hungarian Americans, particularly in behalf of revising the Treaty of Trianon which had dismembered Hungary abroad and which, as all nationalistic Hungarians are likely to repeat, was never ratified by the United States Senate.[89] This organization, however, was not to last. It was ten years later before a more permanent body, the American Hungarian Federation, was finally formed, a body which gave its full support to the American government in World War II.[90] The Federation now has a national office in Washington, D.C., is financed by the larger fraternal organizations, and is the nearest approach to a unified voice for the Magyar people in this country that now exists.[91]

THE PRESS

Like other ethnic groups in America, the Hungarians have had a lively press that has articulated many viewpoints. The first newspaper, the *Magyar Amerika*, was begun in 1879 largely as a national sheet to call for aid on behalf of flood victims in Hungary.[92] Perhaps the most influential of all the newspapers was founded in Cleveland in 1891 by a famous journalist, Tihamer Kohanyi. This was the *Szabadság* * or *Liberty*.[93] The extent of its influence can be gauged from the fact that it became known as dangerous to the autocratic regime in Hungary, especially when its fiery editor printed in the paper forms for voting which could guide the peasants of Hungary in electing leaders who would represent them and not the landlords.[94] [It is an ironical sidelight of history that Kossuth's own son, who was living in Hungary in 1907 and who held an official position in the government, signed an order that banned the *Szabadság* from circulation within the boundaries of that country.[95]] The same tradition exists today under the able and liberal editorial guidance of Mr. Zoltan Gombos.

Another outstanding journal with a more conservative editorial policy is the *Amerikai Magyar Nepszava* (the *American Magyar People's Voice*), founded in 1900 by Geza Berko in New York.[96] In addition to these there is a number of periodicals that serve as the official voice of the fraternal organizations — the *Verhovay Journal*, *The Fraternity*, and several labor papers.[97] In the 1940's there were something like twenty-five Hungarian papers, daily, weekly, or monthly, appearing regularly.[98] Since the first World War these journals have been fairly well united in their opposition to the Treaty of Trianon and on at least some irredentist policies; favorite targets of wrath are the Czechs and the Rumanians, both of whom gained from that treaty at the expense of Hungary.[99] On other issues they have been more divided, particularly in their attitude toward labor and radical movements, though most of them favored a fourth term for President Roosevelt.[100]

During the early part of World War II, the great majority of Hungarian newspapers in the United States advocated an isolationist policy.[101] As the war progressed, more and more of them became openly anti-Hitler,[102] although they naturally expressed satisfaction when Germany showed sympathy for their desire to regain lost lands in Europe. During the same period many of the Magyar newspapers also declared forcibly their opinion that the United States was not winning the war to give Bolshevism a chance in Europe.[103] The alien registration enforced during the war period was regarded

* Pronounced Sobudshog.

as especially un-American by the Hungarian press,[104] and the labor papers particularly were aroused to the plight of Negro and Japanese Americans and urged more substantial justice for both groups as a part of the national effort toward unity.[105]

While political policies were regarded as of primary importance, there were many columns of purely local or immediate interest — church and lodge news, names of financial contributors to churches, and discussions of the obligations of naturalization and citizenship.[106] World War II seemed to have a broadening influence on the topics given space in these newspapers: more columns were devoted to such items as social security, the health of the community, the future of youth, social planning, conservation, and world unity achieved through international cooperation.[107] More and more the Hungarian press has reflected the main currents of American life even though it be through the medium of the Magyar language and expressed in terms familiar to the Hungarian community.

One contribution of the Hungarian colony to American journalism must not be forgotten though it occurred in the later years of the nineteenth century. It was the life and labors of Joseph Pulitzer, who came to the United States in 1864 penniless and without knowledge of English. By 1876 he had become a state Congressman in Missouri. In 1883 he bought the New York *World*, which had lost most of its financial support, and made it a newspaper with a national reputation. Though his methods were the rough and ready ones of the age in which he lived, he finished his life as one of the foremost journalists in the United States. He left in his will a bequest of $2.5 million as the nucleus of a fund that established the Pulitzer School of Journalism at Columbia University.[108]

ACCULTURATION AND HYBRIDIZATION OF CUSTOM

Perhaps the most marked change that has come about in Hungarian institutions has had to do with the church. In Europe it was supported directly by the state, whereas in the United States it had to be maintained by voluntary contributions. Religious freedom as instituted by the Hungarian reform of 1894 did not mean freedom of worship for the individual but the official recognition of various religious groups or denominations by the government. This official approval could be given or withheld, but as soon as it was given, the government would collect a head tax through the religious organization and then take over responsibility for support as a direct result of this recognition.[109]

An interesting sequel to this European policy was the fact that the Protestant branch called the Reformed Church retained its ties to the home church in Hungary; as long as it was simply an integral element of the Reformed Church in Hungary, it was supported from Budapest. As late as 1915, Schaeffer reported that there were twenty-two ministers for Hungarian congregations in the United States who had their salaries paid by the Hungarian government; these congregations had an aggregate membership of 16,000 members.[110] Eventually the Reformed group split into two main divisions: the so-called Free Hungarian Reformed Church, which kept to the older Hungarian controls; and the Reformed Church in America, already organized in the United States, to which Hungarian elements attached themselves.[111] For the most part, all support from abroad ended with the close of World War I.[112]

The Catholic church, however, was organized in a different way, and any Hungarian Catholic congregation immediately had to fit itself into the American diocesan organization. Lutheran congregations also joined synods of their respective territories in America. Neither of these received any support from abroad; they had to make more immediate adjustments to a regime of voluntary contributions.

In America many of the peasant customs were continued not for their own sake, as in Hungary, but for the more utilitarian purpose of supporting the church financially, of erecting new churches, or of paying off church debts.[113] The old vintage festival or *szüreti mulatság* was used in this way under urban conditions, while in Europe it was a part of rural harvest merrymaking.[114] Of course the church is not the only institution to make use of this old festival, for it is one of the most common observances in the Hungarian colony; but the most important function of it today is commercial. The older forms have largely remained but the meaning has changed. The same can be said of the *Bethlehemesek* for which boys parade at Christmas singing carols. The Hungarian churches of Detroit have utilized the occasion for taking up contributions and thus helping swell the income for church purposes, although this was not a part of the old custom in Hungary.[115] The so-called *Kirandulas* or festive picnic to the woods, which was a simple time of fun and jollity in the home country, has become one of the major occasions for commercial enterprise in the American Hungarian colony.[116]

Two of the older customs remaining that do not seem to be used for commercial purposes are the *locsolodas* or Easter Monday celebration, when boys sprinkle girls of their acquaintance with water or perfume, and the *disznotor* or the ceremonial feast after a pig is killed.[117]

More and more, these traditional forms are being lost and their place taken by large celebrations under the auspices of fraternal organizations and churches in which there is a varying mixture of customary observances. Probably the best known celebration of this kind is the annual festival in Kennywood Park near Pittsburgh, a kind of Hungarian Mardi Gras in which many of the old practices are revived, with extensive programs, speeches, Hungarian music, and dancing, especially the *csárdás*. Thousands of Hungarians attend this celebration every year.[118]

VARIABLES IN CLASS STATUS

It has already been remarked that many of the later arrivals from Hungary have come from the intelligentsia. In many respects they have found the adjustment to American life less difficult and have become quickly absorbed into the American community. But it would be a mistake to conclude that the change took place automatically or uniformly for the group as a whole. If the newcomer were a physician or a mechanical engineer, it is usually correct to infer that he would be quickly assimilated. On the other hand, if he were a lawyer, bookkeeper, town clerk, army officer, or educator, it was often a serious problem to find some place in the American scene where his special skill or training could be used to advantage economically.[119]

The consciousness of status which the professional or intellectual brought from Europe often would not allow him to enter an occupation which might be more lucrative but would mean taking a lower place in the social scale. For example, a former lawyer who could not transfer his special knowledge of old Hungarian law to the American environment, was given an opportunity to earn excellent wages in a factory. He could not bring himself to do so, for he would not only have had to take a position lower in the scale than he was accustomed to, but he would also have had to work beside a former peasant. This would have meant a definite loss of self-respect.[120] As a result he took a clerical position that paid him far less.

The European habit of mind decrees that the intellectual should not do manual labor but is entitled to gain a living from those who do labor with their hands. This belief is too deeply ingrained to relinquish at short notice and replace by the less rigid and more democratic casual attitude of the American toward earning a livelihood.[121] Many professionals from Hungary have been able to find employment with newspapers, in steamship offices, private banks, real estate offices, and insurance agencies, and yet many of them report themselves disappointed or disillusioned.[122]

In Hungary the intellectual classes could depend on two unalterable conditions of the status system: a social distance between them and the *nép* or common people which gave them an unquestioning respect from laborers, peasants, and artisans; and secondly, a fixed position below the aristocracy, to whom they also were forced by the rigidities of the system to pay a similar if somewhat grudging respect. In America both of these conditions disappeared and were replaced by a mobility of status in which anyone could forge ahead on the basis of merit. As the intellectual's position vis-à-vis the lower classes became relative rather than absolute, it served to release the long repressed hostilities of the working class.

In the new environment the intellectual no longer had the protected and secure position he formerly enjoyed. A Hungarian laborer might show a certain amount of deference to a Hungarian engineer in a factory, but in social life he might take any occasion to harm the white collar manager or blacken his reputation. So characteristic is this situation that a Hungarian engineer once reported he would advise his personnel manager not to hire "Hunkies" because if they came into the plant, they would "do me dirt" at the earliest opportunity.[123] Thus American conditions have intensified the social distance between the intellectuals and the laboring classes, with the former tending to mingle almost entirely with native-born Americans and to shun the Hungarian community except on special occasions. In fact if a Hungarian doctor who has received his training abroad turns for clients to the Magyar colony in America, it is a sign of failure or an admission of defeat.[124] The truly successful work only with Americans and regard this as a mark of their success.

Perhaps the most "successful" of the Hungarian professionals are engineers, artists, doctors, or musicians (and rarely professors) who have been fortunate in finding a ready place for their skills in American society. Their unquestioned ability and the fact that they move in upper middle class circles where the possession of an accent may be an asset rather than a liability, have served to keep them insulated from the great bulk of lower class Hungarians in the United States.

On the other hand, there is a tiny colony of Hungarian émigrés in New York gathered around the figure of Ferenc Molnar, the most famous Hungarian playwright. These intellectuals, journalists, film and theatrical producers, and musicians seem to remain chiefly within their own circle and are satisfied with this adjustment. A large number of them are refugees from the Nazi policy which was gradually adopted in Hungary up to and including the early part of World War II.[125] But they have no influence in the other Hungarian colonies and do not have many contacts with native Americans either.

In general the professional groups found that, if successful, they were already included near the top of the social scale. There was no clearly defined class above them, as in Hungary, with the possible exception of the very wealthy whose positions were vague and ambiguous. Social climbing has thus taken up a large share of their activities, although it is not too successful and does not usually enable them to reach the top of the ladder.[126] But this tendency is in turn influential on those farther down the status scale in the Hungarian community.

As for the second generation young men, they show two marked tendencies, one downward and one upward. In the former case they turn toward unskilled labor of the kind that brings quick returns and high wages; in the latter they tend in smaller numbers to prepare themselves for the professions. Very few of them show a predilection for skilled labor to the degree found in the first generation group.[127] When they do enter the professional group, they rise from the laboring class and have practically no contact with the Hungarian professionals who come from Europe. At the same time they do not like to associate too much with working-class elements because they feel that they have little in common with them after attaining a higher education. Many of them accept marginal status and mingle with others of their own kind. One, reported by Beynon, took a law degree and then set up a firm in which his partners were both second generation men from other nationalities, one Italian and one Belgian, both sons of laborers.[128] Others find their way into the American community, though perhaps not so high on the status ladder as their compatriots from Hungary. Many of them get a good deal of their practice from the colony at first and thus are constrained to become a part of it, while others gradually sever all connection with Hungarians. A few work their way to positions of high responsibility in political or community activity and are accepted by both groups. On the whole, Hungarians have had little political success as a group and often do not vote for their own candidates.[129]

One thing is certain: the Hungarian in the United States has a highly sensitive status consciousness, or what Remenyi calls "an overstressed conception of . . . dignity of social standing."[130] Much of this is simply transplanted from Hungary into an atmosphere of mobility which allows it free play. A good deal of it is emphasized by the women, who have a higher position in the home than is true of most ethnic groups.[131] They have taken very naturally to the American middle class tendency which gives the woman a position of social responsibility in the home and community, especially as an arbiter of social standing, etiquette, manners, and "making the society page." It is therefore interesting to note the report that there is more intermarriage between Hungarian girls and American boys than between Hungarian boys and American girls, for this seems to be a natural way for the woman to seek a higher status and to raise her position more quickly.[132]

Basically the Hungarians, even the partially assimilated ones, are still an emotional people with a strong sense of honor. Steiner claims that they are less industrious than the Slavs but more intelligent and quick to turn the occasion to their own advantage.[133] Proud of their history and traditions and of the unique place they hold among the polyglot nations of Central Europe, they bring with them a natural dignity which is self assured. Endowed with a passionate love of the arts, music, dancing, and the theater, they have a phrase, *sirva vigad a magyar*, which means "The Magyar's good time is in a tearful laughter." [134] This is true on all levels of society and distinguishes the Magyar from all other ethnic groups.

THE WAR AND ITS AFTERMATH

The second World War placed a considerable strain upon the Hungarian communities in the United States. Since 1918 most of them have been revisionists and nationalists, demanding that the Treaty of Trianon be modified. Hence the promise of the Nazis when they came to power, that many areas would be given back to Hungary, furnished great impetus to Hungarian patriotic feelings in the United States. Although many if not most of the American Magyars were anti-Nazi, they were at the same time prorevisionist and hence tended to excuse the making of "peace" with Germany. This meant that divided loyalties were common and factionalism was intensified; some defended everything the Nazis did, while others, though agreeing that restoration of their areas in eastern Europe was a good move, thought it would be hopeless for Hungary to join with Germany in fighting Yugoslavia or Russia. One *bon mot* that was coined to express the situation in which the Magyars were acceding to the will of the Germans (and yet hoping to outwit them in the end) was, "A Hungarian will sell his country out, but he won't deliver it." That was undoubtedly the way the matter appeared not only to those in Hungary but to Magyars in America.

Perhaps the hardest blow came when Hungarian troops were put into positions of special danger or impending disaster facing the Russians and many thousands of them were slaughtered or taken prisoner — all this in a fight which many if not most Hungarians considered was properly Germany's and not their own. The Magyars in America felt the tragedy of their home country caught in a trap. Today, with their land occupied by Communists and many of their cities in ruins, particularly Budapest, it is felt that the old Hungary is dead. The roots of nostalgia are largely cut, and those who love the old country find themselves hanging in mid-air, culturally speaking. This condition has led to a good deal of tragic cynicism or numbness of feeling, a more devastating experience than the sharp battle of partisanship for which the Hungarian was well prepared.

The Magyars of America now feel that whatever their countrymen in Europe may do, there is little or no hope for them. Although suffering in the homeland has led to an intensification of relief activities, it has also meant, paradoxically, a more poignant awareness of their good fortune in being Americans. Thus it may serve as another, if tragic, influence toward a more complete Americanization.

[CHAPTER 15]

The Yugoslav American: *Exponent of Group Survival*

"PAUL, ARE YOU SURE those men are all right? After all, we have only Antun's word for it."

Mrs. Julinac spoke mildly but there was anxiety in her tone.

"Of course I know," her husband replied angrily. "Don't they come from Djavoko? And wouldn't Antun find out all he could? After all, he came from Vinkovci and that was only a few miles away. He says he knew everyone in Djakovo. How could he miss?"

"But you never told me about any relatives in Djakovo when we were in Croatia and I thought you described them all pretty well."

"If I've told you once, I've told you a dozen times that these cousins are on Franjo's side of the family and you've certainly heard me speak of Franjo. All we know is that his branch was off there somewhere in southern Slavonia. We haven't heard from them in years but they must be there because Franjo said they were. He often spoke of them when we were in Croatia. And now some of them are turning up, that's all. Antun lived near them and testifies that they're my cousins. That's enough for me."

"Well," Mrs. Julinac hesitated. "Perhaps it will be all right. But it does seem odd that so many of your relatives appear every year or two. And when they come, you have to be responsible for them. I have to put them up and feed them for several weeks till they get settled for themselves. I wouldn't mind so much for myself if it weren't for Joey and Dora. They say they can't get any studying done while our greenhorns are here. You want our children to do well in school, don't you, Paul?"

"In school, in school, do you say? When I was their age I could take care of the sheep and goats by myself. I could plow the field and seed it, take care of the oxen, and serve with the militia now and then. What can they do? Read books. What else? Nothing, so far as I can see. Josip hasn't earned a dime since he's been in high school. He always has to go out and play football. Is that an accomplishment? Where we came from, games were for children. If Josip doesn't like it, send him to me. Why shouldn't we take care of our own blood when they come to this land as strangers and depend on us? Have they got anywhere else to turn? Would we want somebody outside the family to help them and have them say that their own cousin wouldn't turn a finger for them? Sure the children can't read their precious books while they're here; if they want to study, let them go to the library or some place where they can get away. To hear them talk, you would think that hearing Croatian was a burden. They don't feel at home right here in our own house that we've saved fifteen years to buy so that they could be comfortable. If they can't have any family feeling, it's up to us. Maybe it doesn't hurt Dora either to do a little extra work around the kitchen for members of her own family line. She could learn a thing or two about family pride and sticking together. That's something apparently that America hasn't taught her. I sometimes wonder if America doesn't destroy it. Where will we be if our family loyalty disappears? Will you tell me that?"

"Well, maybe you're right, Paul. I only know that both Dora and Joey come to me and I don't always know what to tell them. But do you have any plans for Stjepan, Miha, and Jakov? Where will they work? What can they do?"

"Antun says that Jakov is a good carpenter, that he worked for the *gazda* in Djakovo. And Frank told me last week that two of their best cabinet makers at the Godwin Company were killed in an auto accident last week. They both learned their trade in Slavonia. If Jakov can't do as well as either of them, I'd be very much surprised. He should be able to get in there. As for Stjepan and Miha, I'll take them over to the foundry myself. Do you remember when I took Natko down there and they asked me where they could get more workmen like him? I told them then," and here Mr. Julinac grinned broadly, "that I couldn't promise anything until some more of my relatives turned up. Well, here they are. I know they can put on some more unskilled men right now and the foreman will put them on if I say so. So don't worry your head about it, Olga. They'll take care of themselves, and before long they'll even be wanting to pay us back for the few days we've boarded them. Isn't that how it always is?"

"I guess so. Anyhow I'd better go and start to get ready. And won't it be good to hear how things are at home? I wish we could go back and visit some day."

THE DIVERSE CULTURE OF YUGOSLAVIA

The term Yugoslav means South Slav and refers to the people living between Austria and Hungary to the north and Albania and Greece to the south. This group of people are related by ties of language since the Serbo-Croat tongue with its various dialects is the common medium of expression for all.[1] Although social and cultural ties have existed between different elements of the South Slavs for centuries, the group as a whole was not united into a single nation until after World War I when their country was brought together under its present name. From the time of the early Christian era Slavs have occupied this territory, although for most of that period they have been under foreign domination. For the sake of convenience they may be regarded as three main branches, the Serbs, Croatians, and Slovenes from the areas of Serbia, Croatia, and Slovenia.

Serbia occupies the southeastern part of the whole, the Serbs proper having migrated to their present home in the fourth and fifth centuries of our era.[2] Within Serbia there are subordinate or secondary states such as Bosnia, Herzegovina, Montenegro, and a part of Macedonia. Extending from the Hungarian border on the northeast to the Adriatic on the southwest is the section known as Croatia, which includes the states of Slavonia, the Banat-Batchka, and Dalmatia. The original people of Croatia were likewise Slavs, driven south from the Carpathians somewhat later. In fact their name for themselves was Carpati or Hrvati, and in the latter form it is still used today.[3] Finally, in the northwest corner bordering on Austria to the north and Italian territory to the west is Slovenia, which contains the provinces of Carniola, Carinthia, and Styria. Before Yugoslavia was united, each of these three areas had its own capital city: Belgrade in Serbia (now the capital of the country as a whole), Zagreb in Croatia, and Ljubljana in Slovenia.

Any understanding of Yugoslav migration to the United States must take into account the peculiar contribution of Dalmatia, which, while it is usually counted with Croatia proper, is distinguished by a unique history from all other South Slav countries. Whatever the official designation may be, the Dalmatian himself is more likely to claim that he is a Serb than a Croatian if he finds himself in a group who are unfamiliar with the geography of Dalmatia.[4] Otherwise he insists on being recognized as a Dalmatian. Location on the eastern shore of the Adriatic has resulted in maritime occupations that have brought Dalmatia into contact first with Venice and then Italy and other countries of Europe or the Western world. In general this has given Dalmatia an atmosphere of cosmopolitanism not to be found in other parts of South Slav territory. Unlike their countrymen, the Dalmatians are not tied to the soil but know the freedom of the seas. Even though their immigration has not been massive, it has usually been far more influential in leadership than its size would indicate. As a matter of fact, Dalmatia and its contribution to America have been of greater significance on the whole than Serbia, even though in Yugoslavia itself Serbia is of prime importance.

The three major areas of Yugoslav territory have been under the domination of different political regimes, and this has served to differentiate their historical development. The Serbs have been the warriors of the South Slavs and theirs is a bloody history. As early as the eleventh century they established a unified state. By the fourteenth century their kingdom spread from the Danube on the north to the city of Salonica on the Aegean. Following this period Serbia was rent by internal struggles and so weakened that it was forced to succumb to the Turks in the battle of Kossovo (1389) when the entire southern part of the country came under Turkish rule for six centuries.[5] In the meantime the border between northern and southern Serbia became the scene of constant guerilla warfare between Turks and Serbs. By 1815 an independent Serbian kingdom was again established but intermittent warfare did not cease. Both the Serbs and some of the Croatians on the boundary next to the Turks were under military rule and had to be subject to call for the militia at all times. This naturally did not help to develop regular habits of labor among the men; it glorified military virtues at the expense of the agricultural or pastoral.[6] Complicating the picture, Austria penetrated into Serbia during the seventeenth century but later retreated as the Turkish dominions dwindled and the Serbians became dominant again. Serbia became the ground of contention between Austria and Turkey, and both sides employed her guerillas for their own advantage.[7] Since Serbia has extensive mountain regions, groups of brigands called *hajduks* formed outlaw bands in the Robin Hood manner. While their valor and bravery helped to establish the Serbian kingdom, their excesses also glorified violence.[8]

At all events, three chief results of their cultural experience have been (1) continuing contact with the East more than the West, (2) intensifying of clannishness and heroics, and (3) retaining both the Orthodox faith and the Cyrillic alphabet as a part of their social patterns. On the whole they have been more pronounced nationalists than other Yugoslav groups and have had more illiteracy. Even by 1939 it was reported that the Serbs were 60 per cent illiterate, while the Croats had a rate of 28 per cent and the Slovenes 5.5 per cent.[9]

Croatia, on the other hand, has had a somewhat different historical experience. It had a monarchy of its own from the eleventh to the twelfth century but in 1102, because of internal squabbles, elected Koloman the Magyar as king. His title was King of Hungary and Croatia. Later on, the final loss of national independence came with the Hungarian King Lajos or Louis in the fourteenth century.[10] From this time, Croatia was a sister state with Hungary and had a nominal equality which was often fictional. By 1868 Vienna forced the Hungarian-Croatian compromise, which gave Croatia a kind of political, educational, and juristic autonomy while her economic life and finances were managed from Budapest.[11] After this Croatia was not completely Germanized or Magyarized and used her own language in the educational system even though advancement often depended on speaking Magyar or German.

From the medieval period, the Croatians adopted the Roman Catholic faith and thus kept in contact with Western traditions and culture. From the Middle Ages until the twentieth century the intelligentsia was familiar with Latin and Western culture, though the peasants on the whole received it at second hand or not at all.[12] Although Croatia was able to keep some of her aristocracy, her economic vassalage to Hungary hindered her industrial development. The Magyars fixed railroad rates, tariffs, and taxes in their own favor so that industry was centered at Budapest. Up to 1914 Croatia received 44 per cent of her taxes back from the Hungarian capital for internal control of justice and education while the rest went into a so-called joint treasury wholly controlled by the Magyars.[13] An example of the economic difficulties under this arrangement was the Hungarian railroad system, which charged as much for freight from Zagreb to Fiume as from Budapest to Fiume though Zagreb was about halfway between the two points.[14] One Croatian official expressed it to Miss Balch in true peasant language by the phrase, "Our pockets are in Hungarian trousers."[15]

Slovenia, on the other hand, was directly under Austrian control. In the early Middle Ages the Slovenes ruled about half of what later became Austria — up to the Danube on the north and over to the Brenner Pass on the west. In the late eighth century Charles the Great conquered the Slovenes, killed off the aristocracy, and colonized the area with Germans. They thus became an integral part first of the Holy Roman Empire and later of the Austrian Empire. In general the Slovenes have been the Slavic bridge between the West and the southeast Balkans.[16] For centuries the Germans tried to assimilate these Slavs, whom they contemptuously called *Völkerdünger* (ethnic manure) or *Völkersplitter* (ethnic fragments),[17] and would have succeeded if it had not been for the fact that the brief interlude of Napoleon's conquest in 1809 created a new Slavic province called Illyria with its capital city at Ljubljana. There is a Napoleon Square in Ljubljana to this day, with a statue commemorating the province of Illyria. This included not only Slovenia and Dalmatia but parts of Croatia and Serbia as well. Today it is considered by the South Slavs as a true forerunner of the unity of Yugoslavia.

Although the Illyrian province lasted only until 1817, it gave the Slavs of this area a brief respite from Germanization and a chance to revive the use of their own language. Its stimulus to nationalistic feeling among the Slovenes was at least enough to stiffen resistance to Germanization under the later rule of Austria.[18] In order to complete this process, by separating Slav from Slav,[19] Austria divided Slovenia into six different areas with six separate Diets. In only one of these, Carniola, did the Slovenians command a majority in the Diet, but they did not have real control over the school system. This was still largely German, though some concessions were made.[20] The feeling of unity with other South Slavs, however, became more pronounced in the nineteenth century.

CULTURAL PATTERNS OF THE YUGOSLAVS

Although feudalism as an official system was largely gone by the nineteenth century, the customs and habits engendered by it did not disappear so easily. In Serbia, Croatia, and Slovenia, as in most of the Balkan countries, there were two main class divisions, fractionated into smaller groups: there were the *gospoda* or masters, and the *narod* or common people. For the most part this was a division between city men and peasants. These two groups gave each country two modes of existence, two economies, two sets of customs, and two moral codes. The result was often two social worlds at war with one another, with feelings of superiority, honor, or arrogance in the upper class, and resignation, fatalism, or fierce resentment occasionally boiling to the surface in the lower. Truly it was a schizoid culture.[21] The feeling of the peasant toward his urban masters is summed up in a Serbian proverb, "The nearer a city the closer to the devil." [22]

During the nineteenth century the upper class in Serbia was subdivided four ways. All but the top layer existed in Croatia and Slovenia as well. (1) The ruling dynasty and its hangers-on of soldiers and merchants (actually there were two dynasties struggling for supremacy). (2) The army and the police force or gendarmerie — professional soldiers working now for one dynasty and now for another, often at the behest of foreign intrigue and influence after the familiar Balkan tradition. (3) Townspeople of the upper middle class such as professionals, intelligentsia, priests, state employees, and merchants. (4) Village merchants and moneylenders from leading peasant families, usually picked by the government to support the regime.[23] Sometimes in the latter group was the *gazda* or rich peasant (in Russian terms, the *kulak*) who acted as intermediary for the government and turned in confidential reports on the peasants to officials of the regime.[24] The *gazda* differed from other peasants in adopting the culture of unlimited acquisition which was really a part of urban rather than of peasant life.

Since the great majority of the emigrants coming to the United States were of peasant stock, it will be useful to survey briefly the conditions under which they lived. Even by 1918 it was estimated that about 75 per cent of the Slovenians engaged in peasant agriculture, and some 78 per cent of the Croatians.[25] In the early twentieth century something like 82 per cent of the Croatians were engaged in agriculture, chiefly on small plots of land. Out of 400,000 properties, only 930 were medium in size and only 209 large.[26]

The ancient family pattern of the South Slavs was the *zadruga* or communal household. It was really a consanguine family with authoritarian rule and communal distribution. At the head of this large family unit was the patriarchal ruler, the *gospodar* or *stareshina* (the old man). His wife or some other elected woman was the *domachitza* who managed domestic matters while the *stareshina* exerted his authority over the agricultural labor of the household. The patriarch lived in the central house with the other homes of the settlement built nearby. The entire enlarged family, however, ate at the patriarch's house, the men eating together and the women afterward. In one of the homesteads a single large room would be set aside for all the unmarried girls of the family in a kind of dormitory. The usual number of individuals in a *zadruga* was from twenty to thirty and generally it was composed of three generations. When the group became too large, it divided into smaller ones with the young women going into the husband's community. Meats, grains, eggs, and milk were owned by the *zadruga* communally and their distribution was settled by the patriarch. On the other hand, if there were any income from industrial labor, it would be individually owned and managed by the person performing the labor. Each *zadruga* would own something like forty acres or more, and frugal management made it possible to wrest a living from the soil under the strict disciplinary rule and cooperation of the group. This sort of communal living instilled in its members an intense, not to say clannish, family feeling and a habit of thinking in terms of the group rather than of the individual. Even after the breakup of the *zadruga*, a man who formerly belonged or whose family still had the old tradition might be asked, "Whose flock of sheep is that?" To which he would reply, "Ours," but not "Mine." [27] The communal existence of the *zadruga* was relatively passive and the individual would find himself carried along by the group without having to exert too much initiative.[28]

With increased exhaustion of the soil, plant pests, government laws forbidding the pasturing of goats (because they damaged woodlands), laws requiring partitioning of communal property, and the increased urbanization of life, the *zadrugas* began to disappear. It was the dissolution of the *zadruga* that drove many peasants to America in the later nineteenth century, when it became impossible for many men to find available land after they were forced to leave communal households. By 1890 only a fifth of the Croatian population was living in *zadrugas*, and the number constantly dwindled.[29] Strong family solidarity, however, remained as a pronounced cultural trait in the Yugoslav, partly in the practice of hospitality which continued largely unchanged, in family pride, and in clannishness of a fierce, unwavering loyalty. Adamic remarks that nepotism is probably stronger among the Serbs than among any other people.[30]

Among the peasants another communal practice was the *molba* or a kind of "bee" in which neighbors of the same village helped each other with harvesting. It was an unwritten rule that the peasant who was helped should furnish food and drink for all the workers, and the whole affair was semirecreational. In case only two or three neighbors gave their assistance, the communal work was called a *pozajmitza*.[31] This practice of mutual aid was only one of many that led to deeply ingrained group habits of labor and recreation. Extreme poverty also led to enforced cooperation. Frequently two or more peasants owned a plow or a pair of bison together. If they wanted to use them at the same time, they threw dice to determine the outcome.[32] Or in a poor agricultural region, three men would have but one pair of shoes between them, or four men would share the same winter overcoat.[33] Sharing on a scale like this developed mutuality and cooperation as the only possible method of survival.

The South Slavs were accustomed to play together as well as work together. There were many holy days when a round of festivities broke the monotony of toil. Among the old *zadrugas* it was common to have songs and dances in the evening with the younger members of the household taking part.[34] In Serbia and Croatia the peasants joined in a dance known as the *kolo* (circle) and this, too, was a communal affair. Young men and women gathered together in a circle and, with intricate step, kept up a rhythm for hours. As in many peasant communities, the dancing was not by couples.

One writer tells of visiting Skoplye where, near the town, a *kolo* marathon was held in which the girls danced all day. (Sometimes it was even for two or three days with only occasional rest periods allowed.) Continual dancing showed how much endurance the girls had, and this quality gave them marriageability in the eyes of young men.[35] In Croatia and Slovenia music was often played by a tamburica orchestra for dancing. The tamburica is similar to the Russian balalaika and has been called "the oldest stringed instrument in use by any Christian nation." There seems to be some relation between Oriental music and the Slav music of the tamburica orchestra.[36] Slovene music shows Austrian influence while the Croatian has more Magyar gypsy melodies.

Group practices are characteristic not only of the peasants but of the mariners as well. The old custom among the fishermen near Split in Dalmatia was to distribute the proceeds of their catch, one fourth to the boat owner, another fourth to the net owner, and half to the crew.[37] This practice was so common as to constitute a principle of equity.

In the peasant regions patriarchalism was the rule. Women did most of the heavy work, milking the cow or goat, getting food for both family and animals, taking meals to the men in the fields, weaving, mending, baking, striking the laundry on a board, and the like. Often the husband would beat his wife but she could not complain. It was common for her to bear as many as ten children, half of whom died early. In the poorer farm districts, she would often give birth to her infants on a bed of straw without medical or midwife care and then return to work three days later. This meant that many of the peasant women were aged at thirty.[38]

Marriage was arranged chiefly by the parents or at least could not occur without their approval. In Slovenia the *stareshina* was the bridegroom's elder, usually a close relative, who acted as a go-between and kept on the lookout for a likely match with a girl who was a good worker and would bring a fine dowry. He might propose one name after another to the young man; but if one was accepted, it had to receive the parents' blessing. The usual procedure when the son took a wife was for the young man to take over the house of his father and continue the work of the farm, particularly when he was the oldest. The parents signed over the property to him but reserved a room in the old homestead where they could pass the rest of their days.[39] If times were prosperous, the wedding festivities would last three or four days, and otherwise hardly ever less than two.[40] As soon as a young girl could hold a needle, she was expected to start knitting to make clothes for herself and husband which would serve as a dowry.[41] In addition to all the domestic work of the household, women in the more poverty-stricken areas would have to do the plowing with tiny oxen that came up only to their waists.[42]

Since the largest number of Yugoslav immigrants came from Croatia, it may be of some value to depict the karst regions, which are the poorest sections in that country. Karst is a kind of limestone that crops up near the surface or on top of the ground, making it impossible to cultivate. In Croatia there may be mile after mile of these formations with only occasional depressions in the rock where soil can wash in and be planted. These little rounded depressions, sometimes only ten or fifteen feet in diameter, are known as *dols*. As the limestone is constantly eroded by water, many caverns are formed or rivers may disappear underground, to appear several miles away.[43]

In many villages of the karst country there is no water whatever and peasants had to haul it from a distance of one to twenty-five miles. In extreme cases it would take twenty-four hours of labor to get five gallons of water for the family or household. It was not uncommon to see men and beasts fight each other for water. This meant that people would not waste water for the purpose of keeping clean when its prime use was for drinking or cooking. One family, for example, reported to a doctor that they had no water, so they bathed "in sweat and tears."

Throughout the karst region there was often severe hunger, especially in the winter months. Many peasants had the same fare three times a day — *pura* or gruel made of ground corn. Often enough the peasant did not even eat his own corn but had to buy it at the village. Malaria, caused by mosquitoes that bred in stagnant pools, was common and tuberculosis was also of regular occurrence. The calendar of the karst peasant has been described as threefold: hunger in winter, thirst in summer, and floods in spring or fall.[44] The homes were built of rough stone with a hole in the roof instead of a chimney, and this remained closed all winter; a trap door kept out the cold. Better houses were heated with huge stoves of unglazed tile.[45] The windows in these homes were so small that, in case of fire, members of the family could not get out. Cattle were often kept in the same room with the family.[46] Most beds were simply wooden frames with straw or leaves thrown inside and a coat or rug laid over them.[47] In case there were blankets, they were of the roughest sort, Croatian blankets being "almost as shaggy as the original sheep." [48] Many of the family would sleep directly on the floor or on mats, some with stones under their heads. Linen was quite unheard of in the karst country.[49]

The religious life of the peasantry has received little attention from students of the South Slavs. It bears a close resemblance to that in the villages of Czechoslovakia and Hungary which have already been discussed. One difference is that the Orthodox Church is dominant in Serbian territory. The Croatians and Slovenes as part of the westerly division are both pre-eminently Roman Catholic; during the Reformation period, the Slovenes were greatly influenced by Protestantism and most of the Carinthians at that time became Protestants.[50] Eventually this heresy was crushed by the Hapsburgs, and since the movement was not indigenous to Slovenia as it was in Bohemia, traces of this doctrine had disappeared almost completely by the nineteenth century.[51] By the end of the first World War, 171,000 Calvinist Slovenes were reported in the western part of Hungary, but they are so small in number and so insignificant in the tide of immigration that they do not concern this study.

The strong hold of the South Slavic language, however, brought about one important difference in the Catholic ceremony which did not occur farther north: in many Yugoslav Catholic churches, mass was celebrated in the old Slavonic language, just as it was in the

Orthodox Church.[52] This did not mean that the ties with Rome were weaker. Next to the Poles and the Slovaks, the Croatians and Slovenes are perhaps strongest in the Catholic faith. As in other parts of Europe already mentioned, the Yugoslav before coming to America was not accustomed to direct support of his church by voluntary contributions.

With the forms of group and communal living permeating his life, the Yugoslav peasant had strong in-group feeling and loyalty for (1) his family and relatives, (2) his class as opposed to the rulers or city people, (3) his village, (4) his religion, (5) his language and national group. The reverse of the shield was indifference or suspiciousness, sometimes downright enmity, toward outsiders. The nature and extent of family solidarity has already been noticed.

As for class loyalty, the peasant would always play humble before any *gospodar* and affect great ignorance in order to show proper subservience. This attitude was often used in ways which eventually procured him what he wanted, much as it did in the case of the southern Negro's dealings with white bosses. It was simply a defense role which was worn whenever a member of the upper classes was present, and it served the purpose of keeping the *gospodar* at a distance. The peasant's generalization, based on experience, was that no city man ever came to him who did not want something. When the peasant got his own way by such a palpable ruse, he would share his success with his fellows amid roars of amusement.[53] When it is remembered that centuries of dealing with masters of another language and religion left their mark on the Southern Slav, it is not surprising that, for example, the Serbs developed *podvala* (deceit) to defeat the Turks or that this became customary when Serb began to rule over fellow Serb. The Kossovo songs or epics, in which the major defeat of the Serbs at the hand of the Turks was commemorated for centuries, appeared to the Moslems an incomprehensible paradox of the Slav mind, but for the Slavs they constituted a way of keeping fierce patriotism alive under threat of constant danger.[54]

Under continual social pressure, family clannishness reached an all-time high. Serbs from one region were often greatly suspicious of Serbs from another, and still more of the Croats or Slovenes.

Religious differences helped to keep this in-group feeling alive. To a certain degree conditions in Croatia and Slovenia were similar, with enmity directed against the Magyar or the Austrian as well as against each other. In Dalmatia the people were accustomed to think of Austrian taxes as oppressive and to evade them under every pretext. Smuggling was common, as was illicit tobacco raising. Tax collectors feared to go into some backward or isolated regions of Serbia because of possible violence. High taxes on alcohol made illegal liquor production popular in much of Yugoslavia. The Dalmatian fishermen of the Adriatic coast, usually at the poverty line, supplemented their income by continual shipment of contraband goods. In this way they could not only improve their economic standing but also strike at the foreign oppressor.[55]

This in-group attitude of intense loyalty has made it difficult for the three peoples to unite into a single country since World War I and has also served as a divisive force among the immigrants who came to the United States. But it must not be overrated. In the Dinaric Alps both Serbs and Croats fought together against the Turk and worked together on a basis of trust and loyalty. Their common mode of life developed similar characteristics, especially a marked impulsiveness. Their proverb is (in the language of the mountaineer), "One freezes if he thinks too long." This mixed group furnished a large share of the rebels against foreign rule.[56] Furthermore, Croatians and Slovenes, who have a common religious unity and closely related languages, have been cooperative to a marked degree both in Europe and the United States, frequently burying their differences in a common cause. All this, however, does not rule out the more natural loyalty of the Croat for his own institutions and societies, while the same may be said for the Slovene. This will appear more clearly in the discussion of the immigrant colonies below.

In spite of hard, grinding poverty, or perhaps because of it, the South Slav peasant developed art forms still appropriated by sophisticated connoisseurs in continental Europe and the United States. The Croatian peasant costume has been called the most beautiful in Europe with the possible exception of the Serbian. On holy days men and women both wore bright colors with simple but stunning designs.[57] On weekdays it was the custom of the peasants of the plains to wear white even while they were working. Their shirts and blouses were made of homespun linen for wearing qualities. Women and adolescent girls, on the other hand, wore white skirts with aprons and jackets in red, yellow, blue, and green. All this clothing was handmade by the women during the long winter evenings or when there was a lull in the housework. In addition they decorated eggs by the batik method and stitched highly intricate embroideries. Designs were distinctive for each community. For wealthy families individual designs had a significance comparable to a coat of arms elsewhere. Even in rude cottages tables, chairs, and chests would be entirely hand carved, and the beehives would be painted.[58]

Peasant music has already been mentioned; among the Serbians it became a special form of ballad sung with a *gusla* or a sort of one-stringed violin.[59] The singer who regaled his hearers with poems and sagas sung to the minor music of the *gusla* was called the *guslar;* he was usually crippled or blind. In fact the *guslar* was the authentic troubadour of Serbia, except that his purpose was to stir the people by ancient tales of military exploits and thus keep patriotic feeling alive. Pribichevich suggests that this folk poetry, like that of other peasant peoples, is the reverse shield of illiteracy and perhaps a compensation for it.[60] The same could probably be asserted for peasant art in costume, carvings, batik work, embroidery, and music. Certainly the illiteracy was there. Croatia in 1900, at the time when emigration began to increase, had 47 per cent of its men illiterate and 62 per cent of its women.[61]

Nor was this entirely avoidable. While school attendance was theoretically compulsory, homes were widely scattered and it was difficult for children to get to school before adequate transportation systems were devised. There was also a good deal of sex discrimination; parents did not care to send their girls to school but would often let the boys go. One county in 1910 listed 10,601 boys in school and 2,720 girls.[62] The large number of holy days also interfered with school attendance, cutting it still lower.[63] One significant compensation that occurred in various villages was a cooperative venture on the part of the peasants who bought a library for the community and gathered there on winter evenings to listen to some literate member of the village read to them from the writers who understood peasant life — translations of Tolstoy, Turgenev, and Dostoievski.* [64]

FACTORS INFLUENCING IMMIGRATION

The early emigration to the United States consisted chiefly of Dalmatians, who were adventurous wanderers traveling all over the globe from the seventeenth century on. It is even conjectured from the evidence that the Croatan Indians in North Carolina received their name indirectly from Yugoslav settlers on the southern coast in that century.[68] A few priests, noblemen, and refugees from Croatia and Slovenia came during the eighteenth century. The most famous priest to migrate to American shores was Bishop Baraga, a Slovene, who settled among the Chippewa Indians in the midnineteenth century, a scholar who translated the Chippewa dialect into printed form and anticipated some of the more enlightened Indian policies of today by about a century.[69]

Meanwhile many more Dalmatians kept coming in the same period, some of them settling in New Orleans and others in California.[70] The chief attraction for these early sporadic emigrants seemed to be the opportunity to ply their familiar trades in unexploited territory without excessive taxation or the need to bribe petty officials. These Yugoslavs were the first on the American continent to cultivate oyster beds and began their work in New Orleans and the Gulf of Mexico.[71] Others went to the Pacific Coast, where they engaged in deep-sea fishing, establishing themselves as the early pioneers in that occupation. In both Louisiana and the West Coast area these early settlers were called Slovanians, a name that stuck.[72]

Economic considerations stimulated the later migration as well. In the home area the mountainous coast line had been largely stripped of its forests for the piles of Venice, for ships and masts

* The reader may be interested, in passing, to know of three English words that have come into the language from the South Slavs: (1) "Argosy," meaning a cargo of exotic goods, is a corruption of Ragusa (now called Dubrovnik), the great trading port of Dalmatia during the Renaissance; (2) "cravat," which is the French word for Croat; Croatian soldiers who entered French military service in the seventeenth century wore bright-colored neckpieces and this name was eventually transferred to them; (3) "maraschino" was originally the name for a liqueur manufactured from Dalmatian cherries or *marasks*. For references to these three in order, see footnotes 65, 66, and 67.

and buildings. In the nineteenth century a great decline in shipping and commerce led to increasing privation. By 1890 the price of Dalmatian wine was badly depressed. At the same time the Phylloxera, a plant pest, destroyed many vineyards in the interior. Since wine was the chief article of export, this condition brought in its train still more misery and want. The fact that a large number of Dalmatians were traders and seamen gave them many opportunities to hear of specific openings in the United States. It is noteworthy that most Dalmatian emigrants knew precisely where they wanted to go in the new country, in contrast with other Slavs who went vaguely "to America" and made their adjustment after arrival.[73]

In Croatia several conditions helped to hasten the process of departure. Perhaps the first of these was the construction of the first railroad from Karlstadt to Fiume; this displaced a large number of workers who had transported freight by hand or with burros through the mountain passes. By the 1880's many of these displaced freight handlers began to leave for the United States.[74] In the same decade the plague of Phylloxera laid waste many of the old vineyards just as it did in Dalmatia. An abatement of the pest was followed by further invasions in 1900 and 1901.[75] Poverty and overpopulation increased, and the lot of the peasant was not improved by the government regulation prohibiting goat raising. Milk and milk products began to disappear from the diet, leading to a considerable loss of food and a resulting loss of vigor. Taxes were high. The peasant who attempted to improve his economic position could only go to the moneylender of the town and pay him interest of 12 per cent and more, coupled with various restrictions. Such rates kept the borrower constantly in debt.[76]

After some immigration had begun, word of comparatively high wages in the United States began drifting back to Croatia. In the 1870's and 1880's a number of Yugoslavs went to Michigan and northern Minnesota for work in the iron and copper mines.[77] A good many returned home with their savings. To many families it then appeared that sending one member to America might be the only way in which the rest could manage to survive. As one school teacher wrote of the emigration process, Croatia was not free nor in charge of her own national finances and was therefore forced to allow her young men to migrate to a land of strangers in order that the families who remained behind might continue to exist.[78] Income from abroad might make the difference between starvation and satisfactory living.

Matters in Slovenia were essentially similar to those in Croatia, except that depressed conditions were highly concentrated in the indigenous Slavic portions such as Carniola. There was little emigration from Carinthia or Styria where there were more Germans or Austrians, but some districts of Carniola lost as much as 12 per cent of their population in a few years. Among all the Slavic migrants, only the Slovaks show a comparable record.[79] In the ten years from 1893 to 1903 something like 30,500 Slovenes from Carniola left for America, and less than one in fifty of these was female.[80]

NUMBER AND DISTRIBUTION

The United States Census did not report separate nationality immigration of the South Slavs until 1908; before that time all were listed under the general title of Austro-Hungarians.[81] Following the estimate made by J. S. Roucek (which includes Bulgarians, whose number was so small as to cause little inaccuracy) it appears that the number of Yugoslavs entering the United States in the nineteenth century and up to 1930 was 778,877. Many of these returned to their home country, however, so that it is more accurate to give the net figure after 343,935 migrated back. This would leave 434,942; about 98,215 dead and 12,000 Bulgarians should not be counted, which leaves a total of 323,677 by 1930 (in round numbers 325,000). As there has been relatively little migration from Yugoslavia since 1930 as a result of immigration restrictions, this is perhaps the most accurate figure for the first generation in the United States.[82] Ivan Mladineo estimates about 334,500 for the second generation. This brings the total of parents and American-born children to 659,500. If the round number of 700,000 is taken as relatively accurate, it may be broken down into subtotals of 345,000 for the Croatians, 295,000 for the Slovenians, and 60,000 for the Serbians.[83] It is important to note that the dominance of the Serbs, both politically and numerically in Europe, has been reversed in the immigrant colonies. Political hegemony in Europe lessened the need to migrate because of foreign oppression.

The states with the largest number of Yugoslavs are, in order:

Pennsylvania, Ohio, Illinois, Michigan, and New York. Chicago has the most of any urban center, though this honor is also claimed by Pittsburgh. The largest Serb colony is in Pittsburgh. Croatians have their two largest groups in Pittsburgh and Chicago. Cleveland contains the greatest number of Slovenes.[84] A smaller group are employed in the Detroit region, working in auto industries. Something like 40 per cent of the Yugoslavs have been absorbed into mining, chiefly in Pennsylvania. There are a few farm settlements in Minnesota, Colorado, and California.[85]

GROUP ADJUSTMENT TO AMERICAN LIFE

With the exception of the few who settled in Minnesota, Colorado, and California, the great mass of the Yugoslavs came too late to share in the development of agriculture and went directly to industrial and mining areas. Since they came chiefly from peasant areas, few of them had training that would equip them to begin their labor in any skilled category. The Immigration Commission reported in 1906 that 91 to 96 per cent of the Croat immigrants were unskilled.[86] Slovenians and Serbs were essentially similar. They thus began on the lowest level of manual labor because of the language handicap and the American prejudice against foreigners. A few more ambitious tradespeople, especially the Dalmatians, entered the liquor or food business.[87]

True to their background and culture patterns, the Yugoslavs began their initial period with group practices that reinforced the weakness of the individual. A sample colony in the city of New York showed the characteristic cooperation and toleration. Men who migrated without wives or children lived together in groups of relatives or of those who came from the same village and were known to each other at home.[88] A typical organization was found in boardinghouses with male cooks. These households were cooperative, and the name given to each was the *drustvo* (club). Having little or no social contact with native English-speaking Americans or exploited when they did have by employers or politicians, the Yugoslavs declared that they could not board in the American way, each man on his own. This habit was too lonely and thus appeared psychologically impossible to them. Living in the *drustvo* was "more like home." Expenses were equally divided and social intercourse was based on familiar language and ideals. Money disputes were rare since each man had been trained in modes of communal living and seldom questioned the levies which he knew were necessary.[89]

In general there were three types of *drustvo:* (1) those with a male house-boss who was paid for cooking, cleaning, and managing the household; (2) those without a house-boss, where the work was done cooperatively and the men took turns at various jobs; (3) boardinghouses influenced by American standards and headed by a man and his wife who shared the management problems while the wife did the major share of domestic labor.[90] The Serbo-Croatians in the *drustvo* did a great deal of personal borrowing from each other, but it was a point of honor to repay.[91] This system also developed in St. Louis very early; the food bill would be equally divided and the boarder would pay a flat sum of $3 a month for laundry expense. Here the *drustvo* was modeled more after the American pattern with husband and wife in charge (his title being the *burtimbas* and hers the *burtimbasica*). The dominant couple could always make a slight additional profit by purchasing a keg of beer, bottling it, and selling it for ten cents a bottle.[92]

These early colonies around the turn of the century were composed almost entirely of men, and the boardinghouse type of living in a one-sex community undoubtedly encouraged a certain amount of promiscuity.[93] If, however, there were women cooking for the *drustvo,* they were universally respected as members of the in-group.[94] Quarreling and feuding among members of different families or different groups were fairly common, and there was a certain amount of violence. Since the colony was often socially isolated from the rest of the community, a good deal of this conflict passed unnoticed, especially because notifying the police was regarded with abhorrence.[95] Experience with the police in Europe engendered suspicions that took decades to overcome in America.

Women began to appear in the colonies in greater numbers about 1904. Like the Poles and some other Slavic groups, the young male Croatian would often send back to the homeland for a girl he had never seen, on the basis of his parents' choice. His only way to get her was to pay for her passage, and sometimes the young woman might be unwilling to complete the bargain on arrival. In that case she was obligated to return the money for the fare. If some other youth could be found who was acceptable to her, it was customary for him to pay it and thus settle the problem.[96] It was common practice for the males who came to America from the 1880's to 1900 to send home as much as 80 per cent of their wages. As standards of living rose, however, this was gradually reduced until it reached a figure of around 20 per cent.[97]

With the increased number of women in the communities, family life took on more stability and permanency. At the same time the shortage of women favored a considerable number of marriages outside the group. Mihanovich shows that the marriages at the largest Croat church in St. Louis from 1904 to 1935 indicated that 43.2 per cent married foreign-born Croats, 25.7 per cent married native-born Croats of foreign parentage, and 30 per cent married native Americans of other groups.[98] This is probably not unrepresentative of the Yugoslavs as a whole in the United States, though we are handicapped by the lack of accurate studies. Families still followed the patriarchal pattern with a large number of children and an intimacy of relationship that partly reflected social distance from native American homes.[99] This was combined with extensive neighboring within the Slav colony itself.[100]

For the most part the Croatians and other Yugoslavs do not allow their wives to work outside the home because this reflects on the ability of the husband.[101] With regard to younger girls, the customs are more diverse. In Cleveland, Slovenian girls were hired in large numbers for work in a hardware factory and seem to have been allowed considerable freedom.[102] In San Pedro, on the other hand, where Dalmatian fishermen live in large numbers, families would attend dances as a unit and mothers would insist on chaperoning their daughters home. No dates were allowed. Girls married young and the parents preferred not to have them marry "American boys."[103] This may be partly due to the Italian influence among the Dalmatians or to the fact that both Italians and Dalmatians shared a common culture around the shores of the Adriatic. The greater freedom generally characteristic of the Dalmatians seems to apply in greater degree to men than to women.

Group practices were carried over in other ways. Fishermen along the California coast revolutionized the tuna fish industry by introducing large boats during the first World War. Thousands of Yugoslav immigrants have joined their compatriots since 1921, and they carry on their activities in group fashion. Two or three boats go together to Mexico, the Gulf of California, or even as far as Peru for fish. The old method of dividing the catch, already noted, is carried over bodily to the American scene. In addition, the boat owners, who are the upper class or masters, organize themselves into a cooperative which handles business transactions for the individual member, thus taking this responsibility off his hands.[104]

There are also the many mutual benefit societies on the pattern familiar in other cultural groups, scattered from New York to California. These local groups eventually formed into national associations or federations, the Slovenes first in 1904 with the Slovene National Benefit Society (Slovenska Narodna Podporna Jednota), then the Croatian Fraternal Union (Hrvatska Bratska Zajednica) in 1925, and four years later the Serb National Federation (Srpski Narodni Savis).[105] One of the chief motives of these organizations was to prevent the individual from being dependent on charity, a practice which the Yugoslav with his folkways of mutuality heartily detests.[106] They are primarily insurance companies with social and athletic programs for mutual enjoyment.

Like the Hungarians and other central European groups, the leaders and members of these organizations are largely composed of first generation personnel with little formal education and without as much attention to serving younger members as the latter might wish. There is a tendency among all mutual benefit societies, Yugoslav among others, merely to hoard large savings accounts and give little service in terms of second generation needs. The question is fairly raised whether many of them are not therefore in danger of dying out with the first generation.[107] Some have revived by starting vigorous programs in English-speaking lodges for young people. At the same time their value to the older members of the community must not be overlooked. They furnish havens of refuge for like-minded individuals to renew the ties of the homeland, and their halls are the scenes of entertainments, dances, dramatic evenings, and musicals. Tamburica orchestras form a part of the regular activities in all the larger halls devoted to Yugoslav community life.

The close-knit character of the communities retains a social cohesion that serves to keep delinquency and crime to a minimum. Offenses against property are almost nonexistent and in all other categories but one the Yugoslavs have shown a very low rate. That one was violation of the liquor laws, particularly during the prohibition era. Since this was crime by legal definition, a definition which has now been withdrawn, it is to be regarded as a temporary condition. Noted already is the reaction of Serbians, Croatians, and Dalmatians against the high taxes on alcohol by an oppressive government, and resistance against it in terms of individual liquor production. The same attitude was taken toward restrictive measures in the United States so that a high ratio of violations and bootlegging existed among the Yugoslavs in Minnesota, Wisconsin, Missouri, and California. In Spokane, it is estimated that at the height of the prohibition era, something like 80 per cent of the Yugoslavs were engaged in illegal production and marketing of liquor.[108] This waned with the disappearance of the Volstead Act.

Perhaps the general attitude of the South Slav immigrant toward the whole matter of lawbreaking can be summed up in the statement that what was a crime in Serbia, Croatia, or Slovenia was regarded as a crime in the United States. What was regarded as a protest against oppression in the home country had the same status here. The only exception would be found when the unity of the group was threatened. Thus southern Dalmatians from the region of Boka Kotorska practiced the law of blood revenge in Europe; if one of them in this country heard that his brother had been killed in Yugoslavia, he might go home and get revenge after the well-recognized practice there. On the other hand, he might be living in New York or Chicago with a man who had killed a member of his family abroad and continue on friendly terms with him as long as the two were in the United States. If, however, this traditional enemy returned to Dalmatia, he would have to guard himself against possible reprisal from his onetime friend. The principle behind this is expressed in a Dalmatian proverb, "When you're in a strange world, you have to be brothers." [109]

As long as the definition of crime in the European homeland was clear cut, the immigrant felt that he did not dare commit such an act in this country, for then he would be disgraced in Yugoslavia and would not be received back as a member of his family. It was a common experience for a Serb or Croatian not to let his family hear from him if he had a prison sentence but to let them think he was dead so that they would make no further attempt to communicate with him.[110]

Big-time racketeers did not flourish in the Yugoslav colonies; as a matter of record it was the testimony of a Slovenian immigrant, Gus Korach, backed by that of many other Slovenians in Cleveland including Frank J. Lausche, later governor of Ohio, that broke one of the largest "mobs" in that city.[111] And it was Judge Anthony Lucas, a Croatian, who was primarily responsible for pushing through the first compensation law for miners in the state of Michigan after he had been an interpreter many years for the mining company.[112] The hatred for tyranny which the Yugoslav has brought with him from centuries of living under foreign rule has borne fruit in the United States.

CULTURAL AND RELIGIOUS ACTIVITIES

The national halls of the Serbs, Croats, and Slovenes are the center of innumerable clubs, associations, and organizations. Throughout the United States there are something like 128 singing societies, the most important of which is Zora (Dawn), of Chicago. In addition the Yugoslavs have organized forty dramatic societies [113] and a large number of tamburica orchestras, the most famous being the Slavonic Tamburica Orchestra of Duquesne University in Pittsburgh. It is the only college organization of its type.[114] Then there are Kolo dancers in nearly all the larger colonies.[115] Sokol societies also exist in many of the centers for the purpose of physical training.[116] The number of these Sokol organizations is small, however, in comparison with those of the Czechs whose attachment to them is more highly charged with nationalistic feeling.

From the 1880's the Yugoslavs have been publishing newspapers in their own languages for the benefit of those who have learned little English or who want to keep in touch with their own national cause and traditions. The first was the *Srbin Amerikanac* (*Serb-American*), started in San Francisco during the year 1886. The second, founded in the same city, began as *Nas Sloga* in 1892 and changed its name to *Slavjanska Sloga* in 1893. The largest newspaper printed in Serbo-Croatian today in the United States is the *Zajednicar* (*Unifier*), which is the weekly organ of the Croatian Fraternal Union in Pittsburgh. Mr. F. Vukelio is the editor. Some of the other larger newspapers are *Prosveta* (*Enlightenment*) of Chicago, *Enakoprovnost* (*Equality*) of Cleveland, and *Narodnia Glasnik* (*National Herald*) of Pittsburgh.[117] Also worthy of mention is *Hrvatski Svijet* (*World*), a Croatian daily of New York. A majority of the newspapers now carry one or more pages of English for their younger readers.[118] By 1944 there were forty-five Yugoslav publications throughout the country, of which eight are dailies.[119]

In religious activities the South Slavs show only one sign of unity in the three main groups: the celebration of the Feast of St. Cyrrilus and St. Methodius, who are credited with the conversion of the Slavs to Christianity in the ninth century of our era. Both Orthodox and Catholics observe this feast on June 7. For the most part, however, religious lines follow those of nationality and linguistic adherence. The first Yugoslav church in America (if the efforts of Bishop Baraga among the Chippewa be excepted) was founded by Slovenian farmers in Brockway, Minnesota, in 1871. Today there are eighty Roman Catholic churches, thirty-three of which are Croatian and forty-six Slovenian. The Serbs have thirty-eight Orthodox churches or parishes.[120] The parochial school, however, has not had the same strong hold on the Yugoslavs as it has on the Poles; in all, the Slovenians and Croatians have thirty-eight full-time parochial schools with about 16,000 pupils. These are divided almost equally between the two groups.[121] The Serbian Orthodox church in America is organized as a separate diocese with its own bishop in Libertyville, Illinois. He is appointed by the Serbian patriarch of Yugoslavia.[122] Only two Greek Catholic churches are reported for all the Yugoslavs in the United States.[123]

CHANGING PATTERNS IN RECENT YEARS

Since most of the Yugoslav immigrants came to the United States before World War I, the great majority of the first generation are now somewhere between fifty-five and seventy-five years of age[124] and their numbers are much smaller than those of their children. While many still belong to colonies of their own people, they are entering more fully into American patterns of life. This is especially true where their original numbers were small, in Minnesota, Colorado, Louisiana, and some of the West Coast areas. With the possible exception of the fishing communities, the Dalmatians have probably been the most quickly absorbed. There are two reasons for the rapidity of their assimilation: first, they came to America with traditions of individual initiative in enterprise and trade; second, their migration was a "long continued dripping of individuals, not a mass movement." [125] Perhaps their cosmopolitanism and familiarity with other languages may also be given some credit in the process.

As for the other groups, probably the Slovenians came to the United States with more advantages in the way of literacy and education; their entrance into business and professional occupations has thus been accelerated. In the second generation, however, the problem has not been very different for Serb, Croat, or Slovene, and the hold of the older culture on the younger members of the community is slipping away rapidly, perhaps less in the church than in the fraternal or cultural organizations. Since no scientific studies have been made of this process, these trends can be stated only as probabilities. During World War II some 50,000 second and third generation Yugoslavs served in the armed forces of the United States; this has meant still more rapid assimilation into the main stream of American life.[126]

Although all elements of the community firmly supported the cause of the United States against the Central Powers during World War I, there was not quite the same unanimity in the recent war. The division arose because of the split between Croatians and Serbs in the newly organized Yugoslavia, and a reflection of that hostility in America. During the early part of World War II many Croatians in Europe made an early peace with the Axis, and a puppet government under Pavelich was organized. Some of the Croatians in the United States supported this fascist regime while others remained loyal to the Yugoslav government-in-exile. In turn that group supported the Serbian general Mihailovich even after considerable evidence that he collaborated with the Nazis against a still newer champion of Yugoslavia, Marshal Tito. It is probably safe to say that the great majority of Croats and Slovenes in this country still believe in the integrity of Mihailovich and are strongly anti-Tito,[127] though how much of this is natural Catholic aversion to the Communism represented by Tito it is hard to say.

On the other hand a smaller group led by Louis Adamic has vigorously pressed Tito's claims not only during the war while Tito and all Communists were allies but also since the peace when continued complaints of terrorist tactics used by Tito in Yugoslavia have come to the attention of the press. Probably Adamic has been the chief leader of the United Committee of South-Slavic Americans, organized in 1943 for the purpose of giving aid to Tito against the opposition of a lukewarm press in the United States. While it may have been true that this committee brought together a large number of Yugoslavs, it seems questionable to state, as Adamic does, that this was "the majority of the Yugoslav element." [128]

Today it is more likely that the great bulk of Yugoslavs in the United States deeply regret the excesses of the Tito regime, particularly the stronger Catholics. The Serbs are also split on the issue; some of them are anti-Tito because they are anti-Croatian (Tito being a Croatian); others have a natural sympathy with Russian policies because they share the same religious culture in the Orthodox faith. Politically the divisions still exist, though they mean far more to the first than to the second generation. The latter is probably as much uninformed about the whole issue as the average American. To the native American these clashes between political opinions often look like incomprehensible Balkan intrigue, but to those who are torn by honest differences this is simply a reflection of the partisan convictions brought with them from the European homeland and the attempt to think of them simultaneously in Yugoslav and in American terms.

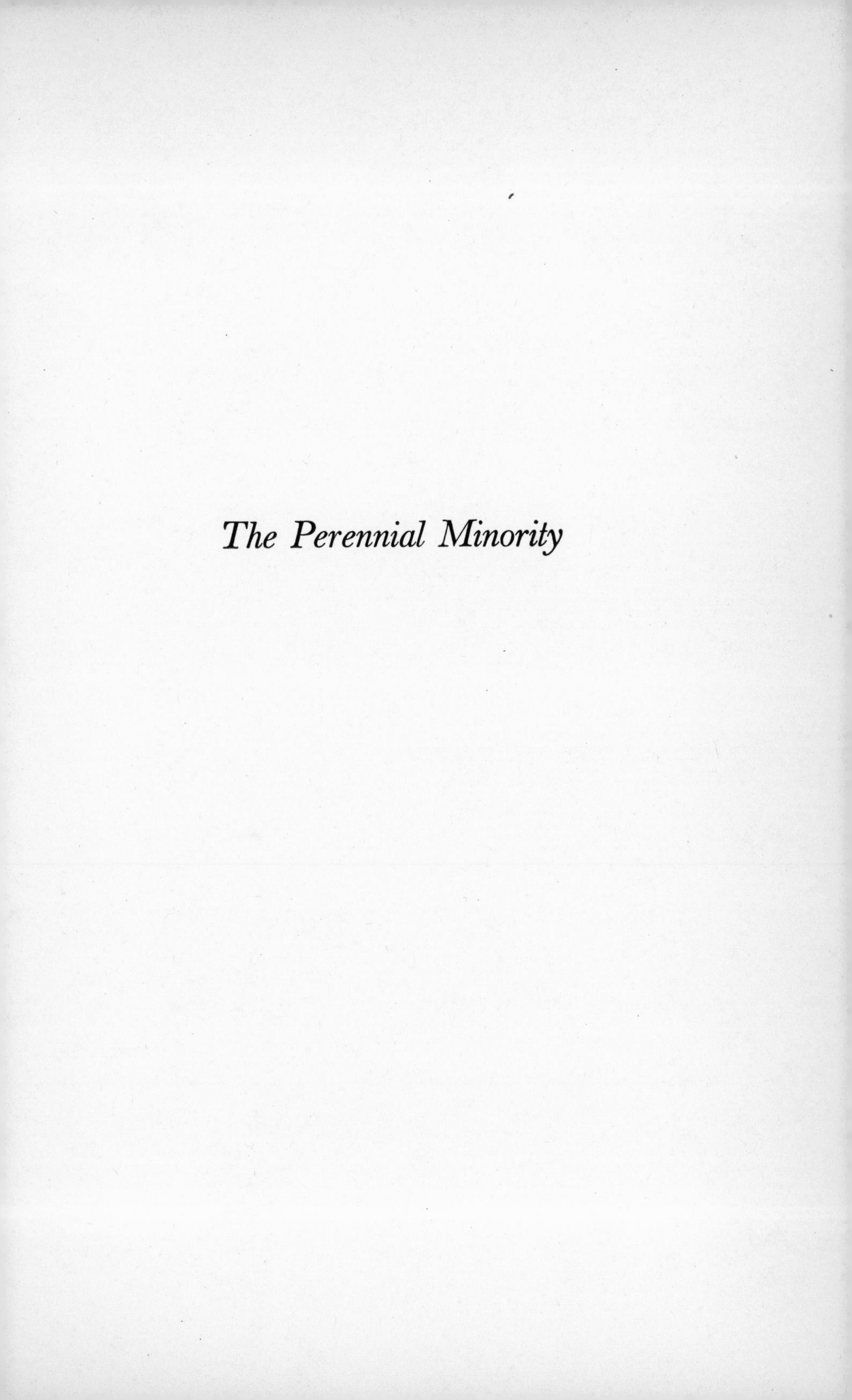

The Perennial Minority

CHAPTER 16

The Jewish Community: *Minority with Bicultural Status*

THE COUNSELLOR turned wearily in his chair. All day the neuropsychiatric cases had been pouring into his office from the hospital and he was nearly at the exhaustion point. New Guinea was no place for man or beast; the heat was unbearably oppressive and the G.I.'s were coming back from the jungle a mass of raw nerves. Suddenly the door opened and a thin, emaciated lad in a rumpled uniform hesitated at the threshold, gazing vacantly at the man behind the desk.

"Come in, corporal. Just take that chair over there."

"Yes, sir," came the automatic response as the young soldier made his way unsteadily to the seat by the window. A twitching movement seemed to spread like a paroxysm over his frame although it was evident he was trying to sit quietly under the gaze of the older man.

"The report here says you haven't been sleeping well, you usually refuse to eat, have severe headaches, and are unable to carry on in the line of duty. Is there any way I could help you?"

Silence.

"You may relax, corporal. Just forget my rank. This is not a cross-examination and nothing we say here will be reported. I am simply here to give you any service that I can."

The expression of dull apathy and hopelessness changed for a moment; a slight flicker of interest appeared and was gone.

"I believe your name is Mangin, isn't it, corporal? Let me introduce myself. Lieutenant Fishberg."

A slow gleam of comprehension in the soldier's eyes changed to a mounting excitement as he finally spoke:

"Are you a Jew?"

"Yes, certainly. Or at least my family is. Of course you might not think I was a very good one. It's been a long time since I went to synagogue."

"No, but you must understand. You know." The words were coming rapidly now. "The others had no idea. How could they? I couldn't talk to anyone. What was the use? They'd have thought I was crazy. Maybe I am. But it wouldn't seem like anything to anybody else and they would have clapped me in the guardhouse. It's a wonder I'm not there now instead of the hospital. But it isn't right, I tell you, it isn't right. It can't go on like this."

"Suppose you start at the beginning. There is plenty of time."

Painfully and incoherently, Corporal Joe Mangin told his story. His parents were strictly Orthodox and had reared him to reverence and obey the traditional laws and ceremonies of the synagogue. He had always wanted to please his parents, and although he became more lax in observance during his high school years, he was always the dutiful son at home. After Joe began working in an office, he met a gentile girl who was the kindest and friendliest person he had ever known, his mother only excepted. For months he thought of her merely as a good friend, more like a sister than anything else. But it did not stop there. Before a year had gone by, he realized suddenly that he could not face the prospect of living without seeing Phyllis every day. But that was impossible, for his parents would call him an apostate if they knew he even thought about a gentile girl seriously. His dilemma was absolute.

Finding no way out, he flung himself furiously into his work, seeing as little of Phyllis as he could and continuing to please his parents by regular attendance at the synagogue on all other occasions except the Sabbath, when he had to work. But there were plenty of other young men in his neighborhood who were nothing but "Yom Kippur Jews," and his parents were well content. Intense concentration on his work soon made him a respected expert in the business office and he found to his great surprise that in another year he was offered a supervisory position in another city with the same firm at a much higher salary. Should he take it? He would probably lose Phyllis if he did. And then a new and wilder idea occurred to him. Would it be possible? What if his parents should find out? But would they? And if he didn't come back, how much difference would it make?

He told his idea to Phyllis, glossing over the difficulties he knew would inevitably appear. Why couldn't they get married in the other city? The only thing that had kept him from asking before was the thought that his parents would make it hard for him. But at that distance he didn't see how they could interfere, and maybe after a while they would get used to the idea and acquiesce. He knew lots of other Orthodox parents that did. And surely his father and mother were just as understanding as the others. Why not try it?

Phyllis agreed. She had always wanted to live away from home and she loved him. They didn't need any more. It was certain to her that her own parents would approve in time because they usually agreed with her wishes. Her mother and father both knew Joe and thought highly of him, except that they both "hoped she wouldn't get serious with a Jew." This ought to be a good way to bring both sets of parents around to their way of thinking. Phyllis agreed that any children of the match could be brought up in the Jewish faith, but she preferred to remain Presbyterian herself. To this Joe gave hearty assent. In a few months their secret marriage took place, a Reform rabbi officiating.

Very little time elapsed before Joe's parents got word of the affair. To the amazement of the young couple, the older Mangins accepted Phyllis without a qualm. One thing that may have helped them to decide was the news that their new daughter-in-law was willing to bring up her children as "good Jews." At any rate, Joe soon got a transfer back to his native city, where his first child was born. Years elapsed and the young son was sent to Hebrew school even though the mother attended the Presbyterian church regularly with her own parents who had now come to think of Joe as their own son in all but religion.

With the coming of the war the Army drafted Joe and he was sent to the Pacific theater. Through the desperate fighting in New Guinea he was fortified by letters from Phyllis telling of the progress made by their son David. Gradually, imperceptibly, the tone of her letters began to change. At first it was only a hint or two; then accusations began. Joe's family were neglecting her. They no longer came to see her and were cold and distant toward her whenever they met. As months went on, she wrote of being with her Christian friends, of church affairs, and of her increasing interest in bringing up David in a more friendly atmosphere.

In the steaming jungle of New Guinea, filled with the terror of sleepless nights under constant fire, Joe became drawn and haggard. If he could only get home, if he could only make them see. The fighting grew hotter while his anxiety grew deeper. At last came the fateful news from Phyllis that she had taken David out of Hebrew school and was putting him in Sunday School. All her fine promises, and now it had come to this! Maybe his father and mother were to blame. But what could he do? Nothing could help but a trip back to the States, and he might as well wish for the moon. He wandered around talking to himself. In the ranks he did wild, foolish things that endangered his company. After his efficiency had been almost totally destroyed by sleeplessness, loss of weight, splitting headaches, and intestinal trouble, he was transferred behind the lines. With only two surgeons and no psychiatrists on hand, all N.P. cases were referred to the counsellor, Lieutenant Fishberg.

Hearing his story, the Lieutenant was able to work out a transfer for the young corporal that permitted a return home for a short visit. Joe's later story was never learned.[1]

In miniature, this brief account of what happened to a single Jew gathers up several components of the problems faced by his minority. In many ways these elements show striking similarities to those of the new immigration in general and yet it has seemed best to consider them as a special case. Although there are inherent dangers in the treatment of the Jewish group by themselves, it is not implied here that their problems differ *in toto* from those of other immigrant communities or that the forces that have played a part in determining their reactions would have resulted in quite a different configuration of culture traits in another group subjected to the same pressures. Least of all is it asserted that the special qualities or characteristics of the group are the result of hereditary factors. Our earlier discussion of the fallacies and misconceptions of race stereotyping should have dispelled any such notion.[2]

The position taken here is simply that the Jewish community represents a unique minority in American life because of the particular history of the group and their peculiar interaction within the social process of Western civilization in the last two millennia. Unless and until the special nature of these conditions is fully understood by the student of minority problems, a comprehensive appraisal of the Jewish group and its relation to American life will be quite impossible.

THE UNIQUENESS OF THE JEWISH COMMUNITY

What, then, are the features that have served to mark off the Jew from his neighbors in European or derivative societies? For the sake of convenience these may be limited to ten major factors:

(1) The religion of the Jews, known as Judaism from the time of their Babylonian exile, has served to distinguish them from their neighbors, particularly after the dispersion in A.D. 70 when their central temple at Jerusalem was destroyed. For the better part of two thousand years they have had a minority religion within Christendom, refusing as a whole to adopt the religious faith of the countries in which they lived. To complicate matters, their religion was not only historically prior to but served as the foundation for the later Christian faith reared upon its superstructure. This made the Jewish group a continual irritant to the Christians surrounding them, a particularly stubborn remnant who refused to accept the Messiah believed in by the great majority and who were (at least in their historic past) charged with the death of that Messiah.

On the other side of the ledger, the Jews themselves clung to their ancient faith as the original and purer form of revealed religion and hence the superior one. Central to this theology was the belief that they were a people especially selected by the Deity to reveal his will to the world. In the words of a renowned scholar of their people, "The Jewish religion without the 'chosen people' is unthinkable." [3] This view further antagonized the Christians by challenging the superiority of their religion.

(2) There was always a highly developed reverence for learning among the Jews, dating from the days of the Talmud in the pre-

Christian era. Even in this ancient period the Talmud taught, "Turn all thou hast into money and procure in marriage for thy son the daughter of a scholar, and for thy daughter a scholar." [4] The learned man was the man of supreme prestige in the community and the Jewish group were "the people of the Book." Whether the genetic effect of the Talmudic injunction was considerable or not, it is difficult to discover; but at least it made certain that the ancestral lines of scholars' families did not die out. And it put the stamp of cultural authority on a preference for intellectual occupations, even though much of the tendency was dissipated in formalistic and legalistic disputation.

(3) Since the dispersion the Jews have had a culture without a land. Unlike the nationality groups that have migrated to the United States, the Jews do not come from a single country but from many. While this has resulted in minor divisions among them,[5] it has not destroyed their essential unity, which has been that of a cohesive culture that disregarded the usual attachments to soil, climate, topography, or political institutions of any locality. The implication is that they have not idolized loyalty to such nationalistic agencies of power as government, imperialism, or military strength. Their very presence is a sort of question mark in relation to chauvinism. On the other hand it has led to serious doubts about their patriotism and has exaggerated their position as strangers in every national home.*

(4) While not strictly a race from the ethnological point of view, the Jews have nevertheless been severely endogamous since the days of the Priestly Code in the Old Testament. This has not prevented the addition of some Mongol and Nordic traits to a group originally a mixture of the Mediterranean and Alpine racial groups [6] but it has resulted in some anthropometric characteristics that frequently distinguish them from the non-Jewish population.[7]

Up to the modern period consanguineous marriages among Jews were relatively frequent, since Jewish law does not forbid, for example, the marriage between an uncle and his niece.[8] This tendency, as long as it lasted (and it is entirely discontinued today), would

* The intent of this paragraph is not to prejudge the case for or against Zionism, which asserts that the Jewish people can no longer exist without their own land. Further discussion of this issue will appear in due course.

heighten the general effect of endogamy in producing a more pronounced type. The result has been not only that the Jews have been regarded by their non-Jewish compatriots as a race but the same idea has persisted in the popular opinion of many Jews themselves. Since a social fiction believed is a social influence with observable results, this conception of a separate race has given rise to a belief in the inheritance of special traits of behavior that are supposed to be specifically Jewish.

(5) Because of their frequent position as sojourners in other cultures the Jewish people have developed a pattern of biculturality.[9] Constantly forced to adapt himself to a society outside of his own, the individual has become accustomed to two coexisting behavior patterns, one for his own group and one for the gentile. Perhaps the most striking form of this bicultural activity has been the use of more than one language at a time. From the fifth century B.C. the Jewish people have been bilingual instead of monolingual. In fact this has resulted in various dialects in which Hebrew has been mixed with other languages such as Persian, Arabic, Ethiopic, Spanish, and German. Coexistent with these has always been a strain of the original Hebrew utilized in worship and in education;[10] by means of this original tongue the continuity of the culture has been maintained. In addition there have always been two sets of etiquette, manners, and custom, one directly derived from the more traditional Judaic way of life, the other reflecting the daily business and commercial interests of life in a gentile community. One or the other of these two habit patterns might dwindle, but it rarely reached the vanishing point. That this resulted not infrequently in a dual ethic is undeniable. A somewhat different end product is what Jessie Bernard has aptly named "cultural schizophrenia,"[11] an alternating pair of emotional loyalties particularly in societies that granted the Jew a generous fund of democratic rights and freedoms.

(6) Perhaps as significant as any historic precipitate in their long cultural experience is the effect of segregation in the ghetto for centuries. Though this was first a policy adopted to preserve the Jewish religion and institutions, and thus a voluntary policy, it later became an enforced status imposed from without by kings, nobles, and city councils throughout Europe.[12] These areas of town or city had high surrounding walls with gates that were closed and barred

at night. Armed guards frequently watched the gates to see that no one went out after dark, on Sundays, or on holy days. During the day a few members of the community within the ghetto would venture outside to transact business, but most of the group, especially women and children, stayed strictly within its confines. Inside were the synagogue, the burial place, and the overcrowded tenements. Seclusion of the Jewish people in these segregated quarters had the effect of social isolation. On the other hand, mobs frequently broke in, slaughtering and burning at the instigation of popular religious leaders, particularly during the Crusades.[13]

Forced by these circumstances to shun the Christians, the group within the ghetto became more provincial, narrow, ignorant, and superstitious, and the religion of the masses, as well as that of many rabbis, became more rigidly set than ever.[14] The social effects of enforced segregation gave rise to an exaggerated cohesiveness and solidarity of the community (to outsiders, clannishness). It meant a temper of mind increasingly uneasy when too far from the organized forms of Jewish institutions and communal activities. Just as it has been remarked that one can take a girl out of the country but not the country out of the girl, so it would be equally true that it might be comparatively easy to take the Jew out of the ghetto but not the ghetto out of the Jew. In times of persecution — even though it affected their fellows in far distant lands — the lines within the Jewish community tightened so that an unbroken front was presented to the host society.[15]

(7) With the advent of the French Revolution and its universalistic ideals of individual civic rights came the sudden emancipation of the Jews. They now became citizens of national states rather than members of a segregated community with special status. Beginning with France in 1806, the movement for emancipation followed Napoleon's armies across Europe. Perhaps its most dramatic episode came in Italy where, as French forces entered city after city, they broke down ghetto gates and burned them, inviting the Jews to come out and enjoy the political privileges of other men.[16] One after the other, various European nations and small states followed the precedent until in the latter part of the nineteenth century the Jews received civic rights like those of other citizens from the Atlantic Ocean to the border of Poland.[17]

This sudden change had a powerful and in some ways a disruptive effect upon the Jewish people as a whole. Even today the emancipation is only a century old, and for many members of the community less than that. The extent of the new-found freedom has been spotty and uneven.[18] Late entrance into Western society has meant a sudden adjustment to the scientific and political revolutions which required centuries of adjustment to become assimilated into the thought patterns of the Christian world. Thus the full impact of the Copernican, Newtonian, and Darwinian world views struck the Jewish community at a single blow.[19]

(8) Unlike other immigrant groups entering the United States, the Jews have come from towns and cities rather than from the land. In medieval times they were legally forbidden to own land. Even though the vested interests of nobles might have prevented this in any case, there were also other reasons: Jews could not take the oath of fealty, and their Sabbath and dietary laws kept them from serving in feudal armies.[20] Their ghetto areas were consequently in relatively large centers of settlement where they developed personality characteristics quite distinct from those of the peasant. They also learned to adapt their trade and commerce to the simple tastes of agriculturalists so as to profit from them. And with the emancipation, life in the cities also incurred full exposure to the rising tide of secularism which took quick root in Jewish groups.

(9) Just as the number of Jews engaged in agriculture was much smaller, so the number in commerce was usually much larger than among non-Jews.[21] As settlers in other lands under foreign domination, they have adopted occupations especially fitting for those who are not natives. During the Middle Ages Christians were forbidden the loaning of money at interest and so banking became a means of subsistence for many Jews.* Since the emancipation came at a time when capitalism was acting as a forced draft on business and commercial occupations, the Jews with long centuries in these pursuits were economically well adapted to the new social climate.[23] At the

* It should be noted that this did not keep Christians from collecting "gifts" or "rent" for the loan of money. With this terminology the Knights Templars became prominent bankers with vaults scattered from Armenia to Ireland. During the Renaissance, gentile bankers in Florence charged "rent" of 25 to 50 per cent per annum.[22]

same time it is incorrect to infer that all or even a majority of Jews were capitalist enterprisers; many of them took up handicraft occupations and became artisans such as dyers, tailors, furriers, diamond cutters, and the like, especially in eastern Europe where the guilds were weaker and the Jews were not excluded.[24]

(10) Last but not least the Jews in the modern world occupy an ambiguous position which prevents them as a group from agreeing on their own status. With the Italian, Pole, or Hungarian this problem does not arise. But the Jew, especially since emancipation, has felt the full force of this ambiguity. Although not a race, he has often referred to himself in racial terms. Though not a nation, he has adopted a new pattern of nationalism in Zionism. Though not exclusively a religion (since many secularized individuals with Jewish parents regard themselves as Jews), he often believes that he should restrict his uniqueness to religion alone. Though emancipated from the ghetto, he often prefers to live in his own community. As one organ of Jewish opinion has put it, "We have not yet determined whether we are to use the term "race," "religion," "nation," or "culture" to clarify the nature of our Jewish entity and identity." [25] Nor is this confusion simply one of the Jewish mind; the mental confusion mirrors the social ambiguity.

It is, of course, incorrect to insist that every one of these characteristics is unique in the Jewish experience. Biculturality appears in one form or another in all minority groups wherever found. Sudden emancipation occurred for the American Negro, though it implied an earlier condition of slavery rather than of parallel segregation. The practice of commercial occupations has occurred among other minority peoples such as Armenians, Parsees, and Scotch (termed by Becker "marginal-trading peoples").[26] We are simply employing the term "unique" in a relative sense as having degrees.[27] And to be more explicit, the organization of these ten factors in Jewish experience has been different from that of any other people.

In the sense of configuration, then, these factors serve to distinguish the historical experience and consequently the personality characteristics of the Jewish community in a way which makes their cultural pattern a recognizable, unique entity. Perhaps the clearest summary of the whole matter has been given by Salomon Reinach in his comment that both Jewish virtues and Jewish faults have come from one or more of six causes: (1) generations of Talmudic education; (2) long persecution; (3) enforced abstention from certain occupations; (4) enforced practice of certain other occupations; (5) the brusque change from oppression to liberty and from misery to riches; (6) the sudden transition from docile faith to a free intellect.[28]

IMMIGRATION TO THE UNITED STATES

While it is incorrect to class the Jews entirely with the new immigration, the great bulk of their migrants have come to America since 1881. There have been five waves or nodal periods:

(1) The colonial period, in which Sephardic Jews from Spain, Portugal, or Holland turned to the new land for fresh opportunities. At first this was only a tiny trickle of immigrants but it kept increasing gradually until 1815, when it rose somewhat more sharply.

(2) A larger wave following the revolutions in Europe around 1848 and continuing until 1877. This group was largely composed of German Jews, some of whom came even earlier.

(3) The largest wave, stimulated by pogroms after 1881 in Russian Poland and the Ukraine, where the migration began. It was continued by other groups from eastern and central Europe, particularly Hungary, Rumania, Slovakia, and Bohemia, and lasted until the first World War.

(4) A large immigration after World War I from most of the same areas as (3) above. The peak came in 1921; immigration laws reduced the number drastically after 1924.

(5) The last wave, following Nazi persecution and during World War II. This did not reach sizable proportions until 1937 and reached its peak in 1939, declining gradually until American entrance into the war. This group consisted largely of German and Austrian Jews with a smaller number of others from central Europe and Poland.*

* This division of immigration periods is simplified for exposition. There are qualifications and reservations to be made. In the first period, by the eighteenth century, a majority of New York Jews were either German or Polish. The second period showed a considerable number of French and English Jews as well as German. Both in New York and Boston a large percentage of eastern European Jews were noted in the 1840's and 1860's; almost half the synagogues of New York were made up of eastern European Jews. Furthermore, some of

Earlier in their history, especially during the Moslem period, some of the Jewish people migrated to Spain (called in Hebrew "Sephard"). From then to the tenth century they prospered and reached a position of eminence. With the victory of Christianity they shared a minority status with the Moors for a time and therefore were conciliated. A few migrated to France and Holland, where they were favorably received. Beginning with the thirteenth century they became victims of increasing discrimination and persecution until the Inquisition of the fifteenth century, when in 1492 they were expelled or given the choice of renouncing their faith. Many left for Portugal and Holland; others renounced their belief and became Christians but secretly practiced the traditional Jewish ceremonies. These latter were called Marranos. It was from these groups that the first immigrants came to the United States.[29] Divided from the rest of American Jewry by ritual and by tradition, the Sephardic group kept itself aloof and refused intermarriage with later comers.[30] (By 1930 the Sephardic Jews formed about 5 per cent of the Jewish population of the world.)

Another and larger group migrated northward from the Levant to the Balkans and eastern Europe, and still another branch proceeded westward to the kingdoms of the Franks. This latter group, especially after the Crusades, traveled farther and farther east until most of them reached Poland and Russia, though some remained behind in Germany. Since the great mass of them had resided in Germany for a time on their eastward journey and had mixed German with Hebrew to form the Yiddish dialect, they were called Ashkenazic Jews (in Hebrew, "Ashkenazi" means German). After the emancipation the group still in Germany gave up their dialect for German and most of Hebrew culture for German culture. On the other hand the eastern Jews of Polish Russia and the Ukraine, who were still living in segregated conditions, kept their culture intact and retained Yiddish as their major tongue. This split in the Ashkenazic group is reflected in the differentiation of the second and

---

those labeled German Jews had come from Bohemia (e.g. the Brandeis family), Hungary, Prussian Poland, Austrian Poland, Switzerland, or Alsace. More careful studies are still needed in the earlier phases of Jewish immigration. See Oscar Handlin, "Our Unknown American Jewish Ancestors," *Commentary* 5:104–110, 1948, esp. p. 105.

third waves of American immigration. (In the 1930's the Ashkenazic Jews formed 92 per cent of the Jewish population of the world.)[31]

After 1848 the number who migrated to the United States increased rapidly. By 1880 there were about 230,000 Jews in the country.[32]

Statistics on Jewish immigration are somewhat inaccurate due to the fact that many arrivals listed themselves as nationals of the country from which they came. Furthermore the basis for enumeration changed with shifting policies of immigration authorities. Between 1881 and 1898 figures were available for Jewish arrivals in the ports of New York, Philadelphia, and Baltimore only. From 1899 to 1907 these statistics were modified to include all ports of entry, and the classification "Hebrew" was added to the "race or nationality" question asked of all immigrants.[33] The Immigration Service explained that "race" would be used "in its popular rather than its strict ethnological sense." [34] For the most part the Jews who registered themselves as "Hebrews" were Yiddish-speaking individuals from eastern Europe; others, like the German, Hungarian, or western European groups, would simply report themselves as nationals of their respective countries. Ruppin calculates that the discrepancy would be from 5 to 10 per cent of the total number of Jews entering.[35]

Between 1899 and 1914 there were 1.45 million "Hebrews" entering the United States, the largest number (154,000) in 1906.[36] After World War I Jewish immigration rose to a peak of 119,000 in 1921 but new restrictive quota Acts decreased the number. After the 1924 quota law the annual average from 1925 to 1933 was about 10,000.[37] Estimates by H. S. Linfield would give the total Jewish immigration for the years 1921–1924 inclusive as 270,282.[38] From 1925 to 1930 the admissions were only 66,089 [39] but by 1933 with the coming of the Hitler government the refugee stream began to pour in. Between 1933 and 1941 the United States took in from 160,000 to 170,000 Jewish refugees.[40]

To summarize for the entire period, something like 2.5 million Jews (net immigration) came to the United States from 1881 to 1942.[41] On the whole they showed a very different pattern from other immigrant groups since most of them did not return to their country of origin. While departure of other immigrants averaged 35 per cent of the admissions, only 5 per cent of the Jewish admissions left again.[42] Having a culture without a land enabled the Jews to transport their institutions with less dependence on national or geographic conditions. Today the estimated Jewish population of the United States is given as five million;[43] this is a conservative estimate based on the 1937 Census of Religious Bodies. Probably 5.5 million would be an adequate round number. Of these about 10 per cent are of native parentage, approximately 50 per cent native of foreign or mixed ancestry, and something like 40 per cent foreign born.[44]

EARLY ADJUSTMENT

While space does not permit an account of the early Sephardic communities, some attention to the early German Jewish settlers is necessary to appreciate the variable nature of adjustment to American life. A tiny minority of German Jews came to America between 1800 and 1848, most of them poor traders seeking better opportunities. They had an Orthodox religious background and came from a semi-ghetto existence where they spoke both Yiddish and German. A large number started their economic careers as peddlers. Their stocks were supplied by two or three Jewish merchants in New York who sold them "Yankee notions," called in the vernacular *kuttle muttle.*[45] Spreading from eastern centers they traveled to the Middle West, particularly Ohio and Illinois. In the larger centers they were often able to form a *minyan* (a group of ten male Jews which constituted the necessary minimum for a congregation) but in many cases this was impossible.

Having come from the smaller towns of southern or northeastern Germany, these Jews clung to their traditional ways of life, established *Landsmannschaften* (societies from the same towns or provinces in the Old World) for sociability and mutual assistance, and kept themselves apart from the older Sephardic group.[46] In Chicago the early German Jews had a number of tailors, dry goods dealers, a tobacconist, a grocer, and several peddlers.[47] Most of them were fairly well established economically when the larger wave came in following the revolutionary movements of 1848.

The new group, poor though they were, were emancipated Jews who looked upon Germany as their mother country, came largely from urban communities, and showed far more sophistication. Having worked side by side with their fellow-Christians in the homeland for a German revolution, they were more socially and politically than religiously conscious.[48] Before long they began to be the dominant influence in the Jewish community and, true to their background, strove for more complete integration within the American scene. In this they were aided by American public opinion, which regarded them as half German and half Jewish. As Buch comments on a German Jew of this period, "The fact that he was half German made him half human being."[49]

Perhaps the most influential institution brought in by the new immigrants was the Reform synagogue. The early demands for reform came from enlightened laymen of the higher middle class in Germany who were most exposed to the results of cultural assimilation. In line with the higher criticism reinterpreting the Bible for Christians of that day, Reform Jews of Germany gave up the notion of literal inspiration of the Scriptures. In their belief the Torah (law) was created by the Jewish people with the aid of divine inspiration but it was not equally binding or valid in all parts nor for every age; along with this was the relegation of the Talmud to a minor place in Jewish tradition.[50]

Even more important were the practical changes in observance approved by Reform rabbinical conferences in Germany. These included religious services in the vernacular with a minimum of Hebrew, the seating of men and women together, the use of the Christian Sunday instead of the old Saturday or traditional Sabbath day, organ music as a part of worship, and approval of intermarriage, with the rabbi officiating. The Messianic hope was to be reinterpreted, prayers for the restoration of the Jewish state were omitted, and dietary laws were no longer considered binding in the modern world.[51] While not all these reforms materialized in the European environment where tradition was more powerful, Reform rabbis entering the United States found themselves less hampered and thus were able to carry through a more positive program.[52]

The most prominent leader of the movement in the new land, Isaac Wise, regarded the synagogue as an Americanizing institution and to that end composed a specifically American Jewish prayer book and ritual of worship which was published in 1857. A more widely used prayer book of the same type was compiled by Reform rabbis in 1894 and has been twice revised since; today it is the official ritual of the American Jewish Reform Congregations.[53] Thus the tendency toward rapid Americanization was hastened by more radical innovators who held to the belief that Jews should become indistinguishable from other Americans in everything but worship and to a minor degree in that. Wirth believes that had it not been for the later Jewish immigration from Poland and Russia, Jewish communities would have lost their distinctiveness and there would have been a more or less complete assimilation after the German model.[54]

It is false to conclude, however, that the influence of German Jewry was exclusively in the direction of the Reform movement and a more modernized religion. Among them were many secularists and at least an equal number of more orthodox believers. They resembled the earlier German Jewish immigrants in the organization of burial societies which often served as the nucleus of communal life, supplementing, where they did not predate, the synagogue itself. These burial societies came into existence for (1) the purchase of cemeteries and selling lots to fellow believers; (2) provision of free burial service, including the ritual preparation of bodies for burial; (3) bestowal of aid to relatives of deceased members if they needed help. As the various members climbed the social scale, the third function gradually disappeared while the others were specialized and secularized in accordance with American customs. Each wave of Jewish immigrants went through the same cycle of burial ground societies.[55]

In addition to these and the *Landsmannschaften*, the newer wave of German Jewish immigrants was largely responsible for the setting up of new agencies like the Young Men's Hebrew Association, which opened classes in English, American history, and civics, and the Hebrew Immigrant Aid Society (H.I.A.S.), which gave financial assistance and counsel to a new flood of Jewish immigrants that began to come after 1881.[56]

Meanwhile the influx of eastern Jews began to change the complexion of the American Jewish community. Pogroms begun in Russia as an official policy of the czarist government started a wave of refugees to the city of Brody in Austrian Galicia. Jewish agencies on the Continent and in England helped several thousand of these to emigrate to America. Prophetic of the nature of this immigration was an incident in which the Alliance Israelite Universelle of Paris wired the refugees that it would send a specified number of their men to New York and received a message in answer, "Would rather starve than leave families." [57] Later studies have clearly shown that the Russian Jewish immigration was chiefly a family affair with a much larger proportion of women and children than was the case with other arrivals.[58] These Russian and Polish Jews came from a ghetto background into a freedom and way of life that were often confusing and bewildering to them.

The habits and customs of the new arrivals set them off sharply both from native Americans and from their German colleagues. The latter often held aloof from the Russian Jews, who were considered inferior. Most of the eastern Europeans wore beards and *paoth* or earlocks,[59] they spoke a dialect that was not true German, and they organized old fashioned *cheders* and *Talmud Torahs* as traditional Jewish schools where ancient rabbinical knowledge was taught.[60] They were far more strict about keeping the Sabbath and the dietary rules. Some of their earlier synagogues were small, attended by rough-and-ready men not averse to fighting when they disagreed among themselves within its precincts.[61] One historian has commented that the Russian Jews were either extremely Orthodox or radicals and revolutionists, since the educated young Jew frequently became a violent atheist in his medieval surroundings.[62]

Something like 26 per cent of the east European Jews (those over fourteen years of age) were illiterate, which was just barely below the figure for all immigrants.[63] The entire group experienced a transition like the original emancipation within the brief space of an ocean voyage to the new land. They had, however, certain initial advantages: 67.1 per cent of the Russian Jews were skilled laborers like tailors, hatmakers, milliners, and shoemakers; only 22.9 per cent were unskilled laborers or servants; the number of professionals was just slightly over one per cent.[64] The large number of skilled workmen helps to explain why so many of them settled in New York where there was an opportunity in the clothing industry particularly.[65]

With increased numbers arriving after 1901 and 1903 following fresh pogroms in Russia, an attempt was made by a new Jewish agency, the Industrial Removal Office (I.R.O.), to settle more of the immigrants away from the Atlantic seaboard. This succeeded in distributing only 79,000 from 1901 until the coming of the war in 1917 stopped all further efforts. Another attempt, called the Galveston Movement, tried to route incomers to Galveston from 1906 to 1908 but was stopped because of a depression.[66] Neither of these recolonizing efforts could compete with the natural economic advantages offered in the eastern industrial centers, and many of the immigrants they helped to move gradually drifted back to the larger cities.[67]

For the east European Jew the problem of adaptation to the freer atmosphere of the American city was more severe than it had been for the Sephardic and German precursors. In both Poland and Polish Russia or the Ukraine the Jews lived chiefly in villages and small towns,[68] and the transition to urban living was both harsh and abrupt. Thousands of them began working in factories and shops where industrialism destroyed both the tempo of living and the habit cadences of traditional religious observance. It was impossible to stop a factory machine several times a day for the regular prayers of Orthodox religion. To avoid this difficulty a number of the older men went into pushcart occupations where they could govern their own time schedule. But this did not satisfy the younger or more ambitious who wanted to get ahead. As one of them states it,

> From the moment I entered the shop my religious interest began to decline. In a year it was practically nil. My "four corners" wore out and were never replaced; my forelocks disappeared; my phylacteries and my prayer books were in exile. I ceased going to the synagogue, first only on week days, later on Saturdays as well. In after years I never entered it but twice a year, at the anniversary of my mother's death and on the Day of Atonement.[69]

Probably hundreds of thousands of eastern European Jews underwent a similar displacement of their religious customs. A simple act like trimming one's own beard or shaving it off would mean distress and anguish not only for the man performing the act but for his entire family who would look upon it as the cutting of an irrevocable link with a sacred past that would not return.[70] The general tendency was to keep "as much as possible" of the older ways when they did not interfere with business or ordinary social contacts. Most of the Orthodox homes eventually gave up the Saturday Sabbath, but dietary laws and the Hebrew education of the young were retained to a greater degree.[71] Since form meant a great deal to the immigrant, frequent quarrels arose in the home over failure to attend Hebrew classes, the eating of nonkosher food, the failure to keep holy days, or a general refusal to attend synagogue services.[72] In the synagogue, adjustments to American ways became visible in the weekly sermon and social activities of clubs after the American manner.[73]

The loss of the ghetto life of the old world made the immigrant seek for a substitute form of solidarity and group life in America. This was found to a limited extent in the *Chevras* or *Vereins*, which were mutual benefit societies with social activities somewhat like those of various nationality groups. The New York Jewish Community Register for 1917–1918 listed 3000 of these societies.[74] Another form of this solidarity was an emphasis on the home, which was modeled after that of their fathers, and on the new forms of the synagogue. Sometimes it expressed itself in neighborly acts to help a Jewish brother in need through direct aid. The first reaction to culture shock was therefore centripetal; [75] later came a transition to more pronounced mobility that broke up the static pattern in line with the European past.

Many of these Jewish families gradually lost contact with their relatives abroad and felt that they had little in common with them any longer. In addition America offered a new freedom of occupation with considerable economic reward. The result was an excessive zeal in vocation which brought about rapid adaptation to American folkways and a corresponding transformation in family life as well as in business.[76] In the old ghetto most parents could not even afford to send their children to school and even less could the younger members of the family learn anything of the great world outside. Now as the older generation moved into positions of higher economic rank, they followed their traditional inclination for learning by supplying it for their children. In many families the parents from eastern Europe actually laid more stress on education than their second generation children did. Often the children took naturally to this program and worked their way up to white collar or professional status, neither they nor the parents realizing that this was only a preparation for serious cultural conflicts in the home. In extreme instances this cultural gap led to a complete severance of all relations between parents and children although the parents had been the first to insist upon higher education for the young.[77]

Another form of conflict appeared in the families where the oldest son took over the business and the whole direction of family life. Since he himself had abandoned a professional career, he often refused to let his brothers go beyond high school. At the same time the older brother in his new-found freedom and greater acquaintance with American business methods might take frequent occasion to criticize sharply the father's "old fashioned" methods of conducting the business, inferring that he (the son) saved the family from impending catastrophe.[78] In common with other immigrant families, the Jewish family of the period showed a sudden change in the fulcrum of discipline as the patriarchal pattern dissolved. The mother frequently took over more and more of the directing functions in line with dominant middle class patterns, while in other cases issues would be settled by an older brother or simply by the clash of personalities.[79]

As the parents became dependent on their children for support in their old age, the latter often attempted to dominate their life in all details, even dictating what associates they should have.[80] Nor in the families where more reason and consideration played their part could the gap between generations be wholly concealed. Economic affluence, if and when attained, could not entirely hide the differences.

TWO INSTITUTIONS

The eastern European group and their descendants, forming by far the great majority of American Jews, have been largely responsible for the creation and expansion of two institutions that have had marked influence on Jewish life. These are the Conservative Synagogue and the Zionist movement.

Although the Conservative branch of Judaism was first organized by German Jewish immigrants who felt that Reform had gone too far, it declined steadily until the influx of Russian Jewish immigrants gave it new life. In Solomon Schecter (a native of Rumania), who was called from Cambridge, England, to the presidency of the Jewish Theological Seminary in New York, the group found a qualified spokesman for a more gradual adaptation of Judaism to urban secular changes.[81] It may be termed a mediating type of religion attempting to conserve (hence its name) traditional elements like ceremony and ritual in such a form as to be recognizable to the more orthodox and yet adapted to the changes in contemporary society. The central conception is not discarding of older elements, as accomplished in the Reform group, but the modification and shaping of them in new ways that preserve traditional forms.

Although the Sabbath cannot be strictly kept in an industrial world, it should, under Conservative theory, be as much as possible a day of rest and study. While not all kosher prescriptions are compatible with changed conditions, they are kept with little modification in reverence for the old law. An official pronouncement of the Conservatives states that it appeals only to those "who have neither accepted the Union Prayer Book nor worshipped with uncovered heads." [82] In general the Conservatives have a wide variety of practices but most of them have introduced the family pew, confirmation, organ music, and the replacement of the Yiddish sermon with English.[83] While Reform Judaism obtains its members from more favorably situated economic groups, Conservatives draw chiefly from the middle classes or those part way up the economic ladder. In general the Conservatives also accepted the idea that the Jews were a people rather than a purely religious group and thus became closely allied with the elements in the Jewish community who led its secular activities.[84]

This means that by and large the Conservative group were prone to consider Zionism favorably; though they shared this with Orthodox congregations,[85] their historical connection was perhaps even closer for reasons peculiar to the American scene. They were drawn from the eastern European group, which has been the seedbed of the Zionist movement from early times. Inasmuch as space forbids more than a brief sketch of the movement here, it is important to note that it had its main origin in the reaction of an Austrian Jew, Theodore Herzl, to the anti-Semitism of the Dreyfus affair in France.[86] He was convinced that although Western nations had professed to accept the Jews, anti-Semitism always lurked close to the surface and in an emergency would quickly undo the work of political freedom. "If we could only be left in peace. . . . But I think we shall not be left in peace."

Herzl believed that whatever national peoples profess, they are either openly or covertly anti-Jewish; to him the long history of Jewish life proved this. But he concluded that the Jews could not be respected like other peoples as long as they were homeless and belonged nowhere. In his view they were really a people, a nation without a home. Until they found a homeland of their own where they could develop their own culture in line with the peculiar Jewish genius, they would never be accepted. As soon as they did, all Jews everywhere could hold up their heads proudly and point to their national home, as the English, the French, or other peoples could. And in time of dire need those who suffered would then have a refuge to which they could turn without apology and with hope.

Although Herzl was not the only leader of the new idea, all the original exponents — Hess, Pinsker, Ahad Ha'am, as well as Herzl — were insistent on the national character of Jewry. Paradoxically every one of the group approached the Jewish problem from a secular angle and advocated a purely secular solution — a national state to be founded in Palestine. After trying hopelessly to interest the Jews of England and western Europe in the idea, Herzl eventually turned to the masses of east European Jews still living in ghettos under the harsh rule of despots. Here his ideal of a national homeland gave positive substance to the old Messianic hope still nurtured by Orthodox Judaism and to the daily prayer for the restoration of Zion to her people.

As these eastern Jews began pouring into the United States, they aroused the interest of a young writer, Emma Lazarus, whose lines, "Give me your tired, your poor," appear on the Statue of Liberty. She came to the conclusion that Europe was no longer a place for Jews to live and even if America could accept many, she could never find room for them all. The only remedy that was not a "temporary palliative" was the reconstitution of "an independent Jewish nationality" in Palestine.[87] Emma Lazarus also pointed out that it was the responsibility of American Jews to ameliorate the suffering of their brothers in Europe and facilitate a movement to Palestine for those who longed to go.[88]

Although this idea was opposed by Reform rabbis, who preferred to think of Judaism as a religion and not a national people, it began to take hold of both secular and religious Jews alike in Orthodox and in Conservative circles. Zionism had the unique quality of appeal to both the pious and the agnostic — to the former because it came as the realization of an age-long dream enunciated by prophecy; to the latter because it gave a feeling of "belonging" with the Jewish people without any religious allegiance and at the same time satisfied a moral urge in a way analogous with Marxism. This latter was probably true of the most outstanding American exponent of Zionism, Justice Louis D. Brandeis, whose support of the synagogue before his interest in Zionism was entirely lacking.[89]

Though Brandeis came from a German Jewish (Bohemian) background, other later leaders of American Zionism have largely belonged to the eastern European group.[90] So influential has the Zionist philosophy been in America that an Elmo Roper poll conducted in September, 1945, showed that of every ten Jews polled, eight favored a Jewish state in Palestine, one was opposed, and one was undecided. Those in the higher income brackets were frequent among the anti-Palestine voters.[91]

A DISTINCTIVE JEWISH ETHOS?

A few attempts have been made to summarize the traits of Jewish culture in the American scene as derivative from life experience. Though their validity needs testing by further observation and research, some are of value as initial hypotheses. To begin with, it is suggested that Jews are little interested in technology or mechanical devices, which are dominant in American culture. They seldom tinker with machinery,[92] and Jewish inventors are rare. They are much more interested in personality and evoking personal response from others. There is a preference for medicine and law rather than engineering (this in spite of their frequent exclusion from that field) and for buying and selling rather than making.[93] While unfamiliarity with sports has been largely overcome in the Jewish community, by and large the adage is still true, "If a Jew tells you he enjoys hunting, do not believe him."[94] Although fishing has become popular, the hunting complex is not a part of the Jewish ethos, possibly because of less participation in American pioneer culture.

Probably proportionately more Jews are used to the mazes of financial transactions than non-Jews. The Jewish artisan or trader from Poland or eastern Europe often comes from a family of traders and has lived in an environment that has sharpened his knowledge of commodities. The Jew who lived with Poles, Rumanians, Ukrainians, or Hungarians knew their tastes and desires and how to satisfy them. His human interest here combined with the trading interest so that in the new country men of these nationalities were frequently forced to seek him out as shopkeeper or even professional.[95]

Another characteristic attributed to the Jew is sobriety and temperateness. He is seldom if ever inebriated and in general disapproves of alcohol and drugs. At the same time he is not puritanical about the pleasures of the body but enjoys a comfortable home, good food, and wine. There is no sense of guilt about having the good things of life. Even in the Middle Ages Rabbi Saadia said that a man who lives on coarse food becomes coarse himself "so that the subtleties of wisdom escape him."[96]

Furthermore self-sacrifice is perhaps rated less highly among Jews than among non-Jews (a trait blending indistinguishably with the unashamed enjoyment of pleasure). It is significant that an arbiter of etiquette in America defines good manners as the toning down of behavior in order not to offend others — a modified form of self-sacrifice. If self-sacrifice is a subordinate element of the culture, as it seems to be among the Jews, this will mean that there is no great urge to make manners conform to such a norm. Hence what to an outsider may seem crass may to the insider be a simple way of expressing the ego.[97]

On the whole, Jews lay less stress on voting than most Americans. Customarily, the Jewish citizens of America have not voted for anything within their own group though special organizations like councils and groups of rabbis may do so. In fact Jewish culture is highly individualistic, so much so that it often appears to the insider more of an anarchy than a community, even though non-Jews see a fictitious unity.[98]

There are also a number of paradoxical and apparently contradictory elements in Jewish behavior, though this may be largely a logical rather than a psychological judgment. The American Jew has simultaneously shown intense practicality and also a high idealism. On the one hand he has clung firmly to tradition while on the other he has produced many startling innovations. He shows an emotional intuitiveness in response and thought which penetrates to the center of argument, and yet his history has shown a never-ending parade of dry and arid controversy about abstractions. Showing a strong commercial sense, he has at the same time been a pronounced philanthropist. Finally in his religion, even from Old Testament times, both universalism and particularism have been blended without the loss of either.[99]

Whether these traits are relatively stable or a passing phenomenon depends largely on the continuation within the American scene of earlier social processes to which the Jews as a whole have made their life adjustment. If it can be shown that acculturation within the American tradition (or any other tradition) effectually removes all those situations and conditions that have served to make Jewish culture distinctive in the past, then the admission that there is such a culture will need to be qualified as a transitional or temporary stage on the road to assimilation. The outcome depends, however, not alone upon the host society but also upon programs and policies adopted by Jewish Americans themselves. The whole issue must here be postponed until anti-Semitism as a social phenomenon receives greater attention in the next chapter.

THE REFUGEE GROUP

During the years 1933 to 1943 between 160,000 and 200,000 Jewish refugees were admitted to the United States.[100] About 60 per cent of these were from Germany and Austria, fleeing from Nazi persecution or expected reprisals.[101] This group differed from earlier immigration waves since it was mainly a middle or upper class movement with a much larger proportion of individuals over forty-five years of age and a greater number of white collar workers, professionals, and intellectuals who competed on higher occupational levels and thus came into direct rivalry with already established native middle class groups. Most of them learned English more rapidly than the earlier immigrants and began to make their contributions to American life immediately.[102] As a whole the group also brought more financial means with them, although restrictions on removing currency from Nazi dominated countries was such that "the amount of money brought from Germany is something that only God and the individual refugee knows." [103] This also meant that at least for a time a large number of the refugees had to adjust themselves to a lower standard of living in contrast with their earlier establishment in the European society.[104] Most refugees were more cosmopolitan in outlook, having been assimilated into the life of their respective countries; the German Jews regarded themselves as Germans, and expulsion was a traumatic experience in which a tremendous adjustment of attitudes became necessary. This problem of reorientation of attitudes was certainly as important as new cultural and occupational adjustments.[105]

Since the refugee group was composed largely of emancipated and secularized Jews, their lack of a separate Jewish culture served to set them off from many earlier arrivals.[106] While the actual number married to non-Jewish individuals is not known, it was almost certainly larger than in earlier Jewish immigration since mixed marriages in Prussia from 1906 to 1930 were over one third of all Jewish marriages.[107] Davie's questionnaire sample from 11,233 refugees also showed that after arrival about 30 per cent of the males married native Americans and 17 per cent of the women did the same. This is a particularly high percentage and shows that the refugees assimilated more rapidly than earlier groups.[108]

Some of the refugees arrived when the serious effects of the depression were still in evidence so that the initial period was fraught with difficulty. Many native Americans felt that the chances of jobs for those already citizens were in serious danger from the "flood" of foreigners coming into the country. In this respect the experience of America paralleled that of a good many European countries. What was often not realized was that this group of immigrants differed considerably from many earlier ones since their advanced technical and professional skills could be more quickly converted into national assets. The Committee for the Study of Recent Immigration from Europe in a study of 158 refugee enterprises found that the actual amount of capital invested in this small percentage of all businesses was between $10 and $12 million.[109] While this may not be typical of all, it nevertheless shows that this type of investment was actually creating jobs rather than eliminating them.

The situation in the professional field was somewhat different. Although the skill of the physician was more readily transferable to a new environment than almost any other, American doctors apparently attempted to take protective measures against competitive practice to a greater degree than comparable professional groups, chiefly through restrictions imposed by local or state medical associations, including increased difficulty in becoming licensed.[110] Lawyers, on the other hand, found a certain inherent obstacle in transferring European concepts and practice into American terms and in spite of some attempt at retraining, most of them apparently went into allied fields such as accounting or business or even industry, nearly always with a consequent lowering of living standards.[111] Many professors and scientists were placed in colleges and universities, with their salaries subsidized for one or two years by philanthropic funds; others found opportunities because of international reputations.[112] The stimulus to American education resulting from the presence of these foreign scholars has been immeasurable, and their technical contributions to the war effort have been frequently heralded.[113]

Artists and writers often found it difficult to carry on in a new language medium. It is interesting to note that more than two hundred rabbis were placed in synagogues throughout the United States during the refugee years.[114] The greater emphasis in Europe upon classical and humanistic training and the more intensive education practiced there often led the refugee to make invidious comparisons with American training that were not always gratefully received. Many American doctors, for example, asserted that the foreign physician too frequently overemphasized former reputation, experience, and superiority of training.[115] It even appears that unfavorable reaction to these natural comments of refugee Jews occurred either because they seemed compensatory or because they were uncomfortably near the mark.

While many of the aid societies attempted in this case as before to distribute the refugees in more widely separated geographical areas, great numbers settled in New York City. Many of the newcomers actually hesitated to leave New York because of a fear of anti-Semitic prejudice in the other parts of the country and proved their assertions by referring to daily news reports.[116] For a time New York City was called "the Fourth Reich" and by 1942 there were nearly 25,000 refugees in the Washington Heights area alone.[117]

Since 1933 about two thirds of the refugees have settled in New York, Philadelphia, Chicago, San Francisco, and Los Angeles.[118] In New York several centers were established where they could carry on a social life of their own, the most important being the New World Club which sponsored the largest newspaper of its kind, the *Aufbau*, with a circulation of 12,000.[119]

A NOTE ON JEWISH POPULATION

As might be expected by the urban concentration of Jewish people, the rate of increase for births is greatly diminishing. Even by the 1930's the marriage rate was everywhere lower for Jews than for non-Jews and the age at marrying was higher.[120] Though demographic studies for the Jewish population as a whole in the United States are only beginning to develop, there is enough evidence from research in individual cities to show the general trend. In Buffalo, for example, the Jewish population pyramid showed each five-year group below the 20-24 level to be lower than the one before it, with a steady decline in the younger age groups.[121] In Pittsburgh the number of children from five to nine years of age was smaller among Jews than among the native white population as a whole.[122] For the most part Jews had smaller families than gentiles in that city.[123] In Chicago the net reproduction rate for the total white population was higher than the Jewish, and Jewish women tended to marry later than non-Jewish.[124]

If these and other studies summarized by Robinson are fairly typical of the Jewish population as a whole, it would seem probable that the birth rate among Jews is somewhat lower than that of the native population among the non-Jews. Factors affecting the rate seem to be urbanization, longer period of education for the young with a consequent later marriage, and a high divorce rate. Although the comparative evidence on the point is not of sufficient volume to be wholly conclusive, it seems probable that the Jewish birth rate has been declining more rapidly than that of other immigrant groups.

On the other hand the Jews probably lose fewer numbers through intermarriage than is commonly believed. In this respect the assimilative process has not proceeded so far as in Germany before the advent of Hitler or in western European countries. Kennedy's study in New Haven shows that the Jews of that city, a fairly well acculturated group, are more endogamous than any other white ethnic group.[125] Even highly Americanized Jewish parents usually oppose what they consider unsuitable marriages, even though they do not actually arrange them,[126] and one indubitable evidence of unsuitability is marriage with a non-Jew.

European experience shows that the smaller the percentage of Jews in large cities, the more marked is the assimilative process. For instance Hamburg (1.75 per cent Jewish) in the 1930's had, after Glasgow, the lowest proportion of Jews, no special residential quarter, and the highest number of mixed marriages in relation to the total. The greater the mass and concentration of the Jewish population, the more this tends to segregate Jews from gentiles even in the same metropolis.[127] Precisely the same factors are operative in the United States, where the tendency toward concentration is sufficiently marked so that about four fifths of all Jews are in cities with over 100,000 population.[128] The fluctuations of the business cycle also affect the problem since there is more intermarriage in periods of prosperity than in those of depression.[129]

Parenthetically it is of interest to notice that intermarriage occurs more often among children of Orthodox families than of other religious groups, even the Reform. When separation comes, there is a preference for a clean break with the strictness of home training.[130] Another noticeable trend where intermarriage does occur is that Jewish males are more likely to take the step than Jewish females, except in Reform circles where the tendency is reversed.[131] But the total number is comparatively small.

JEWISH COMMUNITY ORGANIZATION

While the Jews maintained some sort of separate parochial system of schools during the nineteenth century, today Jewish education is supplementary to public schools which all groups attend. A separate type of schooling distinct from congregations is the *Talmud Torah* which occupies the children four afternoons a week and also on Sundays for instruction in Hebrew, the Bible, Jewish history, holidays, and festivals. Six years are required to complete the course.[132] This type of instruction is carried over from the parochial period, for today about 60 per cent of Jewish education is conducted under the auspices of congregations like the Hebrew Schools of the Conservative Synagogue and the Sunday Religious School of the Reform temple.[133] There is even some discussion of re-establishing a parochial system on the model of the many Yeshivahs in New York where the pupils pursue other academic subjects along with their Hebrew training.[134] Only one fourth of all the Jewish children are receiving this specialized type of education at any one time, though two thirds do receive some sort of Jewish education along with their public school training.[135]

During the early part of the present century, many local clubs were formed for social and recreational purposes in serving younger Jewish people. Some of these were organized after the manner of settlements while others took the form popularized by similar organizations in the Christian community and were called Y.M.H.A.'s or Y.W.H.A.'s. In 1920 the Jewish Welfare Board, which had served Jewish troops overseas, decided to continue its operation by supporting these Y.M.H.A.'s and similar organizations and encouraging other cities to start more of them. By 1945 there were three hundred of these organizations altogether, with the name generally changed to Jewish Center or Jewish Community Center. These are now foci of community interest and arrange recreational, social, educational, and cultural activities for groups of all ages. Most of them are staffed today by trained group workers.[136]

During the latter part of the nineteenth century a number of philanthropic agencies came into existence on both the local and the national level for the purpose of aiding immigrants, the poor, the widowed, or the aged. With the growth of their numbers, the appeals for funds increased and some means had to be found to unify the efforts of all. The result was the establishment of local Jewish Federations or Welfare Funds, beginning with the joint financial campaigns in Boston during 1895. This predated the formation of the Community Chest in other communities by eighteen years.[137] A national coordinating group was formed in 1932 for those community-wide Welfare Funds: the Council of Jewish Federations and Welfare Funds.[138] The training of social workers for service in specifically Jewish agencies is carried on by the Graduate School for Jewish Social Work of New York City, organized in 1925.[139]

The problem of combating anti-Semitism has been met chiefly at the national level, with the community activities derivative. Until recently this task has been performed by four organizations: (1) The American Jewish Committee, first formed in 1906 and supported largely by influential and relatively wealthy citizens from Reform congregations; this group has preferred to work quietly and by means of indirect influence rather than by much more aggressive methods.* [140]

(2) The Antidefamation League of B'nai B'rith,** organized in 1913 to combat anti-Jewish attitudes especially through publications refuting libelous attacks against the Jews; this organization includes members of different strata in the Jewish community.[141]

(3) The American Jewish Congress, which came into existence in 1917, adjourned in 1920, and re-formed in 1922 for the purpose of defending the political rights of Jews in the United States and overseas. It really originated in rebellion against the leadership of the American Jewish Committee and draws its members from middle class groups of Conservative and Orthodox supporters who were Zionists and militant in espousing the Jewish cause.[142] It has recently established a research unit called the Commission on Community Interrelations that sponsors studies on prejudice and discrimination with their effects.[143]

(4) The Jewish Labor Committee, which began in 1933 to organize the efforts of workingmen against the antilabor movements in European countries and has more recently turned its attention to problems within the United States.[144] This is a group of trade unionists or radicals of the noncommunist variety, largely nonreligious.[145]

These four groups have frequently worked quite independently or at cross-purposes with each other but in 1943–1944 they arranged for mutual consultation and division of labor in the National Community Relations Council.[146]

For the relief of Jewish distress abroad, particularly in Europe, the American Jewish Joint Distribution Committee (known as the J.D.C.) united the services of several agencies in 1916 and continued the work up to and including World War II, raising about $200 million dollars by 1946.[147]

* In recent years the pattern has changed to a more aggressive one.

** B'nai B'rith (Sons of the Covenant) is a national Jewish lodge or fraternal organization.

By 1946 the efforts of the J.D.C. were merged with the fund-raising activities for Palestine until all overseas aid came under a coordinating agency known as the United Jewish Appeal. This is the most comprehensive charitable fund-raising agency for all Jews.[148]

While there is great diversity among Zionist organizations, it is possible to mention here only the Zionist Organization of America (the Z.O.A.) with about 200,000 members which is affiliated with the World Zionist Organization, the Mizrachi or Orthodox Zionist group, the Labor Zionists or Poale Zion-Zeire Zion, and the Hadassah or women's organization.[149] In all, about 500,000 Jews in America belong to one Zionist organization or another.[150]

Religious organizations are of two kinds: of congregations and of rabbis. Among Reform Jews the former are united nationally in the Union of American Hebrew Congregations; the rabbis, most of whom are graduates of Hebrew Union College in Cincinnati, belong to the Central Conference of American Rabbis. Conservative congregations are represented in the United Synagogue of America; their rabbis, alumni of the Jewish Theological Seminary of America (New York), call their organization the Rabbinical Assembly of America. Among the Orthodox the congregations are not united in a single group, though the largest and perhaps most representative is the Union of Orthodox Jewish Congregations.* Orthodox rabbis trained at Yeshiva College and the Isaac Elchanan Seminary (New York) belong mainly to the Union of Orthodox Rabbis.[151]

In the religious census of 1936 it was estimated that there were 3700 Jewish congregations, of which about 3000 were Orthodox, 350 Conservative, and 300 Reform. The membership of the Orthodox congregations was about 250,000 (membership being by families rather than individuals), the Conservatives had about 75,000, and the Reform had an aggregate of 65,000. If these family memberships are expanded to include all those affiliated with the synagogues, the total would be about 1.5 million or about one third of all the Jews in the United States in 1936. Accurate statistics have not been gathered since that year.[152]

Another and newer development — less an organization than

* This represents only about 10 per cent of all Orthodox synagogues. Abraham G. Duker, "Structure of the Jewish Community" in Oscar Janowsky, ed., *The American Jew, A Composite Portrait*, New York, Harper, 1942, p. 137.

a movement among Jews — is Reconstructionism, sponsored by Dr. Mordecai Kaplan, a rabbi of the Conservative Synagogue. Dr. Kaplan came to the belief that Judaism was not a religion alone but a civilization (the social scientist would probably use the term culture), an amalgam or organic unity of religion, literature, art, ceremonial, and the common historic memories of peoplehood. Under this theory the secularist or nonreligious Jew would still retain his identity as a member of the Jewish people but could never fully separate himself from his religious past since that is an inescapable part of his historical memory.[153] Thus Dr. Kaplan can plead for an organization of Jewry that speaks with a single voice, even though it is not the voice of the synagogue, and conversely for the representation of the synagogue in all Jewish federations, welfare funds, and community councils.[154] His program calls for a rejuvenation of Jewish religion, art, and social and cultural activities as well as a more complete solidarity of the Jewish community. In his opinion, those who oppose such a program because it is too Jewish are showing "ghetto phobia" of a pathological sort.[155]

Of the two major attempts to unite American Jews, one has occurred at the national level and proved unsuccessful, the other at the local level with somewhat better outcome. The larger one was the convening of the American Jewish Conference in 1943, one quarter of the delegates being appointed by national Jewish organizations and the other three fourths elected by indirect popular vote. Its purpose was to project a program on which all American Jews could unite, but this aim was not recognized when it came to enunciating a policy for Palestine. On this issue the American Jewish Committee, unwilling to adhere to the resolution advocating a Zionist state, formally withdrew. That there were unresolved contradictions between some of the resolutions is clear. At all events the unity hoped for did not materialize.[156]

On the other hand local experience in various cities has evolved a new type of community cooperation for all Jews within a given metropolis. Beginning as a purely advisory and coordinating agency, the new organization, termed The Jewish Community Council, consists of delegates from every type of Jewish organization in the city, from synagogues, welfare societies, lodges, labor groups, educational organizations, and social clubs. By performing the function of community planning, eliminating duplicate services, and coordinating programs for all Jews in a city, the Community Council represents a more cautious first step toward a united Jewry. As an agency it is not empowered to engage in any specific activity without a vote of its representative membership so that it cannot engage in autocratic practices on its own authority. By 1945 there were twenty-five cities in the United States with Community Councils,[157] and the proposal is already being made for a National Council to unify and carry forward the tasks and programs of these local agencies.[158] If this were done it still would not represent a single voice speaking for American Jews until every city had such a Council.

OCCUPATIONAL STRUCTURE

From the very beginning Jewish immigrants entered the United States with a distinctive occupational distribution. From 1900 to 1925 the Jews were 10.3 per cent of all immigrants but about one fourth of all the traders in the immigrant population and about the same proportion of industrial workers.[159] Of the Jewish industrial workers entering the country during the same period, about five sixths were skilled and only one sixth unskilled.[160] The relative advantage which the Jewish immigrant possessed in comparison with other newcomers was a reflection of his European experience. Particularly true was this tendency in the making of clothing since the Jews who entered in the period stated comprised 65.1 per cent of all tailors arriving in the United States.[161]

Since the period of immigration the Jewish population has steadily climbed the ladder of social advancement with other ethnic groups in the community although with more emphasis on the occupations requiring higher education. It seems unquestionable that the Jews are the best educated minority in the United States. Since only 40 per cent of the Jewish population is in New York City, the occupational distribution there cannot be accepted as typical. On the basis of estimates gathered by the Jewish Occupational Council, Nathan Reich concludes that taking the United States as a whole, from thirty-five to forty Jews out of every hundred are in trade or commercial activities, between fifteen and twenty in manufacturing, ten to twelve in the various professions, and the rest in miscellaneous types. He then gives similar figures for the population as a whole;

these show 13.8 per cent in commerce, 26.3 per cent in manufacturing, 6.8 per cent in the professions, and the rest in other occupations.

This would mean that the Jewish population had nearly three times as many in commerce or trade as non-Jews, twice as many in the professions, and a somewhat smaller number in manufacturing.[162] The proportion engaged in trade is much higher outside New York City than within it.[163] In general the denser the Jewish population the greater is the number of industrial workers, and the sparser the population the greater is the group of traders and the intermediate or service occupations.[164] Another factor to be considered is recency of immigration, for in general the more recently arrived the group, the larger is the number of industrial workers.[165] This principle must be modified by the opposite tendency among the somewhat smaller group of refugees.

Occasional references to the "abnormal" economic structure of the Jewish population are only relatively true. Each immigrant group brought with it some cultural accentuation from previous history and these have been reflected in their American experience. The considerable number of Germans engaged in beer brewing, Italians in wine making, or Yugoslavs in fishing are indications of the same trend. Another consideration is that the Jews have been moving up into the same occupations followed by other Americans with the possible exceptions of public service [166] and heavy industry. This gives a clue to the *real* abnormality in Jewish occupational distribution as contrasted with the popular view. For this genuine abnormality results, not from the unique orientation of the group by reason of previous historical experience, as in the case of other immigrants, but from the checkerboard pattern of discrimination in American economic life.

According to the *Fortune* survey of 1936 major industries such as coal, auto manufacturing, rubber, steel, chemical industries, shipping, transportation, shipbuilding, petroleum, aviation, utilities, and machine tools are chiefly non-Jewish. Neither commercial nor investment banking has more than a handful of Jews, and their place in insurance is unimportant.[167] Even in the so-called light industries they are restricted to the distributing function, with the exception of the clothing industry.[168] Many of these industries make a regular policy of excluding Jews from employment, particularly public utilities, telephone, telegraph, and engineering firms.[169] Life insurance companies require a statement of religious affiliation from applicants and decline to give figures on the number of Jewish employees. A check of two large insurance firms in New York City revealed 4200 employees in home offices, of whom forty-five were Jews although the salesmen were quite largely Jewish.[170] Nor is this a mere pre-war phenomenon.

Although the greater use of available man power during the war modified many of these practices, a study made by Albert Weiss of discrimination in Chicago during 1946 showed that thirty-two out of thirty-three employment agencies required applicants to state their religion while twenty-seven of them stated it was more difficult to place Jews than non-Jews. In the same year the four Chicago newspapers increased religious specifications in help-wanted ads over 144 per cent above 1945 (a war year). The businesses or industries showing most discrimination were accounting, advertising, banking, insurance, real estate, railroads, public utilities (clerical divisions), mercantile and managerial occupations, chemical and electrical, machine tools, and metal products.[171]

The question naturally arises: what are the bases of this selective discrimination and what are the factors that determine its appearance in some economic areas but not in others? An analysis by Carey McWilliams supplies at least three hypotheses deserving further research: (1) that Jews are systematically excluded from types of business with artisan backgrounds and the long tradition of family names; (2) that Jews are restricted to the types of enterprise which involve a large factor of risk and less security (and cultural inclination toward this type of occupation cannot be excluded); [172] (3) that prestige patterns in the industries with greater social power determine the pattern of exclusion through the imitation of behavior engaged in by top executives. "The business executive who achieves the Nirvana of membership in the X club selects for his junior executives men who are ascending the socioeconomic ladder in the same fashion. Seeing how the system works, the junior executives apply exclusionist policies in the selection of their assistants, often without being told to do so." [173] The meaning of this analysis would be that the Jew in business is artificially frozen in a marginal position of the economic structure where not only vertical but also horizontal mobility is impossible. If this is the case (and future research may modify one or more of these hypotheses), it would help to explain why Jews have gone in large numbers into other marginal or new occupations unaffected by tradition, such as the theater, moving pictures, and radio, where they have "disproportionate" numbers. The inability to find positions in key industries would also mean an additional pressure to seek a place in the professions, perpetuating the vicious circle already present. Some of these professions are already showing progressively diminishing returns as more Jewish youth engage in them. Fagen has shown, for example, that the Jewish lawyers of New York City find it harder to make a living than non-Jews, that few of them earn large incomes, that they are younger on the whole, have less adequate training, and attend chiefly evening schools. They incline toward individual practice rather than partnership or firm practice.[174]

The issue of discrimination, however, raises more general questions as to the nature of anti-Semitism in the United States and the reaction of Jews both individually and communally to the social prejudices directed specifically against them. This forms the basis of the following chapter.

[CHAPTER 17]

Anti-Semitism and Jewish Personality Reactions

On his first trip through Kansas the young Jewish author was introduced to a native farmer and in the course of the conversation happened to mention that he was Jewish. The farmer looked at him with incredulity and amazement:

"How can that be so? You haven't any horns on your head."

The writer could not believe that he had heard correctly. Yet later he discovered that other Jews had had the same experience, and as he searched the medieval tradition, he found that a common designation of the Jew in the Middle Ages pictured him as in league with the devil, sometimes with horn and tail, sometimes riding a goat, which was the devil's animal. It is also significant that Mephistopheles is so often pictured as curly haired, hooknosed, and swarthy; at times he even wears the Jew badge, which leaves no doubt as to his identity.[1]

Jake had lost his job. The blow fell so suddenly that he was still reeling from it.

"How did it happen?" asked Dave.

"All I know is that the boss called me in and said that the company no longer needed my services."

Dave snorted unbelievingly. "Don't tell me that's all he said."

"Well no; there was more, of course. He said he was disappointed in me; he had always taken me for a truthful man and he was sorry to learn otherwise. I asked him what he meant and he told me that he had just learned I falsified my application when I first came in. That was a pretty serious charge but I could guess what he was driving at. So I said at once, 'You mean about my religion?' He seemed relieved and answered yes, that was it. I told him that I signed up as a Unitarian, that I was a Unitarian then and a Unitarian now; at least that was the church I stayed away from. He didn't seem to enjoy the joke but told me that the application blank referred to my original religious faith. When I asked him if a good many people didn't change their religion, he didn't bother to answer. All he said was that I knew the firm never took on accountants with Jewish backgrounds because so many of the other accountants objected and I must have known that. When I answered that no one ever seemed to notice anything Jewish about me or I would have been fired right away, he let it pass. 'Anyhow,' he said, 'they know it now and that means they won't want you back.' When I wanted to know if my work had been satisfactory, he mumbled something that sounded like yes but I could see that it was no use to press the point. To cap the climax he wouldn't even write me a recommendation. And to think of the overtime I put in for that man! How far does a guy have to run to get away from being Jewish anyhow?" [2]

ANTISEMITISM AND THE AMERICAN TRADITION

Perhaps the simplest way to define anti-Semitism is to call it an attitude of hostility toward the Jew, individually or collectively, together with the various acts, beliefs, or doctrines that express the attitude. As the term is used here, it includes the milder forms of social exclusion from clubs, hotels, or vacation resorts as well as the myth-making activities of the demagogues or the violence which they incite. For purposes of this discussion "anti-Semitic" and "anti-Jewish" will be employed synonymously, although some writers prefer to use the latter for the more temperate expressions of dislike.* On the other hand it seems best to recognize this difference in meaning sufficiently to restrict the use of the *noun* "anti-Semite" to the individual whose attack upon the Jew is so hostile that he has no desire to control it, who in fact prefers to whip up enough feeling

* For example, Maurice Samuel in *The Great Hatred*, New York, Knopf, 1940, pp. 16–17.

so that his psychological state verges upon mania. The difference between the anti-Semite and the one who merely happens to dislike Jews is that the former has a mission, a cause to propagate.

Anti-Semitism, however, is not a single concept but a composite or mosaic. The very fact that it is definable through a negative relation shows that it has a somewhat adventitious unity. Antagonism to Jews may arise from such disparate conditions as envy because they are specially protected by rulers, as they were in Macedon, in Rome, and by the nobles of western Europe; [3] or resentment over the success of some Jews in economic competition; or hostility against unbelievers wearing the *odium theologicum* because they refuse to be converted to Christianity; or derision expressed in the phrase "Christ-killers"; or a reaction against the unassimilated Jew who fails to take on certain forms of etiquette accepted in polite society; or, conversely, resistance to rapid assimilation for fear that the Jew may "run things." Perhaps the crucial element is the identification of the individual Jew with the group so that his characteristics are derivative from that membership, whatever may be the historic justification at the time.

It is impossible to review even briefly the history of anti-Semitism in any short account of it. The tendency existed in the pre-Christian era, when it was largely political and partly cultural; [4] during the late Roman and medieval period, when it was chiefly religious; [5] and in the modern epoch, when it has been both economic and political. Anti-Semitism as a political weapon made its appearance in the latter half of the nineteenth century.[6] Of all the European countries (before Hitler) the only one to employ anti-Semitism as an official state policy was czarist Russia.[7]

The original American tradition had little place for anti-Semitism; the earlier Jewish arrivals were not numerous and took their place in the colonies without exciting much comment. In the first part of the nineteenth century the same relation continued during the immigration of the German Jews. In spite of the bitterness between the North and South during the war of 1861–1865, the Northerners held no special antipathy toward the Jews because of the fact that a prominent Jew, Judah P. Benjamin, was Secretary of the Treasury in the Confederacy.[8] Although it might seem likely that the first major appearance of anti-Semitism coincided with the arrival of the mass of east European Jews, it actually dates from several years before that time.

Recent research has shown that the first overt manifestations of anti-Semitism in America occurred during the 1870's with the simultaneous growth of a financial aristocracy and the increased numbers of German Jews who were taking their places in positions of leadership in the economic structure. Restrictions on Jews in hotels, resorts, clubs, and vacation spots began about this time, reflecting the attempt of native industrialists to prevent social participation of Jews who had climbed higher in the class scale. It did not affect the lower class Jews at all but only those who began to share financial status with the magnates of the period.

It is perhaps characteristic of an open-class society like that of the United States that its first expression of anti-Semitism came not with the advent of Jewish immigrants but only as a brake on their mobility long after their arrival.[9] This pattern of delayed reaction appeared again on a lower economic level after the wave of east European Jews was followed by an increasing number who found their way into white collar occupations and clerical pursuits. By 1910 this new wave of discrimination sprang up and continued to rise steadily. The number of want ads in the newspapers specifying "Christians only" or "gentiles only" rose continually from 1911 to the period after the first World War, when it was joined by Ku Klux Klan agitation as a part of a larger antialien movement. Now it was the middle class that participated in the attempt to restrict Jewish vertical mobility, and evidence points to the fact that a good deal of the propaganda for the limitation of immigration, culminating in the Immigration Act of 1924, was directly aimed at cutting off further influx of the Jews.[10]

During the same period the arrival of Russian émigrés brought to the United States a new ideological element from the land where anti-Semitism had been an official policy. Beginning with the 1920's, the notorious forgery, *The Protocols of the Elders of Zion*, which had been used as a tool for stirring up agitation by the czarist secret police,[11] found a ready acceptance among sections of the American public whose knowledge of history was insufficient for them to recognize its errors. An American industrialist who declared that "history is bunk" was completely won over to the doctrine of the

Protocols that Jews were secretly preparing to enslave the world. Henry Ford subsidized the publishing of these and other myths in the *Dearborn Independent* from 1920 to 1927. His publication, which had a circulation of 700,000, had an immense influence in the midwest, where the Ku Klux Klan had its strongest following.[12] Ford was stopped only in 1927 on threat of a libel suit, after which he publicly apologized.[13]

By this time the terms "international bankers," "Jewish domination of industry," "Jewish radicalism," and other elements of the ideology had become familiar to the American masses. This trend of thought was enlarged in the 1930's by the increasing flood of Nazi propaganda which found the way well prepared and which led to the formation of native anti-Semitic organizations. There came to be 121 of them, under the leadership of Father Coughlin, William Dudley Pelley, Joe McWilliams, and others. The peak of their influence came in 1934 and again in 1940.[14] All these organizations were nationalistic, appealed to a 100 per cent American patriotism, and were antileftist.[15] Tying in with political conservatism, the native anti-Semitic movement attributed the New Deal to "Jewish radicals" and the economic collapse to "Jewish bankers." [16] At the outbreak of the war it was connected with the isolationist appeal when Lindbergh, Wheeler, and John Rankin accused the Jews of using pressure to get the United States into war.[17]

In the meanwhile the social and economic effects on Jewish mobility, particularly after 1920, were great enough to alter the structure of the group. By 1922 an employment agency in Chicago reported that 67 per cent of the requests for employees specified that Jews were excluded. Teachers' agencies in the Middle West in 1925 released the information that nearly 100 per cent of all calls for teachers specified "Protestants only." By 1930 the quota system for Jews had become well established in most eastern colleges and universities, and the process continued into the graduate and professional schools.[18] In the medical schools of New York State the number of Jews enrolled was cut from 241 in 1920 to 108 in 1940.[19] Pressure at the college level has forced Jewish students from New York to range from Rhode Island to Wisconsin to seek admission in state universities and smaller colleges.

Among the chief sources of anti-Semitic indoctrination of the

American child are juvenile literature and the educational materials of church and school. Even in learning Mother Goose rhymes the child repeats such lines as

Jack sold his egg
To a rogue of a Jew,
Who cheated him out
Of half his due.

The Jew got the goose
Which he vowed he would kill,
Resolving at once
His pockets to fill.[20]

In attending church school or receiving religious instruction the American child learns that the Jews were responsible for the death of Christ and that they have rejected him ever since. In many cases he is taught that the Jewish "race" has since had to live under a curse for refusing the Gospel or that Cain symbolizes the Jewish people who put the Saviour to death.[21] The place of the Romans in the Crucifixion is omitted and the fact that Jesus was a Jew who was carrying on many of the prophetic ideas of former Jews is never mentioned.[22]

In public school thousands of American students who may never have seen a Jew get their only picture of him from *The Merchant of Venice*, where Shylock becomes the epitome of Jewish traits. Teachers do not stop to point out to them that probably Shakespeare never knew an individual Jew, that he wrote a play about one because Marlowe had set the fashion, and the plot he used originally had the gentile playing the part he gave to Shylock.[23] The result is that, even apart from the informal influences of the home, average American children have a conditioned predisposition for disliking Jews imposed upon them in the classroom where a stereotyping process is begun. The very word "Jew" is an epithet, an emotion-arousing word which becomes an insult or a social weapon.

As Kallen observes, calling an individual a Pole, a Czech, or a Texan arouses no special hostility or feeling — these words are emotionally neutral. But the term "Jew," because of social conditioning, draws a ring around the individual and sets him off almost visibly as different from others. Its psychological effect is to the auditory nerves almost what the perception of skin color would be to the visual nerves, and it is often bound up with the belief that perceiving the Jew is a normal act of sensory selection.[24]

With all other minorities, a nickname derived from the more formal appellation becomes an epithet; Bohemians become Bohunks, Hungarians become Hunkies, Negroes become niggers, and Japanese become Japs. Perhaps the accidental occurrence that the word "Jew" is monosyllabic is at least the linguistic reason why no other cognomen has been necessary (though others like "kike," "sheeny," etc., have been elaborated). But that the word "Jew" has a derogatory emphasis can be observed from the fact that a gentile conversing with Jewish friends will often refrain from using the term at all until it has been brought into the conversation from the Jewish side. Much of this is the unwitting result of unconsidered educational policies. It simply prepares the way for the ideological anti-Semitism which finds channels all ready for its propaganda.

A CAUSAL ANALYSIS OF ANTISEMITISM

There are writers who maintain that to search for the causes of anti-Semitism is not only futile but deceptive, since it is basically irrational and serves as a mask for something deeper.[25] Its irrationality is evident when the Jew is disliked for being too rich or for being a beggar, for being clannish and for trying to become like the majority, for being a radical or for being too patriotic, for being a coward or for being a martyr.[26]

Perhaps the most common explanation of anti-Semitism in the contemporary world is an economic one. It is already clear that anti-Jewish feeling in America arose simultaneously with the increasing competition of Jewish financiers and tradesmen. There is little doubt that the commercial occupations to which medieval society restricted the Jew gave him a natural advantage with the rise of capitalism, an advantage which his emancipation enabled him to exploit to the full. In a way the same advantages were enjoyed by the Quakers and the Huguenots, neither of whom attracted special antagonism in spite of their striking financial successes. Why then was the Jewish businessman singled out for opprobrium while the Quaker or Huguenot received little attention? Is the cause of this differential treatment economic?

Bergman asks the reader to imagine a tenant becoming irate with his Jewish landlord who has been somewhat unscrupulous. If the tenant loses his temper and begins to berate all Jews, is his anti-Semitic attitude brought about by the economic situation (such as the refusal to give more heat or to redecorate), or is the immediate event only the occasion for the expression of dislike? Would the tenant do the same if the landlord were Irish, German, or Welsh? If the answer is no, then economic conditions may be the cause of this *particular* quarrel though they do not explain why the tenant is against all Jews. Economic competition is therefore not a sufficient explanation of anti-Semitism since it deals only with the immediate occasions of its expression.[27] And certainly other situations are just as likely to give rise to it (as for example if a Jewish boy charms a girl away from a gentile). Of course in a society dominated by pecuniary values the conditions are more often apt to be economic than otherwise. In the Middle Ages, on the other hand, the antagonism was more religious and theological; in the fourth century, even more so.[28]

The opposite side of the shield is the psychoanalytic approach. This represents anti-Semitism as only one of countless compensatory mechanisms in which the individual projects his own difficulties and conflicts upon a scapegoat. According to the Freudian theory everyone struggles with repressed impulses from the Id, tendencies toward cruelty, murder, and unfettered sexuality. These dynamic urges are so deeply hidden from consciousness that the person is unaware of them and does not know of their existence, though dreams and other symptoms of everyday behavior make them apparent to the initiated observer. Strangely enough the individual's own unconscious processes are considered foreign to himself — and so are the Jews. Anything foreign has an uncanny quality, just as the murderer or one who commits incest is uncanny because the individual has felt such impulses within himself and has repressed them.

In the same way any alien person or group must be uncanny also, must be murderous, grasping, sensual — in fact, be catalogued with all the evil qualities that have been repressed. By projecting these characteristics upon the alien group the individual gets rid of any implication that they can be his own; he frees himself from the burden of his own impulses by attributing them to others, and by his hostility to others shows a similar hatred for the sins to which he has a secret inclination. By finding a scapegoat against whom aggression is allowable he rids himself of his own potential crimes by attacking the "criminal" without mercy. All is fair in war.[29]

This explanation also has a good many elements of plausibility except to those who reject the pseudophilosophical and unverifiable mechanisms of the unconscious as unscientific. But if, for the sake of argument, they are allowed to stand, there are still difficulties. The same arguments may be urged for other pathological explanations in the same vein, such as Ben Hecht's picture of the "Anti-Semitic Goon" who is at the bottom of the economic ladder, is dissatisfied with himself and the world, and so comes to believe that death to all Jews will relieve him of the burden of his internal misanthropy; or his "Man with a Nowhere Ticket" who is frustrated by the complexity of a world he cannot understand and therefore turns to a crusade against the Jews who, he discovers in a secret meeting, are trying to dominate the world. Here he finds a way to combat his own loneliness and bewilderment in a confused world, a welcome tangible that somehow simplifies everything.[30]

All these analyses have one thing in common: they explain by indirection. Anti-Semitism does not bear its meaning within itself but can be understood only as the external manifestation of repression or frustration, the rationalization of a disordered mind or the socially directed hate of the self-hater. That the descriptions of the more venomous or pathological anti-Semite ring true can hardly be denied. On the other hand they give little indication of how this explanation would apply to the milder forms of anti-Jewish dislike among individuals who appear to need no such bolstering of their ego, whose status is secure enough to need little reinforcement. While the analysis may be applied to them and the assertion made that they are *really* insecure and have more self-distrust than appears on the surface, this statement often has little evidence to support it, except the very fact of anti-Semitism itself, which would make the argument circular. Nor does it quite explain why the Jewish group rather than some other alien community is chosen as the scapegoat to receive the repressed hostility of the individual. Any minority would serve. In fact the "analysis by indirection" is also used to explain any or all hatred toward every conceivable group which can be identified as somehow different from the dominant society and hence would clarify the genus (like xenophobia or fear of the stranger) without at the same time differentiating the species (more specific antagonism toward Jews as such).

Another variant of the indirect approach to anti-Semitism appears in the account by Maurice Samuel, who maintains that the fierce hatred of the Jew in the modern world is actually a substitute for an attack on Christ and Christianity. Christ was a Jew who brought to a focus many of the earlier Judaic teachings: of fairness, justice, and benevolence as opposed to the unabashed search for power. But secretly, Western man has always resented this curb on his natural impulses and while he cannot admit this openly, should he attack Christianity directly as Nietzsche did, he nevertheless feels that he can oppose the ideals of charity and kindness by an attack on the Jews who gave birth to Jesus and thus to his demands.

The dread of Christ and his doctrines which is concealed by external adherence to the church manifests itself in a kind of secret sympathy for those who deny all morality and in an attack on the people who produced a religious leader requiring an undivided allegiance to admittedly hard virtues.[31] While this explanation has considerable plausibility, it applies chiefly to the Nazi or fascist type of anti-Semitism, to the myth makers, rabble rousers, and demagogues who organize movements. Samuel himself begins by distinguishing this from the more temperate "anti-Jewishness," to which he pays no more attention after his initial distinction.[32] Nor does he attempt to show that his analysis applies to any forms before the twentieth century; it would certainly have no validity at all before the Christian era although anti-Semitism existed at that time.

The following answer to the question will seem deceptively simple, yet we may confidently assert that anti-Semitism is basically sociological. It may exist on an elementary level or it may be elaborated and intensified by innumerable historic and ideological currents that mingle with it on a secondary level. Thus the sociological answer will have much in common with both the psychoanalytic and the economic explanation and overlap with them while it yet remains more fundamental than either. In the last analysis the group preference for homogeneity is an irreducible datum revealed by anthropology and sociology in all societies. Whether it be a local group, a tribe, or a nation, the society which has coherence is sufficiently organized to have *esprit de corps* and a conception of itself as a working unit with common purposes, values, and social patterns of behavior.[33] Where newcomers are admitted it is with the tacit assumption that they too will accept and adopt the ways of life that constitute the homogeneous pattern of the society. But only after they have become completely assimilated are they fully accepted. Self-effacement thus becomes the price of full participation in the culture.

Since the Diaspora the Jews have been the one minority in the Western world that has been unwilling to pay this price because their religious beliefs would not permit it. This has been true in Egypt, the Roman Empire, Spain, and the countries of northern and eastern Europe. For this reason they can be called "the perennial minority." The one offense that the many dominant societies of Europe and America could not condone has been the unwillingness of the Jews to become assimilated in this one respect. It should be clear by this time, however, that this factor accounts for only the elementary level or what might be called "folk" anti-Semitism. Once this initial dislike of the unlike has been established and ingrained by centuries of experience, it develops into an irrational attitude of hostility which has a quasi-independent existence of its own and leads to an unfriendly interpretation of any and all actions of Jews, even the attempt to become assimilated that might have been welcomed at first.

It follows that where the unity of society is unachieved, where a plurality of cultural and religious elements is unavoidable, the position of the Jews has been less fraught with peril. This was true in the later Roman Empire, where all religions were given state recognition; or in Spain, when the presence of the Moors gave the Jews greater freedom; or in the Europe of the Dark Ages before the coherence of the later medieval world view was fully attained. It is also significant that with the recurring attempt of Germany under Nazi domination to reach a monolithic unity under totalitarian conceptions, the Jews suffered most of all.

It is precisely in the countries of western Europe (including England), where a certain amount of internal diversity has been encouraged as a part of the folk ideal of democracy, that the Jewish community has been most protected and most secure. It might seem at first glance that Soviet Russia was an exception to this general rule since it has outlawed anti-Semitism under a dictatorship. But it must be remembered that the Soviet policy is a centralized political unity with the widest latitude given to languages and folk customs so long as they do not interfere with this unity.

Once this primary variety of anti-Semitism has taken sufficient root in any population, it may lie dormant or become intensified. In periods of rapid social change or transition when the structure of society undergoes considerable modification, it appears in more virulent form, as in the Crusades of the Middle Ages, in the growth of industrialism (which, coupled with emancipation, made the Jews more conspicuous in the role of commercial leaders), or in economic depressions. Many writers have noticed its recurrence when the middle class are increasingly pauperized and look about for a scapegoat on which to fix the blame for their plight.

The crisis theory of the growth of anti-Semitism does not apply, however, to revolutionary epochs; in such periods the Jew is included with other underprivileged groups and improves his position with the rest. This liberty is bought at the cost of being more conspicuous during reaction when it is possible for conservatives in power to single him out. Naturally the Jewish community is in sympathy with libertarian movements and, when the reaction comes, finds itself pointed out as a special culprit.

At least one writer finds the root of all modern anti-Semitism in political conservatism, maintaining that when one scratches the skin of an anti-Semite, he will find a reactionary.[34] While a good case can be made for this theory since the Emancipation, it hardly furnishes a complete account of the whole tendency in earlier periods. Like other economic and political theories, it deals with anti-Semitism on what we have called the secondary level; unless the channel had already been dug by centuries of experience in which the Jew had been regarded as an unassimilated element, it would hardly result in the more virulent forms. The existence of this primary channel makes it possible for social and political leadership to foster and nourish anti-Semitism as a weapon whereby it may gain political power. That this tendency is deep rooted may be seen from the fact that an ancient Jewish sage of the third century made the profound observation, "He who persecutes Israel becomes a chief." [35]

A corollary of the sociological explanation is that anti-Semitism becomes more dangerous and violent in its secondary than in its more elemental form, since in the secondary type it is deliberately fostered by exaggerating the differences that already exist. At such periods anti-Semitism may often be directly out of line with official church or national policy, but the masses, whipped to fury by popular leaders, take matters into their own hands.* Often the strategy or financial backing, however, comes from more well-to-do circles.

JEWISH REACTION TO ANTISEMITISM: GENERAL TRAITS

Since the great majority of American Jews have an east European background, their mode of life must be evaluated in terms of a constant response to the more or less official anti-Semitism of Poland and Russia. State legislation in those areas regulated most of their public affairs, economic behavior, legitimation or identity papers, military service, place of residence, and rules for changing domicile. The Jewish attitude toward the police who enforced these regulations was similar to that of the Czechs to the dominant Germans, the Poles to the dominant Russians, or the Yugoslavs to the dominant Austrians or Hungarians. Police and law were identified with the op-

* In the twelfth and thirteenth centuries both popes and bishops, kings and nobles attempted to protect the Jews from persecution and declared that violence was not to be used against them. It was the lower clergy, especially three popular leaders, Peter the Hermit, Volkmar, and Gottschalk who inflamed the masses with a desire to wreak vengeance on the Jews.[36] In the twentieth century Pope Pius XI clearly stated, "Antisemitism is a movement in which we cannot, as Christians, have any part whatsoever. . . . Spiritually we are Semites." With encouragement from the Vatican, Catholic priests in Italy taught Hebrew to Jewish children out of touch with Jewish schools, in 1939. During the war it was estimated that 7000 Roman Jews owed the saving of their lives to the Vatican. When Italy was occupied by the Germans, and the Nazis prohibited the ritual slaughter of cattle and poultry for Jews, the Pope ordered Jewish slaughterers into Vatican City, where they performed their services so that food could be stored for the Jews there.[37] In the same period the German Catholic hierarchy stood out against the Nazis. Yet simultaneously both Austrian and German Catholics joined the Nazis by the thousands, and Father Coughlin was promoting a quasi Nazi brand of anti-Semitism in the United States, which gave it semiofficial sanction in Catholic eyes. Morris Lazaron reports a member of the lower clergy in the Catholic church in America who told his parishioners they should not work for Jews because the Jews were Communists and thus enemies of the church.[38]

pressor, who often made it difficult if not impossible to carry on normal business occupations without threading a maze of rules and regulations specifically adapted to curtail these operations in favor of the majority. Group survival usually demanded methods of evasion and shrewd practice often declared by outsiders to be unethical and unfair; one could hardly afford to be scrupulous if he was to live.

For example, a Russian law had it that Jews might not live in a village. Administratively the community in which a group of Jews were living might be called a "town." Yet if the officials arbitrarily decided on a certain day to make it a village, the law required that all Jews must leave. They were then forced to choose between leaving or bribing the police, and the latter was often an easier policy.[39] The Jew felt no more compunction about this self-defensive act than the Czech, Pole, or Yugoslav who suffered similar restrictions. The main difference is that the Jews had been forbidden to engage in agricultural occupations and thus had to carry on their economic life in rather narrow channels of trade and handmade goods. Generations of experience in developing business methods that would yield a profit even under the most stringent conditions, learning how to keep the letter of the law while evading some of its provisions, and practicing mutual aid among his fellow Jews for the bare purpose of survival gave the immigrant to the United States a rough and tumble tradition of commercial practice.

The early Jewish community in America was coherent enough and united enough to constitute a perfect grapevine for keeping track of bargains to be had anywhere. Bernard suggests that as the men of the *Vereins* or *Landsmannschaften* gathered together, the talk was often of business so that the discussions furnished the younger members with a kind of information later disseminated in much more academic fashion by business schools.[40] All these traits are related directly or indirectly to the group response to anti-Semitism abroad and the carry-over into a freer American atmosphere where such methods could produce more rapid results. Since there are no studies of business failures in which gentile and Jewish firms are compared, it is impossible to report whether the "Jewish business acumen" was widespread or limited to only a few. The practices described above actually existed and the common stereotype of the Jewish businessman makes them appear typical. Yet proof is lacking.

Probably a sizable minority of Jews from eastern Europe developed these survival practices, and their visibility in America made them seem typical of Jews in general. The main point for the discussion here is that this was one notable response to anti-Semitism.

In addition to dynamic aggressiveness among some of the Jewish traders, many also developed a technique of indirection which appeared to contradict it. Being members of a minority group easily identifiable, they have not allowed this aggressiveness to become overt because it would leave them unprotected before the attacks of the outsider. In order to be successful they have preferred to utilize more devious ways of self-protection, to employ subterfuge, alternately yielding and then pressing an advantage with diplomacy born of long practice.[41] In this respect their psychology has a certain similarity to feminine traits in response to the more brutal and direct methods of the male in Western culture. Is it fanciful to suggest that like the female the individual Jew frequently shows a greater interest in people than in things, in practical, rule-of-thumb psychology, in contacts and personal responses? [42] Is this one reason why the psychology of women has received so much elucidation from Jewish writers and thinkers, particularly Freud and the psychoanalytic school?

Parkes contends that another response which has been deeply imbedded in Jewish life as a result of centuries of experience with hostile surroundings is a certain disputatiousness and love of argument. As he states it, the gentile is sometimes bewildered to find that the reasoning of his Jewish neighbor often puts emphasis or stress on issues that seem to have little significance to the non-Jew. One of these elements is the immense importance the Jew often places upon legality and formal rights rather than upon "fair play." The historian might be tempted to attribute this to many centuries of Talmudic education, but this is not the whole of the story.

Parkes claims that for generations in Europe the very existence of the Jewish community was dependent upon a system of rights carefully defined in the law, upon special privileges which were the result of deliberate negotiation. National peoples living in their own territory had no such experience and were willing to leave rights to lawyers.[43] Thus the ability to argue in terms of formal rights had distinct survival value for the Jewish community and led to facility in reasoning that became widespread. This is one of the factors that also helped to give the Jewish student certain initial advantages in schooling but which often set him off from other students because of his unwillingness to concede an argument that might be readily acceptable to gentiles in the classroom.

Parkes' observation hardly takes into account the different strata in the Jewish community, even in England where he applies it, certainly not in the United States. Surely the disputatiousness of the Czech workman as remarked above (Chapter 13) is equal to that of any other group, and in the working class there seem to be similar tendencies in all nationality groups. And among shopkeepers or businessmen the diplomatic traits already mentioned would tend to inhibit argument.

The writer's observation, coupled with desultory reports from others familiar with the Jewish community, leads to the hypothesis that the most striking cases of Jewish disputatiousness come not from the business or industrial groups but from students, intellectuals, and professionals who have recently made a fantastic leap in social status and show the strain resulting from it. For this group Parkes' elaborate historical explanation seems quite unnecessary.

The persistent antagonism which the Jew has met from the outside world is nevertheless fraught with uncertainties; it has an inconsistency of its own which is reflected in a basic uncertainty of response. The individual Jew is never sure whether a hostile act is directed toward him as an individual or is directed against the group of which he is a member; hence he develops a watchfulness or sensitiveness that can be easily hurt, and what appears to be an attitude of looking for trouble that is characterized by the well-known phrase "chip on the shoulder." Or this attitude may be exaggerated into a compensatory pride or intensified egoism which may in turn provoke more hostile acts. It often means, too, an increased awareness of the mistakes and errors of other Jews, since the group as a whole is judged by them. In spite of his insistence to outsiders that generalization is impossible and that an individual should be judged purely on the basis of his own qualifications, that no individual is representative of a group, etc., he nevertheless tends to be highly sensitive to the actions of a "bad" Jew and inordinately proud of the accomplishments of an outstanding leader.[44]

The group awareness developed in Jewish psychology and the ever-present watchfulness to see how the behavior of the group is regarded by others also lead to an immense amount of criticism of other individual Jews. This criticism is so highly developed that it often makes Jewish community life a welter of conflicting cross-purposes and heightens the natural individualism which is so characteristic of the community itself. Class distinctions, national background, religious affiliation, Jewish loyalty or lack of it, support of Jewish charities, radicalism, conservatism, Zionism, or anti-Zionism, all come in for caustic comments. This is no less true of the behavior traits that make Jews conspicuous to non-Jews, and perhaps no one complains more bitterly about the boisterousness of individual Jews than other Jews.[45] Since humor is an accepted outlet, this criticism takes the form of the self-derisive jokes and stories about various Jewish types by comedians who thus make a virtue out of necessity for psychic relief.[46]

As the Emancipation gradually brought the Jews more and more into participation with the gentile world and as the edge of the older segregation was blunted, anti-Semitism was often modified into a newer form of "tolerance." But this very tolerance, as the Jew was keenly aware, masked a sense of superiority on the part of the person who asserted it. The distinction between full acceptance and the partial or grudging acceptance so often characteristic of the "tolerant" person led not to gratitude but to an increasing defiance of the very group which had made overtures of friendship. This reaction appears to a greater or lesser degree in other minority groups and therefore calls for no special comment, except to note that it sets up another vicious circle that may increase the anti-Semitism of the tolerant.

Much of the so-called "clannishness" in Jewish life is a direct reaction to the various discrimination policies in American social institutions. The Immigration Act of 1924 had the effect of closing the door permanently to the only escape from east European conditions, thus accelerating the Zionist movement even more. Increased exclusion of Jews from clubs, fraternities, and vacation resorts resulted in a growing number of Jewish institutions to take their places. Jewish employers who themselves preached the doctrine of nondiscrimination have found themselves forced to take over more and more Jewish employees simply because the latter could not find positions open elsewhere, and thus to discriminate against gentiles by indirection.[47]

Leaders with talents of organization and administration who have found it impossible to exercise them in the broader social scene have turned to utilize their gifts in Jewish community organization. The same tendency has occurred in the field of social work, where the many Jewish agencies offer opportunities for a large number who cannot utilize their capacities elsewhere. The parallel or "clannish" society in this, as among other minorities, is a natural response to limiting conditions. There is evidence to show that this tendency becomes more marked in the life of the Jewish individual with the advance of age. A study by Adeline Harris and Goodwin Watson of Jewish and gentile children around twelve years of age in New York schools brings out the pattern in early years.

Harris and Watson discovered that the choice of friends in their own class was quite similar when the two groups were compared; but outside of school gentile children chose only 6 per cent of their friends among Jews while Jewish children chose 28 per cent of their friends among gentiles. Even allowing for the fact that the number of potential gentile friends must have been larger, this study would indicate that Jewish children in their early years begin with more friends in the out-group than do gentiles and thus are not noticeably clannish to begin with.[48] Jessie Bernard at least suggests by her study that this tendency persisted into high school, where the young people grouped themselves according to spontaneous likings; but with the college period, when either dating or parents were concerned, adults stepped into the picture and polarized their children into Protestant, Catholic, or Jewish groups.[49] The fraternity and sorority pattern accentuated the process.

A threat of any kind to the Jewish community as a whole sends many members back to it with an increased feeling of solidarity which links them to their past. The rise of Nazism in Germany increased the participation of many secularized Jews in the activities of Judaism, synagogue worship, or Jewish social service and welfare activities. Edward Sapir, the Yale anthropologist, for example, confessed that with the coming of Hitler he went back to the Hebrew studies of his youth "through a kind of irrational sentiment" which he had believed foreign to himself.[50]

In some cases the danger is felt to be more immediate, as in Yankee City, for instance, where the death of three Jewish elders reduced the daily congregation of Jews to less than a *minyan*. Although a large share of the Jewish community had not attended synagogue up to that moment, they then bestirred themselves, raised $10,000 in a few weeks, purchased a Protestant church vacated through a merger, and used it for a new synagogue which would unite their efforts. The entire movement was engineered by a group of young men who had been conspicuous for lack of interest in the organized religious life of Judaism.[51] This single drive revitalized the entire life of the Jewish community in Yankee City.

The impact of discrimination against the Jews has resulted in a curious and sometimes contradictory set of attitudes vis-à-vis the Negro. In urban areas where the Negro moves in, the Jews move out rapidly in much the same fashion as the dominant community but in contrast to the Irish, who resist invasion, and the Italians, who offer very little resistance.[52] The fact that he shares minority status with the Negro serves to set up ambivalent attitudes in the individual Jew, together with certain guilt feelings and anxiety. On the one hand is the tendency to identify himself with another group whose position is also insecure, while on the other hand there is a desire to detach himself from a group receiving more discrimination than his own.

Although the majority of Jewish community leaders take on the first pattern, with full realization that minority issues require a unified approach to their solution, many others (probably less integrated with their own group) take the opposite path and identify themselves with the dominant white gentile in order to receive recognition and a more secure place in accepted society. Significantly enough, the Jew is more shielded from the full impact of anti-Semitism in the South, where anti-Negro prejudice is greater and where the hostility of the community is channeled away from the Jews. In spite of this greater protection, a considerable number of southern Jews show strong anti-Negro attitudes in which they may even outdo the southern white in their declaration of anti-Negro antagonism.[53] Elsewhere the number of younger Jews who are sensing the parallels between the Negro struggle for status and their own, is increasing and a marked interest is developing in Negro problems.

JEWISH REACTION TO ANTISEMITISM: SPECIAL STUDIES

The scientific studies of personality traits that have compared Jews with non-Jews are both few in number and somewhat conflicting in results. Since there has been little in the way of concerted effort to solve the problem, it is possible to present only a few of the findings representative of the whole and to indicate the need for further research. Although it might be expected that Jewish groups, as a result of their atypical experience, might show a greater incidence of mental disorders, Malzberg has shown that both in New York and in Massachusetts Jews have a smaller proportion of admissions to mental hospitals than non-Jews.[54]

In a comparison of foreign-born groups he shows that both Jewish males and females had a lower rate of admissions than other white foreign-born groups, though the female rate exceeded the male.[55] The Jews were the only foreign-born group showing a higher female than male incidence, all the others showing the reverse.[56] The functional psychoses (schizophrenia and the manic-depressive syndrome) are relatively more prevalent among Jewish psychotics than among any other foreign whites.[57] In comparison with native white males, Jewish males had an incidence of only 1.1 per 100,000 for alcoholic psychoses, while native whites had a rate of 10.8.[58] When Jewish foreign-born females were compared with native white females, the former had a greater incidence of admissions for several psychotic groups; they were proportionally higher by 66.1 per cent for senile psychoses, 44.2 per cent for manic-depressive, and 58.5 per cent for schizophrenia cases.[59] It is unfortunate that there is no similar study of the second generation, more marginal Jewish group.

With respect to neurotic traits the evidence is not so clear. Three studies comparing Jewish college students with gentiles of similar background show the Jews to have a somewhat higher maladjustment score or higher rating on traits showing mild deviation. Sward and Friedman found Jewish college students at the University of Pittsburgh, Western Reserve, and the University of Minnesota with somewhat higher neurotic averages (and significantly higher among Jewish women than among Jewish men). At the same time they found little correlation between these scores and those of the Jewish students' own parents.[60] A more intensive study by Sward of paired Jewish and gentile students at Western Reserve University showed the former to have higher scores in (1) gregariousness or social hunger, (2) humility and sensitiveness, (3) drive and aggressiveness, (4) emotionality or instability, especially anxiety states. These traits, as Sward points out, are significantly like those of a child with domineering parents.[61] Another study by Sukov and Williamson at the University of Minnesota on entering freshmen both Jewish and non-Jewish, showed the former with higher neurotic scores relative to morale, law, education (women only), and general maladjustment.[62]

On the other hand there is also evidence of little significant difference between the two groups. Even in the Sward and Friedman study first mentioned, the authors make it clear that the divergence of Jews from non-Jews is not large.[63] In one of the tests given by Sukov and Williamson (the Bell Adjustment Inventory) there were no significant differences at all between Jews and gentiles, and the divergences within each group were greater than those between the two groups.[64] A later study by Sperling of students at the City College of New York showed no significant differences between Jews and non-Jews in emotional stability, social acceptability, superiority-inferiority, objectivity, or family relationships. Furthermore, Jews scored higher in extroversion and political liberalism and lower in religious interests, were educationally accelerated about three fourths of a year, and showed higher intelligence scores.[65]

The weight of evidence from these studies does not permit any generalizations with respect to major neurotic trends among Jews, even though they may be suggestive. Since all the studies are of college students, excepting one comparison with adults, it is not only too small but too selective a sample.

After making a study of sixty-seven Jewish boys in summer camp as compared with ninety-one non-Jewish in another camp where the boys had a similar socioeconomic background, Fred Brown discovered no differences in neurotic scores but found the Jewish boys reliably higher in "play preferences, fantasy life, ambitions, adjustment to the group, choices of books and movies, and in their ability to accept responsibility." Referring to Malzberg's analysis showing the higher incidence of functional rather than organic psychoses among Jews, Brown then proposes a hypothesis that the incidence of neuroticism increases among Jews as the person comes into participating contact with adult social realities. He explains this by the greater thrust toward unlimited intellectual achievement in Jewish homes which gives the child an illusory sense of "limitless vertical mobility." During the early years at school this makes for good adjustment but when the time comes for choosing a vocation and the individual discovers that discrimination limits this mobility sharply, disillusionment follows, with anxiety states, depressions, and the like. The drive toward achievement continues by momentum, resulting in "overreaction and compensatory behavior." The later number of functional psychoses represent a further stage of the process and show the conflict between a powerful vertical thrust and a restricted social ceiling.[66] This hypothesis has considerable plausibility if it be applied to the actual number of neurotics and psychotics in the group, though not if it implies that this number is greater than it is among non-Jews, since that is yet to be proved. But Brown's conception suggests interesting lines of research for further corroboration.

The account would be incomplete without the observations of Kurt Lewin on the reaction of Jews to external pressure. He shows that the marginality of Jewish group life differs somewhat from that of other minority groups in that the Jew may not only be uncertain about the group he is entering (with all the self-consciousness, inhibition, or overreacting implied) but that he is also uncertain about the group he is leaving and his position relative to it. Whether he belongs to the Jewish community, how much he belongs, or where he stands with respect to it are questions that cannot be adequately decided and therefore receive different answers.

On the other hand those Jews whose action is in terms of membership within their own group (where this is a matter of somewhat rigid loyalty predominating over others) tend toward unbalanced action since there is no labile quality that enables them to proceed smoothly from one group requirement to another.[67] In ghetto days social pressure was applied to Jews as a whole but the individual had a certain protection against disruptive psychological tendencies because of group reinforcement; today he feels this pressure more as a relatively isolated individual and therefore is more exposed. The pressure of anti-Jewish feeling is accordingly increased to the extent that the person lacks integration within his own group.[68]

Lewin also shows that a person who has almost reached a goal operates at a particularly high tension, for instance, the prisoner who attempts escape a few days before release or the boy in a reformatory who regresses in behavior just prior to his time of leave. This is because he already feels himself a member of the group outside and strains tensely to join it. Somewhat the same tendency is operative among those Jews who are almost but not quite accepted in the gentile world. One symptom of this is general restlessness, of which the most productive form is overwork. Evidence is given that Jews in Palestine lose this restlessness a few months after arrival.* [69] Furthermore the conflict situation increases as the boundary between the minority and the dominant group becomes weaker; hence it is likely to be greatest for younger members of wealthy families, especially since these youths have as yet had no chance to prove their individual merit and achieve self-confidence in that way.[70]

On the other hand there are individuals who want to leave the group and have no loyalty to it but because of social prejudice are forced to stay in it. Such persons will then try to get away from anything Jewish and give a low evaluation to habits, attitudes, or customs that appear Jewish. Though staying as far from Jewish life as the gentile world will permit, these persons will be in a continual state of frustration and tension, which is then directed not against the dominant group that has higher status but against the Jews themselves or against the individual himself as a Jew. This "negative chauvinism" is really the same, basically, as the familiar phenomenon of Jewish "self-hatred" which receives so much attention from Jewish writers.[71] Part of this phenomenon results from the acceptance by the individual of outsiders' views concerning his own group.[72] As he enters the competitive race for success, he may desire to be judged on his merits and conclude that the less conspicuously Jewish he appears the better;

* A somewhat different report has been relayed to the writer by a former army officer stationed in the Middle East who observed a Jewish professional he had known in Germany. This professional showed intense ambition while in Europe but lost his drive in Palestine. Increased group security may thus lessen anxiety at the expense of initiative.

he can see no virtue whatever in carrying the added millstone of Jewishness about his neck when it so often proves embarrassing to him. Thus he tends to accept the common stereotype of Jews even though by his actions he attempts to fight against it. As Pelcovits states the problem, he forgets that Jews are people.[73]

It is also significant that privileged groups are centripetal, while underprivileged are centrifugal. Members of the former seek to remain within and find the center of the group a basic value, while members of the latter often try to escape. Thus organizing the underprivileged group becomes highly difficult because it has so many members with negative balance whose chief aim is to leave the group rather than try to promote its interests. This diversity of aims and the consequent plurality of goals has already been noticed and will receive attention below in the discussion of Zionism.

Another aspect deserving attention is what Lewin calls the "leader from the periphery." Often the person who has become successful in his business or profession has done so in such a manner as to bring him into more direct contact with the dominant majority than with the Jewish group itself. When the time comes for someone to mediate between the two groups, this individual may be designated either by the Jews because of his influence with gentiles or by the gentiles because they are aware of his Jewish connections. However, this same leader is often lukewarm in his attitude toward the Jews because he does not want to imperil his position with the majority. He thus confines his leadership activities to keeping Jews from being too "conspicuous" and in many cases actually opposes the rise of other Jews to positions of prominence (such as sending a Jew to the Supreme Court bench) for fear it will raise the Jewish question in the minds of the majority.[74]

These peripheral leaders, while they have the advantage of constant acquaintance with outsiders, may, because of their position, tend to exaggerate negative attitudes toward Jews; on the other hand their lack of solidarity with Jews, while obvious enough, may not be so great as their critics insist. Although their influence on the Jewish group may be potentially disruptive, it may also have prevented a certain amount of ill-considered and hasty action. It seems true, as Lewin suggests, that strong group solidarity can prevent self-hatred because then the Jew will no longer regard himself in terms of an unfriendly majority; [75] yet this thesis overlooks the impersonal forces of assimilation that tend to reinforce the centrifugal tendencies within the Jewish group as a part of a larger social process.

ZIONISM AND ANTISEMITISM

It is impossible to discuss all the political and economic factors in the Palestine question without devoting a whole volume to the problem, but the ideological issues deserve some comment as they bear on the question of Jewish status. Although the great majority of American Jews favor some sort of national homeland in Palestine, it is probable that not more than a third are actively engaged in programs which involve Zionist aims; [76] perhaps this is also true so far as participation in Jewish community organization is concerned.

It has already been pointed out that the earlier immigrants, the German Jews, in their program of Reform Judaism tended to stress assimilation as the chief answer to the problem of anti-Semitism. Today it is being urged in Jewish circles that assimilation is a false answer to the problem of status, since it failed most lamentably in the very area where the Jews were most assimilated, namely, Germany. If such a program can be followed by the ruthless war of extermination against Jews as it was among the Nazis, the inference is that it cannot succeed elsewhere. More than ever the Zionist insistence that the Jews are a "people" or "nation" has taken hold as a philosophy, with the corollary that establishment in Palestine of a Jewish commonwealth would serve to normalize relations between Jews and citizens of other nations. To all those Jews living outside of Palestine, the presence of their own people on their own soil, represented in embassies and international bodies officially and not on sufferance, thus points the way to a natural type of protection, a feeling of national pride, and a refuge or haven in time of distress elsewhere. Particularly among east European Jews the notion that a Jewish homeland will restore "self-respect" since it is based on the same national realities accepted by citizens elsewhere, has come to be almost a self-evident axiom.

From the first, Zionism in America was opposed by the American Jewish Committee and by Reform elements. At the opposite end of the scale a small group of ultra-Orthodox Jews opposed it on the ground that the Palestinian restoration was supposed to be the work of the Lord following the millennium. For man to usurp this task was blasphemy. A number of Jewish charitable organizations have also opposed the program for various reasons. Although the American Jewish Committee gradually modified its stand, other groups have not. A sizable number of Jews who have remained outside the organizations, ignore the issue entirely or are indifferent.

Perhaps the most vociferous antagonism to the national state in Palestine comes from a new organization calling itself the American Council for Judaism. Rabbi Elmer Berger, the outstanding leader of the movement, has pointed out that instead of saying assimilation failed in Germany, it is more true to say that democracy did not succeed since Germany never digested the democratic ideal.[77] He asserts that wherever democratic freedoms are truly established, the Jews also live in freedom; and where they are insecure, not only the Jews but all minorities are insecure. Thus it is the view of the American Council that the only way in which the Jew can find acceptable status in the modern world is for him to identify himself with the nation in which he lives in every way except that of religion. There is no reason why a Jew cannot be a good Englishman, Frenchman, Belgian, or Hollander. In fact this program has worked remarkably well in countries like those of western Europe where democracy has been firmly established; it has even been true in Russia and Yugoslavia as well.[78]

Berger claims that until Jews adopt the philosophy that they are citizens of those countries in which they live, and accept those countries as their homelands, they cannot expect to be welcome anywhere.[79] He attacks the Zionist program because for him it implies that the Jews want special and segregated status; he contends that this is a step backward toward the medieval ideal, a claim that the "Jewish people" have rights as a group which are somehow different from those of other minorities. At the same time he charges that the present official leaders of Jewry are separatists who try to retain a "medieval" control of intellectual pursuits, press releases, recreation, social and political affairs,[80] giving them such responsibility for leadership that the non-Zionist is everywhere forced to be on the defensive since his view is not the "official" one.[81] The result is that the simple "garden-variety Jew" has no spokesman and no voice in the councils of Jewry. Berger denies that Jewish nationalism has ever been the expression of the hopes of Jews in America or anywhere else.[82] He urges that special pleading for Jews is never effective and that it will result in more antipathy to them. In fact the Zionists, as he sees them, accept the basic principle of anti-Semitism that a special Jewish people actually exists.[83]

As for Palestine, the American Council for Judaism supports increased immigration into that area but believes that the erection of a specifically Jewish state is the very policy that inflames Arab opposition, especially since the Zionists accept the United Nations proposal for partition as only provisory and openly declare that a Jewish state embracing all of Palestine is still their ultimate aim.[84] As an alternative plan the American Council urges a special United Nations trusteeship for Palestine, with eventual self-government in which both Jews and Arabs will be included.[85]

While the American Council for Judaism admittedly speaks for a minority of United States Jews, having grown to a membership of only 8000 in two years,[86] it nevertheless has become highly vocal. Since the position of its members is very similar to that of early Reform Jews and since they include mostly Reform elements in their group,[87] there is a tendency on the part of Zionists to call all individuals holding these and similar opinions "assimilationists."

There seems little doubt that Steinberg had this group in mind when he asserted that assimilationists believe that a Jew "as he is" is not so desirable as he would be if he were a gentile, that they believe the Jews should abandon their special traditions and dissolve themselves into outer society and even seek to lose themselves thereby. Steinberg then charges that such doctrines can lead only to further self-reproach and self-hatred, an intensifying of feelings of inferiority already too prevalent among the Jews.[88] This clearly seems an overstatement when Berger emphasizes the need for Jews to respect their own religion in precisely the way that Christians do theirs and when he prefers the terms "emancipation" and "integration" to "assimilation."[89]

It is interesting that proponents of both sides accuse each other of being responsible for the death of innocents in Europe. Zionists assert that if those in favor of emancipation had taken Zionism a little more seriously, many Jews who perished during the Nazi extermination would now be living in Palestine.[90] On the other hand those holding the point of view of the American Council urge that the Zionists are unwilling to have the Displaced Persons go anywhere except to Palestine and have therefore failed to give the Stratton Bill popular support or to supply money and aid for any of them who wish to come to America.[91]

While to the outsider this may at first appear a minor tempest in a minority teapot, it is really the struggle of two competing philosophies of considerable importance for the future of the Jews in America. In an attempt to evaluate the background of the American Council for Judaism, Mordecai Grossman found in a representative sample that all the respondents but one belonged to Reform Judaism and that they all came from upper middle class groups with higher incomes and high intellectual attainments.[92] The great majority questioned held that the word "Jew" always has a religious meaning and never any other.[93] If there are cultural implications, they are derivable from the religious ethos.

At the same time Grossman notes that this position is not always consistently held and that "in an unguarded moment" many admit that a person may lose his Jewish religious affiliation and still remain a Jew.[94] Thus there is an opposition between their conscious definition of what is meant by a Jew and their unconscious or habitual ways of viewing the problem.[95] Nearly four times as many respondents preferred the "melting pot" ideal as a design for America rather than "cultural pluralism," although there was lack of clear definition on this point.[96] The majority wanted some curtailment of Jewish communal life in America [97] and insisted that Jewish education should be entirely under religious rather than secular auspices; in addition they opposed Talmud Torahs and parochial schools.[98] In fact another term for the Council and its adherents might be "minimal" Jews, and the Zionists, together with all those who personally support the nationalist ideal, could be called "maximal" Jews.

To the outsider, and particularly to the sociologist, the program of the American Council will definitely make a great appeal. Typical of this general view is that of J. O. Hertzler who insists that the bicultural relationship of the modern Jew runs counter to national assimilation and that, under present conditions, becoming one with a people involves giving up old loyalties or wanting to be something else at the same time. He states it very bluntly when he declares, "The loyalty of the Jew, when confined to Jews, is tribal; when applied to general relations, it is universal." [99] It is perhaps typical of this view also that Hertzler should assert that if anti-Semitism is to cease, the Jew himself will have to do most of the changing.[100] The implication is that any other loyalty the Jew may have besides that of religious loyalty will undoubtedly increase anti-Semitic attitudes. Integration must be wholehearted or it is not integration at all. It is inferred that the larger group has the right to make this demand or that under conditions of American society unidirectional assimilation is inevitable.

Our study takes the position that Hertzler's thesis is too simple, in fact oversimplified, if anthropology and its findings are seriously accepted. Is it the only rational conclusion that the uniqueness of any culture when it comes into continuous contact with another larger one is to merge with the latter and become obliterated (even if religion itself be excluded)? If so, it means an insistence upon cultural monism instead of cultural pluralism as the only possible outcome. If divided loyalties are not permitted in the Jewish community, what about the countless divided loyalties of the person in any secondary culture which continue to make divergent demands every hour of the waking life? Or what of the divided loyalty of the individual who prefers internationalism to a narrow nationalism? Must we insist that he give up one or the other or else take the consequences of being eliminated under the steam roller (whether it be that of internationalism or nationalism)? Is one really incompatible with the other at all times and in all relations?

This raises the issue of consistency, an issue to which the anthropologists have also given considerable attention. Here the answer is plain that cultures, like personalities, often carry certain inconsistencies within them and that the tension resulting therefrom may be a prelude to fresh solutions of problems hitherto considered insoluble (provided only that these inconsistencies do not affect the value core of the culture).[101] The principle of freedom which is an integral part of the American ethos could then not only allow plural loyalties but might well insist upon them. To restrict Jewishness to religion is, as Grossman well says, an arbitrary procedure. "One is entitled to be selective with regard to his own Jewishness. . . ." [102]

To do that selecting for him is simply to practice cultural imperialism, which in turn proves to be ultimately impossible. Thus if many Jews find their Jewishness in language, customs, and folkways which are not specifically religious, and proceed to make of them a national ideal which is fulfilled in the aspirations of a Jewish Palestine (and it seems that this is one fateful outcome of anti-Semitism), the result can then be accepted by the social scientist as a perfectly natural one that shows a continuing growth; it is then one alternative among many cultural responses. It may be the type which reinforces the sense of belonging for many Jews in a way that nothing else can offer. Since Zionism has become a mass movement while the process initiated by the American Council with its upper class membership lacks that character,[103] it is visionary to insist that the Zionists must give up their ideal in order to become good Americans.

The same principle cuts both ways. It presumes that the integrationalists have an answer to anti-Semitism which is equally satisfactory for themselves and that Zionists who misrepresent their position or call them "quislings" (as has been done in the author's hearing) are also violating the principle of cultural pluralism. If there is room for cultural diversity within the American pattern, it goes without saying that there should be similar room within Jewish culture. It is likely that if this diversity continues, the conflict of ideals may produce a revitalized ideology to deal with anti-Semitism.

Certainly the nationalism of Zionism is different in many important respects from the nationalism of citizens in other countries; the very fact that the Jewish state in Palestine has been, so to speak, manufactured or brought into existence by Jews all over the world, makes it quite unique; thus Zionism has an entirely different character from the loyalty a citizen has to a nation in which he was born by accident of birth. It is questionable whether the same loyalty can be felt in both cases. How can one be a national of a country he helped to create? Unless he goes there to live (and the majority of Jews, most of whom are now in the United States, certainly will have no desire to do so) will he actually think of himself as in some sense a citizen of that "homeland"? In what sense will a consul or ambassador of Jewish Palestine be able to speak for him if he is a citizen of another country? This would raise the question posed by the Japanese and Germans long ago, and the United States has a traditional hostility to dual citizenship. Or in what sense does the American Jew have more "self-respect" or "dignity" because of the creation of a Jewish state? That the east European Jew may have on the Continent is probably the case; but the acceptance of the eastern European ideology in the American scene has created certain anomalies.*

In certain respects the Zionist ideal has been romantic — like the view that after marriage all will be happy "ever after." Certainly the attempted creation of a Palestinian state has clearly shown that this does not settle all Jewish problems at a stroke; in fact it simply begins a new chain of causes and effects, and new difficulties that were not faced before. The Zionists themselves are coming to recognize this when their Action Committee states, "Any solution for Palestine cannot be considered as a solution of the Jewish problem in general." [104] Is it perhaps not more realistic to conclude that there is no single solution to the problem of anti-Semitism and to allow several alternatives to be attempted at the same time?

If the principle of cultural pluralism has any validity at all, it should

* The psychological atmosphere from which Zionism comes is a fusion of certain ideas accepted and repeated so often that they appear self-evident to those Jews who assert them:

(1) By anti-Semitism is meant the virulent European variety.
(2) Assimilation did not prevent Hitlerism in Germany. Hence it is a failure anywhere.
(3) Those who disagree that the Jews are fundamentally a nation are really anti-Semitic.
(4) Jewish nationhood by its very nature includes all Jews, whether in Europe or in the United States.

David Bernstein shows convincingly that each of these assertions is untenable; that the most prevalent form of American anti-Semitism is basically the anti-foreignism directed against more recently arrived immigrants, which weakens with time; that the crisis of Hitlerism was due to lack of democratic convictions, not to Jewish assimilation; that being a Jew may result from diverse factors — being defined by gentiles as Jewish, accepting Jewish culture, identifying oneself with Jewish religion, or defining Jewishness as nationhood. Since there are Jews who accept some of these views and not others, it is idle to assert that nationhood embraces all Jews. It may do so normatively for the Zionist but not actually and objectively. Bernstein's conclusion, in line with the proposition advanced here, is that no conception of Jewishness can have validity unless it "will permit the individual Jew to make as much or as little of his background as he wishes." David Bernstein, "Jewish Insecurity and American Realities," *Commentary* 5:119–127, 1948.

be applicable within the Jewish community as well as outside. While this may be confused with a laissez-faire policy, it can be regarded as an active, not merely a passive, principle. There are of course more concrete measures in which the entire Jewish community can join in an open and concerted effort to abate anti-Semitism, and these will be considered in more detail below when dealing with programs and policy. In the meanwhile it is neither defeatism nor a counsel of despair to insist that the price of being a Jew is the facing of at least a minimal amount of anti-Semitism [105] just as being a member of contemporary urban society involves everyone in the problem of poverty. While poverty may never be entirely eliminated, there are many ways in which society may reduce it so that it will no longer endanger the welfare of the community. Even so with anti-Semitism.

When Peoples Meet

[CHAPTER 18]

Minority Patterns of Adjustment:
Uniformities and Variabilities

THE HALL was crowded. One after another the speakers presented their arguments from the platform, now and then arousing ripples of applause from the audience as they touched on common aims: the outlawing of restrictive covenants, professionalizing police forces, joining of religious forces to combat prejudice, the immediate need for a state F.E.P.C. law. Excitement rose even higher as the chairman announced that the meeting was now open for discussion from the floor. Hands shot up all over the room, and the chair recognized a well-dressed man apparently in his middle forties, who began speaking rapidly.

"This meeting shows how much can be accomplished if we all get together," he declared. "Until all groups that feel the lash of discrimination work as a team, they cannot expect to be heard. I myself am a Jew. My parents came from Poland and we have lived in this city for twenty years. Yet there have been many times when we did not feel that we belonged. But until recently we did nothing about it until this organization came along. We are just beginning to realize — and I say this to all of you Negroes in the audience — we are all in the same boat. If the speakers said anything this afternoon, that was it. Whenever . . ."

Henry got up from his seat at the back of the hall and almost ran for the door. Outside he hurried down the flight of steps and out into the fresh air, his whole body trembling. On the sidewalk he nearly collided with another Negro, who pushed him roughly and then laughed.

"What got into you, Henry? Cops after you?"

"Who do you think . . .? Oh hello, Frank! Naw. Something worse. Couldn't take it any longer. You know about the interracial meeting upstairs?"

"Yeah, sure."

"Well I got out of there as fast as I could for fear I'd shoot off my big mouth and say something I shouldn't. When I left, Finky was playing the grand slam about how we Jews and you Negroes were all in the same boat. Can you tie that? He can ride in any train he wants to all over the country, stay practically anywhere he pleases, get waited on in any store with no trouble, eat in any restaurant, and all that. I'd like to see any of us brown boys trying the same thing. Maybe we wouldn't get lynched but we certainly would get set clear back on our heels. How can he tell us we're all in the same boat? He's white, ain't he? Does he or any other white man know what the score is? Can he compare the struggle of his people with ours? It seems pretty tame to me. Is he a hypocrite or is he just ignorant? I can't for the life of me figure out which. But I know one thing: when he says we're all in the same boat, it just won't make sense. Maybe I shouldn't boil over the way I do but I'll tell you, Frank, if I hadn't left that hall when I did, I might have said something that could of broken up the meeting. I mean it." [1]

In X-ville another meeting was under way. This one was under the auspices of the National Urban League. The program dealt with housing for Negroes, and many facts regarding the slums in which Negroes were forced to dwell had been presented. A small scattering of whites was in the room and before long one of them asked permission to speak.

"I came here this evening at the invitation of your chairman, Mr. Brown. My name is Mr. Bren and I run the corner drugstore at Fifteenth and Jackson, right near the area you have been talking about. Some years ago many of my people lived there; we came from Yugoslavia. This meeting has interested me a great deal because I know that section of town so well and have watched it change for fifteen years. As I sat here listening to the discussion, I remembered how many of us used to live down there and how a good many of us were able to move to better parts of the city.

And I wondered whether our experience may not be of some value to you.

"As soon as we had enough immigrants together we formed a fraternal union, the Zajednica. We didn't have much to live on in those days but each of us would contribute a few cents to a dollar a week to the organization for an insurance policy. Others put theirs into a building and loan fund that gradually grew with the years. In ten, fifteen, or twenty years, each family head had enough put away to make a down payment on a house, and then he would ask the building and loan branch of the society to show him a few sites where he could build. Before long most of us were able to get new homes, though it took a long time to get started. Wouldn't it be possible for the Urban League to start a building and loan fund for Negroes so they could do the same thing? Nothing can take the place of thrift, and I think that whether it is business or home building, thrift is the basis of everything. What do you think, Mr. Chairman?"

Jack Brown cleared his throat. This was going to be difficult. There were so many things to say he hardly knew where to begin. When he did, the words came slowly.

"There is a lot of sense in what you're saying, Mr. Bren. I'm sure that all of us here tonight are glad that you could tell us of your experience and how the Yugoslavs were able to get ahead. I would be the last one to discount the value of thrift. Only many of our people have saved up some money and then found that they couldn't buy out of the neighborhood because real estate dealers wouldn't let them. Nor would any banks or savings and loan companies give any loans to Negroes outside of this restricted area which is already built up so that it is impossible to squeeze another house in. And perhaps it is harder for our people to practice thrift than it was for you in your day. Most of them are at the bottom of the economic ladder, you know, and their jobs don't leave them much after food and rent are paid for."

"But one dollar a week or fifty cents a week would do it," cut in Mr. Bren. "We used to have poor jobs too but part of it we never spent; we always put it away."

"What you say is probably true. But your people were not the last hired and the first fired. They never worked in the South for years without a cent to their name, carried by the commissary and getting used to being without money. They never knew what it was to be slaves and have all the family upkeep off their shoulders while they worked so that somebody else could get rich. It's hard to develop habits of thrift that way, you know. There are a lot of things we can learn from the nationality groups in this country, but we have to learn them in our own way and at our own tempo. And like everyone else we have to learn it the hard way. Considering our obstacles, I think that we have moved ahead pretty far." [2]

These examples and many others which might be cited, give evidence of the uneven pace of adjustment among minority groups. The constant emphasis given through these pages to the concrete setting and life experience of each minority has not been so much to focus interest on differences as to make them appear inherent or permanent. It has been rather to stimulate a sense of reality in regard to the problems of minorities, to see them as functions of historic experience.

TYPES OF DISCRIMINATION

In our first chapter it became apparent that minority groups emerge as the end product of power relations in which a dominant group prevents the full participation of the minority in the culture through stereotypes, ideology, persuasion, folkways, etiquette, or enacted law. Where any of these techniques involve overt behavior, they are forms of discrimination; the psychological anticipatory set which calls these overt reactions into being may be called prejudice. Only in exceptional cases may one be present without the other since they are mutually implied.

It has also been shown that minorities typically arise through conquest, slavery, immigration, or a shift in political boundaries.[3] The historical realities of any one of these will determine what feature or characteristic of the subordinated group can serve to set it off from the dominant group. Around this feature cluster a set of stereotypes which simplify the identification of the group and tend to connect every individual in it with the label and its accompanying beliefs.

The most common form of identification is the visual, perhaps because of the fact that sense perception is primarily optical; there is psychological evidence that visual imagery is the most common type of all.[4] Thus if visible differences between the minority and the dominant group exist, they are given a pre-eminent place in the construction of a stereotype, which is nothing but the image that enables individuals to treat all members of a class as essentially the same.[5] Thus where racial differences are present and are easily visible, the identification of individual with group reaches its apex, so that discrimination unerringly reaches its mark. Other things being equal, we should then expect that discrimination would be most marked where racial differences are more obvious. To some extent this is true; we have already seen that lighter-colored Mexicans can often find accommodations or receive service in restaurants where darker-colored ones cannot, and that segregation bears less heavily on the Mexican community than on the Negro.[6]

But other things are not equal. The mode whereby a minority undergoes a change to subordinate status also affects the discrimination pattern. Thus those who have experienced either conquest or slavery bear an additional historical handicap which is then translated into a sharper separation between themselves and the dominant majority. So it becomes clear that the Indian and the Negro are most thoroughly segregated from native whites, since they have a visible racial distinctiveness as well as a lower status due to more violent subordination through the power relations of conquest and slavery. The segregation of the Indians on reservations is almost absolute, while that of the Negroes in the South is sufficient to make possible certain features of a parallel culture.[7]

Of the four racial groups discussed above, the Japanese are probably next as victims of discriminatory practice. The major segregation experienced by them was the temporary condition of relocation resulting from the hostilities of the war, and it terminated with the peace. The fact that no European minority identified with an enemy country had to undergo a comparable even if temporary internment, indicates that the racial difference in this case was crucial.[8]

While the Mexican thus appears to have suffered the least discrimination of the four racial groups considered here, the contrast between him and individuals of ethnic minorities from Europe is sufficiently great to constitute almost a difference in kind. The majority of Mexican Americans are still in a socioeconomic position so tightly circumscribed that there is little or no chance to rise above it. The job ceiling for most Mexicans is low and rigid.[9]

Turning from the racial groups to the new immigration from Europe, the observer might suppose that there is little differentiation. As the minorities of audibility rather than visibility, they have for the most part entered the country to swell the ranks of unskilled labor, with language and customs that distinguished them from older arrivals. As they learned American speech, participated in the folkways of the native population, and climbed up the economic ladder, they lost their original marks of difference. There seems to be no single criterion to determine which nationality group experienced most discrimination. Probably a compound of several factors was responsible: dominance of unskilled labor, enforced slum housing, colony living, and lateness of arrival, all combined, would determine discriminatory practice.*

In this respect the Italian group probably faced more serious problems of overcrowding, poverty, and lower paid occupations.[10] But this was true only for the mass and not necessarily for all individuals; certainly many Poles, Slovaks, Hungarians, or Croatians contended with difficulties of equal urgency. At the other end of the scale, however, it seems reasonable to conclude that the Czechs had fewer discriminations to meet; their arrival was earlier and they entered the economic system nearer the top because so many of them were skilled workmen.[11]

On the other hand, if all European groups are considered and not merely those with national backgrounds, it becomes apparent that the Jews were subject to greater discrimination; their divergence from the religious norm was greater, and this often took a visible form — the celebration of holidays at times when other elements of the population were working, or attendance at synagogues markedly different from churches, or observance of dietary customs that sometimes made them conspicuous. Probably these factors rather than the occasional visibility of the Jews rendered them visible and made it possible for the dominant majority to segregate them more decisively than it did the national groups. That they became a special target for discrimination is shown by the fact that they alone, of all European groups, share with racial minorities the odium of

* Lateness of arrival alone would be an inadequate criterion. On this basis the refugees of the 1930's and 1940's would suffer most, but they certainly did not.

restrictive covenants and unfair employment practices that prevent them from exercising free choice of occupation.[12] One reason for this is probably the popular but erroneous idea that they constitute a distinct racial group of their own, and racial distinction implies some segregation.

Minority adjustment is therefore partly a function of the variation in the intensity of the discrimination process. The group (which means the individuals within it) face a definite pattern of social separation and willy-nilly accommodate themselves to its operation. Their attitudes, feelings, beliefs, and actions are slowly but definitely molded in the direction or shape of the discriminatory pattern; some of the characteristics resulting from this come to be known through the stereotyping process as inherent rather than as imposed traits.

Where discrimination is not legally enforced (as in anti-intermarriage laws or court injunctions to carry out restrictive covenants), it may be quite as potent in the folkways. Thus it may become customary to admit no "foreigners" or people whose names are not markedly Anglo-Saxon into exclusive clubs or societies or political organizations. Professional societies, university faculties, or teachers' agencies may function smoothly by means of tacit agreements that exclude all those whose ancestors did not come from the older immigration even though such agreements have proved quite unworkable for athletic teams. It is an interesting thesis, and one which perhaps deserves more careful study, that the increasing number of Slavic or Italian names in sports may be partly a result of their exclusion from upper class pursuits, and at the same time their participation in athletics is an important agency promoting assimilation.

VARIABILITY IN ADJUSTMENT, ACCULTURATION, AND ASSIMILATION

While it has been necessary to portray the adjustment of minorities within the primary framework of discrimination as our basic orientation, it is now time to present these other contingent factors more clearly. Although none of these operates in isolation from the others or from discrimination itself, each may be treated separately for convenient analysis. In general the rate of acculturation and assimilation (involving acceptance) is a function of many variables, of which seven are selected here.

(1) The first of these is position. By this term we signify the locus in social space assigned to the group at a given time. For example, a relatively isolated position such as the one occupied by Indians on the reservation may be contrasted with the position of the manual laborer in a Slovak coal mining community; the immigrant group in the latter case (because of its place in the scale of occupations) is partly but not wholly removed from many concerns of the community. Thus while "position" overlaps with "status," it is not synonymous with it.[13]

It may be ventured that the more isolated the position, the slower will be the rate of adjustment; the more these positions alter to increase the contacts with the dominant group, the greater will be the tendency toward assimilation. This is more apparent among the European minorities as their infiltration into new economic occupations brings them into increasing contact with the older American stock. This process cannot be considered by itself, however, but only in the broader framework of discrimination noted above; thus the altered position of the rural southern Negro after he migrates to a northern city may also bring an increased amount of mingling with whites and yet the visibility pattern allows the dominant group to restrict contacts to more impersonal ones. Accordingly changes in position occur most freely among the European groups, somewhat less among the Jews (who may be included within them), and still less among Japanese, Negroes, and Mexicans.* In general, change to a more central position allowing for contacts will accelerate the rate of assimilation even when it is retarded by racial discrimination. For most European migrants this change in position becomes the agency of almost automatic social advancement.

(2) Divergence in culture patterns. Let us advance the hypothesis that the basic American culture pattern in the past has been dominantly middle class, individualistic, and Protestant, with adherence to ideals of monogamy, the romantic ideal in marriage, and

* Arranging the racial groups on a scale is problematical. Probably the most extensive changes during World War II occurred among the Japanese (relative to the size of the group). Selected groups among Negroes and Mexicans made quite as radical alterations in position.

sentimental attachments between members of the same family. Divergence from this dominant pattern set off any group which did not conform to it as "outsiders" barred from participation with "nice people." This exclusion effectively retarded assimilation.

In the new immigration the group which approached this pattern most consistently, the Czechs, have advanced rapidly enough so that their position as a minority has dwindled to the vanishing point.[14] Perhaps their chief divergence was in religious tradition but though most of them were nominally Catholics upon arrival, their defection from Catholicism was rapid and the secularist norm sponsored by the freethinkers could be traced back historically to at least partially Protestant sources.[15] Perhaps most significantly they were dominantly middle class on arrival, at least more so than other groups in the new immigration. They came in family groups and for the most part had an ideology characteristic of the business community in America.

Another subgroup showing relatively rapid assimilation into American life would be the Magyar professionals who entered the United States shortly after World War I. While it may be questioned whether they had middle class ideals because of the sharp separation of white collar workers from the *nép* or people in Hungary, yet the nearest analogy in American terms would be the upper middle class group composed of the financial semiaristocracy. Here the change in position was perhaps least, for it was a transfer from an urban white collar occupation in Hungary to a similar one in the United States.[16]

With the exception of a certain percentage of the Jews, most other migrants from Europe deviated from the major culture pattern of the United States as depicted above. Practically all were former peasants and unskilled; this put them in the working class, where they began as units of utility for American industry.

As for the racial minorities, probably the Indian with his folk culture, simple, rural, and communal, showed most deviation from the basic American pattern. Not even the heroic attempts to alter it by the Dawes Act had the least success. Somewhat less deviant, yet considerably different from the American, was the Japanese culture with its marked communal activity, Oriental religion, and formal family behavior. The predominance of maternal family behavior among the Negroes also tended to set them off from the general culture pattern although at the same time they conformed to the Protestant tradition; perhaps the social definition of Negro labor as menial was even more important. Certainly it was for the Mexican since the great majority of the Latin Americans performed unskilled tasks.

On the surface the romantic ideal may seem to be of little consequence in defining the dominant American culture pattern, and yet it is more important than is generally recognized. Certainly the absence of free choice in selecting a marriage partner is one of the characteristic features of many minority subcultures. Among the racial minorities this is especially marked among the Japanese and to a lesser degree among the Mexicans, and nearly all European ethnic groups came to America with the tradition of arranged marriages.

One of the chief sources of conflict between first and second generation Americans came with the selection of a marriage partner. The younger group felt keenly that it was not "American" to allow the parents to determine a mate. And when the older generation had its way, the rate of assimilation diminished; as long as the immigrants themselves controlled their children after the traditional European pattern, they were different and hence not "American." The parents, when uncontrolled by their children's wishes or by American culture norms, usually preferred endogamy and group distinction.

(3) Socioeconomic status, as distinct from "position," is another element that helps determine the degree of acceptance by the wider society. To the extent that the members of a minority group are day-laborers or menial workers, a stereotype of the group as a whole arises. This in turn prevents individual members from attaining a higher economic status even when prepared for it. The result is the well-known "job ceiling" for Negroes and Mexicans, the resistance to upgrading by members of unions, or the hostility shown by white collar workers and professionals when their ranks are swelled by rising, ambitious members of minority groups.

This process operates more openly where the subordinate group is racially visible or identifiable and is present in considerable numbers. On the other hand when only one or two individuals at a time are involved, as was sometimes the case with Japanese during the war, fewer barriers are encountered. Then again it appears in more muted form in the case of European nationals identifiable by name, language difficulties, or marked group affiliation; here also job opportunities in the higher brackets are severely restricted. Status operates less potently today than it did twenty years ago because the second and third generation children are largely indistinguishable from other Americans. That the stereotype was not without its effect is evident, however, in the difficulty experienced by the ethnic member in participating in the "private culture" as distinct from the "public culture" of American life; there was little opportunity, for example, to learn what American home life was like though there were constant contacts with school, court, law, or economic institutions.

The public definition of the foreigner as a menial and a cultural deviant also prevented the meeting of leaders from the dominant group with outstanding members of the minority, since the latter were regarded as belonging to a lower socioeconomic status.[17] In a still more subtle way, preferred occupations (automatically conferring status) within the larger middle class group have been denied to a number of Jews prepared for these vocations even though they were unmistakably middle class.[18]

(4) A commonly neglected factor is a high sex ratio. Since this involves the problem of intermarriage, it appears most noticeably among the minorities from Europe among whom non-Caucasians are largely absent. No single inclusive generalization regarding the sex ratio is adequate, however. It is false to assert that the higher the sex ratio (more males than females) the greater the rate of intermarriage, since a preponderance of males often resulted in the boardinghouse complex which effectively insulated the males from American family culture and kept alive the desire to send abroad for wives at the first opportunity.

It was only among the Italians that this institution appeared weakly developed so that intermarriage in the early period was a marked trend.[19] Among Poles, Hungarians, and Yugoslavs, all of whom developed distinctive boardinghouse institutions for males, one-sex living accentuated the tendency toward endogamy instead of retarding it.[20] Conversely the Czechs, who migrated chiefly in family groups, were quickly assimilated, with intermarriage more characteristic of the second generation.[21]

This variability may be explained in terms of other factors already mentioned such as cultural and socioeconomic similarity, showing that the general process of assimilation is a function of variables. On the whole the sex ratio seems less significant in hastening or retarding the rate of assimilation than many other factors, largely because its significance is masked by other more potent ones. Most important of these, perhaps, is the tendency for intermarriage to be a delayed reaction. Galitzi shows that three phases of assimilation normally follow in the same order: economic, cultural, and biological.[22] Since intermarriage does not occur until the last stage of the process, the effect of the sex ratio is minimized simply because it becomes more equalized with the passage of time.

A short addendum on the general subject of intermarriage may be of some interest in this connection. Barron asserts that it occurs most frequently among ethnic groups, somewhat less so between religious groups, and least between racial groups.[23] Where a diversity of groups is present, endogamy is normal and exogamy is usually prohibited.[24] Interracial marriage never exceeds the rate of 1.2 per hundred whether legal or not.[25] Indians have a higher incidence of intermarriage than Negroes, and the Japanese rate is more variable; but all groups show variability with change of locale.[26] So far as the European groups are concerned, there is a tendency for ethnic lines to be submerged in the identity of religious affiliations. Single nationality churches favor endogamy, while mixed nationality churches favor intermarriage.[27] Where interracial marriages occur, they are more often a mating of Negro men and white women, although the number of Negro women exceeds that of Negro men.[28]

(5) In general the greater the dispersion of the group, the more rapid is the rate of assimilation, provided that the minority is numerically small. This is equivalent to saying that where groups are concentrated in larger numerical ratios, they tend to face inward and thus preserve culture, institutions, customs, and in-marriage. When the groups are large, segregation is most likely to be adopted by the dominant group as well. While segregation is applied more often to racial groups, it can also be observed where the differences

are largely those of culture and variation in custom, as among Jews, Italians, Slovaks, Croatians, or Slovenes.[29]

On the other hand if the dispersion is such that the individual stands alone, there is pronounced deculturation of his older traits as well as rapid acculturation in terms of new ones. This places a greater strain upon the personality and creates the problem of marginality which will receive more attention below. The process of dispersion is especially well illustrated by the Mexicans who, as they take up residence farther from the border, tend to decrease in the size of their settlements and to become more rapidly Americanized, at least in the areas where they take up permanent residence.[30] The migratory workers are another problem entirely.

Of the European groups most widely dispersed in smaller numbers, perhaps the best illustration would be the Dalmatians from Yugoslavia, whose individualistic habits have also brought them into more direct line with the dominant patterns of American culture.[31] Other instances would be the northern Italians and some of the Czechs.[32] Since most other ethnic groups have largely settled in colonies, the dispersion process has had less effect, though the Japanese after relocation furnish another minor example.[33]

In connection with dispersion the factor of mobility in general hastens the adoption of customs and folkways of the dominant group. There are, however, complicating elements. When groups of families travel together and have only external contacts with American culture through habitual use of technological devices, the employer-employee relationship, and occasional brushes with the law, the assimilative process is weak or almost absent. Such is the case with the Mexican migratory workers. In the past, mobility had relatively little effect as an agency of assimilation when individuals migrated from colony to colony with only minimal contact on the journeys between, provided the status of the colony to which they went was approximately equal to the one they left. Such was the case of the Hungarians as they shuttled to and fro from coal fields to industrial areas somewhat after the manner of their migratory habits in Europe.[34] Again it is the lone individual or the smaller group that feels the effect of mobility more than larger concentrated masses: the early German Jews came alone or in widely scattered families, as did many of the Czechs before 1880 and Negroes before the great migration following World War I.* [35]

(6) Urbanization must not be neglected as an influence leading toward rapid absorption of the dominant pattern. This process, which usually acts as a powerful solvent for divergent cultures and traditions, is somewhat limited in effect since it was precisely in the cities where the greatest concentrations of minority colonies were to be found — the Polonia, little Italy, little Tokyo, little Hungary, or little Bohemia. These colonies served to arrest the pace of amalgamation through centripetal tendencies of group solidarity, serving as a temporary protection before the later plunge into the strange and unknown surroundings outside.

But in spite of the modifying force of colony living, the wage earners were obliged to meet constantly with the dominant group in factories, streetcars, busses, crowds, stores, elevators, and subways. They became subject to the mass influences of political campaigns, advertising, newspaper headlines, radio programs, and movies. American mass culture had its greatest influence in the urban environment. As secondary contacts of impersonal groups predominated over the primary, the individual became subjectively isolated and lonely while externally he moved in larger and larger crowds. Intimacy became replaced by mass thrills, beliefs instilled by suggestion and propaganda, gratifications by the vicarious satisfactions of crowd enthusiasms, crazes, fads, and "the latest thing." Mannheim has called this process "negative democratization" and points out that its operation is most visible in the larger cities.[36]

Mass culture has one indubitable advantage for the newcomer: it is easy to imitate. The gag, the popular song, the posturings of movie heroes or heroines, slang, wearing gaudy clothes, conversation at the tabloid level on tabloid subjects fresh with each passing day —

* After this period, and especially during World War II, the larger migration of Negroes was to a situation of constantly increasing freedom in employment, restaurants, parks, theaters, and other places of amusement. The sudden release from the repressive social control of the rural South precipitated many outbursts of turbulent behavior with open hostility toward whites. As might be expected, this provoked an equally strong reaction. Tension situations of this sort were smoothed over or denied by friends of the Negro. The Negro press carried some articles and editorials on the importance of deportment, at the time.

all these become a sign that one is "American." On this common ground all minorities meet with the native American on his own terms since they have access to the same popular novels, theater entertainment, mass spectacles, and the music of dance bands. Though some observers may call these the superficialities of American life, it is these very traits that make their way most easily into the subcultures to bend them into a more facile conformity. Randolph Bourne called them "the influences at the fringe" or "the flotsam and jetsam of American life." [37]

Urbanization hastens the acceptance of these features whether among Negroes, Italians, Poles, or Jews; for all the minorities they become the badge of "belonging" to the wider society. They can be adopted without intimacy, regardless of segregation, discrimination, diversity of origin, or visible differences. The traits of negative democratization fostered by city life are the great levelers of culture. Perhaps only the Indian has escaped them.

On the other hand there have been little knots of Poles, Italians, Czechs, Slovaks, and Yugoslavs who have formed agricultural communities along the lines of older traditions in order to preserve the more distinctive features of European customs and cooperative practice. These groups have resisted the broader features of Americanization, often for longer periods. In the absence of urban acceleration of uniformity in terms of a general common denominator, they have maintained a certain conservativeness and independence of outlook.[38]

(7) Another feature usually studied in terms of urban settlement is ecological organization. The spatial position of minority groups in the city is usually determined by the advice of friends or neighbors who have preceded the migrant and by the economic resources which he brings to the new setting. Because of his initial inability to pay any but the lowest rent, the newcomer in a minority must locate his place of residence in areas that have been abandoned by other low-income groups after their flight to better residential sections. This has meant that in cities like Chicago and others with a predominantly radial pattern they have begun their sojourn in the new environment within an area of transition near the center of the city and have followed the preceding wave on its way toward the outskirts.[39]

In other cities where the pattern has been more variegated they have clustered together in areas with natural disadvantages like heavy industry, railroad yards, docks, or deteriorated housing.[40] Not infrequently these were the very locations in which vice, non-family living, delinquency, and inadequate city services tended to destroy neighborhood interest in the improvement or care of property. Other things being equal, the longer the residence the less "residential coherence" there will be;[41] but this tendency is modified by factors such as large numerical size of the minority or racial distinctiveness.

In general the trend toward middle class apartment and one-family residence areas is parallel with the vertical mobility of groups, especially those from European backgrounds. Among racial minorities such as the Negro this differentiation tends to take place *within* a segregated area so that class lines are reflected to some degree by "better" and "worse" neighborhoods in Negro sections, e.g., in the lower south side in Chicago or the Sugar Hill development in Harlem. The strength of residential cohesion depends in turn upon some of the other variables such as recency of arrival, intensity of control exercised by religious organizations, and potency of the cultural subsystem. Thus the latest arrivals among the European immigrants still show the pattern of "little Italy" in many American cities. Where church and parochial school have most control, there are still numerous residential aggregations of Poles, Slovaks, Hungarians, and Yugoslavs, as well as of Orthodox Jews. Again, the cultural cohesion of other Jewish groups has helped to maintain fairly marked concentration even outside the original area of settlement.

A RECENT ASSIMILATION HYPOTHESIS

It will be instructive to compare these factors with an alternative set proposed by Warner and Srole. Dividing all groups into five racial types, they present

1. Light Caucasoids
2. Dark Caucasoids
3. Mongoloid and Caucasoid mixtures with Caucasoid appearance
4. Mongoloid and Caucasoid mixtures that appear Mongoloid
5. Negroes and all Negroid mixtures

They then take religion and language as the two most important differentiating factors. This gives six parallel cultural types:

1. English-speaking Protestants
2. Non-English speaking Protestants
3. English-speaking Catholics and non-Protestants
4. Catholics and other non-Protestants speaking an affiliated Indo-European tongue
5. English-speaking non-Christians
6. Non-Christians who do not speak English

If each racial type then has its six parallel cultural types, the scale of subordination would be least for racial type 1 (light Caucasoids) who were English-speaking Protestants; then racial type 1 combined with cultural type 2 (Protestants who do not speak English); etc. The same process would be repeated with racial type 2 (dark Caucasoids) and so on down to racial type 5 (Negroes and all Negroid mixtures).

There are certain disadvantages in drawing distinctions as fine as this. For example, would it be correct to state that in racial type 5 the English-speaking Protestants would be less subordinate than English-speaking Catholics? This is doubtful, particularly in areas where Catholics have taken in large numbers of Negroes, as in New Orleans. It could even be asserted that a considerable number of Negroes might be attracted to Catholicism in that area as a protective measure or for the higher status it affords. Again, to take another illustration, it is questionable whether an English-speaking Jew (cultural type 5) would be more subordinate in American society than a Sicilian Catholic (cultural type 4) or, for that matter, whether a German-speaking Jew (cultural type 6) would either. The rate of dispersion, divergence from the dominant cultural norm mentioned above, ecological position, and occupational status would all tend to influence the outcome. There is a certain artificiality in typologies erected on the basis of fixed elements such as language and religion; for when the attempt is made, these apparently static elements eventually turn out to be variables, i.e., as they enter into permutations they alter their quality.

On the other hand the criteria which Warner and Srole present for subordination and social distance are more functional. They are (1) freedom of residential choice; (2) freedom to marry out of one's own group — although it is not clear how much this results from weakening of endogamous ties or from lessening of discrimination externally imposed; (3) amount of occupational restriction; (4) strength of attitudes in the host society preventing participation in associations and cliques; and (5) the amount of social mobility allowed for the members of a racial or ethnic group.

The elements which Warner and Srole set up to determine the strength of the cultural or racial subsystem are (1) the power of the religious organization over its members, and its divergences from Protestant norms; (2) separate schools and the extent of their social control; (3) political unity of the group; (4) economic unity of the group; and (5) the number and power of ethnic associations. Among the European groups we have already seen that these factors operate most powerfully among Italians, Poles, lower-income groups among the Hungarians, and in most strata of the Croatians and Slovenes. Solidarity among the Jews is most characteristic because of items one and five. In the Negro group it is largely item five which unites them, though three and four are growing; the resemblance to number one is decreasing. The Japanese Americans are more like the Negroes except that the political unity of the rising Nisei is much greater. On the other hand the solidarity of the Mexican Americans is more passive, due almost wholly to common cultural traditions or customs but not to any of the factors mentioned by Warner and Srole. Outside pressure has not produced any large number of ethnic associations among them and they are weakly organized.

Finally Warner and Srole give a "timetable" of assimilation which they contend is dependent on (1) the time taken for the entire group to disappear as a recognizable unit; (2) the proportionate number of people who drop out of a group in each generation; and (3) the amount and kind of participation permitted by the members of the dominant society. While the first item seems tautological, the other two can be roughly measured and seem valid.[42]

The categories which Warner and Srole introduce are suggestive enough to warrant more empirical testing; it may be that no successful chart can go beyond the minute differences they record. For our purpose here it has appeared more useful to select somewhat different and broader criteria which are treated as variables rather than as categories.

COMMON MINORITY TRAITS

It has become apparent that each of the minorities considered here shared certain characteristics as a result of divergent backgrounds. Three of these deserve mention.

(1) Customary patterns of behavior due to unique historical experience in the past. Whether it was the proud Indian preliterate in the dignity of a tribal ceremony or the urbane, sophisticated Jewish refugee escaping from the threat of a concentration camp; whether the patient, plodding Slovak with his memories of past persecution or the restless, questioning Negro whose grandmother regaled him with stories of plantation life never revealed to the white man — all had a set of memories, habits, and attitudes different from the dominant majority. There was an unwavering loyalty to the group and its way of living as an indelible heritage, and, except for the Negro, this was often identified with the native language or idiom.

(2) Status as cheap labor and its accompanying disadvantages. It is true that this did not always appear until the minority member was brought into interaction with the dominant culture, but its chief roots lay in the divergent past. With the possible exception of a number of Czechs and Jews, the great mass of minority group members began their period of adjustment as unskilled, poorly paid hands utilized to erect a civilization in many ways foreign to them, whose purposes and benefits they only gradually began to share.

(3) A family pattern which deviated from that of the dominant majority. In the case of the Negro the high frequency of the maternal family and its blunted institutional controls were socially inherited from slavery and a semicaste system. With all other groups the patriarchal feature was probably more strongly emphasized than it was among native white Americans; this resulted in the partial seclusion of women, especially in Italian and Mexican homes. In nearly all it implied stern and rigorous discipline from the father, unquestioning obedience of the children, a subservient wife and mother, and economic management controlled by the male head of the household.

In addition to the traits due to divergent backgrounds, there are others which developed as reactions to prejudice, discrimination, and exclusion from participation. Perhaps the most important are:

(1) Resistance to change and the formation of cultural subsystems to cushion the shock of disruptive social forces that threatened to tear the web of habits, folkways, and attitudes already built up. Among the Indians this took the form of stubborn adherence to living in the open and the maintenance of dances, ceremonials, and religious observances distinctly their own, even though they were forced to use the white man's tools and language. For the Mexican it meant retaining his modes of socializing or of worship and continued preference for his regular diet of tortillas and frijoles. For Japanese and European immigrants it meant residential concentration, with countless benefit and welfare organizations or culture societies that furthered the conserving of older memories and ways. The nationality societies served to protect ethnic groups from sudden changes arising from the initial shock of contact with a new culture. Cooperative endeavor reinforced group morale even while it served to insulate the minority group temporarily from the outsider.

Paradoxically the immigrant press, which was a potent organ in the cultural subsystem, also served to introduce the newcomer to the wider world which he discovered only vicariously in its pages. It urged upon him the necessity of citizenship, of learning the English language and American ways, and of fitting himself for a larger place in the surrounding American civilization. Thus even in the attempt to retain his own folkways the immigrant was ambivalent: he *also* wanted to "belong" to his new country. He first began this latter process in and through his own subsystem. It is almost as though he said, "I want to belong too, but I must do it in my own way and at my own pace, accompanied by those who come from my past and will support me by going forward with me." Politically, socially, and economically the immigrant began with solidarity but gradually began to lose it as he became a more active participant in the common stream of American life. Today many of his organizations are becoming weaker, he is losing his political consciousness,* and his press is gradually disappearing.

* Exceptions occur, of course, where colonies here and there maintain solidarity. The Poles of Milwaukee certainly keep Congressman O'Konski in office, and the Italians of Rhode Island have strongly supported Governor Pastore.

In this respect, the Negro has followed the opposite course. Beginning with a mass of unorganized individuals who had little common heritage except the negative status of slavery, he has gradually built up a group consciousness which is reaching an organized form. Far from waning, his newspapers, organizations, and political demands are attaining increased strength and power. And paradoxically, too, he is using this new solidarity in a desperate attempt to dissolve it, as the attack on segregation will undoubtedly do if it is successful. To a lesser extent the same course is being pursued by the Japanese American and by the Mexican. Thus we see that the cultural subsystem becomes an agent of acculturation and assimilation caught in the larger impersonal trend which Sumner called "the strain toward consistency." What often begins as a form of resistance to change, particularly among ethnic groups, becomes the vehicle of change.

(2) In making his adjustment to the dominant group the minority member first borrows the tools, techniques, and behavior associated with material culture or technology. Even though he did not accept the industrial habits of the white man, the Indian found himself forced to use firearms, horses, plows, knives, and utensils. Today the Mexican soon learns that he is expected to work by the clock and not by the job. The Japanese merchant or hotelkeeper finds that he must learn the American method of accounting. The Yugoslav fisherman employs diesel engines to power his boats. Since accepted business and industrial habits are necessary for survival, the new arrival must either learn them or fail to satisfy his most elementary need. Etiquette, manners, or the niceties of social conduct and hospitality can wait for second place.

(3) The subordination of cultural to economic adjustment is reinforced by uneven acquaintance with the dominant culture. A common example of this is differential experience with the private family life of native white Americans. Minorities like the Negroes and Japanese, a large number of whose members are employed as domestic servants, come into direct contact with the family life of employers in a more intimate way. Although this might be expected to hasten the adoption of family folkways observed by them, the process has not been so simple. Among the Negroes the domestics usually come from lower class strata and therefore from families of the most di-

vergent types, as already noted.[43] Since their major loyalties and values come from association with their own people, and successful imitation of the employer would often require far more income than they can obtain, acculturation is retarded. Segregation of the races not only prevents normal social intercourse that would hasten the adoption of dominant culture patterns but also removes the natural rewards of conformity as long as vertical mobility is prevented. For instance, unless there are clear and unmistakable advantages accruing to the Negro when he adopts the family or work patterns of the dominant whites, he will see little reason to do so. Yet in spite of these obstructions, prestige gains will sometimes have their influence, particularly among the "strivers," who adopt the mobility patterns of the middle class most wholeheartedly.

Among the Japanese the background of a semirigid feudal class system is such that no one in a lower class tries to act above his station; therefore direct contact of Japanese domestics with dominant family patterns has not served to change their own to any great degree or at least the results have been delayed. It is only with the second generation or the children who mingle freely in public schools with comrades from homes having a different background that the unique customs and folkways of minority homes are brought into question and repudiated. Among all immigrants this probably occurs least frequently among the Mexicans, who are more rigidly segregated and have less opportunity for higher education. In all immigrant groups, however, it is rare for first generation members to sense the subtle difference between one home and another until their children point out discrepancies. On the whole, then, all minority groups show uneven adaptation to the private culture elements in American society. In-marriage, a common phenomenon in all subsystems, accentuates the retention of divergent folkways and customs.

(4) The reaction of minorities to exclusion and discrimination may follow obvious and direct patterns somewhere between the two extremes of apathy and protest but tending to cluster round these two poles. Where experiences of an entire lifetime have imposed conformity or accommodative patterns, acquiescence and resignation become a part of the personality structure as they do with many Indians or southern lower class Negroes. In cases where more easy-

going or complaisant habits have been learned in another culture before arrival in the United States, adaptation to the more rigorous American pattern may also result in a passive subservience and visible apathy, though for a different reason. Something of this sort has occurred among the Mexicans of the Southwest. In contrast there are subsystems that develop a fierce pride and group solidarity which are highly resistant to outward pressure. A response of dynamic aggressiveness then develops, as we have seen in the case of the Japanese and the Jews. Although a similar pattern might be expected in the case of the Hungarian, it is modified by the heartiness and cheer of his sociability.

On the other hand the protest motif has increased among more submerged groups like the Negro on account of the discrepancy between constantly rising status and the continuing number of "incidents" in which civil and economic rights are denied. Organs of Negro opinion have given these such wide publicity that restlessness and militant protest have become endemic among middle and upper class Negroes. The masses have also been caught up in the current.[44] On the whole it is "felt" or "perceived" discrimination that causes most unrest. Since the number of Japanese Americans is too small to have much political influence, the most effective protest movements and organizations have come from the Negroes and Jews, both of whom are sufficiently large minorities to make their opinion felt. In the fight for antidiscrimination measures, leaders from these two groups have been most numerous.

(5) Then there are indirect responses when full participation in the dominant culture is denied; the most characteristic of these are compensatory behavior, marginality, constant watchfulness, etc. While all minority groups show this mode of reaction, yet it seems to be the nationality groups of the new immigration that show this pattern to a greater degree than the more direct one of apathy or protest. It is quite possible that immigrants from Bohemia, Slovakia, Italy, Poland, Hungary, and Yugoslavia were at least dimly aware that their own home countries restricted immigration, that the newcomer was present on sufferance, that they were in America, so to speak, on trial. Being less conspicuous than the minorities of high visibility and coming from a peasant background of considerable subservience to upper class landlords, it was more natural for them

to minimize attention to themselves and to strive for concealment and indistinctness. The task of adapting themselves to American culture was full of contradictory elements: it called for economic initiative at the same time that it demanded hasty relinquishment of the greenhorn role. Thus the problem was obscure and indefinite, demanding a more veiled technique. Compensations for this inner conflict were many. They took such multiple and diverse forms as blatant Americanism (to hide one's past origins), old country nationalism (something the native American cannot share), social climbing, nostalgia for the past, looking down on later arrivals, changing one's name, changing one's religion, hypersensitiveness, self-consciousness, hypercriticism, feelings of inferiority, feelings of superiority, obsessive goals, detachment, and many others.

As two cultures come into close contact with each other, the figure of the "marginal man" appears. He is an individual who leaves one social group for another without being fully accepted (or feeling unaccepted) in the group of his new allegiance.[45] Thus he is on the borderline of two groups, unwilling to go back or repelled when he does so; at the same time he finds no satisfactory adjustment in the group to which he would like to belong, even when his qualifications are such as to gain him admittance. Though the first generation immigrant who came to America during adult years was rarely assimilated,[46] the problem of marginality appeared more distinctly in younger immigrants or second generation children.

Probably the Japanese have the largest proportion of this second generation group.[47] While their racial visibility resulted in stereotypes that pushed them back into their own group, their higher education and quick acceptance of American ways helped to offset this initial disadvantage so that they could compete with Caucasians on the same ground. It seems likely that the gap between generations was as marked among the Japanese as in any American minority, heightening the marginality of the Nisei. The uncertainty of their position was especially evident in the relocation centers, where their ambivalence became painfully clear. In the postwar period many of them were in economic positions of considerable security and yet they revealed a kind of basic anxiety about the future, a feeling of having lost their moorings.

Among the second generation European immigrant group there

are two incompatible standards, one in the home, the other in society at large. The younger person may be embarrassed socially because of things he learned "wrong" at home, things he has to cover up by quick thinking and action. In this culture cleavage he has had to decide where his loyalties were. If the American community gave him more security he decided against his parents but could not be sure of acceptance. Today it is only too easy to accept the evaluation of American society about "foreignness" and to be ashamed of the poor impression parents make outside their cultural setting. By obtaining better positions or occupations than the parents, the children may obtain more power and then detach themselves entirely from parental control.

In fact this pattern of surpassing the parents has become so pervasive that Margaret Mead calls it a fundamental feature of American life in general since "we are all third generation," at least figuratively.[48] Parents are caught in the same marginal problem and find it impossible to inculcate the old loyalties in their children without arguing with themselves.[49] The marginal man may thus take over new ways, new foods, new habits, and new loyalties in a desperate effort to belong but find paradoxically that even though he changes his name, occupation, modes of thought, and ideas, he is not yet firmly rooted in the dominant group. His life is spent in turmoil, in apprehension, in uncertainty and doubt. If an artist, he may channel these tensions into creative expression, often finding both relief and acceptance at the same time. But this path is open to few. Most marginals pursue endlessly the phantom of belonging.

Among the Negroes the mulatto has been identified by Stonequist as the marginal person, because he is more white than colored and still is unaccepted by white society.[50] However, Myrdal has shown that on the whole it is less the color situation than the class status that creates the difficulty. It may be successfully questioned whether the mulatto is continually conscious of his racial affiliation with the dominant whites, and certainly there is much advantage for him to remain in Negro society, where he frequently has a privileged position.[51] To the more careful observer it appears that the educated Negro rather than the mulatto is the true marginal man of colored society. The discrepancy between his training and his opportunity, the strain to achieve some measure of recognition in his profession irrespective of his color, the need for constant communication with those who share his function in the community, and the comparison between the free and easy association of whites with each other contrasted with his need for caution so as "not to embarrass anybody," serve to stress his truly marginal position.

It would be false to leave the impression that the marginal man is always maladjusted or that his peculiar position involves a permanent state of unhappiness. He is not only a keen critic of sham idealism in American life because of his sensitiveness; he is also likely to have a more objective attitude toward diverse cultural values and then to contribute this objectivity to society at large. The dynamism of the culture conflict which he has interiorized saves him from the complacency and self-satisfaction of those who have never openly faced the problem of competing loyalties; he is therefore stimulated to incessant activity, and his lack of balance will then be only a prelude to new achievements.[52] The inventions of Michael Pupin, the stage directing of Elia Kazan, the eloquent prose of W. E. B. DuBois, and the expressive dancing of Sono Osato might have been forever lost without the tension of marginality.

(6) The centrifugal force operative on all minorities, drawing them into the orbit of the dominant society in terms of individual rather than group achievement, has resulted in intraminority conflicts over policies and personalities. This clash of forces has produced a considerable amount of factionalism which is more accentuated in the relatively permanent minorities like the racial groups or the Jewish community. In the vanishing minorities of the new immigration, however, the discord over policies is more largely confined to those of the first generation; the second and third no longer have a sufficient interest to take sides. The battles of Czech freethinkers against Catholics, the Polish feud between clericals and anticlericals, or even the Italian disagreement between fascists and antifascists are losing their importance. It is true that Yugoslavs still show a few flare-ups in the battle of pro-Tito and anti-Tito forces, and yet this occurs more often in the first generation than in the second.*

The peculiar relation of the minority to the wider society, whereby

* Exceptions here follow the same trend as in voting habits (above, pp. 468–469). The tighter the organization of the colony, the more uniform the behavior of first and second generations.

a leader of the subculture may be recognized as a representative of his group because of individual achievements, has led to similar tendencies in all minorities. The Mexican *explotador*, the Italian *prominenti*, the colored "white man's nigger," the "haolified" (Americanized) Japanese, and the eminent Jewish leader who is far removed from the realities of his own people, all show the continual pull of the dominant culture upon them and the distrust which arises within their own groups when such leaders attempt to speak in their name. This distrust and suspicion are then attached to all policies or programs that in any way might be identified with such unpopular leaders, and charges such as "selling out" or "betrayal" fill the air.

The relatively low status of minority groups in the community creates a special sensitiveness to prestige values in the subsystem; in benefit societies, lodges, clubs, churches, and organizations of all kinds there is exaggerated emphasis upon titles of office and the trappings of power. In a sense this is only another of the compensatory factors operating in the minority group in which lack of acceptance by native white Americans increases the jockeying for power within the subsystem. Political divisions centering around personalities of minor prominence often help to fill the pages of foreign language newspapers, the Negro press, or Jewish periodicals.

The more mature personalities enjoy these as the spice of life in a humdrum world, but to the antagonists themselves and their supporters all is deadly earnest. Outsiders who look on may be amused and contemptuous of these apparently petty bickerings without seeing that they are a by-product of the minority situation, an attempt to recapture a sense of importance denied by the dominant society. Yet the same tendencies operate among any individuals whose security system is threatened or nonexistent; it is not confined to minority groups though it may appear somewhat more conspicuously there.

(7) In all minorities there is a deviate occupational distribution, usually at first in the ranks of unskilled and low paid labor. With the vanishing minorities of southern and eastern Europe, this is gradually disappearing in favor of a wider spread of economic activities. There are still major businesses, however, that will not employ Jews, and there are types of openings that remain relatively closed — executive jobs, sales executive positions, and many clerical

occupations, not to speak of professional schools which could prepare Jews for more advanced opportunities. Racial groups are the subject of differential wage practices and thus find that even when they perform the same labor, they receive a lesser compensation.

The proportion of menial and unskilled jobs is still greatest among Mexicans, Negroes, and other racial groups. The job ceiling or discrimination on the job prevents these groups from rising into supervisory positions or receiving the training that would fit them for professional occupations. The many wartime advances made under the F.E.P.C. are gradually being lost as discriminatory practices gain in intensity [53] and as devices for evading regulations are developed. Only those states that have adopted laws prohibiting discriminatory policies in employment have been able to conserve these improvements, and this means that the great majority of minority workers are still unprotected. The folkways of discrimination reinforce the stereotype of inferiority as applied to the minority and thus freeze minority members into artificial occupational distribution.

MINORITY DIFFERENCES

There is little space to devote to the many interesting variations among the subcultures as they develop in the United States. However, many of the reactions and culture patterns developed by minority groups result from the conjunction of these differences with the multiple features of American life. Considerable space might be given to the variation in sex ratio — the high preponderance of males among the Japanese, Italians, Slovaks, and Poles, down to the low proportion among the Negroes. The gap between generations would make another interesting study, with the Japanese showing the most pronounced pattern, while Mexicans and new generation immigrants follow.

It would be significant to trace the divergences in the delinquency pattern — to show that it is relatively small among Japanese and Jews, and to note a higher female ratio among Negroes and an almost nonexistent female rate among Mexican and European groups. It might be important to trace the decreasing influence of the ethnic press and the increasing part played by the Negro and the Jewish press. Some of the major differences in economic traditions and folkways could be shown by delineating the importance of the benefit and insurance societies among the European and Japanese groups and the relative absence of these organizations among Negroes, Indians, and Mexicans. The significance given to the class structure could be brought out by a comparison of the Hungarians with the Negroes to show how prestige patterns operate in the most diverse groups in parallel ways.

The variant rate of intermarriage — least among racial groups and the Jews, most among European middle class groups — would bring out another feature of the multiple pattern. A study of family solidarity — so strong among Yugoslavs and Jews, more weakly developed among Negroes and Mexicans — would be a fruitful study of contrasts. The differences in religious devotion (with Polish, Slovak, and Orthodox Jew showing the most pronounced loyalty to religious institutions) and the consequent effect on assimilation would be another interesting aspect of adjustment. These and many other factors can only be hinted at here, though they should give impetus to more thorough study of group relations. Before some of our minorities vanish entirely, it is to be hoped that such features as these will evoke more thorough research as a contribution toward a better understanding of American life.

TYPICAL AMERICAN PATTERNS

On the other hand it must be emphasized that all minorities are also inescapably American and have therefore appropriated to a greater or lesser degree the ways of living that are characteristic of the population as a whole. All are caught in the tide of vertical mobility, the search for advancement, for gradual improvement of economic opportunities, as they rise in the class scale. Segregation has been unable to prevent this since the wider pattern cannot be successfully withheld from any minority that shares in the educational system, the political process, and economic life. A part of this rise in status is the familiar American one of changing residence to fit the pocketbook, thus giving objective evidence of changing position in the social scale.

All the minorities, with the possible exception of the Indian, have shown the familiar decrease in the birth rate with urbanization.*

* Until the Indian shares urban culture, his fertility pattern will resemble that of American rural society.

Their divorce and crime rates approximate, year by year, to the more typical "native white" pattern. One by one all the members of the subcultures are approaching equalitarian habits of family living so that their private culture is becoming less distinguishable from that of other major groupings. And in spite of obstructions they are also participating more fully in the political life of the nation and bid fair to become some of its most politically conscious citizens.

Even though the distinguishing marks of racial origins may tend to set many of them off from the vast majority, their places as citizens are increasingly more secure and their vote is following the typical two-party division in the political arena. There seems little evidence that they are tending to form special pressure blocs of their own, except as this may further their chances to participate freely in economic, educational, and political fields. The danger of exclusive group loyalties will be dissipated as these wider opportunities become available.

[CHAPTER 19]

Prejudice and Its Reduction

THE NIGHT was clear and cold. Through the dingy window of the local café a murky light shone dully. With a grinding of brakes, an automobile with four men wrapped in mackinaws came to a halt on the narrow pavement as the driver announced, "Well, this seems to be the only eating place in town."

"Looks good enough for me," said Mario. "I'm so hungry that I could eat the glass right out of that window."

"O.K., boys, let's give it a try," grinned the agent as he swung himself out of the left door. "I wouldn't mind a little ham and eggs myself."

Leading the way, he marched across the sidewalk to the door, followed in rapid succession by the others. The latch clicked as a warm wave of air swept across the faces of his olive-skinned companions. Like a team the four men made for the counter and sat down. A sallow, partly bald, middle-aged man with a dirty apron approached at a slow, unwieldy pace.

"What do you want?" he asked.

The leader responded, "I want a cup of coffee. What the other boys want I don't know. Maybe sandwiches."

The proprietor frowned, "I don't serve Mexicans," he answered shortly.

"Look," said the agent, "we've just gone over to Mr. X's place and these boys are going to help him harvest his cotton. Your place doesn't look so elegant to me that you can't afford to serve us all a cup of coffee."

"I'll give *you* what you want," replied the owner, "but I'm telling you I don't serve Mexicans."

"In that case," said the agent, "I guess you don't serve me either."

Slowly the four men rose and walked to the door. Again the latch clicked, they filed out, and the slam of the door echoed throughout the tiny café. In the darkness all started to speak at once.

"Did you see the way that guy looked at us? Maybe we're just criminals and don't know it."

"Must be a crime to work around here. I notice the Anglos want us fast enough when they're in a hurry to get the cotton in. But when it comes to feeding time they want us somewhere else."

"Say, why should we go over to X's anyway? If that's the way we're going to be treated around there, we might as well stay away. This is the nearest town and we would have to spend our week ends in this Godforsaken hole. What could we do here? Probably the cops would run us in and we wouldn't even collect our wages."

"Good idea! *I'm* not coming back."

"Nor I."

"Count me in too."

The next day, farmer X missed his laborers. Not until weeks later, when his cotton crop had deteriorated, was he able to find other hands for the work. He noticed that his neighbors were having the same difficulties. That summer laborers were scarce in the county. For some reason that no one seemed to explain, all the Mexicans wanted to work somewhere else.[1]

The door of the registrar's office swung open as a diminutive girl with finely chiseled features and a pleasant smile looked about her uncertainly.

"My name is Miss Barr. The secretary said you would see me."

Mr. Trevithick looked up from the papers on his desk and said heartily, "Come in, Miss Barr. I have just been looking over your record. It is very good indeed. No doubt you are interested in enrolling for liberal arts?"

"That's right, sir. I've been thinking about psychology as a major. You know I hope to become a social worker some day."

"Excellent. Excellent," replied the admissions representative. "If you will look over our graduate courses, I think you will find that we have a school of social work that ranks high in the country. Do you think that psychology is the best way to prepare yourself?"

"Well, I have been talking with some of the workers in the city and though some of them say one thing and some another, most of them confess that they would like to have had more psychology than they did in college."

Mr. Trevithick arranged his tie absently and brushed a fleck of dust from his pin striped suit. "It sounds as though you have done some investigating on your own. Tell me, why do you want to come to our school instead of going elsewhere?"

A shadow crossed Miss Barr's face, then her lips set in a firm line. "Perhaps this is the wrong thing to say, sir, but I cannot afford to go anywhere else. You see, my family live here in the city and if I go to school here, we can manage it without too much trouble. And I believe the college can give me what I want — what I need," she added hastily.

"Hm, yes," replied the counselor. "We always encourage local students to come. We depend a lot on our constituency here in the city, of course. You seem to have done well in high school (John Hancock, wasn't it?). We have had some high grade students from Hancock."

"Yes sir, that's my school."

"I think you ought to do well here." Mr. Trevithick paused, scratched his left ear, and looked at the papers on his desk. "Oh, by the way, what is your church affiliation? We have no record of it here."

"Jewish."

"Oh."

Silence fell for a few minutes while the counselor fidgeted with a pencil. "Have you ever thought about business, Miss Barr? With your record, you could go far in that line."

"No, I haven't really thought much about it. You see, my first love is social work."

"It is? Hm, I see." Mr. Trevithick rose to let her know the interview was over. "Glad to have met you, Miss Barr. Sorry that we cannot take you in at this time."

The pair walked to the door with the girl making no comment.

"Why don't you try getting into business, Miss Barr? Your people always do so well in it."

"Good-bye." [2]

AN ANALYSIS OF PREJUDICE

These two examples serve to illustrate how prejudice operates to separate one group from another. Our discussion will concern itself mainly with prejudice of this sort which functions as a method of exclusion; but if the term "prejudice" is clearly understood, it will appear that we are dealing with a restricted sense of the term and not with all forms of prejudice.

To be exact, one's irrational preference for or liking of anything is just as much a prejudice as hostility or aversion. Prejudice is essentially an attitude * for or against anything — a person, group, idea, or object — held without rational or empirical investigation and/or in open disregard of evidence. The very word means *pre-judgment*, which implies decision prior to examination. Theoretically one may have a neutral attitude (one which is neither for nor against) but this is only a limiting case. The great bulk of prejudices fall into either positive or negative categories. Like all attitudes, prejudice is a tendency predisposing an individual toward a specific mode of behavior and is basically an emotional orientation. Psychologically it fuses an affective response with an idea of a simplified sort (often a stereotype). Social training determines how this ideational content will operate in terms of group pressure.

Thus a man with a prejudice for blondes may seek an introduction to a golden haired girl in ordinary circumstances but inhibit this tendency when his brunette sister is with him. That his prejudice is irrational could be shown by the fact that he continues to have a marked fondness for a blonde who is known to be fickle, deceitful, or cruel and defends her against all detractors. This would be a positive prejudice. A simple case of the opposite kind would be a dislike of sea food by a person who refused to give it a fair trial. Probably the negative connotation of the word "prejudice" is more common than the positive, but an exact definition must include both, so long as prejudgment operates.

"Antipathy" and "bias" are often coextensive with prejudice but are not identical with it. In general, antipathy is an attitude of hostility or aversion to something; thus it is always negative.

* An attitude is an established readiness which is learned and which determines the response of an individual in a selective way.[3]

Prejudice is not. Furthermore, antipathy may arise from interpersonal relations so that it is directed toward an individual rather than a group. As we shall see, the type of prejudice usually present in intergroup conflict is seldom of this sort. Again, antipathy may be the result of study and research, as when a person delves into Thomism or Marxism and emerges with a definite dislike of either philosophy. This could not be called a prejudice unless it could be proved that the student failed to examine the issues with an objective frame of mind. In social experience it is often true, as Fairchild contends, that antipathy results from direct contact which precipitates dislike for an entire group.[4] (The function of the social context is highly important in determining this result, as research has shown.)

"Bias" is a broader term than "antipathy" because it refers to any selective attitude, positive or negative. It shares this wider connotation with prejudice, which may also be for or against, as already noted. The main difference is that bias need not involve prejudgment. Sometimes it does so but in other instances it does not; by very definition, however, prejudice always includes a prejudgment. In the broadest possible sense, all attitudes are biased because they are oriented for or against something. For the limiting cases where they are neutral or indifferent, they are still selective in a moderate sense. Bias simply indicates partiality, a personal like or dislike, a food preference, enjoyment of violence, aristocratic leanings, or a general antagonism toward foreigners. The philosopher and the scientist have their bias as well as the most narrow-minded provincial, though the former reach their attitudes after more reflection and rational thought.

The term "bigot" applies to a prejudiced person who is usually unwilling or unable to examine his own attitudes and compare them with objective evidence. Thus the terms "bigoted" and "prejudiced" have the same referent, i.e., attitudes predetermined by forgotten experiences, or persons having such attitudes.

Some classification of terms is necessary before explaining how they will appear in this discussion. The above analysis should supply a basis for what follows and the context should now give an adequate idea of those cases where the meanings of related terms overlap. Theoretically prejudice may be either positive or negative, but from here on we shall confine ourselves to prejudice *against* something. In the most general terms prejudice can be directed against anything whatever: a tax policy, constitutional government, atheism, or red hair. But in this sense it is too blunt a tool for our purposes. In the context of minority problems, prejudice refers to hostile attitudes toward groups. To be more specific: prejudice in this chapter signifies those predetermined attitudes of animosity toward social groups which stereotype all members as hateful or obnoxious.

The incident about Mexican workers, related above, illustrates a prejudiced attitude according to our definition. The café owner regarded all Mexicans in the same category as individuals to be shunned; individual differences were entirely disregarded. Whether the Mexican was a criminal, a musician, a saint, or an unskilled worker, the attitude was the same. "We don't serve Mexicans."

The bigot regards the ideas compounded with these attitudes as fully justified by the behavior of the disliked group. Without explicitly stating the fact, all discussions of prejudice in social psychology, sociology, and intercultural education restrict themselves to this limited scope. In general when we employ such terms as "hostility," "antagonism," "aversion," and "antipathy," it will be in terms of group-directed prejudices and those only; when a broader meaning is implied, it will be stated implicitly or made clear by the context. And from here on, "prejudice" will mean group prejudice.

It follows from this definition that prejudice which is group directed is also group conditioned. It has often been remarked that the infant or young child shows no prejudice, but this is not the result of pristine purity or innocence; it lies rather in the intense absorption with himself which characterizes his early development. In the early years it is not only impossible to have an aversion for outer groups, it is equally impossible to have a feeling of belonging to one's own group. Only when ego development reaches the stage where identification is possible, only when there is a "we–they relationship" can either group loyalty or its obverse, group prejudice, arise.[5] On the other hand antipathy may be a common experience. Any source of conflict which serves to block or impede free expression of the impulsive life will give rise to antipathy, whether the source be a parent, a sibling, or a child in another family or from another racial or cultural group.[6] For the child the fact that such a person has frustrated a natural desire is reason enough for the antipathy. But it does not place the other person in a group category so that others from the same group are automatically included in the dislike. *Conflict originates in personal-social relations;* * *prejudice in culturally defined relations.*[7]

HOW PREJUDICE IS LEARNED

Like every other attitude, prejudice must be learned. As soon as the child is able to identify himself with his own group, he learns that there are "others" who do not qualify for acceptance. In some cases he has this impressed upon him directly and forcibly:

> "Ma," said Johnny, "that little nigger boy wants to play ball with us. We told him he couldn't play but he says he can. Dan seems to think it's all right. Why can't he play with us? He says he's a good pitcher and we need a pitcher."
>
> "Now listen, Johnny, you can't play with him because he's black. Do you understand? You shouldn't play with nigger kids because they aren't as good as you are. Now don't be mean to him. Just go on back and tell him to go home and not try to play with you any more." [8]

On the other hand the teaching may be more indirect and suggestive. At dinner time the youngster may hear his father say, "I met Mr. Stern today. You know he is certainly different from most Jews. Frank said that he gave twice as much to the community chest as he was asked to and told the boys to keep it quiet. I guess Sam Stern could show the rest of these yids a thing or two — if they'd only let him."

Both of these examples, while true to life, nevertheless throw doubt on the popular opinion that prejudice is a result of contact with a different group and the inevitable reaction to difference. Researches in social psychology show clearly that prejudice results from contact with attitudes rather than with groups.[9] The social definition of the other group which is appropriated before contact, or at least simultaneous with it, determines what the group *means*. Following this, the stereotype of the group becomes the most convenient classification of any member belonging to it. Desiring approval of the parents, the child accepts their attitudes and opinions

* Personal-social relations arise from social interaction which is not defined in terms of cultural habits. See Kimball Young, *Social Psychology*, 2nd ed., New York, Crofts, 1944, p. 9.

as natural and right, whether they apply to the next door neighbor, to political affiliation, or to the characteristics of Italians, Poles, or Japanese.

Studies of children in kindergarten and the early grades show that they are already aware of group differences and social definitions that single out negative traits in minorities to which they do not belong. An extended research in Philadelphia shows the white Protestant children replying freely to questions about Negroes with such responses as "They kill people," "They carry knives," "They are always fighting," "They're black and it won't come off." The projective method used with these children evoked the following response about an old, bearded man: "He's an old man; you've got to buy something in his store"; "They talk funny"; "They sell all kinds of stuff"; "They sell Jewish crackers, bread"; "They cheat you." And a picture of two boys coming out of a synagogue and confronted by three boys across the street elicited this response from a Negro boy, "They're going to wait for them to come out of there and then they're going to beat them up." A white boy shown a picture of white boys playing ball while a Negro child looks on is asked, "Would he [the Negro boy] want to be white?" He replies, "Yes, because white boys do more things than colored — more gooder things." [10]

The observer must be careful, however, not to confuse these reactions with fully developed prejudice. Lasker's early study showed clearly that many children of this age who used such epithets as "wop," "nigger," or "Jew" had little awareness of their meaning except that they served to taunt and insult others.[11] They should be understood as *power words* which produce quick reactions and thus draw attention when nothing else will. During the preschool years the process of prejudice formation seems to be largely a matter of imitation without much definite structure, a result of passive learning which lacks reinforcement from the child's own group loyalties.

This interpretation also tallies with Horowitz' research in which children were shown photographs in pairs, one colored and one white and asked which they would like to have for playmates, classmates, etc. He found that prejudice at the kindergarten level was weak but tended to increase steadily with age, proceeding from more sporadic forms to well-structured ones.[12] Lasker showed clearly that prejudice did not take the form of open antagonism, cruelty, systematic ridicule, or unfairness until the early years of school.[13] Weatherford suggests that group or race prejudice does not become fully formed until the child comes into open competition or rivalry with a colleague who is clearly defined as belonging to another group (for example, in athletics).[14]

The studies so far mentioned were conducted in northern cities. Effects vary somewhat with environment, as Horowitz showed in another study of children in a border state. Here he discovered that race prejudice was more firmly set, even in first grade children, than ideas of sex, age, or economic status. In these tests, the younger children reported that they gained their attitudes from parents, but the older ones did not. Apparently the children in later grades forgot the source of their attitudes and rationalized them successfully.[15]

Blake and Dennis examined children in a more or less typical Southern rural school and found that those in the lower grades had only negative stereotypes of the Negro like "bad" and "dirty" while in the higher grades both negative and positive ideas were mingled, i.e., it was possible for the children at that age to characterize the Negro as happy-go-lucky, cheerful, or more religious than whites.[16] In their report on prejudices of Harvard, Radcliffe, and Dartmouth undergraduates, Allport and Kramer found that most of them say that their prejudices took form between the ages of six and sixteen, especially in the age group from twelve to sixteen.[17] No claim is made about the accuracy of these estimates.

Unfortunately none of the studies so far published have dealt directly with children in controlled situations where the competitive element can be compared with a noncompetitive one. Most of the research strongly suggests that competition may be the precipitating factor (the element that crystallizes a previous misty dislike), and we offer this as the most likely hypothesis. It is well established that prejudice is not innate but learned like any other attitude, that it is more often caught from parents (at least in the preschool stage) than from playmates and teachers, and that it proceeds from a vague and undifferentiated form to a clear-cut pattern. Finally it results more from contact with other attitudes than with clearly defined groups and as the children get older, develops a greater set of rationalizations to account for it.

THE STRENGTH OF ATTITUDES

Since the 1930's there have been several attempts to measure attitudes (prejudice among them) by the use of attitude scales. Perhaps the best known of these are the Thurstone,[18] Likert,[19] and Guttman [20] methods. It is not possible here to review these in detail; the interested reader will find adequate information in the footnotes just mentioned.

On the basis of these techniques or simpler ones investigators have sought to measure the attitudes of subjects toward various ethnic or racial groups in the community. For example, Merton found that religious groups could be ranked in terms of the most unfavorable toward Negroes, then the next most unfavorable, and so on. The ranking (among 679 college students in five colleges during 1938–1939) was: Catholics, Protestants, Jews, no religious affiliation.[21] Allport and Kramer reached a somewhat similar conclusion when they found that prejudice against the Negro was greater among 420 college students in the following order among religious groups: Catholic, Protestant, no religious affiliation, Jewish.[22]

It is worth comment that the general method of measuring attitudes employed by most of the studies made in the 1930's and 1940's (represented by the two given above) attempts to measure the *amount* of prejudice, i.e., whether a given individual has *more* or *less* of it. Although many interesting results have been reported on this basis, they are limited in scope and are sometimes conflicting in their answers. F. Tredwell Smith, for example, reports that men college students are more favorable to the Negro than women college students, while Allport and Kramer discover that women students are less prejudiced (toward Negroes as well as Jews) than men college students.[23] Other discrepancies like this occur, and while they may indicate only the inadequate range of the data investigated, they still leave one question unanswered: even if we know the relative *amount* of prejudice held by the individual, how can we be sure that it plays a dominant part in his behavior?

The only investigator who has approached this problem with clear recognition of its importance is Hartley. He has given to ethnic attitudes the term "salience," borrowed from the German psychologist Stern. Salience may be called the emphasis upon a like or a dislike. It is clear that one person may show more prejudice on an attitude scale than another and yet may give it little expression in his everyday behavior if he is occupied with useful activities that drain off his interests through other channels. Another person who shows much less prejudice on an attitude scale may nevertheless be aggressive in displaying it at the first provocation.[24]

Hartley shows that there is far greater ethnic salience, for example, in the case of newspaper advertisements for domestic workers than there is for commercial and industrial positions. This is explained by the fact that greater intimacy of contact is required for the domestic worker but is not so likely to occur in the commercial world. Yet curiously enough there is not the same consistency of salience in the advertisements for sharing apartments or furnished rooms. Salience was also measured in terms of students' tendencies to group pictures according to ethnic attributes or to use ethnic designations on successive descriptions.[25] The results are meager, however, and are far more suggestive than conclusive. They point the way for the testing of this hypothesis in terms of life situations so that salience can be correlated not only with personality traits as measured in a testing situation but in response to ethnic groups of different sorts, with factors like competition, rivalry, subordination, and superordination carefully controlled.

The conception of salience is of highest importance for our knowledge of prejudice because it points to an unexplored area, namely, the strength of attitudes in terms of the frequency of their expression. An attempt to present a preliminary analysis of this problem has been given by Doob, who distinguishes in any attitude three types of strength: (1) afferent habit strength, or the strength of the bond between the stimulus and the response; (2) efferent habit strength, or the bond between attitude as internal stimulus and the response pattern; (3) drive strength, or the extent to which the tension is not satisfied until some sort of reward is obtained.[26] The first two of these might be designated by "stimulability" and "excitability." The third, however, seems to be dependent upon and not separate from the other two. Drive strength as defined by Doob can be expressed only in or through stimulability or excitability and could be expressed as the intensity of one or the other.

The real question is therefore not how much prejudice an individual has but the intensity with which he expresses it, the extent to which it is a driving force in his personality. This leads naturally to another aspect of prejudice which has so far been disregarded.

PSYCHODYNAMICS OF PREJUDICE

In the discussion about anti-Semitism above, it was pointed out that one explanation for its appearance was on the basis of repressed hostility. Both the members of the psychoanalytic school and many popular writers who have taken over the vocabulary and ideology of the Freudians have tried to show that prejudice is a projection of these antisocial urges upon some group or "scapegoat" which, because of its visible differences, could be singled out as a potential threat. On this theory the individual who is insecure cannot admit to himself that his insecurities are the result of his style of life or the result of inner conflicts which render him powerless. He therefore feels the need to account for his insecurity as the result of anxieties created by others, especially those who are different from himself, who work for values that he actively dislikes, or who in some way threaten his status (or appear to do so).

The psychoanalysts of the newer school point out that in a competitive society like our own, success can be achieved only by competing with rivals, and that by the very nature of the system only a few individuals can reach the pinnacle of success. That means that the rest are "more often defeated than victorious" so that competitive society creates continual frustration for those who accept its demands. Very few can accept the fact that society as a whole is organized to frustrate their drive for security — the problem is too vast to be visualized. Consequently it must be whittled down to manageable size, and this is done by attributing the frustration to human scapegoats. "Thus intolerance is the consequence on the one hand of the pressure of anxiety and frustration and on the other hand of the absence of suitable controls which would prohibit their discharge through intolerance." [27] On this basis prejudice is a function of maladjustment, of a psychopathological condition; the person living in social isolation is therefore especially liable to be motivated by this type of prejudice.[28]

Two major questions are raised by this interpretation: (1) Can all or even most prejudice be explained by asserting that its origin is in neurotic tendencies? (2) If not, how much validity does the psychoanalytic theory have?

The answer to the first question seems to be a flat no. Refutation of the argument could follow several lines of evidence. In the first place, the above use of the word "intolerance" as a synonym for prejudice is an example of overstatement. It is already clear from the discussion of salience that intolerance is a particularly virulent form of prejudice or one with great drive strength.* Does it apply to the attitudes of the child in the early grades? Or to adults who have a mild aversion to, or dislike of, Italians, Japanese, Mexicans, or Jews? Common usage would hardly apply the term "intolerant" to those whose prejudice shows so little salience.

Then is prejudice always a function of insecurity? If so, why do Levinson and Sanford find that the higher the income of the father the greater the proportion of anti-Semites? Or that anti-Semitic students are those who have least conflict with their parents? [29] (It is not denied that economic insecurity often has a bearing on prejudice.) Another way of testing this hypothesis would be to discover whether there was any correlation between prejudice in children and neurotic or maladjustment scores. A recent careful statistical study by Melvin Seeman on grade school children in an Ohio city shows "no reliable relation between adjustment and prejudice" whatever.[30] He calls the psychoanalytic theory "the mental hygiene point of view" and asserts that though it has been accepted as a set of axioms, tests conducted to confirm it have been uniformly inconclusive so far.[31] And he states that the result of his own study, specifically undertaken to confirm or deny the mental hygiene point of view, discovered that the pattern of group interaction of the prejudiced person was not significantly different from that of the unprejudiced in his own group, i.e., he does not show pronounced negativism, heightened aggression, or a deviant view of himself nor is he regarded as queer by his own group.[32]

This evidence is especially significant for younger groups; it has not yet been sufficiently tested for adults, and it is possible that it may have more validity for them. But so far what we actually have is a series of propositions that apply to clinical cases, erected into a

* Some writers employ the terms "intolerance" and "prejudice" synonymously. This seems too far from common usage, for the reasons given above.

theory and applied without qualification to the population as a whole. Until this is accepted as a hypothesis and not as a generalization based on verified data, social science will not advance another step in the direction of control.

The second question was: what validity does the psychoanalytic theory have? Is it entirely useless? Here one must proceed with caution because actual data are lacking in the scientific records. Going back to Bettelheim's argument that persons living in social isolation are highly sensitive to prejudice and scapegoat reactions, we find that, as a psychoanalyst, he suggests that there may be social differentiating factors that make individuals especially prone to prejudice of a high salience.[33] The sociologist would agree that "the social isolates are . . . the most fertile ground for the seed of group hatred."

Studies of native fascist movements both in the United States and in Germany have shown that many of their followers come from lower middle class groups, who are basically insecure and therefore susceptible to projective and displacement mechanisms. However, too many of the inferences made in these studies have transferred clinical psychology uncritically to the interpretation of group phenomena without empirical study of the groups themselves.[34] What is needed is actual research in these hate groups with the same meticulous care and attention to detail that has been given to the study of criminal gangs or inmates of penitentiaries. If social psychology or sociology ever attempts this task (say by the participant-observer method à la John Roy Carlson with a scientific technique), the results would help to answer the question: to what extent is the strength (or salience) of prejudice correlative with social maladjustment, economic insecurity, loss of status, or abnormal family situations?

Let us present a cautious hypothesis for testing. The general level of prejudice (the strength of prejudice in the "public" as judged by overt expression) is low in salience but may be given more dynamic potency by added insecurity, whether it be economic or status centered. The psychoanalytic theory may thus be valid in explaining the variation in prejudice-intensity but not of prejudice in general. It seems fairly clear that prejudice has a function, namely, to separate in-group from out-group.[35] In MacIver's words,

"The anti-image is the defensive-offensive response of the threatened interest, whether it be economic or political or cultural on any level. It is an ideological device to evoke in the group a fighting consciousness of its separateness and superiority." [36]

SOCIAL COMPONENTS OF PREJUDICE

It is important to depict the growth of hostile reactions in the individual or the stereotypes resulting from early training in childhood, but this by itself is insufficient. Immediately the question will be raised: if the child learns prejudice from suggestion or direct teaching of parents and intimate acquaintances, how did the latter learn it? It is quite inadequate to reply that they learned these attitudes from *their* parents and so on *ad infinitum*. To do so would be to explain the phenomenon in a single linear dimension rather than as the result of a complex set of variables, as it is. It is therefore necessary to examine the social dimensions which bear on the parents and their parents.

Roughly speaking, the society in which prejudice arises displays *group factors* and *process* (or pervasive) *factors*. Being a by-product of conflict, prejudice appears more often where groups are multiple and diversified, with conflicting demands on the role of the individual. Evidence seems to show that where a society is homogeneous or largely based on the older bonds of kinship, internal divisions are kept to a minimum, friction is reduced, and hostility is directed more toward deviant individuals than toward groups. On the contrary a society which has a multiplicity of secondary groups and is highly differentiated, makes conflicting demands on its members, who then begin to vent their antagonisms upon members of other groups *as members*.[37]

Within such a society certain groups are more important than others in terms of power relations, as has already been pointed out in Chapter 1. Typically there is a "dominant group," defined as one whose historical language, traditions, customs, and ideology are normative for the society; it should be added, of course, that this dominant group is also in position to control the major institutions of the society by means of concerted action and to reinforce its pre-eminence in such ways as ranking individuals for social stratification, determining occupational roles, and perpetuating cultural values. In this sense the dominant group acts as an integrating influence on the society.[38] Prejudice arises when any one of these functions is obstructed or hindered because it conflicts with the stable system already achieved.

In addition to these group relations there are more pervasive ones that permeate the entire social atmosphere. Most important of all these is simply social change. In a static society there may be differences of status but as long as they are fixed and rigid, as long as they are continued from one generation to the next by a process of traditional transmission along with other mores and folkways, the conflict is kept to a minimum and, with it, prejudice.* It is largely where the pattern is fluid and change threatens the stable relationships already fixed by the realities of power that status becomes uncertain and prejudice becomes intensified.[39] Since social change is at a maximum in differentiated societies, the social scientist would regard the two factors of secondary society and rapid social change as simply the obverse of each other, correlative elements in the same situation.

Sudden changes in terms of geographical or territorial mobility may intensify conflict when the numerical position of two groups may be rapidly altered by migration. Thus reports of increased hostility to Negroes in the San Francisco area during war and postwar years have reflected the impact of such changes. Earlier race riots in St. Louis and Chicago and contemporary ones in Detroit illustrate the same principle.

Vertical mobility also plays a conspicuous role in setting the stage for prejudice. As chances for success decrease in the social order, any rise in the economic or social position of groups or individuals labeled as "outsiders," foreigners, race groups, or those who can be defined by visibility factors, occasions negative reactions and increased solidarity on the part of the dominant group.

Another pervasive element that defines the social relations in which prejudice appears is the presence of ideals. We have already noted in Chapter 1 that the so-called "American dream" of equality, opportunity, and democracy of which Myrdal makes so much, enters as a dynamic factor into the prejudice situation. This is of enough

* Rural areas of the South seem to be an exception to this rule since they are *more* static than urban areas even of the same region.

importance to lead two students of the problem to insist that it must be incorporated into the basic texture of prejudice itself. Thus Grosser and Korchin give the following definition: "Group prejudice is a common attitude of hostile nature whose manifestations conflict with some aspects of the basic value framework of the society in which they occur." * [40]

Perhaps it should also be indicated that the social situation is particularly susceptible to prejudice in periods of what Durkheim called *anomie*. By this is meant those epochs in which social disorganization is prominent, in which institutional controls are losing their grip, or in which the relations between effort and reward are greatly altered. The most prominent example of this, of course, is an economic depression in which the scramble for bare existence becomes intensified to the extent that ordinary controls are lacking; at such a time anxiety mounts, while the predictability of institutions or the behavior of others is being lost.[41]

Under these conditions perversion of the usual thought patterns is manifest and mass behavior increases as individuals share their misery or misfortune. Lacking an explanation for the rapid deterioration of position, the masses also seek for an interpretation that will satisfy them, *a pursuit of meaning* in Cantril's terms. This they find most readily in the systematized utterances of paranoid leaders, who always flourish during such periods. But these leaders operate through channels already laid down in the familiar thought pattern of childhood; they do not concoct new explanations. They merely give additional force to the vague suspicions already engendered by secondary learning and crystallize these into convictions backed by powerful emotional drives.

Another dimension of the group situation becomes apparent when it is reflected that each society has appropriate or group-approved channels for aggression. It would take us too far afield to consider the early growth of the aggression pattern, but the important feature in this context is the role of the culture in directing the aggression developed by the individual in his early primary-group relationships. In this respect, John Dollard has given an amusing but essentially

* This does not mean that the "American dream" increases prejudice but that it enters as a component into the social definition of prejudice in American culture.

accurate definition of culture when he calls it "an arbitrary inheritance of problem solutions" for any given generation.[42]

Early experience teaches the individual that it is quite impossible to express antagonism toward members of the group on which he depends for subsistence and affectional support. Therefore not only is the deflection of this aggression to an out-group necessary psychologically but the person learns, from the cultural rules and patterns expressed by the in-group, where he may direct them without fear of reprisal. At least this is possible in the dominant group, though among minorities such deflection of hostility is attended by even more danger, since it may lead to violence or to denial of position, status, or economic opportunity. It then reverts to his own in-group and we have "self-hatred," or a form of inverted prejudice.*

A social component of prejudice in the American scene is suggested by a syndrome of traits discovered by Frenkel-Brunswik and Sanford in their studies of the anti-Semitic personality. A constant recurrence of certain factors in a cluster indicates that prejudice appears in connection with conventional religion, nationalism, and exaggerated moral strictness. The number of times these traits occurred together was highly significant. The anti-Semitic subjects give religion a utilitarian touch, admire most patriots or figures of power, and are highly insistent on etiquette and honesty.[43]

The element of nationalism, when one considers the widespread use of the phrase "100 per cent American" or the use of "American" for insiders and derogatory terms for outsiders, is evidence of the thesis that the "very American American" is likely to be a bigoted personality. If the data gathered by Frenkel-Brunswik and Sanford are at all representative, the "American" would not be a "zoot-suiter" or live in a "bad part of town," would not be of "lower class people" or live in slums. "Americans" would rather be the ones who are typically "nice" people, who have money, good clothes, possessions, and power or who have "right" attitudes and standards (as defined by someone like them). Prejudice often accompanies a particular philosophy of life identified with middle-class, conventional, power-loving attitudes.

* See Chapter 18 on anti-Semitism, above.

THE CONFLICT SITUATION

Enough has been indicated to show that the social dimensions of attitude appear in the context of conflict. It is not even enough to assert that an in-group vs. out-group situation sufficiently describes the basic social configuration, because before this distinction can become an important influence, there must be differentia of power involved, i.e., one group must have more or less control over the society. (A limiting but rarely appearing case would be two absolutely equal groups, evenly matched in all respects, a condition possible chiefly in theory.) While the extent to which this difference of power is perceived may vary from heightened consciousness to bare awareness, it is perhaps the essential ingredient in the social situation where prejudice develops. This is the element of truth in the Marxian theory or any other which emphasizes the competitive culture in which prejudice develops. The conflict theory of prejudice throws doubt upon the explanation of it as group conformity without emphasizing *why* the group is motivated to *bring* pressure on its members (as Lasker tends to do). It is true that the individual finds it expedient to conform to the prevailing attitudes, myths, and stereotypes in the prevailing mores, to be like the group-approved pattern; but the pattern itself is distinctly a weapon used in the service of power against another group defined as menacing.

It is clear from the conflict situation that whether the group is subordinate or dominant, prejudice will be an accepted way of reacting to the other group. If subordinate, the group will be victims of an exploitative situation and react with resentment, anger, and an image of the dominant group that represents it as a monster. Prejudice is not a function of dominant groups alone. In addition to the anti-Negro, anti-Mexican, anti-Japanese, and anti-Semitic forms of prejudice developed for protective measures by an Anglo-Saxon, Protestant, white dominant group there is also antiwhite and antigentile prejudice of considerable force, as has already been suggested in the review of minorities above. The extent to which it may be "justified" is of secondary interest here. But at least it may be indicated that where a plurality of subordinate groups is present in a culture, some of the prejudice in each minority may be deflected from the dominant group to another disadvantaged group.

The history of ethnic minorities indicates how often a prejudice retained from the European environment has continued in the American scene; residual Slovak hatred of Hungarians or Polish antagonism toward Germans and Russians has continued unabated for long periods and made it possible for employers to play these groups off against each other. In a somewhat different fashion, anti-Semitism has developed among Negroes as a surreptitious means of fighting against whites with the weapons of the dominant gentile. Or in another context, the Japanese returning to the West Coast were frequently able to displace Mexicans who had temporarily captured their positions during the war and this led to Mexican prejudice against Japanese. Here and there it has been possible to show rationally that these interminority conflicts and prejudices were really functions of the larger dominance-submission pattern, but this has not always been successful. Since the type of dominance varies with each group, there are even those who maintain that this brings about a situation that differs not only in degree but in kind.*

Although the field of prejudice reactions within minority groups is a fascinating area of study, it must be confessed that it has received little scientific examination. Furthermore it may be urged that with reduction of prejudice in the dominant group, there will be a corresponding reduction of the same phenomenon in the more disadvantaged group while the reverse is obviously not the case. For these reasons more attention will be devoted to that of the dominant group in this discussion.

Ichheiser suggests that the situation in which prejudice arises is usually marked by conflict of (1) interests, (2) values, (3) personality types.[44] Although the last of these is not so clearly observable for empirical study, the former two are of great significance. Wherever there is intergroup conflict it is likely to involve both, although it is probable that in ethnic conflicts the divergent values occupy the forefront of attention.

* Cox, for example, distinguishes "intolerance" from "race prejudice," applying the former to the attitude held by gentiles to Jews, while the latter characterizes the attitude of whites to Negroes. In his view, the intolerant group insists upon assimilation and conversion; but the race-prejudiced group *refuses* assimilation. In the view adopted here, this may be called a genuine distinction but only one between two varieties of prejudice. Cf. Oliver C. Cox, *Caste, Class, and Race*, New York, Doubleday, 1948, pp. 394ff.

To say that prejudice arises from conflict of interests is to assert that there are definite gains or rewards for prejudiced attitudes. In American society the chief are probably economic and status gains. If by social definition the Mexican, the Oriental, the foreigner, or the Negro is put in the category of a group that can "live on less," then a differential wage is justified and profits can be increased. Or if the Jew can be defined as a person who pushes every advantage unfairly in order to eliminate the gentile from competition and who is therefore excluded from clubs, hotels, medical schools, or professional opportunities, the gentile can reap his gains undisturbed.

A good many leftist writers have inferred from this that by eliminating the forms of competition so characteristic of the capitalistic system, prejudice itself might be reduced to the point where it would no longer constitute a serious threat to society. Thus Cox asserts that under a socialistic form of economic organization, the relations between people of different color would be "significantly modified." Or to go farther, he contends that race prejudice can never be wholly removed under a capitalistic system because the latter is inherently exploitative.[45] Yet if socialism would largely eliminate race prejudice, we might expect such elimination to occur in a country which has perhaps gone further in socialistic practice than any nation outside the Soviet Union, namely Australia. The socialization of industry in Australia, however, has not appreciably reduced the prejudice against the aboriginal population; in fact the attitude toward the native population is still typically that of the colonial, a situation quite unmodified by the change in economic system.

If other examples are needed, a glance at the Soviet Union shows that the official policy or ukase of the government has hardly been sufficient to alter many of the basic anti-Semitic prejudices there. Even during the war anti-Semitism appeared in Moscow intelligentsia groups, and the postwar period saw an increase of anti-Semitism in Russian Turkestan after the appearance of many Jewish refugees. There has also been removal of all Jewish diplomats who might represent Russia in foreign countries. It is true that anti-Semitism shows an obvious increase in the Ukraine but this can be attributed largely to Nazi propaganda.[46]

The truth of the matter is that prejudices become part of the mores and folkways which persist through many economic systems. Certainly anti-Semitism as a form of group prejudice was in many ways stronger under a medieval economy than under a capitalistic one.* If the reference is to race prejudice alone, it is true that this developed *pari passu* with capitalism; but it did so unevenly (for example, it has scarcely appeared in France) and where capitalism gives way to another economic system, race prejudice will probably continue in the folkways, as in Australia, unless specific efforts are made to eradicate it.

Moreover it appears that a good deal of prejudice is fictitious competition. To the extent that another group is defined as different, visible, or recognizable, the competition of any member will be defined as the *group's* competition. But where a member of the out-group becomes a working member of a shop, office, or crew without attention being called to his group membership, prejudices as a function of competition may disappear entirely. This may be true even when the member of the out-group has a high visibility and belongs to a different racial category which cannot be concealed.

Among merchant seamen of the National Maritime Union it was discovered that the more often white crews had shipped with Negroes, the less prejudiced they were, regardless of their previous geographical origin.[47] Part of this may have been due to union training against prejudice, which emphasized the importance of regarding a member of another race as simply a person without label. Where the label is erased or disappears through gradual contact (as among the nationality groups whose assimilation made it less and less possible to single them out), prejudice goes with it. Perhaps prejudice has a suspicious likeness to Bernard Shaw's definition of love as "the exaggeration of the difference between one woman and another." By substituting the word "group" for "woman" the parallel becomes clear.**

* A natural objection here is that this involved a maximum of discrimination and not prejudice, since the latter was not perceived as such. Even this may be questioned since Trachtenburg's study (footnote 1, Chapter 18) shows that the persecution of the Jews in medieval times directly conflicted with the Christian value norms as enunciated by the Popes and the hierarchy.

** The observant reader will note that this appears to contradict one of the main contentions of this volume, i.e., that groups *are* different, that their background, cultural history, and position vis-à-vis the dominant majority are clues

Since conflict over status in American society is so inextricably intertwined with conflict over economic matters, it seems unnecessary to treat this aspect separately. In a few cases the two factors may appear independently, as in those areas where "old families" have status regardless of their economic position. But in these cases the groups with status are really minorities attempting to act like dominant groups with the aid of most members of the community who adopt the prevailing folkways and ideology. Prejudice in this case takes the form of pure snobbishness.

In the conflict situation prejudice may begin as a mild reaction. As it becomes crystallized or culturally channeled into group-approved patterns, it passes from a mere implicit reaction to a clearly observable form of behavior in discrimination. And where the conflict becomes intensified by competition, "incidents," or sudden change in the numerical ratio between groups, it passes into physical violence, riots, or gang warfare.[48] But neither discrimination nor group violence is understandable except on the basis of pre-existing prejudice.

It must be clearly recognized that the dynamic power of aggression

---

to understanding their behavior and their dominant values. In a way it is useless to gloss over this fundamental difficulty because it lies at the basis of all discussions of minority problems. Any treatment of them must begin with a polarity — difference and similarity. It is precisely the same issue faced by the anthropologist who insists upon the variability of culture and yet concludes that the same personality types and the same "basic human nature" appear everywhere. Both are true but not on the same level of discourse. When an anthropologist emphasizes the similarity of all human groupings, he is speaking largely of the potentialities involved; if a human infant from any culture is reared in another culture, it will behave like members of the host society. There is no reason to believe that if the organism is normal to begin with, it cannot adapt itself to any social environment whatever; its intelligence cannot be assumed to be inferior because of the color of skin or slant of eye. On the other hand, when diversity is emphasized, it refers to another dimension, namely, a set of learned behavior patterns. People brought up in two divergent social systems will start from different premises and presuppositions; their accent and cadence, their style of life, and their modes of action will vary. Thus when they come into a different society, they will learn and adapt themselves in terms of their already learned symbols and patterns. By doing so they will bring into the host society a variety and richness that will prevent a dead-level uniformity. An insistence upon the "right to be different" is therefore the basis of the doctrine of "cultural pluralism." But this does not deny the original similarity of potential.

is in some ways stronger than the tame satisfactions of promoting harmony and good will. Group unity and cohesion are attained most easily by means of directed attack against an enemy. This is clearly observable in wartime, but it has its counterpart during periods of peace when aggression is turned toward internal groups. Davidson states the case well:

> Another sorry but serious thesis for the popularity of prejudice springs from the fact that to the average person antagonism is more attractive, more exciting, than good will and friendliness. You will certainly be the center of more interest at a party by promising to "dish out the dirt" than by reporting a catalogue of praiseworthy deeds. We sense a not too unpleasant thrill at hearing malicious gossip about even our best friends. We hanker to do forbidden things and envy those bold enough to traverse the sanctions that keep us from complete freedom. And to envy some one is to wish him ill. This mechanism makes antagonism a pleasure and approval a bore. A campaign of hatred and vilification is always more exciting than one of endorsement.
>
> If the average man starts with a neutral attitude towards all races, he is more likely to be whipped into interest by the exciting, flattering blasts of the preacher of prejudice than by the more modest presentation of apostles of good will. The former offers membership in a master-group, revenge against those stigmatized as responsible for his difficulties, and all the thrill of the chase with the added condiment of human quarry; while the unprejudiced offer only the unexciting doctrine that one individual is no better than another, that we have only ourselves to blame for our failures, and that we belong to a universal brotherhood. Since those who would destroy prejudice have not dramatized their program, victory by default goes to the more articulate peddler of hatred.[49]

It may then be suggested that prejudice has a powerful hold on the public because of the conventional, impersonal, and routine features of everyday existence which restrict the expression of certain outlawed emotions. When, however, the culture provides for an accepted channel for these dangerous emotions — fear, suspense, hatred, revenge, envy, malice, suspicion, and dread — it gives to prejudice and its expression a thrill and sense of participation that is superior even to the vicarious satisfactions of movie-going, where the same emotions are released.

For this reason there are purveyors of prejudice as there are purveyors of movies or peep shows, burlesques, and yellow journals. The organizers of hate groups or fomenters of antagonism, whether demagogues, politicians, or editors, find they have touched a responsive chord. Their constant use of testimonials from individuals who have been "awakened" or have "seen the light" is based upon sound emotional realities. How much these leaders are coolly and deliberately playing on feelings and attitudes that are simply mechanisms of power or how much they actually share in the emotional release of their followers is not always clear. But the evidence would suggest that they cannot remain entirely outside the circle of mass enthusiasm, even though they must have a certain amount of objectivity in order to employ their techniques skillfully. A highly successful use of prejudice to further vested interests can be noted in California, where the peak of anti-Japanese agitation has come at election times, with dozens of Congressmen gaining their seats as a result.[50] And examination of their own convictions and attitudes suggests that many of them received quite as much satisfaction from the agitation as their followers.

NEGLECTED ASPECTS OF PREJUDICE

The discussion so far may seem to have assumed that prejudice is directed against *all* members of an out-group. This is far from the case. There are always "exceptions." And the function of the exception appears to be rationalization or the proof of broad-mindedness. The prejudiced person may not merely admit but insist on the personal merit of an individual Mexican, Italian, Jew, or Negro, his cleanliness, good manners, refinement, and intelligence. The way in which this is stressed leaves no doubt that it is unfortunately not typical and that other members of these groups are "beyond the pale." It is possible for the stereotype to remain even though the prejudiced person is acquainted with an individual of the out-group who does not conform to the conviction about *all* members of the particular group. He is then characterized as exceptional, but he has no influence on the prejudice. This is shown by the fact that a chance meeting with another individual who does conform to the stereotype will appear to be proof or demonstration of its validity. Thus the statement, "Some of my best friends are Jews," carries with it the implicit correction, "but they are exceptional — not like the usual run."

The most important element of prejudice is the potent hostility or aversion connected with it, not the fixity of the stereotype. The latter may consist of multiple elements quite incompatible logically. For example, the stereotype of Jews may carry with it contradictory elements such as ostentation and miserliness. Therefore if an affluent Jew makes a large contribution to charity, it is proof of the ostentatiousness of Jews; if, however, he gives less than a gentile in the same income bracket, it is evidence of the miserliness of his people. Regardless of behavior, the prejudice is "justified."[51] Levinson and Sanford showed that the same individuals who asserted that the Jews tried to mix too much with gentiles were the same as those who contended that they were too clannish and kept to themselves too much.[52] Likewise the southern white who asserts that there "is no race problem" because the Negro knows his place, may in the next breath explain that considerable force is needed to keep him there.[53]

Gregory tested this in another way by having subjects rank nationalities by preference, rate photographs of members of these nationalities, identify the photographs with the various nationalities, and give reasons for their identification. He found that the identification of the photographs was about equal to chance distribution but that the disliked photographs were uniformly linked with disliked nationality groups.[54] This suggests that the outlines of the stereotype have no clear lines and that the real constant is the emotional antagonism involved. The stereotype appears to have fluid boundaries which alter with the situation.

MacIver also reports that social images are not as fixed or static as the term "stereotype" implies. He points out that on one day the American may picture the French as a nation of degenerates and on the next as marching with the United States in the van of civilization. Then he concludes that these social images have a "changeful relativity" and that in this very fact lies the hope of social education.[55] Unfortunately his analysis seems to regard these realities in terms of cognitive elements without taking into account the underlying affective dynamisms.

The exponents of the "mental hygiene school" have emphasized the importance of projection as an essential element of prejudice. While this is undoubtedly important in many cases, Ichheiser has performed a unique service by showing that another form of false social perception is often confused with it. He calls this second form the "mote-beam mechanism." The two may be distinguished as follows: in projection we attribute to others certain characteristics of our own that we keep well concealed (such as hostility, egoism, carelessness, laziness, or heightened sexuality); in the mote-beam mechanism, however, we perceive "characteristics in others which we do not perceive in ourselves" and thus perceive "those characteristics as if they were peculiar traits of the others."

Ichheiser suggests that if the term "projection" is to be used properly, it should imply that the content of the perception is false and that therefore individuals who engage in it attribute to other persons characteristics which are not there. On the other hand, the mote-beam mechanism as such would not imply that the content of the perception is false (such characteristics may truly be found in the out-group) but that the inference is false (namely, that the characteristics truly observed do not belong to the observer). Thus in the mote-beam mechanism the observer sees the other person or group "in a false perspective" which excludes himself. True projection would then be pathological and a source of paranoid development to be treated by abnormal psychology, while the mote-beam mechanism would be a more universal quality of group life which does not imply anything abnormal and hence belongs to the province of social psychology or the sociology of knowledge. It follows that recognition of the mote-beam mechanism would lead the observer not to say, "Look how prejudiced they are" but rather "They are as prejudiced as all other people including ourselves, although the content of their prejudices seems to be somewhat different."[56] An analysis of this kind gives further evidence for the conclusion that most prejudice is not abnormal or pathological since instances of projection are far rarer than cases of the mote-beam mechanism.

Another feature of prejudice too often disregarded is that it forms a part of an equilibrium of forces both within the individual and within the group. As Kurt Lewin states the problem, "Some forces support each other, some oppose each other. Some are driving forces, others restraining forces. Like the velocity of a river, the actual conduct of the group depends upon the level . . . at which the conflicting forces reach a state of equilibrium. To speak of a certain culture pattern . . . implies that the constellation of these forces remains the same for a period or at least that they find their state of equilibrium at a constant level during that period." [57]

If this is true, then prejudice is supported and reinforced by other attitudes and emotions, by feelings of adequacy, moral conceptions, political loyalties, religious beliefs, and many others. It is not an isolated element that can be eradicated from the internal structure of the personality, leaving the rest of the configuration unchanged. In the same way it has its position as a part of the group process, where it is embedded in power relations, status feelings, conformity, group fears, institutional patterns, and the like. An attempt to alter it may be regarded as a threat to the harmony or equilibrium of group life which has been achieved after careful balancing and accommodation of factors. For this reason an indirect attack which alters the meaning of an entire social configuration may often be more successful than a direct challenge to the isolated prejudice itself.[58]

This immediately suggests that prejudice is not a unitary phenomenon since the content of the attitude expressed will differ in one context or another. To follow up the conception of equilibrium, it is surely significant that Harlan found his southern students less prejudiced toward Jews than the northern ones in a southern situation.[59] It is a plausible hypothesis in keeping with our observations on anti-Semitism above that the actual level of conflict is lower in the South where there are few Jews but many Negroes; that the hostility directed against the latter may have been compensated for by a raising of the level of tolerance for Jews. If this is the case, we might even assert that anti-Semitism in the South is significantly different from the anti-Semitism of the North.

Another line of evidence in the same direction is Ichheiser's discovery that anti-Negro and anti-Jewish prejudices are conceived in terms of different threats — one the fear of the gangster and the other the fear of the swindler.[60] But it is not proved that these two forms of prejudice are always unrelated; Allport and Kramer found (with Harvard, Radcliffe, and Dartmouth students) that the persons who were more afraid of swindlers turned out to have higher prejudice scores in general. Thus anti-Semitic prejudice in this case proved to include anti-Negro prejudice.[61] While it is still unproved that prejudice is entirely unitary, further research may show certain significant correlations. However, it seems likely that any program designed to combat prejudice cannot assume a uniform character but must take into account the social field in each case.

Finally, one of the most subtle phenomena in intergroup relations so frequently overlooked is that there can be prejudice against prejudice. Those who are relatively free from antigroup hostility frequently develop new hostilities of which they seem complacently unaware. Since their early training and education have prepared them for a realistic view of group differences combined with relatively rational standards of merit which they apply to individuals regardless of race, color, and national or religious affiliation, they are subject to a certain blindness with regard to their own aggressive impulses, often denying that they exist. In Davidson's words, they are "proportionately gratified by the implication that they belong to a well-adjusted emotional elite. Nor should we forget the hysterically conspicuous 'tolerance,' a sluice through which a person whose own life has been insipidly ungratifying pours himself onto platforms in which 'racial equality' is a prominent plank. Here he can divert his aggressiveness toward those who reject his philosophy instead of toward those of different national or racial breed." [62]

Although these individuals are willing and eager to point out the environmental forces that have created differences within social groups, they seem entirely blind to those that produce prejudice itself and they prefer to blame, malign, or attack in the very area where understanding is most needed. Many, for example, are quite unaware that cultural pluralism includes the culture of the prejudiced. Intolerance of intolerance is in many ways an admirable trait but it often precludes the fact-finding, objectivity, and understanding necessary for a strategic attack on the citadels of prejudice.

REDUCING PREJUDICE

It is possible to diminish the role of certain attitudes so that they play a weaker part in the personality and in the group. Perhaps the most useful analysis of this process comes from Doob. In his view there are four possible ways in which an attitude may be weakened: (1) by diminishing the stimuli that evoke it; (2) by regulating the attitude so that it is aroused less frequently; (3) by setting up stronger competing drives; (4) by punishing the overt behavior induced by the attitude.[63] Though it is impossible to review all these methods in detail, yet they furnish a highly convenient way of summarizing the various efforts put forth to combat prejudice.

The first method, repugnant to most believers in democracy ("ship 'em back where they came from," "let them keep to themselves and we won't have any trouble," "distribute them evenly throughout the country and you'll find the problem solved," "let them learn our ways of doing things and then we'll accept them"), is nevertheless a by-product of the more impersonal forces of acculturation and assimilation. The gradual disappearance of European national minorities in the process of accepting American culture has eventually made these groups less and less conspicuous. As language, customs, and culture patterns take on a more familiar form, the stimuli that would normally evoke prejudices are reduced. The numerical distribution of Japanese Americans following the relocation experience has worked in the same direction. To the extent that segregation is possible, this is the grain of truth underlying the policy, namely, that separation of groups will prevent contact and thus diminish the stimuli that call forth prejudice. The only comment to make on this policy here is that segregation is advocated not to *combat* prejudice but to *support* it. Furthermore it may be questioned whether segregation in a modern era of intense mobility, more efficient transportation, and industrial concentration is at all feasible.

In connection with the other methods, it is interesting to compare them with Goodwin Watson's classification of the efforts being made to promote greater unity within the United States.[64] He lists seven techniques: exhortation, education, participation, revelation (exposé), negotiation, contention, and prevention. On the basis of Doob's analysis we might then combine the two somewhat as follows:

(2) Regulating the attitude so that it is aroused less frequently
- a. Exhortation
- b. Education
- c. Revelation (as Watson uses it, really a form of education adapted locally)
- d. Participation

(3) Setting up stronger, competing drives
- a. Negotiation (mediation)
- b. Prevention
- c. Participation
- d. Contention (often political)
- e. Exhortation
- f. Education
- g. Revelation

(4) Punishing the overt behavior induced by the attitude
- a. Contention (political)

This outline is useful to show that an accepted method (like education) may have two functions: (1) to keep prejudiced attitudes to a minimum, and (2) to set up strong countermotives which will eliminate prejudice by indirection. Likewise, exhortation may be regarded purely in its negative function of regulation or suppression of unfavorable attitudes or in its positive function of appealing to values that will call forth a different sort of response. Is it significant that three out of four methods suggested by Doob are negative? Certainly his first (diminishing stimuli that evoke the attitude), his second (regulating the attitude so that it is aroused less frequently), and the fourth (punishing overt behavior) are all forms of negative control. If we compare these with the techniques mentioned by Watson, it becomes clear that the latter can be interpreted either positively or negatively. Revelation (exposé) and contention are perhaps the only purely negative methods on his list.

The reason for the discrepancy in Doob's categories as compared with those of Watson is that the latter are concerned with reducing both discrimination and prejudice, while Doob's refer primarily to control of subjective attitudes. Since this volume deals with both problems, it is only fair to state here that the division of the field into the two sections is only provisionally useful. For purposes of analysis it is necessary to review the problem of prejudice apart from that of discrimination; but when methods and techniques for controlling the two are considered, the artificiality of the dichotomy becomes apparent at once. The whole question of controlling or reducing prejudice must be considered in the next chapter along with strategic considerations for combating discrimination.

CHAPTER 20

Programs and Policies for Minority Problems

"WHY DON'T YOU come and join us some time?"

"I don't know. Maybe it's because I'm not sure just what you're trying to do. Of course I'm in sympathy with your aims but I don't quite see how to go about it."

Ann smiled. "It's really very easy. How would you like to come over to Friendship House next week and get into one of our meetings? That's the best way to find out."

"Well, I think I'll try it once. What you say appeals to me anyhow," responded Frances. "What night is it?"

"Monday would be the best time. Come over about eight o'clock."

When Frances timidly ventured into the parlor of the Friendship House of Chicago, she found Ann at the door waiting for her. People were drifting in by twos and threes, some colored and some white. Many of them seemed to be acquainted with each other, for greetings were exchanged. Ann introduced Frances to a Negro couple who said they lived just around the corner, then to a white lawyer and his wife. Before she had finished talking with them, the room was filled and the meeting was called to order. A young priest took charge and, after opening the meeting with a prayer, introduced the speaker who addressed the group on the liturgy of the Christmas cycle, the meaning of the symbolism, and how it fitted in with the pattern of Catholic life. At the close of his remarks, which took about thirty-five minutes, the meeting was thrown open to questions, most of them asked by whites. Until this point in the program not a word was said about the interracial issue, but before completing the answers to questions, the speaker referred to the connection between liturgy and everyday life, together with its importance in solving the problem of racial relationships.

Coffee and cookies were served and then the speaker suggested that everyone join in the singing of Advent hymns and ecclesiastical chants. Several members passed printed sheets of words, and since there were not enough to go around, colored and white looked on together and sang the hymns in unison. As one of them phrased it later, "If there is any race consciousness present, it now yields to voice consciousness, providing everyone with a very enjoyable time."

No problems were solved, no policies uttered, no programs urged. The mixed group, however, came together on the religious plane. As the couples began to file out, Ann asked Frances, "How did you like it?"

"I don't know. It did make a deep impression on me. Perhaps I never thought about Catholic doctrine having anything to do with Negroes before. Yet I don't know why I didn't. What's that paper you have in your hand, Ann?"

"Oh, this is a new meditation for some of our meetings. Would you like to see it?"

"Of course."

Frances bent over the mimeographed sheet and read these words:

> We condemn You again to death, O Christ, when we hate Negroes, Jews, or the members of any race.
>
> We condemn you to death when we condemn our brother, the Negro, to death. . . .
>
> Living death, yes! The moments tick into minutes, the minutes into hours, hours to days, to weeks, to years. And every moment of his existence the Negro suffers a thousand deaths, of doubt, fear, insult, ridicule, violence, rejection, to find out if he can get a meal, get on a train, get into a hotel. Two things all men need — food and shelter; and we deny Negroes these.
>
> We turn You away, O Christ, from our hospitals because we say, "It is not yet time to admit Negroes."
>
> And this is what we are really saying: "It is not yet time to admit You, O Christ.". . .
>
> It is You again that we have condemned to death, O Christ, in our foul treatment of Your brothers, because they are our brothers too, in You, sealed with your blood.

For a moment Frances was silent. Then she spoke.

"Well, the connection seems clear enough. One cannot believe in Christ and his church and allow such things to go on. How does one become a member of the lay apostolate?"

"You must have a letter from your priest and turn in your application soon. Within a month they will choose probationers for this year. You will not be asked to take the vow of poverty but must voluntarily accept the state of being poor. Friendship House, if it accepts you, will furnish you room and board and five dollars a month. You will have a two-months' indoctrination course in the ideals and objectives of our program. Then you will be put on for the official probationary period the first year, during which they will give you training in Negro history, race relations, cooperatives, rural work, labor history and unionism, housing, health, recreation, and adult education. In addition to this will be training in crafts or skills along the line of your own aptitudes, and a layman's theology course. You will be expected to live among the people you serve, eat simple food, and identify yourself with your Negro neighbors. In due time you will be given responsibility in one of the special fields you have trained for, so as to work in the settlement. Let me warn you that there is a large turnover of staff and they are becoming more strict about screening out all candidates who will not continue with the work."

"Ann, I can't decide now, but I'm going home and talk it over with Dad and Mother. And Father Callahan. I can see the need. Whether I can measure up to it, I don't know." [1]

Sonya Shevich was in trouble. How many times would she have to tell the immigration authorities, and how could she make them listen? Again and again she repeated that she was born in Russia and in 1913 had been brought to Chicago by her parents, where both of them died. In 1917 she returned to Warsaw and married a Polish subject who was killed in the Russian revolution. Being trained as a nurse, she went to France and then Indo-China in the line of professional duty. It so happened that she was in the Philippines when the Japanese attacked, and immediately she offered her services to the American Red Cross. When the Japanese came, she helped some of her patients escape to the jungle, where they were finally rescued by invading Americans. The Army personnel insisted that she come to the United States but she could get nothing except a temporary permit. Now she was back in Chicago, her old home. Why couldn't she stay? The only answer she got from the officials was, "Sorry. But the law's the law. Your permit runs out next month and we can't get it renewed."

Then a friend told her of the services performed by the Immigrants' Protective League. Eagerly she sought their office. The report they gave her was a bit discouraging; yet there was hope. It would cost her a good deal of money; in fact she would have to borrow some. But she was informed that if she had a pre-examination, left the country for Canada, and then re-entered the United States, she could be accepted on a permanent basis and later on she could take out her first papers. Sonya decided that it was the only way out. She would be in debt for some time and the Government would be put to more expense on her behalf, but what could one do? Immigration laws were strict and the public was apathetic. At least she had a chance. But when would the laws catch up with the many cases of her kind? [2]

These examples show the wide diversity of programs in only two representative samples of literally hundreds of organizations in the field of intergroup relations throughout the nation. Some are religious, some educational, some political, some in the field of labor — the list is endless. Charles S. Johnson enumerates seventy-five of these on a national basis,[3] with innumerable others on a statewide basis; some, like the Catholic settlement house and the Immigrants' Protective League mentioned above, are purely local in their reach. It is not the purpose of this chapter to list these organizations by name. Some already have been mentioned in passing, and the interested reader can easily find the data for himself.[4] It is more important here to evaluate the work now being done in terms of goals and aims on the one hand, and means of accomplishment on the other.

PREJUDICE, DISCRIMINATION, AND CONFLICT

In the discussion of prejudice, it was possible to give a psychological analysis of the various ways in which prejudice as an attitude could be controlled.[5] The reduction of prejudice, however, is not only a subordinate (though important) task, but a direct attack upon prejudice may result in wasted effort and continual delay if it is not a part of a wider and more comprehensive plan. The most thoughtful students of the problem agree that since prejudice is a subjective reaction, it is less amenable to social control than overt expressions; being a private experience, it yields more quickly to indirect methods if only for the reason that attitudes or feelings can be concealed. This does not mean that it is impossible to affect prejudices by various techniques that are being developed, especially in the public schools; some of the results from experiment in the field are in fact most encouraging. It merely signifies, if military terminology be allowed, that the ways and means of modifying prejudice can be considered a tactical operation within a larger strategy. MacIver, for example, asserts that it is much more effective to "challenge conditions" than private emotions. Objective situations like differential wages, closed economic opportunities, denial of the franchise, inadequate housing, and the like are clearly visible, and a change in the discriminatory system will inevitably have its effects.[6]

Watson likewise maintains, for example, that it is more effective to attack something tangible, such as segregation, than prejudice itself, for when the walls of segregation break down, the resulting contact will help to dispel prejudice in a more natural way.[7] The breaking of barriers in war industry, the operation of F.E.P.C., and the mingling of races in the C.I.O. unions serve to illustrate how this actually happens. However, attacking segregation narrows the method to the level of one specific kind of discrimination rather than to discrimination itself. By making this technique primary, Watson elevates a specific method to the level of a general principle. His examples are more valid in the North than in the South, where no responsible leader would suggest that a frontal attack on segregation would be the most feasible policy.

As C. S. Johnson has convincingly shown, the South insists upon the general policy of separation of the races and regards public homage to it as a matter of principle, even when occasional violations occur in practice. Responsible southern Negro leaders have accepted this situation as a framework for their operations and have not pressed the issue so long as there were other tangible programs on which they could unite — equalizing teachers' salaries and educational expenditures, enlarging job opportunities, and the like. Even though the Negro may not accept segregation in principle, Johnson asserts that "both groups should cease to demand what is for the present impossible" and proceed to other issues that require their efforts.[8] It is still discrimination that is being attacked, but hardly segregation itself.*

Thus with all due respect to the many leaders of Negro opinion in the North who maintain that "the race problem is a national problem and must be solved on a national basis," the fact remains that every policy must be oriented to a specific social "field" and in terms of a realistic understanding of the stresses and strains within the system where it operates.[9] It therefore seems more plausible to assert that a challenge to discrimination is the basis of strategy rather than an attack on segregation; that is, if we are discussing the nation as a whole.

This is also in line with Myrdal's observations on the "rank order of discriminations" which he has outlined in his work on the Negro. In observing race relations, he listed the items which were held to be the most significant in the interaction between the races, in order of importance for southern whites. They were:

(1) The bar against intermarriage
(2) The insistence on separation of races in "social" or recreational interests; "social equality"
(3) Separation in schools, churches, and transportation
(4) Denial of the franchise
(5) Discriminations in legal and court procedures
(6) Discrimination in economic matters, jobs, housing, securing property, salaries, credit, public relief

* It may be conjectured that the revolt of the southern Democrats in 1948 as a result of President Truman's Civil Rights program was largely due to this direct challenge. That policy proposed four items: (1) an antilynching bill, (2) a permanent F.E.P.C. on a federal basis, (3) an antipoll tax bill, and (4) the abolition of "Jim Crow" in schools, transportation facilities, and restaurants.[10]

The first three have always aroused bitter resentment in the South, but it is quite possible that they *alone* might have led to the usual filibuster tactics in the Senate without precipitating a repudiation of the Democratic presidential candidate. The direct attack on segregation in the Civil Rights program, however, brought forth instant resentment and retaliation. It is not impossible that a temporary decline in harmonious race relations in the South reflected a reawakened solidarity and loyalty to the *status quo* below the Mason and Dixon line. Segregation is still the symbol of stability in race relations throughout the Solid South.

In his opinion the rank order of importance for the Negro was almost exactly the reverse of this. Myrdal's list is only suggestive; it has no statistical evidence to support it. Yet it has received fairly wide commendation. If its findings are correct, the items in number six, having to do with employment, remuneration, securing of credit, and better vocational opportunities are still major forms of discrimination which can be attacked without arousing the same determined opposition as items near the top of the scale.[11]

The question might fairly be raised whether, in the social system of the South, a planned program to reduce prejudice might not actually be more effective than one directed against segregation. From the evidence now available a fairly good case could be made for this hypothesis which would contradict Watson's position completely. On the other hand it would leave the basic truth of MacIver's thesis untouched if Myrdal's rank order of discrimination is accepted.

Since prejudice and discrimination frequently arise from conflict of interests between privileged and underprivileged groups, some writers state the chief goal of policy in dealing with minority problems as merely a reduction of conflict itself. This, however, is to oversimplify the issue. Is it not assumed that reduction in prejudice, in discrimination, and in conflict may all occur together? Is this true? For long-range objectives, perhaps; but Williams has clearly shown that in short-run programs one of these aims may come into conflict with another. Any attempt to eliminate discrimination will almost certainly meet with some resistance and therefore an initial increase in conflict. Or on the other hand an attempt to minimize conflict may be a means of perpetuating long-standing patterns of discrimination.[12]

VALUES AND PLANS OF ACTION

This leads to the reflection that the plurality of values in modern society is such that the promotion of one may lead to a decrease in the enjoyment of another. In fact this is quite inevitable and involves the very nature of selection itself, after the well known principle that all determination is negation. If there is to be more freedom for some citizens, there must be less for others; if there is to be more contact between groups, there will be less opportunity for the development of unique qualities. On the other hand if there is more insistence on the values of diverse beliefs and cultural traditions, the less chance there will be for homogeneity of culture.

In general, values are not absolutes but only hypostatized cultural situations selected from the welter of a total cultural pattern and given preference over another set of situations. It is true that these situations are imagined rather than actual, but their relevance is judged on the basis of empirically observed conditions. Nevertheless they always involve a selection of one pattern in preference to another, with the assumption that this can be translated into actuality at a minimal cost to other preferred patterns. Since the ability to regard the difficulties and obstacles of implementing results, or the concrete realities implied by the selection, is limited, constant revision and reshaping of the value goal occurs. Thus there may arise unanticipated effects, boomerang effects, and a threat to other values already held as a result of narrow adherence to any single goal. Many escape from this by stating the value so broadly that it loses most of its concrete reference and serves no longer to guide action in the short run. In this latter case, the value tends to be absolute but unrelated. It is already clear from the above example that this process occurs when the value goal becomes a "harmony" or a minimum of conflict. When harmony is considered apart from the more concrete experiences of translation into actuality (like "keeping one's place"), it may be emotionally satisfying; but as soon as it appears that an attempt to conserve harmony will perpetuate traditional patterns of discrimination, the dilemma is laid bare.

For this reason the value goal of programs and policies for minority problems will not be stated here in words such as "justice," "fair play," "harmony," and the like but in terms of the general issue laid down in our total analysis, i.e., as a concrete pattern of events relative to the situation in which minorities arise. Making this goal explicit, we would then state it as follows: the aim of programs and policies in minority problems is to create a situation in which members of minority groups will be enabled to pursue the same sort of goals in fulfillment of life purposes as are now pursued by members of the dominant group. At a minimum this will involve a decreasing number of hindrances placed in their path by the society as expressed in mores, laws, or institutional structures; at a maximum it would eliminate nearly all obstructions to this end and assume also a subjective conviction on the part of the great mass of informed citizens that such a policy is necessary for the full utilization of the human resources of American society.

This proposition is in line with the basic ideals of American society as expressed in its notions of democracy, equality of opportunity, and freedom for self-realization. It also satisfies Myrdal's requirement of stating valuations as explicitly as possible instead of leaving them in the realm of obscure assumptions. As he so clearly asserts, such an expression of valuation is neither a priori nor self-evident nor absolutely valid. It has the character of a hypothesis. Yet it seems to the present writer to be the hypothesis on which the "social control" of prejudice, discrimination, and conflict is founded in resolving minority problems.[13]

A corollary of this initial value premise is needed when the question is raised: why? If it be asked why our society should desire a situation in which individual members of minority groups would have the opportunity to participate on the same basis as all members of the American community in the pursuit of their life goals, the answer will be in terms of national welfare and national unity. That this may be an undue restriction of value goals may be urged by a good many idealists who require a more universal aim in order to escape from the provincialism of a narrow nationalism. Their objections have considerable cogency but they require an answer on the basis of social realities. Ideally speaking, the final goal might well be the welfare of humanity in general. For those who accept this as a primary goal, there is no immediate conflict, since the value norm can be stated in these broad terms.

But from the standpoint of actual group loyalties as they exist, the potency of the national welfare and the national unity is such as to serve for an actual rallying point; it is better to employ a focus of values that is accepted than one that is not recognized. And if it can be shown that the denial of equal opportunity to minority groups is a threat to the strength and welfare of the nation, there is a powerful appeal that cannot be denied.[14] Secondarily, the idealist may realize that the type of unity and strength this would give the nation is more in keeping with the ultimate unity of humanity which is his permanent goal.

CLASSIFICATION OF THE FIELD

To clarify the situation in which action programs operate, it is convenient to separate social problems into two main types: emergency problems and tractable problems.[15]

Emergency problems are those in which a crisis arises, where a tangle of circumstances forces an immediate decision on responsible administrators. At this stage it is too late to alter the conditions that gave rise to the emergency. In a lynching, a riot, gang warfare, or violence of any kind between groups, it is useless at the moment to ask what preventive measures would have checked the trouble at the source. Immediate action is imperative. There is no breathing space for weighing the merits and demerits of alternative policies. The solution (if solution it may be called) demands coercive action or a makeshift operation sufficiently adequate to halt the emergency.

In the crisis it is rare for action to be based on rational planning or carefully selected evidence. The situation is too fraught with conflict. Officials must run the risk of making decisions which intensify the conflict in the short run. Nevertheless the risk is clearly less dangerous than inaction, because neglect may result in a social disaster. Law and order thus take precedence over other values at this point.

Tractable problems are those in which the need for immediate action is less urgent. Haste gives way to deliberation, and coercion to more strategic considerations. Time permits research, the marshaling of evidence, and comparison of alternative methods. Analysis of causal or conditioning factors allows some control of crucial elements; time also allows measurement of results before and after a program is adopted, so that its effectiveness is subject to testing. Thus the researcher and planner have sufficient leeway to develop a body of theory and to formulate a satisfactory relation between means and ends in applying theory to practice. As experiments develop, there is also time for modifying hypotheses and methods or for considering combined modes of attack and their efficacy.

Those who are concerned with tractable problems can regard the hasty solutions adopted during an emergency as rough equivalents of laboratory experiments which pile up cumulative evidence on the efficacy of future action in similar contingencies.[16] A long-range research program may also make it possible to compare various modes of action in crucial situations in order to guide administrators in preparing for sudden decisions. If adequate long-range methods are already in force, the sudden measures necessary for a contingency may not arouse the same initial resistance or conflict.

The body of theory developed in the study of day-to-day problems can then be enlarged to include preventive measures to avert future crises or to give a new orientation to leaders who habitually wait for crucial situations to arise before taking action.

The distinction between emergency and tractable problems permits two inferences. (1) The difference between them is one of degree rather than kind. Job and housing discrimination may be a real emergency for a Negro migrant from the South but not equally compelling for an Interracial Commission. In a way, each major problem has both an emergency context and a more remote context. (2) The two types of problems require greater integration in the future. By this we mean that the methods developed in the study of tractable problems should eventually become applicable to emergency problems.

The first inference suggests that there may be a conflict continuum on which the various methods, programs, and policies may be located. There are certain lines of action that provoke more conflict in pursuit of the value aim stated above (minority opportunity on the same basis with the dominant group). Combining this continuum with Williams' analysis that there are only two broad techniques involved — altering the situation, and appealing to values [17] — we would then have:

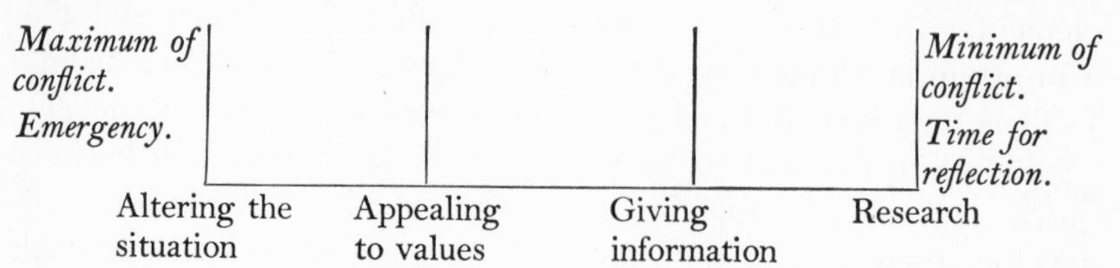

By stating this as a continuum one can avoid the impression that by engaging in one of these forms of action he is not engaged in the others. For example, there is no clear line of demarcation between appealing to values and giving information. It is possible to present information so academically or apathetically that it will have little appeal to values, but a composite type of education (and many believe the most successful one) combines the two features. Instead of making a special category for education, therefore, it will be recognized that education can be weighted on the side of its appeal to values or to the simple presentation of facts and generalizations.*

The various programs and policies adopted in the field of minority problems will then be included under one of these categories, though the actual organizations operating in the field usually employ two or more approaches without always being aware of the full implications in their lines of action. Therefore when the work of these organizations is mentioned under any of these headings, it does not imply that their operations do not include others. In fact, before concluding we shall share even more deeply Deming's conviction that research and action should be combined or integrated for the various purposes at hand.

So far as possible each of the four main categories — altering the situation, appealing to values, giving information, and research — will be treated subordinately in terms of the conflict continuum. The discussion of each category will begin with programs most closely allied with emergency behavior and proceed to those that deal with minimal conflict situations. There is no claim, however, that these situations are categorized irreproachably. It must be remembered that what may be regarded as an emergency by a minority group — the loss of jobs or inability to procure them — may not be regarded by the society as a whole as an emergency situation. This difference in the frame of reference must be constantly borne in mind and reference will be made to it on occasion.

ALTERING THE SITUATION

Among those emergency situations calling for direct action in minority problems are riots, disorders, attempted violence, and the

* One difficulty that arises from this classification can be predicted in advance. Some forms of appeal to value, such as exhortation or the reiteration of ideals, may be no closer to action that alters the situation than pure research. This peculiarity of emotional excitement to become dissipated without action is simply a unique characteristic of the affectional life that spoils the beautiful symmetry of the diagram. All that is claimed here is a certain rough justification for our classification. It seems more useful than others in spite of such exceptions.

like. These are predicaments calling for immediate action by the members of the community designated to repress violence and bring about civil order. There is little time for argument or for balancing one course of action against the other when a police officer in a squad car receives radio messages from headquarters informing him that a riot crowd has formed at the corner of 23rd Street and Harrison Avenue and that he must get there in a hurry. But experience has shown that guidance and training of the police in the professional standards of their vocation, based on research, can endow them with techniques far more effective than the indiscriminate swinging of billy clubs.

One manual on the subject analyzes three stages in the formation of a mob and suggests measures appropriate for each. In the initial stage, it is recommended that the incident be isolated and curiosity seekers be discouraged from entering the area. During the second stage of collective excitement the program calls for removal of key individuals and an adequate show of force to discourage further participation. At the third stage ("social contagion") the police are urged to make a greater show of force and to mobilize reserves, keep a cordon around the affected spot, and have a loud-speaker system for encouraging the crowd to break up. The impression to be left with the crowd is that the police are always in control of the situation; by this means, the actual use of force is often made unnecessary.[18] Areas of tension in a city are carefully pointed out and the need for special vigilance explained.[19]

In the training of police for this special responsibility there are many approaches: officers must understand the rise of bigotry, how rumors start and multiply, the need for public confidence in the fairness of police officers,[20] the growth of prejudice, basic facts about racial and cultural groups and their modes of behavior,[21] and the use of situations where police have informal relations with school children so that the latter have opportunity to observe equal consideration for children of all races, nationalities, or creeds.[22] The relation of law and administrative controls to minority problems requires examination, as do the statutes of a given state which bear on the problem.[23] Preventive policing, the distribution of personnel, press relations, and cooperation with other agencies working to lessen tension need emphasis.[24] In one of the manuals prepared for these purposes a shrewd technique for revealing the irrationality of prejudice is employed. It shows how many people have the stereotyped idea of police officers themselves that "cops as a group are stupid, brutal, and crooked. This is certainly harmful. It undermines public confidence in the police and makes it hard for them to do a good job of law enforcement." [25]

Equally important is the administrative policy of a police organization in hiring able personnel from minority groups. The effectiveness of Negro police officers in controlling crime within their own group is becoming widely recognized. Although no figures are available for this practice in the North, it has received attention below the Mason and Dixon line, where at last report forty-one cities employed 196 uniformed Negro policemen, twenty-five plainclothes men, and seven Negro policewomen.[26] The number is much larger than this if the District of Columbia and Missouri are added.[27] Reports from various areas of the South testify to the more adequate enforcement of the law as a result of using Negro personnel.[28]

Another means of altering the situation is the use of political and legal pressures. These take so many forms that it is impossible to summarize them here. Perhaps the most militant organization in this field is the N.A.A.C.P., which has initiated suits in the courts for equalization of employment, housing, educational opportunities in the schools and colleges, and state F.E.P.C. laws.[29] In the same category is the Commission on Law and Social Action of the American Jewish Congress which, in addition to the above practices, also sponsors state group-defamation statutes and laws prohibiting bias in the entrance requirements of universities and professional schools.[30]

In the North the chief line of political action is now directed to the passage of state F.E.P.C. bills to lessen discrimination in employment because of race, creed, or national origin. By 1948 six states had enacted such a law: New York, New Jersey, Indiana, Wisconsin, Massachusetts, and Connecticut. Of these states only New York, New Jersey, and Massachusetts provided for enforcement with legal penalties.[31] The President's Committee on Civil Rights recommended the passage of state laws for this purpose, as well as federal legislation.[32] The National Community Relations Advisory Council has been espousing a national F.E.P.C. law and has prepared a manual for all those interested in supporting such legislation.[33] Organizations are gradually accumulating a body of information on the actual operation of state F.E.P.C. legislation. On the positive side is the well-established fact that at least up to the spring of 1948 court action was unnecessary in the enforcement of F.E.P.C. provisions since negotiation and mediation proved sufficient to end discriminatory practices; [34] testimony of business leaders indicated that the law did not place an undue burden on employers.[35]

On the negative side was the lack of publicity given to the settling of cases by state commissions so that the public did not learn their accomplishments. Furthermore, minority groups feared that commissions dismissed too many charges on want of evidence, or they distrusted work that was carried on behind closed doors.[36] Those who expected immediate and decisive changes as a result of state F.E.P.C. laws were often disillusioned when the pattern of discrimination changed slowly, when employers and labor unions required continual education, and when the public was uninformed. For instance, almost a year and a half elapsed after the passage of the Massachusetts F.E.P.C. Act before the state commission organized a survey of the vocational opportunities in Springfield that were available for members of minority groups. The survey itself required several months; in addition, integration of minority workers required many more months after the facts were revealed.[37]

Besides state legislation dealing with discrimination, there has also been an attempt to deal with the problem at the local level. For instance, the Chicago City Council passed an ordinance making discrimination in industrial employment on grounds of race, color, creed, or nationality a misdemeanor.[38] There seems to be a consensus of opinion among well-informed leaders in intergroup relations, however, that the local attack is somewhat less effective than a state-wide program.

A few of the recommendations of the President's Committee on Civil Rights include a new department of civil rights in the Department of Justice, with a similar organization in each state; a national antilynching act; legislation enabling wartime evacuees to make claims for property losses; granting suffrage to Indian citizens of New Mexico and Arizona; modification of naturalization laws to permit granting of citizenship without regard to race, color, or national origin; enactment by the states of legislation outlawing restrictive covenants; and the prohibition of discrimination in transportation.[39]

It is perhaps significant that the Committee on Civil Rights did not propose antidefamation statutes; instead, they suggested that all groups that attempt to influence public opinion should be required to register pertinent facts about their organizations.[40] While it may be natural for groups subject to defamation to press for legal measures of redress, authorities point out the difficulties involved in criminal sanctions. The New Jersey statute making group libel a crime has been invalidated as unconstitutional and an abridgment of free speech. The disadvantage of such a law is that it could prevent public discussion of issues that need airing.

If group libel were confined only to racial and religious groups, the question would arise: who is the proper person to sue? If any individual in such a group could sue, many others might follow. Nor is there one organization in any minority group that could speak officially for all. Furthermore, if group libel were applied narrowly to only a few groups, others like the C.I.O., savings banks, cooperatives, or railroads could ask for the same privilege to be extended to them. Oftentimes vague issues would have to be decided by judges or juries swayed by the same prejudices as the defendant. There are many levels of opinion in ordinary courtroom procedure; how is it certain that the right one will be adopted? If it is a matter of determining the truth or falsity of a charge, this should be decided by a qualified body of experts rather than by a court. The use of criminal prosecution may also make a martyr out of the defamer. Thus where it is possible, defamatory tactics can be met more effectively outside the law through other methods of voluntary organizations which expose the activities of the libelers. Conciliatory programs or preventive measures are preferable.[41] At least this appears to be the judgment of responsible social scientists who have examined the issue.

It is important to urge another cautionary qualification for those who support legislation to prohibit discriminatory policies in educational institutions subsidized in whole or in part by public funds or allowed tax exemption. Briefly it is this: such legislation should not in any way determine the fitness of candidates to meet educational standards; this is rightly the province of the institutions themselves. The law, to be effective, should simply be directed to the determination of the weight of evidence on the question: has discriminatory practice been followed or not? [42]

In all cases of political and legal pressures, it is obvious that the most militant action will be taken by members of the disadvantaged groups who suffer the inequities of discriminatory policies. On the tactics employed by these "contenders," as Watson calls them, two comments are in place. First, while their hammer-and-tongs technique may arouse a reactive hostility among certain sections of the public, they have definite value in keeping the issue before the people and in putting pressure in the right places; they undoubtedly produce results unattainable by other means. One head of a Mayor's Committee on Human Relations reported to Watson that militant Negro organizations gave them more impetus in carrying out their program than anything else could have done.[43]

The second comment is that minority leaders have the responsibility to see that protest techniques are channeled into plans that will bring the most permanent advantage. If possible, natural resentment of their groups should be guided so that it will not be dissipated either in rash behavior with boomerang effects or in a self-righteous moral superiority so often reiterated that it provokes withdrawal, indifference, or counterresentment from people whose support is needed. When every emergency is announced as the greatest crisis in civilization, there is a compelling temptation to dismiss an individual case as a matter of overwrought nerves. Prejudice exists in all groups, and both sides of a controversy need to learn the best methods of controlling it.[44]

Another method of altering the situation is that of negotiation, mediation, or conciliation. Sometimes this is applied by making contacts with the "right people," keeping things out of the newspapers, or working through "inside" channels to smooth over a situation. The list of negotiators is long and cannot be attempted here. Watson mentions school administrators as especially prone to this form of operation; in many cases they may even deny that conflict situations have arisen.[45] Wealthy members of minority groups who have influence in the community because of their position are often found in this camp; an amusing instance was the affluent minority leader who said that his main problem was finding someone to replace him when he died.[46] It is quite natural that as minority members become more well-to-do they join the ranks of the mediators. The chief weakness of this method, as Watson surveys it, is that compromise may eventually be considered a valuable end in itself rather than a means of making new gains.[47] Another defect is that the role of mediator is so often pragmatic and "common sense" that it fails to employ research to test its effectiveness. On the constructive side, however, are the objectivity of the mediator and his ability to reduce tension and get ingenious compromises accepted.[48]

Perhaps the most notable examples of this mediating role are the so-called Mayors' Committees. These are official bodies brought into existence by formal or informal action of a mayor to lessen the tension between groups in an urban area. Although Watson speaks of "hundreds of cities" with such committees,[49] the American Council on Race Relations in its directory of local public agencies in race relations lists only twenty-eight.[50] The discrepancy appears to hinge on their actual functioning. In a good many cases they are appointed as a gesture of good will, are given no funds, and serve only on ceremonial occasions. On the other hand the twenty-eight listed by the American Council on Race Relations are more definitely geared into political or community functions and therefore operate with a good deal of effectiveness. For example, only ten out of the twenty-eight are given no operating funds by city or county, and only eleven have no staff. Most of them receive public funds for operating expenses and often a regular budget.*

* A list of the twenty-eight is as follows:

1. Fresno Council for Civic Unity, Fresno, Calif.
2. Citizens Committee for Latin American Youth, Los Angeles, Calif.
3. Los Angeles Committee on Human Relations, Los Angeles, Calif.
4. Mayor's Committee on Civic Unity of San Francisco, San Francisco, Calif.
5. Mayor's Committee on Racial Tolerance, New Britain, Conn.
6. Mayor's Advisory Committee on Negro Affairs, Savannah, Ga.
7. Mayor's Commission on Human Relations, Chicago, Ill.
8. Galesburg Brotherhood Commission, Galesburg, Ill.
9. Peoria Council on Human Relations, Peoria, Ill.
10. Rockford Interracial Commission, Rockford, Ill.
11. Mayor's Committee on Race Relations, Indianapolis, Ind.
12. Brookline Community Relations Committee, Brookline, Mass.

It is perhaps significant that only thirteen of these committees specify research as one of their functions.[51] Other activities most often listed include direct negotiation, making official reports and recommendations, publishing information, and improving public relations. Less frequently mentioned are legislative activity and in-service training programs for public employees. A number of these committees have released publications with special information about their own communities; among these are Chicago, Detroit, Los Angeles, Cambridge, Minneapolis, Buffalo, and New York. Functions of the various committees vary with political realities, the mayor's support, and the aggressiveness of appointed officials. Watson's comment that the Mayors' Committees do not originate pressure but are useful in transmitting it is perhaps a fair estimate.[52] However, it is certain that many executives of these committees have a much larger view of their function in the community. In 1948, some of these leaders organized the "National Association of Intergroup Relations Officials" to coordinate efforts in the field, to operate more closely with state commissions (which are growing in number), and also to work with citizens' committees.[53]

At the state level there are parallel commissions in at least twenty-five states. While these organizations are still younger than those of the cities and have somewhat less experience, their work is analogous to that of the Mayors' Committees. Representatives from twelve of these state commissions met in Chicago on November 13, 1947, to bring about more concerted action, especially for new state

---

13. City of Cambridge Civic Unity Committee, Cambridge, Mass.
14. Lynn Community Relations Committee, Lynn, Mass.
15. City of Detroit Interracial Committee, Detroit, Mich.
16. Mayor's Council on Human Relations, Minneapolis, Minn.
17. St. Louis Race Relations Commission, St. Louis, Mo.
18. Passaic Community Welfare Commission, Passaic, N.J.
19. Board of Community Relations, Buffalo, N.Y.
20. Intercultural, Interracial Committee of Mt. Vernon, Mt. Vernon, N.Y.
21. Council for Unity of New Rochelle, New Rochelle, N.Y.
22. Mayor's Committee on Unity of New York City, New York, N.Y.
23. Mayor's Friendly Relations Committee, Cincinnati, O.
24. City of Cleveland Community Relations Board, Cleveland, O.
25. Board of Community Relations of the City of Toledo, Toledo, O.
26. Mayor's Committee on Good Will, Philadelphia, Pa.
27. Civic Unity Committee, Pittsburgh, Pa.
28. Mayor's Committee on Interracial Relations, Milwaukee, Wis.

legislation in line with the recommendations of the President's Committee on Civil Rights. The group set up a continuation committee headed by Martin H. Bickham, chairman of the Illinois Commission, and it appears that this will be the nucleus of a more permanent organization.[54]

Examination of the reports published by Mayors' Committees and State Commissions shows evidence of multiple activities but little awareness of the strategy involved, the focalizing of effort, the precise use of research, or the evaluation of programs already under way. As the movements mature, these issues will need more clarification and testing by objective means. Coordination of official committee efforts with voluntary organizations will also require more careful delimitation of fields of activity.

Mediating organizations operating for the benefit of immigrants and their children are such associations as the American Committee for the Protection of the Foreign Born, the American Federation of International Institutes, the Immigrants' Protective League, and the Pan-American Good Neighbor Forum. These organizations assist recent immigrants in acquiring American citizenship, finding lost relatives in Europe, sending for kinsfolk and friends abroad, preventing injustices in deportation procedure, setting up language schools, training for citizenship examinations, and the like.[55] The Interpreter Releases of the Common Council for American Unity constitute a thorough information service on immigrant problems and are kept thoroughly up to date.

In addition to interpretative and negotiating functions, these organizations have also interested themselves in legislation to admit many of Europe's displaced persons into the United States, especially under the Stratton Bill which was introduced into Congress in 1947. They have publicized such data as the number of displaced persons (800,000 in all) who refuse to return to their countries of origin for fear of political reprisals. They have analyzed the ethnic backgrounds of the displaced persons, shown that most of them are Poles, Yugoslavs, and natives of Baltic states, with a minority of about 170,000 Jews. Under the terms of the Stratton Bill, a total of 400,000 of these displaced persons would be admitted into the United States during a four-year period. This would be less than the unfilled quota from 1940 to 1946 (914,762 persons).[56] Furthermore, such organizations have supported bills that would give the people of any race the right to become naturalized citizens.[57]

Parenthetically it is interesting to observe that many Negroes oppose any lifting of restrictions on immigration because it is likely to interfere with their labor opportunities. For instance, W. O. Walker, editor of the *Cleveland Call and Post*, an outstanding Negro newspaper, writes, "The Negro for his own protection must oppose any change in the immigration policies of this nation. The Negro problem in this nation will never be solved so long as a predominantly large number of our people live in the cotton belt. The only hope they have to leave the peonage farms and the semislavery conditions under which most of them now live, is for there to be available to them job opportunities in other sections of the country." [58] This is only one example of the cross-purposes often involved in minority policies.

A highly effective method of altering the situation has been taken over from personnel practices in industry and business, where workers have organized contacts on a natural vocational basis so that minority workers are integrated into new jobs. Much of this has been initiated by unions, particularly the United Auto Workers and other strong C.I.O. organizations and the National Maritime Union. Experience has shown, however, that the policy of integration cannot succeed without the cooperation of both labor and management. Where there is semi-isolation of these two groups, it is possible for either to assert convincingly that no change is possible so long as the other is recalcitrant.

Wartime experience has shown that integration can take place without serious repercussions when certain practical steps are carried out. Haas and Fleming list these as (1) self-education and conviction on the part of management and policy-enforcing officials; (2) the taking of a firm position by management when a new policy is adopted; (3) informing and securing the cooperation of any labor organization with which a company has an agreement; (4) a program of education for workers, especially the supervisory staff; (5) careful selection and screening of the first minority workers who are given positions, and careful placement in departments where foremen and supervisors are in charge; (6) careful follow-up and fullest integration.[59] An experiment carried on successfully at the

National Smelting Company of Cleveland, showed the constant vigilance needed to keep the program running smoothly.[60] Watson shows that the *fait accompli* method appears to have the best chance of success: the policy is firmly announced and a vote is not taken beforehand.[61] Living and working together without segregation changes attitudes, but association on a basis that assumes inferiority only makes prejudices deeper.

It is pertinent here to deal with the valid point made by Fairchild that contacts with other groups do not necessarily lead to liking them. He asserts, and with reason, that extended association may similarly lead to aversion or antipathy.[62] What Fairchild omits is experimental evidence to clinch his point. What we need to know is *under what conditions* will aversions arise when the number of contacts is increased? Is it true in recreational situations? Educational? Vocational? Nonvocational? Impersonal? Intimate or personal contact? His bare statement does not suffice for the answer.

Actual reports from social scientists investigating diverse social fields indicate that mingling in work situations is more likely to bring about reduction in prejudice and acceptance of minority members than other types of contact.[63] Even here, however, it is necessary to qualify the findings. If the six factors mentioned by Haas and Fleming are missing, the nature of the social field will be entirely different. Unless the social climate has been *prepared* for acceptance of differences, integration and the increasing contact of groups in vocational settings may actually increase hostility when there is notable visibility of a group by reason of physiognomy, dress, or behavior patterns expressing deviation of values. If preparation is lacking, the old uninformed, preconceived notions will determine the social definition of the newcomers, and the sense of competition will be heightened. Then hostility will naturally increase.[64]

The conclusion seems to be that it is *unprepared* and *casual* contacts that carry with them the greatest possibility of increasing antagonism.* This hypothesis is exactly in line with the conclusions advanced by Harlan in his study of anti-Semitism among southern

* Allport and Kramer also note that indiscriminate contact is less effective in reducing prejudice than equal-status contact. "Some Roots of Prejudice," *Journal of Psychology* 22:9–39, 1946, p. 37.

students, and so far it has remained unchallenged.[65] The inference from this conclusion may be paradoxical and yet it seems valid: that unless employers and workers are willing to prepare for vocational integration beforehand (so as to remove stereotypes, minimize differences, and emphasize similarities), contacts on the job may bring increased hostility or aversion to minority members. Success thus depends on the value-premises of those either observing the situation or arranging to bring it into existence. If the value-premises do not allow for a prearranged attempt to deal with prejudices before they become overt, the result will naturally be more antagonism. The general tenor of Fairchild's remarks reveals a probable adherence to such a set of value-premises, and under those axioms his results are of course valid. Under the opposite set of value-premises, hostility has actually been reduced to a noticeable extent.

Watson, in his survey of the action field, asserts that it is important to work directly in those areas where conflict is greatest and the need for mitigating hostility is at a maximum. Particularly important are those sections of the community where anti-Semitic, anti-Negro, and antidemocratic forces find social antagonisms easy to exploit; such areas are likely to be the scene of gang activity. A program which reduces tensions in the regions where aggression is openly admired will operate where the need is greatest.[66]

In line with this suggestion the Commission on Community Interrelations of the American Jewish Congress has initiated programs in Chicago with the aim of bringing gang activities into a cooperative framework and thus contributing toward greater intergroup understanding. Although the pattern of the first experimental ventures is tentative, several principles emerge for future guidance. The adult group-worker who begins his work with gangs must accept the conflict group for what it really is. He must get himself accepted as not in league with the "cops" or other authorities. He must be a participant-consultant who has enough skills and enough understanding so that his suggestions for fun-activities are more attractive than those already adopted by the group. Once such a program is under way and there is confidence in the leader, methods of working out intergroup contacts may cautiously be suggested and some will be tried. The neighborhood dance, in which several clubs of different racial or ethnic composition hire a hall and by pooling their resources finance a large-scale affair, is one example of such an enterprise. An experiment of this sort in Chicago was followed up by a canoe trip, in which the representatives of various groups sponsoring the dance came together for outdoor recreation. Eventually the parents and adults can be brought into various planning activities until the neighborhood takes on a more convincing community spirit. The new atmosphere can then allow for an increasing number of intercultural and mutual recreational and planning activities.[67]

Other forms of contact in leisure time or in recreational settings continually increase as Boy Scouts and Girl Scouts conduct interracial camps,[68] or when field trips are sponsored under religious, social, or educational auspices. Perhaps the most influential organization arranging field tours is Reconciliation Trips, Inc., of New York City. The director, Clarence V. Howell, conducts interested groups from the entire eastern seaboard on planned excursions to minority centers, including the Chinese, Indian, Japanese, Italian, Russian, Syrian, Jewish, Spanish American, and Negro. The organization arranges its tours so that the first impression emphasizes the achievements of the group visited.[69] If such trips are to be effective, leaders must emphasize what the two groups share in common; if this point is neglected, familiarity may simply accentuate the differences that divide the groups and an increase in social distance may result.[70] Care is also needed to prevent conspicuous behavior in neighborhoods where sensitiveness is at a maximum. The counsel of experienced social workers or anthropologists could greatly increase the effectiveness of such visits.

An interesting variant of the field trip is the arrangement that has been made for Negro children from Harlem to spend a summer in Vermont as the guests of the white children and their parents who belong to the parish of the Rev. A. Ritchie Low.[71] Catholic Interracial Councils also organize to bring together educated white and colored Catholics, chiefly for religious purposes.[72] The Department of Race Relations of the Federal Council of Churches (Protestant) reports interracial committees "established in many strategic communities," though their activities are not clearly outlined.[73] It is estimated that the various intergroup committees, forums, and councils number several hundred.[74]

CHAPTER 21

Programs and Policies for Minority Problems: *Concluded*

APPEALING TO VALUES

THE DIVIDING line between "appealing to values" and "changing the situation" is a shifting one. The former assumes loyalty to certain ideal patterns of fair play, democracy, and equality as expressed in religious or secular terms. The emphasis is essentially positive since it stresses consensual agreement. But in exceptional cases it becomes negative and militant.

For example, leaders may organize opposition against "hate groups" or demagogues, who are represented as threatening the American way of life. The Friends of Democracy, Inc., headed by Leon M. Birkhead, is perhaps the most prominent organization in this field. His group has promoted campaigns against such figures as Father Coughlin, Gerald L. K. Smith, Merwin K. Hart, and other leaders of the same kind. The chief contention of the Friends of Democracy is that the terms "American," "patriot," and "constitution" are employed by individuals and groups that actually undermine the basic principles of the Constitution. The Friends of Democracy sponsor a direct propaganda attack on native fascists, expose their methods, and assail their ideas as subversive of democracy.

The chief investigator of the group, John Roy Carlson, has written *Under Cover* and *The Plotters* to substantiate their stand.[75] Other organizations that have used an "exposure" technique against individuals and groups stirring up hatred against minorities have been the Anti-Defamation League of B'nai B'rith and the American Jewish

Committee. The publication of such a book as *Must Men Hate?* by Sigmund Livingston, in which the calumnies of the anti-Jews are carefully answered, is one type of appeal that has been employed.[76] The somewhat melodramatic title has called forth unfavorable comment, though the tone of the work is judicious and rational.

Some groups have also used aggressive methods by organizing demonstrations against meetings where prominent agitators have attempted to inflame public opinion against ethnic or racial groups. Although these forms of mass action have occasionally (as in Los Angeles) rallied many persons to affirm democratic principles,[77] there is still no agreement as to the value of this method. Some assert that it gives even more publicity to the hate movements and helps them get their message before the public; others feel that the crystallization of attitudes and convictions of those engaging in mass action is sufficient justification for demonstrations.[78]

Obviously, peacetime techniques cannot be based on what was successful in wartime. Those who believe that mass action is justified claim that the "silent technique" might have been effective during the war when the appeal to national unity had more potency for morale but that this method cannot be transferred to a situation when divergent interests become more powerful. Many have criticized the Anti-Defamation League for collecting dossiers on influential leaders who were supporting undercover movements but keeping the dossiers confidential in preference to giving them wide publicity.[79]

Another method of appealing to values is being developed through experimental techniques tested by social psychologists on the staff of the Commission on Community Interrelations of the American Jewish Congress (henceforth referred to as the C.C.I.). The experiment began with a study of personal incidents, in which a bigot made a slurring remark about a minority as a whole when he was frustrated by a member of that group. Careful testing showed that a derogatory statement in public produces a small but reliable change in the prejudice of bystanders. By bringing in from the street various pedestrians chosen at random and letting them observe staged incidents of this kind, C.C.I. discovered that two types of answer to the bigot were most effective: first, the appeal to the notion of individual differences ("all Jews aren't alike"); second, the emphasis on American traditions ("America is made up of all races and religions, and everybody should get the same square deal").

While observers showed no preference for one type of reply, testing showed that the "American tradition" appeal was more effective in producing a change in attitude. Moreover, the replies were better liked if delivered in a calm, quiet manner, though this did not seem to affect the attitude.[80] In a sense this method may appear to be a way of altering the situation, and that alone. It is significant, however, that it accomplishes the change through an appeal to the ideal patterns of democracy. This incidentally agrees with the value-premise just stated.[81] The results of the C.C.I. study are highly reliable because of the scientific care and scrupulousness employed.

Another fundamental attempt to appeal to values appears in the various programs of intercultural education promoted through the public schools. Since these are not merely ways of presenting information but of affecting attitudes and emotions as well, they are included here. Any discussion of intercultural education must take into account its varied and sometimes discordant aims. Certain discrepancies appear when these aims are carefully stated. Some of them are: (1) showing that behavior differences among groups are not inherited but are the result of cultural training; (2) indicating the wide variations in behavior of different human groups; (3) cultivating a respect for diversities as a means of social enrichment; (4) minimizing the differences in values and emphasizing shared aims; (5) showing the historic reasons for prejudice, and its dangerous effects; (6) learning to work and play with members of other groups as a natural result of the democratic way of life. The list is not exhaustive but presents the major objectives.[82]

It is clear that breaking down barriers between groups requires the assertion of the basic similarity and essential oneness of all peoples and the underlying capacity for inventiveness, creativity, and achievement of any individual regardless of skin color, slant of eye, or physiognomy. On the other hand the teacher attempts to awaken appreciation of cultural values different from one's own. Here it seems that unity disappears. If the teacher really succeeds in transmitting this idea, she must develop awareness of the composite character of American society and its advantage in preventing a dead-level uniformity.

It is probably the experience of most teachers dealing with intercultural problems that the first of these two approaches is more effective when dealing with race and race differences, while the second is a more adequate weapon against intolerance directed at ethnic and religious groups. Watson quotes a Negro leader in Newark as saying that problems of his racial group were really the opposite of those stressed by Jewish organizations. He asserted that the Negro group desired to have barriers broken down between themselves and the whites, while the Jews wanted to preserve their separateness vis-à-vis the gentiles.[83] It is noticeable that scholars who approach minority problems from the standpoint of an ethnic base (like Louis Adamic or J. S. Roucek) tend to view the chief goal of minority programs as a more or less complete acceptance of cultural pluralism (in which the diversity of peoples is regarded as an asset rather than a handicap).[84] Neither of these authorities gives any space to anthropological or psychological studies of race differences in his publications. Conversely, Negro writers devote no attention to cultural pluralism.

The dilemma of intercultural education is therefore keeping a balance between stressing similarities on the one hand and differences on the other. If the former receive too much attention, pupils may come to expect an identity in groups which later experience contradicts. Then comes the risk of secondary disillusionment. The opposite emphasis, on differences, may bring an increased awareness of the exotic or strange elements in the culture of ethnic minorities so that their basic identity is not appreciated.[85] The cultural or anthropological approach is necessary for resolving the difficulty since it shows clearly that the identities of human nature lie in its potentialities, while differences result from cultural history. The training of teachers in the intercultural approach therefore requires a thorough use of cultural anthropology until its principles are fully apprehended.

Three of the major organizations which are most active in the field of intercultural education are the Council Against Intolerance in America, the Bureau for Intercultural Education, and the American Council on Education. The first of these publishes *American Unity*, a monthly educational guide, suited chiefly to the elementary grades, that provides illustrative material for use in formulating lesson plans in the public school. The Bureau for Intercultural Education issues the *Intercultural News*, a monthly magazine of wide circulation which presents articles by specialists in social science and education, book reviews in the field of intergroup relations, and discussions of school and community programs that use successful techniques in intergroup relations. It also prints an annual list of publications on intercultural education, most of them pamphlets that can be obtained at minimal cost from the Bureau.

The Bureau's most recent publication, *Intercultural Attitudes in the Making*, offers illustrations of effective policies at different school levels, with suggestions on extending them into community activities.[86] The Bureau has also conducted many experimental studies within public school systems of the East and of the Middle West. One of these programs is a joint venture with the Research Center for Group Dynamics formerly at the Massachusetts Institute of Technology.[87] In addition to these activities, the Bureau plans summer workshops for teachers preparing themselves to utilize the intercultural approach in their special fields.

One of the former directors of the Bureau, Dr. Stewart G. Cole, relinquished his office in order to become the director of the Pacific Coast Council on Intercultural Education which began its work in 1943 and became incorporated in 1946. Up to March, 1948, the Pacific Coast Council sponsored summer workshops at the University of California, Stanford University, the University of Southern California, and the University of California at Los Angeles, as well as school–community in-service workshops in many cities. Furthermore it initiated a three-year experiment in intercultural education for the San Diego public schools, enlisting the services of specialists in anthropology, sociology, psychology, and education. The Pacific Coast Council also developed a three-year experiment in preservice teacher education in cooperation with the California State Department of Public Instruction and the seven state colleges of Southern California.[88]

The American Council on Education has conducted experimental programs in seventy-two school systems from coast to coast and a number of summer workshops under the direction of Miss Hilda Taba.[89] A special effort inaugurated in 1945 by the A.C.E. (entitled

The Project on Intergroup Education in Cooperating Schools) obtained the assistance of eighteen school systems in revising curricula for intergroup education and for reshaping school activities to serve as a laboratory for human relations.

All these projects are in communities with a heterogeneous population of various racial, religious, or nationality backgrounds. The A.C.E. has supplied consultants for setting up the programs, but the eventual aim is to transfer these to local responsibility after an initial period.[90] A list of workshop papers and classroom planning units available at small cost is also published by the American Council,[91] as well as a study which evaluates 267 textbooks in terms of teaching materials in intergroup relations.[92] So far, the most complete survey of "promising practices in intergroup and intercultural education in the social studies" has been a volume, *Democratic Human Relations*, edited by William Van Til of the Bureau for Intercultural Education and by Hilda Taba of the American Council on Education.[93]

The most widely publicized of the intercultural programs is probably the so-called "Springfield Plan." Dr. John Granrud, Superintendent of Schools at Springfield, Massachusetts, inaugurated the policy in 1939. At that time a few teachers in the Springfield schools were already experimenting with intercultural education in a limited way; it remained to enlarge and expand the work already begun and to establish it on a more systematic basis.[94] Beginning with the social studies program, largely at the junior high school level (for example, a unit on "the contributions of older civilizations to present democratic procedures"),[95] teachers and supervisors extended the use of curricular materials in "democratic living" to the lower elementary grades and up to the high school level. Emphasis throughout was on citizenship and the values of learning to live together; the appeal to values was integral to this process and received a great deal of attention. For example, at the elementary school level certain "concepts and understandings" basic to citizenship are listed as follows:

Pride in and love of American things such as symbols of our country — flag, national anthem, American eagle, Statue of Liberty

A concept of what the community offers and an understanding of one's duty to it

A concept of what the early settlers and pioneers contributed to American culture, and an urge to add to this heritage

An understanding of our likenesses and differences

An evaluation of the lives of great Americans and what they have contributed to our living

An understanding of what the government does for us and of one's duty to it [96]

As the program expanded, two leading features appeared: (1) organizing pupil groups and the school program democratically and (2) increasing the use of community history and resources to implement the growth of citizenship behavior.

One school illustrated the practice of democratic organization through an incident which followed a play written and produced by elementary pupils themselves. After the production, two or three of the Negro children approached a teacher with the complaint that a Negro child had been made the villain of the piece and they considered this unfair. Then the student council gravely considered the matter. The authors of the play asserted that they had no intention of slurring any group in the school. So the group asked the Negro pupils what would satisfy their demands. Eventually the children's council decided that if the authors of the play appeared in every classroom and declared that they did not consider the effects of the play on Negro children and had no intention to run them down, the whole matter would be cleared up. The juvenile authors carried out the decision, the Negro children were satisfied, and the whole school had an object lesson in the unintended effects of prejudice.[97]

As for the use of community resources, an event in a junior high school class studying the nationalities of the city helped to crystallize a new project. Here a Chinese boy, who had been trying to write in English about his own parents' background, slowly began to trace Chinese characters alongside his English essay. One of the nearby children observed it and called the others to see what was happening. Excitedly they asked the teacher, "Why can't we all do that, i.e., write our part in English and then the rest [or parallel story] in the language of our parents at home?" This began the project. Children went back to their homes eager for parents' help. Finally they completed a book, *The School Speaks*, in which stories of their own families were given in English with a parallel rendition in Chinese, Czech, French, German, Greek, Dutch, Italian, Yiddish, Polish, Swedish, and Syrian.[98]

Another class put together a similar book depicting the folk music of the countries represented in their junior high school. In the more advanced years of the high school, two special courses, "Public Opinion and How It Is Influenced" and "The High School Town Meeting," have also been applied by the students to their own situation in the city of Springfield. Their discussion of community prejudices led to new types of thinking, as when one commented that his grandmother told him he should not associate with foreigners but now he thought of them only as Americans. After commenting that adults were more prejudiced than younger people, another student said bluntly that the adults could not live forever.[99]

Before long the citizenship program spread to evening classes in adult education. There a special course called "The New Citizen in Our Community" gave adults the same understanding of the contributions of new citizens as younger students obtained in the public schools. "I Am an American Day" featured the naturalization ceremony of these citizens when each was presented with an official greeting and welcomed as an honored citizen now qualified and accepted as an "active participant in the government for, of, and by the people."[100]

An incomplete sketch of this kind can suggest only a few features of the intercultural program at Springfield. Mention could be made of the integration of teachers from different racial, nationality, and religious groups into the public school system; the use of many subjects to emphasize intercultural goals; the celebration of Christian and Jewish rituals together in December; the use of maps; the hospital project; the interfaith council; and many others.[101] An evaluation of the program in school and community has not been made by any scientific agency. Yet a casual visit to the city by the writer in 1948 resulted in the following impressions:

(1) There is sufficient awareness of the intercultural program in the schools so that political representatives now feel the necessity of approving it publicly.

(2) Unsolicited opinion furnished by a prominent Negro leader testifies to the fact that a pattern of friendship and acceptance of

colored students exists not only in the elementary grades but also in the high school.

(3) The intercultural program is operating far more successfully in some schools than in others. The problem of securing cooperation and understanding among all teachers in thirty-eight schools of different levels is recognized as a serious one. Most of the examples of the program in action have come from a few outstanding schools in the system.

(4) Negro youth of the city who are prepared for white collar or clerical positions usually go to other cities to find work opportunities. There is still some discrimination in employing members of recently arrived immigrant groups.

(5) On the level of clubs and associations there is little mixture of old residents with newer arrivals of different race, nationality, or religion. A start has been made in the Parent-Teacher groups. Service clubs do not make a practice of admitting Jews, so that the latter have formed a club of their own. In 1948, one of the businessmen's luncheon clubs admitted a Jewish rabbi but no Jewish businessmen.

(6) The implications of the Massachusetts Fair Employment Practices law for the city of Springfield receive little attention in the high school citizenship classes although its relevance to the school program as a whole could be made highly significant.

(7) More than a year after the passage of the Massachusetts Fair Employment Practices Act, the local committee in Springfield, working with the state commission, prepared a survey of industrial opportunities for those of racial, nationality, and religious groups excluded from employment in years past. After this study was made, it was to serve as an entering wedge for introducing minority workers into various industrial establishments. It appeared likely that this process would take a year or two after the initial study began. In the meantime discriminatory practices remained and many young people left the community to find employment.

(8) The city of Springfield is still more or less typical of northern urban centers in the use of restrictive covenants limiting the sale of property to certain favored groups in different areas. There is, however, an interesting difference on the level of verbal utterances about the subject. Leading lawyers of the city, when questioned, deny that such covenants exist. This may be due to an increased

awareness of the problem stimulated by the intercultural program of education. However, the Negro population of Springfield is well aware of the far-reaching influence of restrictive covenants from personal experience of attempting to buy property.[102]

Our summary of the Springfield situation, superficial as it is, nevertheless shows that reduction of intergroup prejudice and discrimination is not a miracle that comes about as a result of an educational program. Even after such a policy has been practiced for many years, the resulting conditions measured in terms of minority group experience may be only slightly altered, outside of the school atmosphere itself. The main purpose in presenting the Springfield situation is neither to debunk nor to expose. It is rather to emphasize the fact that even under the most favorable conditions, where the attitudes of an entire school generation or more are permeated with understanding and mutuality, *democratic practice as defined in our value norm is only in its beginning*. Responsible leaders both in Springfield and in other communities attempting similar measures know this, but it is important that the fact become more widely understood by the public at large. Minority groups need this knowledge to avoid unnecessary disillusionments. Whatever successful experiments have been made, the goal is far from realization.

Another type of approach using appeal to values has been sponsored by various organizations. These range all the way from action programs based on religious attitudes to pure exhortation as a method of emphasizing ideal patterns. At the action end of the scale are such projects as the Interracial Clinics conducted by the Department of Race Relations of the Federal Council of Churches in various cities throughout the country. The Department calls a conference of church community leaders and, under the leadership of Dr. George Haynes or some other member of the staff, local people make a survey of community conditions with regard to housing, education, recreation, and employment. Returning to the conference, members of the group present their findings and map out a program of action. Leaders utilize press and radio in drawing public attention to the issues. The program to be adopted is put in the hands of a continuation committee who have responsibility for carrying out the details. Six months later Dr. Haynes or one of his coworkers returns to check on accomplishments.[103]

Among the Roman Catholics, the Catholic Interracial Councils have engaged chiefly in educational or religious work. The Los Angeles Council has been most aggressive in campaigns for specific issues like the opening of hospitals to Negro or non-Caucasian nurses and physicians, the restoration of Japanese Americans to civil service positions, the passage of legislation to prohibit restrictive covenants, challenging the discriminatory policy of the Teamsters' Union, and the like.[104]

It is sometimes overlooked that in the South, where church attendance and interest appears to be higher than in other parts of the United States, a great religious motivation can be tapped. Experience would lead one to believe that the majority of the leaders in southern interracial activities have received an initial impetus in this direction from religious teaching. In the last few years both Catholic and Protestant churches below the Mason and Dixon line have been making progress toward unsegregated meetings, conferences, and programs. Significantly these programs have been moving more rapidly in the youth groups than among adults.[105]

For the most part the work of the churches has proceeded through conferences and committees or in education with a religious emphasis. Groups of various types studying interhuman relations have organized, and church publishing houses have printed an enormous amount of literature for distribution. No one has measured the effects of this educative process, and the observer may fairly raise the question of how effective a pamphlet on race discrimination, on the achievements of race leaders, or on Mexican migrants could be in the hands of an untrained Sunday School teacher or leader of a young people's group. It seems likely that these educational appeals are relatively impotent when not employed by those whose previous education and experience give them the background to employ the materials adequately. And the number is likely to be small. Likewise, careful perusal of the various programs adopted by church leaders among the Catholics show that most of their programs, though wide in scope, depend largely upon the clergy for leadership with only occasional (though sometimes effective) lay leadership. Nearly all the Catholic activities are educational in nature rather than direct programs of social action; a much smaller group attempts to influence members of the church by actual "interracial living" [106] — like the example given at the opening of the previous chapter.

Protestant churches also sponsor Race Relations Sunday and Brotherhood Week programs, usually accompanied by an exchange of pulpits between a white and a Negro minister, or a Protestant minister and a Jewish rabbi. These programs have stimulated a certain mild interest in minority problems but have not been followed by action of an organized nature. Watson shows the main weaknesses of the exhortative method so far as it applies to religious appeals: preaching and emphasis on codes of conduct have little permanent effect; they reach only the "saved"; they too often emphasize good will and achievement but evade unpleasant issues that need to be faced; they leave individuals with their reservations still untouched. Continual expressions of good will may eventually come to be a substitute for behavior in behalf of the ideal.[107]

Nevertheless the significance of religious belief as a motivating force cannot be discounted entirely. The initiation of action programs depends on motive, conviction, decision, and sacrifice. Without scientific method, the program may very well be so weak and ill considered that it can have no permanent value. Yet the adoption of new techniques in human relations "involves sacrifice, and science . . . is powerless to induce men to make sacrifices." * [108] Accordingly, a refusal to utilize the motivating force of religion or the rejection of religious exhortation as a method implies neglect of a potent social lever for action in an area where energy is often not persistent enough to continue a program through disappointments, frustrations, and secondary disillusionments.

It is admittedly difficult, if not impossible, to measure the effectiveness of an appeal to religious values. Unquestionably many of the preachments of fervid oratory are far removed from realistic life situations; yet even though the weakness of meetings, conferences, and the passing of resolutions is obvious, there remains a residue of aroused conviction resulting from religious appeals that will not be rejected by the social scientist who is objectively aware of the fulcrums of social power.

* The statement is rhetorical, of course. Its significance is that "pure" science has little power to motivate individuals for action beyond the field of investigation.

Allied with specific church organizations is the National Conference of Christians and Jews that was formed in 1928. This association has grown to national and international scope, with a budget of $1.45 million in 1946–1947.[109] Beginning as a committee on good will between Jews and Christians, the National Conference has become a coordinating agency for the promotion of harmonious relations between members of different faiths, extending its program to cover all aspects of intergroup relations. Although it has retained its original functions of bringing together on the same platform Catholic, Protestant, and Jewish religious leaders (emphasizing the conference approach), it has expanded into the educational field by sponsoring a number of significant experimental projects throughout the country.

Originally the appeal to religious values was paramount in the N.C.C.J.; its emphasis was positive, seeking to build respect and understanding between members of various religious groups. During the mature stage, when it sponsored a greater variety of projects, the early emphasis was still salient, though dependence on research methods and techniques became more fundamental. To the general public its chief purpose still appears to be the fostering of cooperation among religious groups, but a more careful analysis of the organization reveals that it has become one of the most important fund-raising associations in the field of human relations and that the subsidizing of educational and community projects has gradually become its main function.

For example, the N.C.C.J. furnished part of the funds for the original educational program in Springfield, Massachusetts. By 1947 it sponsored intergroup education in eighteen public school systems in the United States under the American Council on Education and its program noted above. At the same time it financed the College Study in Intergroup Relations under the direction of Professor Lloyd Allen Cook in twenty-one colleges and universities engaged in teacher training. The main aim of the College Study is to stimulate institutions of higher education to deal more adequately with intergroup relations both on the campus and in the preparation of teachers to initiate programs devoted to more democratic practices in the public schools.[110] Between 1941 and 1947 the N.C.C.J. also sponsored thirty-six summer workshops in which teachers in public school systems could prepare themselves for increasing effectiveness in intercultural education.

Among religious organizations N.C.C.J. provides a Religious News service with Protestant, Catholic, and Jewish news items ordinarily neglected by the daily press. It supplies speakers for 150 Protestant summer conferences (rabbis, Negroes, or Nisei leaders), conducts institutes for Protestant clergymen and religious educators, and aids in the preparation of lesson materials for religious education programs.

So far as community agencies are concerned, N.C.C.J. aids in preparing programs for clubs and associations of all sorts; it conducts a nursery and play school in New Haven for children of all races and creeds; it has presented over eighty radio programs weekly and has acted as consultant for the Superman program in channeling its facilities for brotherhood. It also presents awards to radio stars and persons contributing to national unity each year; it has helped produce a number of films, including an annual one for Brotherhood Week; and it has called conferences of writers to discuss ways of improving intergroup relations through the medium of short stories, novels, and plays.

Another project has been a subsidy to the Advertising Council of America for various publicity channels contributing to national unity. Posters entitled, "Did You Make This Kid Cry?" "The Best Team State Ever Had" (diverse ethnic origins), "The Atom Bomb Is Just a Peashooter Compared to This" (whispering campaign), "But Who Cares?" (pictures of singers and stage stars of different races and religions), "Who's a Bigot?" (self-quiz on prejudiced thinking), and "Typhoid Mary" (spreading germs of hate) are examples. A sponsor's name appears on each sheet, and the posters are large enough to attract immediate attention.[111]

It is significant that N.C.C.J. does not engage directly in any action programs, though its consultative capacity has presented an opportunity to mediate between groups in tension situations. Apart from the educational programs sponsored by the organization its main reliance has been upon meetings, conferences, mass propaganda, and persuasion, features common to the religious approach mentioned above.

Some observers have pointed out that the N.C.C.J.'s cooperation with the Jewish community is largely with the Reform element rather than with the Conservative or Orthodox groups who are probably more representative of that community as a whole. Whether this is due to the fact that the Reform group has more wealth and can give more support to the program or whether the Reform element is more cooperative, it is difficult to say. No doubt both of these considerations have some influence; at the same time it is likely that a relatively small group of Jews (numerically speaking) is actively engaged with the program. On the Catholic side it would appear that top figures in the hierarchy appear less often on N.C.C.J. programs than lesser figures. Since there is some reluctance on the part of Catholic prelates to speak authoritatively for any cooperative program with other religious groups, this may be unavoidable.

At all events the continual emphasis on minimal agreement is necessary for the N.C.C.J. program; under these conditions, a certain air of superficiality is perhaps inevitable. As long as the organization must stress adventitious unity it must accept the lowest common denominator of consensus and engage in considerable fulsome praise. In this atmosphere it becomes easy to evade unpleasant realities. The N.C.C.J. is engaged in building more mutuality, more harmonious relationships, more friendship and good will for diverse groups in America. In the attempt to get more supporters for its cause it has avoided making enemies if possible. It seldom attempts to expose crying evils or to deflate the pretensions of superiority on the part of the white Anglo-Saxon gentile. In emphasizing good behavior and proper etiquette it therefore evades situations that involve contention or conflict. This does not mean that the N.C.C.J. fails to accomplish results but that its program has the defects of its qualities. Any visit to meetings sponsored by N.C.C.J., particularly among religious organizations, will reveal this quality clearly.

As for the mass persuasion methods sponsored by the N.C.C.J., it is even more difficult to determine their effectiveness. Evidence from social psychology suggests that prejudiced people respond to antiprejudice propaganda by evasion, misunderstanding, derailment of understanding, or actual reversal of the message.[112] Such propaganda is not entirely ineffective but it gets results chiefly when the attitude of the individual is already structured in favor of the message presented or when it is ambiguous enough so that there is no resistance.[113] Propaganda appeals make few, if any, converts. For maximum effectiveness such propaganda should be coupled with control of the channels of mass communication, should attain saturation of protolerance symbols, and should indicate the cruciality of the situation. Otherwise radio deafness sets in.[114]

Since none of these conditions is possible under present radio, newspaper, and advertising processes, propaganda messages of tolerance and good will must compete with romantic love, murder, war scares, and the advantages of X soap powders. For the great mass of individuals whose attitudes are already structured in a direction favorable to prejudice, the tendency to evasion is almost irresistible and the diversion to other channels will provide the escape. Results will therefore be minor. Social psychologists, recognizing this problem, have endeavored to formulate factors that might serve to indicate "potential effectiveness," since actual results are difficult to measure. These items of potential effectiveness are: (1) getting attention, (2) holding attention, (3) having the item liked, (4) comprehension, and such items as ability to recall, repeat, or engage in social behavior called for by the propaganda.[115] Since a call to action is not sponsored by N.C.C.J.'s programs (writing to Congressmen, voting for a given measure), the ability to test effectiveness is greatly lessened. Watson specifically suggests that less time and effort be devoted to such items as pamphlets, posters, radio programs, and meetings unless they are the prelude to specific commitment for a specific constructive policy.[116] Changes in policy could be made more adequately if they were preceded by scientific testing and evaluation.

Another appeal to values emphasizes what losses, injuries, and disadvantages accrue to the nation as a result of the disunities and tensions brought about by prejudice and undemocratic practices. Southern liberals have frequently referred to the economic cost of discrimination to the South in schools, transportation, and employment. The President's Committee on Civil Rights devoted two pictorial illustrations to effects of excluding minority workers — the inefficient use of our labor force, a lessening of purchasing power and lowered consumer demand, reduced production, and a lowered standard of living for all.[117] The untoward consequences of American discrimination at home or the constant embarrassment faced by diplomats and military leaders in foreign countries can be used to good advantage, perhaps more today than in previous years when the importance of foreign policy received less attention than it has since World War II. If these issues are brought home directly in the educational system and through the channels of public opinion, they may awaken patriotic motives of compelling force, not merely an external obligation to give something "abstractly owing to an unesteemed fellowman." [118]

Finally it is important to link the desired behavior with prestige symbols. It is a truism in sociology and social psychology that behavior is molded by the system of social rewards; if prejudice and discrimination are followed by approbation, they can never be uprooted. A greater use of public awards for those who have made distinct contributions to better human relations, together with attendant publicity, can do much to popularize the cause. In the past the awarding of the Spingarn Medal and the Willkie Award, and the public recognition given to figures of film, stage, and radio by the N.C.C.J. have been steps in this direction. Each local program dealing with human relations could easily adapt this to its own community. If a local committee gave such awards not merely to national figures but to unpretentious citizens who make more humble contributions, it would firmly impress the concepts of better intergroup relations into the thinking of every citizen.

GIVING INFORMATION

Many assume that the method of giving information is noncontroversial, that it has a quiet objectivity entirely unruffled by conflict. While this is generally true, it hardly applies to the techniques of exposing unsavory situations unknown to the average citizen. There is no large community where investigation cannot disclose anti-Semitic, antiforeign, or anti-Negro sentiment in forms that come as a surprise to most of its citizens.

When, however, an organization that makes a practice of exposing prejudiced attitudes does not hesitate to name names, including many prominent business and civic personages, white and Negro, Jew and gentile, repercussions are likely to become serious. The public may also come to regard the organization as anything but respectable. Two prominent associations of this kind on the national level are the Friends of Democracy and the Anti-Defamation League of B'nai B'rith, mentioned above.[119] Organizations with local scope are the Civil Rights Federation of Detroit and the Chicago Action Council, which have been specially militant in exposing antidemocratic forces in their own cities.[120] Individual newspapers have sometimes engaged in bringing to light the activities of undercover groups that attempt to exploit hatred and prejudice, such as the Chicago *Sun*, which publicized the work of the Gentile Cooperative Association, or the Cleveland *Press* when it exposed the Columbians in Atlanta, Georgia.[121]

This method of giving information has its value partly because it is congruent with the familiar pattern of sensationalism in metropolitan journals and hence is accepted. Journalistic exposure of hate groups has been the means of lowering their prestige and weakening their influence. When civic groups disclose discriminatory practices of prominent citizens, the method runs the risk of increasing tension and conflict, at least temporarily. The proponents of this approach are quite aware of this and are confident that conflict is not only unavoidable but sometimes salutary. Such militant opinion is not shared by the negotiators or mediators, who often try to tone down these attempts.

From the standpoint of strategy it is probably fortunate that organizations which make a habit of exposing hate groups or prejudice in high places are not coordinated with other efforts in the community. Although it may be true that a concerted effort in behalf of better human relations is a crying need, aggressive groups that publish information of this kind are doubtless more effective on a free-lance basis. Only in this way can they operate without the hampering restrictions which would undoubtedly be placed on them if their efforts were coordinated with more "respectable" organizations; and the latter can also disclaim all responsibility for the excesses of zeal which might embarrass them.

In disseminating information two general types of survey are effective. The first of these could be designated as a participating survey, in which the individuals doing the fact-finding are those who have a definite stake in the outcome. They are members of the community making the study, and develop considerable interest during the course of investigation in the eventual use of their findings.

A participating survey becomes a prelude or stimulus to action that alters the situation. The prime example of this type is the action-research developed by Lippitt and Radke of the Research Center for Group Dynamics and continued under the sponsorship of the Commission on Community Interrelations of the American Jewish Congress and its research director, Isidor Chein.[122] The other type may be called the traditional or academic survey. This is purely objective and is linked to no community action whatever; at its conclusion the findings, of course, may be used as a solid basis of information revealing where the most important areas of difficulty are. Oftentimes these areas are not precisely those that the uninitiated could predict, and the results of the survey may modify the original picture with which hasty reformers began. An illustration of this is the research carried on in South Chicago under the direction of Professor Blumer investigating the relations of tension between Negroes and Jews.[123]

Perhaps the best example of the participating type is the community self-survey initially developed by President C. S. Johnson of Fisk University and later simplified in practice by the Commission on Community Interrelations (C.C.I.). The purpose of this method is to avoid the natural resistance which citizens so often show when an "outsider" investigates local discrimination. The resident who is unacquainted with the effects of prejudice at home may question the results or claim that an "outsider" who "does not know the community" has no authority. In some cases the citizen has a vested interest in existing practices and therefore tries to discredit the report or bury it. Such reactions can be kept to a minimum when members of the community plan the survey and conduct the investigation with a social scientist in a purely consultative role. They know community problems in general but are curious enough to look for more exact information or to ask how their city compares with others having similar problems. The larger the number of citizens participating, the greater will be the awareness of the issues to be faced and the greater the motivation to act on the basis of well-established knowledge.

The following cities have engaged in participating surveys: San Francisco, Pittsburgh, Minneapolis, Montclair, N. J., and "Northtown," an unidentified city of the northeast section of the United

States.[124] A sponsoring committee from the city takes responsibility for planning and for expense; it solicits the participation of prominent citizens and workers who actually do the interviewing. In Minneapolis this committee was the Mayor's Council on Human Relations. In Northtown it included representatives from influential organizations such as the Chamber of Commerce, the Ministers' Association, the labor councils, the League of Women Voters, the Council of Jewish Organizations, and the N.A.A.C.P. Depending on the scope of the survey, a variable-sized group of social scientists cooperate as technical consultants. In San Francisco and Pittsburgh, five social scientists were employed in each case; in Montclair only one.[125]

The simplified treatment in the Northtown survey indicates in graphic form how the method is used. There the committee reduced the problem to five areas of community life in which discriminatory practices occurred: employment, housing, education, public facilities, and organizations. The investigators developed two indices for each of these categories, one dealing with *differential treatment* and the other with *exclusion*. For example, in housing, an index of the differential treatment indicated the quality of housing obtained by minority group members compared with that obtained by the dominant group for the same rent. Exclusion, on the other hand, referred to the number of sections in the community which barred minorities absolutely. The research called for separate indices for Negroes and Jews since an "average" would be meaningless for either group.

A comparison will indicate the results. With the earnings of the dominant group at the norm of 100 per cent, Negroes earned 27.5 per cent less than dominant group members at the same point of earning potential (for the same type of work requiring the same skill). Similar differentials appeared in housing. A map showed graphically the areas of total and partial exclusion for both Jews and Negroes.[126]

An agreement at the outset of the investigation usually stipulates that no individual or organization engaging in discriminatory practice will be identified by name; the aim of the survey is to give an accurate picture of general conditions in the city. Even though the committee eventually publicizes the report as a whole, they single out no one for unfavorable attention. The sponsoring group and the interviewers finally organize, digest, and publish the report and secure ample accounts in press and radio. By this time the community as a whole is aroused to the magnitude of its own problem. Conviction growing out of participation is the most powerful reaction resulting from the survey. As yet, the translation of aroused attitudes into action that eliminates discriminatory practices lags behind the new impetus. Official cooperating bodies are loath to get down to cases and apply pressure; yet without this pressure accomplishments are few. A follow-up or continuation committee on a less official basis may have responsibility for this task, but lack of power often makes it ineffective.[127] The parallel with interracial clinics under the Department of Race Relations of the Federal Council of Churches is clear,[128] except that the community self-survey obtains broader participation so that a larger cross-section of the community is involved and becomes convinced that action is needed. Until actual community changes occur, however, critics will ask why the term "action" is used to denote this type of research.

Social scientists sometimes deprecate education also. They point out that factual and scientific knowledge about race frequently has no immediate effect on action. They can hardly deny, however, that this knowledge serves as a standard norm on the subject. Deviation then becomes conspicuous. Alpenfels indicates one effective way to present such norms when she reports (from a questionnaire) fifty recurrent fallacies on race expressed by elementary school children.[129] A carefully planned curriculum to dispose of these fallacies is a very definite need at all levels of public school education.

Experience has shown that constant pressure to add new courses to the curriculum (such as anthropology in the high school) meets with too much resistance from teachers, who are already bombarded from all sides by those who believe the course of study needs more of this or more of that. In Springfield, Massachusetts, where an experimental course in anthropology was tried in the high school, teachers discovered that the same results could be obtained without a new curriculum by introducing proper items into courses in civics, biology, health, literature, history, and vocational guidance.[130] In the field of history there is also opportunity for presenting material about minority groups in American life and their contribution since colonial times.[131] In addition, of course, there are teacher training courses and workshops already mentioned above. In higher education, the College Study in Intergroup Relations, under Lloyd Allen Cook's direction, is probably the most effective program.[132]

Adult education can also increase awareness of minority problems and intergroup relations. Colleges and universities, church organizations, libraries, labor unions, and specialized groups like the Pacific Coast Committee on American Principles and Fair Play or the Pan-American Good Neighbor Forum, have made an important beginning. Watson outlines the types of courses and literature offered to the public in these programs.[133] Labor unions have developed especially significant programs for their own members because they deal with the realities of vocational situations in which all their members directly engage.

Elsewhere adult education programs seem to reach chiefly the individuals who come with an initial interest and therefore are already inclined favorably toward intercultural education. As in many other cases, more women's groups participate than men's organizations. The women's clubs, the League of Women Voters, church study groups, and even the social agencies, show a preponderance of women studying these questions. As this process is continued, it may perpetuate one of the culture patterns already characteristic of American society in a direction fatal to intercultural education. By this we mean that the female sex (beginning with the mother) is often regarded in the role of moral teacher. Eventually these ideals become concessions to feminine demands but masculine society divests itself of them when by itself.[134] So far the adult education programs have not captured the citadels of male behavior, the business clubs, Lions, Rotary, Kiwanis, etc. Neglect of these channels not only perpetuates indifference but helps to engender downright resistance to human relations programs as a woman's game.

In the field of publications there are hundreds of books and pamphlets available for educating the public on issues of race and cultural differences. The Public Affairs Pamphlets such as *Races of Mankind*, children's books like Eva Knox Evans' *All About Us*, or popular works like Dorothy Baruch's *Glass House of Prejudice* have had rather wide circulation. Yet the average bookstore, even with a large nonfiction stock, rarely carries such titles and certainly none of the more scientific works on the subject. Local committees attempting to arouse interest in intergroup relations have not enlisted the support of the bookbuying public or the booksellers. The latter would certainly cooperate in any movement that increased sales.

There is also no indication that adult educators for rural groups have ever given much attention to programs of this nature. The farm population of the United States includes at least thirty million in the open country and twenty-seven million more who live in essentially rural conditions.[135] The National Opinion Research Center reported in 1945, in a nation-wide sample of farmers, that 75 per cent opposed anything like an F.E.P.C. law, while only 57 per cent of the businessmen polled opposed it.[136] Even though this is not conclusive evidence, it does at least suggest that the pressure of rural opinion on legislative bodies may be such as to retard any legislation dealing with discrimination, whether at the federal or at the state level. Although complaints are issued from time to time that business elements oppose such legislation powerfully, one seldom hears any comment on the antagonism of the farm population to these measures.[137] This is perhaps typical of the urban myopia of both political leaders and social scientists. At any rate, programs of intercultural education in township and consolidated schools and in the programs of granges, lodges, cooperatives, and farm organizations generally have an open field for the future.

RESEARCH

The amount of study devoted to race relations and intercultural problems in the past ten years has been steadily growing. Today the literature is enormous. Most of the investigations have been descriptive, concerned chiefly with maladjustments, social disorganization, conflict, tension, and problem areas. Drake and Cayton's portrayal of Negro Chicago, Ruth Tuck's analysis of Mexican-Anglo conflict, Raper's study of lynching, Dorothy Krall's treatment of conflicting attitudes in the foreign born and their children, Odum's investigations of race situations in the South, Dollard's different approach to the same theme, Myrdal's work on "the American dilemma," and many others, have centered attention on points of friction, unresolved hostilities, or continual frustrations. The importance of these researches in revealing problem areas cannot be minimized, and their number will undoubtedly grow in the future.

On the other hand preoccupation with maladjustment, absorbing as it may be, has not given sufficient information about the way in which these phenomena may be controlled. As Donald Young has said, this is roughly analogous to an engineering study "about defective timbers and flawed girders while ignoring the qualities of sound materials." [138] Although the need for new cross-sectional studies of discrimination and prejudice will continue in the future, social action requires an even greater number of researches that evaluate programs and policies for lessening tension or methods which increase the areas of opportunity for minority group members.

In addition to the descriptive studies there is a growing place for what Chein calls conditional research, i.e., research that has for its chief aim the discovery of conditions which determine events (sometimes called the causal approach).[139] The aim of this research is more accurate prediction and control. As the research worker determines the causes of certain types of prejudice, differential treatment, or exclusion, he gradually discloses ways and means of altering situations and of manipulating circumstances.

The chief danger of this method from the scientific point of view is that it may be so narrowly determined by a particular problem or set of problems that it reflects the exclusive interest or bias of the investigator. When this happens, the answers are too limited in scope to be of any value for the advancement of systematic knowledge.* From the practical point of view the disadvantage may be that the problem will be too closely allied with community interests simply to assure ready acceptance of the results. Unless the community's definition of its own problems is basic, the investigator may fail to get cooperation. While the risks involved are sufficiently great, experience has shown that conditional research, if properly handled, may produce significant results.

In general, conditional research is of two types, action research and evaluative research. Action research may be defined as a type of investigation in which individuals and groups cooperate with the

* It is partially a question of predominant motive. If the motive is getting quick results, scientific accuracy and objectivity will suffer.

social scientist in studying the patterns of behavior in their own community so as to become aware of new social implications, redefine the situation, and voluntarily accept new values and modes of action in dealing with the problems surveyed. This definition, while it describes the main functions of the investigation, attributes to it certain features that shade off into evaluative research. The main point of difference is that the latter is carried on almost entirely by the social scientist himself in an effort to analyze the effectiveness of action programs instituted by others, without the aim of initiating new ones. Evaluative research has its chief goal in analysis, with the secondary aim of improving already existing programs and policies.

The way in which these two types fuse into each other can be illustrated by Chein's account of the four subtypes of action research. They are (1) the diagnostic — examination of "incidents" so as to observe the precipitating conditions; (2) the participant action — like the community self-surveys already noted; (3) the empirical — in which the researchers act and then record the results; this method is used for observing the effects of certain procedures in handling gangs; (4) experimental or controlled research on the utility of various action techniques. In this last type we are already in an area where the social scientist operates alone and have passed over the line to the evaluative kind of research.[140]

MacIver divides the evaluative type into two major subdivisions. In the first, the observer examines a specific unified program affecting various aspects of community life, like the Springfield plan. By means of testing, comparing short-run with long-run effects, observing how the program operated with other forces in the community working in the same or opposite direction, he can then make a more exact evaluation. The second type involves an examination of the program adopted by a specific action organization such as the N.C.C.J., a Mayor's Committee, or the like. Its aims are to weigh methods and techniques, learn how the organization coordinates its program with objectives, what determines the choice of projects, and how well they are carried out.[141]

In addition to the types of research there are different kinds of problems to be investigated. Two broad divisions of this field, as already suggested, are: (1) attitudes and values and (2) actual social situations. Examples of the first category appear in our chapter on prejudice, above. Illustrations of the second would be such studies as that of Koenig on ethnic factors in industry,[142] Pittman's summary of the factors involved in building an interracial church,[143] or Brameld's review of minority situations in public education.[144] Here again there is no absolute dividing line between the two problem types but a scale with each one serving as a polar opposite. It is impossible to review here the studies made, but convenient summaries are already available.[145]

Finally there is also the question of orientation. Research may be oriented in two possible directions: toward amelioration (practical results) or toward the advancement of theory. Neither social scientists nor leaders of intercultural programs have sufficient data for answering many simple questions authoritatively. Watson lists sixteen of these practical issues to which scientific answers are needed, and the list could be multiplied indefinitely. To mention a few, reliable data are needed on the subgroups and subcultures from which fascist leaders and movements come; the exact conditions under which contact between different ethnic or racial groups increases or decreases cooperation; radio programs and how they affect social action; practical effects of cooperating with official as compared with private militant organizations; techniques of integrating different racial groups in organizations, industries, camps, schools, etc.[146]

On the theoretical side there is need for testing such hypotheses as Myrdal's principle of cumulative causation; [147] or the proposition that it is chiefly individuals in the relatively "upper" class positions who have sufficient security to work actively for innovations in interracial or interfaith programs; [148] the commonly held hypothesis that general economic security is the primary goal in reducing intergroup hostility and that other programs are ancillary to it; [149] the notion that simultaneous attack on all forms of discrimination may actually increase hostility so that it is more effective to begin with "items of lowest negative symbolic potential"; [150] the examination of the concept of cultural pluralism and the conditions under which it may make a valid appeal or may bring about increased anxiety; [151] conditions under which the appeal to conscience augments emotional tension or conflict; [152] and many others. The best summary of these theoretical problems is contained in Williams' work already noted.[153]

A general summary of the types of research needed may then be represented graphically as follows:

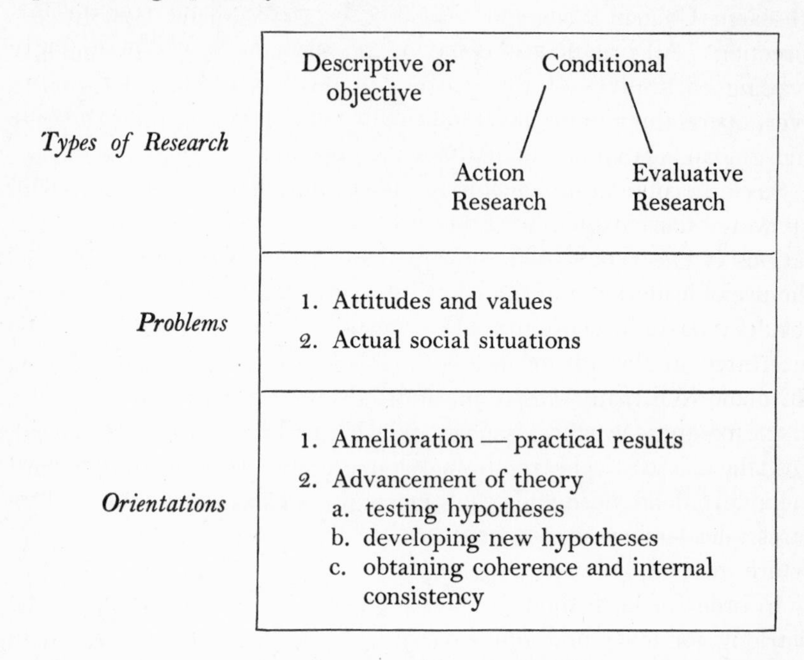

Types of Research
Descriptive or objective
Conditional
Action Research
Evaluative Research
Problems
1. Attitudes and values
2. Actual social situations
Orientations
1. Amelioration — practical results
2. Advancement of theory
a. testing hypotheses
b. developing new hypotheses
c. obtaining coherence and internal consistency

The importance of such an outline is chiefly to clarify issues: every investigator about to select a problem and the methodology with which he will work could advantageously ask himself at the outset what type of research he is employing, the extent to which his major problem is one of attitudes and values or the study of actual situations, the way in which his inquiry could be employed for practical results on the one hand and the advancement of theory on the other. Clear awareness of these issues will not only increase the likelihood of more adequate analysis and final results but it will also extend the coordination of research effort so that a more concerted attack will be possible.

A central clearing house to which all research projects (with methodology) would be submitted in advance might be useful in avoiding trivial problems, checking assumptions, defining variables, placing studies in line with previous efforts to get cumulative evidence, and relating all factors so as to test or advance systematic theory. This directive administration, properly applied, need not assume too much authoritarian control. Prior submission of all research efforts to a recognized body such as the Social Science Research Council [154] would probably be a successful step in this direction. All organizations having research staffs are increasingly availing themselves of the services of the S.S.R.C.; others, however, operate in a more isolated fashion and thereby lose the stimulus and guidance possible under this arrangement.

Since the amount of research in intergroup problems is continually growing, there would be great value in annual or biennial publications of two types: (1) surveys of successful action programs for the use of leaders in interracial or intercultural programs, with tested results if possible; (2) surveys of research, chiefly for social scientists interested in the advancement of theory. If studies like those of Rose and Williams were continually revised and brought up to date in the theoretical field, the labor of scholars would be tremendously lightened. And if a survey like Watson's were repeated and enlarged biennially, field workers, officials, social workers, church representatives, and leaders of minority organizations would be able to correlate their efforts more successfully.

In order to keep their programs more effective, all organizations working for unity and democratic relations in intergroup life could improve their techniques through periodic analyses of their policies by research experts. A powerful campaign bearing the slogan, "No program without testing," could fertilize action with fact-finding. Unless and until community leaders become research minded, they will miss a cardinal opportunity.

[CHAPTER 22]

Epilogue: *Things to Remember*

AFTER TRAVERSING a long road, let us turn and survey our climb. In all the twists and turns, can we see any evidence of a single direction? Many steps of the way will be forgotten but the major landmarks should be familiar. Partial though our study has been, let us summarize in tentative form our findings on minority issues.

NATIONAL UNITY

The distinctiveness of American society is in its diversity, in the many ethnic and racial strains which make up its total pattern. It is not a theory which we confront but a reality. Walt Whitman was asserting a literal and not merely a poetic truth when he called America a "nation of nations." In MacIver's terms, we are a multigroup community.

This condition carries with it potentialities for strength or weakness. If the various cultural strands of our national life are bound together in the cable of unity, no power will be sufficient to break it. If the cords are separated, hostile elements without or within can break any one of them or rub them together until friction brings disintegration. Benjamin Franklin saw a similar peril when he coined his famous phrase, "We must all hang together, or assuredly we shall all hang separately." The plural groups in his day were colonies with different geographical, economic, and cultural interests. Neglect of common concerns brought these colonies to the brink of anarchy but they rallied in time to achieve a workable consensus in the Constitution. It was not a perfect harmony they achieved; there were still bickerings, arguments, and quarrels.

Sectional disagreements even led to a civil war in which the national unity was severely tested; scars from that conflict still show but the unity remains.

Since that time the field of social action has shifted. America began to engage in a colossal experiment with racial and cultural groups who became the new pluralities. Today the major problem is not sectional differences * but rather those of race, creed, and nationality. At the same time we have forged powerful weapons of social science to help us understand what these diversities mean and what they do not mean. Absolute agreement between groups is too much to expect today, just as it was when the Constitution was written. What we can expect, therefore, is not an obliteration of differences, but acceptance of them within a common framework of cooperation. This is what started our nation on an upward course, and it can do the same thing again.

The war against the Axis showed our vulnerability to division within our own ranks. Racist theories of the Nazis, false though they were (neither the "Aryan" nor the "Jewish" race existed except as social fictions for inflaming public opinion), nevertheless took root in the United States while we were fighting the proponents of those theories abroad. Our indigenous differences, our own brand of intolerance and discrimination, furnished an opening wedge for exploitation by propaganda, one which Hitler boasted could be used to defeat us. The chief reason this Nazi policy was unsuccessful is that when our national life was in peril, the American people rallied sufficiently to cover up their differences "for the duration." As one commentator acutely observed, America was fighting a total lie in the name of a half-truth.

The national crisis provided a gain which peace had failed to give. Divisiveness and conflict, prejudice and discrimination, do not grow without social compensations. An emergency like the war furnished a system of social rewards for unity which prevented social bigotry from gaining too much headway — unless it coincided with fear of the enemy, and then it gained fresh strength as it did in the case of Japanese relocation. The temporary flare-up over enemy aliens of European extraction showed that antiforeign feeling still existed in

* And the most pronounced sectional differences which do occur (like the Dixiecrat revolt) are themselves closely related to the racial issue.

the American public, but without the issue of race differences it soon died down.

With the end of the war the internal divisions appeared again; the national F.E.P.C. was scrapped, increased discrimination against employment of Jews appeared, and antialien sentiment grew strong enough to prevent the admission of displaced persons in spite of unfilled immigration quotas. Conflicting policies with the Soviet Union began to arouse an increasing hostility toward communism on every hand. Since it happened that the Soviets had an official antiracist policy, attempts to establish racial equality in the United States were attacked as communistic. The Soviets have made excellent capital of this in Oriental countries where the fear of totalitarianism is vague and uncertain but hatred of racialism and colonial exploitation are an ever-present reality. Informed observers today assert that purely on the race issue the peoples of the Orient would favor Soviet Russia rather than the United States in case of a showdown between the two nations.

The treatment of minorities in the United States has therefore become of world concern. It is out in the open. It can no longer be concealed. Discrimination in all its forms has become an explosive issue in modern society; it not only threatens the safety of our nation but it has international repercussions. Our diplomats abroad are continually embarrassed when other nationals point to the discrepancy between American ideals and American practice. As the United States enters the arena of world politics, it becomes the task of every citizen to see that the solidarity of the national life is strengthened and that considerations of common welfare override the narrow interests and exclusiveness of any group.

The national tradition of America has welcomed the contributions of all peoples and has sought to create an environment where no group would have special privilege. It is becoming abundantly clear that when any minority suffers disadvantages because of exclusion from social participation, there is common loss and injury to the entire nation. As Booker T. Washington once put it, "No man can hold another in the ditch without getting down there with him." The injuries which the nation has suffered in disease, poverty, loss of buying power, lowering of educational standards, and increasing tensions can no longer be afforded. Fair play and opportunity to advance on merit are not only part of the American creed, they are indispensable to the survival of a democratic people in the long run.

STRAIGHT AND CROOKED THINKING

Social perception is often a result of mass impressions which twist and deform reality. Too frequently the citizen regards minorities through a haze of half-truths, stereotypes, myths, and rationalizations of power. Armed with this distorted image (inferior, lazy, shiftless, greedy, uncanny, foreign, or outsider), he then regards all members of the group as the same. If he meets a person of the minority who fits the stereotype, that confirms his opinion; if he meets a dozen or more who fail to match the specifications, he concludes that they are concealing their "true" character. Or he treats them as "exceptions" which do not affect the general rule.

Social science, on the other hand, views minority groups as disadvantaged groups who have had differential cultural conditioning. Part of their early training accentuates culture traits that differ from the dominant pattern in America, e.g., strict chaperonage of girls among Italians and Mexicans, a large number of maternal families among Negroes, marked family solidarity among the Yugoslavs, or intense emphasis on kinship honor among Hungarians and Japanese. But usually these are not the traits which receive most attention in the stereotype or distorted image. *Popular clichés about minorities more often seize upon traits that result from the disadvantage of minority status itself.*

Thus the ignorance and shiftlessness of some Negroes are regarded as inherent traits, although the amount expended for Negro education is only one third to one fifth of that expended for whites. Negro college graduates continue to do unskilled labor in large cities and find up-grading practically impossible. Or the Jew is called a cutthroat competitor at the same time that he is denied opportunities in major industries. When he enters marginal occupations or those with a large factor of risk, the established gentile merchant who receives complaints that his prices are too high can smile and say, "Of course, you can always get these things cheaper at the 'kike's' down the street." Some members of ethnic minorities who are unable to participate in the broad stream of American life because of exclusion policies become frustrated and seek revenge through illegal operations, crime, black-market activities, or racketeering. Small as their numbers are, they confirm the stereotype of immigrants as criminal. The popular stigmas placed upon minorities are often a little like binding a man with a stiff rope and then calling his contorted motions unnatural.

Evidence from anthropology, psychology, and history shows that there are no pure races, that inherent group differences in intelligence are unproved, and that racial dominance in civilization is a transient phenomenon. The ability factor seems to be a constant in all races, while achievement and behavior patterns are variables. It may be easy to accept such propositions but it is difficult to think in terms of them. The person with astigmatism finds that the world looks different when glasses correct his vision. There are no social glasses which can be prescribed, but it may be useful to suggest certain exercises which may eventually correct faulty group perception.

One helpful practice is to notice that the diversities in behavior within groups are as great as the diversities between them. By watching for variations and contrasts between different members of racial minorities, an observant witness will gradually come to see that so-called "exceptions" are more common than he supposed and that no simplified image can do justice to the multiform impressions he receives.

Another exercise closely related to the one just mentioned is to make distinctions in describing any member of a racial group. Instead of speaking of a Negro, for example, it would clarify thinking to specify "a lower-class Negro," "a Negro intellectual," "a Negro politician," or "a Negro skilled worker." Continual practice in these appreciations of difference will increase one's power of estimation and comparison and automatically correct stereotyped thinking.

It goes without saying that the same techniques can be applied to members of ethnic communities from any cultural background. The differences between a pious Orthodox Jew, a secular Zionist, a Jewish radical with a lower-class background, a liberal Jew with a middle-class upbringing, or even a Jew from New York City as compared with one from upstate New York, can be very striking. As one becomes accustomed to thinking in terms of political, socioeconomic, and religious difference within minority groups, his social vision becomes sharpened.*

American provincialism is likely to exaggerate the gap between a group speaking English and one using some other language. With regard to the nationality groups it is useful to remember that use of a foreign tongue is often an evidence of social stability; that the marginals or second-generation individuals have greater problems of divided loyalties and increased disorganization than members of a foreign-language colony who speak a native tongue of some other country. The resentment which many monolingual Americans show when they hear languages other than English spoken is a reaction due not to social knowledge but to ethnocentrism. In view of present social realities it is probably utopian to expect English-speaking Americans to learn other languages in order to understand subordinate groups with status which seems lower than their own; but the few who have made the attempt report increased awareness and understanding.

Broader knowledge of the psychosocial traits of individuals having minority status will show that there are certain reactions which appear in greater or lesser measure for all. There may be cowed submission, oversensitiveness (with a "chip on the shoulder" attitude), heightened aggressiveness, clinging to one's own group for security, concealed ambition which works in secret, exaggerated thrift, or moral arrogance. The psychologist might explain some of this as the interaction of basic personality types with the subordinate status situation characteristic of minorities. Passive types of individuals will be more likely to adopt traits of submission, introverted types a greater sensitiveness, highly active types a more pronounced aggressiveness, and so on.

The wall of concealment which often surrounds a subordinate community is a protective device which prevents others from imposing on them; whatever this initial distrust of outsiders may be, it is relaxed as soon as it becomes apparent that there is no real threat. Those who plan to concern themselves with intercultural relations

* This elementary procedure destroys a major stereotype at the peril of substituting a minor one. New simplified images of the "Negro politician" or "Jewish intellectual" may then arise. The process is incomplete until the individual is regarded as such. But the first step toward this is conceiving the minority group pluralistically rather than as a homogeneous mass.

must expect to be on probation for a trial period of testing. This is a new experience to many whose primary assumption up to that time has been that the minorities are on trial. After an early period of accommodation, relations will be easy and natural.

Sometimes the novice in the field will be disturbed because minorities do not "control" their own members, many of whom seem highly irresponsible. It must be remembered that subordination of a group in a highly competitive society results in increased rivalries and jockeying for power. Thus there is no one who can speak for all Negroes, all Italians, all Mexicans, or all Jews, and no organization which can exercise control over an ethnic group. The situation becomes clarified by asking a parallel question such as: "Why don't Protestants control their own radicals?" or "Why don't the Anglo-Saxons do something about their criminal element?" The real answer is that social control is a function of norms accepted by members of the society as a whole, and the fact that certain individuals do not have loyalty to them may indicate a failure of that society to give them adequate reason to be loyal. But it is not a function of any particular segment of the society to impose these norms.

There are those who approach the whole matter of intercultural understanding cautiously and gingerly; at the first sign of disillusionment, they withdraw to their old beliefs and forms of behavior. One of the most common shocks they may encounter is the discovery that members of minorities are frequently prejudiced against others. Many Poles, Negroes, Italians, and Japanese are anti-Semitic; many Jews are bitterly anti-Negro. The implied question in the mind of the person who confronts this unpleasant fact is, "If these persons who suffer discrimination are ready to show prejudice themselves, why should I remain unprejudiced myself or cooperate with a group which has been unable to do what it asks me to do?" To some this may be a matter so elementary that it calls for no discussion; but to others it is a source of real puzzlement.

Usually the question can be answered on the same level by posing an analogous question: "Should one cooperate with an Anglo-Saxon Protestant group for any cause if any members show prejudice toward other races or cultural communities?" Put in this way the question seems to lose its point. Even yet, however, it does not touch the real issue as the social scientist sees it.

There are perhaps two reasons why interminority prejudice is fairly common. One may be illustrated by the frustration-aggression hypothesis. Any group that is frustrated by subordinate status may find itself, because of power relations, unable to express its resulting aggression on the dominant group. As a result, that aggression is displaced to some other group which is regarded as having lower status in the society, so that hostility can be safely displayed toward it. The other reason may be called status-identification. If higher status is identified with the displaying of prejudice toward others, then the best way to capture that higher position is to show the same prejudice. If being "American" seems to involve contempt for Jews, a Negro or Japanese American may identify himself with the "American" ideology by showing that he can be as prejudiced as anyone else. On the other hand if a Jew is a resident in the South and being a "Southerner" involves feelings of superiority or hostility toward Negroes, he will sometimes outsouthern the Southerner in showing that he belongs. In both cases this identification has the added advantage of drawing attention away from a possible subordinate status which the individual is trying to escape. A good deal of interminority prejudice is therefore a distorted attempt to escape from prejudice by prejudice.

Parenthetically we may add that this situation cannot change basically until the definition of "American" or higher class status is itself changed. As long as it is "American" to avoid, distrust, neglect, or maintain social distance from minorities, there will also be interminority prejudice simply because all minority members want to become "good" Americans. The section above on national unity indicates that there is another American tradition.

Perhaps it is not out of place to notice here that ethnic and racial groups often adopt American culture in a distorted form. These culture patterns are not original in their groups but are a result of adopting ways of behavior from the dominant group and developing them in a segregated or parallel community. Sometimes the historical occasion for adopting a segment rather than a whole is obscure; for example, it is not clear why so many Negroes play bridge with one deck rather than two decks of cards. This is a trivial instance, of course. In others there appears to be a more satisfactory explanation — the Ghost Dance religion of Plains Indians was an adaptation of Christian messianism to the needs of a submerged people looking for supernatural salvation from exploitation and suffering. At times a minority has taken over a prestige pattern in such a way as to elaborate it, like conspicuous consumption in dress or highly formalized dinner parties that appear among both ethnic and racial groups. Any sudden rise in status results in parvenu behavior, whatever the group. We might call this compensatory identification.

The American habit of "joining" is accentuated among many minority groups which have innumerable clubs, societies, and associations. Often the form is accepted while the meaning differs. In nationality groups the meaning seems to be connected with the nostalgic revival of old home memories and the congeniality that goes with them, as among Hungarians or Yugoslavs. With Negroes congeniality also plays a considerable role, but there is still another dimension; club activity is often a substitute for political activity which is frequently denied by the wider society. Myrdal's description of Negroes as "exaggerated Americans" will also apply to other ethnic groups. Thus the compensatory response elaborates the dominant pattern of American culture in an attempt at identification. Or it may simply take over the American complex and use it in the service of parallel minority needs, as Jewish Community Centers have adapted the methods of group work of their special clientele.

PREJUDICE

It is important to remember that prejudiced persons are usually unconscious of the influences which have affected their thinking. They have learned their prejudices but forgotten how or where they learned them. Most of them regard their hostilities as well justified by the misconduct of minority groups and regard their antipathies as the result of experience with those groups. Social science has produced sufficient evidence to show that prejudice is nearly always a result of contacts with attitudes rather than contact with groups, whatever popular opinion may be. It has also shown that where personal or social insecurities are increased, prejudice also increases, usually with no awareness on the part of the prejudiced person as to the role that uncertainty and inadequacy have played in the process. Unhappiness, frustration, and disappointment from any source will give greater urgency to prejudices already held. This is also true of prejudices held by members of minority groups themselves, since social psychologists have noted that the persons who feel most victimized have a tendency to develop displaced hostility toward disadvantaged groups.

The chief function of prejudice is to separate group from group so that one may have an added advantage in competition or rivalry. It enables the prejudiced group to gain more power or to retain the power it has; through prejudice it can control the social situation without law or overt political expression but through the pervasive force of custom. It also supplies group-approved channels for aggression, either verbal or physical.

Prejudice is found significantly related to certain philosophies of life; it appears in connection with an authoritarian outlook and also with the conception of life as a jungle or as a war of all against all. A narrow nationalism, flag-waving, and "one-hundred-per-cent Americanism" nearly always go hand in hand with prejudice. Anti-Negro feelings appear to be highest among Roman Catholics, less among Protestants, and lowest among Jews or those with no religious affiliation.* Among middle-class individuals prejudice is connected with keeping certain conventions, the fear of losing status, and hence the danger of associating with people defined as "not nice." In upper classes prejudice is chiefly related to fear of infiltration by "outsiders" who have every qualification for high position except birth and hence are on the point of entering the charmed circle. Since there is a relatively smaller group of Negroes in this category than of those having foreign parentage, anti-Semitism and antiforeignism occur more frequently than racial prejudice. Exceptions may appear when the foreigner is a professional and appears singly rather than with others of the same nationality. In such cases a foreign accent may positively be an asset rather than a liability. Examples occur among Hungarians, Spanish Americans, and Japanese.

Perhaps the most potent weapon for attacking prejudice consists in making provision for natural contacts between groups of approximately the same social level in vocational or social situations where members of both pursue a common goal; the habit of cooperation is worth more than exhortation or argument because it focuses at-

* At least, among college student samples.

tention on areas of agreement rather than disagreement and allows understanding to proceed at its own pace. A basic supplement to this behavior pattern is intercultural education which brings out the basic similarity of potential in all groups while it explains differences as simply the result of diverse cultural history.

BEHAVIOR TOWARD MINORITY MEMBERS

Grace Abbott of the Children's Bureau once remarked, "All children are treated alike only if all children are treated differently." Every parent will recognize the truth of this statement, but its application goes far beyond the family to the related areas of criminology, social work, and the treatment of minorities. As there is need for parents to apply wisdom in recognizing and utilizing the individual differences in their own children, there is analogous social wisdom in approaching members of minority groups in terms of their own cultural patterns. A social worker in an Italian area once asserted that it was impossible to have a Father and Son Banquet in his area because the gap between generations was too great and patriarchal dominance so compelling that the easy camaraderie between parent and child necessary for such an occasion was lacking. Other techniques of equal value were needed as alternatives.

A basic minimum for guidance is the making of decisions *with* a minority group, not *for* it. Any other attitude is resented as patronizing, though the persons who entertain it are blandly unaware of the implication. Programs of indiscriminate good will can heighten the very tensions they attempt to diminish when they are one sided or lack the feeling for social realities.

One very common mistake of the sentimentalists is to assume a fervent heartiness in the presence of minority members, a cordiality which is so obviously forced that it embarrasses and alienates others because it is pitched in a false key. Dorothy Parker gives a classic illustration of this in her short story, "A Study in Black and White." The compensatory vehemence of well-meaning people shows clearly that it conceals subjective prejudice by going to the opposite extreme. The psychologists call this reaction-formation. Minority differences, whatever they may be, do not call for a specially prepared etiquette but for natural simplicity and unaffected behavior. Again the family analogy clarifies the situation. The parent may be as natural with an aggressive as with a shy and withdrawn child, though the orientation will be somewhat different for each.

But analogies are dangerous. The dominant group does not stand *in loco parentis* to minorities, though the relations of power frequently give it an administrative position in evaluating claims and counterclaims of rivals for attention. If, remembering the lessons of history, the dominant group recognizes the provisional nature of its status, it will find it easier to become aware of mutual understanding on a reciprocal basis. This awareness, however, can be an informed one which perceives the unique flavor of diverse cultural traditions as an asset to be used. The aim is not a kindly tolerance — the reader may have noticed that the term is avoided in these pages — but realistic appreciation.

Eventually wider loyalties to the community as a whole, to the nation, and to the larger world take precedence over restricted group-thinking. Oddly enough these universal demands cancel out segmental interests of intermediate groups and allow individuals to meet face to face on a personal basis. This final stage of meeting persons as they really are, not merely as members of a group, has a value that surpasses the intermediate stage of cultural pluralism. It must be experienced to be appreciated.

SOCIAL ACTION

For those who feel an urgent need for action in the field of intergroup tensions, certain guiding principles may be valuable. Perhaps the most adequate starting point is a realistic appraisal of the community and of one's own capacities.

In rural communities there may be no agencies directly concerned with the problem, and new beginnings may be necessary. Even here it is probably more effective to utilize associations or institutions already functioning than to start with a totally new organization. Intercultural education in the schools or a study of minority problems in church or grange is a convenient place to begin. Even better, if the situation allows, is a study of a minority group in the community, a discovery of their first appearance, data on origins, places of settlement, their progress, and their contribution to the community. Effective contact with leaders of the group will smooth the way to this sort of survey. Bringing in minority leaders from other communities for community functions in music, recreation, or social get-togethers is another natural way to commence. One project usually suggests others.

In urban areas, on the other hand, there will already be dozens of organizations at work in the human relations field. Prudence suggests initial cooperation with some one of these agencies in line with one's own interests. The associations mentioned in Chapters 20 and 21 above will indicate the range of activities present. As a means of sustaining initial interest the availability of *Common Ground* or some analogous publication summarizing new developments in the field is of great value. For the more scientifically minded there are other periodicals such as *Race Relations* (Fisk University), *Phylon* (Atlanta University), *Commentary* (the American Jewish Committee), and the various publications of the American Council on Race Relations, the American Council on Education, and the Bureau of Intercultural Education.

Unless the individual is blessed with unusual executive ability, it will probably be wiser for him to work through established channels than to set up new ones at the present time. If organization is his bent, a period of initial probation with agencies already in the field may suggest new tactics that will be fruitful on a local or national scale. Eventually questions of unified approach to human relations problems will arise; strategy will call for division of labor in some fields, and concerted effort in others.

Before planning extensive programs, it is well to recall that research is a prerequisite to effective action; without the testing of results no one can be sure precisely what is being accomplished. It is therefore highly important that every influence be used to see that evaluation of programs and policies be made periodically. Suggestions of this kind are included in Chapters 20 and 21.

The principles to recall in social action are: (1) Adapt tactics to community traditions and realities; awareness of the "social field" is highly significant. (2) Strike at tangibles first, e.g., housing, employment, and visible evidences of discrimination, before attacking prejudice directly.

ORIENTATION

We need a new philosophy of differences. Anthropology and history, sociology and psychology, are slowly revealing that human beings like plants and animals may have individuality without any implication of superiority or inferiority. Who can say that a Winesap or Greening is inherently inferior to a Jonathan or a Delicious? Or superior? It all depends on what they are good *for*.

In human society the physical differences are far less than they are between domesticated species of botanical or zoological types; it cannot be proved that races or peoples are at different levels of physical development or that racial differences have any significant social import. Racial changes are far more rapid than popular opinion assumes, and it is becoming clear that cultural achievements have no basis in racial characteristics. It is what men learn (culture) that distinguishes one from another, and this learning process creates the only differences that count.

Under three conditions cultural differences appear as a threat: (1) in primitive or socially isolated groups having limited familiarity with any ways of life not their own; (2) where one group establishes social dominance over another and regards any deviation from its ways as a menace to the system of power; or (3) where personal or group anxieties, frustrations, or insecurities create inner tensions so ominous that there is unwillingness to acknowledge them. Under these conditions individuals or groups prefer to project their fears on others, if they are different enough to be recognized. It is the scapegoat mechanism. If any one of these or a combination of them is powerful enough, the phenomena of ostracism, social distance, discrimination, or segregation will appear.

A secondary effect prolongs the initial impact of these fears when they enter the ideological stage and are taught from one generation to another. Thus those who learn prejudices may themselves be far removed from the original situation which was defined as a threat, yet they retain the same basic viewpoint. Other things being equal, those who have learned such attitudes and beliefs without being markedly affected by any of the three above conditions are most amenable to a new view of the situation. Thus individuals who have a considerable range of diverse contacts, who have sufficient social status to feel secure, and who are relatively untroubled by neurotic difficulties are least likely to regard social and cultural differences as a menace. They can define the situation as one of equality in differences because their interests stand less in their way.

They are capable of seeing that common concerns can be pursued, not by imposing agreement (as the insecure want to do) but by adult behavior which finds cooperation within differences a new level of behavior.

Gradually it occurs to such minds that cultural variations have a special value of their own, that the idiomatic flavor of each group is an ingredient of the savory dish we call civilization. To insist that the salt and the pepper and the tomatoes and the rice must be served separately or not at all is a form of stupidity.

Leaving analogies behind, we are gradually beginning to learn that the breaking down of any one of the three basic conditions of social disunity is a major contribution to mutual respect and co-operation. Social isolation is not dead. It is reinforced by educational systems which make it appear that only a limited group of people has contributed the major values to American society. It is perpetuated by religious teachings that arouse hostility for other faiths. It is continued by class conventions which ignore or depreciate anything outside their rigid circle. And it is crystallized and institutionalized by economic, political, and social practice based upon fear of outsiders. Social isolation is gradually breaking down, however, under the impact of urbanization, mobility, and increased contact among peoples. But impersonal forces alone cannot accomplish the destruction of all divisive barriers; gradually it is becoming clear that the mingling of peoples and cultures cannot be left to chance but that it can be guided so as to eliminate fears and to increase mutuality.

In America the political traditions of the Constitution sanction only one type of social dominance — that based on merit and ability. There is therefore a powerful reagent operative for the dissolving of other forms of social authority. There is implicit in the democratic way the realization that social domination of any other type is temporary and unstable. Even those who enjoy special privileges in American society based on wealth, class, religious or racial position, recognize that a turn of the wheel may leave them in a less favored position. There is nothing in the Constitution or the early documents of American history which intimates that social dominance shall be restricted to Caucasians, Anglo-Saxons, gentiles, or Protestants. The artificiality of any such authority is clear. It is then possible in this favorable social climate to press vigorously for political and economic measures to assure the rise of leaders with the greatest merit, regardless of race, creed, color, or national origin.

The spearhead of the attack is not directed so much against any particular dominant group as it is against unearned privilege itself. It was Tom Johnson who once remarked that privilege is the real corrupter of men, and the truth of his statement is painfully apparent. Until economic and political inequities are altered so that privilege can be kept to a minimum, differences between groups will still be defined as a menace. First-class citizenship cannot be enjoyed as long as any substantial part of the nation are second-class or third-class citizens. Neither science nor religion nor American political beliefs sanction permanent subordination because of the accident of birth. States and municipalities are trying to correct the inequities that occur by passing laws and statutes that prevent artificial domination of this kind.

Mental health is a third condition of successful group integration. The public is becoming increasingly conscious of the emotional disorders and breakdowns that appear to be endemic in contemporary society. Various authors stress different reasons for the high incidence of these mental disorders — competitive culture, conflict of basic values in society, rapid social change, rigid morality, lax morality, and many others. It is clear that many conditioning factors are responsible and that no single theory can do justice to all. It is not out of place to suggest, however, that the insecurities and neurotic patterns of our time are in part subjective reflections of the conflicts arising from the struggle to *maintain* social isolation and social dominance. If these two features were brought into proper social balance, therapy itself would be given tremendous impetus.

Individual treatment can hardly be eliminated, however. Preventive action is necessary so that persons from childhood on can develop adequate security feelings, self-knowledge, consistency, and realistic life-goals. The individual needs that peculiar balance which requires him to satisfy the demands of the group while maintaining enough emancipation from it to assert independence. Without this balance he is submerged and smothered by his group loyalty or else he becomes an irresponsible fanatic without any binding group ties.

Since social change is so pervasive and continuous, only the flexible and liberated personality with insight into himself and his social relations can hope to escape intolerance and fear.

A concerted attack on these three fronts will do more in the long run than any passive study of group differences. Habits of action alter thinking more effectively than the presentation of facts or values. Action comes before thought. This book will be of little worth except as a gateway to community action in which ethnic and racial diversities lose their power to be divisions and become a crucial opportunity to create a wider and richer unity than our nation has yet achieved. The goal is still, "one nation, indivisible, with liberty and justice for all." But now with enlarged meaning.

NOTES

CHAPTER 1. MINORITIES — A "PROBLEM"?

1. See A. J. Toynbee, *A Study of History*, London, Oxford University Press, 1935, I, 211 ff., for a discussion of the Protestant inclination toward attitudes of racial superiority.
   Stewart Cole shows the prevalence of Anglo-Saxon attitudes and beliefs: "Intercultural Education" in *One America*, ed. by Francis J. Brown and J. S. Roucek, New York, Prentice-Hall, 1945, p. 561.
2. See H. I. Priestley, *The Coming of the White Man*, History of American Life Series, vol. I, New York, Macmillan, 1929.
3. Now of course, "American." Europeans on the Continent have accepted the British assertion that "Americans" do not speak "English," and H. L. Mencken seems to have confirmed this suspicion.
4. See pp. 11 ff., for a further discussion of this concept.
5. See W. G. Sumner, *Folkways*, Boston, Ginn, 1906, and W. G. Sumner and A. G. Keller, *Science of Society*, New Haven, Yale University Press, 1927, vol. I, chap. 15 for a fuller account.
6. This is fully documented in the volume by W. Lloyd Warner, R. J. Havighurst, and M. B. Loeb, *Who Shall Be Educated?* New York, Harper, 1944.
7. See Kimball Young, *Social Psychology*, 2nd ed., New York, Crofts, 1944, chap. 11.
8. J. T. Adams, *The Epic of America*, Boston, Little Brown, 1941, Epilogue. For a fuller and more critical account see Gunnar Myrdal, *An American Dilemma*, New York, Harper, 1944, vol. I, chap. 1.
9. C. H. Cooley, *Social Organization*, New York, Scribner, 1929, p. 236.
10. *Ibid.*, chap. 19.
11. Robert S. Lynd and Helen M. Lynd, *Middletown in Transition*, New York, Harcourt Brace, 1937, pp 71 ff. Also W. F. Ogburn and M. F. Nimkoff, *Sociology*, Boston, Houghton Mifflin, 1940, pp. 309 ff.
12. *Ibid.*, pp. 330 ff.
13. Carl R. Fish, *The Rise of the Common Man*, History of American Life Series, vol. IV, New York, Macmillan, 1927, pp. 112–116.
14. Cf. above, p. 7
15. Chapter 2 will give fuller consideration to this issue.
16. Technically "American" refers to a native of North or South America. Since "United States" has no adjectival form, this study will employ "American" to mean any individual living in the United States who claims the protection of its laws.

CHAPTER 2. WHAT IS A RACE?

1. C. Goring, *The English Convict*, 1913; quoted by Otto Klineberg, *Social Psychology*, New York, Holt, 1940, pp. 206–207.
2. These two types are adapted from W. M. Krogman, "The Concept of Race" in *The Science of Man in the World Crisis*, ed. by Ralph Linton, New York, Columbia University Press, 1945; Krogman's article, "An Anthropologist Looks at Race," *Intercultural Education News*, November 1945, pp. 1–2; and Ralph Linton, *The Study of Man*, New York, Appleton-Century, 1936, chap. 2. Krogman presents what we have termed the *general* conception, and Linton the *specific*. In order to keep the results uniform, we have followed Linton's list of races in both cases, though Krogman includes a somewhat

variant list with South Baltic and Dinaric races in the Caucasian stock. For this and other discrepancies, see text following this section.

3. Ales Hrdlička, *The Old Americans*, Baltimore, Williams and Wilkins, 1925.
4. The example comes from A. Goldenweiser, *Anthropology*, New York, Crofts, 1937, p. 16.
5. M. F. Ashley Montagu, *Man's Most Dangerous Myth: the Fallacy of Race*, 2nd ed., New York, Columbia University Press, 1945, pp. 31–32.
6. W. M. Krogman, "The Concept of Race," p. 43.
7. *Ibid.*, p. 49.
8. Franz Boas, *Changes in Bodily Form of Descendants of Immigrants*, New York, Columbia University Press, 1912.
9. H. L. Shapiro, *Migration and Environment*, New York, Oxford University Press, 1939, pp. 198, 187–188.
10. Marcus Goldstein, *Demographic and Bodily Changes in Descendants of Mexican Immigrants*. A Publication of the Institute of Latin-American Studies, Austin, Texas, The University of Texas, 1943, pp. 16 and 19.
11. For examples see A. C. Haddon, *The Races of Man and Their Distribution*, New York, Macmillan, 1925. Cf. remarks on the Beaker-Folk, pp. 30–31.
12. W. M. Krogman, "The Concept of Race," p. 53.
13. *Ibid.*, p. 46.
14. Melville Jacobs, "Jewish Blood and Culture," in Isacque Graeber and Steuart H. Britt, *Jews in a Gentile World*, New York, Macmillan, 1942, p. 49.
15. Summarized in Otto Klineberg, *Characteristics of the American Negro*, New York, Harper, 1944, pp. 270–272.
16. Lyle Owen, "Your Million Fathers," *Common Ground*, Summer 1944, pp. 3–8.
17. Montagu, *op. cit.*, p. 39.
18. Julian S. Huxley and A. C. Haddon, *We Europeans*, New York, Harper, 1936, p. 99.
19. *Idem.*
20. W. M. Krogman, "The Concept of Race," p. 45.
21. Carleton S. Coon, "Have the Jews a Racial Identity?" in Graeber and Britt, *op. cit.*, p. 33.
22. Huxley and Haddon, *op. cit.*, pp. 142, 149.
23. Melville Jacobs, "Jewish Blood and Culture" in Graeber and Britt, *op. cit.*, p. 52.
24. Montagu, *op. cit.*, pp. 225–226.
25. *Ibid.*, p. 223.
26. Huxley and Haddon, *op. cit.*, p. 150.
27. Coon, *op. cit.*, p. 35.
28. For a discussion of fallacious theories which cannot be summarized here cf. Louis L. Snyder, *Race: A History of Modern Ethnic Theories*, New York, Longmans Green, 1939. For a thorough account of genetic principles involved cf. Gunner Dahlberg, *Race, Reason and Rubbish*, trans. by Lancelot Hogben, New York, Columbia University Press, 1942.
29. For the results of race crossing cf. Montagu, *op. cit.*, chap. 8, "The Creative Power of Race Mixture."
30. For an account of this case and a picture of Fung Kwok Keung, cf. Amram Scheinfeld, *You and Heredity*, New York, Stokes, 1939, p. 354.

CHAPTER 3. RACE AND CULTURE

1. This illustration is adapted from Kimball Young, *Personality and Problems of Adjustment*, New York, Crofts, 1940, pp. 439–441.
2. Quoted in E. B. Reuter, *The American Race Problem*, New York, Crowell, 2nd ed., 1938, p. 76. See C. C. Brigham, *A Study of American Intelligence*, Princeton, Princeton University Press, 1923.
3. Otto Klineberg, ed., *Characteristics of the American Negro*, New York, Harper, 1944, p. 36, table 3.

4. C. C. Brigham, "Intelligence Tests of Immigrant Groups," *Psychological Review*, 37 : 158–165, 1930. Summarized in Klineberg, *op. cit.*, p. 75.

5. Brigadier General Arthur G. Trudeau, "Army Experience and Problems of Negro Education," *Education for Victory*, U.S. Office of Education, Federal Security Agency, vol. 3, No. 20, April 20, 1945, pp. 13–16.
Quoted in Paul Witty, "New Evidence on the Learning Ability of the Negro," *Journal of Abnormal and Social Psychology* 40 : 401 ff., October 1945.

6. Trudeau, *op. cit.*, p. 14, quoted in Witty, *op. cit.*, pp. 403–404.

7. See a summary of the findings in M. H. Krout, *Introduction to Social Psychology*, New York, Harper, 1942, pp. 207–212; also G. M. Whipple, ed., *Intelligence, Its Nature and Nurture*, 39th Yearbook, National Society for the Study of Education, Bloomington, Ill., Public School Publishing Co., 1940.

8. B. S. Burks, "The Relative Influence of Nature and Nurture Upon Mental Development," 27th Yearbook, National Society for the Study of Education, Bloomington, Ill., Public School Publishing Co., 1928, pp. 219–316.

9. Read Bain, "Personality Development and Marriage" in *Marriage and the Family*, ed. by Howard Becker and Reuben Hill, Boston, Heath, 1942, p. 128.

10. Gee, Wilson, and Corson, *Rural Depopulation in Certain Tidewater and Piedmont Areas of Virginia*, Monograph of the University of Virginia, 1929, p. 102. The Gist, Pihlblad, and Gregory study is summarized in Noel P. Gist and L. A. Halbert, *Urban Society*, New York, Crowell, 1941, pp. 282–284.

11. Noel P. Gist and Carroll D. Clark, "Intelligence as a Selective Factor in Rural-Urban Migrations," *American Journal of Sociology* 44 : 55 ff, July 1938.

12. P. A. Sorokin and C. C. Zimmerman, *Principles of Rural-Urban Sociology*, New York, Holt, 1929, pp. 573 and 582. Also C. C. Zimmerman, "Migration to Towns and Cities," *American Journal of Sociology* 32 : 450–455.

13. See Otto Klineberg, *Race Differences*, New York, Harper, 1935, p. 197.

14. *Idem.*

15. *Ibid.*, pp. 185–187.

16. Otto Klineberg, "Racial Psychology" in *The Science of Man in the World Crisis*, ed. by Ralph Linton, New York, Columbia University Press, 1945, p. 71.

17. W. W. Clark, "Los Angeles Negro Children," *Educational Research Bulletin*, Los Angeles City Schools, 1923. Summarized in Klineberg, *Race Differences*, p. 183.

18. Otto Klineberg, *Race Differences*, pp. 176–177.

19. F. H. Hankins, *The Racial Basis of Civilization*, New York, Knopf, 1931, p. 326.

20. Klineberg, *Race Differences*, pp. 193–194.

21. *Ibid.*, p. 194.

22. *Ibid.*, pp. 155 and 159.

23. Ralph Linton, *The Study of Man*, New York, Appleton-Century, 1936, p. 53.

24. Otto Klineberg, ed., *Characteristics of the American Negro*, p. 68.

25. Otto Klineberg, *Race Differences*, p. 177.

26. See Louis Snyder, *Race: A History of Modern Ethnic Theories*, New York, Longmans Green, 1939.

27. Richard T. La Piere and Paul R. Farnsworth, *Social Psychology*, New York, McGraw-Hill, 1936 First Edition, p. 261.

28. A. J. Toynbee, *A Study of History*, London, Oxford University Press, 1934, II, 232–233.

29. *Ibid.*, I, 239–240.

30. *Ibid.*, I, 175–177.

31. *Ibid.*, I, 232.

32. See Linton, *The Study of Man*, chap. 3.

33. *Ibid.*, p. 55.

34. W. E. B. Du Bois, *Black Folk Then and Now*, New York, Holt, 1939, pp. 12–13, 44–46, 65.

35. A. J. Toynbee, *op. cit.*, I, 233–234.

36. Franz Boas, "An Anthropologist's Credo," *The Nation*, 147 : 201–204, 1938.

CHAPTER 4. THE AMERICAN INDIAN

1. Cf. Willard Price, *Japan's Islands of Mystery*, New York, John Day, 1944.
2. Cf. M. J. Herskovits *et al.*, *Acculturation*, New York, Augustin, 1938.
3. C. T. Loram and T. F. McIlwraith, eds., *The North American Indian Today*, University of Toronto–Yale University Seminar Conference, Toronto, University of Toronto Press, 1943, pp. 8–9.
4. H. L. Shapiro, "The Mixed Blood Indian" in *The Changing Indian*, ed. by Oliver La Farge, Norman, Oklahoma, The University of Oklahoma Press, 1942, p. 20.
5. W. W. Beatty, "Training Indians for the Best Use of Their Own Resources" in La Farge, *op. cit.*, p. 129.
6. C. B. Glasscock, *Then Came Oil*, New York, Bobbs-Merrill, 1938, p. 147.
7. *Ibid.*, p. 148.
8. *Ibid.*, p. 263.
9. Clark Wissler, *Indians of the United States, Four Centuries of Their History and Culture*, New York, Doubleday Doran, 1940, pp. 241–242.
10. Ralph M. Linton, "Land Tenure in Aboriginal America" in La Farge, *op. cit.*, pp. 44–45, 49–50.
11. Henry Elkin, "The Northern Arapaho of Wyoming" in Ralph Linton, ed., *Acculturation in Seven American Indian Tribes*, New York, Appleton-Century, 1940, p. 253.
12. Loram and McIlwraith, *op. cit.*, p. 7.
13. Clark Wissler, "The American Indian" in *One America, The History, Contributions and Present Problems of Our Racial and National Minorities*, ed. by Francis J. Brown and J. S. Roucek, New York, Prentice-Hall, 1945, p. 22.
14. Julian H. Steward, *Basin-Plateau Aboriginal Socio-Political Groups*, Smithsonian Institution, Bureau of American Ethnology, Bulletin 120, Washington, D.C., Government Printing Office, 1938, pp. 253, 258–259.
15. Ralph Linton, "Land Tenure in Aboriginal America" in La Farge, *op. cit.*, p. 43.
16. John H. Provinse, "Cultural Factors in Land Use Planning" in La Farge, *op. cit.*, p. 61.
17. *Ibid*, p. 60.
18. Louis Balsam, "Some Economic Problems of the Indian in the United States" in Loram and McIlwraith, *op. cit.*, p. 209.
19. Loram and McIlwraith, *op. cit.*, p. 6.
20. Grenville Goodwin, *The Social Organization of the Western Apache*, Chicago, University of Chicago Press, 1942, p. 536.
21. R. S. Woodworth, "Racial Differences in Mental Traits," Atlanta University Publications No. 20, Atlanta, Atlanta University Press, 1916, quoted in W. F. Ogburn and M. F. Nimkoff, *Sociology*, Boston, Houghton Mifflin, 1940, p. 191.
22. E. R. Embree, *Indians of the Americas*, Boston, Houghton Mifflin, 1939, p. 152.
23. Wissler, *Indians of the United States*, chap. 21, "The Mystery of the Indian Mind."
24. Cf. Walter Prescott Webb, *The Great Plains*, Boston, Ginn, 1931, chap. 4.
25. *Ibid.*, p. 52 ff.
26. H. I. Priestley, *The Coming of the White Man, 1492–1848, A History of American Life*, vol. I, New York, Macmillan, 1929, pp. 119 and 129.
27. John Collier, "United States Indian Administration as a Laboratory of Ethnic Relations," *Social Research* 12:265–303, September 1945, p. 270.
28. Priestley, *op. cit.*, p. 128.
29. Wissler, *Indians of the United States*, p. 259.
30. *Ibid.*, pp. 268–269.
31. *Ibid.*, p. 265.
32. *Ibid.*, p. 267.
33. *Idem.*
34. *Idem.*

35. Byron Brophy, "The American Indian and Government" in Brown and Roucek, *op. cit.*, p. 441.
36. *Ibid.*, p. 442.
37. Loring Benson Priest, *Uncle Sam's Stepchildren, The Reformation of United States Indian Policy, 1865–1887*, New Brunswick, Rutgers University Press, 1942, pp. 5–6.
38. *Ibid.*, p. 6.
39. Allan Nevins, *The Emergence of Modern America, 1865–1878, History of American Life*, vol. 8, New York, Macmillan, 1927, p. 107.
40. *Idem.*
41. John Collier, "Policies and Problems in the United States," in Loram and McIlwraith, *op. cit.*, p. 142.
42. Carey McWilliams, *Brothers Under the Skin*, Boston, Little Brown, 1943, p. 64.
43. Loring B. Priest, *op. cit.*, chap. 3.
44. *Ibid.*, p. 212.
45. Carey McWilliams, *op. cit.*, p. 60.
46. Oliver La Farge, *As Long As the Grass Shall Grow*, New York, Alliance Book Corporation, Longmans Green, 1940, p. 27.
47. *Ibid.*, p. 30.
48. *Ibid.*, p. 34.
49. *Ibid.*, p. 30.
50. Clark Wissler, *op. cit.*, p. 282.
51. *Ibid.*, p. 241.
52. *Idem.*
53. J. G. Townsend, "Problems of Health Among the Indians of the United States" in Loram and McIlwraith, *op. cit.*, p. 225.
54. *To Secure These Rights*, The Report of the President's Committee on Civil Rights, Washington, U.S. Government Printing Office, 1947, p. 71; and Townsend, *op. cit.*, pp. 227, 232.
55. J. G. Townsend, "Indian Health, Past, Present and Future" in La Farge, *The Changing Indian*, pp. 32–33.
56. Grenville Goodwin, *op. cit.*, pp. 156–163 *passim.*
57. Frank Lorimer, "Observations on the Trend of Indian Population in the United States" in La Farge, *The Changing Indian*, p. 13.
58. La Farge, *As Long As the Grass Shall Grow*, pp. 13–17. Also *Sun Chief, The Autobiography of a Hopi Indian*, ed. by Leo Simmons, New Haven, Yale University Press, 1942, chap. 5.
59. Gordon Macgregor, "Indian Education in Relation to the Social and Economic Background of the Reservation" in La Farge, *The Changing Indian*, p. 118.
60. *Ibid.*, p. 120.
61. *Ibid.*, pp. 122–123.
62. Linton, *Acculturation in Seven American Indian Tribes*, p. 490.
63. *Ibid.*, p. 485.
64. *Ibid.*, p. 499.
65. Natalie E. Joffe, "The Fox of Iowa" in Linton, *Acculturation*, pp. 260, 270–271.
66. Linton, *Acculturation*, pp. 515–516.
67. Henry Elkin, "The Northern Arapaho of Wyoming" in Linton, *Acculturation*, pp. 231–232.
68. *Ibid.*, pp. 238–239.
69. *Ibid.*, p. 233.
70. *Ibid.*, pp. 247–248.
71. Ruth Underhill, "Some Basic Cultures of the Indians of the United States" in Loram and McIlwraith, *op. cit.*, p. 25.
72. Edward A. Kennard, "The Use of Native Languages and Cultures in Indian Education" in La Farge, *The Changing Indian*, p. 114.
73. Underhill, *op. cit.*, pp. 27–28.
74. Cf. Laura Thompson and Alice Joseph, *The Hopi Way*, Chicago, University of Chicago Press, 1945, and Simmons, *op. cit.*
75. Mark A. Dawber, "Protestant Missions to the Indians in the United States" in Loram and McIlwraith, *op. cit.*, p. 98.
76. Gordon Macgregor, in La Farge, *The Changing Indian*, p. 126.
77. *Ibid.*, p. 124.
78. J. C. McCaskill, "Problems of Administration of Law and Order Among

Indians of the United States" in Loram and McIlwraith, *op. cit.*, p. 257.

79. Allan G. Harper, "Indian Land Problems in the United States" in Loram and McIlwraith, *op. cit.*, pp. 172–173.
80. La Farge, *As Long As the Grass Shall Grow*, p. 65.
81. *Ibid.*, pp. 65–66.
82. Collier, *op. cit.*, p. 276.
83. *Ibid.*, pp. 278–279.
84. *Ibid.*, p. 278.
85. *Ibid.*, p. 276.
86. La Farge, *As Long As the Grass Shall Grow*, p. 78.
87. *Idem.*
88. Collier, *op. cit.*, p. 279.
89. Collier, "Policies and Problems in the United States" in Loram and McIlwraith, *op. cit.*, pp. 149–150.
90. La Farge, *As Long As the Grass Shall Grow*, pp. 85–86.
91. Theodore H. Haas, "The American Indian in Recent Perspective," *Race Relations, A Monthly Summary of Events and Trends*, Nashville, Tenn., December 1947–January 1948, p. 58.
92. Ward Shepard, "Land Problems of an Expanding Indian Population" in La Farge, *The Changing Indian*, p. 78.
93. Collier, *op. cit.*, p. 277.
94. Cf. O. K. Armstrong, "Set the American Indians Free!" *Reader's Digest*, August 1945, p. 49.
95. *Idem.*
96. *Ibid.*, p. 50.
97. John H. Provinse, "Cultural Factors in Land Use Planning" in La Farge, *The Changing Indian*, p. 60 ff.
98. Armstrong, *op. cit.*, p. 50.
99. Gordon Magcregor, *Warriors Without Weapons*, Chicago, University of Chicago Press, 1946, pp. 41, 148 ff.
100. Haas, *op. cit.*, pp. 51–52.
101. Macgregor, *op. cit.*, p. 148.
102. Louis Balsam, in Loram and McIlwraith, *op. cit.*, p. 217.
103. J. G. Townsend, in Loram and McIlwraith, *op. cit.*, p. 239.
104. Priest, *op. cit.*, p. 252.
105. Byron Brophy, in Brown and Roucek, *op. cit.*, pp. 446–447.
106. Priest, *op cit.*, p. 173.
107. Haas, *op. cit.*, p. 51.
108. Loram and McIlwraith, *op. cit.*, p. 349.

CHAPTER 5. NEGRO CULTURE

1. For the distinction between meaning and form in anthropology, see Ralph Linton, *The Study of Man*, New York, Appleton-Century, 1936, pp. 403 ff.
2. See Chapter 3, above.
3. See Chapter 2, above.
4. Linton, *op. cit.*, pp. 41–42.
5. Chapter 2, p. 29 above.
6. Melville J. Herskovits, *The Myth of the Negro Past*, New York, Harper, 1941, p. 296.
7. *Ibid.*, p. 90.
8. See Chapter 4.
9. See Chapter 9, below.
10. See below, p. 87 for qualifications of this statement.
11. See below, Chapter 10.
12. Richard Hofstadter, "U. B. Phillips and the Plantation Legend," *Journal of Negro History* 29:119, April 1944.
13. E. B. Reuter, *The American Race Problem*, 2nd ed., New York, Crowell, 1938, p. 106.
14. *Ibid.*, p. 124.
15. E. F. Frazier, *The Negro Family in the United States*, Chicago, University of Chicago Press, 1939, p. 21.
16. E. R. Embree, *Brown America*, New York, Viking, 1931, pp. 10–11.
17. See Herskovits, *op. cit.*, chap. 11.
18. Quoted in Herskovits, *op. cit.*, p. 276.
19. Ida Ward in her *Introduction to the Ibo Language*, quoted in Herskovits, *op. cit.*, p. 323, note 41.

20. Herskovits, *op. cit.*, pp. 146, 268, 271.
21. *Ibid.*, p. 140.
22. *Ibid.*, p. 148.
23. *Ibid.*, pp. 198–202 and Frazier, *op. cit.*, pp. 255 ff.
24. N. N. Puckett, *Folk Beliefs of the Southern Negro*, Chapel Hill, University of North Carolina Press, 1926, pp. 102 ff. Also Herskovits, *op. cit.*, p. 206.
25. Herskovits, *op. cit.*, p. 161.
26. Puckett, *op. cit.*, p. 10.
27. Some masters, of course, opposed giving Christianity to the slaves. See W. D. Weatherford and C. S. Johnson, *Race Relations*, Boston, Heath, 1934, chap. 10, pp. 187 ff — but this attitude did not continue. See also Gunnar Myrdal, *An American Dilemma*, 2 vols., New York, Harper, 1944, II, 859.
28. C. S. Johnson, *The Shadow of the Plantation*, Chicago, University of Chicago Press, 1934, chap. 5. Also Myrdal, *op. cit.*, II, chap. 40.
29. Herskovits, *op. cit.*, p. 222.
30. Weatherford and Johnson, *op. cit.*, p. 211.
31. Johnson, *op. cit.*, pp. 151–152.
32. Herskovits, *op. cit.*, pp. 214–217.
33. Hortense Powdermaker, *After Freedom*, New York, Viking, 1939, pp. 259–260.
34. See above, note 27.
35. Myrdal, *op. cit.*, II, 861.
36. See Benjamin E. Mays and J. W. Nicholson, *The Negro's Church*, New York, Institute of Social and Religious Research, 1933.
37. Myrdal, *op. cit.*, II, 862.
38. *Ibid.*, pp. 860–861.
39. *Ibid.*, pp. 864–865.
40. St. Clair Drake and Horace R. Cayton, *Black Metropolis*, New York, Harcourt Brace, 1945, p. 415.
41. Leopold von Wiese, *Systematic Sociology*, adapted and amplified by Howard Becker, New York, Wiley, 1932, pp. 306–307.
42. Herskovits, *op. cit.*, pp. 132–133.
43. See above, p. 88 of this Chapter.
44. U. B. Phillips, *American Negro Slavery*, New York, Appleton, 1918, pp. 341–342.
45. James Truslow Adams, *The American: The Making of a New Man*, New York, Scribner, 1943, p. 135.
46. Herbert Aptheker, *American Negro Slave Revolts*, New York, Columbia University Press, 1943, chaps. 9–15.
47. *Ibid.*, p. 141.
48. *Idem.*
49. *Ibid.*, pp. 141–142.
50. W. E. B. Du Bois, *Black Reconstruction*, New York, Harcourt Brace, 1935, chap. IV, "The General Strike," especially p. 71.
51. Claude Bowers, *The Tragic Era*, Boston, Houghton Mifflin, 1929, p. 308.
52. Du Bois, *op. cit.*, p. 387.
53. *Ibid.*, p. 225.
54. C. S. Johnson, *Patterns of Racial Segregation*, New York, Harper, 1943, p. 83.
55. Powdermaker, *op. cit.*, pp. 113–114.
56. *Ibid.*, p. 116.
57. Johnson, *Patterns of Racial Segregation*, p. 89.
58. Drake and Cayton, *op. cit.*, chap. 16.
59. Herskovits, *op. cit.*, pp. 167–169.
60. Karl Lamprecht, *Deutsche Geschichte*, Berlin, P. Gaertner, 1902, 3rd ed., I, 96; and Paul Lacroix (Pierre Dufour) *History of Prostitution*, trans. by Samuel Putnam, New York, Covici-Friede, 1931, pp. 661–662, 675, and 697.
61. Herskovits, *idem.*
62. Herskovits, *op. cit.*, pp. 180–181.
63. *Ibid.*, pp. 169–170.
64. Stated by E. F. Frazier, *op. cit.*, pp. 55, 57.
65. Du Bois, *op. cit.*, pp. 11–12.
66. Herskovits, *op. cit.*, p. 178.
67. Charles E. King, "The Negro Maternal Family: A Product of an Economic and a Culture System," *Social Forces* 24:100–104, October 1945.
68. *Ibid.*, p. 101.

69. Frazier, *op. cit.*, pp. 45–46, note 9.
70. *Ibid.*, p. 46, note 11.
71. U. B. Phillips, *Life and Labor in the Old South*, Boston, Little Brown, 1929, p. 204.
72. *Idem.*
73. *Idem.*
74. *Ibid.*, p. 205.
75. King, *op cit.*, p. 101.
76. Otto Klineberg, *Characteristics of the American Negro*, New York, Harper, 1944, pp. 263–264.
77. *Ibid.*, p. 264.
78. Frederick Douglass, *My Bondage and My Freedom*, New York and Auburn, 1855, p. 59, quoted in Herskovits, *op. cit.*, pp. 127–128.
79. King, *op. cit.*
80. Frazier, *op cit.*, pp. 126–131 and King, *op. cit.*, pp. 100 and 102.
81. Johnson, *Shadow of the Plantation*, pp. 66–67, and King, *op cit.*, pp. 102–103.
82. King, *op. cit.*, p. 103.
83. Powdermaker, *op. cit.*, p. 149.
84. Johnson, *Shadow of the Plantation*, pp. 39–40.
85. King, *op. cit.*, p. 102.
86. Powdermaker, *op. cit.*, p. 157.
87. Reuter, *op. cit.*, p. 206.
88. Frazier, *op. cit.*, pp. 461–464.
89. Johnson, *Shadow of the Plantation*, pp. 32–33.
90. King, *op. cit.*, p. 102.
91. Frazier, *op. cit.*, pp. 461 and 469 ff.
92. Drake and Cayton, *op. cit.*, p. 531.
93. Frazier, *op. cit.*, p. 115.
94. Drake and Cayton, *op. cit.*, pp. 564 ff. and 587 n.
95. Powdermaker, *op. cit.*, pp. 201–204.
96. King, *op. cit.*, pp. 103 and 104.
97. Klineberg, *op. cit.*, p. 366.
98. Drake and Cayton, *op. cit.*, pp. 498–499.
99. *Ibid.*, p. 496.
100. Margaret Brenman, "The Relationship between Minority Group Membership and Group Identification in a Group of Urban Middle Class Negro Girls," Journal of Social Psychology 11:171–197, 1940, p. 192.
101. Margaret Brenman, *The Personality of Urban Negro Girls*, p. 13, Carnegie-Myrdal Study, The Negro in America, 1940. This study is found in the Schomburg Collection of the New York Public Library and the author acknowledges his indebtedness to Dr. L. D. Reddick, former Curator of the Collection, for this and all other references below from the Schomburg Collection.
102. Drake and Cayton, *op. cit.*, p. 500.
103. *Ibid.*, p. 502.
104. *Ibid.*, p. 503.
105. Cf. Embree, *op. cit.*
106. Klineberg, *op. cit.*, pp. 368–369.
107. Drake and Cayton, *op. cit.*, p. 506.
108. *Ibid.*, p. 514.
109. *Ibid.*, p. 515.
110. *Idem.*

CHAPTER 6. THE SOUTHERN NEGRO

1. Paraphrased from an interview in *Lay My Burden Down*, ed. by B. A. Botkin, Chicago, University of Chicago Press, 1945, p. 253. This series of interviews, quoted from former slaves and telling of their reactions to Emancipation, is a highly revealing and significant document on southern mores.
2. Howard W. Odum, *Southern Regions of the United States*, Chapel Hill, University of North Carolina Press, 1936, pp. 55 ff.
3. Personal-social conditioning is the result of personal interaction not necessarily structured by cultural patterns. See Kimball Young, *Social Psychology*, 2nd ed., New York, Crofts, 1944, pp. 9–10.
4. John M. Maclachlan, "Normal Social Controls in the Mississippi Delta Plan-

tation Community" in Appendix II, p. 3, of Arthur Raper, ed., *Race and Class Pressures*, Carnegie-Myrdal Study, The Negro in America, 1940. Schomburg Collection.

5. Clarence E. Cason, "Middle Class and Bourbon" in *Culture in the South*, ed. by W. T. Couch, Chapel Hill, University of North Carolina Press, 1934, p. 483.
6. Hortense Jones, "Women Criminals in Atlanta, August, 1939" in Appendix II, p. 6, of Raper, *op. cit.*, Schomburg Collection.
7. Ralph J. Bunche, *Conceptions and Ideologies of the Negro Problem, A Research Memorandum.* Carnegie-Myrdal Study, The Negro in America, 1940, pp. 100–101. Schomburg Collection.
8. Richard Sterner, *The Negro's Share*, New York, Harper, 1943, p. 60.
9. See Gunnar Myrdal, *An American Dilemma*, New York, Harper, 1944, I, 594–595.
10. Ralph J. Bunche, *op. cit.*, p. 97.
11. Hortense Powdermaker, *After Freedom*, New York, Viking, 1939, p. 119.
12. Myrdal, *op. cit.*, I, 612.
13. *Idem.*
14. For this and other instances see Howard W. Odum, *Race and Rumors of Race*, Chapel Hill, University of North Carolina Press, 1943, pp. 34–35.
15. Rupert B. Vance, "The Profile of Southern Culture" in Couch, *op. cit.*, p. 36.
16. G. W. Forster, "Southern Agricultural Economy in the Postwar Era," *Southern Economic Journal* 13:65–71, July 1946.
17. Charles W. Ramsdell, "The Southern Heritage" in Couch, *op. cit.*, p. 11.
18. Odum, *Southern Regions of the United States*, p. 39.
19. *Ibid.*, p. 41.
20. *Ibid.*, p. 43.
21. *Ibid.*, p. 73.
22. *Ibid.*, p. 77.
23. Rupert B. Vance, *All These People, The Nation's Human Resources in the South*, Chapel Hill, University of North Carolina Press, 1945, p. 18.
24. *Ibid.*, p. 92.
25. *Ibid.*, p. 131.
26. *Idem.*
27. *Ibid.*, p. 233. These figures include both the Southeast and Southwest but it appears that the ratio in the Southeast is not substantially changed by the shift in statistical base; N. P. Gist and L. A. Halbert, *Urban Society*, 3rd ed., New York, Crowell, 1948, estimate given on p. 231.
28. Study by H. C. Hofsommer, quoted in Vance, *op. cit.*, p. 229.
29. *Ibid.*, p. 234.
30. Myrdal, *op. cit.*, I, 254.
31. *Ibid.*, pp. 256–259.
32. Vance, *op. cit.*, p. 244.
33. *Ibid.*, pp. 245–246.
34. James M. Stepp, "Southern Agriculture's Stake in Occupational Freedom," *Southern Economic Journal* 13:46–52, July 1946, p. 48.
35. *Ibid.*, p. 47.
36. See G. W. Forster, *op. cit.*, pp. 67–68.
37. See Keith Hutchinson, "King Cotton in a Balloon," *Nation* 163:129, August 3, 1946.
38. Robert W. Harrison, "Land Improvement *vs* Land Settlement for the Southeast," *Southern Economic Journal* 12:30–38, July 1945, p. 32.
39. "State Reports," in *Southern Economic Journal*, July 1946. (Especially for Georgia and Alabama, pp. 85 and 87.)
40. Dillard B. Lasseter, "The Impact of the War on the South and Implications for Postwar Developments," *Social Forces* 23:20–26, October 1944, pp. 20–21.
41. Myrdal, *op. cit.*, I, 285–286.
42. Vance, *All These People*, p. 233.
43. Myrdal, *op. cit.*, I, chap. 8.
44. *Ibid.*, I, 188.
45. C. S. Johnson, *Patterns of Racial Segregation*, New York, Harper, 1943, p. 86.
46. See table, *idem.*
47. *Ibid.*, p. 87.
48. *Ibid.*, p. 84.
49. *Ibid.*, pp. 73–75.

50. *Ibid.*, pp. 71–72.
51. *Ibid.*, p. 46.
52. *Ibid.*, p. 50.
53. *Ibid.*, pp. 26–29.
54. Charles S. Mangum, Jr., *The Legal Status of the Negro*, Chapel Hill, University of North Carolina Press, 1940, pp. 139–140.
55. Walter Chivers, "A Study of the Numbers Racket As It Affects the Lives of Negroes in Atlanta, Georgia" in Raper, *op. cit.*, Appendix IV, p. 8. Schomburg Collection.
56. *Ibid.*, pp. 14–15.
57. See Myrdal, *op. cit.*, I, 330–332.
58. *Ibid.*, I, 650.
59. Johnson, *op. cit.*, p. 34, and Myrdal, *op. cit.*, I, 525.
60. Johnson, *ibid.*, p. 33.
61. *Idem.*
62. Myrdal, *op. cit.*, I, 552, note a.
63. *Ibid.*, I, 535–536.
64. *Idem.*
65. Raper, *op. cit.*, pp. 14–18. Schomburg Collection. Summary in Myrdal, I, 538 ff.
66. Myrdal, *op. cit.*, I, 523–524.
67. W. J. Cash, *The Mind of the South*, New York, Knopf, 1941, p. 33.
68. *Ibid.*, p. 43.
69. Myrdal, *op. cit.*, I, 560.
70. Donald R. Taft, *Criminology*, New York, Macmillan, 1942, p. 152.
71. Myrdal, *op. cit.*, I, 553, and II, 966 ff.
72. Raper, *op. cit.*, pp. 37–40. Schomburg Collection.
73. John Dollard, *Caste and Class in a Southern Town*, New Haven, Yale University Press, 1937, chap. 12, pp. 267 ff.
74. *Ibid.*, p. 274.
75. Allison Davis, Burleigh B. Gardner, and Mary R. Gardner, *Deep South, An Anthropological Study of Caste and Class*, Chicago, University of Chicago Press, 1941, pp. 44 ff.
76. *Ibid.*, pp. 46–47 and 527 ff.
77. Dollard, *op. cit.*, chaps. 6–8.
78. Cf. Hadley Cantril, *The Psychology of Social Movements*, New York, Wiley, 1941.
79. See E. B. Reuter, *The American Race Problem*, New York, Crowell, 1938 ed., p. 369.
80. See John Dollard and others, *Frustration and Aggression*, New Haven, Yale University Press, 1939, p. 31.
81. Davis, Gardner, and Gardner, *op. cit.*, pp. 427–428.
82. Reuter, *op. cit.*, p. 369.
83. W. E. B. Du Bois, *Dusk of Dawn*, New York, Harcourt Brace, 1940, pp. 263–265.
84. For an account of this migration see Chapter 7 below.
85. C. S. Johnson, "The Present Status of Race Relations in the South," *Social Forces*, October 1944, p. 28. This article reviews the entire situation objectively.
86. For this and other similar instances see Florence Murray, "The Negro and Civil Liberties During World War II," *Social Forces*, December 1945, pp. 211–216. For subsequent voting see Chapter 8 below and footnotes.
87. Odum, *Race and Rumors of Race*, Part II.
88. Murray, *op. cit.*, p. 212.
89. Johnson, "The Present Status of Race Relations in the South," p. 30.
90. A full account is given in James A. Dombrowski's article, "The Southern Conference for Human Welfare," *Common Ground*, Summer 1946, pp. 14–25.
91. For the wartime record, see note 89 above. For Monroe killings see *Cleveland Call and Post*, August 24, 1946, p. 1.
92. *Idem.*
93. *Idem.*
94. *Idem.*
95. Dombrowski, *op. cit.*, p. 17.
96. *Cleveland Call and Post*, August 24, 1946, p. 8A.
97. See articles by Eugene Segal in the *Cleveland Press*, beginning November 11, 1946.

CHAPTER 7. THE NORTHERN NEGRO

1. "The Negro in the North During Wartime," *Journal of Educational Sociology*, January 1944.
2. Rupert B. Vance, *All These People*, Chapel Hill, University of North Carolina Press, 1945, pp. 118–120.
3. *Ibid.*, p. 120.
4. Gunnar Myrdal, *An American Dilemma*, New York, Harper, 1944, I, 197.
5. St. Clair Drake and Horace R. Cayton, *Black Metropolis*, New York, Harcourt Brace, 1945, p. 88.
6. See Chapter 6 above, note 23.
7. Howard W. Odum, *Southern Regions of the United States*, Chapel Hill, University of North Carolina Press, 1936, p. 477.
8. For a fuller account of this development see Robert C. Weaver, *Negro Labor, A National Problem*, New York, Harcourt Brace, 1946, chap. 9.
9. L. D. Reddick, "The New Race Relations Frontier," *Journal of Educational Sociology* 19:129–145, November 1945, p. 137. The author is indebted to Dr. Reddick directly for this reference.
10. *Idem.*
11. Release for the Department of Commerce, Bureau of the Census for March 4, 1945, p. 1. These data and other information about Negro war migration have been kindly supplied by Mr. Joseph R. Houchins, Specialist, Negro Statistics, the Bureau of the Census.
12. Weaver, *op. cit.*, p. 91.
13. Release by Bureau of the Census, March 4, 1945, p. 2.
14. *Idem.*
15. "Racial Aspects of Reconversion," Publication of the National Urban League, 1133 Broadway, New York 10, N.Y., issued August 10, 1945. This reference was also supplied by Mr. Joseph Houchins. (See above, note 11.)
16. Weaver, *op. cit.*, p. 91.
17. For a clarification of the South-North-West quandary see L. D. Reddick, *op. cit.*, pp. 130–131.
18. This ideology has been most clearly outlined by Howard W. Odum in his *Race and Rumors of Race*, Chapel Hill, University of North Carolina Press, 1943, pp. 42–43, from which this account has been paraphrased and altered. The term subordination as contrasted with segregation is suggested by Drake and Cayton, *op. cit.*, p. 113.
19. Drake and Cayton, *op. cit.*, p. 119.
20. T. J. Woofter, *Negro Problems in Cities*, New York, Doubleday Doran, 1928, p. 42, and Konrad Bercovici, *Around the World in New York*, New York, Appleton-Century, 1924, p. 216.
21. Woofter, *idem.*
22. Harold Gibbard, *Residential Succession: A Study in Human Ecology*, unpublished doctoral dissertation, University of Michigan, 1938, p. 163, quoted in Gist and Halbert, *Urban Society*, New York, Crowell, 1941, p. 191.
23. Bercovici, *op. cit.*, pp. 216–218.
24. Woofter, *op. cit.*, maps on pp. 40–51.
25. *Ibid.*, p. 100. In Cleveland, the Negro section is known as the "Central Area."
26. Drake and Cayton, *op. cit.*, p. 27, and Woofter, *op. cit.*, p. 102.
27. *The Central Area Social Study*, Research Committee, The Welfare Federation of Cleveland, 1944, pp. 44–45.
28. Carey McWilliams, "Critical Summary," *Journal of Educational Sociology* 19:187–197, November 1945, pp. 191–192.
29. Robert W. O'Brien, "Profiles: Seattle," in *ibid.*, pp. 146–157, p. 148.
30. Joseph James, "Profiles: San Francisco," in *ibid.*, pp. 166–178, p. 170.
31. Edwin C. Berry, "Profiles: Portland," in *ibid.*, pp. 158–165, p. 160.
32. Dorothy J. Liveright, "Tuberculosis Mortality Among Residents of 92 Cities of 100,000 or More Population, 1939–41," U.S. Public Health Reports, July 21, 1944, pp. 942–955.
33. *Vital Statistics Rates in the United*

States, 1900–1940, quoted in *The Central Area Social Study* (Cleveland), p. 109.

34. Frank W. Notestein, "Differential Fertility in the East North Central States," *Milbank Memorial Fund Quarterly* 16:184–185, April 1938.
35. Drake and Cayton, *op. cit.*, p. 202, note 2.
36. *The Central Area Social Study* (Cleveland), pp. 117–118.
37. See above, Chapter 5.
38. Myrdal, *op. cit.*, I, 438–439 and Charles S. Mangum, *The Legal Status of the Negro*, Chapel Hill, University of North Carolina Press, 1940, chap. 18.
39. Myrdal, *op. cit.*, I, 492–493.
40. *Ibid.*, p. 491.
41. *Ibid.*, p. 492.
42. Margaret Brenman, *The Personality of Urban Negro Girls, Three Research Memoranda*, Carnegie-Myrdal Study, The Negro in America, 1940, p. 15. Schomburg Collection.
43. Editorial in *Cleveland Call and Post*, September 28, 1946.
44. Myrdal, *op. cit.*, I, 493.
45. Drake and Cayton, *op. cit.*, p. 348.
46. *Ibid.*, p. 353.
47. Adam Clayton Powell, Jr., *Marching Blacks*, New York, Dial Press, 1945, p. 155.
48. *Ibid.*, pp. 161–162.
49. See Chapter 8 below for a more extended discussion of Negro agitation.
50. Myrdal, *op. cit.*, I, 493–497 and Drake and Cayton, *op. cit.*, pp. 353–354 and 359–360. An exception to this would be the New York City Negroes, who were offered favors by Tammany as early as 1900. See Claude McKay, *Harlem, Negro Metropolis*, New York, Dutton, 1940, pp. 125 ff.
51. For De Priest's rise to power see Drake and Cayton, *op. cit.*, pp. 360–370.
52. Myrdal, *op. cit.*, II, 1329, note 69.
53. Ralph J. Bunche, *A Brief and Tentative Analysis of Negro Leadership*, Carnegie-Myrdal Study, The Negro in America, 1940, pp. 2 and 197. Schomburg Collection.
54. C. S. Johnson, *The Negro in American Civilization*, New York, Holt, 1930, p. 114.
55. *Ibid.*, p. 116. See Also Sterling D. Spero and Abram L. Harris, *The Black Worker*, New York, Columbia University Press, 1931, and Horace R. Cayton and George S. Mitchell, *Black Workers and the New Unions*, Chapel Hill, University of North Carolina Press, 1939.
56. Myrdal, *op. cit.*, II, 1298–1299.
57. Weaver, *op. cit.*, p. 15.
58. *Ibid.*, chap. 5.
59. *Ibid.*, table, p. 80.
60. Drake and Cayton, *op. cit.*, p. 328.
61. See *National News Views*, 4th Quarter 1944, published by the Joint Labor-Management Committee of the National Smelting Company, Cleveland, Ohio.
62. Cf. *ibid.*, p. 1, a letter from a Negro technical sergeant in New Guinea to the National Smelting Company regarding their antidiscrimination policy.
63. *The Central Area Social Study* (Cleveland), p. 132.
64. Drake and Cayton, *op. cit.*, p. 384.
65. *Ibid.*, pp. 604–605.
66. *Ibid.*, pp. 73–74.
67. See diagram in *ibid.*, p. 711, and discussion pp. 711–712 and 524 ff.
68. For a discussion of the more precise use of the class concept see *ibid.*, pp. 787–790.
69. Margaret Brenman, "The Relationship Between Minority Group Membership and Group Identification in a Group of Urban Middle Class Negro Girls," *Journal of Social Psychology* 11:171–197, 1940, pp. 182–183.
70. Drake and Cayton, *op. cit.*, chap. 20.
71. Brenman, *The Personality of Urban Negro Girls*, p. 8. Schomburg Collection.
72. Drake and Cayton, *op. cit.*, pp. 611 ff.
73. *Ibid.*, p. 616.
74. *Ibid.*, p. 583.

75. Brenman, *The Personality of Urban Negro Girls*, p. 39. Schomburg Collection.
76. Drake and Cayton, *op. cit.*, pp. 608–609.
77. *Ibid.*, pp. 611 ff.
78. *Ibid.*, p. 615.
79. *Ibid.*, pp. 655–656.
80. *Ibid.*, pp. 661–662.
81. *Ibid.*, p. 689.
82. Brenman, "The Relationship Between Minority Group Membership and Group Identification," pp. 182–183.
83. Drake and Cayton, *op. cit.*, pp. 496–497.
84. Otto Klineberg, ed., *Characteristics of the American Negro*, New York, Harper, 1944, p. 366.
85. Drake and Cayton, *op. cit.*, p. 531.
86. *Ibid.*, p. 537.
87. *Ibid.*, pp. 534, 548.
88. *Ibid.*, p. 698.
89. *Ibid.*, p. 530.
90. *Ibid.*, p. 552.
91. *Ibid.*, p. 557.
92. *Ibid.*, p. 558.
93. *Ibid.*, p. 553.

94, 95, and 96. *Ibid.*, pp. 550–560 *passim.*

CHAPTER 8. NEGRO MILITANCY

1. This is paraphrased from Adam Clayton Powell, Jr., *Marching Blacks*, New York, Dial Press, 1945, chap. 6.
2. Karl Mannheim, *Man and Society in an Age of Reconstruction*, New York, Harcourt Brace, 1940, p. 130.
3. Kimball Young, *Social Psychology*, 2nd ed., New York, Crofts, 1944, p. 409.
4. Mannheim, *op. cit.*, p. 125.
5. *Ibid.*, p. 132.
6. *Idem.*
7. *Idem.*
8. See Chapter 5 above, especially note 46, the reference to Herbert Aptheker, *American Negro Slave Revolts*, New York, Columbia University Press, 1943.
9. See W. E. B. Du Bois, *Black Reconstruction*, New York, Harcourt Brace, 1935, and the more glamorized account in Howard Fast, *Freedom Road*, New York, Duell, Sloan and Pearce, 1944.
10. W. D. Weatherford and C. S. Johnson, *Race Relations*, Boston, Heath, 1934, p. 489.
11. *Negro Digest*, November, 1946, pp. 47–51.
12. Booker T. Washington, *Up From Slavery*, Chicago, Burt, 1901, pp. 221–222 and 223.
13. W. E. B. Du Bois, *The Souls of Black Folk*, Chicago, McClurg, 1929 ed., p. 51.
14. *Idem.*
15. See F. G. Detweiler, *The Negro Press in the United States*, Chicago, University of Chicago Press, 1922, p. 61.
16. *Idem.*
17. Gunnar Myrdal, *An American Dilemma*, New York, Harper, 1944, II, 837.
18. See W. E. B. Du Bois, *Dusk of Dawn*, New York, Harcourt Brace, 1940, pp. 87–95.
19. *Ibid.*, pp. 309 ff.
20. *Ibid.*, p. 193.
21. Ralph J. Bunche, *Conceptions and Ideologies of the Negro Problem, A Research Memorandum*, Carnegie-Myrdal Study, The Negro in America, 1940, p. 96. Schomburg Collection.
22. St. Clair Drake and Horace Cayton, *Black Metropolis*, New York, Harcourt Brace, 1945, p. 530.
23. See Myrdal, *op. cit.*, p. 837.
24. See for example, *The Urban League of Cleveland*, Twenty-eighth Annual Report, 1945, p. 6. This and other material from the Cleveland Urban League were very kindly supplied by Mr. Sidney Williams, former Executive Director.
25. "Succeed on Your Job," pamphlet prepared by the Urban League of Cleveland.

26. In the passage from Drake and Cayton (note 22 above) there is no mention whatever of the Urban League receiving contributions from upper class Negroes.
27. Du Bois, *Dusk of Dawn*, pp. 245 ff.
28. Roi Ottley, *New World A-Comin'*, Boston, Houghton Mifflin, 1943, p. 73.
29. Detweiler, *op. cit.*, p. 178.
30. *Ibid.*, p. 179.
31. *Ibid.*, p. 180.
32. Ottley, *op. cit.*, p. 71.
33. *Ibid.*, p. 73.
34. *Ibid.*, p. 75.
35. *Ibid.*, pp. 75–76.
36. *Ibid.*, p. 75.
37. *Ibid.*, pp. 79–80.
38. Du Bois, *Dusk of Dawn*, p. 278, and Myrdal, *op. cit.*, II, 749.
39. Myrdal, *op. cit.*, II, 748.
40. Ottley, *op. cit.*, chap. 7.
41. *Ibid.*, p. 99.
42. Myrdal, *op. cit.*, I, 313; Drake and Cayton, *op. cit.*, pp. 295–296, where it is called "Spend Your Money Where You Can Work" campaign.
43. Myrdal, *op. cit.*, II, 1261.
44. Personal communication with Mr. Sidney Williams (see note 24 above), who was instrumental in the St. Louis Movement.
45. *Ibid.*, and Myrdal, *op. cit.*, II, 1261.
46. Personal communication from Mr. Sidney Williams.
47. Ottley, *op. cit.*, p. 290.
48. See above, Chapter 7, p. 135.
49. A. Philip Randolph, "March on Washington Movement Presents Program for the Negro" in *What the Negro Wants*, ed. by Rayford W. Logan, Chapel Hill, University of North Carolina Press, 1944, pp. 144–145.
50. Ottley, *op. cit.*, p. 292.
51. Drake and Cayton, *op. cit.*, pp. 745–746.
52. Randolph, *op. cit.*, p. 135.
53. Doxey A. Wilkerson, "Freedom Through Victory in War and Peace" in *What the Negro Wants*, p. 210.
54. Myrdal, *op. cit.*, II, 1006. For an account of Negro morale during the war see C. S. Johnson and Associates, *To Stem This Tide*, Boston and Chicago, Pilgrim Press, 1943.
55. See article by F. D. Patterson of Tuskegee in *Negro Digest*, March 1946, pp. 75–77.
56. L. P. Edwards, *The Natural History of Revolution*, Chicago, University of Chicago Press, 1927, p. 35.
57. See Myrdal, *op. cit.*, I, chap. 1, pp. 8 ff.
58. See article by Carey McWilliams, "How the Negro Fared in the War," *Negro Digest*, May 1946, pp. 67–74.
59. For a vigorous disclaimer of this policy see Claude McKay, "Don't Blame Segregation" *Negro Digest*, January 1946, pp. 51–54.
60. See *Tab* for October 1946, p. 16, and Annual Report of the Cleveland N.A.A.C.P. for 1945, p. 5. The latter is supplied through the courtesy of Mr. Charles P. Lucas, Executive Secretary of the Cleveland Branch of the N.A.A.C.P.; see also a symposium, "Should Negroes Accept Jim Crow Hospitals?" in *Negro Digest*, March 1946, pp. 73–77, where President Patterson of Tuskegee takes an affirmative position.
61. Seymour J. Schoenfeld, *The Negro in the Armed Forces*, Washington, D.C., Associated Publishers, 1945, chap. 5.
62. *Ibid.*, chap. 4.
63. Johnson and Associates, *op. cit.*, p. 61.
64. B. T. McGraw and Frank S. Horne, "The House I Live in," *Opportunity*, Summer 1946, p. 126.
65. Fern Marja, "Co-racial Camp," *Negro Digest*, April 1946, pp. 41–42.
66. Stanley High, "Black Omens," *Saturday Evening Post*, May 21, 1938, p. 66.
67. Drake and Cayton, *op. cit.*, p. 115.
68. *Ibid.*, pp. 114 and 201.
69. Drake and Cayton, *op. cit.*, p. 417.
70. *Ibid.*, p. 115.
71. See *Pittsburgh Courier*, Ohio State Edition, October 19, 1946, page 1 on Republican leaders for an example.

72. McWilliams, "How the Negro Fared in the War," p. 73.
73. For a documented legal description, see Charles Mangum, *The Legal Status of the Negro*, Chapel Hill, University of North Carolina Press, 1940.
74. Drake and Cayton, *op. cit.*, pp. 182–190.
75. *Negro Digest*, February 1946, p. 36.
76. *Idem.*
77. See Carey McWilliams, "The House on 92nd St.," *The Nation*, June 8, 1946; and William E. Hill, "Racial Restrictive Covenants," *Opportunity*, Summer 1946, pp. 119 ff.
78. "The Negro Wants First Class Citizenship" in Logan, *op. cit.*, p. 14.
79. Earl Brown, "On the Eve of Violence," *Headlines and Pictures*, September 1946, pp. 5–6.
80. W. G. Carleton, "Ballot Revolution in Dixie," *Negro Digest*, August 1946, p. 66.
81. Brown, *op. cit.*, p. 13.
82. John H. Burma, "The Negro, Citizen Second-Class," *Opportunity*, Winter 1946, pp. 3–4.
83. McWilliams, "How the Negro Fared in the War," p. 71; and see below, Chapters 20–22.
84. Samuel M. Strong, "Negro-White Relations As Reflected in Social Types," *American Journal of Sociology*, July 1946, pp. 24, 29, and 30.
85. *Ibid.*, p. 26.
86. *Ibid.*, pp. 24–25.
87. *Ibid.*, p. 26.
88. *Ibid.*, p. 26; Drake and Cayton, *op. cit.*, p. 394, note.

CHAPTER 9. MEXICANS AND SPANISH AMERICANS

1. Thorstein Sellin, *Culture Conflict and Crime*, New York, Social Science Research Council, 1938, table, p. 77.
2. *Problems of a Changing Population*, Washington, D.C., National Resources Planning Board, 1938, p. 224.
3. *Sixteenth Census of the United States*, Series P–15, No. 1, June 9, 1942.
4. H. I. Priestley, *The Coming of the White Man*, History of American Life Series, New York, Macmillan, 1929, pp. 19–20.
5. Carolyn Zeleny, *Relations Between the Spanish-Americans and Anglo-Americans in New Mexico, A Study of Conflict and Accommodation in a Dual-Ethnic Relationship*. Dissertation for the Ph.D. degree in Sociology, Yale University, 1944, pp. iv and 124. The author is indebted to Miss Zeleny for the use of this unpublished manuscript.
6. Carey McWilliams, *Brothers Under the Skin*, Boston, Little Brown, 1943, p. 128.
7. *Idem.*
8. Zeleny, *op. cit.*, p. iv.
9. Quincy Guy Burris, "Latin Americans" in *One America*, ed. by Francis J. Brown and Joseph S. Roucek, New York, Prentice-Hall, 1945, p. 347. It should be noted that this figure includes those from South and Central America and the West Indies, but this hardly affects the general accuracy of the estimates, since the three groups named are only 5 per cent of the total throughout the country. In the Southwest their proportion is probably less. Cf. *ibid.*, p. 346.
10. *Ibid.*, p. 346.
11. Preston E. James, *Latin America*, New York, Odyssey Press, 1942, p. 596.
12. *Ibid.*, p. 597.
13. Zeleny, *op. cit.*, p. 29.
14. *Ibid.*, p. 38.
15. *Ibid.*, iv.
16. Ruth Tuck, *Not With the Fist, Mexican-Americans In A Southern City*, New York, Harcourt Brace, 1946, p. 67.
17. *Ibid.*, p. 65.

18. Zeleny, *op. cit.*, p. iv.
19. *Idem.*
20. McWilliams, *op. cit.*, p. 128.
21. Zeleny, *op. cit.*, pp. 211–247.
22. McWilliams, *op. cit.*, p. 128.
23. Zeleny, *op. cit.*, p. 324.
24. *Ibid.*, p. 339.
25. See Chapter 4 above.
26. George L. Sanchez, *Forgotten People, A Study of New Mexicans*, Albuquerque, N.M., 1940, p. 61.
27. *Ibid.*, p. 60.
28. Sigurd Johansen, "Family Organization In a Spanish-American Culture Area," *Sociology and Social Research* 28:123–131, 1943.
29. Sanchez, *op. cit.*, p. 64.
30. Charles P. Loomis, "A Cooperative Health Association in Spanish-Speaking Villages," *American Sociological Review* 10:149–157, 1945.
31. Sanchez, *op. cit.*, pp. 66–67.
32. *Ibid.*, p. 24.
33. *Ibid.*, pp. 31–32.
34. Zeleny, *op. cit.*, p. 295.
35. Sanchez, *op. cit.*, p. 31.
36. *Ibid.*, p. 32.
37. *Ibid.*, p. 75.
38. Zeleny, *op. cit.*, pp. 201–205.
39. *Ibid.*, p. 275.
40. *Ibid.*, pp. 290–292.
41. *Ibid.*, pp. 306–329.
42. *Ibid.*, p. 327.
43. *Ibid.*, p. 329.
44. *Ibid.*, p. 330.
45. E. D. M. Gray, *The Spanish Language in New Mexico, A National Resource*, Bulletin of the University of New Mexico, 1912, quoted in Zeleny, *op. cit.*, p. 299.
46. McWilliams, *op. cit.*, pp. 144–145.
47. Tuck, *op. cit.*, p. 56.
48. Manuel Gamio, *Mexican Immigration to the United States*, Chicago, University of Chicago Press, 1930, p. 10.
49. *Ibid.*, pp. 7–8.
50. James, *op. cit.*, p. 602.
51. *Idem.*
52. Manuel Gamio, *The Mexican Immigrant, His Life Story*, Chicago, University of Chicago Press, 1931, pp. 187, 205, 214–215, 217, 259.
53. Gamio, *Mexican Immigration to the United States*, pp. 22–23. Henceforth referred to as *Mexican Immigration.*
54. *Ibid.*, p. 165.
55. *Ibid.*, p. 27 and Tuck, *op. cit.*, p. 60.
56. Tuck, *idem.*
57. *Ibid.*, p. 58.
58. Gamio, *Mexican Immigration*, p. 11.
59. E. S. Bogardus, "Current Problems of Mexican Immigrants," *Sociology and Social Research* 25:166–174, 1940–1941.
60. Tuck, *op. cit.*, p. 60.
61. Gamio, *Mexican Immigration*, chap. 3, and Tuck, *op. cit.*, chap. 3.
62. Tuck, *op. cit.*, esp. pp. 79 ff.
63. *Ibid.*, p. 68.
64. *Idem.*
65. Gamio, *Mexican Immigration*, p. 42.
66. Tuck, *op. cit.*, p. 83.
67. Norman D. Humphrey, "The Changing Structure of the Detroit Mexican Family, An Index of Acculturation," *American Sociological Review*, 9:622–626, esp. p. 625.
68. Tuck, *op. cit.*, p. 84.
69. *Ibid.*, p. 84.
70. *Ibid.*, pp. 84–85.
71. *Ibid.*, p. 85.
72. Norman S. Hayner, "Notes on the Changing Mexican Family," *American Sociological Review* 7:489–497, esp. pp. 489–490.
73. Tuck, *op. cit.*, p. 85.
74. *Ibid.*, p. 76.
75. *Ibid.*, pp. 79–81.
76. Gamio, *Mexican Immigration*, p. 111 passim.
77. Tuck, *op. cit.*, p. 81.
78. Gamio, *Mexican Immigration*, p. 41.
79. Tuck, *op. cit.*, p. 81.
80. *Ibid.*, pp. 80 and 132.

81. Gamio, *Mexican Immigration*, p. 148.
82. Tuck, *op. cit.*, p. 89.
83. Gamio, *Mexican Immigration*, pp. 41–42.
84. Tuck, *op. cit.*, p. 99.
85. See life histories in Gamio, *The Mexican Immigrant*, chap. 3.
86. Tuck, *op. cit.*, p. 97.
87. *Ibid.*, p. 125.
88. Humphrey, *op. cit.*, p. 626.
89. Tuck, *op. cit.*, p. 131.
90. *Ibid.*, pp. 125 and 131.
91. *Ibid.*, p. 118.
92. *Idem.*
93. *Idem.*
94. *Ibid.*, pp. 133–134.
95. *Ibid.*, p. 137.
96. Agnes E. Meyer, "Southwest Farms Encourage Child Labor, Illegal Entry," *Pan American News*, August 1, 1946, p. 3.
97. *Idem.*
98. Cf. *Mexican Migratory Workers of South Texas*, Washington, D.C., Federal Works Agency, Work Projects Administration, Division of Research, 1941, esp. the map p. 29.
99. Henry Hill Collins, *America's Own Refugees, Our 4,000,000 Homeless Migrants*, Princeton, Princeton University Press, 1941; and Carey McWilliams, *Ill Fares the Land; Migrants and Migratory Labor in the United States*, Boston, Little Brown, 1942.
100. Carey McWilliams, "Mexicans to Michigan," *Common Ground* 2:5–18, Autumn 1941.
101. Interviews with members of the Mexican American community at Lorain, Ohio.
102. Tuck, *op. cit.*, p. 133.
103. Humphrey, *op. cit.*, p. 626.
104. Tuck, *op. cit.*, p. 117.
105. *Ibid.*, p. xii.
106. Gamio, *Mexican Immigration*, p. 53.
107. H. T. Manuel, *Comments on the Education of Spanish-Speaking Ancestry in Texas*, Mimeographed Report, Conference on the Problems of Education Among Spanish-Speaking Population of our Southwest, Santa Fe, New Mexico, 1943, p. 1.
108. *Idem.*
109. McWilliams, "The Forgotten Mexican," *Common Ground* 3:65–78, 1942–1943, p. 69.
110. See this chapter above p. 182 and *Committee Reports* of the Conference on Educational Problems in the Southwest with Special Reference to the Educational Problems in Spanish-Speaking Communities, Santa Fe, N.M., 1943, pp. 9–10 (Mimeographed).
111. McWilliams, "The Forgotten Mexican," p. 69.
112. Pauline R. Kibbe, *Latin Americans in Texas*, Albuquerque, University of New Mexico Press, 1946, p. 132.
113. *Idem.*
114. For a fuller account see McWilliams, "The Zoot-Suit Riots," *New Republic* 108: 818–820, 1943; and "Los Angeles Pachuco Gangs," *New Republic* 107:76–77, 1943.
115. Tuck, *op. cit.*, p. 214.
116. *Idem.*
117. Donald R. Taft, *Criminology*, New York, Macmillan, 1942, pp. 88–89.
118. Tuck, *op. cit.*, p. xiii.
119. *Ibid.*, p. 102.
120. *Ibid.*, p. 90.
121. *Ibid.*, p. 92.
122. *Ibid.*, pp. 139–142.
123. Daniel L. Schorr, "'Reconverting' Mexican-Americans," *New Republic*, September 30, 1946, pp. 412–413.
124. Burris, *op. cit.*, p. 351.
125. Tuck, *op. cit.*, p. 222.
126. *Ibid.*, p. 218.
127. *Ibid.*, p. 219.
128. Robert C. Jones, "Mexican Youth in the United States," *The American Teacher*, 28, No. 6:11–15, March 1944, p. 14.
129. Tuck, *op. cit.*, p. 148.
130. *Ibid.*, pp. 146–147.
131. *Ibid.*, p. 147.
132. *Ibid.*, pp. 169–171.

133. *Ibid.*, p. 171.
134. Jones, *op. cit.*, p. 15.
135. Tuck, *op. cit.*, p. 135.
136. *Ibid.*, pp. 132, 135.
137. *Ibid.*, p. 137.
138. Jones, *op. cit.*, p. 15.
139. Tuck, *op. cit.*, pp. 160–161.
140. Tuck, *op. cit.*, pp. 161–162.
141. *Ibid.*, p. 160.
142. *Ibid.*, p. 162.
143. Cf. *The Lulac News* for April 1946, pp. 5 ff.
144. *Ibid.*, p. 15.
145. *Pan American News*, Denver, Col., August 1, 1946, p. 1. Copies of the Pan American News were furnished through the courtesy of Mrs. Helen Peterson, Secretary, The Community Service Clubs.
146. Cf. *Alianza*, Tucson, Arizona, for February, April, June, and September–October 1946.
147. Robert C. Jones, *Mexican War Workers in the United States*, Washington, D.C., Pan-American Union, 1945, pp. 2–3.
148. *Ibid.*, p. 2.
149. *Ibid.*, p. 39.

CHAPTER 10. JAPANESE AMERICANS

1. Excerpt from student manuscript of Mary Furusho (Baldwin-Wallace College), October 22, 1945. In author's files.
2. John F. Embree, *The Japanese Nation, A Social Survey*, New York, Farrar and Rinehart, 1945, p. 10.
3. *Idem.*
4. *Ibid.*, pp. 9–10.
5. *Ibid.*, p. 10.
6. *Ibid.*, p. 11.
7. Ruth Benedict, *The Chrysanthemum and the Sword, Patterns of Japanese Culture*, Boston, Houghton Mifflin, 1946, pp. 99–101.
8. *Ibid.*, p. 115.
9. *Ibid.*, pp. 103–104.
10. *Ibid.*, p. 52.
11. *Ibid.*, pp. 52–55.
12. *Ibid.*, pp. 115–116.
13. *Ibid.*, pp. 133–135.
14. *Ibid.*, p. 141.
15. *Ibid.*, pp. 145–147.
16. Frederick S. Hulse, "A Sketch of Japanese Society," *Journal of the American Oriental Society* 66:219–229, July–September 1946, p. 219.
17. Benedict, *op. cit.*, pp. 48–49.
18. Hulse, *op. cit.*, p. 223.
19. Benedict, *op. cit.*, p. 233.
20. *Ibid.*, pp. 254, 273–274, 288.
21. *Ibid.*, p. 223.
22. *Ibid.*, p. 151.
23. *Ibid.*, p. 222.
24. Hulse, *op. cit.*, p. 221.
25. Carey McWilliams, *Prejudice, Japanese Americans: Symbol of Racial Intolerance*, Boston, Little Brown, 1945, p. 79.
26. *Ibid.*, pp. 79–80.
27. *Ibid.*, p. 80.
28. Hulse, *op. cit.*, p. 221.
29. Robert Park and Herbert A. Miller, *Old World Traits Transplanted*, Society for Social Research, University of Chicago, New York, Harper, 1921, pp. 167–168.
30. *Ibid.*, p. 170.
31. H. P. Fairchild, ed., *Immigrant Backgrounds*, New York, Wiley, 1927, pp. 189–190.
32. Benedict, *op. cit.*, p. 293.
33. McWilliams, *op. cit.*, pp. 16 ff.
34. *Ibid.*, p. 81.
35. Fairchild, *op. cit.*, p. 195.
36. Quoted from a letter in J. F. Steiner's article, "Some Factors Involved in Minimizing Race Friction on the Pacific Coast," *Annals of the Ameri-*

can Academy of Political and Social Science 93:116–120, 1921, p. 117.

37. James D. Phelan, "Why California Objects to the Japanese Invasion," *Annals*, p. 17.
38. E. K. Strong, Jr., *Japanese in California*, Stanford University Publications, University Series, Education-Psychology, vol. I, no. 2, Stanford University, Stanford University Press, 1933, p. 116.
39. Col. John P. Irish, "The Japanese Issue in California," *Annals*, *op. cit.*, p. 75.
40. Fairchild, *op. cit.*, 191.
41. B. J. O. Schrieke, *Alien Americans, A Study of Race Relations*, New York, Viking, 1936, pp. 15 and 23.
42. Yamato Ichihashi, *Japanese in the United States*, Stanford University, Stanford University Press, 1932, pp. 4–5.
43. *Ibid.*, pp. 81–82 and 89.
44. *Ibid.*, pp. 88–89.
45. *Ibid.*, p. 87.
46. *Ibid.*, pp. 44–45.
47. Forrest E. LaViolette, *Americans of Japanese Ancestry, A Study of Assimilation in the American Community*, Toronto, Canadian Institute of International Affairs, 1945, p. 10.
48. Ichihashi, *op. cit.*, pp. 68–69.
49. Carey McWilliams, *Brothers Under the Skin*, Boston, Little Brown, 1943, p. 151.
50. Annual Report of the U.S. Commissioner-General of Immigration, 1908, pp. 125–126.
51. Ichihashi, *op. cit.*, p. 57.
52. LaViolette, *op. cit.*, p. 13.
53. McWilliams, *Brothers Under the Skin*, chap. 2, pp. 97 ff.
54. H. A. Millis, *The Japanese Problem in the United States*, New York, Macmillan, 1915, p. 23.
55. McWilliams, *Prejudice*, pp. 40 ff.
56. Maurice R. Davie, *World Immigration, with Special Reference to the United States*, New York, Macmillan, 1936, p. 323.
57. Ichihashi, *op. cit.*, p. 63.
58. Davie, *op. cit.*, pp. 323–324.
59. Ichihashi, *op. cit.*, p. 196.
60. Constantine Panunzio, *Immigration Crossroads*, New York, Macmillan, 1927, chap. 7, "Grave Consequences."
61. P. J. Treat, *The Far East*, New York, Harper, 1928, pp. 216–217.
62. McWilliams, *Prejudice*, p. 68; and *Brothers Under the Skin*, p. 153.
63. LaViolette, *op. cit.*, pp. 5, 11–12, 39, and 152 ff.
64. *Ibid.*, pp. 19 ff.
65. *Ibid.*, pp. 24–25.
66. *Ibid.*, pp. 49–51.
67. *Ibid.*, pp. 111–115.
68. R. H. Ross and E. S. Bogardus, "Four Types of *Nisei* Marriage Patterns," *Sociology and Social Research* 25:63–66, 1940–1941.
69. LaViolette, *op. cit.*, pp. 119–120.
70. LaViolette, *op. cit.*, p. 120.
71. *Ibid.*, 122.
72. *Ibid.*, 128.
73. *Ibid.*, 132.
74. E. K. Strong, Jr., *The Second Generation Japanese Problem*, Stanford University, Stanford University Press, 1934, pp. 177–179.
75. *Ibid.*, pp. 185–189.
76. Dorothy Swaine Thomas and Richard S. Nishimoto, *The Spoilage, Japanese American Evacuation and Resettlement*, Berkeley and Los Angeles, University of California Press, 1946, p. 2.
77. Park and Miller, *op. cit.*, p. 179.
78. B. Schrieke, *op. cit.*, pp. 42–43. The statement on the discontinuance of the *gakuins* has been furnished the writer by Dr. Frank Herron Smith, of the Protestant Church Commission for Japanese Service.
79. LaViolette, *op. cit.*, pp. 65–66.
80. *Ibid.*, pp. 66–68.
81. *Ibid.*, p. 68.
82. *Ibid.*, p. 38.
83. *Ibid.*, p. 37.
84. McWilliams, *Prejudice*, p. 84.

85. McWilliams, *Brothers Under the Skin*, p. 164.
86. *Ibid.*, p. 166.
87. McWilliams, *Prejudice*, p. 86.
88. Leonard Bloom, "Familial Adjustments of Japanese Americans to Relocation: First Phase," *American Sociological Review* 8:551–560, table on p. 553.
89. LaViolette, *op. cit.*, pp. 151–157.
90. *Ibid.*, p. 155.
91. S. Frank Miyamoto, "Immigrants and Citizens of Japanese Origin," *Annals* 223:107–113, September, 1942, p. 110.
92. War Relocation Authority, Great Lakes Area, News Letter, May 15, 1946, p. 4.
93. Miyamoto, *op. cit.*, p. 111.
94. McWilliams, *Prejudice*, p. 114.
95. *Ibid.*, 112.
96. *Ibid.*, p. 138.
97. Bradford Smith, "The Great American Swindle," *Common Ground*, Winter 1947, pp. 34–38, esp. p. 35. Also cf. Toru Matsumoto, *Beyond Prejudice*, New York, Friendship Press, 1946, p. 21.
98. See Mine Okubo, *Citizen 13660*, New York, Columbia University Press, 1946, p. 35. This pictorial account of evacuation, with drawings, is unusually vivid.
99. Thomas and Nishimoto, *op. cit.*, p. 22.
100. *Ibid.*, p. 27.
101. Okubo, *op. cit.*, p. 128 and 143; also Leonard Bloom, *op. cit.*, p. 558.
102. Alexander H. Leighton, *The Governing of Men*, Princeton, Princeton University Press, 1945, p. 95.
103. Thomas and Nishimoto, *op. cit.*, p. 21.
104. See copies of their publication *The Pacific Citizen* (edited by Larry Tajiri, in Salt Lake City) from 1945 on for clear evidence of their growing strength.
105. Thomas and Nishimoto, *op. cit.*, p. 44.
106. Leighton, *op. cit.*, p. 123.
107. Bloom, *op. cit.*, p. 559.
108. Jim Yamada, "Report from Poston," *Trek*, June 1943, p. 36. *Trek* was a relocation periodical published at Topaz Relocation Center in Utah.
109. Bloom, *op. cit.*, pp. 558–560.
110. *Idem.*
111. LaViolette, *op. cit.*, p. 175.
112. Thomas and Nishimoto, *op. cit.*, pp. 57, 62–63, 85, 88–91, and 94–95 with 350–358.
113. *Ibid.*, pp. 58–59, note.
114. *Pacific Citizen*, October 12, 1946, p. 3, "Federal Judge Raps Treatment of *Nisei* Group During War," and October 26, 1946, p. 1, "Civil Liberties Union Files Suit for Restoration of Rights Renounced by *Nisei* in Camp."
115. Supplied by Prof. Miyakawa.
116. Thomas and Nishimoto, *op. cit.*, p. 35.
117. *Idem.*
118. Yamada, *op. cit.*, p. 36. For a graphic documentary of one school see M. L. Ramsdell, "A Star is Something to Steer By," *Antioch Review*, 6:78–98, Spring 1946.
119. Matsumoto, *op. cit.*, pp. 58–59.
120. Berta Choda, "A Counselling Program in a Relocation Center," *The Family* 27:140–145, June 1946, p. 140.
121. Taro Katayama, "State of the City," *Trek*, December 1942, p. 10.
122. *Idem.*
123. Leighton, *op. cit.*, p. 141.
124. Katayama, *op. cit.*, pp. 10–11.
125. Matsumoto, *op. cit.*, chap. 5.
126. Dillon S. Myer, "Japanese American Relocation: Final Chapter," *Common Ground*, Autumn 1945, p. 61.
127. *Ibid.*, p. 66.
128. Bill Hosokawa, "From the Frying Pan," *Pacific Citizen*, September 14, 1946, p. 5.
129. W.R.A. Great Lakes Area News Letter, *op. cit.*, p. 4.
130. *Pacific Citizen*, December 21, 1946, pp. 4–5.
131. *Ibid.*, p. 11.
132. *Ibid.*, pp. 4–5.
133. Mary Furusho, student manuscript.

134. For actual examples see Bradford Smith, "Legalized Blackmail," *Common Ground* 8, No. 2:34–36, 1948.
135. S. Frank Miyamoto and Robert O'Brien, *A Survey of Some Changes in the Seattle Japanese Community Resulting from the Evacuation* (Mimeograph), 1947. The writer is indebted to Professor Miyamoto for making this document available.

CHAPTER 11. ITALO-AMERICANS

1. Adapted from an assimilation study by Orrie Van de Visse in Cleveland, Ohio.
2. See Chapter 2 above.
3. Constantine Panunzio, *Immigration Crossroads*, New York, Macmillan, 1927, pp. 34–36.
4. *Ibid.*, pp. 33 and 36.
5. The expression comes from the Democratic platform of 1856. *Ibid.*, pp. 28–29.
6. *Ibid.*, p. 29.
7. *Ibid.*, p. 43.
8. *Ibid.*, pp. 44–45.
9. *Ibid.*, p. 45.
10. *Idem.*
11. See table in M. R. Davie, *World Immigration, with Special Reference to the United States*, New York, Macmillan, 1936, p. 52, and discussion in chaps. 3 and 4.
12. *Ibid.*, p. 376.
13. See Louis Adamic, *A Nation of Nations*, New York, Harper, 1944, Preface.
14. *Ibid.*, p. 7.
15. Davie, *op. cit.*, table, p. 107.
16. Edward Corsi, "Italian Immigrants and Their Children," *Annals* 223:100–106, September 1942, p. 100, n. 2.
17. Davie, *op. cit.*, p. 66.
18. See table in F. J. Brown and J. S. Roucek, *One America*, New York, Prentice-Hall, 1945, p. 9.
19. *Ibid.*, p. 259.
20. Antonio Stella, *Some Aspects of Italian Immigration to the United States*, New York, Putnam, 1924, p. 13.
21. *Ibid.*, p. 12.
22. See Max Ascoli, "The Italian Americans" in R. M. MacIver, ed., *Group Relations and Group Antagonisms*, New York, Harper, 1944, p. 32.
23. Francis J. Brown, "Italian-Americans" in Brown and Roucek, *op. cit.*, p. 263.
24. Corsi, *op. cit.*, p. 100.
25. Brown and Roucek, *op. cit.*, p. 263.
26. Corsi, *op. cit.*, p. 101.
27. Konrad Bercovici, *On New Shores*, New York, Century, 1925, pp. 86–87.
28. Robert F. Foerster, *The Italian Emigration of Our Times*, Cambridge, Harvard University Press, 1919, pp. 382–383.
29. Giovanni E. Schiavo, *The Italians in Chicago, A Study in Americanization*, Chicago, Italian American Publishing Co., 1928, p. 41.
30. *Ibid.*, p. 52.
31. Leonard Covello, *The Social Background of the Italo-American School Child, A Study of the Southern Italian Family Mores and Their Effect on the School Situation in Italy and America.* Ph.D. Thesis, New York University, 1944, pp. 22–23.
32. *Ibid.*, p. 44.
33. *Ibid.*, pp. 54–55.
34. *Ibid.*, p. 144. Also cf. Jerre Mangione, *Mount Allegro*, Boston, Houghton Mifflin, 1942, p. 263.
35. Foerster, *op. cit.*, p. 57.
36. *Ibid.*, p. 65.
37. *Ibid.*, pp. 66–67.
38. Covello, *op. cit.*, pp. 108, 144.
39. *Ibid.*, p. 105.
40. *Ibid.*, p. 88.
41. *Ibid.*, p. 95.
42. *Ibid.*, p. 78.
43. *Ibid.*, p. 84.

44. Paul Radin, *The Italians of San Francisco, Their Adjustment and Acculturation*, Abstract from the S.E.R.A. Project, Cultural Anthropology, San Francisco, 1935, p. 43.
45. Foerster, *op. cit.*, pp. 77 and 81.
46. Covello, *The Italians in New York City*, MS., 1947. The author is indebted to Dr. Covello for this and other important documents.
47. Davie, *op. cit.*, p. 112.
48. Foerster, *op. cit.*, p. 50.
49. Davie, *op. cit.*, p. 111.
50. Carl Wittke, *We Who Built America*, New York, Prentice-Hall, 1940, p. 437.
51. Covello, *Italians in New York City*, p. 3.
52. Covello, *Social Background*, p. 95.
53. *Ibid.*, p. 126.
54. *Ibid.*, p. 74.
55. *Ibid.*, pp. 115–116.
56. *Ibid.*, p. 111.
57. *Ibid.*, p. 113.
58. *Ibid.*, p. 82.
59. *Ibid.*, pp. 97, 223.
60. *Ibid.*, p. 122.
61. *Ibid.*, pp. 123–124.
62. *Ibid.*, p. 137.
63. Foerster, *op. cit.*, p. 102.
64. Covello, *Social Background*, p. 236.
65. *Ibid.*, pp. 237 and 247.
66. *Ibid.*, pp. 240–241.
67. *Ibid.*, p. 241.
68. *Ibid.*, p. 270.
69. *Ibid.*, p. 272.
70. *Ibid.*, p. 282.
71. *Ibid.*, p. 274.
72. *Ibid.*, p. 292.
73. *Ibid.*, p. 294.
74. *Ibid.*, p. 249.
75. *Ibid.*, pp. 242–243.
76. Phyllis H. Williams, *South Italian Folkways in Europe and America*, New Haven, Yale University Press, 1938, pp. 81 and 83.
77. Covello, *Social Background*, p. 332.
78. *Ibid.*, p. 323.
79. *Idem.*
80. *Ibid.*, p. 306.
81. *Ibid.*, p. 339.
82. *Ibid.*, p. 374.
83. *Ibid.*, p. 349.
84. *Ibid.*, p. 347.
85. *Ibid.*, p. 346.
86. *Ibid.*, p. 338.
87. *Ibid.*, pp. 340–341.
88. *Ibid.*, p. 341.
89. *Ibid.*, p. 330.
90. *Ibid.*, pp. 328–329.
91. *Ibid.*, p. 348.
92. *Ibid.*, p. 363.
93. Foerster, *op. cit.*, p. 85.
94. Covello, *Social Background*, p. 294.
95. *Ibid.*, pp. 295–296.
96. *Ibid.*, pp. 296–297.
97. Covello, *The Italians in New York City*, p. 13.
98. Williams, *op. cit.*, pp. 9–11.
99. *Ibid.*, p. 9.
100. Covello, *Social Background*, p. 265.
101. Foerster, *op. cit.*, p. 96.
102. Covello, *Social Background*, pp. 394–397.
103. *Ibid.*, p. 393.
104. Foerster, *op. cit.*, p. 460.
105. Covello, *Social Background*, p. 399.
106. *Ibid.*, p. 390.
107. *Idem.*
108. *Ibid.*, p. 402.
109. Foerster, *op. cit.*, p. 97.
110. Covello, *Social Background*, p. 165.
111. J. J. Blunt, *Vestiges of Ancient Rites and Customs in Modern Italy and Sicily*, London, John Murray, 1823, quoted in Antonio Mangano, *Sons of Italy*, New York, Missionary Education Movement, 1917, pp. 76–77.
112. Williams, *op. cit.*, p. 136.
113. Bruno Roselli, "The Italians" in H. P. Fairchild, ed., *Immigrant Backgrounds*, New York, Wiley, 1927, pp. 108–109.

114. Williams, *op. cit.*, p. 143.
115. *Ibid.*, p. 144.
116. *Idem.*
117. *Ibid.*, pp. 108, 138, and 151.
118. Covello, *Italians in New York City*, p. 17.
119. Covello, *Social Background*, p. 213.
120. *Ibid.*, p. 208.
121. Mangione, *op. cit.*, p. 71.
122. Williams, *op. cit.*, pp. 140–141.
123. Roselli, *op. cit.*, pp. 106–107.
124. R. E. Park and H. A. Miller, *Old World Traits Transplanted*, Chicago, Society for Social Research, University of Chicago, 1925, p. 10.
125. Mangione, *op. cit.*, p. 195.
126. Gaetano Mosca, "Mafia" in *Encyclopedia of the Social Sciences*, New York, Macmillan, 1937, X, 36–37.
127. Schiavo, *op. cit.*, p. 29.
128. Foerster, *op. cit.*, p. 425n.
129. *Ibid.*, p. 422.
130. Covello, *Social Background*, p. 144.
131. Schiavo, *op. c t.*, p. 29.
132. *Ibid.*, p. 19.
133. Foerster, *op. cit.*, p. 434.
134. Pascal D'Angelo, *Pascal D'Angelo, Son of Italy*, New York, Macmillan, 1924, p. 83.
135. Foerster, *op cit.*, p. 425n.
136. *Ibid.*, pp. 435–436 and Roselli, *op. cit.*, p. 89.
137. Mangione, *op. cit.*, p. 146.
138. Eloise Griffith, "A Social Worker Looks at Italians," *Journal of Educational Sociology*, 5:172–177, 1931, p. 175.
139. David Efron, *Gesture and Environment*, New York, King's Crown Press, 1941, chap. 3.
140. Irvin L. Child, *Italian or American? The Second Generation in Conflict*, New Haven, Yale University Press, 1943, pp. 33–34.
141. Davie, *op. cit.*, p. 225.
142. *Ibid.*, p. 467.
143. D'Angelo, *op. cit.*, p. 112.
144. Schiavo, *op. cit.*, pp. 36–37.
145. Niles Carpenter, *Immigrants and Their Children*, Washington, D.C., Census Monograph VII, 1927, pp. 234–245.
146. Julius Drachsler, *Democracy and Assimilation*, New York, Macmillan, 1920, pp. 121–122.
147. Konrad Bercovici, *On New Shores*, New York, Century, 1925, p. 86.
148. W. F. Whyte, "Race Conflicts in the North End of Boston," *New England Quarterly* 12:623–642, December 1939, pp. 626–627.
149. Radin, *op. cit.*, p. 92.
150. Philip M. Rose, *The Italians in America*, New York, Doran, 1922, p. 61.
151. Park and Miller, *op. cit.*, p. 146.
152. *Ibid.*, pp. 147–148.
153. Child, *op. cit.*, p. 23.
154. W. C. Smith, *Americans in the Making*, New York, Appleton-Century, 1939, pp. 100–101.
155. Giovanni Schiavo, *The Italians in Missouri*, Chicago and New York, Italian-American Publishing Co., 1929, p. 65.
156. Radin, *op. cit.*, p. 16.
157. Schiavo, *The Italians in Chicago*, p. 125.
158. *Idem., passim.*
159. *The Italians of New York, A Survey Prepared by Workers of the Federal Writers Project, W.P.A. in the city of New York*, New York, Random House, 1938, pp. 54–55.
160. *Idem*, and E. H. Sutherland, *Principles of Criminology*, Philadelphia, Lippincott, 1939, 3rd ed., pp. 124–125.
161. W. H. Seabrook, *These Foreigners*, New York, Harcourt Brace, 1938, p. 168.
162. Panunzio, *op. cit.*, p. 262.
163. Foerster, *op. cit.*, pp. 398–399.
164. Adamic, *op. cit.*, p. 34.
165. Roselli, *op. cit.*, p. 104.
166. Schiavo, *The Italians in Chicago*, p. 75
167. Williams, *op. cit.*, p. 147.

168. Child, *op. cit.*, p. 34 and Roselli, *op. cit.*, pp. 104–105.
169. Williams, *op. cit.*, pp. 146–147.
170. Schiavo, *The Italians in Chicago*, pp. 107–108. For a similar list see Davie, *op. cit.*, p. 504.
171. *Interpreter Releases, An Information Service on Immigration, Naturalization, and the Foreign-born*, Common Council for American Unity, 224 Fourth Ave., New York City, Vol. 20, No. 11, Series C, No. 4, March 23, 1943, p. 84.
172. Corsi, *op. cit.*, p. 104.
173. Child, *op. cit.*, p. 46.
174. Information furnished by Mrs. Domenic Grillo, Cleveland, Ohio.
175. Child, *op. cit.*, p. 33.
176. Rose, *op. cit.*, p. 87.
177. Covello, *Social Background*, pp. 455, 457–458.
178. *Ibid.*, pp. 470–497.
179. *Ibid.*, p. 452.
180. John J. D'Alessandre, *Occupational Trends of Italians in New York City*, Bulletin No. 8, Casa Italiana Educational Bureau, Columbia University, 1935, p. 4.
181. *Ibid.*, pp. 7 and 9.
182. *Ibid.*, p. 13.
183. Bercovici, *op. cit.*, p. 85.
184. Radin, *op. cit.*, p. 59.
185. Bercovici, *op. cit.*, pp. 90 ff. and Seabrook, *op. cit.*, pp. 158 ff.
186. Bercovici, *op. cit.*, pp. 87–89.
187. For names, see Seabrook, *op. cit.*, pp. 117–120 and Corsi, *op. cit.*, p. 101.
188. Schiavo, *Italians in Chicago*, p. 116.
189. Covello, *The Italians in New York City*, p. 19.
190. *Ibid.*, pp. 22 and 23.
191. *Idem.*
192. Schiavo, *Italians in Chicago*, pp. 86–89.
193. Corsi, *op. cit.*, p. 102.
194. *The Italians of New York*, chap. 10.
195. Covello, *Social Background*, p. 503.
196. Rev. John V. Tolino, "The Future of the Italian American Problem," *Ecclesiastical Review* 101:221–232, 1939.
197. See E. V. Stonequist, *The Marginal Man*, New York, Scribner, 1937.
198. From a case history sent to the author by letter with the request that the identity remain unrevealed.
199. Child, *op. cit.*, pp. 71–72.
200. *Ibid.*, pp. 113–116.
201. *Ibid.*, pp. 146–149.
202. *Ibid.*, pp. 179–184.
203. See criticism by Mary Bosworth Treudley in "An Ethnic Group's View of the American Middle Class," *American Sociological Review* 11:715–724, 1946, pp. 721–722.
204. Noel P. Gist and L. A. Halbert, *Urban Society*, New York, Crowell, 1941, p. 191.
205. Covello, *Social Background*, p. 551.
206. Corsi, *op. cit.*, p. 103.
207. *Ibid.*, p. 103.
208. *Ibid.*, p. 104.
209. Jeanette Sayre Smith, "Broadcasting for Marginal Americans," *Public Opinion Quarterly* 6:588–603, 1942, p. 589.
210. J. S. Roucek, "The Foreign Language and Negro Press" in Brown and Roucek, *op. cit.*, p. 376.
211. Two figures are given for this: 695,363 and 665,000. The first is in *Interpreter Releases*, p. 28, the other in Corsi, *op. cit.*, p. 105n.
212. Corsi, *op. cit.*, p. 105n.
213. *Idem.*
214. *Ibid.*, p. 103.

CHAPTER 12. POLISH AMERICANS

1. Adapted from Edward Urban, "Two Worlds," *Common Ground* 3, No. 2: 91–94, 1943.
2. M. R. Davie, *World Immigration*, New York, Macmillan, 1936, p. 124.
3. Emily Balch, *Our Slavic Fellow Citi-*

zens, New York, Charities Publication Committee, 1910, p. 21.
4. Quoted in Balch, *op. cit.*, p. 21.
5. Balch, *op. cit.*, pp. 10–11.
6. William Seabrook, *These Foreigners*, New York, Harcourt Brace, 1938, p. 236.
7. Balch, *op. cit.*, p. 28.
8. See Louis Adamic, *Nation of Nations*, New York, Harper, 1944, chap. 12.
9. Miecislaus Haiman, *Polish Past in America, 1608–1865*, Chicago, Polish Roman Catholic Union Archives and Museum, 1939, p. 1.
10. Paul Fox, *The Poles in America*, New York, Doran, 1922, pp. 58–59.
11. Statement kindly supplied by Mr. Z. Dybowski, editor of the *Polish Daily News*, Cleveland, Ohio.
12. Cf. Chapter 18 below.
13. Fox, *op. cit.*, p. 58.
14. E. G. Olszyk, *The Polish Press in America*, M.A. Thesis, Milwaukee, Marquette University Press, 1940, p. 8.
15. Fox, *op. cit.*, pp. 61–62.
16. F. J. Brown and J. S. Roucek, *One America*, New York, Prentice-Hall, 1945, p. 137, and Stefan Wlosczewski, *History of Polish-American Culture*, Trenton, N.J., White Eagle Publishing Co., 1946, chap. 1.
17. Olszyk, *op. cit.*, p. 7.
18. See Chapter 11 above.
19. Olszyk, *op. cit.*, p. 7.
20. Florian Znaniecki, "The Poles" in H. P. Fairchild, ed., *Immigrant Backgrounds*, New York, Wiley, 1927, p. 201.
21. Fox, *op. cit.*, p. 60.
22. Lee Weilop Metzner, "Polish Pioneers of Kewaunee County," *Wisconsin Magazine of History* 18 : 269–80, March 1935.
23. W. I. Thomas and Florian Znaniecki, *The Polish Peasant in Europe and America*, New York, Knopf, 1927, I, 160–161.
24. *Ibid.*, p. 144.
25. *Ibid.*, p. 88.
26. *Ibid.*, p. 96.
27. *Ibid.*, pp. 92 and 95.
28. *Ibid.*, pp. 93–94.
29. *Ibid.*, pp. 107–110.
30. *Ibid.*, pp. 123–124.
31. *Ibid.*, pp. 149 and 286.
32. Information very kindly supplied the writer by Father J. W. Solinski, Berea, O.
33. Sister Mary Remigia Napolska, *The Polish Immigrant in Detroit to 1914*, Chicago, Polish Roman Catholic Union Archives and Museum, 1946, p. 64.
34. Thomas and Znaniecki, *op. cit.*, p. 285.
35. *Ibid.*, p. 143.
36. *Ibid.*, p. 275.
37. *Ibid.*, pp. 144–145.
38. *Ibid.*, pp. 133–134.
39. *Ibid.*, p. 141.
40. Balch, *op. cit.*, pp. 135–137.
41. *Ibid.*, pp. 228–230.
42. *Ibid.*, p. 231.
43. *Ibid.*, pp. 135–137.
44. Brown and Roucek, *op. cit.*, p. 137.
45. W. I. Thomas and F. Znaniecki, *The Polish Peasant in Europe and America*, Boston, Richard G. Badger, 1920, V, 33.
46. Thomas and Znaniecki, *op. cit.*, V, 29n and 67n.
47. Ed Falkowski, "Polonia to America," *Common Ground* 2, No. 1 : 28–36, 1941, p. 30.
48. *Idem.*
49. Thomas and Znaniecki, *op. cit.*, V, 103.
50. Falkowski, *op. cit.*, p. 30.
51. Thomas and Znaniecki, *op. cit.*, V, 63–64.
52. Napolska, *op. cit.*, p. 96.
53. Falkowski, *op. cit.*, p. 30.
54. Thomas and Znaniecki, *op. cit.*, V, 64.
55. *Ibid.*, p. 44.

56. Rev. Joseph Swastek, "The Poles in South Bend to 1914," *Polish-American Studies* 2:79–88, July–December 1945, p. 81.
57. Napolska, *op. cit.*, pp. 43–44.
58. Swastek, *op. cit.*, p. 82.
59. *Ibid.*, p. 81, and cf. also Constantin Symonolewicz' review of Rev. Francis Bolek's "The Intellectual Movement Among Polish-Americans," *Polish-American Studies* 2: 52–53, January–June 1945, p. 53.
60. Napolska, *op. cit.*, p. 65.
61. *Ibid.*, p. 66.
62. *Ibid.*, p. 83.
63. *Ibid.*, pp. 90–92.
64. Balch, *op. cit.*, Appendix 26, p. 477.
65. Fox, *op. cit.*, p. 93.
66. Quoted in Fox, *idem.*
67. Olszyk, *op. cit.*, pp. 25–26.
68. Thomas and Znaniecki, *op. cit.*, V, 65, and William Seabrook, *op. cit.*, p. 271.
69. *Poles of Chicago, 1837–1937, A History of One Century of Polish Contribution to the City of Chicago, Ill.* Chicago, Polish Pageant Inc., 1937, p. 150.
70. Thomas and Znaniecki, *op. cit.*, V, 117.
71. *Ibid.*, p. 113.
72. *Ibid.*, p. 117, and *Poles of Chicago*, p. 153.
73. Olszyk, *op. cit.*, p. 17.
74. *Poles of Chicago*, p. 6.
75. Thomas and Znaniecki, *op. cit.*, V, 122.
76. *Ibid.*, pp. 122–123.
77. Father Kruszka, quoted in Olszyk, *op. cit.*, p. 10.
78. Thomas and Znaniecki, *op. cit.*, V, 125.
79. Olszyk, *op. cit.*, pp. 16–17.
80. *Poles of Chicago*, p. 6.
81. Fox, *op. cit.*, p. 91.
82. "Preserving a Cultural Heritage," *Common Ground* 1, No. 4:116–117, 1941.
83. *Poles of Chicago*, pp. 159–160, and Swastek, *op. cit.*, p. 87.
84. Olszyk, *op. cit.*, p. 12.
85. *Ibid.*, p. 13.
86. *Ibid.*, p. 15.
87. *Ibid.*, p. 18.
88. *Ibid.*, p. 16.
89. *Ibid.*, p. 17.
90. *Ibid.*, p. 43.
91. *Ibid.*, pp. 48–49.
92. *Ibid.*, pp. 45, 48.
93. *Ibid.*, pp. 19–21.
94. *Ibid.*, pp. 35–40.
95. *Ibid.*, p. 64.
96. Konrad Bercovici, *On New Shores*, New York, Century, 1925, pp. 86–87.
97. D. D. Everett and F. Everett, "Black Acres," *National Geographic Magazine* 80:631–652, November 1941.
98. *Ibid.*, pp. 635, 651.
99. Edmund de S. Brunner, *Immigrant Farmers and Their Children*, Garden City, N.Y., Doubleday Doran, 1929, p. 216. This chapter on Sunderland, Mass., gives a summary of the Polish community and institutions as found in New England.
100. *Ibid.*, p. 221.
101. Seabrook, *op. cit.*, p. 263.
102. *Ibid.*, pp. 261–262.
103. Rev. Joseph Swastek, "What is a Polish-American?" *Polish-American Studies*, vol. I, ed. by Constantin Symonolewicz, New York, Polish Institute of Arts and Sciences in America, 1944, p. 38.
104. *Ibid.*, p. 38.
105. *Ibid.*, p. 37.
106. Seabrook, *op. cit.*, p. 259.
107. Napolska, *op. cit.*, pp. 69–70.
108. *Ibid.*, p. 39.
109. *Ibid.*, pp. 39–40.
110. Falkowski, *op. cit.*, p. 33.
111. *Ibid.*, p. 34.
112. Seabrook, *op. cit.*, p. 281.
113. *Ibid.*, p. 292.
114. Seabrook, *op. cit.*, pp. 289–290.

115. Thomas and Znaniecki, *op. cit.*, V, 221.
116. *Ibid.*, pp. 256–266.
117. *Ibid.*, pp. 319, 336, 338–339.
118. Lola Kinel, "Jozefa Kudlicka," *Common Ground* 1, No. 2:35–39, 1941, p. 38.
119. *Idem.*
120. Niles Carpenter and Daniel Katz, "A Study of Acculturization In the Polish Group of Buffalo," *University of Buffalo Studies*, vol. 7, June 1929, No. 4, pp. 103–133, p. 109.
121. *Ibid.*, p. 128.
122. *Ibid.*, p. 123.
123. *Idem.*
124. *Ibid.*, p. 124.
125. *Ibid.*, p. 125.
126. *Ibid.*, pp. 116 and 120.
127. Dr. Karol Wachtl, *Polonja w Ameryce*, Philadelphia, Polish Star Publishing Co., 1944, pp. 420, 422. This and relevant passages from Dr. Wachtl's work were kindly translated for the writer by Father J. W. Solinski.
128. Swastek: "What is a Polish-American?" p. 38.
129. *Ibid.*, p. 39.
130. Samuel Stouffer, "Trends in the Fertility of Catholics and Non-Catholics," *American Journal of Sociology* 41, No. 2:143–166, September 1935.
131. Gilbert Kelly Robinson, "The Catholic Birth Rate: Further Facts and Implications," *American Journal of Sociology* 41:757–766, May 1936, pp. 757–758.
132. "The Spirit of Poles in America," *Survey* 40:720–21, September 28, 1918, p. 721.
133. Brunner, *op. cit.*, p. 225.
134. Wachtl, *op. cit.*, p. 72.
135. Statement contributed by Father J. W. Solinski.
136. E. S. Bogardus, *Essentials of Americanization*, Los Angeles, University of Southern California Press, 1919, p. 150.
137. J. S. Roucek ed., *Central Eastern Europe*, New York, Prentice-Hall, 1946, chap. 18.
138. These figures were very kindly supplied by Mr. Z. Dybowski.
139. *Polish-American Congress Bulletin*, Chicago, February 1947, p. 17.
140. Wachtl, *op. cit.*, pp. 429 and 430.

CHAPTER 13. CZECH AND SLOVAK AMERICANS

1. See below pp. 307–8 ff. of this Chapter.
2. Milan W. Jerabek, *Czechs in Minnesota*, M.A. Thesis, University of Minnesota, 1939, pp. 9–10 (quoted from Count Lutzow, *Bohemia*, pp. 206, 218, and 228).
3. Kenneth D. Miller, *The Czechoslovaks in America*, New York, Doran, 1922, p. 35.
4. *Ibid.*, p. 13.
5. Emily Greene Balch, *Our Slavic Fellow Citizens*, New York, Charities Publication Committee, 1910, p. 78.
6. Eleanor E. Ledbetter, *The Czechs of Cleveland*, Cleveland, Cleveland Americanization Committee, 1919, p. 8.
7. Balch, *op. cit.*, p. 77.
8. Peter B. Yurchak, *The Slovaks, Their History and Traditions*, Whiting, Indiana, Rev. John J. Lach, 1946, pp. 41 and 149.
9. Balch, *op. cit.*, p. 85.
10. Yurchak, *op. cit.*, p. 66.
11. Miller, *op. cit.*, p. 37.
12. Yurchak, *op. cit.*, pp. 147–148.
13. Balch, *op. cit.*, p. 96.
14. *Ibid.*, p. 111.
15. *Ibid.*, p. 69.
16. *Ibid.*, pp. 73–74.
17. Jerabek, *op. cit.*, pp. 31–34.
18. *Ibid.*, p. 39.
19. Balch, *op. cit.*, p. 70.
20. Jerabek, *op. cit.*, p. 45.
21. Balch, *op. cit.*, p. 72.

22. Jerabek, *op. cit.*, p. 28.
23. *Ibid.*, pp. 19–20; Social conditions, pp. 16–19.
24. *Ibid.*, p. 16.
25. *Ibid.*, p. 21.
26. *Idem.*
27. Jakub Horak, *The Assimilation of Czechs in Chicago*, Ph.D. Dissertation, University of Chicago, 1920, p. 95.
28. Jerabek, *op. cit.*, p. 22.
29. Horak, *op. cit.*, pp. 111, 117.
30. *Ibid.*, pp. 114 and 123.
31. Balch, *op. cit.*, p. 78.
32. Horak, *op. cit.*, pp. 12–13.
33. Balch, *op. cit.*, p. 81; Thomas Capek, *The Czechs (Bohemians) in America*, Boston, Houghton Mifflin, 1920, p. 29; J. S. Roucek, "The Passing of the American Czechoslovaks," *American Journal of Sociology* 39:611–625, 1934, pp. 612–613.
34. Balch, *op. cit.*, p. 78.
35. Conrad Bercovici, *On New Shores*, New York, Century, 1925, p. 39.
36. Rose Rosicky, *A History of Czechs (Bohemians) in Nebraska*, Omaha, Czech Historical Society of Nebraska, 1929, pp. 25, 185, *passim.*
37. *Ibid.*, p. 26.
38. Capek, *op. cit.*, p. 49.
39. Jerabek, *op. cit.*, p. 60.
40. Capek, *op. cit.*, p. 112.
41. Edmund deS. Brunner, *Immigrant Farmers and Their Children*, Garden City, N.Y., Doubleday Doran, 1929, pp. 183–212, *passim.*
42. Russell W. Lynch, *Czech Farmers in Oklahoma* (Ph.D. Thesis, Columbia University), *Bulletin, Oklahoma Agricultural and Mechanical College*, vol. 39, no., 13, Stillwater, Okla., 1942, pp. 34–105, *passim.*
43. Bercovici, *op. cit.*, pp. 40–53, *passim.*
44. *Ibid.*, p. 48; and Jerabek, *op. cit.*, p. 134.
45. Roucek, *op. cit.*, p. 614.
46. Bercovici, *op. cit.*, p. 53.
47. Capek, *op. cit.*, p. 96; Miller, *op. cit.*, p. 76.
48. Miller, *idem.*
49. Miller, *op. cit.*, p. 57.
50. Capek, *op. cit.*, p. 70.
51. Bercovici, *op. cit.*, pp. 39–40.
52. Ledbetter, *op. cit.*, p. 8.
53. Balch, *op. cit.*, p. 76; and Jerabek, *op. cit.*, p. 86.
54. Jerabek, *op. cit.*, p. 60; and Capek, *op. cit.*, p. 112.
55. Capek, *op. cit.*, p. 125.
56. Conrad Bercovici, *Around the World in New York*, New York, Century, 1924, p. 369.
57. *Ibid.*, p. 371.
58. *Ibid.*, p. 376.
59. Miller, *op. cit.*, p. 74.
60. *Idem.*
61. *Ibid.*, p. 75.
62. Horak, *op. cit.*, pp. 22–28, *passim.*
63. *Ibid.*, p. 30.
64. Capek, *op. cit.*, p. 72.
65. *Ibid.*, p. 73.
66. Bercovici, *Around the World in New York*, p. 370.
67. *Idem.*
68. Roucek, *op. cit.*, p. 615.
69. Capek, *op. cit.*, p. 84.
70. *Ibid.*, pp. 103 and 112.
71. *Ibid.*, p. 103.
72. Miller, *op. cit.*, p. 66.
73. Horak, *op. cit.*, p. 34.
74. *Ibid.*, pp. 34–36.
75. *Ibid.*, pp. 37–38.
76. Roucek, *op. cit.*, p. 615.
77. Horak, *op. cit.*, p. 31.
78. Bercovici, *Around the World in New York*, p. 387.
79. Edward A. Steiner, *From Alien to Citizen*, New York, Revell, 1914, p. 175.
80. Capek, *op. cit.*, p. 77.
81. *Ibid.*, p. 78.
82. *Ibid.*, p. 254.
83. *Ibid.*, pp. 258 and 263.
84. *Ibid.*, p. 259.
85. *Ibid.*, p. 263. A complete list of or-

ganizations may be found here and on p. 264.

86. Jerabek, *op. cit.*, p. 122.
87. Horak, *op. cit.*, p. 113.
88. Capek, *op. cit.*, p. 263.
89. Capek, *op. cit.*, pp. 165, 170–171, and 185.
90. Capek, *op. cit.*, pp. 128, 129, 165, 170–171, 185.
91. *Ibid.*, p. 624.
92. F. J. Brown and J. S. Roucek, *One America*, New York, Prentice-Hall, 1945, p. 153.
93. Miller, *op. cit.*, p. 71; and Roucek, "The Passing of the American Czechoslovaks," p. 616.
94. Roucek, *ibid.*, p. 618.
95. Balch, *op. cit.*, p. 86.
96. *Ibid.*, pp. 93–94.
97. P. R. Radosavljevich, *Who Are the Slavs?* Boston, Gorham Press, 1919, p. 107.
98. Balch, *op. cit.*, p. 85.
99. *Ibid.*, p. 96.
100. *Ibid.*, p. 98.
101. P. V. Rovnianek, "The Slovaks in America," *Charities* 13:239–244, December 1904, p. 242.
102. Balch, *op. cit.*, p. 89.
103. *Ibid.*, pp. 89–93.
104. Rovnianek, *op. cit.*, p. 244.
105. E. Ledbetter, *The Slovaks of Cleveland*, Cleveland, Cleveland Americanization Committee, 1918, p. 31.
106. Yurchak, *op. cit.*, p. 24, n. 7.
107. Miller, *op. cit.*, pp. 71–72.
108. Balch, *op. cit.*, p. 95.
109. Yurchak, *op. cit.*, pp. 146–151.
110. Ledbetter, *The Slovaks of Cleveland*, p. 7.
111. Yurchak, *op. cit.*, pp. 161–162.
112. *Ibid.*, pp. 165–166.
113. Mary Lydia Zahrobsky, *The Slovaks in Chicago*, M.A. Dissertation, University of Chicago School of Social Service Administration, 1924, pp. 6–7.
114. Sarka B. Hrbkova, "Americans of Czechoslovak Descent," *Survey* 46: 361–368, June 11, 1921, p. 361.
115. Balch, *op. cit.*, p. 106; Roucek, "The Passing of the American Czechoslovaks," pp. 612–613.
116. Zahrobsky, *op. cit.*, p. 10.
117. *Ibid.*, pp. 7–8.
118. Yurchak, *op. cit.*, p. 183.
119. Balch, *op. cit.*, p. 108n.; this is not proved by sociological analysis, however. It may be a mere conjecture.
120. *Ibid.*, p. 107.
121. Zahrobsky, *op. cit.*, p. 14.
122. Balch, *op. cit.*, p. 100.
123. Zahrobsky, *op. cit.*, p. 8.
124. Yurchak, *op. cit.*, v, Introduction.
125. Ledbetter, *The Slovaks of Cleveland*, p. 10.
126. Zahrobsky, *op. cit.*, p. 9.
127. *Ibid.*, p. 10.
128. Ledbetter, *The Slovaks of Cleveland*, p. 11.
129. Zahrobsky, *op. cit.*, p. 21.
130. *Ibid.*, p. 18.
131. *Idem.*
132. Brown and Roucek, *op. cit.*, p. 147.
133. Rovnianek, *op. cit.*, p. 240.
134. Miller, *op. cit.*, pp. 67–68.
135. *Ibid.*, pp. 53 and 60.
136. Zahrobsky, *op. cit.*, p. 51.
137. Yurchak, *op. cit.*, p. 170.
138. Rovnianek, *op. cit.*, p. 240.
139. Ledbetter, *The Slovaks of Cleveland*, p. 24.
140. *Slovak Record*, March 1944, p. 12.
141. Zahrobsky, *op. cit.*, p. 45.
142. *Ibid.*, pp. 33–34.
143. *Ibid.*, p. 39.
144. Miller, *op. cit.*, p. 72.
145. Zahrobsky, *op. cit.*, p. 57.
146. Roucek, "The Passing of the American Czechoslovaks," p. 618.
147. Miller, *op. cit.*, p. 88.
148. *Ibid.*, p. 64.
149. Zahrobsky, *op. cit.*, p. 61.
150. Rovnianek, *op. cit.*, p. 242.
151. *Idem.*
152. Zahrobsky, *op. cit.*, p. 26.

153. Yurchak, *op. cit.*, p. 170.
154. Zahrobsky, *op. cit.*, p. 62.
155. Yurchak, *op. cit.*, p. 170.
156. Roucek, "The Passing of the American Czechoslovaks," p. 619.
157. Rovnianek, *op. cit.*, pp. 240–242.
158. *Ibid.*, p. 242.
159. Yurchak, *op. cit.*, p. 25.
160. *Ibid.*, pp. 64–66.
161. Miller, *op. cit.*, p. 49.
162. Roucek, "The Passing of the American Czechoslovaks," pp. 624–625.
163. Miller, *op. cit.*, p. 109.
164. Capek, *op. cit.*, pp. 267–268; Yurchak, *op. cit.*, p. 189.
165. Capek, *op. cit.*, p. 275.
166. *Ibid.*, pp. 268–269.
167. Yurchak, *op. cit.*, p. 210; and Alois R. Nykl, "Czechoslovakia or Czecho-Slovakia?" *Slavonic Review* 22, December 1944, pp. 99–110.
168. Brown and Roucek, *op. cit.*, p. 154.
169. Nykl, *op. cit.*, p. 106.
170. Brown and Roucek, *op. cit.*, pp. 154–155.
171. Thorsten V. Kalijarvi, "Central-Eastern European Minorities in the United States," *Annals* 232, March 1944, p. 150.
172. Reported to the writer by Dusan Ruppeldt, a Slovak student from Bratislava completing part of his higher education in America during 1947.
173. E. Beneš, "Postwar Czechoslovakia," *Foreign Affairs* 24 : 397–410, April 1946, p. 403.
174. *American Czechoslovak Flashes*, vol. 1, No. 7, May 15, 1947, p. 1.
175. Yurchak, *op. cit.*, pp. 188–259.
176. Nykl, *op. cit.*, p. 107.

CHAPTER 14. HUNGARIAN AMERICANS

1. Edmann Doane Beynon, *Occupational Adjustments of Hungarian Immigrants in an American Urban Community*, Ph.D. Thesis, University of Michigan, 1933, p. 38.
2. *Ibid.*, p. 139.
3. *Ibid.*, p. 17.
4. Dominic G. Kosary, *A History of Hungary*, Cleveland and New York, The Benjamin Franklin Bibliophile Society, 1941, p. 6.
5. *Ibid.*, pp. 7–8.
6. Joseph Remenyi, "The Hungarians," in H. P. Fairchild, ed., *Immigrant Backgrounds*, New York, Wiley, 1927, pp. 73–74.
7. Beynon, *op. cit.*, p. 18.
8. Julian S. Huxley and A. C. Haddon, *We Europeans*, New York, Harper, 1936, p. 176.
9. V. D. Barker, "Foundations of Magyar Society," *Slavonic Review* 11 : 388–396, January 1933, p. 389.
10. Remenyi, *op. cit.*, p. 73.
11. *Idem.*
12. Barker, *op. cit.*, p. 388.
13. Remenyi, *op. cit.*, p. 74.
14. Beynon, *op. cit.*, pp. 87–88.
15. *Ibid.*, p. 89, and Barker, *op. cit.*, p. 389.
16. Beynon, *op. cit.*, p. 88, and Remenyi, *op. cit.*, p. 77.
17. Beynon, *op. cit.*, p. 86.
18. *Ibid.*, pp. 93–96.
19. Remenyi, *op. cit.*, p. 74.
20. Beynon, *op. cit.*, p. 97.
21. *Ibid.*, p. 100.
22. Remenyi, *op. cit.*, p. 79.
23. Beynon, *op. cit.*, pp. 105–108.
24. *Ibid.*, p. 109.
25. *Ibid.*, p. 156.
26. *Ibid.*, p. 119.
27. Barker, *op. cit.*, p. 391.
28. *Ibid.*, p. 394.
29. For a more complete account see Geza Kende, *Magyarok Amerikaban* (*Hungarians in America*), 2 vols., Cleveland, Szabadság, 1927. The author

is indebted to Mr. Stefan Papp and Miss Mary Papp of Cleveland for the translation of relevant passages, and to Mr. Zoltan Gombos, editor of the *Szabadság* for a copy of this work.

30. Cf. the account in Kende, *op. cit.*, vol. I, chap. 15.
31. M. R. Davie, *World Immigration*, New York, Macmillan, 1936, p. 120.
32. Zoltan Gombos, ed., *Hungarians in America*, Cleveland, Szabadság, 1941, p. 11. The writer is indebted to Mr. Gombos for a copy of this important work.
33. *Idem.*
34. Joseph Kenneth Balogh, *An Analysis of Cultural Organizations in Pittsburgh and Alleghany County*, Ph.D. Thesis, University of Pittsburgh, 1945, p. 19.
35. *Ibid.*, p. 23.
36. Gombos, *op. cit.*, p. 11.
37. The writer is indebted for this term to the Rev. Andor Leffler of Cleveland, Ohio.
38. Beynon, *op. cit.*, p. 18.
39. *Idem.*
40. Davie, *op. cit.*, p. 120.
41. Balogh, *op. cit.*, p. 14.
42. *Idem.* Roucek says expert opinion would place the number as low as 300,000 to 400,000. Cf. J. S. Roucek, "Hungarian Americans" in F. J. Brown and J. S. Roucek, *One America*, New York, Prentice-Hall, 1945, p. 215.
43. Endre Sebestyen, "The Magyars in America," *Hungarian Quarterly* 7: 228–246, 1941, p. 233.
44. Huldah F. Cook, *The Magyars of Cleveland*, Cleveland, Cleveland Americanization Committee, 1919, p. 8.
45. *Ibid.*, p. 11.
46. Beynon, *op. cit.*, p. 32.
47. *Ibid.*, p. 34.
48. *Ibid.*, p. 27.
49. *Ibid.*, pp. 22–24.
50. *Ibid.*, p. 24.
51. Davie, *op. cit.*, p. 121.
52. "Are We Benefiting from Hungarian Immigration?" *Review of Reviews* 33:354–356, March 1906, p. 356.
53. Beynon, *op. cit.*, p. 165.
54. Gombos, *op. cit.*, p. 5, and Remenyi, *op. cit.*, p. 78.
55. Beynon, *op. cit.*, pp. 35–36.
56. *Ibid.*, p. 36.
57. Charles E. Schaeffer, "The Magyars in Hungary and in America," *Missionary Review* 38:367–368, May 1915, p. 367.
58. Remenyi, *op. cit.*, p. 79, and Sebestyen, *op. cit.*, pp. 238–239.
59. Beynon, *op. cit.*, p. 46.
60. Louis H. Pink, "The Magyar in New York," *Charities* 13:262–263, December 3, 1904, p. 263.
61. Beynon, *op. cit.*, p. 39.
62. Balogh, *op. cit.*, p. 33.
63. Rev. Alex Harsanyi (from collected papers), "Protestants in Hungary and in the United States," *Missionary Review* 36:595–596, August 1913, p. 595.
64. E. A. Steiner, *On the Trail of the Immigrant*, New York, Revell, 1906, pp. 246–247.
65. Schaeffer, *op. cit.*, p. 367.
66. Beynon, *op. cit.*, p. 43.
67. Balogh, *op. cit.*, p. 23.
68. *Ibid.*, p. 25.
69. Steiner, *op. cit.*, p. 249.
70. Gombos, *op. cit.*, p. 327.
71. Balogh, *op. cit.*, p. 96.
72. *Ibid.*, p. 16.
73. Gombos, *op. cit.*, p. 225.
74. Balogh, *op. cit.*, pp. 33 and 35.
75. *Ibid.*, pp. 38–39.
76. *Idem.*
77. *Ibid.*, p. 43.
78. *Ibid.*, pp. 47–48.
79. *Ibid.*, p. 33.
80. *Ibid.*, p. 47.
81. *Ibid.*, pp. 33, 35, and 51.
82. *Ibid.*, p. 39.
83. *Ibid.*, p. 61.
84. *Ibid.*, p. 64.
85. *Idem.*

86. *Ibid.*, p. 74.
87. Kende, *op. cit.*, chap. 26.
88. Gombos, *op. cit.*, p. 15.
89. *Idem.*
90. *Ibid.*, pp. 15–17.
91. Sebestyen, *op. cit.*, p. 237.
92. Kende, *op. cit.*, vol. II, p. 31.
93. Gombos, *op. cit.*, p. 20.
94. Kende, *op. cit.*, vol II. pp. 474–475.
95. *Ibid.*, p. 472.
96. Roucek, *op. cit.*, p. 220.
97. Balogh, *op. cit.*, pp. 80–90.
98. Roucek, *op. cit.*, p. 220.
99. Balogh, *op. cit.*, p. 87.
100. *Ibid.*, p. 92.
101. *Ibid.*, p. 91.
102. *Ibid.*, p. 92.
103. *Ibid.*, p. 93.
104. *Ibid.*, p. 97.
105. *Ibid.*, p. 95.
106. *Ibid.*, p. 102.
107. *Idem.*
108. Gombos, *op. cit.*, pp. 10–11.
109. The writer is indebted to Mr. Zoltan Gombos for clarification of this point.
110. Schaeffer, *op. cit.*, p. 367.
111. Balogh, *op. cit.*, p. 25.
112. Interview with Mr. Zoltan Gombos.
113. E. D. Beynon, "The Hungarians of Michigan," *Michigan Historical Magazine* 21 : 89–102, January 1937, p. 101.
114. *Idem.*
115. *Idem.*
116. *Idem.*
117. *Ibid.*, p. 102.
118. Balogh, *op. cit.*, p. 26.
119. Beynon, *Occupational Adjustments*, p. 158.
120. *Idem.*
121. *Ibid.*, p. 159.
122. Beynon, "Social Mobility and Social Distance among Hungarian Immigrants in Detroit," *American Journal of Sociology* 41 : 423–434, January 1936, p. 427.
123. *Ibid.*, p. 430.
124. *Ibid.*, 428.
125. See *New Yorker* profile on Ferenc Molnar, third article, Spring 1946.
126. Beynon, "Social Mobility," pp. 432–433.
127. Beynon, *Occupational Adjustments*, p. 168.
128. Beynon, "Social Mobility," p. 433.
129. *Ibid.*, pp. 430–431.
130. Remenyi, *op. cit.*, p. 80.
131. Lois Rankin, "Detroit Nationality Groups. Hungarians," *Michigan History Magazine* 23, no. 2 : 146–153, 1939, p. 151.
132. Beynon, *Occupational Adjustments*, p. 39.
133. Steiner, *op. cit.*, p. 250.
134. Joseph Remenyi, "Hungarian Humor," *Slavonic and East European Review* 21 : 194–210, March 1943, p. 203.

CHAPTER 15. YUGOSLAV AMERICANS

1. *The Southern Slavs, Land and People*, The Southern Slav Library, London, Nisbet, 1916, p. 5. The author is indebted to Mrs. Paula Mihal of Cleveland for this source.
2. Vlaho S. Vlahovic, *Two Hundred and Fifty Million and One Slavs*, New York, Slav Publications Inc., 1945, p. 66.
3. M. S. Orenstein, "The Servo-Croats of Manhattan," *Survey* 29 : 277–286, December 12, 1912, p. 278.
4. Contributed in private interview by Mr. Vlaho S. Vlahovic.
5. Vlahovic, *op. cit.*, pp. 66–67.
6. Emily Greene Balch, *Our Slavic Fellow Citizens*, New York, Charities Publication Committee, 1910, pp. 160–161.
7. Dinko Tomasic, "Sociology in Yugoslavia," *American Journal of Sociology* 47 : 53–69, July 1941, p. 53.
8. *Ibid.*, p. 56.

9. Stoyan Pribichevich, *World Without End, The Saga of Southeastern Europe*, New York, Reynal & Hitchcock, 1939, p. 257.
10. Paul R. Radosavljevich, *Who Are the Slavs?* 2 vols., Boston, Gorham Press, 1919, vol. II, p. 198.
11. Bogumil Vosnjak, *A Dying Empire, Central Europe, Pan-Germanism and the Downfall of Austro-Hungary*, London, Geo. Allen & Unwin, 1918, pp. 81–82. Mrs. Paula Mihal of Cleveland also kindly supplied this volume from her library.
12. Tomasic, *op. cit.*, p. 60.
13. *The Southern Slavs*, p. 37, and Vosnjak, *op. cit.*, pp. 81–82.
14. Balch, *op. cit.*, p. 157.
15. *Ibid.*, p. 190.
16. Vosnjak, *op. cit.*, pp. 63–64.
17. *Ibid.*, p. 71.
18. *Ibid.*, p. 67, and Radosavljevich, *op. cit.*, II, 199.
19. *The Southern Slavs*, p. 61.
20. *Idem.*
21. Pribichevich, *op. cit.*, p. 243.
22. *Ibid.*, p. 246.
23. Tomasic, *op. cit.*, p. 58.
24. Pribichevich, *op. cit.*, p. 317.
25. Vosnjak, *op. cit.*, p. 84.
26. Balch, *op. cit.*, p. 179.
27. Radosavljevich, *op. cit.*, II, 145–146.
28. Balch, *op. cit.*, p. 162.
29. *Ibid.*, pp. 163, 178.
30. Louis Adamic, *The Native's Return, An American Immigrant Visits Yugoslavia and Discovers His Old Country*, New York, Harper, 1934, pp. 229–230.
31. Clement Simon Mihanovich, *Americanization of the Croats in St. Louis, Mo. during the Past Thirty Years*, M.A. Thesis, St. Louis University, 1936, pp. 16–17.
32. Adamic, *op. cit.*, p. 216.
33. Pribichevich, *op. cit.*, pp. 253–254.
34. Radosavljevich, *op. cit.*, II, 145.
35. Adamic, *op. cit.*, p. 215.
36. Vlaho S. Vlahovic, *Yugoslavs in America, Their Achievements and Contribution*, unpublished manuscript, pp. 195, 198–199. These and other passages in the manuscript are furnished by courtesy of Mr. Vlaho S. Vlahovic, former editor of the *Slavonic Review.*
37. Adamic, *op. cit.*, p. 173.
38. Pribichevich, *op. cit.*, pp. 258–259.
39. Adamic, *op. cit.*, pp. 37–60.
40. *Ibid.*, p. 53.
41. Balch, *op. cit.*, p. 166.
42. *Ibid.*, p. 177.
43. *Ibid.*, p. 158.
44. Pribichevich, *op. cit.*, pp. 253–256.
45. Balch, *op. cit.*, p. 164.
46. *Ibid.*, p. 165.
47. Pribichevich, *op. cit.*, p. 257.
48. Balch, *op. cit.*, p. 165.
49. Pribichevich, *op. cit.*, p. 257.
50. Balch, *op cit.*, p. 149.
51. Vosnjak, *op. cit.*, pp. 64–65.
52. *The Southern Slavs*, p. 6.
53. Pribichevich, *op. cit.*, pp. 314–315.
54. Adamic, *op. cit.*, p. 249.
55. Nicholas Mirkovich, "Yugoslavs and Criminality," *Sociology and Social Research*, 25 : 28–34, September–October 1940, p. 33.
56. Pribichevich, *op. cit.*, p. 302.
57. Sir Arthur Evans, quoted in *South Slav Herald*, December 1–16, 1938. These and other copies of the *South Slav Herald* quoted were supplied by the courtesy of Mrs. Jeanette Cahill and Mrs. Paula Mihal of Cleveland, Ohio.
58. Adamic, *op. cit.*, pp. 268, 272.
59. Vlahovic, *Yugoslavs in America*, p. 199.
60. Pribichevich, *op. cit.*, p. 353.
61. Balch, *op. cit.*, p. 167.
62. *Ibid.*, p. 168.
63. *Ibid.*, p. 169.
64. *Idem.*
65. Adamic, *op. cit.*, p. 152.
66. Vlahovic, *Yugoslavs in America*, p. 202.

67. *The Southern Slavs*, p. 29.
68. Louis Adamic, *A Nation of Nations*, New York, Harper, 1944, p. 235.
69. *Ibid.*, pp. 237–238.
70. *Ibid.*, p. 239.
71. Ivan Mladineo, ed., *Narodni Adresar, Hrvata, Slovenaca-Srba. The National Directory of the Croat-Slovene-Serb Organizations, Institutions, Business, Professional and Social Leaders in the United States and Canada*, New York, Ivan Mladineo (privately published), 1937, p. viii. The author is indebted to Mrs. Jeanette Cahill for making this reference available.
72. *Idem.*
73. Balch, *op. cit.*, p. 194.
74. *Ibid.*, p. 175.
75. *Ibid.*, pp. 176–177.
76. *Ibid.*, p. 179.
77. Adamic, *A Nation of Nations*, p. 240.
78. Balch, *op. cit.*, p. 184.
79. *Ibid.*, p. 153.
80. *Idem.*
81. J. S. Roucek, "Yugoslavs Under the Stars and Stripes," *South Slav Herald*, April 17, 1935, p. 2. This is substantially the same article that appeared under the same authorship as "The Yugoslav Immigrants in America," *American Journal of Sociology* 40:602–611. It will be quoted here for convenience from the former source.
82. *Idem.*
83. *Idem.* Some Yugoslav newspapers in the United States have given much higher figures but the tendency of all foreign language publications to overestimate such statistics is well known.
84. *Idem.*
85. *Idem.*
86. Quoted in Mihanovich, *op. cit.*, p. 26.
87. *Ibid.*, p. 27.
88. Orenstein, *op. cit.*, p. 279.
89. *Ibid.*, pp. 279–280, 286.
90. *Ibid.*, p. 280.
91. *Ibid.*, p. 279.
92. Mihanovich, *op. cit.*, p. 27.
93. Orenstein, *op. cit.*, p. 282.
94. *Idem.*
95. *Ibid.*, p. 283.
96. Balch, *op. cit.*, p. 185.
97. *Ibid.*, p. 304.
98. Mihanovich, *op. cit.*, pp. 42–43.
99. Mirkovich, *op. cit.*, p. 30.
100. See articles by M. S. Logan such as "Without Benefit of Clergy," *Common Ground* 5, No. 2:66–72, 1945; or "On My Father's Mountain," *ibid.* 6, No. 1:67–73, 1945.
101. Mihanovich, *op. cit.*, p. 49.
102. Balch, *op. cit.*, p. 355.
103. Bilyanna Niland, "Yugoslavs in San Pedro, California," *Sociology and Social Research* 26:36–44, September–October 1941, p. 42.
104. *Ibid.*, pp. 37–39.
105. Vlahovic, *Yugoslavs in America*, pp. 274–275.
106. *Ibid.*, p. 279.
107. *Ibid.*, pp. 279–280.
108. Mirkovich, *op. cit.*, p. 31.
109. Interview with Mr. Vlaho S. Vlahovic.
110. Vlahovic, *Yugoslavs in America*, pp. 290–291.
111. Adamic, *Nation of Nations*, pp. 243–246.
112. Vlahovic, *Yugoslavs in America*, pp. 232–234.
113. *Ibid.*, p. 255.
114. *Ibid.*, pp. 197–198.
115. *Ibid.*, p. 257.
116. F. J. Brown and J. S. Roucek, *One America*, New York, Prentice-Hall, 1945, p. 163.
117. Vlahovic, *Yugoslavs in America*, pp. 239–243.
118. *Ibid.*, p. 240.
119. Brown and Roucek, *op. cit.*, p. 164.
120. Vlahovic, *Yugoslavs in America*, p. 249.
121. *Idem.*
122. *Ibid.*, p. 248.
123. Brown and Roucek, *op. cit.*, pp. 161–162.
124. Adamic, *Nation of Nations*, p. 247.

125. Balch, *op. cit.*, p. 194.
126. Adamic, *Nation of Nations*, p. 247.
127. Interview with Frank Suhadolnik, formerly librarian of the Intercultural Library, Cleveland, Ohio.
128. Adamic, *Nation of Nations*, p. 247.

CHAPTER 16. THE AMERICAN JEW

1. Adapted from a case history by Saul Hofstein, "Counseling with Jewish Soldiers," *Jewish Social Service Quarterly* 22 : 259–273, June 1946.
2. Cf. Chapters 2 and 3 above.
3. Salo W. Baron, *A Social and Religious History of the Jews*, 2 vols., New York, Columbia University Press, 1937, vol. I, p. 3.
4. Quoted in Arthur Ruppin, *The Jews in the Modern World*, London, Macmillan, 1934, p. 261.
5. See below, p. 393.
6. Ruppin, *op. cit.*, pp. 8–10.
7. Isacque Graeber and Steuart H. Britt, *Jews in a Gentile World, The Problem of Anti-Semitism*, New York, Macmillan, 1942, article by C. S. Coon, p. 35.
8. Ruppin, *op. cit.*, p. 262.
9. This term comes from Jessie Bernard, Graeber and Britt, *op. cit.*, pp. 265 ff.
10. Mordecai Kaplan, *Judaism as a Civilization*, New York, Macmillan, 1934, p. 193.
11. Graeber and Britt, *op. cit.*, p. 265.
12. Louis Wirth, *The Ghetto*, Chicago, University of Chicago Press, 1928, pp. 18 ff and 29 ff.
13. Cf. Joshua Trachtenberg, *The Devil and the Jew*, New Haven, Yale University Press, 1943, p. 168.
14. Wirth, *op. cit.*, p. 92.
15. See Chapter 18 for an elaboration of this issue.
16. Cecil Roth, *A Bird's Eye View of Jewish History*, Cincinnati, Union of American Hebrew Congregations, 1935, p. 320.
17. For a brief summary see Wirth, *op. cit.*, pp. 114–115.
18. G. W. Rabinoff, "The Role of the Organized Jewish Community in Jewish Life in America," *Jewish Social Service Quarterly* 22 : 202–208, June 1946, p. 203.
19. Milton Steinberg, *A Partisan Guide to the Jewish Problem*, New York, Bobbs-Merrill, 1945, p. 184.
20. Doris Jeanne Kaphan, *Adjustment Problems of German-Jewish Refugees*, M.A. Thesis, Columbia University, 1939, p. 7.
21. Ruppin, *op. cit.*, p. 130.
22. Miriam Beard in Graeber and Britt, *op. cit.*, pp. 381–382.
23. Sombart's theory that the Jews were largely responsible for modern capitalism has been pretty well demolished. Cf. reference 22, above.
24. Ruppin, *op. cit.*, pp. 133–134.
25. *Reconstructionist*, June 23, 1944.
26. See H. E. Barnes and Howard Becker, *Contemporary Social Theory*, New York, Appleton-Century, 1940, pp. 31–35.
27. For a similar use cf. John F. Cuber, *Sociology*, New York, Appleton-Century, 1947, pp. 174–175.
28. Quoted in Stoyan Pribichevich, *World Without End*, New York, Reynal and Hitchcock, 1939, p. 220.
29. Cf. Roth, *op. cit.*, chaps. 21–22.
30. Wirth, *op. cit.*, p. 137.
31. Ruppin, *op. cit.*, p. 10. For a discussion of the forced movements of the Ashkenazi see A. J. Toynbee, *A Study of History*, 6 vols., London, Oxford University Press, 1934, vol. II, 240–248.
32. Ruppin, *op. cit.*, p. 48.
33. Max Feder, *An Evaluation of the Contemporary Jewish Immigration to the United States (1880–1942)*, M.A. Thesis, Columbia University, 1942, p. 2.
34. "The Classification of Jewish Immigrants and Its Implications. A Sur-

139. Karpf, *op. cit.*, p. 119. For a more comprehensive account of the many Jewish agencies see especially chapters 6–8 of Karpf's work.

140. H. L. Lurie, "Developments in Jewish Civic and Protective Activity in the United States," *Proceedings of the National Conference of Jewish Social Welfare*, New York, National Conference of Jewish Social Welfare and Jewish Social Service Quarterly, 1939, p. 14. Also Steinberg, *op. cit.*, p. 209.

141. Lurie, *idem*, and Steinberg, *idem*.

142. Lurie, *op. cit.*, p. 15, and Steinberg, *idem*.

143. See bulletin of the Commission on Community Interrelations, April 1946.

144. Lurie, *idem*.

145. Steinberg, *idem*.

146. *Ibid.*, p. 208.

147. Edidin, *op. cit.*, p. 175.

148. *Ibid.*, p. 176, and Steinberg, *op. cit.*, p. 206.

149. The Hadassah was not originally Zionist but an organization promoting better medical facilities in Palestine. For an account of its increasing dominance by Zionists cf. Berger, *op. cit.*, p. 141.

150. Edidin, *op. cit.*, p. 190.

151. Karpf, *op. cit.*, pp. 52–55.

152. Estimate by Mordecai Grossman and transmitted to the writer through the courtesy of the American Jewish Committee, November 18, 1947.

153. For a full account see his *Judaism as a Civilization*, and Steinberg, *op. cit.* chaps. 9 and 11.

154. Mordecai Kaplan, "The Organization of American Jewry," *Proceedings of the National Conference of Jewish Social Service and the Jewish Social Service Quarterly* 1935, pp. 67–68; and Mordecai Kaplan, "The Implications of the World Situation for Jewish Cultural Life in America," *Jewish Social Service Quarterly* 17:38, September 1940.

155. Kaplan, "The Organization of American Jewry," p. 63.

156. For two opposing views of the problem cf. Steinberg, *op. cit.*, pp. 210–211, and *Information Bulletin of the American Council for Judaism*, editorial of September 1, 1944.

157. Edidin, *op. cit.*, pp. 263 ff.

158. Steinberg, *op. cit.*, p. 216.

159. Jacob Lestchinsky in Graeber and Britt, *op. cit.*, pp. 406–407.

160. *Idem.*

161. *Idem.*

162. Nathan Reich, "Economic Trends," in Janowsky, *op. cit.*, p. 165.

163. *Ibid.*, tables, pp. 163 and 164.

164. Lestchinsky in Graeber and Britt, *op. cit.*, p. 409.

165. Reich in Janowsky, *op. cit.*, pp. 166–167.

166. *Ibid.*, p. 173.

167. Editors of Fortune, " Jews in America," New York, 1936.

168. *Idem.*

169. Dorothy Goldstein, *The "Disproportionate" Occupational Distribution of Jews and Their Individual and Organized Reactions*, M.A. Thesis, Columbia University, 1941, p. 14.

170. *Ibid.*, p. 32. This preceded the passage of the New York F.E.P.C. law, which has modified the practice.

171. Albert J. Weiss, "Post-War Employment Discrimination," *Jewish Social Service Quarterly* 23:396–405, June 1947, pp. 404–405.

172. Ruppin, *op. cit.*, pp. 206–207.

173. Carey McWilliams, "Does Social Discrimination Really Matter?" *Commentary* 4:408–415, November 1947, pp. 413–415. The first of these three factors is suggested by Riesman in the *Public Opinion Quarterly*, Spring 1942, as McWilliams states, p. 410. For an expansion of this view see Carey McWilliams, *A Mask for Privilege: Anti-Semitism in America*, Boston, Little Brown, 1948, chap. 6.

174. Melvin M. Fagen, "The Status of Jewish Lawyers in New York City," *Jewish Social Studies*, vol. 1, No. 1, 1939, p. 104.

CHAPTER 17. ANTI-SEMITISM AND JEWISH DERIVATIVES

1. Adapted from Joshua Trachtenberg, *The Devil and the Jew, The Medieval Conception of the Jew and Its Relation to Modern Antisemitism*, New Haven, Yale University Press, 1943, pp. 226 and 227n.
2. Adapted from A. J. Weiss, "Post War Employment Discrimination," *Jewish Social Service Quarterly* 23: 396–405, June 1947, p. 403.
3. Cf. Koppel S. Pinson, ed., *Essays on Anti-Semitism*, New York, Conference on Jewish Relations, 1946, section by Ralph Marcus, "Antisemitism in the Hellenistic-Roman World," p. 62; and Hannah Arendt, *Privileged Jews*, New York, Conference on Jewish Relations, 1946, pp. 7 ff.
4. Cf. Marcus in Pinson, *op. cit.*, pp. 62–70.
5. Cf. Solomon Grayzel, "Christian-Jewish Relations in the First Millennium" in Pinson, *op. cit.*, pp. 79–92, and Trachtenberg, *op. cit.*, parts 2 and 3.
6. See article, "Anti-Semitism," by Benjamin Ginzburg in *Encyclopedia of the Social Sciences*, New York, Macmillan, 1937, II, 119–125.
7. Cf. Mark Vishniak, "Antisemitism in Tsarist Russia" in Pinson, *op. cit.*, pp. 121–144.
8. Jacob J. Weinstein, "Anti-Semitism" in Oscar Janowsky, ed., *The American Jew, A Composite Portrait*, New York, Harper, 1942, p. 186.
9. Carey McWilliams, "How Deep Are the Roots?" *Common Ground* 7, No. 4, Summer 1947, pp. 3–11. Enlarged in his *Mask for Privilege* Boston, Little Brown, 1948, chaps. 1 and 2. Note pp. 24 ff.
10. Carey McWilliams, "How Deep Are the Roots? II," *Common Ground* 8, No. 1, Autumn 1947, pp. 3–15, and *Mask for Privilege*, p. 21.
11. For an exposé of the Protocols see John S. Curtiss, *An Appraisal of the Protocols of Zion*, New York, Columbia University Press, 1942.
12. McWilliams, *Mask for Privilege*, pp. 34–35.
13. Weinstein in Janowsky, *op. cit.*, p. 190. Ford's apology was followed by the employment of Fritz Kuhn the German-American Bund leader and an acceptance of the Grand Order of the Great Eagle from the Nazis. Cf. McWilliams, "How Deep Are the Roots, II," *Common Ground* 8, No. 1, Autumn 1947, p. 9.
14. Donald S. Strong, *Organized Anti-Semitism in America*, Washington, American Council for Public Affairs, 1941, pp. 146–147.
15. *Ibid.*, p. 15.
16. Weinstein in Janowsky, *op. cit.*, p. 193.
17. McWilliams, *A Mask for Privilege*, pp. 45–46.
18. *Ibid.*, pp. 10–11.
19. Ben M. Edidin, *Jewish Community Life in America*, New York, Hebrew Publishing Co., 1947, p. 144.
20. Sigmund Livingston, *Must Men Hate?* New York, Harper, 1944, p. 4.
21. *Ibid.*, pp. 6–9.
22. *Ibid.*, p. 9.
23. *Ibid.*, pp. 12–17.
24. Horace M. Kallen, "The National Being and the Jewish Community" in Janowsky, *op. cit.*, p. 272.
25. Z. Diesendruck, "Antisemitism and Ourselves" in Pinson, *op. cit.*, p. 43.
26. I. W. Wechsler, "Some Remarks on the Psychology of Antisemitism" in Pinson, *op. cit.*, p. 37.
27. Shlomo Bergman, "Some Methodological Errors in the Study of Antisemitism," *Jewish Social Studies* 5: 43–60, January 1943, pp. 45–46.
28. Solomon Grayzel in Pinson, *op. cit.*, pp. 86 ff.
29. See Otto Fenichel, "Elements of a Psychoanalytic Theory of Anti-Semitism" in Ernst Simmel, ed., *Anti-*

Semitism, a Social Disease, New York, International Universities Press, 1946, pp. 16 ff.

30. Ben Hecht, *A Guide for the Bedevilled*, New York, Scribner, 1944, pp. 257–264.
31. Maurice Samuel, *The Great Hatred*, New York, Knopf, 1940, chaps. 4 and 11.
32. *Ibid.*, pp. 17 ff.
33. Ralph Linton, *The Study of Man*, New York, Appleton-Century, 1936, chaps. 7 and 20.
34. Stanley High, "Jews, Anti-Semites and Tyrants," *Harpers* 185:22–29, June 1942.
35. Pinson, *op. cit.*, p. vii.
36. Trachtenberg, *op. cit.*, pp. 165–168.
37. Pinson, *op. cit.*, pp. 6–7.
38. Morris S. Lazaron, *Common Ground, A Plea for An Intelligent Americanism*, New York, Liveright, 1938, p. 283n.
39. James Parkes, *An Enemy of the People, Anti-Semitism*, New York, Penguin Books, 1946, p. 101.
40. Jessie Bernard, "Biculturality: A Study in Social Schizophrenia," in Isacque Graeber and S. H. Britt, *Jews in a Gentile World, The Problem of Anti-Semitism*, New York, Macmillan, 1942, p. 267.
41. I. S. Wechsler in Pinson, *op. cit.*, p. 38.
42. Cf. Chapter 13 above, p. 311.
43. Parkes, *op. cit.*, p. 124.
44. Diesendruck in Pinson, *op. cit.*, p. 44.
45. *Ibid.*, p. 45.
46. *Ibid.*, pp. 45–46.
47. Albert J. Weiss, "Post War Employment Discrimination," *Jewish Social Service Quarterly* 23:396–405, June 1947, p. 403.
48. Adeline Harris and Goodwin Watson, "Are Jewish or Gentile Children More Clannish?" *Journal of Social Psychology* 24:71–76, 1946.
49. Bernard in Graeber and Britt, *op. cit.*, pp. 285–286.
50. *Proceedings, Third Annual Meeting of the New England Conference of Jewish Communal Agencies, New Haven, Conn. April 25–26, 1936*, New York, Council of Jewish Federations and Welfare Funds, October 1936, p. 11.
51. W. Lloyd Warner and Leo Srole, *The Social Systems of American Ethnic Groups*, Yankee City Series, New Haven, Yale University Press, 1945, pp. 205–209.
52. Noel P. Gist and L. A. Halbert, *Urban Society*, 2nd ed., New York, Crowell, 1941, p. 191.
53. Kenneth B. Clark, "Candor About Negro-Jewish Relations," *Commentary* 1:8–14, February 1946, p. 13.
54. Benjamin Malzberg, "New Data Relative to Incidence of Mental Disease Among Jews," *Mental Hygiene* 20:280–291, 1925 (?), p. 283.
55. *Ibid.*, p. 287.
56. *Idem.*
57. *Ibid.*, p. 291.
58. *Ibid.*, p. 290.
59. *Idem.*
60. Keith Sward and Meyer B. Friedman, "*Jewish Temperament*," *Journal of Applied Psychology* 19:70–84, 1935, p. 77.
61. Keith Sward, "Patterns of Jewish Temperament," *Journal of Applied Psychology* 19:410–423, 1935, pp. 412–413 and 421.
62. May Sukov and E. G. Williamson, "Personality Traits and Attitudes of Jewish and Non-Jewish Students," *Journal of Applied Psychology* 22:487–492, 1938, p. 490.
63. Sward and Friedman, *op. cit.*, p. 82.
64. Sukov and Williamson, *op. cit.*, p. 492.
65. Abraham P. Sperling, "A Comparison Between Jews and Non-Jews with Respect to Several Traits of Personality," *Journal of Applied Psychology* 26:828–840, 1942, p. 839.
66. Fred Brown, "A Note on the Stability and Maturity of Jewish and Non-Jewish Boys," *Journal of Social Psychology* 12:171–175, 1940, *passim.*
67. Kurt Lewin, "Psycho-Sociological Problems of a Minority Group,"

Character and Personality 3:175–187, March 1935, pp. 177–178.

68. *Ibid.*, p. 182.
69. *Ibid.*, p. 185.
70. *Ibid.*, p. 186.
71. Kurt Lewin, "Self-Hatred Among Jews," *Contemporary Jewish Record* 4:219–232, June 1941, p. 225. See also N. A. Pelcovits, "What About Jewish Anti-Semitism?" *Commentary* 3:118–125, February 1947, where the "flight from Jewish identity" receives considerable attention.
72. Kurt Lewin, *ibid.*, p. 226.
73. Pelcovits, *op. cit.*, pp. 120–121.
74. Kurt Lewin, "Self-Hatred Among Jews," p. 228.
75. *Ibid.*, p. 230.
76. See Chapter 17 above, pp. 426–427.
77. Elmer Berger, *The Jewish Dilemma*, New York, Devin-Adair, 1945, p. 25.
78. Elmer Berger, *Emancipation, the Rediscovered Ideal*, Philadelphia, The American Council for Judaism, 1945, p. 1.
79. *Ibid.*, p. 4.
80. *Ibid.*, p. 7.
81. *Ibid.*, p. 2.
82. *Idem.*
83. Berger, *op. cit.*, pp. 191, 194.
84. Elmer Berger in *The Council News*, published by the American Council for Judaism, September 1947, p. 1. The author is indebted for this and other literature of the Council to Rabbi Elmer Berger.
85. *The Council News*, October 1947, p. 1. See also the article by Morris S. Lazaron, "Palestine and the Jew," *Christian Century* 64:1401–1422, November 19, 1947.
86. Berger, *The Jewish Dilemma*, p. 242.
87. Mordecai Grossman, *Opinions of Leaders of American Council for Judaism on Jewish Integration and Group Survival. A Questionnaire Study*, (mimeographed), n.d., p. 3.
88. Milton Steinberg, "Current Philosophies of Jewish Life in America" in Janowsky, *op. cit.*, pp. 208–210.
89. Berger, *The Jewish Dilemma*, p. 164.
90. Milton Steinberg, *A Partisan Guide to the Jewish Problem*, New York, Bobbs-Merrill, 1945, p. 239.
91. Article, "New Yorker Who Fled From Reich Answers Zionists," *The Council News*, October 1947, pp. 1 and 3.
92. Grossman, *op. cit.*, p. 4.
93. *Ibid.*, p. 11.
94. *Ibid.*, p. 13.
95. *Ibid.*, p. 15.
96. *Ibid.*, p. 29.
97. *Ibid.*, p. 36.
98. *Ibid.*, p. 38.
99. In Graeber and Britt, *op. cit.*, p. 75.
100. *Ibid.*, p. 98.
101. Linton, *op. cit.*, p. 358.
102. Grossman, *op. cit.*, p. 71.
103. *Idem.*
104. Quoted in *The Council News*, September 1947, p. 1.
105. I. S. Wechsler in Pinson, *op. cit.*, p. 39.

CHAPTER 18. MINORITY ADJUSTMENTS

1. Suggested by Kenneth B. Clark, "Candor About Negro-Jewish Relations," *Commentary* 1:8–14, February 1946, pp. 12–13.
2. From an actual occurrence related to the writer.
3. See Chapter 1, p. 6.
4. Floyd L. Ruch, *Psychology and Life*, new ed., Chicago, Scott Foresman, 1941, p. 388.
5. For a more extended discussion of the stereotype see Gardner Murphy, *Personality*, New York, Harper, 1947.
6. See above, Chapter 9, pp. 190 ff.
7. See above, Chapters 5 and 6.
8. See above, Chapter 10.

9. See above, Chapter 9.
10. See above, Chapter 11.
11. See above, Chapter 13.
12. See above, Chapters 16 and 17. Also Loren Miller, "Covenants for Exclusion," *Survey Graphic* 36:541 ff., October 1947, p. 542.
13. The use here is analogous to R. E. Park, "The Concept of Position in Sociology," *Publications of the American Sociological Society* 20:1–14, Chicago, 1926.
14. See article by Joseph Martinek, "Czechoslovakian Ingredient in the Melting Pot," *American Czechoslovak Flashes*, October 15, 1947.
15. See above, Chapter 13.
16. See above, Chapter 14.
17. See above, Chapter 12, p. 273.
18. See above, Chapters 16 and 17.
19. See above, Chapter 11.
20. See above, Chapters 12, 14, and 15.
21. See above, Chapter 13.
22. Christine A. Galitzi, *A Study of Assimilation Among the Roumanians in the United States*, New York, Columbia University Press, 1929, pp. 165–167.
23. Milton L. Barron, *People Who Intermarry, Intermarriage in a New England Industrial Community*, Syracuse, Syracuse University Press, 1946, p. xi.
24. *Ibid.*, p. 21.
25. *Ibid.*, p. 332.
26. *Ibid.*, pp. 332 and 342.
27. *Ibid.*, pp. 330 and 343.
28. *Ibid.*, p. 332.
29. See above, Chapters 11, 13, 15, and 17.
30. See above, Chapter 9.
31. See above, Chapter 15.
32. See above, Chapters 11 and 13.
33. See above, Chapter 10.
34. See above, Chapter 14.
35. See above, Chapters 7, 13, and 16.
36. Karl Mannheim, *Man and Society in an Age of Reconstruction*, New York, Harcourt Brace, 1940, p. 85.
37. From Randolph Bourne, *The History of a Literary Radical*, New York, Huebsch, 1920, quoted in Alain Locke and B. J. Stern, eds., *When Peoples Meet*, New York, Progressive Education Association, 1942, p. 730.
38. See above, Chapters 11, 12, 13, and 15.
39. See Paul Cressey, "Population Succession in Chicago, 1898–1930," *American Journal of Sociology* 44:59–69, July 1938.
40. W. Lloyd Warner and Leo Srole, *The Social Systems of American Ethnic Groups*, New Haven, Yale University Press, 1945, chap. 3.
41. *Ibid.*, p. 51.
42. *Ibid.*, pp. 288–292.
43. See above, Chapter 5.
44. See above, Chapter 8.
45. See definition by E. V. Stonequist in *The Marginal Man*, New York, Scribners, 1937, pp. 2–3.
46. Dorothy Krall, *The Second Generation Immigrant in America, With Special Reference to Problems of Adjustment*, Doctoral Dissertation, Yale University, 1937, section III, 7.
47. *Ibid.*, II, 30.
48. Margaret Mead, *And Keep Your Powder Dry, An Anthropologist Looks at America*, New York, Morrow, 1943, chap. 3.
49. Krall, *op. cit.*, V, 25.
50. Stonequist, *op. cit.*, p. 25.
51. Gunnar Myrdal, *An American Dilemma, The Negro Problem and Modern Democracy*, 2 vols., New York, Harper, 1944, I, 699; II, 1385–1386.
52. W. C. Smith, *Americans in the Making, The Natural History of the Assimilation of Immigrants*, New York, Appleton-Century, 1939, pp. 239–242.
53. *To Secure These Rights, The Report of the President's Committee on Civil Rights*, Washington, U.S. Government Printing Office, 1947, p. 59.

CHAPTER 19. PREJUDICE

1. Adapted from Pauline R. Kibbe, *Latin Americans in Texas*, Albuquerque, University of New Mexico Press, 1946, pp. 178–179.
2. From a true incident related to the writer.
3. This is a simplified version of the more elaborate definition of attitude given by Muzafer Sherif and Hadley Cantril in *The Psychology of Ego Involvement*, New York, Wiley, 1947, p. 5.
4. Henry Pratt Fairchild, *Race and Nationality as Factors in American Life*, New York, Ronald Press, 1947, p. 86.
5. Sherif and Cantril, *op. cit.*, p. 102.
6. Kimball Young, *Social Psychology*, 2nd ed., New York, Crofts, 1944, pp. 259–260.
7. *Ibid.*, p. 259.
8. Adapted from Gil Sanford, "Shall We Teach Prejudice?" *American Unity*, January 1948, p. 3.
9. Gardner Murphy and R. Likert, *Public Opinion and the Individual*, New York, Harper, 1938, p. 136.
10. From an unpublished study by Marian Radke and Helen Trager under the joint auspices of the Research Center for Group Dynamics and the Bureau of Intercultural Education. The author is indebted to Dr. Radke for making this study available. For a preliminary report see Helen G. Trager and Marian Radke, "Early Childhood Airs Its Views," *Educational Leadership* 5:16–24, October 1947. Thanks are due to Miss Caroline Emery for transcribing the notes from Dr. Radke's studies.
11. Bruno Lasker, *Race Attitudes in Children*, New York, Holt, 1929, pp. 4–6.
12. E. L. Horowitz, *The Development of Attitude Toward the Negro*, Archives of Psychology, No. 194, New York, Columbia University Press, 1936.
13. Lasker, *op. cit.*, pp. 4–6.
14. W. D. Weatherford and C. S. Johnson, *Race Relations, Adjustment of Whites and Negroes in the United States*, Boston, Heath, 1934, p. 67.
15. E. L. Horowitz and R. E. Horowitz, "Development of Social Attitudes in Children," *Sociometry* 1:301–338, 1938.
16. Robert Blake and Wayne Dennis, "The Development of Stereotypes Concerning the Negro," *Journal of Abnormal and Social Psychology* 38:525–531, 1943.
17. G. W. Allport and Bernard M. Kramer, "Some Roots of Prejudice," *Journal of Psychology* 22:9–39, 1946, especially pp. 21–22.
18. L. L. Thurstone and E. J. Chave, *The Measurement of Attitude*, Chicago, University of Chicago Press, 1929.
19. Rensis Likert, *A Technique for the Measurement of Attitude*, Archives of Psychology, No. 140, New York, Columbia University Press, 1932.
20. Louis Guttman, "A Basis for Scaling Qualitative Data," *American Sociological Review* 9:139–150, 1944. A brief summary of these methods may be found in Arnold M. Rose, *Studies in the Reduction of Prejudice*, (mimeographed), Chicago, American Council on Race Relations, 1947, Section IV, pp. 3–9. The student who wishes to have a more thorough and detailed critique will find it in an article by Quinn McNemar, "Opinion-Attitude Methodology," *Psychological Bulletin* 43:289–369, 1946.
21. Robert K. Merton, "Fact and Factitiousness in Ethnic Questionnaires," *American Sociological Review* 5:13–28, 1940.
22. Allport and Kramer, *op. cit.*, p. 27.
23. F. Tredwell Smith, *An Experiment in Modifying Attitudes Toward the Negro*, New York, Teachers College, Columbia University, 1943; and Allport and Kramer, *op. cit.*, p. 30.
24. Eugene Hartley, *Problems in Prejudice*, New York, King's Crown Press, 1946, p. ix and chap. 5.
25. *Ibid.*, pp. 104–116.

26. Leonard W. Doob, "The Behavior of Attitudes," *Psychological Review* 54: 135–156, 1947.
27. Bruno Bettelheim, "A Scientific Approach to the Problem of Prejudice," Public Relations Workshop 1946, Chicago, American Council on Race Relations, 1947, p. 35.
28. *Ibid.*, p. 36.
29. D. J. Levinson and R. N. Sanford, "A Scale for the Measurement of Anti-Semitism," *Journal of Psychology* 17: 339–370, 1944.
30. Melvin Seeman, *Some Personality Correlates of Prejudice*, Unpublished Doctoral Dissertation, Ohio State University, 1947. The author is indebted to Dr. Seeman for making this manuscript available. Reference is to chap. 11.
31. *Ibid.*, chap. 11, p. 11.
32. *Ibid.*, chap. 11, p. 12.
33. See above, note 28.
34. Erich Fromm, *Escape from Freedom*, New York, Farrar & Rinehart, 1941, pp. 163–164.
35. Young, *op. cit.*, p. 258.
36. R. M. MacIver, "The Power of Group Images," *American Scholar* 14:220–224, Spring 1945.
37. George H. Grosser and Sheldon J. Korchin, *Some Theoretical Aspects of Group Prejudice and Conflict, A Study Based on the Work of the Committee on General Theory as part of the Seminar on Group Prejudice and Conflict*, held jointly by the departments of Psychology and Sociology, Harvard University, Fall Term, 1944–1945, p. 3.
38. *Ibid.*, p. 4.
39. Robin M. Williams, *The Reduction of Intergroup Tensions, A Survey of Research on Problems of Ethnic, Racial, and Religious Group Relations*, New York, Social Science Research Council, 1947, p. 59.
40. Grosser and Korchin, *op. cit.*, p. 2.
41. *Ibid.*, p. 10.
42. John Dollard, "Hostility and Fear in Social Life," *Social Forces* 17:15–26, 1938, p. 15.
43. Else Frenkel-Brunswik and N. Nevitt Sanford, "The Anti-Semitic Personality: A Research Report" in Ernst Simmel, ed., *Anti-Semitism*, A Social Disease, New York, International Universities Press, 1946, chap. 6, esp. pp. 108–111.
44. Gustav Ichheiser, "The Jews and Anti-Semitism," *Sociometry* 9:92–108, 1946.
45. Oliver C. Cox, *Caste, Class and Race*, New York, Doubleday, 1948, pp. 345–346, and 477.
46. Harry Schwartz, "Has Russia Solved the Jewish Problem?" *Commentary* 5: 128–136, 1948.
47. Ira N. Brophy, "The Luxury of Anti-Negro Prejudice," *Public Opinion Quarterly* 9:456–466, 1946.
48. Grosser and Korchin, *op. cit.*, p. 22.
49. Henry A. Davidson, "The Anatomy of Prejudice," *Common Ground* 1 No. 2: 3–12, Winter 1941.
50. Carey McWilliams, *Prejudice. Japanese Americans: Symbol of Racial Intolerance*, Boston, Little Brown, 1944, pp. 3, 25, 44, 235.
51. Davidson, *op. cit.*, p. 6.
52. Levinson and Sanford, *op. cit.*, *passim.*
53. Gunnar Myrdal, *An American Dilemma, The Negro Problem and Modern Democracy*, 2 vols., New York, Harper, 1944, I, 31.
54. W. S. Gregory, "A Study of Stereotyped Thinking: Affective Reactions to Persons as the Basis for Judging Their Nationality," *Journal of Social Psychology* 13:89–102, 1941.
55. MacIver, *op. cit.*, p. 221.
56. Gustav Ichheiser, "Projection and the Mote-Beam Mechanism," *Journal of Abnormal and Social Psychology* 42:131–133, 1947.
57. Kurt Lewin and others, *Authority and Frustration*, Studies in Topological and Vector Psychology III, University of Iowa Studies; Studies in Child Welfare, vol. XX, Iowa City, University of Iowa Press, 1944; essay — "Constructs in Psychology and Psychological Ecology," pp. 3–27. Note esp. p. 19.
58. Ronald Lippitt and Marian Radke,

"New Trends in the Investigation of Prejudice," *Annals of the American Academy of Political and Social Science* 244:167–176, 1946, p. 171.

59. Howard H. Harlan, "Some Factors Affecting Attitude Toward Jews," *American Sociological Review* 7:816–827, 1942, p. 822.

60. Gustav Ichheiser, "Fear of Violence and Fear of Fraud," *Sociometry* 7:376–383, 1944; and Allport and Kramer, *op. cit.*, p. 33.

61. Allport and Kramer, *idem.*

62. Davidson, *op. cit.*, p. 5.

63. Doob, *op. cit.*, p. 143.

64. Goodwin Watson, *Action for Unity*, New York, Harper, 1947, chap. 3.

CHAPTERS 20 AND 21. INTERGROUP PRACTICE

1. Personalized and adapted from Rev. Thomas J. Harte, *Catholic Organizations Promoting Negro-White Relations in the United States*, Ph.D. Dissertation, Washington, D.C., Catholic University of America Press, 1947, chaps. 3 and 4.

2. Adapted from Adena M. Rich, "Current Immigration Problems," *Social Service Review* 21:85–106, 1947, p. 98.

3. Charles S. Johnson, "National Organizations in the Field of Race Relations," *Annals of the American Academy of Political and Social Science* 244:117–127, 1946, p. 117.

4. *Idem*, and *Directory of Agencies in Race Relations*, Chicago, Julius Rosenwald Fund, 1945. A shorter list may also be found in Goodwin Watson, *Action for Unity*, New York, Harper, 1947.

5. See Chapter 19, esp. pp. 507 ff.

6. From a typewritten report on the efficacy of organized effort in group relations (pre-publication manuscript). The writer is indebted to Professor MacIver for making this manuscript available before publication. It will henceforth be referred to as MacIver MS. All references are to Chapter 10 of the document. Published as R. M. MacIver, *The More Perfect Union*, New York, Macmillan, 1948.

7. Watson, *op. cit.*, p. 64.

8. Charles S. Johnson and associates, *Into the Main Stream, A Survey of Best Practices in Race Relations in the South*, Chapel Hill, University of North Carolina Press, 1947, pp. vi–viii.

9. Robin M. Williams, *The Reduction of Intergroup Tensions, A Survey of Research on Problems of Ethnic, Racial and Religious Group Relations*, New York, Social Science Research Council, 1947, p. 47.

10. *New York Times*, Sunday, March 7, 1948.

11. Gunnar Myrdal, *An American Dilemma, The Negro Problem and Modern Democracy*, 2 vols., New York, Harper, 1944, I, 60–61.

12. Williams, *op. cit.*, p. 40, n. 6.

13. See Myrdal, *op. cit.*, II, appendix 2.

14. MacIver Ms. p. 8.

15. Suggested by W. Edwards Deming, "On an Application of Statistical Philosophy to Democracy," *Approaches to Group Understanding*, ed. by Lyman Bryson, Louis Finkelstein, and R. M. MacIver, Sixth Conference on Science, Philosophy, and Religion, New York, Harper, 1947, pp. 424–429, esp. 426–428.

16. *Ibid.*, p. 428.

17. Williams, *op. cit.*, p. 17.

18. Joseph D. Lohman, *The Police and Minority Groups*, Chicago Park District, 1947, pp. 80–86.

19. *Ibid.*, p. 4.

20. Gordon W. Allport and others, *A Tentative and Partial Manual for Police Training on the Subject of Minority Groups*, (mimeographed), Boston, 1944, pp. 2–4, 11–16, 24–25. The writer is indebted to Professor Allport for a copy of this manual.

21. *A Guide to Race Relations for Police Officers*, Police Training Bulletin,

pamphlet, Department of Justice, State of California, 1946, pp. 15–27.

22. Joseph T. Kluchesky, *Police Action in Minority Problems*, pamphlet, New York, Freedom House, 1945, p. 6.

23. Lohman, *op. cit.*, chap. 6, and appendices A and B.

24. J. E. Weckler and Theo. E. Hall, *The Police and Minority Groups*, pamphlet, Chicago, International City Managers' Association, 1944, pp. 10–18.

25. *A Guide to Race Relations for Police Officers*, p. 15.

26. *The New South*, 2, No. 10, October 1947, p. 1.

27. Johnson, *op. cit.*, pp. 52 ff.

28. See special issue of *The Negro South*, 2, No. 9, October 1947, where actual cases are cited.

29. See their monthly publication, *The Crisis*.

30. See the American Jewish Congress' bimonthly publication, *Law and Social Action*. See also their *Survey of Application for Admission Forms in Current Use by Liberal Arts Colleges Throughout the Country*, prepared by the Commission on Law and Social Action, revised, October 28, 1947. In New York State there has been increasing agitation for an antidiscrimination law in education. Because the matter has received widespread national attention, the Association of American Colleges appointed a Committee on Minority Groups in the Colleges. Their report, made in 1947, was adopted as the policy of the Association. Relevant passages are, "Colleges should lead, not follow the thinking of society... It is our conviction... that the problem of discrimination should be solved by education and voluntary action and not by coercive legislation... It would place in the hands of the state a threat to the freedom of colleges now independent of political control." They suggest a commission under the auspices of the Association of American Colleges to hear complaints, and investigate and report the facts annually to the Association. No recommendation is made for action after such a report is filed. Information furnished through the courtesy of Chancellor W. P. Tolley of Syracuse University, chairman of the Committee on Minority Groups in the Colleges.

31. *State F.E.P.C. What the People Say*, pamphlet, Chicago, American Council on Race Relations, 1947, Analysis II.

32. *To Secure These Rights*, The Report of the President's Committee on Civil Rights, Washington, D.C., U.S. Government Printing Office, 1947, pp. 167–168.

33. *F.E.P.C. Manual*, New York, Committee on Employment Discrimination of the National Community Relations Advisory Council, n.d.

34. See *Annual Report* of the Massachusetts Fair Employment Practices Commission, November 20, 1947; and Herbert R. Northrup, "Proving Ground for Fair Employment," *Commentary* 4:552–556, December 1947; and *Providence Evening Bulletin*, February 5, 1948.

35. *Boston City Reporter*, published by the Frances Sweeney Committee, September 1947, p. 2.

36. Northrup, *op. cit.*, pp. 554–555.

37. Information supplied through the courtesy of Miss Alice Halligan of the Springfield Public Schools, member of the Springfield Fair Employment Practice Council, appointed in 1947 under the chairmanship of Mr. Roger L. Putnam, former mayor of Springfield.

38. Watson, *op. cit.*, p. 120.

39. *To Secure These Rights*, pp. 151 ff.

40. *Ibid.*, p. 164.

41. These opinions are expressed at greater length in Zechariah Chafee, Jr., *Government and Mass Communications, A Report from the Commission on Freedom of the Press*, Chicago, University of Chicago Press, 1947, I, 116–144. MacIver concurs in this opinion by stating, "No expression of opinion should be outlawed merely on the ground that it is defamatory of or prejudicial to any social group,

whether ethnic, racial or other. Still less should any censorship be set up to check such expression of opinion." MacIver Ms. p. 25.

42. MacIver Ms. p. 25.
43. Watson, *op. cit.*, p. 94.
44. MacIver Ms. p. 19.
45. Watson, *op. cit.*, p. 88.
46. *Ibid.*, p. 89.
47. *Ibid.*, p. 92.
48. *Ibid.*, pp. 91–92.
49. *Ibid.*, p. 7.
50. *Directory of Local Public Agencies in Race Relations*, 1948, 2nd ed., (mimeographed), Chicago, American Council on Race Relations, 1948.
51. The original directory listed twelve but Mr. F. W. Baldau, executive director of the City of Cleveland Community Relations Board, adds the name of his organization to the list. The writer is indebted to Mr. Baldau for calling attention to this directory and for supplementary information furnished by his office.
52. Watson, *op. cit.*, p. 8.
53. Personal communication from Mr. F. W. Baldau.
54. Information supplied through the courtesy of Dr. Martin H. Bickham, Chairman of the Illinois Inter-Racial Commission.
55. For concrete examples see "The Common Council At Work," *Common Ground* 8, No. 1:101–104, Autumn 1947.
56. "Pass the Stratton Bill," *Nation* 64:674, 1947. For negative comment see H. P. Fairchild, "Shall We Suffer More Émigrés?" *Saturday Review of Literature* 30:16 ff., May 24, 1947, reviewing M. R. Davie's *Refugees in America*, quoted above, Chapter 16.
57. Cf. "The Common Council At Work," p. 102.
58. Editorial "Down the Road," *Cleveland Call and Post*, August 24, 1946. See further editorial comment, "Immigration a Threat to Negro Migration," *ibid.*, August 2, 1947.
59. Francis J. Haas and G. James Fleming, "Personnel Practices and Wartime Changes," *Annals of the American Academy of Political and Social Science* 244:48–56, 1946.
60. Abraham Rubin and George J. Segal, "An Industrial Experiment," *Annals* 244:57–64, 1946.
61. Watson, *op. cit.*, p. 71.
62. H. P. Fairchild, *Race and Nationality as Factors in American Life*, New York, Ronald Press, 1947, p. 188.
63. See Ira N. Brophy, "The Luxury of Anti-Negro Prejudice," *Public Opinion Quarterly* 9:456–466, 1946.
64. Williams, *op. cit.*, p. 54.
65. Howard H. Harlan, "Some Factors Affecting Attitude Toward Jews," *American Sociological Review* 7:816–827, 1942, pp. 822 ff.
66. Watson, *op. cit.*, pp. 145–146.
67. Charles E. Hendry, Russell Hogrefe, and Edward Haydon, "Gangs," in W. H. Kilpatrick and William van Til, eds. *Intercultural Attitudes in the Making*, New York, Harper, 1947 (Ninth Yearbook of the John Dewey Society), chap. 6.
68. Williams, *op. cit.*, p. 23.
69. Communication from Clarence V. Howell, Director.
70. Williams, *op. cit.*, p. 70.
71. A. Ritchie Low, "Invitation to Vermont," *Common Ground* 6, No. 4: 44–52, 1946.
72. Harte, *op. cit.*, pp. 29 ff.
73. *Twenty-Five Major Accomplishments in Twenty-Five Years 1922–1947*, pamphlet edited by the Department of Race Relations of the Federal Council of Churches of Christ in America, 1947.
74. Williams, *op. cit.*, p. 23.
75. For an interesting account of these activities see A. J. Liebling, "Democracy's Friend," a profile in *The New Yorker*, July 26, 1947, August 2, 1947, and August 9, 1947.
76. Sigmund Livingston, *Must Men Hate?* New York, Harper, 1944.

77. Watson, *op. cit.*, p. 123.
78. See Solomon A. Fineberg, "Checkmate for Rabble Rousers," *Commentary* 2:220–226, 1946, and "How to Fight Rabble Rousers: A Discussion," *Commentary* 2:460–466, 1946.
79. Watson, *op. cit.*, pp. 81 and 123.
80. Cf. Sidney Katz, "How to Squelch a Bigot," *Negro Digest* 6, No. 4:62–69, February 1948, reprinted from *Magazine Digest*, Toronto, Canada. For an account of the scientific method involved, cf. John Harding, Abraham Citron, and Claire Sellitz, "Personal Incidents; A Study of the Effectiveness of Various Types of Answers to Anti-Minority Remarks," paper read at the Fifty-Fifth Annual Meeting of the American Psychological Association, September 9–13, 1947, Detroit, Mich. Mimeographed by the Commission on Community Interrelations of the American Jewish Congress (C.C.I.). For this and other data on the work of the C.C.I. the writer is indebted to Isidor Chein, research director of the organization.
81. See above, pp. 14–15.
82. For a more complete summary see Kilpatrick and van Til, *op. cit.*, chap. 1 "Basic Principles in Intercultural Education," by W. H. Kilpatrick.
83. Watson, *op. cit.*, p. 96.
84. Louis Adamic, *Nation of Nations*, New York, Harper, 1946, and F. J. Brown and J. S. Roucek, *One America*, New York, Prentice-Hall, 1945, parts IV and V.
85. Williams, *op. cit.*, p. 64.
86. Kilpatrick, *op. cit.* Publication list available at 1697 Broadway, New York, 19, N.Y.
87. See Chapter 19, note 10, above.
88. The writer is indebted to Dr. Stewart G. Cole for this information. See also *Race Relations, A Monthly Summary* 4, No. 3:83–85, October 1946. (Published at Fisk University, Nashville, Tenn.)
89. *Education for Better Human Relations*, pamphlet, New York, National Conference of Christians and Jews, n.d. The N.C.C.J. supplies a considerable share of the funds for the various projects of the American Council on Education. Information furnished through the courtesy of Dr. E. R. Clinchy, director of N.C.C.J.
90. The writer is indebted to Miss Hilda Taba for supplying the data regarding the activities of the American Council on Education.
91. Can be obtained from the American Council on Education, 437 W. 59th St., New York 19, N.Y.
92. *Education for Better Human Relations.*
93. *Sixteenth Yearbook of the National Council for the Social Studies*, Washington, D.C., 1945.
94. Clarence I. Chatto and Alice L. Halligan, *The Story of the Springfield Plan*, New York, Barnes and Noble, 1945, p. 6.
95. A revised copy of this unit for grade 7 is now available in mimeographed form at the Springfield Public Schools. The writer is indebted to Miss Evelyn T. Holston, General Supervisor of Junior High Schools in the Springfield schools for this and other documents presenting study units in the system.
96. *Citizenship*, Springfield Public Schools, mimeographed analysis for use of teachers. The writer is indebted to Miss M. O. Pottenger, General Supervisor of Elementary Education of Springfield schools for this and other materials on the work of the elementary grades.
97. Miss Alice Halligan, Director of Guidance, Springfield Public Schools, supplied this illustration.
98. Chatto and Halligan, *op. cit.*, pp. 56–59.
99. *Ibid.*, p. 82.
100. *Ibid.*, p. 106. Also see official greeting and welcome for new citizens printed at Springfield, Mass., for "I Am An American Day," May 20, 1945. A list of courses in all grades and in adult education appears in abbreviated form in the pamphlet, *To Parents, A Message*, printed in 1944. Fur-

nished through the courtesy of Miss Evelyn T. Holston. These interviews were all arranged through the courtesy of Dr. Alden H. Blankenship, Superintendent of Schools, Springfield, Mass., to whom the author is greatly indebted.

101. For a more detailed picture see Chatto and Halligan, *op. cit.*, and Alexander Alland and James Waterman Wise, *The Springfield Plan*, New York, Viking, 1945.

102. Information obtained through personal interviews, not all official or arranged.

103. See Watson, *op. cit.*, pp. 84–85 and 132–133 and pamphlet, *The Work of the Department of Race Relations of the Federal Council of Churches*, Interracial Publication No. 60, 1945.

104. Harte, *op. cit.*, pp. 48–49.

105. C. S. Johnson, *op. cit.*, pp. 283–312 and chap. 11.

106. Harte, *op. cit.*, pp. 156–157.

107. Watson, *op. cit.*, pp. 27–30.

108. Karl W. Deutsch, "Problems of Justice in International Territorial Disputes" in *Approaches to Group Understanding*, p. 240.

109. Willard Johnson, "N.C.C.J. in Action," mimeographed report November 1947, p. 8.

110. See monthly bulletins mimeographed by the College Study in Intergroup Relations, Lloyd Allen Cook, Director, Wayne University, 5272 Second Ave., Detroit 2, Michigan.

111. Available at Advertising Council, Dept. T–24, 11 W. 42nd St., New York City. Other information concerning N.C.C.J. can be found in Willard Johnson, *op. cit.*; in the pamphlet, "Education for Better Human Relations"; and in *Conference, the Magazine of Human Relations*, all obtainable through N.C.C.J., 381 Fourth Ave., New York 16, N.Y.

112. E. Cooper and M. Jahoda, "The Evasion of Propaganda, How Prejudiced People Respond to Anti-Prejudice Propaganda," *Journal of Psychology* 23:15–25, 1947.

113. Samuel H. Flowerman, "Mass Propaganda In The War Against Bigotry," *Journal of Abnormal and Social Psychology* 42:429–439, 1947, p. 431.

114. *Ibid.*, pp. 430–431.

115. *Ibid.*, pp. 434–437.

116. Watson, *op. cit.*, p. 30.

117. *To Secure These Rights*, p. 142.

118. MacIver Ms. p. 10.

119. See above, pp. 534 ff.

120. Watson, *op. cit.*, pp. 78 and 81.

121. *Ibid.*, p. 80, and articles by Eugene Segal in the *Cleveland Press*, beginning November 11, 1946.

122. Ronald Lippitt and Marian Radke, "New Trends in the Investigation of Prejudice," *Annals of the American Academy of Political and Social Science* 244:167–176, 1946. Also below, footnote 126.

123. Watson, *op. cit.*, p. 83.

124. John Harding, "Community Self-Surveys, A Form of Combating Discrimination," *Congress Weekly*, March 5, 1948.

125. *Idem.*

126. Margot Haas and Stuart Cook, "The Use of the Community Self-Survey in Combating Discrimination," paper read at the Fifty-Fifth Annual Meeting of the American Psychological Association, September 9–13, 1947. Mimeographed by C.C.I.

127. Harding, *op. cit.*

128. See above, p. 543.

129. Watson, *op. cit.*, p. 31.

130. Interview with Clarence I. Chatto, Principal of Classical High School, Springfield, Mass.

131. As in Louis Adamic, *Nation of Nations.*

132. See above, footnote 109.

133. Watson, *op. cit.*, pp. 36–44.

134. Geoffrey Gorer, "The American Character," *Life*, August 18, 1947, p. 96.

135. J. H. Kolb and E. S. Brunner, *A Study of Rural Society*, Boston, Houghton Mifflin, 1946, p. 9.

136. *Opinion News* of the National Opinion Research Center, December 1945.
137. An exception is William G. Mather, "The Rural Church Situation as Seen by a Social Scientist," *Town and Country Church*, February 1948, reprint of an address delivered at the National Convocation on the Church in Town and Country, Rochester, N.Y., November 4, 1947.
138. Donald Young, "Techniques of Race Relations," *Proceedings, American Philosophical Society* 91:150–161, April 1947.
139. Isidor Chein, Stuart W. Cook, and John Harding, "The Field of Action Research," mimeographed by the C.C.I., 1947.
140. *Ibid.*
141. MacIver Ms. pp. 4–5.
142. S. Koenig, "Ethnic Factors in the Economic Life of Urban Connecticut," *American Sociological Review* 8:193–197, 1943.
143. R. H. Pittman, "Building an Interracial Church," *Sociology and Social Research* 29:297–303, 1945.
144. Theodore Brameld, *Minority Problems in the Public Schools*, New York, Harper, 1946.
145. For attitudes and values the most complete summary is Arnold M. Rose, *Studies in Reduction of Prejudice*, Chicago, American Council on Race Relations, 1947. Mimeographed. For social situations a less complete summary (mixed with items of the attitude category) is given in Williams, *op. cit.* There is need for a still more comprehensive summary of this type.
146. Watson, *op. cit.*, pp. 152 ff.
147. Myrdal, *op. cit.*, I, 75 ff.
148. Williams, *op. cit.*, p. 59.
149. *Ibid.*, p. 62.
150. *Ibid.*, p. 63.
151. *Ibid.*, p. 64.
152. Kurt Lewin and Paul Grabbe, "Conduct, Knowledge and Acceptance of New Values," *Journal of Social Issues* I, No. 3:53–64, August 1945, p. 59.
153. Williams, *op. cit.*, particularly chaps. 2 and 3.
154. Social Science Research Council, 230 Park Ave., New York 17, N.Y.

INDEX